opposing viewpoints®

SOURCES

male/female roles

opposing viewpoints®
SOURCES

male/female roles

David L. Bender, *Publisher*
Bruno Leone, *Executive Editor*
M. Teresa O'Neill, *Senior Editor*
Bonnie Szumski, *Senior Editor*
Janelle Rohr, *Senior Editor*
Lynn Hall, *Editor*
Julie S. Bach, *Editor*
Thomas Modl, *Editor*
William Dudley, *Editor*
Robert Anderson, *Assistant Editor*

Karin E. Wandrei, DSW, *Consulting Editor*
Clinical Coordinator, Zonta Children's Center, San Jose, California
Private Psychotherapy Practice, Oakland, California

greenhaven press, inc.
San Diego, CA

ISBN 0-89908-534-2
ISSN 0897-7372

"Congress shall make no law . . . abridging the freedom of speech, or of the press."

First amendment to the US Constitution

contents

foreword

"It is better to debate a question without settling it than to settle a question without debating it."

Joseph Joubert (1754-1824)

The purpose of Opposing Viewpoints SOURCES is to present balanced, and often difficult to find, opposing points of view on complex and sensitive issues.

Probably the best way to become informed is to analyze the positions of those who are regarded as experts and well studied on issues. It is important to consider every variety of opinion in an attempt to determine the truth. Opinions from the mainstream of society should be examined. But also important are opinions that are considered radical, reactionary, or minority as well as those stigmatized by some other uncomplimentary label. An important lesson of history is the eventual acceptance of many unpopular and even despised opinions. The ideas of Socrates, Jesus, and Galileo are good examples of this.

Readers will approach this anthology with their own opinions on the issues debated within it. However, to have a good grasp of one's own viewpoint, it is necessary to understand the arguments of those with whom one disagrees. It can be said that those who do not completely understand their adversary's point of view do not fully understand their own.

A persuasive case for considering opposing viewpoints has been presented by John Stuart Mill in his work *On Liberty*. When examining controversial issues it may be helpful to reflect on his suggestion:

> The only way in which a human being can make some approach to knowing the whole of a subject, is by hearing what can be said about it by persons of every variety of opinion, and studying all modes in which it can be looked at by every character of mind. No wise man ever acquired his wisdom in any mode but this.

Analyzing Sources of Information

Opposing Viewpoints SOURCES include diverse materials taken from magazines, journals, books, and newspapers, as well as statements and position papers from a wide range of individuals, organizations, and governments. This broad spectrum of sources helps to develop patterns of thinking which are open to the consideration of a variety of opinions.

Pitfalls To Avoid

A pitfall to avoid in considering opposing points of view is that of regarding one's own opinion as being common sense and the most rational stance and the point of view of others as being only opinion and naturally wrong. It may be that another's opinion is correct and one's own is in error.

Another pitfall to avoid is that of closing one's mind to the opinions of those with whom one disagrees. The best way to approach a dialogue is to make one's primary purpose that of understanding the mind and arguments of the other person and not that of enlightening him or her with one's own solutions. More can be learned by listening than speaking.

It is my hope that after reading this anthology the reader will have a deeper understanding of the issues debated and will appreciate the complexity of even seemingly simple issues on which good and honest people disagree. This awareness is particularly important in a democratic society such as ours where people enter into public debate to determine the common good. Those with whom one disagrees should not necessarily be regarded as enemies, but perhaps simply as people who suggest different paths to a common goal.

The Format of SOURCES

In this anthology, carefully chosen opposing viewpoints are purposely placed back to back to create a running debate; each viewpoint is preceded by a short quotation that best expresses the author's main argument. This format instantly plunges the reader into the midst of a controversial issue and greatly aids that reader in mastering the basic skill of recognizing an author's point of view. In addition, the table of contents gives a brief description of each viewpoint, allowing the reader to identify quickly the point of view for which he or she is searching.

Each section of this anthology debates an issue, and the sections build on one another so that the anthology as a whole debates a larger issue. By using this step-by-step, section-by-section approach to understanding separate facets of a topic, the reader will have a solid background upon which to base his or her opinions. Each year a supplement of twenty-five opposing viewpoints will be added to this anthology, enabling the reader to keep abreast of annual developments.

This volume of Opposing Viewpoints SOURCES does not advocate a particular point of view. Quite the contrary! The very nature of the anthology leaves it to the reader to formulate the opinions he or she finds most suitable. My purpose as publisher is to see that this is made possible by offering a wide range of viewpoints that are fairly presented.

David L. Bender
Publisher

introduction

"It is nearly impossible to determine just when sex-role learning begins."

•Marcia Lassell & Norman M. Lobsenz

One day each year the men and the women of the Greek village of Monoklissia observe an ancient custom. For twenty-four hours they trade places. The men remain on their farms or in their houses to cook the meals, take care of the children, milk the cows, and do the other routine household chores. Their wives, meanwhile, gather at the taverna in the village square to gossip, play cards, and drink the potent *retsina* wine of the region. Any man found on the streets of Monoklissia during that time period risks the traditional punishment: a thorough soaking in the town fountain.

In our times, in our towns, men and women are also "trading places"—not just for twenty-four hours but for the years ahead. Freed from the strictures of generations of cultural conformity, both sexes are increasingly choosing life-styles that suit their needs and their skills rather than the dictates of society. Women in large numbers are taking their places in occupations once monopolized by men. In turn, many men are beginning to share equally with women in homemaking and child care, and some are even choosing to stay at home and be house-husbands. Women are learning that it is not unfeminine to be assertive, and men are learning that it is not unmasculine to be dependent. Both women and men are taking advantage of the full range of options they can now choose from in the emotional and intimate areas of their lives. They are deciding to marry later, or not at all; to live with a lover, who may be of either sex; to have children or to be a nonparent.

Unlike the Monoklissians, those who resist or challenge these changes in the social structure, or who do not take them seriously, or who do not grasp the significance of their sweeping effects, risk no

Marcia Lassell & Norman M. Lobsenz, *Equal Time: The New Way of Living, Loving, and Working Together.* New York: Doubleday & Co., 1983. Reprinted by permission.

mere dunking. Their destiny is considerably more serious. For their human relationships will flourish or suffer depending on how well they understand and deal with the new definitions of masculinity and femininity; and on how effectively they apply these new definitions to such matters as intimacy, commitment, trust, fidelity, and conflict in the context of being husband or wife, mother or father, coworker, friend, or lover.

No Empty Ritual

"Ladies' Day" in Monoklissia is an annual charade that probably represents a dim, anemic vestige of some lusty pre-Christian ritual that honored the Mother Goddess. But the changing and merging of sex roles in American life during the past decade is no empty ritual. The resulting shock waves have been felt by every woman and man, regardless of her or his chosen life-style. Most of the changes, of course, have occurred in the roles of women. But when women change their definitions of femininity and the kinds of behavior that are appropriate to the female sex role, men will also change. Every couple constitutes a single emotional "system." And since there are no signs that women and men are any less emotionally involved with each other than they ever have been, changes that affect one sex must necessarily lead to changes in the other.

Such a major social transition (especially one so basic) carries enormous potential for both good and ill. On the one hand, the prospect of anything new or different tends to promote anxiety. Old ways, like old clothes, are familiar and therefore reassuring, even though they may be unfashionable, uncomfortable, or no longer functional. So we postpone coming to grips with change; and when we do, we do so, for the most part, reluctantly. Firm convictions and deeply imbued ways of behaving are slow to change, if at all, despite our best intentions and most sincere efforts.

On the other hand, change has the advantage of exposing us—or forcing us to expose ourselves—to ideas and feelings, to skills and achievements, and to ways of relating that hold the promise of greater emotional fulfillment. In short, change offers a man and a woman the opportunity to help each other grow and, perhaps more important, to enjoy each other's growth. Many people, still hemmed in by outdated or prescribed roles, are dimly trying, and failing, in both areas.

Heading for Trouble

If the quality of a relationship is linked to how well partners agree on their roles, then many women and men are headed for trouble. One recent survey showed that out of more than thirty different complaints that spouses registered when filing for divorce, conflict over sex roles ranked second among husbands and eighth among wives.

It is hardly surprising, then, that we believe the overriding task for women and men today, and in the years immediately ahead, is to learn how to rebuild their partnerships so as to *benefit* from the sex-role changes that have taken place. This means couples must take a whole new look at each other, deal with a host of unexpected feelings and reactions, find fresh paths to mutual joy. . . .

For generations women and men have measured themselves against "ideal" characteristics appropriate for each sex. There have always been certain traits considered desirable for women and certain others approved for men. As far as we can tell, there probably always will be. It is not, therefore, that we have emerged into a "roleless" society but, instead, that our definitions of feminine behavior and masculine behavior are changing in important ways.

Masculine and feminine traits traditionally lay at opposite ends of a continuum, so that some of the approved characteristics for women were specifically *not* approved for men and masculine traits were taboo for women. In this way, masculinity and femininity were defined as opposites. If aggressiveness was considered masculine (and it usually has been), a woman who exhibited aggression was judged to be unfeminine; since feminine traits usually included submissiveness and modesty, these characteristics were considered undesirable in a man. Men who showed traits considered peculiarly feminine were labeled "sissies." Women who were competitive or dominant—both stereotypical male traits—often were said to be "castrating" or to have "unresolved gender problems."

Teaching Sex Roles

These "bipolar" stereotypes became so entrenched in our society that each generation carefully taught the next generation that there were "good" and "bad" ways for boys and girls to behave. Accepted patterns of femininity and masculinity were translated into family responsibilities and work roles with equal care. Boys grew into men who were taught it was their role to represent the family in the community and the world of work. Girls grew up expecting to nurture the family by tending to its physical and emotional needs. Men managed their families' economic interests by controlling access to the outside world; women controlled men's access to affection, sex, and nurturance (unless men found these resources outside the home). The implication of these "opposite" roles was that if men were powerful in the family's interface with the world, then women could not be. Similarly, if women were dominant in controlling the family's emotional resources, then men could not be. Perhaps the most significant aspect of changing sex roles is how these stereotypes have been challenged. As large numbers of women have entered the labor market, for example, it has become more acceptable for assertiveness to be included in definitions of femininity. As men are more and more involving themselves with child care, nurturance has come to be seen as an acceptable masculine trait and function.

"For generations women and men have measured themselves against 'ideal' characteristics appropriate for each sex."

As ideas have changed of what women should be and do, and what men should be and do, we've learned that the sexes have not been cast by evolution in totally separate molds. Research is breaking important new ground in showing us how the sexes differ and how they are alike. There are the obvious differences in physiological equipment. But while anatomy is *not* destiny, there are important biological differences that cannot be denied—mainly in the form of the sex hormones and their effects, and in the actions of the chemical transmitters that spark neural impulses in the brain. Current research highlights other sex differences that may be biological, or may be learned, but are nonetheless very real. We know, for instance, that women and men respond differently to sounds, visual stimuli, tactile sensations, and problem-solving challenges. (But "different" does not mean one sex's reactions are necessarily "better" or "worse" than the other's.)

The research of Stanford University psychologists indicates that while the sexes are equal in general intelligence, they seem to process information differently. By the age of ten or eleven girls excel in verbal ability, and boys suffer more from such language problems as stuttering and reading disabilities. Conversely, by adolescence, boys seem to excel in mechanical skills, mathematics, and the kind of spatial reasoning essential to map-reading and other scientific endeavors. (But by adolescence, girls—and educators—have already been "taught" that boys are better in these fields, and thus this "difference" becomes a self-fulfilling prophecy.)

Moreover, studies of brain structure and development suggest that many—if not most—of these cognitive differences may be due in part to the fact that girls mature physically earlier than boys. For example, the right side of the brain is the center of spatial reasoning, among other factors, and the left is the center of language skills. In early maturers the two sides have less time to specialize. Since both halves of the female brain share these and other tasks, women may be able to integrate more information and process it faster. (Some experts feel this may account for what has been called woman's "intuition.")

Unfortunately, such biological differences have been used to distort the fact that literally from infancy we are culturally conditioned to prescribed sex roles. Harvard University biologist Richard Lewontin speaks for many researchers when he says that the determining influence in the development of a person's sexual orientation is that people "are called 'boys' and 'girls' from the day they are born." In a classic experiment, subjects were asked to describe the behavior of a group of newborns. When the infants were dressed in blue diapers (the conventional color for boy babies), the observers said that they were "very active." When the same infants were presented in pink diapers, the subjects commented on their "gentle" behavior. And when the babies were put into yellow diapers the observers, according to Lewontin, "got upset. . . . They started to peek inside the diapers to see their sex."

Physiological Differences?

In sum, then, the sciences are telling us that while there are physiological differences between the sexes, they are far fewer than we once thought; that the differences ought to be relatively unimportant in setting the pattern of our social and sexual roles; and that the similarities between women and men are greater than the common wisdom ever believed or admitted. The fact is that there are sex-linked chromosomes in *every* cell of our bodies, and their physical effects are widespread and profound. At the same time, how we judge the rightness or wrongness, propriety or impropriety, of male and female behaviors is the result of social learning. To force the issue of whether heredity or environment, biology or culture, is more important in determining sex roles is like forcing the issue of which blade of a scissors cuts the cloth more effectively.

The real issue for women and men in day-to-day living is not what makes particular people behave in particular ways, but how constructively we respond to that behavior: to give our partner a sense of human dignity, a chance for joy, and the freedom and energy to achieve his or her goals in life. The task is not merely to substitute new rules in relationships for the old rules; the task is to get rid of rules and open new horizons.

"Studies show that from the earliest days of life girls are responded to more quickly when they cry than boys are."

The new information about how a woman and a man differ from yet resemble each other has, paradoxically, left most people both wiser and more confused. Let's look for a moment at just one issue basic in the debate over sex-role function that we referred to earlier: whether women are born to be nurturers and men born to be protectors and providers, or whether these roles are learned rather than innate and therefore capable of modification and change.

Both positions have been argued passionately if not always eloquently. Those who speak for innate differences base their case on the fact that each gender has its specific reproductive function, and for hundreds of thousands of years has specialized in doing what each does best. Others cite the role of prenatal hormones, which some scientists believe predispose males to be more aggressive than females. Combined with the knowledge that on the average men are physically larger and stronger than women, the conclusion has been drawn that males are indeed "programmed" to protect and provide. By the same token, women, since they give birth to and nurse children, are assigned the role of nurturer.

But these and other gender differences have been called irrelevant by those who say that such stereotyped sex roles are chiefly the result of child-rearing practices, the educational system, the media, and other sources of socialization. Reproductive differences, they claim, are of secondary importance; that women bear and nurse children is not the crucial factor. Instead, it is the fact that women have always been culturally charged with the responsibility of child care that spells the major difference between the roles of women and men in our society.

Resolving Opposing Views

A major obstacle to resolving these opposing views is that it is nearly impossible to determine just when sex-role learning begins. Studies show that from the earliest days of life girls are responded to more quickly when they cry than boys are. Mothers increase the amount of attention they give to a fussy baby girl and are more likely to interpret her crying as fear. They reduce the amount of attention they give to boy babies because they perceive *their* cries as a show of anger. Does this maternal behavior subtly program girls to learn to be more nurturant and boys to be more aggressive?

Infants cannot label such differential treatment as "the way girls should be treated" and "the way boys should be treated." But by the time children can walk and talk, they know quite clearly what sex they are, and by the age of three they have learned many of the "proper" masculine and feminine ways to behave. Yet we still cannot say with any certainty whether these behaviors are the result of biological predisposition, of direct instruction, of subtle social learning, of a child's amazing ability to imitate the behavior of parents and other adults important to them, or (most likely) from a combination of all of these. It is a chicken-and-egg puzzle. Do boys prefer to play with cars and guns because they are by nature aggressive, or do parents give them such toys because the parents think boys *should* be aggressive, or because cars and guns have come to be considered the *right* toys for boys? Do girls play with dolls because they are innately nurturant, or because they are early on encouraged to play with dolls and assume the nurturant role?

New Ways To Relate to Each Other

Most women and men today seem to have decided that it will be a long time, if ever, before these questions are finally answered. What is more important, they say, is to find new ways of relating to each other—ways that will free them from those aspects of traditional sex roles that limit personal growth and interpersonal intimacy, and at the same time let them keep hold of those aspects that provide important emotional rewards. Pressured (or eager) to change in some areas of their lives, and wanting to remain unchanged in others, women and men are fumbling for workable solutions to the unexpected and unfamiliar conflicts this dilemma is causing. For example:

• As women increasingly move into once male-dominated fields of work, and men are increasingly involved in domestic responsibilities, what feelings are aroused and what power balances are upset? What happens between a couple when she earns more than he does? When she gets a promotion and has a higher career status than he does? When he must move because she has been offered a better job? When their work separates them geographically? When her new bargaining power in their partnership entitles her to a stronger role in decision making?

• Trust has always been a key ingredient in a couple relationship. In the past it focused on a woman's trust in her man, since he had more

independence and mobility in the world outside the home. Today the emphasis is on *mutual* trust, and how a couple can build and keep it in the face of woman's growing freedom.

• Friendship between the sexes is raising questions that disturb many women and men. Are non-sexual, non-romantic friendships possible? Can they stay platonic? What functions do they serve? What problems do they cause? How can they be protected?

• Having children, not too long ago an almost automatic choice for most couples, is now a complex decision to make. Is the price of being a parent (including the loss of a working woman's income and the possible handicap to her academic or professional progress) too high? Should couples wait to have children? How long? Do they want children at all? Does one partner want a child, but not the other? Do children strengthen a marriage or do they add to its stresses?

These are but a few of the key areas where sex-role changes are making it necessary for women and men to learn new ways of being together and growing together. There are no facile answers to the problems involved in balancing the best of the past with the best of the present and future. On the one hand, sex stereotypes—deeply rooted in religion, education, economics, and countless generations of family history and ritual—are slow to die. A man today still usually identifies himself in terms of the world outside his home: his work, his school, the organizations he belongs to, his practical accomplishments. A woman still tends to identify herself (even now, twenty years after the women's movement raised her consciousness) as a daughter, a wife, a mother. Moreover, the changes that have been evoked have aroused more rage and created more conflict than anyone anticipated. . . .

"Neither sex, having traded conventional certainties for unorthodox options, quite knows how to deal with the other."

Advances by women (they've reaped more benefits from sex-role changes so far than men have), plus slowly growing acceptance of the new human environment by men, have lessened the climate of hostility. In the decade between 1970 and 1980, for instance, the number of women and men who favor the new sex-role patterns has substantially increased. According to a Roper poll, more than half of the women and men questioned in 1970 said they did not support efforts to strengthen the status of women; in 1980 fewer than one quarter opposed the idea.

Yet the truce that exists is an uneasy one. Neither

sex, having traded conventional certainties for unorthodox options, quite knows how to deal with the other. Thus, the critical issue for today and for the years ahead is sharply defined: How can women and men successfully come to grips with the changes that are taking place in their roles and relationships and still retain the positive qualities—trust, intimacy, emotional security, mutual respect—that make it possible for them to live together, love together, work together, grow together.

"Women manipulate male sexual desire in order to teach men the long-term cycles of female sexuality and biology on which civilization is based."

Gender Roles Are Necessary

George Gilder

The crucial process of civilization is the subordination of male sexual impulses and biology to the long-term horizons of female sexuality. The overall sexual behavior of women in the modern world differs relatively little from the sexual life of women in primitive societies. It is male behavior that must be changed to create a civilized order.

Men lust, but they know not what for; they wander, and lose track of the goal; they fight and compete, but they forget the prize; they spread seed, but spurn the seasons of growth; they chase power and glory, but miss the meaning of life.

In creating civilization, women transform male lust into love; channel male wanderlust into jobs, homes, and families; link men to specific children; rear children into citizens; change hunters into fathers; divert male will to power into a drive to create. Women conceive the future that men tend to flee; they feed the children that men ignore.

Women's Superiority

The prime fact of life is the sexual superiority of women. Sexual love, intercourse, marriage, conception of a child, childbearing—even breast-feeding—are all critical experiences psychologically. They are times when our emotions are most intense, our lives are most deeply changed, and society is perpetuated in our own image. And they all entail sexual roles that demonstrate the primacy of women.

The central roles are mother and father, husband and wife. They form neat and apparently balanced pairs. But appearances are deceptive. In sexual terms, there is little balance at all. In most of these key sexual events, the male role is trivial, even easily dispensable. Although the man is needed in intercourse, artificial insemination has already been

used in hundreds of thousands of cases. Otherwise, the man is altogether unnecessary. It is the woman who conceives, bears, and suckles the child. Those activities that are most deeply sexual are mostly female; they comprise the mother's role, a role that is defined biologically.

The nominally equivalent role of father is in fact a product of marriage and other cultural contrivances. There is no biological need for the father to be anywhere around when the baby is born and nurtured. In many societies the father has no special responsibility to support the specific children he sires. In some societies, paternity is not even acknowledged. The father is neither inherently equal to the mother within the family, nor necessarily inclined to remain with it. In one way or another, the man must be *made* equal by society. . . .

In primitive societies men have the compensation of physical strength. They can control women by force and are needed to protect them from other men. But this equalizer is relatively unimportant in a civilized society, where the use of force is largely restricted by law and custom. In successful civilized societies, man counterbalances female sexual superiority by playing a crucial role as provider and achiever. Money replaces muscle.

Sexual Parity

If society devalues this male role by pressing women to provide for themselves, prove their "independence," and compete with men for money and status, there is only one way equality between the sexes can be maintained: Women must be reduced to sexual parity. They must relinquish their sexual superiority, psychologically disconnect their wombs, and adopt the short-circuited copulatory sexuality of males. Women must renounce all the larger procreative dimensions of their sexual impulse.

This is precisely what sexual liberals advocate.

From MEN AND MARRIAGE by George Gilder. Copyright © 1986 by George Gilder, used by permission of the publisher, Pelican Publishing Company. Inc.

They assiduously deny that women have a maternal instinct and assert women's "right" to adopt male sexual attitudes and ape male sexual drives. At the very same time they argue that men can find sexual fulfillment in "nurturant" activities like child-rearing.

Whether "instinctive" or not, however, the maternal role originates in the fact that only the woman is necessarily present at birth. Only the woman has a dependable and easily identifiable connection to the child—a tie on which society can rely. No matter how "equally" the functions of child-rearing are distributed, the man will always know that the woman's role with the children was more important, more organically indispensable. There is no way the man can share in the euphoria that many women feel—along with the pains—when pregnant, for it is a sensation of warm separateness and independent fulfillment. There is no way that men can share in the "mothering hormone" that many authorities believe the woman secretes in childbirth. There is no way the man with the bottle will experience the sense of sexual affirmation and sensual fulfillment felt by the woman with a child at her breast.

Boys' and Girls' Development

The man's dependence on women begins in his earliest years. A male child is born, grows, and finds his being in relation to his own body and to the bodies of his parents, chiefly his mother's. His later happiness is found in part on a physiological memory. Originating perhaps in the womb itself, it extends through all his infant groping into the world at large, which begins, of course, in his mother's arms. In trusting her he learned to trust himself, and trusting himself he learns to bear the slow dissolution of the primary tie. He moves away into a new world, into a sometimes frightening psychic space between his parents; and he must then attach his evolving identity to a man, his father. Almost from the start, the boy's sexual identity is dependent on acts of exploration and initiative.

Throughout the lives of men we find echoes of this image, of a boy stranded in transition from his first tie to a woman—whom he discovers to be different, and perhaps even subtly dangerous to him—toward identification with a man, who will always deny him the closeness his mother once provided. At an early age he is, in a sense, set at large. Before he can return to a woman, he must assert his manhood in action. The Zulu warrior had to kill a man, the Mandan youth had to endure torture, the Irish peasant had to build a house, the American man must find a job. This is the classic myth and the mundane reality of masculinity.

Female histories are different. As Margaret Mead observed: "The worry that boys will not grow up to be men is much more widespread than the worry

that the girls will not grow up to be women, and in none of of these South Seas societies [that she studied] does the latter fear appear at all." A girl's sexuality normally unfolds in an unbroken line, from a stage of utter dependency and identification with her mother through stages of gradual autonomy. Always, the focus of female identification is clear and stable.

Anthropologist Ashley Montagu has reported evidence that women treat girls and boys differently from the time of birth, fondling and caressing the girls more and making them feel more a part of their initial environment. The mothers may unconsciously recognize that girls can enjoy a continuous evolution of identity with their mothers, while boys relatively soon must break this primary tie. . . .

Men's and Women's Sexual Identity

Male sexual consciousness comes as an unprogrammed drive. Nothing about the male body dictates any specific pattern beyond a repetitive release of sexual tension. Men must define and defend the larger dimensions of their sexuality by external activity.

As a physical reality, the male sexual repertory is very limited. Men have only one sex organ and one sex act: erection and ejaculation. Everything else is guided by culture and imagination. Other male roles, other styles of masculine identity, must be learned or created. The most important and productive roles—husband and father in a durable marriage—are a cultural invention, necessary to civilized life but ultimately fragile.

"The prime fact of life is the sexual superiority of women."

A woman is not so exclusively dependent on copulation for sexual identity. For her, intercourse is only one of many sex acts or experiences. Her breasts and her womb symbolize a sex role that extends, at least as a potentiality, through pregnancy, childbirth, lactation, suckling, and long-term nurture. Rather than a brief performance, female sexuality is a long, unfolding process. Even if a woman does not in fact bear a child, she is continually reminded that she can, that she is capable of performing the crucial act in the perpetuation of the species. She can perform the only act that gives sex an unquestionable meaning, an incarnate result.

Thus, regardless of any anxieties she may have in relation to her sexual role and how to perform it, she at least knows that she has a role of unquestionable importance to herself and the community. Whatever else she may do or be, she can be sure of her essential female nature.

On this point the sexes do not understand each other. Women take their sexual identity for granted. They assume that except for some cultural peculiarity, men might also enjoy such sexual assurance. Women are puzzled by male unease, by men's continual attempts to prove their manhood or ritualistically affirm it. Judith Hole and Ellen Levine, in the *Rebirth of Feminism*, show typical female complacency when they call sexual identity "an almost immutable fact," like "the location of one's head." Seymour Fisher's elaborate research of female sexuality for the National Institute of Health confirms this greater security of women: "It was my conclusion, after reviewing all available studies," Fisher writes, "that the average woman is more 'at ease' with her own body than is the average man. . . . Her body 'makes sense' to her as one of the prime means to become what she wants to become." This assurance about sexual identity leads to a certain impatience with men.

Throughout the literature of feminism there runs a puzzled complaint: "Why can't men *be* men and just relax?" The reason is that, unlike femininity, relaxed masculinity is at bottom empty, a limp nullity. While the female body is full of internal potentiality, the male is internally barren (from the Old French *bar*, meaning man). Manhood at the most basic level can be validated and expressed only in action. A man's body is full only of undefined energies—and all these energies need the guidance of culture. He is therefore deeply dependent on the structure of the society to define his role. In all its specific expressions, manhood is made, not born. . . .

Man's Sexual Insecurity

In general, therefore, the man is less secure sexually than the woman because his sexuality is dependent on action, and he can act sexually only through a precarious process difficult to control. Fear of impotence and inadequacy is a paramount fact of male sexuality. For men the desire for sex is not simply a quest for pleasure. It is an indispensable test of identity. And in itself it is always ultimately temporary and inadequate. Unless his maleness is confirmed by his culture, he must enact it repeatedly, and perhaps destructively for himself or his society. Particularly in a society where clear and affirmative masculine activities are scarce, men may feel a compulsive desire to perform their one unquestionable male role. It is only when men are engaged in a relentless round of masculine activities in the company of males—Marine Corps training is one example—that their sense of manhood allows them to avoid sex without great strain.

Under most conditions, young men are subject to nearly unremitting sexual drives, involving their very identities as males. Unless they have an enduring relationship with a woman—a relationship that affords them sexual confidence—men will accept almost any convenient sexual offer. This drive arises early in their lives, and if it is not appeased by women it is slaked by masturbation and pornography. The existence of a semi-illegal, multibillion-dollar pornography market, almost entirely male-oriented, bespeaks the difference in sexual character between men and women. One can be sure that if women passionately wanted porn, it would be provided. Though sexual liberals have denied it so often as to thoroughly confuse each sex about the feelings of the other, the fact is that women lack the kind of importunate, undifferentiated lust that infects almost all men.

"Only the woman has a dependable and easily indentifiable connection to the child."

This view is strongly confirmed by a cross-cultural study of 190 different societies made by Clellan S. Ford and Frank A. Beach. Males almost everywhere show greater sexual aggressiveness, compulsiveness, and lack of selectivity. Over the whole range of human societies, men are overwhelmingly more prone to masturbation, homosexuality, voyeurism, gratuitous sexual aggression, and other shallow and indiscriminate erotic activity. Male sexuality is a physical drive and a psychological compulsion. This voracious need can rise to a pitch at the slightest provocation; it demands nothing but an available body; at its height it aspires less to a special love than to an orgiastic rut.

Women's Sexual Security

In virtually every known society, sex is regarded either as a grant by the woman to the man or as an object of male seizure. In most societies, the man has to pay for it with a gift or service. Although women are physiologically capable of greater orgasmic pleasure than men—and thus may avidly seek intercourse—they are also much better able to abstain from sex without psychological strain. In the United States the much greater mental health of single women than single men may be explained in part by this female strength. But greater sexual control and discretion—more informed and deliberate sexual powers—are displayed by women in all societies known to anthropology. Indeed, this intelligent and controlled female sexuality is what makes human communities possible.

This difference between the sexes gives the woman the superior position in most sexual encounters. The man may push and posture, but the woman must decide. He is driven; she must set the terms and conditions, goals and destinations of the journey. Her faculty of greater natural restraint and selectivity makes the woman the sexual judge and executive, finally appraising the offerings of men, favoring one and rejecting another, and telling them what they must do to be saved or chosen. Managing the sexual nature of a healthy society, women impose the disciplines, make the choices, and summon the male efforts that support it.

The Foundation of Civilization

Modern society relies on predictable, regular, long-term human activities, corresponding to the sexual faculties of women. The male pattern is the enemy of social stability. This is the ultimate source of female sexual control and the crucial reason for it. Women domesticate and civilize male nature. They can jeopardize male discipline and identity, and civilization as well, merely by giving up the role.

"Males almost everywhere show greater sexual aggressiveness, compulsiveness, and lack of selectivity."

The female responsibility for civilization cannot be granted or assigned to men. Unlike a woman, a man has no civilized role or agenda inscribed in his body. Although his relationship to specific children can give him a sense of futurity resembling the woman's, it always must come through her body and her choices. The child can never be *his* unless a woman allows him to claim it with her or unless he so controls her and so restricts her sexual activity that he can be sure that he is the father. He cannot merely come back nine months later with grand claims. He must make a durable commitment.

Even then he is dependent on the woman to love and nurture his child. Even in the context of the family, he is sexually inferior. If he leaves, the family may survive without him. If she leaves, it goes with her. He is readily replaceable; she is not. He can have a child only if she acknowledges his paternity; her child is inexorably hers. His position must be maintained by continuous performance, sexual and worldly, with the woman the judge. The woman's position, on the other hand, requires essentially a receptive sexuality and is naturally validated by the child that cannot ordinarily be taken away. The man's role in the family is thus reversible; the woman's is unimpeachable and continues even if the man departs.

The man's participation in the chain of nature, his access to social immortality, the very meaning of his potency, of his life energy, are all inexorably contingent on a woman's durable love and on her sexual discipline. Only she can free the man of his exile from the chain of nature; only she can give significance to his most powerful drives.

The essential pattern is clear. Women manipulate male sexual desire in order to teach men the long-term cycles of female sexuality and biology on which civilization is based. When a man learns, his view of the woman as an object of his own sexuality succumbs to an image of her as the bearer of a richer and more extended eroticism and as the keeper of the portals of social immortality. She becomes a way to lend continuity and meaning to his limited erotic compulsions. . . .

Without a durable relationship with a woman, a man's sexual life is a series of brief and temporary exchanges, impelled by a desire to affirm his most rudimentary masculinity. But with love sex becomes refined by selectivity, and other dimensions of personality are engaged and developed. The man himself is refined, and his sexuality becomes not a mere impulse but a commitment in society, possibly to be fulfilled in the birth of specific children legally and recognizably his. His sex life then can be conceived and experienced as having specific long-term importance like a woman's.

Obviously the most enduring way to make this commitment is through marriage. . . .

The Role of Marriage

Marriage is not simply a ratification of an existing love. It is the conversion of that love into a biological and social continuity. The very essence of such continuity is children—now fewer than before, but retained far longer within the family bounds. Regardless of what reasons particular couples may give for getting married, the deeper evolutionary and sexual propensities explain the persistence of the institution. All sorts of superficial variations—from homosexual marriage to companionate partnership—may be played on the primal themes of human life. But the themes remain. The natural fulfillment of love is a child; the fantasies and projects of the childless couple may well be considered as surrogate children.

A man without a woman has a deep inner sense of dispensability, perhaps evolved during the millennia of service in the front lines of tribal defense. He is sexually optional. Several dominant males could impregnate all the women and perpetuate the tribe. It is this sense of dispensability that makes young men good fighters, good crusaders, good martyrs. But it also weakens the male ability to care deeply and long and stunts young men's sense of the preciousness of human beings. Because the woman has always been directly responsible for infants and almost always exclusively responsible, she is dubious about the dying and killing that have surrounded male activities.

Once the man marries he can change. He has to change, for his wife will not long have him if he remains in spirit a single man. He must settle his life, and commit it to the needs of raising a family.

He must exchange the moral and spiritual rhythms of the hunt for a higher, more extended mode of sexual life. He must submit, ethically and sexually, to the values of maternal morality and futurity.

Marriage and Society

When the man submits to female sexuality, therefore, he not only adopts an ethic of long-term responsibility for the life and death matters of his own children's upbringing but he also adopts a new perspective on life and death itself. His life is no longer so optional, because his wife and children depend on him. Thus individual life assumes a higher value within the monogamous marriage than it does in a male group.

As a social institution, marriage transcends all individuals. The health of a society, its collective vitality, ultimately resides in its concern for the future, its sense of a connection with generations to come. There is perhaps no more important index of the social condition. It is the very temperature of a community. A community preoccupied with the present, obsessed with an immediate threat or pleasure, is enfevered. A social body, like a human body, can run a very high fever for short periods in order to repel a specific threat or to meet an emergency, a war or domestic crisis. But if it finds itself perpetually enfevered, it begins to run down and can no longer provide for the future. Its social programs can fail to work, its businesses can fail to produce, its laws can become unenforceable. The will and morale and community of its people can founder. A society, apparently working well, can stand impotent before its most important domestic and external threats and opportunities. . . .

"Women domesticate and civilize male nature."

The ideology of the sexual liberationists sees society as a male-dominated construct that exploits women for the convenience of men. In evidence, they cite men's greater earning power, as if economic productivity were a measure of social control rather than of social service. But it is female power, organic and constitutional, that is real—holding sway over the deepest levels of consciousness, sources of happiness, and processes of social survival. Male dominance in the marketplace, on the other hand, is a social artifice maintained not for the dubious benefits it confers on men but for the indispensable benefits it offers the society: inducing men to support rather than disrupt it. Conventional male power, in fact, might be considered more the ideological myth. It is designed to induce the majority of men to accept a bondage to the machine and the marketplace, to a large

extent in the service of women and in the interests of civilization.

Any consideration of equality focusing on employment and income, therefore, will miss the real sources of equilibrium between the sexes. These deeper female strengths and male weaknesses are more important than any superficial male dominance because they control the ultimate motives and rewards of our existence. In childbearing, every woman is capable of a feat of creativity and durable accomplishment—permanently and uniquely changing the face of the earth—that only the most extraordinary man can even pretend to duplicate in external activity.

The Economy of Eros

Women control not the economy of the marketplace but the economy of eros: the life force in our society and our lives. What happens in the inner realm of women finally shapes what happens on our social surfaces, determining the level of happiness, energy, creativity, morality, and solidarity in the nation.

These values are primary in any society. When they deteriorate, all the king's horses and all the king's men cannot put them back together again.

George Gilder is a conservative economist and social critic whose books include Wealth and Poverty *and* Sexual Suicide.

"The achievement of manhood [is] defined by . . . the extent and success of man's domination of woman as wife, as supporter, as servant, but primarily as sexual object/victim."

Gender Roles Are Oppressive

Haunani-Kay Trask

It is through a radical exploration of women's hidden body—the body of flesh and feeling, the body of insight and imagination, the body of material and symbolic reality—that contemporary feminists have come to define the causes of women's subordination to men. In the eloquent brevity of Adrienne Rich, female oppression is grounded in

> . . . the *sexual understructure* of social and political forms . . . a familial-social, ideological, political system in which men,—by force, direct pressure, or through ritual, tradition, law and language, customs, etiquette, education, and the division of labor determine what part women shall or shall not play, and in which the female is everywhere subsumed under the male.

Crucial to Rich's understanding is the notion of an inclusive system of power founded in the primacy of men, as a group, over women, as a group. This system has been called patriarchy. But here, patriarchy does not signify merely the power of the father, as in Freud's symbolic anthropology or in recent feminist works. Rather, patriarchy conveys the power of an entire sex-based class, men, over another sex-based class, women. And it is sexuality and sexual institutions, as Catharine MacKinnon has noted, that are the "primary social sphere" of male power.

Patriarchy and Sex

Such a sense of patriarchy allows for matrilineal and patrilineal descent, for differences in economic and technological development, for changing ideals, symbols, and myths regarding women. There is, in other words, the conception of "nature, law, the family, and roles as consequences not foundations" of women's subordinated state. The essential characteristic is the pervasive power of men over

women's sexuality. . . .

The "sexual understructure" is nothing but the forced exchange of women "mined for their natural resources (sex and children)." Fraternal organization leads to military organization *for the purposes of rape.* Patriarchy ("politics") as brutal domination ("gang bang"); sexuality as violation, love as domination; sexual politics. Eros (love-life, symbolized by sex) is perverted by Thanatos (aggression-death, symbolized by war). The battleground of patriarchy *is* the body of woman.

Rape and Male Power

In her monumental history of rape, Susan Brownmiller recounts the "deadly serious" game of patriarchy, locating the *original* act of subjugation in man's violation of woman's body. Behind the social contract, the tribe, the brotherhood, is rape, the first and most basic expression of "power over."

> It seems eminently sensible to hypothesize that man's violent capture and rape of the female led first to the establishment of a rudimentary mate-protectorate and then sometime later to the full-blown male solidification of power, the patriarchy. As the first permanent acquisition of man, his first piece of real property, woman was, in fact, the original building block, the cornerstone, of the "house of the father." Man's forcible extension of his boundaries to his mate and later to their offspring was the beginning of his concept of ownership. Concepts of hierarchy, slavery, and private property flowed from and could only be predicated upon the initial subjugation of woman.

Brownmiller [has] taken the pulse of patriarchy: fraternal organization and the achievement of manhood are defined by, and depend upon, misogyny; upon the extent and success of man's domination of woman as wife, as supporter, as servant, but primarily as sexual object/victim. Thus the reality of man's hatred and fear of women is told through the record of patriarchal crime—sexual slavery, incest, clitoridectomy, infibulation,

Haunani-Kay Trask, *Eros and Power: The Promise of Feminist Theory.* Philadelphia, PA: University of Pennsylvania Press, 1986. Reprinted with permission.

footbinding, prostitution, witch hunts, child molestation, even rape within marriage. The sexual understructure is protected by patriarchal violence.

Exogamy

The link between exogamy and rape is clear. Given its origins and purposes, exogamy means much more than kinship. For women, exogamy is a regulated form of transfer of their bodies and its products. Beyond the mate-protectorate, exogamy simply means that a certain man has exclusive rights to the body of a certain woman. The fundamental, social significance of these rights accounts for the definition of rape (customary and legal) as a crime of property rather than a crime of violence. Historically, rape has never been viewed as a violation of the person. It has always been seen as a violation of one man's property (woman) by another man. This, and not money or land, explains why marriage is a property relationship. Institutionally, marriage has protected a man's right to his wife's body. Historically, marriage is but one socially acceptable form of rape.

"Historically, marriage is but one socially acceptable form of rape."

In anthropological terms, the impact of the exchange of women, their objectification as gifts, is clear: men control women, sexual dominion is anchored in social structure. Lévi-Strauss has argued: "The reciprocal bond basic to marriage is not set up between men and women, but between men and men by means of women, who are only the principle occasion for it." The relationship between women and men is that between gift and giver, object and owner. Regardless of women's valuation (and women are enormously valued because they reproduce the species), they remain the *objects* of exchange. In terms of power, the relationship between men and women is forever unequal, freighted with oppression; it is the ancient bondage between ruler and ruled. . . .

A Prized Possession

And so it is that women are the lifeblood of a people, their magical symbols of immortality. Women are defined and confined by their power to bring forth. Before the discovery of paternity, woman was the only certain source of life. Once paternity was known, she became the most prized possession of men. On women's place in agrarian societies, sociologist Meda Chesney-Lind has written:

> They are used to form alliances between different patriarchal units and produce progeny for these particular kinship groups. Thus, in settled agrarian society, women's childbearing capacity dictates their

status. . . . Women became, in a sense, sexual property within an almost universal patriarchal system.

This function does not alter in industrial societies, despite the family's changed structure (from extended to nuclear) and diminished productivity (from a center of production to a center of consumption). Thus, in linking groups and ensuring heirs, women are enslaved to the species.

Institutionalized Motherhood

And this enslavement is culturally instituted. Despite the obvious burdens of maternity, woman's bondage to man is only facilitated, not foreordained, by her biology. Painfully, woman's historic condition reflects a pool of oppression. Subordination is blatant (as in institutional oppression—exclusive female child-care), yet insidious (as in psychological oppression—over dependence). From infancy, socialization processes point to motherhood as the supreme aim of woman's life. Religion, popular mythology, and the language of patriotism nourish an "inevitable" choice. Finally, through a confluence of forces—legal, economic, and educational discrimination; sociopolitical exclusion; ideological justification—motherhood becomes an institutional reality. "Biological" mothering *engenders* "emotional" mothering: an anguished because unrelieved source of love and self-sacrifice for the child, the man, the nation. Adrienne Rich has pointed out:

> Institutionalized motherhood demands of women maternal "instinct" rather than intelligence, selflessness rather than self-realization, relation to others rather than the creation of self. . . . Patriarchy would seem to require, not only that women shall assume the major burden of pain and self-denial for the furtherance of the species, but that a majority of that species—women—shall remain essentially unquestioning and unenlightened. On this "underemployment" of female consciousness depend the morality and the emotional life of the human family. . . .

The deplorable effect is that strong women are rendered psychologically and economically dependent. In patriarchal culture, strength is destructive, dependence crippling. But in the mother's relationship with the child, strength is generative, dependence supportive. There is an essential conflict between the mother-child unit, and the larger patriarchal family of which it is part. Under a system of sexual dominion, repudiation of our "mother" values is necessary for the embrace of our "father" values. . . .

The connection between parental conflict, the legacy of each new generation of mothers and fathers, and the persistence of exogamy is clear. As long as women are exchanged, the "kingdom of the fathers"—the public realm—passes to the sons. The "sacred calling of the mothers"—the domestic realm—is bequeathed to the daughters. The sexual division of labor, writ large, is precisely this division between the "kingdom of the fathers" and the "sacred calling of the mothers." In sociological terms, exogamy reveals that women are not *true* inheritors; they serve only as the bloodline *between* inheritors.

Western Civilization

For many anthropologists, exogamy is the cornerstone of Western civilization, the basic organizational form from which all other cultural forms radiate. If this is accurate, then exogamy enables Western civilization. Rephrased: without the objectification, sexual constraint, and systematic exchange of women, Western civilization would be impossible. Freud's theory recapitulated in Lévi-Strauss's anthropology: the oppression of women is necessary for Western civilization.

But the question remains: What kind of civilization? If it is true that women are *always* subordinated to men, that social authority always belongs to men, then Western civilization, *as we know it,* has been patriarchal. Therefore, the wellsprings of patriarchy must be the grounding of this civilization. Sexual dominion, the power of men over women, is not merely an agent of culture, it is the origin and conduit of culture. . . .

While no single cultural form can be said to supersede all others in significance, the sexual division of labor approaches central importance. For here, where tasks and achievements divide between the sexes, differences come to have unequal consequences, and thereby exaggerated expression.

"Woman's bondage to man is only facilitated, not foreordained, by her biology."

Because of tremendous cultural diversity in the actual tasks assigned by sex, anthropologists generally agree that it is the *fact* of the sexual division of labor, rather than its specific form, which is required by human groups. According to Lévi-Strauss, "the sexual division of labor is nothing else than a device to institute a reciprocal state of dependency between the sexes."

Power Imbalance

Considering men's primary cultural status and the psychological effects of inequality, Lévi-Strauss's claim of reciprocity is doubtful. Men and women may need each other, and this need may be elaborated and justified through the division of labor, but the uneven social valuation which attaches to labor arrangements renders any judgment of reciprocity false. Moreover, the anthropological definition of reciprocity (an exchange of equally

valued objects) does not apply between men and women. Reciprocity applies only between men, because they are the exchangers of women. . . . The resulting power imbalance precludes true reciprocity in all but the most creative and "care-full" of relationships. Thus is the division of labor, like wisdom and love, everywhere unequally valued for men and for women. Margaret Mead argues: "One aspect of the social valuation of different types of labor is the differential prestige of men's activities and women's activities. Whatever men do—even if it is dressing dolls for religious ceremonies—is more prestigious than what women do and is treated as a higher achievement."

Enforcing Heterosexuality

But if the state of dependency is hardly reciprocal between the sexes, the resulting socioeconomic unit of one woman and one man does serve a particular organizing purpose. The sexual division of labor splits the sexes into exclusive categories (GENDER) while forbidding same-sex unions (HOMOSEXUALITY). The argument has been constructed by Gayle Rubin. In tracing the logic of the organization of sexuality, Rubin notes that homosexuality is not simply prohibited, nor is heterosexuality simply encouraged. Specific cultural forms appear in considerable variety, such as cross-cousin marriage, mandatory (but temporary) homosexual unions, bridewealth (which enables both men and women to take same-sex spouses), and gender transformations replete with cross-sex privileges. Despite variations, however, the norm is everywhere protected: exclusive gender divisions and heterosexual unions. The protection of those norms suggests that they are far from naturally occurring products of our biology. Needing the cultural reinforcement of the sexual division of labor, they appear to be carefully ensured social prescriptions. "If biological and hormonal imperatives were as overwhelming as popular mythology would have them, it would hardly be necessary to insure heterosexual union by means of economic interdependency."

Rubin's insight points to the related nature of patriarchal imperatives. The sexual division of labor (particularly female child-care) exacerbates biological differences between the sexes, thus creating gender. In turn, gender identifies the sexes as separate yet complementary. Not only is heterosexuality ensured, but homosexuality is proscribed. . . .

Repressing Personality

Psychologically, the command of exclusive gender identity necessitates the repression of natural similarities and an exaggeration of natural differences. In terms of personality development and expression, this means a denial of "feminine" behavior in men and "masculine" behavior in women, however these categories are culturally defined.

> The division of the sexes has the effect of repressing some of the personality characteristics of virtually everyone, men and women. The same social system which oppresses women in its relations of exchange, oppresses everyone in its insistence upon a rigid division of personality.

The *social* rule of gender division creates the *psychological* rule of personality division. Patriarchal social organization is supported by repressive psychologies in both women and men. Polarized and unequal personalities (gender) facilitate internal control, safeguarding the patriarchal order more effectively than any external force....

Women's Oppression

Rubin and [Juliet] Mitchell have suggested that the domination of men, and the socioeconomic and psychic oppression of women are directly traced to the organization of human sexuality. Biology is transformed by the sexual division of labor, currently expressed through the modern nuclear family. Psychically, the enculturation of the human infant involves a complicated unconscious journey (pre-Oedipal and Oedipal stages) which occurs under patriarchal conditions (asymmetrical parenting). These conditions and the consequent resolution of psychic processes are inherently oppressive to women, even while women's mediating function in civilization is valued.

"The sexual division of labor . . . exacerbates biological differences between the sexes, thus creating gender."

Structurally, exogamy guarantees the objectification and exchange of women and the sociopolitical authority of men. Meanwhile, the sexual division of labor (particularly institutionalized motherhood) reproduces exclusive and asymmetrical gender, thereby ensuring heterosexuality. "Masculine" and "feminine" identities are imprinted on our unconscious through the incest taboo, giving psychic force to cultural norms. Finally, women's sexuality is constrained lest the entire system collapse from a repudiation of men's power. Gayle Rubin has argued:

> From the standpoint of the system, the preferred female sexuality would be one which responded to the desire of others, rather than one which actively desired and sought a response.... What would happen if our hypothetical woman not only refused the man to whom she was promised, but asked for a woman instead? If a single refusal were disruptive, a double refusal would be insurrectionary. If each

woman is promised to some man, neither has a right to dispose of herself. If two women managed to extricate themselves from the debt nexus, two other women would have to be found to take their place. As long as men have rights in women that they do not have in themselves, it would be sensible to expect that homosexuality in women would be subject to more suppression than in men.

In the West, the roots of male control which Rubin describes attain their first growth within the triangle of the nuclear family. Apart from reproducing and socializing children, the family is the main form through which women participate in collective life. Here, the sexual division of labor appears as a justification for the restriction of women to certain tasks, reified as "domestic" contributions. Here too, women's erotic/reproductive characterization encourages their primary responsibility for the "emotional" life of family members. And as the public world becomes ever more impersonal and brutal (as Thanatos triumphs in the abuse of the environment, the slaughter of the weak, and the proliferation of destructive technology), the family beckons as a haven—tense, contradictory, and traumatic, but a haven nevertheless.

Consisting of two parents and their children, the family as we know it today is but the latest form of the sexual understructure. That is, social structure has evolved from extended kinship systems into relatively isolated nuclear units: the modern family.

The Two Realms

This historical change underlies the commonplace and scholarly observation that women's lives are defined by the family. The anthropological argument that women's sphere is primarily the domestic realm while men's sphere is primarily the public realm supports our larger social sense that women are attached to the family and invest more of their time and take more of their emotional and creative satisfaction from the family than men do. This is partly explained by women's historical responsibility for child-care, which occurs within the family (while the child-tending responsibility itself is explained by the sexual division of labor). But women's restriction to the family is also explained by their systematic and near total exclusion from authority and achievement in the public realm.

Nevertheless, the obvious perception of women's symbiotic association with the family tends to obscure the exact institutions responsible for women's oppressed, subordinate condition. The family is not the final cause of women's subjugation. Rather, the family is but the form, the shell which surrounds and enables the "sexual understructure."

Haunani-Kay Trask is a feminist author and professor of American Studies at the University of Hawaii, Manoa.

"Babies, male and female, arrive in the world with built-in differences that go beyond genitalia."

Male/Female Biological Differences Are Significant

Kathy Keeton

Chances are very good that the first thing anyone ever wanted to know about you was your sex. Boy or girl? For most of us, it's the first question that comes to mind when we hear of a pregnancy. After all, we need to know so we can tell what color crib sheets and sleepers to buy as gifts—or the value and type of fruit, jewels, or livestock to give, depending on your culture. But there's more to it than that. The very fact that we consider different gifts appropriate for boys and girls is a clue to our deeper purpose in asking the question. We expect the answer to temper our behavior and attitudes toward the child and our expectations of it.

I sense that a warning click sounded in some of your minds just then. Different expectations. Sexism, you're probably thinking. And you're partly right, because that's half the story. Every human culture fosters myths and attitudes about men and women that reinforce the status quo and help to mold individuals into roles that in the past served to keep the society stable. Obviously, many of these roles are outmoded today and long overdue for change. . . .

Biological Differences

As we break away from the old stereotypes, the attitudes and expectations we bring to the birth of a boy or girl in the future will undoubtedly change. But I want you to understand that even when all the social and professional barriers have fallen, the question "boy or girl?" will still have meaning. Our expectations, as I pointed out, are only half the story. Babies, male and female, arrive in the world with built-in differences that go beyond genitalia. Sex, even with the absence of sexism, affects the way each of us perceives the world and behaves in it. That's basic biology, not sexism. . . .

The study of biological and other sex differences is being carried out on many fronts by anthropologists and psychologists, who catalog human behavior, neuroscientists, who probe the brain, and endocrinologists, who trace the action of hormones in the body. It's still a very young science; its findings are often controversial. But in the past two decades, a clear theme has emerged: Every child is born with innate biases or preferences, predisposed to pay more attention to some sights and sounds than to others, to react to certain happenings more strongly, to learn some things more easily. And we can spot these biases even before babies outgrow their cribs. . . .

By the time he's four to six months old, a boy baby is more interested in looking at objects, geometric patterns, and blinking lights than at people's faces. He may smile for you when you coo and grin at him, but he'll smile just as readily at a brightly patterned mobile hanging over his crib. In contrast, a girl baby saves most of her smiles and baby-noises for faces that smile and make noises back to her. By about four months of age she can tell one person's face from another. (These are statistical averages. Few babies are going to fit these averages in all respects.)

Different Perceptions

As their senses mature, boys and girls begin to experience the same world in quite different terms. The same sounds appear much louder to her than to him, and she's more sensitive to touch, odors, and, possibly, taste. His eyesight is sharper in the light, while hers is more sensitive in the dark.

No infant, boy or girl, is independent enough to like being left alone. But in the secure presence of a parent or sitter, boys and girls do behave differently. The average girl spends more time smiling, playing, and interacting with the adult while the average boys crawls off to explore. As they get older, she talks more, and he makes more noise. He spends more time roughhousing and trying to dominate other boys. If new children join the playgroup, she's more likely to take an interest in them. He develops better mechanical and spatial skills, but she learns to read more quickly and speak more fluently.

As they grow, of course, children also get feedback from their parents and from the larger world. This is where those attitudes and expectations I mentioned earlier come in. And this socialization process, as psychologists call it, can exert quite different pressures on girls and boys. Every woman I know can remember hearing "that's a boy's toy" and "girls don't . . ." pronouncements. I certainly did. I know some of you must feel that your life has been shaped more by such influences than by your own inclination. But it's important to understand that you *did* come into the world with a unique agenda. Every child does. That's why boys and girls don't necessarily respond to social influences in the way we might expect.

Infant boys, for instance, get a lot more attention from their mothers than do baby girls. They get held, played with, talked to, and smiled at more than girls. So why do boys like objects more than faces? Why aren't *they* the ones who develop the more fluent speech? . . .

Every child sets up a novel pattern of interactions with the world. Each response she receives is filtered back through her perceptions, and classified and stored. The process is what we call *learning*, and it indelibly alters her growing brain, revamping nerve connections, adjusting chemistry, further biasing her future perceptions, values, sensibilities, thoughts, and behaviors.

The end result of this interaction for any child is a uniquely individual brain. And if the child is a girl, the result is a female brain that, on average, will be quite distinct from its male counterparts.

The Female Brain

Once again, I sense shudders among some of you reading this. Female brain. Female nature. I'll admit these concepts have been abused all too often, and we don't have to go far back in history for examples. The nineteenth-century craniologists and phrenologists collected human brains and measured them meticulously in their ludicrous efforts to prove the common wisdom that men were smarter than women (and European gentlemen smartest of all, of course). Much of this flourishing science of the Victorian era was pressed into questionable service to justify keeping women in their traditional places. Women's biology, it was said, made them too emotional and suggestible to vote or hold office, too delicate to participate in vigorous sports, and too frail of nerve to attend medical schools. . . .

These abuses of science make it easier to understand why early twentieth-century reformers

abandoned biology altogether and embraced the notion that society alone makes us what we are. In emotion, intellect, temperament, and behavior, they declared, we arrive in this world empty, all with the same capacity to be filled by education and training. It was a heady, progressive notion, and in practice I'm sure it was far more humane than the extreme and misguided version of biological determinism that preceded it. The early women's movement picked up the same theme: Men and women want, need, and value the same things. Give us the same opportunities and we'll make the same choices in work and lifestyle and accomplish the same things that men do.

Not the Same

The trouble with this idea is that it's wrong. It assumes that men and the institutions they've created are the human norm that women, once "liberated," will rise up to. It implies, for instance, that the legion of women now marching out of business schools should put on dress-for-success suits and fit right into the male corporate structure without making changes or disrupting business as usual. And it says that once the paths men have followed into science, math, and engineering careers are fully opened to women, equal numbers of women will flock at men's heels, settling into traditionally male jobs without causing a ripple.

"A female brain . . . will be quite distinct from its male counterparts."

But presenting our sons and daughters with exactly the same experiences—computer or piano lessons, soccer or ballet practice, astronomy clubs or babysitting—will not necessarily cause them to value and pursue the same careers, or to behave alike even if they enter the same fields. . . . It's time we recognize that girls and boys do *not* come into the world empty. They bring their unique abilities, or agenda. And if we want girls to enter eagerly into fields now dominated by men, we have to make it clear they they can manage corporations, manipulate genes, or design interplanetary space probes without mimicking the style or sensibilities of the men who preceded them.

Male and female brains—they are different, although not in ways the would support most of the sex stereotypes of the past. The distinction is certainly not one of intelligence, for the average female brain is as smart as the average male brain by whatever test we use to measure it. The difference lies in questions of values, interests, style, and motivation. Scientists have barely begun to figure out how and why, but throughout your lifetime you're going to hear a lot more about this research. I hope as you read these accounts of genes and hormones, brain circuitry and behavior, here and in the future, you won't fall into the old trap of thinking that "different" is a value judgment. "Different" does not mean "superior" or "inferior," and denying biology is not the way to shake off the myths that have accumulated about female nature. . . .

The Adam Principle

If you were raised with the biblical myth of Adam's rib you might still have the impression that women are afterthoughts, or variations recast from an original male theme. But the Bible got the story backward. The original human plan, body and brain, is female. Males are actually the makeovers. All mammalian life begins as female. Let me take you through the process and show you what we know about how an embryo—from its sex organs to its brain—ends up feminine or masculine. . . .

Two X chromosomes cause an embryo to begin developing as a female. An X and Y set in motion the development of a male. The egg always carries an X, so it's the X or Y contributed by the sperm that makes the difference. Notice how tentatively I said "set in motion the development of a male." The pairing of X or Y chromosomes is only the first step in a chain of events that has to go off smoothly in order to produce an individual we'd recognize as a male or female.

Every embryo starts life prepared to develop into a female. Within it are two clusters of cells that, left to themselves, will develop into ovaries. The job of the Y chromosome is to interfere with this feminine development plan and cause the embryonic clusters to develop into testicles. . . .

Once testicles have formed, they take charge of the masculinizing process, blocking development of another embryonic structure that would have become the womb and turning out testosterone, which spurs the development of sperm ducts and male sex organs.

So it takes a nine-month remodeling effort to make a male. Scientists call this the Adam principle— although it reverses the Adam and Eve tale. If anything interferes with the work of the H-Y antigen or the testosterone, the fetus reverts to its original female development pattern.

Now, all kinds of things can go wrong, with chromosomes, or the H-Y antigen, or hormones. An embryo may end up with only one sex chromosome, or multiple Xs or Ys. (An embryo with a single X can live, but a single Y cannot—another sign that the Xs carry the essential core of the human being.) Any one of tens of thousands of genes carried by the chromosomes may be defective, leaving the embryo with too much or not enough of various hormones, or even unable to use the hormones it makes. Sometimes the problem is not in the embryo itself.

The mother may use hormones or drugs that leave their mark on her growing child. . . .

There's much more going on here than who gets a penis or a womb. During the first few months of embryonic life a whole marvelous choreography commences as the heart begins to beat, the brain forms, nerve cells reach out for connections, tiny shoots stretch into limbs, and a recognizably human face takes shape.

"Denying biology is not the way to shake off the myths . . . about female nature."

The testosterone that begins to flood the male fetus at this stage stamps its mark not only on the reproductive organs but also on the developing brain. It may bias how belligerent the child will be, what hand he'll write with, how easily he learns to read, perhaps even whether he'll be attracted to male or female sex partners when he grows up. (Bias, remember, not preordain.)

Only twenty years ago those statements would have brought outraged cries of heresy from many scientists. Today, the evidence is overwhelming. That surge of testosterone during fetal life, and perhaps even in first three months after birth, virilizes certain pathways in the brain as it develops. If the hormone isn't there in sufficient proportions, the female plan reasserts itself over body and brain. Testosterone can actually be picked up by nerve cells and carried inside, where it may influence which genes are turned on, what proteins are produced, and thus perhaps how the cells grow and make connections. The issue that's still controversial is exactly what impact this hormonal stamping has on attitudes and behavior.

Animal Evidence

I'll tell you a little bit about animals first, because that's where the research began and it's also where the most dramatic evidence for inborn sex differences comes from. The links between hormones and behavior in animals have been growing stronger since the early part of this century, even before we began looking into the brain itself for physical clues. The strongest evidence comes from the fact that we can take female animals such as rats, guinea pigs, dogs, sheep, or monkeys and cause them to behave, sexually and otherwise, like males simply by injecting testosterone into them while still in the womb or during a critical period soon after birth. Males, likewise, can be made to act like females by castration before or shortly after birth.

If you inject testosterone into a pregnant rat or monkey early, while the external sex organs of the offspring are forming, you'll get hermaphrodites—chromosomal females with male sex organs and behavior. (This happens to some human females, too, and shortly I'm going to talk about what it does to them.) Later in the pregnancy or shortly after birth, the hormone injections will affect only behavior, not appearance. So what does a hermaphrodite or a "tomboy" rat or monkey act like? The most obvious change is in sexual behavior: these virilized females tend to position themselves for mounting, as males do, rather than crouching and presenting, as their sisters do.

But the hormone effects also show up in nonsexual behaviors, too. Perhaps it's hard for you to imagine that male and female rats have different personality traits and abilities that can be measured, but they do. Males are generally better at learning to run mazes. Females learn more quickly how to heed a warning signal that allows them to avoid electric shocks by running from one enclosure to another. And when you put female rats into large open spaces, they're more active and exploratory, less fearful than males. Hormones can cause shifts in all these behaviors. Female monkeys given testosterone before birth are judged tomboyish because they engage in more chasing, threatening, and rough-and-tumble play than do other females.

The Hypothalamus

Now for the brain itself. The strongest connections between prenatal hormones, the brain, and behavior have been found in an area of the brain where you might expect males and females to differ—the hypothalamus, a part of the limbic system or "emotional brain," which we share with all mammals.

"We can take female animals . . . and cause them to behave, sexually and otherwise, like males simply by injecting testosterone into them."

The hypothalamus is the master controller of our hormones. It stimulates the pituitary gland at the base of the brain to release hormones that regulate sperm or egg production, menstruation in women, sex hormone production, and sexual arousal. The hypothalamus also regulates body temperature, blood pressure, and appetite. This is the part of your brain responsible for that speechless, sweaty, heart-fluttering feeling of love at first sight or the adrenaline surge and rising blood pressure of fear or stress.

Some of the effects of testosterone on this part of the brain are hard to dispute, since they're necessary to run the different reproductive machinery of males and females. Before birth, for instance, testosterone resets the biological clock of the hypothalamus so that it will regulate hormone flows along a male schedule instead of in the cycling pattern of females. Testosterone also seems to affect nearby brain pathways that bias our sexual and courtship behaviors. And some scientists now believe it also biases our attentions, perceptions, aggression levels, social styles, and parenting tendencies. . . .

The Cerebral Cortex

So that's the hypothalamus. But what about the "higher" parts of the brain, the cerebral cortex, where learning and memory take place? Well, some of the most dramatic work that's happened there has been done with canaries. Now I realize the canary is even more removed from us on the evolutionary tree than are rats and other mammals, but it has a forebrain that's equivalent to our cortex. Only male canaries are supposed to sing, and males have clusters of nerve cells in their forebrains that are three to four times larger than the ones in females. But, as one may suspect, a dose of hormones will enlarge the clusters in the female's brain and suddenly she sings too.

A structural difference has also been found in the rat cortex, although it produces nothing as splendid as song. In rats, just as in humans, the cortex is divided into two hemispheres, right and left. The right hemisphere is thicker in males, the left in females. And this sex difference in the cortex can be altered with the same hormone doses that alter the hypothalamus.

I'm going to turn now to our own brains. Obviously it would be unthinkable to do these sorts of experimental hormone injections and brain transplants on human babies, so, as a consequence, our knowledge about *direct* links among hormones, brain structure or function, and our own behavior is more limited. What we do know can be divided into three catagories: First, we know some connections between prenatal hormone exposure and later behavior, without knowing the parts of the brain involved. Second, we know some actual physical differences between male and female brains, without knowing how the differences got there and what impact they have on behavior. We also have evidence that male and female brains process the same input through different pathways and with different efficiencies. And third, we've found some universally observed differences in the way men and women, on average, think and behave. . . .

First, how does our exposure to hormones in the womb influence our behavior? Since we wouldn't think of experimenting directly on people to find the answers, scientists have studied instead some of nature's own experiments—those in-between individuals we discussed earlier for whom fetal life didn't go normally.

The most valuable insights have come from girls with a genetic defect called adrenogenital syndrome that causes their own adrenal glands to churn out abnormally high levels of testosterone. Their exposure to this testosterone begins early in fetal life, so the girls are physically virilized to some degree. They usually have an incomplete penis or else very ambiguous sex organs. [Researcher John] Money and Anke Ehrhardt, a clinical psychologist who is now at Columbia College of Physicians and Surgeons, wondered whether this unusual exposure also influenced the girls' attitudes and behavior. (By the way, I'd better clarify here that all women produce testosterone, just as all men produce estrogen. The sex hormones were labeled male and female when they were first isolated in the 1920s, but it's quite misleading. The difference between normal men and women is not which hormones they secrete, but the ratios.)

Before 1950, the kind of behavioral study Money and Ehrhardt wanted to do wasn't possible. There was no treatment for these girls. The flood of testosterone continued to masculinize and distort their bodies, sometimes bringing them to puberty as early as three years of age. Since they couldn't grow up being treated like normal girls, it was meaningless to compare their attitudes and behavior with that of the other girls around them. In the United States today, however, such girls are usually diagnosed at birth. Drug treatments are available to prevent further virilization, their genitals are surgically feminized if necessary, and they're raised as normal girls. But their brains retain the testosterone imprint.

Tomboys

The result, Money and Ehrhardt found, was a group of girls who proudly regarded themselves as tomboys and were regarded as such by friends and families. They preferred athletic, outdoor play and competitive team sports that, until recently, were still considered the domain of boys. "They liked boys to permit them to play on their baseball, football, and other teams, but they did not become dominant or assertive to an extent that would not be tolerated by boys," Money wrote. They were not "assaultive or violent" but they weren't "timid in self-defense," either. They preferred jeans to dresses. "They neglected the dolls they possessed or else gave them away," he noted. They were either indifferent about or actively avoided "rehearsing parentalism in doll play and playing house with friends . . . and when they became older, baby-sitting." They envisioned themselves growing up to have independent careers, with roles as wives and mothers secondary. "In teenage they reached the

dating and romantic stage three to nine years later than their age mates," Money found. . . .

I want to say something about the word *tomboy*. I'm using it for the same reason John Money used it in this context. People know what you're talking about when you say it. But it's a misleading word. It implies there are exclusively male traits and exclusively female traits, and girls who display male traits are tomboys. That's a false dichotomy. As Money says, the only noninterchangeable abilities are that males can impregnate and the females can menstruate, gestate, and lactate. And you don't even have to do any of those to qualify as a man or woman. (Money thinks science will make even these roles interchangeable by the end of the century.) The traits we call tomboyish are really part of the normal range of female characteristics, and most of us who grew up that way suffered no disease. Adrenogenital children have a disease, but their preference for jeans and sports is not pathological. In fact, since every baby develops under the influence of a slightly different mix of hormones, that in itself may be the source of a lot of the individual variations in temperament we see in both men and women.

"We've found some universally observed differences in the way men and women, on average, think and behave."

But the question remains, just what do prenatal hormones do to our behavior? They certainly don't turn us into robots with preset responses to life. Life experiences may even erase their impact entirely. Ehrhardt has pointed out that some adrenogenital girls aren't tomboyish at all. Here's how Money and many others in the field of sex differences have come to think about hormones: Certain capacities such as the ability to learn a language, nurture our young, or fight when our life is endangered are wired into all humans as part of our genetic legacy. What hormones do is to adjust the "biostat," the thresholds at which some behaviors will be triggered in each individual. A key difference between the sexes is therefore the way similar behaviors are organized and elicited—for example, what catches our attention, what we respond to most, the range of our response, and its intensity, what we learn most easily.

We already know that prenatal hormones organize and sensitize our sex-related traits, the ones that are activated at puberty by a new surge of hormones. For instance, biological events that take place at the beginning of the second trimester of pregnancy determine whether you grow a beard or start to menstruate when you reach puberty. It's probable that some of our most fundamental behavioral traits are organized in the same way.

Money has come up with a list of *nine basic kinds of behavior* that can be related to hormonal changes. The list isn't set in concrete, and he's the first to say it may need to be revised as more research is done on us and our fellow primates:

1. High activity levels and expenditure of energy, especially in athletics and muscular work
2. Competitive rivalry and assertiveness, especially for "a higher rank in the dominance hierarchy of childhood"
3. Roaming and territory- or boundary-mapping or marking (perhaps seen in the way boy babies crawl off to explore)
4. Defense against intruders and predators.

These first four are more prevalent or more easily triggered in males.

5. Guarding and defense of the young
6. Nesting or homemaking
7. Parental care of the young

These second three are more prevalent or more easily triggered in females.

8. Male or female style of sexual rehearsal play
9. Method of sexual arousal (Dependence on erotic images is most prevalent in men, dependence on touch and physical stimulation in women.)

Aggression

This is a much more realistic way of looking at human nature than is dividing all our traits into two separate camps. Aggression, for instance, used to be considered a male trait (and by default women were considered passive). There's no question that men commit most of the mayhem in any culture, no matter what other nontraditional division of labors they've adopted. Even among the Tchambuli people of New Guinea, where anthropologist Margaret Mead found that the women fished and conducted business while their men danced, adorned themselves, and gossiped, men were still the headhunters. Men everywhere fight most of the wars, commit most of the murders.

Now we realize, however, that aggression is a potential the sexes share. What makes men and women different is the sort of provocation they'll respond to, and the intensity and duration of their rage. Men are much more likely than women to get worked up to fighting level over honor, tradition, or territory. Start a far-off war or invoke the honor of long-dead patriots, and young men will flock to recruiting stations to get their share of the glory. Make the threat personal, to child or loved one, and woman can react with violence as fierce as any man's. . . .

Now the second area we know something about is actual physical differences between men's and women's brains. There are structural differences, although we don't know how they develop. And there are also differences in the ways male and female brains function. Circumstantial evidence seems to point to these differences to account for women's advantage in verbal ability, social savvy, and intuition, and for men's superior mechanical and spatial skills.

"Circumstantial evidence seems to point to these [brain] differences to account for women's advantage in verbal ability, social savvy, and intuition, and for men's superior mechanical and spatial skills."

I am referring to the largest portion of our brains, the cerebral cortex. This is the "thinking" part of the brain, the seat of mind and consciousness. The cerebrum is divided into two hemispheres, right and left, connected by a large bundle of nerves called the corpus callosum. I'm quite sure you've heard popular accounts about right brain/left brain differences; that is, men are right-brained, women, left-brained. Well, it's not that simple at all. The package just doesn't fit together that way. Every normal person uses both sides of the brain for almost every intellectual or perceptual process. (Jerre Levy, who's been in the forefront of this work for many years, says that the "reality of the human brain . . . is contentious, misleading, complex, and flirtatious." I think she said it with more awe than frustration because it's a marvelous puzzle on which to spend a lifetime.). . .

Our basic understanding of how the right and left brain operate came out of the work of Nobel Laureate Roger Sperry and his group, including Levy, at the California Institute of Technology in the 1960s. To test the competencies of each hemisphere, the team used a machine that separated the field of vision so that the left eye was presented with a different image than the right. The left eye sends its input to the right hemisphere, the right eye to the left. To make sure they were testing the talents of each side of the brain individually, the researchers worked with so-called split-brain patients. These were people whose corpus callosa had been surgically severed in a last-ditch effort to relieve devastating epileptic seizures. Their hemispheres couldn't "talk" to one another, so during the test each side of the brain was on its own.

From the results a *basic theory* emerged: In almost all right-handers and two-thirds of left-handers, the left brain specializes in speech and language, the understanding of symbols and abstract complexities. It is rational, analytical, and attentive to detail. The right brain specializes in visual-spatial tasks, including rapid pattern analysis, but it's also good at recognizing melodies, interpreting tone of voice, recognizing faces, "getting" jokes, and appreciating metaphor. It is intuitive and holistic, specializing in synthesizing things into global form.

Much has been learned since then, especially from newer tests using normal individuals whose right and left brains interact. Levy, who is now at the University of Chicago, says that it now seems possible that each hemisphere may have both analytic and synthetic skills. The two sides of the brain may split up the work based on the nature of the task at hand. Under this theory, the work of detailed analysis would be assigned to the hemisphere that's not able to put together the big picture. For instance, when Levy used verbal test material, no matter which side of the brain received it, "it was the normal left hemisphere that manifested holistic processing. The right hemisphere exhibited feature-by-feature analysis." If the incoming information were spatial, then presumably the left side would pick apart the details while the right side put together "the emergent synthesis.". . .

Sex Differences

When we try to figure out the differences in how male and female hemispheres operate, the puzzle becomes even more complex. Sex differences do show up in the kinds of experiments I've just described. The pattern of electrical activity and blood flowing through the brain while a man or woman is performing various tasks is different. The results could reflect variations on how specialized each hemisphere is, what functions each side is best at, the speed with which each side processes information, or how closely the right and left hemispheres work together in men and women.

Levy proposed more than a decade ago that a woman's brain may be less "lateralized," less tightly organized than a man's. In other words, verbal functions like speaking and understanding what others say aren't centralized in a single area of women's brains the way they are in men's. This could explain why men are more likely than women to lose their ability to speak coherently after a stroke on the left side of the brain, or to suffer deficits in spatial ability after the right side is damaged.

The major sex difference that's been found in the structure of the human brain also fits nicely with the possibility that women's brains are less specialized and have greater integration and communication between the two sides than men's brains. A team of scientists reported just three years ago that the back end of the corpus callosum is broader and larger in women than in men, even before birth. The greater size of this nerve cable could indicate that women have more pathways for interaction between the hemispheres.

More recently, Levy has also suggested that men and women may use the same sides of their brains for different purposes. Each hemisphere may specialize in different skills for each sex. Men, for instance, excel at spatial tasks like rotating three-dimensional images in their heads and picturing what they look like on all sides. That's considered a right hemisphere specialty. Women's right hemispheres apparently aren't as specialized in this skill, but they appear to be more highly specialized than men's in understanding emotion and discerning the meaning of facial expressions. (Martin Safer, at Catholic University, suggests we may have another advantage in understanding emotion, too, because after our right brain has interpreted the image, it gets better help from our left side in putting a verbal label on it—happy, sad, angry. Perhaps this is why we're better able to put our own emotions into words, too.). . .

Another possibility is that the differences in our right and left brains may be the result of our experiences in the world. Of course that doesn't rule out the likelihood that prenatal hormones influence this process in an indirect way. Diane McGuinness, of Stanford University, proposes that inborn sex differences in the hypothalamus and the rest of the "emotional brain" bias our perceptions and the things that grab our attention, and thus influence what we learn.

"The pattern of electrical activity and blood flowing through the brain while a man or woman is performing various tasks is different."

"One of the functions of the brain is to sift out from all of the possible signals impinging on the senses those events that are most meaningful and useful," she says. "Therefore, if males and females have different inherent tendencies, or predispositions, they will pay attention to different events." And this takes us all the way back to babies in their cribs, the way they respond to people and objects, the way they perceive sound, touch, and odor, the way they choose to spend their time. I mentioned earlier that there's a third category of male/female differences we know something about but can't yet link directly to genes, hormones, or brain structures. I'm talking about widely observable differences in the values and interests of girls and boys, men and women—the kind that seem to start in the crib.

We don't even know what makes human beings social animals, so we certainly don't know where to look in the brain yet to see why girls enter the world more interested in people and social situations than are boys. "Where," McGuinness asks, "do we find the object/person distinction in the brain? Nobody can answer that question. What makes dogs, wolves, people, and chimpanzees need to live in social groups and develop complex structures of mutual aid and support? And leopards or solitary orangutans—why don't they like to live in groups? Where is that going on in the brain?"

This question is complicated by the fact that being "social" isn't a category of things that girls are and boys aren't. "Men need the buffering of the group, but they prefer to act somewhat more independently as long as that stability is in place," McGuinness notes. "Men *are* vulnerable. You take the support and the structure away and they seem to fall apart. They fall apart from divorce and bereavement more than women do. But once the social structure is in place they seem to have much less talent for really being in tune. For empathy. And we don't know why that is.". . .

"Men and women may use the same sides of their brains for different purposes."

She and other researchers are continuing to ask questions like these as they probe our brains and our behavior and examine anew questions like how our inherent emotions, including empathy, affect the development of our moral behavior. I'm excited by this work. I foresee great payoffs in terms of our self-understanding and self-respect.

Kathy Keeton is president and co-founder of Omni, *a monthly science magazine.*

"Although biology may influence behavior, neither genes nor hormones lead to specific actions in any simple, direct way."

Male/Female Biological Differences Are Exaggerated

Carol Tavris and Carole Wade

Of all the perspectives on sex differences and sex roles, perhaps none is as susceptible to oversimplification, distortion, and political misuse as the biological one. Consider, for example, these incidents:

1. In a talk to a college audience, James Neely, a surgeon turned self-appointed authority on sex differences, reviewed some complicated research findings on male-female brain differences. Physiology, concluded the doctor, equips men and women for specific kinds of work. Men's brains give them the analytic acumen to be lawyers. Women can do well at some professions too, but their brains also happen to suit them beautifully for housework.

2. Argentina's military junta launched an invasion of the Falkland Islands in a sovereignty dispute with Great Britain. British Prime Minister Margaret Thatcher immediately dispatched troops in a successful campaign to regain control of the islands. In the United Nations, Panamanian Foreign Minister Jorge Illueca, who supported the Argentines, got up to explain that Thatcher's belligerence could be attributed to "the glandular system of women."

3. In a book called *The Compleat Chauvinist*, Edgar F. Berman maintained that women are intellectually inferior and emotionally unstable. . . . Some sample chapter titles from his book: "The Brain That's Tame Lies Mainly in the Dame," "Testosterone, Hormone of Champions," and "Meno: The Pause That Depresses."

Biology and Politics

You can see why many people who hope for greater equality between the sexes are less than enthusiastic about the biological perspective. For centuries the sexual status quo was defended with arguments that women's inferior position was God-given or instinct-driven. Today, too, those who regard sex differences as natural and necessary are apt to feel that the basic features of femininity and masculinity are somehow wired in at birth, with experience playing only an auxiliary role. People's positions regarding biology and their political preferences are intertwined: Although some people who emphasize biology also advocate sex-role equality, a conservative position is more typical. And although some feminists emphasize and even extol the biological differences between men and women, most tend either to minimize sex differences or attribute them solely to social learning. . . .

Biological theorists trace sex differences to the brain, that unassuming, pinkish-gray, squishy mass of tissue where every thought, emotion, and nonreflexive act originates. However, different theorists approach sex differences in the brain from different angles and at different levels of analysis. They can be divided conveniently into four subgroups:

1. Sociobiologists, sometimes called Darwinian psychologists, are more interested in the evolutionary history of our species than they are in the firing of specific neurons or the flow of specific hormones. . . .

2. A second group, composed of endocrinologists, physiologists, physiological psychologists, and other researchers, focuses on how sex hormones produced before birth influence behavior and personality after birth. Their work includes laboratory experiments with animals and clinical observations of human beings who have prenatal hormone abnormalities.

3. A third group, also composed of both medical and social scientists, examines how sex hormones produced after the onset of puberty affect mood, behavior, and mental functioning.

4. Finally, a fourth group studies the brain itself.

Some researchers directly examine brain tissue taken from animals; others infer human sex differences in brain organization from people's performance on various perceptual or mental tasks. . . .

Sex Chromosomes

In human beings the female ovum and the male sperm each possess twenty-three chromosomes, threadlike bodies that contain genetic material. When ovum and sperm get together to form a fertilized egg cell, the result is forty-six chromosomes, aligned in twenty-three pairs. One of these pairs determines the sex of the embryo: it consists of an X chromosome from the mother and either an X or a Y chromosome from the father. The sex chromosome from the father determines the sex of the child. If he contributes an X, the child has two Xs and is a girl; if he contributes a Y, the child has an X and Y and is a boy. The X chromosome is much larger than the Y and carries more genetic material. . . .

"Findings from animal studies may or may not hold true for people."

The sexual differentiation of the embryo proceeds like a relay race, to use John Money and Anke Ehrhardt's simile. The first lap, at six weeks, is run by the genes. If the embryo is genetically male (XY), the testes begin to form; if it is genetically female (XX), the ovaries will appear a few weeks later. Once the testes or ovaries have developed, they take over for the second lap: The sex hormones that the gonads manufacture determine which set of internal reproductive structures and external genitals the embryo will have. In males the dominant sex hormones are called *androgens*. The most potent androgen is *testosterone*. In females the major sex hormones are *estrogen* and *progesterone*. Researchers used to think that these hormones belonged exclusively to one sex or the other, but now they know that everyone has some of each. Males produce some estrogen in the testes and adrenal glands, and females produce androgens in the ovaries and the adrenal glands.

Nature's plan, in a nutshell, is that the embryo will become a female unless two extra factors make it male. The first is the Y chromosome, which turns the embryo's unisex gonads into testes; if the Y is lost, the fetus will become a female with Turner's syndrome. The second is the male sex hormone testosterone. If the testes cannot produce this hormone, the result is not a neuter organism but one with female genitals. As far as endocrinologists can tell, the anatomical development of the female fetus does not require the female hormone. All that is necessary is the absence of male hormones.

Animal studies suggest that there is a second critical period, after anatomical gender has been determined, when the presence of testosterone influences the development of the brain. Experiments with rats and guinea pigs show that testosterone during this period affects the hypothalamus, which is responsible, among other things, for controlling the pituitary gland. In adults the pituitary gland in turn stimulates the ovaries to release eggs and secrete estrogen and the testes to produce androgens. It turns out that no matter what the original genetic sex of a rat happens to be, if it gets a dose of testosterone at the critical period (which for rats is during the first few days after birth) its brain will always be sensitive to male hormones and insensitive to female ones. If it does not get testosterone at this period, its brain later will be sensitive to female hormones. There are striking effects on the animal's sexual behavior.

In nonhuman primates, as in human beings, the critical period for sexual differentiation occurs before birth, so experiments have to be done with fetuses. In the early 1960s a group of researchers injected testosterone into pregnant rhesus monkeys and thereby produced "masculine" female offspring. These females, the researchers observed, threatened other monkeys more than normal females do; they initiated more rough-and-tumble play; they were less likely to withdraw when another monkey approached them; and their sexual behavior was much like that of males. Apparently rhesus monkeys are born with a hormonally determined predisposition toward certain sex-typed behaviors.

Of course . . . findings from animal studies may or may not hold true for people. Fortunately for science, it has been possible to make use of some of nature's errors to understand better the relative contributions of hormones and experience to human behavior.

Hermaphrodites

On rare occasions during fetal development, the hormone system goes wrong and produces a *hermaphrodite,* an organism that has both male and female tissue. True hermaphrodites have one ovary and one testicle, or a single organ containing both types of tissue. The external genitals are usually ambiguous in appearance—the individual has what could be a very large clitoris or a very small penis. (Remember that the genitals develop from the same original tissue in the embryo.) A *pseudohermaphrodite* has only one set of gonads—testes or ovaries—but its external genitals are either ambiguous looking or in actual conflict with its internal system. Thus it may have ovaries and a penis. True hermaphroditism is extremely rare in human beings; in this century only about sixty cases have been reported worldwide. Most of the cases in medical literature, including the ones to be described here, are pseudohermaphrodites. Following the practice of most writers on this subject, we will use the term *hermaphrodites* to refer to both kinds.

In genetically female human fetuses hermaphroditism usually occurs for one of two reasons. First, the female fetus may produce too much androgen because of a malfunction of the adrenal glands. This error occurs too late to affect the internal organs but in time to change the appearance of the genitals, and the baby is born with the *adrenogenital syndrome*. Doctors can suppress the further production of androgens after birth by administering cortisone. . . .

The Tomboy Survey

Money and Ehrhardt (1972) investigated a group of twenty-five hermaphrodites who were genetically female and who had undergone corrective surgery on their enlarged genitals and had been raised normally as girls. Those with the adrenogenital syndrome had received cortisone therapy as well. Money and Ehrhardt matched these androgenized girls, who ranged in age from four to sixteen at the time of the study, with a control group of normal girls who were similar in age, IQ, socioeconomic background, and race. They interviewed all the girls and their mothers and gave them many psychological tests.

Although the androgenized girls definitely considered themselves female, Money and Ehrhardt judged them more likely than the controls to regard themselves as tomboys, to play outdoor sports and games, to wear pants and shorts instead of dresses, and to prefer "boys' toys" to dolls. Most of the androgenized girls were unenthusiastic about babysitting and taking care of small children, and unlike the control girls they were more concerned about their future careers than with marriage. However, they were no more aggressive than the girls in the control group, and they showed no special pattern of cognitive skills. In general their behavior was not terribly unusual for little girls. Since the original report, some of the girls have grown up, married, and had children, and they have turned out to be good mothers.

As for the reported tomboyism, critics point out that Money and Ehrhardt relied heavily on interview data, which are notoriously susceptible to distortion and bias. True, the girls described themselves as tomboys and their mothers reported them to be very energetic and active. But we do not know whether an impartial observer would have noticed behavioral differences between the androgenized girls and the control girls. In addition, although the researchers attributed the self-reported tomboyism to a masculinizing effect of the male sex hormone on the fetal brain, upbringing could also have played a role. That is, the mothers of the androgenized girls may

have reacted to their energy with the attitude, "Well, yes, she's very active, but that's probably natural, considering the extra dose of androgen she got before birth," while the mothers of the controls may have discouraged the same behavior as too masculine.

Hermaphrodite Twins

Finally, in one other type of hermaphrodite study, researchers compare pairs of hermaphrodites who are born with the same physical condition but who are assigned to different genders. In one case the doctors and parents decide the child is to be reared as a boy; in the other they decide the child should become a girl. One child goes home in a blue blanket and the other in a pink one. If prenatal hormones are the strongest influence on gender identity, one of these decisions is right and the other is tragically wrong. But if environment is more critical, the success of either decision rests on the consistency with which the parents raise the child.

Money and Ehrhardt have described several such pairs. For example, two genetically female hermaphrodites, both born with the adrenogenital syndrome, had surgery early in life to correct their enlarged clitorises. But whereas one was feminized and raised as a girl, the other underwent "penis repair" and was raised as a boy. According to Money and Ehrhardt, both children grew up secure in their respective gender roles. The girl was somewhat tomboyish, but she appeared attractively feminine to those who met her. The boy was accepted as male by other boys and expressed a romantic interest in girls.

"Studies show that fetal hormones do not determine one's gender identity in any automatic way."

Such studies show that fetal hormones do not determine one's gender identity in any automatic way. Money and Ehrhardt, whose other work tended to demonstrate the power of prenatal hormones over environmental influences, wrote, "Matched pairs of hermaphrodites demonstrate conclusively how heavily weighted is the contribution of the postnatal phase of gender-identity differentiation. To use the Pygmalion allegory, one may begin with the same clay and fashion a god or a goddess.". . .

Examining Brains

All of the studies discussed so far have directly or indirectly sought sex differences in the brains of men and women. It is time to ask what these differences might be.

One way to approach this question is to examine

the brains of male and female organisms in the laboratory. Research using human brain tissue is just now beginning. In the first study to report a structural sex difference in the human brain, physical anthropologists Christine de Lacoste-Utamsing and Ralph L. Holloway (1982) dissected fourteen autopsied brains and found that a section of the tissue connecting the two cerebral hemispheres (the splenium of the corpus callosum) was larger and more bulbous in females than in males. This finding has been replicated with brains from human fetuses that ranged from 26 to 41 weeks of development. In another study a second difference has emerged. In the human brain the ratio of parietal cortex volume to frontal cortex volume is larger in the left hemisphere than in the right—and this left-right difference seems more pronounced in females than in males. . . .

"Most brain researchers emphasize that their speculations are just that."

Improved techniques may make it possible to study structural brain differences in living persons in the near future. However, except for the studies just described, the bulk of the direct research on the brain to date has been done with animals. Sex differences have been found in many brain regions, but they are concentrated in areas known to be involved in reproduction. Here are some of the key findings from this highly technical area:

1. Specific receptors for sex hormones exist in the cells of various brain regions in a number of species. When hormones pair up with receptors during a critical period in brain development, they direct nerve cell growth in ways that depend on the sex and species of the animal. The resulting nerve cell structures appear to be permanent. Curiously, in rats testosterone seems to influence brain development in a male direction after the hormone has been converted by the rat's body to estrogen, usually thought of as a female hormone. Sex hormones also influence the production of neurotransmitters, chemical messengers that allow brain cells to communicate with one another. Sex differences in amounts of neurotransmitters and neurotransmitter enzymes in rat brains have been reported by several researchers.

2. In male rats synaptic connections (connections among neurons) in the preoptic area of the hypothalamus are denser than in females.

3. When slices of brain tissue from the hypothalamus of a newborn mouse are treated with testosterone the cells produce more and faster-growing outgrowths.

4. Male rats have larger and more numerous nerve cells in the preoptic area of the hypothalamus than female rats do. But if you give females testosterone or castrate males shortly after birth they develop brain structures more characteristic of the other sex.

5. In male rats the right half of the cerebral cortex is significantly thicker than the left in most areas; in females the opposite tends to be true, though most of the left-right differences in thickness are not significant. But if you remove a female's ovaries at birth you can reverse the pattern, and if you castrate a male at birth reversal occurs in most of the cortical areas involved.

Lateralized Brains

In another approach to the study of brain differences, people do various perceptual or mental tasks, and from their performance the researcher infers what parts of their brains are most active or are working most efficiently. Several researchers believe that the brains of males are more *lateralized* than those of females; that is, they believe that when males do certain tasks they are more likely than females to rely on one side of the brain more than the other. For example, when different words are presented simultaneously to the two ears, right-handed people generally discriminate words presented to the right ear a bit more accurately—indicating superior word perception in the left hemisphere of the brain. In men, this right-ear advantage is reportedly stronger than it is in women. This particular sex difference has not shown up in studies of children, but another one, involving vision and the sense of touch, has. Right-handed children, aged six to thirteen, touched pairs of objects that were hidden from view, using the right hand for one object and the left for the other. The objects had meaningless shapes and could not be easily labeled. Then the children tried to pick the shapes out of a visual display. There were no sex differences in overall accuracy, but the boys did better with objects they had touched with their left hands (and presumably processed with their right hemispheres), while girls did equally well with both hands.

Such results could simply be due to differences in how hard males and females try on a particular task, or to differences in the strategies they use. But many brain researchers think the findings can be explained physiologically: Male brains are said to function more *asymmetrically* than female brains. In female brains, various perceptual processes are presumably represented more equally in the two sides of the brain. . . .

The apparent male-female difference in brain lateralization may be due to different rates of neurological maturation. Many researchers believe girls mature more quickly than boys, although the evidence on this is ambiguous. Lateralization takes many years to develop. If maturation begins earlier in girls it may also end earlier, and this may cut the lateralization process off sooner in girls than in boys. . . . However, the exact course of lateralization during childhood for *either* sex is a matter of scientific dispute.

Two Questions

Now for not one, but two, $64,000 questions:

1. Do anatomical sex differences in animal brains (and possibly in human brains) have anything to do with lateralization differences in human beings?

2. Do reported brain differences have anything to do with sex differences in verbal ability, mathematical ability, spatial-visual ability, cognitive style, temperament, or any other human trait or ability?

The answer is the same for both questions: *No one has the foggiest idea.* The brain findings are intriguing in their own right, but at this point no one is quite sure what they mean. What is the psychological implication of larger or smaller cells in the preoptic area of the brain, either for rats or for people? What are the advantages or disadvantages of a larger splenium in the corpus callosum? If lateralization is less complete in females, what difference does it make? Is lateralization good for people, bad, or beside the point?

Speculation vs. Fact

Like all creative scientists, researchers in this area have offered speculations that go beyond their data—some more freely than others. One hypothesis is that the two brain hemispheres communicate more rapidly and efficiently in women than in men because of lateralization differences. This could enhance a female's ability to integrate sensory information in complex situations and pick up details that men might miss or ignore. Men, in contrast, may be able to home in on just those items of information that are relevant for a particular problem, and ignore distractions. Why should these differences have developed? Possibly because they were needed for the specialized roles that males and females played in hunting-and-gathering times. Males presumably needed to focus in on spatial-visual tasks, such as computing the trajectory of a spear. Females presumably needed cognitive flexibility to respond quickly to five demanding children, a pig roasting on the fire, and sundry threats to her offspring. . . .

However, most brain researchers emphasize that their speculations are just that. They admit that the link between physiology and psychology is still missing—that connections between brain structure and sex differences in behavior or personality are, as [Jerre] Levy put it, "intuitive rather than scientifically proven." Unfortunately, though, it is the speculations rather than the careful caveats that tend to make headlines. Thus an article in *Science '82* proclaimed in a subtitle that sex differences "start in

the genes, trigger the hormones, shape the brain, and direct behavior"; another, in that venerable scientific journal *Cosmopolitan,* breathlessly began: "Flash: Authorities now say nature, *not* nurture, makes him thump and thunder while you rescue lost kittens and primp." Readers can easily get the mistaken impression that links between hormones, brain differences, and psychological or behavioral differences are established fact.

Evaluating the Biological Perspective

The evidence for some biological influence on some sex-typed behavior is substantial enough to warrant serious attention, even though the findings from animal studies are more conclusive than those from studies of people. Biological determinists make us confront the fact that biologically speaking, men and women are not exactly alike, and they probe the logically possible relations that may exist between biological and psychological differences. Their work reminds us that we are not disembodied minds.

However, although biology may influence behavior, neither genes nor hormones lead to specific actions in any simple, direct way. Cultural variability shows that our bodies are not straitjackets for personality. And research reveals that experience and learning can override biological factors to a remarkable degree: Hermaphrodites with the same physical condition can successfully be assigned to different genders. . . .

"Research reveals that experience and learning can override biological factors to a remarkable degree."

As a child develops, many interactions between biological potential and the environment are possible. Jacquelynne Parsons (1980) pointed out that neurological immaturity may make boy infants more irritable than girls. Adults may regard this behavior as naughtiness and even punish it; in response, boys may become aggressive. Or, because boy babies are born with stronger neck muscles than girls, adults may think they are stronger all over and handle them less gingerly; as a result, boys may become somewhat more active than girls, and eventually more aggressive. In other words, the way a particular biological attribute manifests itself in life depends on how a child is trained and treated by others. And conversely, life experiences affect the way neurons grow and connect with one another in the brain.

Looking for political and social implications in biological research is a little like reading tea leaves: You are apt to find whatever you are hoping for. Biological determinists are fond of pointing out that inborn spatial-visual differences might account for superior male performance in architecture and geometry. But then, why not leave the sewing to men, too? After all, following a dress pattern requires plenty of spatial-visual ability. Similarly, biological theorists often argue that because women have verbal skill and social sensitivity they are great at raising children and hosting cocktail parties. But might not these same skills make them top-notch politicians, journalists, ambassadors, and disarmament negotiators? . . .

Reductionism

Because all researchers tend to become immersed in the viewpoint of their own field, some biological researchers tend to exaggerate sex differences or even assume differences that have not been documented. Unfamiliar with the psychological literature, they busy themselves constructing theoretical mountains out of empirical molehills. Or, as we have seen, they leap from findings on brain cells to complex behavioral differences, a logically invalid approach known as *reductionism*. Biologists always say they recognize the importance of learning. But a scientist whose research is designed to show that hormones can make a female rat behave like a male, or a male rat behave like a mother, is naturally going to think that a biological approach to behavior is the most interesting and useful one. Similarly, most learning theorists say that of course biological dispositions matter, but a scientist whose research is designed to show that people are amazingly malleable depending on their experience or environment naturally tends to pooh-pooh biological arguments. Like the blind men who tried to describe an elephant, each of these research traditions is capturing just one piece of the total picture.

Carol Tavris and Carole Wade are professors at San Diego Mesa College. Their book The Longest War *examines the study of sex differences.*

Male Dominance Is Natural

Steven Goldberg

That anyone doubted it, was astonishing from the start. All experience and observation seemed to attest to the presence of core-deep differences between men and women, differences of temperament and emotion we call masculinity and femininity. All analyses of such differences were, it seemed obvious, empty or incoherent unless they saw the differences as related to substrative differences between men and women, differences that gave masculine and feminine direction to the emotions and behavior of men and women. The question to be answered, it seemed, was how these substrative differences manifest themselves on a social and institutional level—not whether the differences exist.

An Indefensible Hypothesis

Yet there it was. A generation of educated people was jettisoning the evidence of both experience and intellect in order to propound a clearly indefensible hypothesis: emotional and behavioral differences between men and women, and the social expectations associated with them, are primarily the result of environmental factors to which physiology is of little relevance. Proponents supported this view with arguments ranging from the confused to the misrepresentative. Individuals who are exceptions were invoked as somehow refuting the possibility of physiological roots of behavior, a maneuver that makes about as much sense as arguing that a six-foot-tall woman somehow demonstrates the social causation of height. Myths about matriarchies were introduced as historical evidence, an approach that would justify a belief in cyclopses. The primary argument supporting this view, an argument accepted even in college textbooks, was the

Published by permission from Transaction Publishers, "Reaffirming the Obvious" by Steven Goldberg, SOCIETY, Volume 23, No. 6, September/October 1986. Copyright © 1986 by Transaction Publishers.

argument that emotional and behavioral differences between men and women were caused primarily by socialization.

The central problem with this approach is that it does not explain anything; it merely begs the question: Why does not one of the thousands of disparate societies on which we have evidence reverse male and female expectations? Why does every society from that of the Pygmy to that of the Swede associate dominance and attainment with males? To say that males are more aggressive because they have been socialized that way is like saying that men can grow moustaches because boys have been socialized toward that end. There is no outside experimenter for society, setting up whatever rules seem desirable. Possible social values are limited by observation of reality; if male physiology is such that males have a lower threshold for the elicitation of dominance behavior, then social expectations denying this cannot develop.

Ten years ago it was not clear to all that there had never been a society reversing the sexual expectations I discuss. Social science texts, out of ignorance or tendentiousness, misrepresented ethnographic studies and asserted the existence of societies that reversed the sexual expectations. Recourse to the original ethnography on every alleged exception demonstrated beyond the possibility of reasonable dispute that not one of the thousands of societies (past and present) on which we have any sort of evidence lacks any of three institutions: patriarchy, male attainment, and male dominance.

Patriarchy

All societies that have ever existed have associated political dominance with males and have been ruled by hierarchies overwhelmingly dominated by men. A society may have a titular queen or a powerful queen when no royal male is available; there were more female heads of state in the first two-thirds of the sixteenth century than the first two-thirds of the twentieth. An occasional woman may gain the highest position in a modern state; the other eighteen ministers in Golda Meir's cabinet, and all other Israeli prime ministers, were male. In every society from the most primitive to the most modern—whatever the yardstick—it is the case that political dominance, in particular, and hierarchical dominance, in general, are overwhelmingly in the hands of men.

Whatever the nonmaternal roles that are given highest status—whichever these are and whatever the reasons they are given high status in any given society—these roles are associated with males. A modern example describes the situation that obtains in every society: if being a medical doctor is given high status (as in the United States), most doctors are male; if being an engineer is given high status and being a doctor relatively low status (as in the Soviet Union), then most engineers are male and most nonhierarchical doctors may be female. There are societies—although modern societies, by their nature, could not be among them—in which women perform objectively far more important economic functions while working harder and longer outside the home than do men. Indeed, save for political and hierarchical leadership, internal and external security, and nurturance of the young, every task is seen as male in some societies and female in others. However, in every society that which is given highest status is associated with men. It is tempting to explain this as a residue of male political dominance, but this view gets things backwards. Male roles do not have high status because they are male; nor do high-status roles have high status because they are male. Many male roles have low status and many low-status roles are male. High-status roles are male because they have (for different reasons in different societies) high status; this high-status motivates males to attain the roles—for psychophysiological reasons—more strongly than it does females (statistically speaking). Social expectations conform to limits set by this reality.

Male Dominance

The emotions of both males and females of all societies associate dominance with the male in male-female relationships and encounters. The existence of this reality is evidenced by the ethnographies of every society; the observations and statements of the members of every society; the values, songs, and proverbs of every society; and, in our own society, also by feminists who abhor this reality and incorrectly attribute it primarily to social and environmental causes. We might argue that in the family the women of some or all societies have greater power, attributable to either a male

abdication or a female psychological acuity that enables women to get around men. But the question relevant to universality is why both the men and women have the emotional expectation of a male dominance that must be gotten around.

The social sciences have discovered precious few nontrivial institutions that are both universal and sufficiently explicable with direct physiological evidence. The three institutions I discuss require explanation and this explanation must be simple. I mention this in anticipation of the inevitable, however wrongheaded, criticism that any physiologically-rooted theory is simplistic, determinist, or reductionist. Were we to attempt to explain variation in the forms of these institutions in physiological terms, an explanation would, in all likelihood, be simplistic. Physiology is in all likelihood irrelevant to differences between, say, American patriarchy and Arabic patriarchy. An explanation sufficient to explain the universal limits within which all variation takes place, if it is to be at all persuasive, requires a single factor common to, and imposing limits on, all societies that have ever existed. Indeed, the very extensiveness of the cross-cultural variation in most institutions emphasizes the need to explain why the institutions we discuss always work in the same direction. No reality is inevitable simply because it is universal, but when an institution is universal we must ask why. If the reason for universality is a physiological factor giving direction to the motivations that make us what we are, then we must entertain the possibility that the institution is an inevitable social resolution of the psychophysiological reality.

"All societies that have ever existed have associated political dominance with males."

It is not possible here to catalog the inadequacies of parsimonious nonphysiological explanation in a world that is replete with societies in which women work harder and longer outside the home at more economically important (but lower-status) tasks; in which male physical strength seems uncorrelated with male hierarchical dominance in human beings and in species ethologically and experimentally investigated; and in which modernization and technology affect the institutions we discuss in their form, but not significantly in their strength. (Modernization and technology set upper and lower limits on the strength of male dominance. No modern society could impose on women the limitations imposed by a traditional Moslem society or some primitive societies, nor is any modern society likely to give women the status they receive in certain primitive societies that accord very high status to the maternal role men cannot attain). Alternative explanations, while they correctly look below socialization for a nonquestion-begging factor, are internally illogical, discordant with the empirical evidence (ethnographic, experimental, and medical) or implausible in the extreme. They all simply ignore the enormous mass of direct physiological evidence. They also ignore the fact that plausibility would require we posit a physiologically-rooted explanation on the basis of the ethnographic evidence alone, even if we had no direct evidence of the physiological mechanism whatsoever.

The Physiological Evidence

The direct physiological evidence comes from the study of normal men and women, human hermaphrodites (whose behavior mirrors the sex of hormonalization when this conflicts with sex of anatomy and socialization, an extraordinarily difficult thing to explain without reference to physiology), and the experimental study of other mammals similar to us with respect to the system being studied. These latter studies are of the type routinely used to test food and drugs—research that few find objectionable until they dislike the implications of a particular line of research. These various lines of inquiry all indicate the same thing.

Differences between the male and female endocrine/central nervous systems are such that—statistically speaking—males have a greater tendency to exhibit whatever behavior is necessary in any environment to attain dominance in hierarchies and male-female encounters and relationships, and a greater tendency to exhibit whatever behavior is necessary for attainment of nonmaternal status. Using somewhat unrigorous terms, we might say that males are more strongly motivated by the environmental presence of hierarchy, by a member of the other sex, or by status to do what is necessary to attain dominance. It is irrelevant whether we conceptualize this as a lower male threshold for the release of dominance behavior, a greater male drive for dominance, a greater male need for dominance, or a weaker male ego that needs shoring up by attainment of dominance and status. It is the reality of the male-female difference that matters, not the model used to explain the difference that any model must explain. Likewise, it is irrelevant why our species (and those from which we are descended) evolved the psychophysiological differentiation; all that matters for an explanation of universality is that the differentiation exists.

No one has difficulty conceptualizing this in practice. We speak of the ''aggressive businessman'' and, to use examples of other tendencies, ''the maternal instinct'' and ''women's intuition.'' Many people seem to have trouble picturing the psychophysiological differentiation on a more abstract level. I suspect that this is owing to an unfortunate tendency to think in terms of a hydraulic analogy that sees people as containers of drives and emotions whose release is determined by various valve settings and channel widths. An analogy that much more clearly captures the role of environment as cue and arena for the physiologically-rooted tendency is the analogy of iron and a magnet. Iron does not have a need or drive to find a magnet, but it does have—built into its physical makeup—a tendency to respond to a magnet when there is one in the immediate environment. Similarly, the tendencies I discuss are best conceptualized as built-in tendencies to respond with particular emotions to specific environmental cues (hierarchy, a member of the other sex, status, an infant).

''Males are more strongly motivated by the environmental presence of hierarchy, by a member of the other sex, or by status to do what is necessary to attain dominance.''

Physiology does not determine the actual behavior required for dominance and attainment in any given society: that is socially determined. What physiology accounts for is the male's greater willingness to sacrifice the rewards of other motivations—the desire for affection, health, family life, safety, relaxation, vacation and the like—in order to attain dominance and status. This model makes clear why physiology need not be considered in a causal analysis of the behavior of a given individual exception. At the same time physiology is necessary for an analysis of the existence on a societal level of the universal institutions I discuss. Even the effects of virtually pure physiology expect many exceptions (as the six-foot-tall woman demonstrates). Dominance motivation no doubt has other causes—experiential and familial—in addition to the physiological causes and, for the exception, these may counteract the physiological factors.

The Statistical Reality

When we speak of an entire society, the law of large numbers becomes determinative. The statistical, continuous, and quantitative reality of the male's greater dominance tendency becomes concretized on the social level in absolute, discrete, and qualitative terms. The statistical reality of the male's greater aggression becomes in its pure and exaggerated form: ''men are aggressive (or dominant); women are passive (or submissive).'' This leads to discrimination, often for the woman who is an exception and occasionally for every woman. Discrimination is possible precisely because the statistical reality makes the exception an exception, exposed to the possibility of discrimination. The six-foot-tall girl who wishes she were short lives in a world of boys who are praised for being six feet tall.

As long as societies have hierarchies, differentiated statuses, and intermixing of men and women, they will possess the only environmental cues necessary to elicit greater dominance and attainment behavior from males. In utopian fantasy a society lacking hierarchy, status, and male-female relationships may be possible, but in the real world it is not. In the real world, societies have cultures. These cultures will value some things more than others and—particularly in the modern, bureaucratic society—some positions more than others. If male physiology is such that males are willing to sacrifice more for these things and positions, they will learn what is necessary and do what is necessary—whatever that may be in any given society—for dominance and attainment. There are other necessary conditions: it is not only gender that keeps a black woman from ruling the Republic of South Africa. Nevertheless, within any group possessing the other necessary conditions, dominance will go to those most willing to sacrifice for dominance and status (and social values will lead to such expectations).

Criticisms of the psychophysiological explanation of universality invariably couple the logical fallacy of "explaining" universality by differentiated socialization with a confusion of economic cause with economic function. This is equivalent to claiming that people eat because McDonald's has to make money. There is not a scintilla of evidence that modernization or any other social, economic, or technological change significantly reduces the percentages of males in upper hierarchical and status positions or the feelings of male dominance. What modernization can, on occasion, change dramatically is attitude towards these institutions. For some behavior, attitude is the determinative causal factor (premarital sexual behavior, for example) and, in such cases, changes in attitude become changes in behavior. All the evidence indicates that patriarchy, male attainment, and male dominance are not to any significant extent a function of attitude, but rather of the way we are constructed. Changes in attitude will affect how happy we are with what we are, but with reference to the institutions I discuss they will not affect what we are.

Differences in Thinking

The male-female differentiation that I have discussed is the one for which the evidence is by far the most overwhelming. There are other differences that may well be functions of endocrine-central nervous system differentiation. The stereotype that sees logically abstract thinking as "thinking like a man" and psychological perception as "woman's intuition" without question reflects empirical realities; it is only the cause of these realities that is open to question. A score on the SAT mathematics aptitude section that puts a girl in the ninetieth percentile among girls places a boy in only the sixty-eighth percentile among boys; among mathematically-precocious students (thirteen years old), a score of 700 is thirteen times more likely to be attained by a boy than by a girl (with equal numbers of boys and girls with similar mathematical backgrounds taking the test). There also seems to be a linear relationship between the importance of logical abstraction to an area and the percentage of those at the highest levels who are men; there has never been a woman at the highest level of mathematics, chess, or composing music (which is not thought of as a macho enterprise), while there have been many women of genius in literature and the performing arts. Women's psychological acuity is more difficult to test, but no less real. There are no doubt ad hoc social explanations of these sexual differences (however implausible), but the mere invocation of the suppression of women is not one of them. Such explanations fail to explain why the effects of suppression have been so much more devastating in areas for which logical abstraction is a necessary condition than in areas in which it is not. Whether or not the differences observed in the stereotype are functions of physiological development is still an open question, but one for which a positive answer is far more likely than contemporary ideology would acknowledge. . . .

"Alternative explanations . . . all simply ignore the enormous mass of direct physiological evidence."

The differences in dominance tendency and cognitive style I have discussed go far toward covering the core tendencies represented in our stereotypes of men and women. Assuming that we remember that a stereotype is a statistical generalization that must be considered apart from its subjective value judgment (which is often negative) and its explanation of the association of group and behavior (which is often incorrect), we see that the sexual stereotypes now so derided turn out to be basically correct.

Steven Goldberg is an associate professor of sociology at City College of the City University of New York. His writings include the book, The Inevitability of Patriarchy, *and articles in many journals.*

"Males are not dominant by nature. . . . In one sense, patriarchy is an attempt to make male dominance a 'natural' fact."

Male Dominance Is Cultural

Marilyn French

In the beginning was the Mother; the Word began a later age. The single universal covering primate and ungulate (hoofed) species, indeed all mammals and much other animal life as well, is that the core of society, the center of whatever kind of social group exists, is mother and child. Such a social organization is called *matrifocal* or *matricentric.* These terms are not the same as *matriarchal,* a word formed by analogy with *patriarchal,* which denotes leadership (from the Greek root *arche,* meaning *chief,* and *archein, to be first, to rule*). A matriarchy would thus be a society in which mothers rule in the same way fathers have ruled for the past few thousand years. There is no evidence that a matriarchy ever existed on earth. A society in which someone rules is factitious, manufactured: a person or group decides that one person shall dominate and others obey. Matricentric societies are spontaneous, organic; the mother cares for the baby until it is able to move about easily by itself, find food, and protect itself without her. The mother "rules" by greater experience, knowledge, and ability, but the intention of her "rule" is to free the child, to make it independent.

The matricentric nature of animal life has not been interesting to anthropologists until recently. Despite clear evidence to the contrary, generations of thinkers have assumed male dominance in all living forms. The Greeks believed the "ruler" of the beehive to be a male. Medieval bestiaries show the lion as king of the jungle, even though the male lion does not often kill but is dependent upon the female. The primary interest of researchers in the past has been to find in other species affirmation of the rightness of current human arrangements. It is now known, however, that "the mother-offspring

group is the universal nuclear unit of mammalian species," and that primate societies are "matrifocal almost by definition." Not all adult mammals have a full society; some come together only during courtship. But even among the so-called solitary species, the mothers tend the young with great attention for prolonged periods. The mother feeds her offspring from her body, carries the infant with her, and even after it is weaned, she shares her food with it. In the process she teaches it what is good to eat and how to obtain it, teaches it about the environment, its graces and its perils, and teaches it the paths of movement through the environment that she learned from her mother. . . .

Animal Dominance

Because of the centrality of females in mammal species, one might conclude that mammal females are dominant. The term *dominance* is extremely murky, however, for several reasons. First, although the words are sometimes used interchangeably, *dominance* is different from *domination;* the former refers to an inherent quality which may be natural (like personality, beauty, intellect) or acquired (like rank, office, the aura of wealth) but which is part of a person for a period of time and which influences the behavior of others. Domination is the willful use of power (of whatever sort) to countervail or annul the will of others. Dominance seems to exist in certain species; the existence of domination among animals is more questionable. The behavior of hamadryas baboon "alpha" males has been interpreted as domination of females. However, that human form of domination known as *authority*—the power to control others reinforced by an assertion of a moral right to control—does not exist among primates or other animals. . . .

Finally, the conception of dominance is complicated by human associations with the term. Many people believe that males are more aggressive than females, larger, and stronger, and they assume that greater size and strength lead inevitably to male coercion and oppression of females. But male mammals are not always larger or stronger than the female of their species; second, greater size does not necessarily lead to domination. Sexual dimorphism—a difference in form and size between the two sexes—does not lead to the dominance or domination of the larger sex in species that lack pair bonding, and that includes most ungulates and primates....

Symbol vs. Reality

In the beginning was the Mother; the Word began a new era, one we have come to call patriarchy. The word, a symbol, an arbitrary and abstract entity, can give reality to something nonexistent, invented, imagined. That women have babies is a reality (although it may not always be one; experiments with DNA and ex utero conception may alter it); they also generally take care of them. We may choose to see birth and mother love as great powers—as do people in simple cultures—or as vulnerabilities, sources of weakness and dependency—as do people in complex cultures like our own. However we see them, the facts remain.

"There are cultures and situations in which males are not dominant."

Male dominance is not a reality in this sense. It is not necessary. There are cultures and situations in which males are not dominant. Men are not always stronger than women, nor does the rule of might lead to male dominance per se, but to the domination of certain individuals, males and females (unless females are purposely excluded by consensus of the males), over all others. Rule of might overlaps with male dominance but is not identical with it. Males are not dominant *by nature,* or they would *always* be dominant, in the way females *always* have the babies. In one sense, patriarchy is an attempt to make male dominance a "natural" fact.

Patriarchy is, however, a reality in our world, so much so that many people cannot imagine any other way of organizing human life. They believe humans have *always* organized themselves as they do now in the West. To analyze patriarchy, it is necessary to look at its origin; but to do that, one must first allow the possibility that it *had* one, that some form of male superiority or supremacy has not been a permanent fixture of protohuman and human life....

Structure of Matricentry

The structure of matricentry was loose: families clustered around a mother or set of mothers (sisters), who had strong bonds with their children, especially with daughters, who probably remained with the mother throughout her life. Men were marginal in the matriliny; the closest bond for men was with their mates and the children of their sisters.

Most of the work of the group was done by women, as it still is in simple societies. They took responsibility for their children and, by extension, for the entire group. They provided most of the food, built the houses, and were the primary educators of the young. Again, men were marginal. They may have helped with certain heavy tasks; they may have hunted and provided meat. Both contributions were valued, but men had far more free time than women. They devoted much of this free time to caring for their weapons and for the instruments used in their hunting cults, from which they probably excluded women.

A degree of distance had opened between humans and their environment as a result of increasing controls exercised over nature, controls that led humans to feel alien from nature. A sense of separation frequently arouses hostility, regardless of which party was responsible for the separation. Distance and strangeness arouse fear, which causes enmity. In addition, nature had always been feared as well as loved; the sun can be an enemy, and rain can be a friend. Once people were planting their own crops, their relationship with nature became even more fraught with anxiety: a drought or a storm can wipe out weeks of labor. If the habit of wandering to gather food had been broken, bad weather could present a group with the prospect of a hungry season.

Finally, the discovery of the male role in procreation must have been of extreme importance to the attitudes of matricentric groups. The male role can be interpreted as a controlling one: a "shudder in the loins" that brought ecstasy to a man was all that was required of him to procreate: the woman bore the entire burden after that. Possibly men began to see women not as miraculous bearers of babies but as the soil, as a mere receptacle (so it may have seemed) for male seed which by itself engendered the new growth.

The Idea of Control

Over centuries, perhaps, these ideas led to the emergence of a new value: *the idea of control.* The idea of control is not the same as the exercise of control. A small child exercises control when it first walks or speaks; animals exercise control when they build nests or dams, when a chimpanzee, say, uses a digging stick. But they do not abstract control itself as a value. To value control, *power-over,* means that any form of control seems a good simply because it is a control. It is valued simply because it exists more than for what it accomplishes or creates.

Because men believed they had the controlling role in procreation, and because the gods of their hunting cults were in some sense already controlling gods, men began to worship a transcendent deity, a god who was not part of nature, like the old immanent goddess, but who had power over nature without being part of it. A transcendent god is not subject to what he creates; he controls it without participating in it. The mere idea that such a power could exist is astonishing, for early people must necessarily have been aware that any manipulation reverberates not just on the object but on the subject as well.

It seems likely therefore that the new value was established slowly and shakily; possibly a small group of men held it as their secret, a mystery/hunting-cult god of power. Adherents of the new god would have defined themselves in the god's image: that is, they would have identified themselves with their deity, as beings separate from and with control over nature. In addition, the idea of control is contagious: if a person is interested in power without reference to any other value, he or she will be able to gain power relatively easily over those who are not interested in it. For example, if two people mate, and one wants power over the other, domination, and the other wants love, the former will perceive all acts of the latter in terms of conquest or submission. Whatever the latter does will be turned into part of a contest. The person who wants love will have only two options—to abandon the relation entirely or to play the game. The same thing is true on a larger political scale: if one state desires power over other states, states which wish to live in peace and freedom will be overrun. They have to learn to value power or be eradicated. . . .

Man's Biological Disadvantages

It is not to be imagined that women accepted subordinate status peaceably. Moreover, it is difficult for any human group to prove it is transcendent. Men do not, of course, have any more control over nature than women do. If men's physiological functions are less visible than those of women, who menstruate, get pregnant, and lactate, men are equally limited by their greater vulnerability to death and disease in every decade of life, and their inability to control their own sexual organ. Indeed, the marginality of the male is biological. This unpleasant fact is the equivalent of the unpleasant fact that women bear the burden of racial continuation. Males are more fragile than females throughout life. Although more males than females are conceived—110 to 100—and more are born—104 to 100—by the second year of life the sexes are numerically equal, and men die younger than women in every subsequent decade of life. A famished woman is more likely spontaneously to abort a male than a female fetus.

There are natural reasons for this imbalance. In times of hardship the purposes of the species—

survival and continuation—are served by the production of more females than males. Human females carry their young for many months; they give birth to one at a time, as a rule; and they must devote themselves rather completely to the feeding, protection, and education of the young for many years before the children are capable of independent survival. The continuation of the species requires that many females survive to produce and raise the young, and that they limit their pregnancies.

"The more isolated a culture remains, the more likely it is to be egalitarian."

However, a single male can impregnate many females: there is need—and room—for only one cock in a barnyard. Matricentric social structure reflected this biological situation. The new structure, early patriarchy, was not a modification but a reversal of this arrangement and its morality. In positing that men were superior to nature and women, it was reversing traditional values. Women's generative processes, once seen as superior to men's, were degraded, diminished precisely because of their supposed closeness to nature. The marginality of men in the work life of matricentric groups was reinterpreted, seen as freedom, a life of volition. To accomplish these reversals of traditional values, it was not necessary to change anything in the life people led. Rather like women meeting in consciousness-raising groups in the 1960s, men may have spoken together secretly at cult meetings, rethinking the attitudes they inherited. Change came later. When the cults were large and strong enough to attempt to impose their attitudes on the group, men's larger musculature may have provided them with their single unanswerable argument. But before men could be willing to use their strength in this way, they must have been convinced that only by dominating women could they prove themselves "men," according to the new definition. . . .

Patriarchy is not universal, nor is male dominance. The more isolated a culture remains, the more likely it is to be egalitarian. An egalitarian group, the Tasaday, was found in the jungles of the Philippines some years ago; another recently discovered group is the Waorani, an Amazonian people in eastern Ecuador. They have lived in isolation for thousands of years, and after eight years of research among them, anthropologists report they are completely egalitarian, although they have a fixed division of labor. But most societies endow men with some kind of superiority over women. There are degrees of male dominance, however. Discussion of these degrees will lead into a discussion of the reversals of value that occurred in the creation of patriarchy. . . .

Defining "male dominance" is complicated by two factors: first, even societies in which men are not aggressive toward women, or in which women have some worldly power, manifest what Susan Carol Rogers has called the "myth of male dominance." That is, in many cultures the men and women seem to have made a bargain: women agree to call men more important, and allow them to monopolize public authority and prestige, while they, running the household, the farm, or small shop, possess most of the real power in village life. Such a bargain was probably at the root of male superiority, and is common enough even in modern households in industrial nations. It is enshrined in a joke about division of responsibility in a family: she makes the small decisions—how to spend their money, where they should live, how the children will be educated; while he makes the large ones—such as should the United State recognize Communist China.

Second, since those of us who study this problem come from male-dominant cultures in which the standard for everything (except gynecological functions) is male, we carry our standards with us in investigating other cultures. Even some feminists seem to perpetuate this standard, and judge equality as the achievement by women and minorities of what males already possess. Such a perspective is inadequate in perceiving the moral and sociopolitical structures of certain societies.

A more useful standard in describing varied societies might be an examination of the kinds and degree of controls exerted over nature. It is likely that the more highly control is valued in a given society, the greater will be its regard for males and the more intense will be its diminishment of females—even in societies in which women are associated with the tame (culture) and men with the wild (nature). (This is because in such societies, women are part of the tame only because men have confined them within it, men having taken over women's "wildness.") Moreover, there are different kinds of controls. In some societies, control is purely mystical; nature is brought into line symbolically, through rituals alone. In others, controls are physical but simple: the land is cultivated, animals are domesticated, houses are built to endure for an extended period. And in some, both physical and "spiritual" controls are exercised. In patriarchy, both are used and bolstered by institutionalization. . . .

Controlling Institutions

Patriarchal cultures control women, exclude women, and attempt to control all those things women produce—from children to manufactures. They attempt to take over as their own the very physical functioning of women's procreation, by assigning children to men and diminishing the role of women in procreation. They do this through *the word*: that is, by decree and institutionalization—the

setting up of independent hierarchical structures devoted to control in a particular field or area. Not only unequal degrees of status but also the ideas that sustain and perpetuate male control over females are institutionalized in patriarchy. Thus the fundamental nature of patriarchy is located in stratification, institutionalization, and coercion. Stratification of men above women leads in time to stratification of classes: an elite rules over people perceived as "closer to nature," savage, bestial, animalistic; it legitimizes its rule by claiming to be more in control than others and closer to "God," which essentially means less connected to nature and the flesh—which is why it is a contradiction for women to be numbered among the elite, and one reason why they have been so severely controlled within that class. Control is achieved through institutions: it is decreed that certain people may own property, or pass laws, or receive education, and institutions are created to perpetuate such decrees. An institutionalized society requires coercion because it is oppressive, and because it is factitious. If there were in fact a group of humans who were *in every way naturally superior* to other humans, they would *rule automatically*; they would not require force to maintain supremacy.

"To create a male-superior culture, all that is needed is a perception that there is a difference in volition between women and men."

To create a male-superior culture, all that is needed is a perception that there is a difference in volition between women and men. If *it seems* that women are bound by nature to work, to take responsibility for others, and to provide; that men are not so bound but may choose to work or not, then it seems that men are in some way a privileged group. If women are willing to grant men special praise for what they do to contribute to the group—instead of simply refusing to share with those who do not contribute—that praise could easily, over time, be institutionalized into status. The "Big Man" systems that exist in the highlands of New Guinea, for instance, are devices that prevent the buildup of wealth, that perpetuate sharing and division of wealth. Under such systems women as well as men produce goods which are passed in a system of exchange as gift giving. Men derive great status and praise from giving huge feasts, and thus sharing with others; men possess political prestige. Women do not, although their labor has contributed to the feasts. In our own world and time, it is frequently seen that women offer inordinate praise, flattering the strength or cleverness of men who are in any way helpful, while the labor and helpfulness of women is often taken for granted. . . .

The Essential Question

The essential question about the origin of patriarchy is why people should have altered an ancient and revered way of life. Patriarchy did not arise after three million years of peaceful hominid and human life because men suddenly became more aggressive, or suddenly decided to oppress women. Either the new values held by the men's cults themselves changed behavior or some change in the human situation seemed to require a new adaptation, which was available in a moral change that had to have occurred earlier: the positing of control as a value superior to the old values of fertility, continuation, and sharing. The fundamental nature of this new morality is explicit in the Old Testament, in the opening of Genesis, which propounds the principles of patriarchy. The gift of the male god to man is *dominion* over nature. The old values are still present—humans are to replenish as well as subdue the earth. But man is to have dominion also over woman. The key word is dominion: power-over, control.

Greek Thought

Once control was elevated and nature demoted in the morality of humans, forms developed to foster and transmit power. The distinction in status between men and women was institutionalized. In Greek thought the private was distinguished from the public realm. The private is the realm of animality—of nature—and of *necessity*. It is the realm of women. The public realm is created in *freedom,* is the domain of the human, and transcends the first. It is the realm of men. Although some men—indeed most men—are relegated to the private realm, the *idea* of the distinction exalts all men. Aristotle distinguished between free male citizens and women, children, mechanics, and laborers, who comprised the ''necessary conditions'' of the state. Free males inhabited the *polis;* activities within it were defined as existing outside the realms of nature and necessity; the private realm was seen as the sphere of unfreedom.

In the *Symposium,* Plato's hierarchy of virtue and rationality places women midway between men and beasts; Socrates specifically compares symbolic fatherhood—homosexual love between men, the creation of thought, poetry, and law—to biological fatherhood and asks, ''Who would not prefer such fatherhood to merely human propagation?'' The association of women with nonvolition—necessity—and nature persists in Western thought. Both Hegel and Marx view childbearing as a nonvolitional activity and, moreover, one that precludes women from thinking about their experience.

The forbidden fruit woman ate, causing the fall, is in Hebrew *jadah*—knowledge, penetration, power, possession. It may well be that women took the first bite, the first set of steps into this new realm of control, but men took the second. And in time control superseded natural values; as it did, men superseded women in value. By the twentieth century we have reached the point where an anthropologist can claim ''it is natural for man to be unnatural.''. . .

''The essential question about the origin of patriarchy is why people should have altered an ancient and revered way of life.''

Because patriarchal values and perspectives are so pervasive and seem to be universal, many people believe them to be inevitable. Such thinkers discount the existence of cultures which entertain different values and live in ways far removed from those of the West. They may argue that such cultures are becoming extinct because of the superiority or the invincibility of Western patriarchy. They may also remain unpersuaded by the projection of a matricentric world based on fragmentary evidence, or hold that if such a world existed, it perished in the face of a morality that was necessary to the development of ''civilization.''

Yet no one can deny that the world has changed greatly over the millennia, or that humans created the changes; and that, therefore, humans are capable of altering their ways of thinking and living. Thus to call patriarchy inevitable is essentially to choose it, to choose not to attempt to alter the human course.

Marilyn French is a well-known novelist and literary critic whose books include The Women's Room.

Prehistoric Matriarchies Prove Sex Roles Are Cultural

Riane Eisler

In the nineteenth century, archeological excavations began to confirm what scholars of myth had long maintained—that goddess worship preceded the worship of God. After reluctantly accepting what no longer could be ignored, religious historians proposed a number of explanations for why there had been this strange switch in divine gender. A long-standing favorite has been the so-called Big Discovery theory. This is the idea that, when men finally became aware that women did not bring forth children by themselves—in other words, when they discovered that it involved their sperm, their paternity—this inflamed them with such a new-found sense of importance that they not only enslaved women but also toppled the goddess.

Today, new archeological findings—particularly post-World War II excavations—are providing far more believable answers to this long-debated puzzle. For largely due to more scientific archeological methods, including infinitely more accurate archeological dating methods such as radiocarbon and dendrochronology, there has been a veritable archeological revolution.

As James Mellaart of the London University Institute of Archeology writes, we now know that there were in fact many cradles of civilization, all of them thousands of years older than Sumer, where civilization was long said to have begun about five thousand years ago. But the most fascinating discovery about these original cultural sites is that they were structured along very different lines from what we have been taught is the divinely, or naturally, ordained human order.

One of these ancient cradles of civilization is Catal Huyuk, the largest Neolithic site yet found. Located in the Anatolian plain of what is now Turkey, Catal

Riane Eisler, "Our Lost Heritage: New Facts on How God Became a Man." This article first appeared in THE HUMANIST issue of May/June 1985 and is reprinted by permission.

Huyuk goes back approximately eight thousand years to about 6500 BCE—three thousand years before Sumer. As Mellaart reports, this ancient civilization "is remarkable for its wall-paintings and plaster reliefs, its sculpture in stone and clay . . . , its advanced technology in the crafts of weaving, woodwork, metallurgy . . . , its advanced religion . . . , its advanced practices in agriculture and stockbreeding, and . . . a flourishing trade. . . ."

But undoubtedly the most remarkable thing about Catal Huyuk and other original sites for civilization is that they were *not* warlike, hierarchic, and male-dominated societies like ours. As Mellaart writes, over the many centuries of its existence, there were in Catal Huyuk no signs of violence or deliberate destruction, "no evidence for any sack or massacre." Moreover, while there was evidence of some social inequality, "this is never a glaring one." And most significantly—in the sharpest possible contrast to our type of social organization—"the position of women was obviously an important one . . . with a fertility cult in which a goddess was the principal deity."

Founded on False Assumptions

Now it is hardly possible to believe that in this kind of society, where, besides all their other advances, people clearly understood the principles of stockbreeding, they would not have also had to understand that procreation involves the male. So the Big Discovery theory is not only founded on the fallacious assumption that men are naturally brutes, who were only deterred from forcefully enslaving women by fear of the female's "magical" powers of procreation; the Big Discovery theory is also founded on assumptions about what happened in prehistory that are no longer tenable in light of the *really* big discoveries we are now making about our lost human heritage—about societies that, while not ideal, were clearly more harmonious than ours.

But if the replacement of a Divine Mother with a

Divine Father was not due to men's discovery of paternity, how did it come to pass that all our present world religions either have no female deity or generally present them as "consorts" or subservient wives of male gods?

To try to answer that question, let us look more carefully at the new archeological findings.

Logic would lead one to expect what ancient myths have long indicated and archeology has since confirmed: that since life issues from woman, not man, the first anthropomorphic deity was female rather than male. But logical or not, this position was hardly that of the first excavators of Paleolithic caves, some of whom were monks, such as the well-known Abbé Henri Breuil. They consistently refused to see in the many finds of twenty-five-thousand-year-old stylized female sculptures what they clearly were: representations of a female divinity, a Great Mother. Instead, the large-breasted, wide-hipped, bountiful, and often obviously pregnant women these men christened "Venus figurines" were described either as sex objects (products of men's erotic fantasies) or deformed, ugly women. Moreover, in order to conform to their model of history as the story of "man the hunter" and "man the warrior," they refused to see what was actually in the famous cave paintings. As Alexander Marshack has now established, not only did they insist that stylized paintings of tree branches and plants were weapons, they sometimes described these pictures as backward arrows or harpoons, chronically missing their mark! They also, as Andre Leroi-Gourhan noted in his major study of the Paleolithic, insisted on interpreting the already quite advanced art of the period as an expression of hunting magic, a view borrowed from extremely primitive contemporary societies like the Australian aborigines.

Neolithic Civilizations

Although Leroi-Gourhan's interpretation of the objects and paintings found in Paleolithic caves is in sexually stereotyped terms, he stresses that the art of the Paleolithic was first and foremost religious art, concerned with the mysteries of life, death, and regeneration. And it is again this concern that is expressed in the rich art of the Neolithic, which, as Mellaart points out, not only shows a remarkable continuity with the Paleolithic, but clearly foreshadows the great goddess of later Bronze Age civilizations in her various forms of Isis, Nut, and Maat in Egypt, Ishtar, Lilith, or Astarte in the Middle East, the sun-goddess Arinna of Anatolia, as well as such later goddesses as Demeter, Artemis, and Kore in Greece, Atargatis, Ceres, and Cybele in Rome, and even Sophia or Wisdom of the Christian Middle Ages, the Shekinah of Hebrew Kabalistic tradition, and, of course, the Virgin Mary or Holy Mother of the Catholic Church about whom we read in the Bible.

This same prehistoric and historic continuity is stressed by UCLA archeologist Marija Gimbutas, whose monumental work, *The Goddesses and Gods of Old Europe,* brings to life yet another Neolithic civilization: the indigenous civilization that sprang up in the Balkans and Greece long, long before the rise of Indo-European Greece. Once again, the archeological findings in what Gimbutas termed the civilizations of Old Europe not only demolish the old "truism" of the "warlike Neolithic" but also illuminate our true past, again showing that here, too, the original direction of human civilization was in some ways far more civilized than ours, with pre-Indo-Europeans living in far greater harmony with one another and the natural environment.

Barbarian Invasions

Moreover, excavations in Old Europe, like those unearthed in other parts of the ancient world, show that what brought about the onset of male-dominance both in heaven and on earth was not some sudden male discovery. What ushered it in was the onslaught of barbarian hordes from the arid steppes and deserts on the fringe areas of our globe. It was wave after wave of these pastoral invaders who destroyed the civilizations of the first settled agrarian societies. And it was they who brought with them the gods—and men—of war that made so much of later or recorded history the blood-bath we are now taught was the *totality* of human history.

"The first anthropomorphic deity was female rather than male."

In Old Europe, as Gimbutas painstakingly documents, there were three major invasionary waves, as the Indo-European peoples she calls the Kurgans wiped out or "Kurganized" the European populations. "The Old European and Kurgan cultures were the antithesis of one another," writes Gimbutas. She continues:

> The Old Europeans were sedentary horticulturalists prone to live in large well-planned townships. The absence of fortifications and weapons attests the peaceful coexistence of this egalitarian civilization that was probably matrilinear and matrilocal. . . . The Old European belief system focused on the agricultural cycle of birth, death, and regeneration, embodied in the feminine principle, a Mother Creatrix. The Kurgan ideology, as known from comparative Indo-European mythology, exalted virile, heroic warrior gods of the shining and thunderous sky. Weapons are nonexistent in Old European imagery; whereas the dagger and battle-axe are dominant symbols of the Kurgans, who, like all historically known Indo-Europeans, glorified the lethal power of the sharp blade.

So while we are still commonly taught that it was

to Indo-European invaders—such as the Aechaean warriors, celebrated by Homer, who eventually sacked Troy—that we owe our Western heritage, we now know that they in fact did not bring us civilization. Rather, they destroyed, degraded, and brutalized a civilization already highly advanced along wholly different lines. And, just as the factuality of how these truly savage peoples demoted both women and goddesses to the subservient status of consort or wife has now been established, the fact they brought in warfare with them is also confirmed.

Verifying Myths

Once again, as when Heinrich Schliemann defied the archeological establishment and proved that the city of Troy was not Homeric fantasy but prehistoric fact, new archeological findings verify ancient legends and myths. For instance, the Greek poet Hesiod, who wrote about the same time as Homer, tells us of a "golden race," who lived in "peaceful ease" in a time when "the fruitful earth poured forth her fruits." And he laments how they were eventually replaced by "a race of bronze" who "ate not grain" (in other words, were not farmers) and instead specialized in warfare ("the all-lamented sinful works of Ares were their chief care").

Perhaps one of the most fascinating legends of ancient times is, of course, that of the lost civilization of Atlantis. And here again, as with the once only legendary city of Troy, archeological findings illuminate our true past. For what new findings suggest is what the eminent Greek scholar Spyridon Martinatos already suspected in 1939: that the legend of a great civilization which sank into the Atlantic is actually the garbled folk memory of the Minoan civilization of Crete and surrounding Mediterranean islands, portions of which did indeed disappear into the sea after unprecedented volcanic eruptions sometime after 1500 BCE.

First discovered at the turn of this century, the once unknown Bronze Age civilization of ancient Crete has now been far more extensively excavated. As Nicolas Platon, former superintendent of antiquities in Crete and director of the Acropolis Museum, who excavated the island for over thirty years, writes, Minoan civilization was "an astonishing achievement." It reflected "a highly sophisticated art and way of life," indeed producing some of the most beautiful art the world has ever seen. Also in this remarkable society—the only place where the worship of the goddess and the influence of women in the public sphere survived into historic times, where "the whole of life was pervaded by an ardent faith in the goddess Nature, the source of all creation and harmony"—there was still "a love of peace, a horror of tyranny, and a respect for the law."

And once again, it was not men's discovery of

their biological role in paternity that led to the toppling of the goddess. It was another, final Indo-European invasion: the onslaught of the Dorians, who, with their weapons of iron, as Hesiod writes, brought death and destruction in their wake.

So the revolution in norms that literally stood reality on its head—that established this seemingly fundamental and sacrosanct idea that we are the creations of a Divine Father, who all by Himself brought forth all forms of life—was in fact a relatively late event in the history of human culture. Moreover, this drastic change in direction of cultural evolution, which set us on the social course that in our nuclear age threatens to destroy all life, was certainly not predetermined or, by any stretch of the imagination, inevitable. Rather than being some mystical mystery, it was the substitution of a force-based model of social organization for one in which both the female and male halves of humanity viewed the supreme power in the universe not as the "masculine" power to destroy but rather as the "feminine" power to give and nurture life.

"New archeological findings verify ancient legends and myths."

Another popular old idea about this change was that it was the replacement of matriarchy with patriarchy. But my research of many years shows that matriarchy is simply the flip side of the coin to the *dominator* model of society, based upon the dominance of men over women that we call patriarchy. The real alternative to patriarchy, already foreshadowed by the original direction of human civilization, is what I have called the *partnership* model of social relations. Based upon the full and equal partnership between the female and male halves of our species, this model was already well-established a long time ago, before, as the Bible has it, a male god decreed that woman be subservient to man.

Resisting Knowledge

The new knowledge about our true human heritage is still meeting enormous resistance, with traditional "experts" from both the religious and academic establishment crying heresy. But it is a knowledge that, in the long run, cannot be suppressed.

It is a knowledge that demolishes many old misconceptions about our past. It also raises many fascinating new questions. Is the real meaning of the legend of our Fall from Paradise that, rather than having transgressed in some horrible way, Eve should have obeyed the advice of the serpent (long associated with the oracular or prophetic powers of the goddess) and *continued* to eat from the tree of knowledge? Did the custom of sacrificing the first-born child develop after the destruction of this earlier world—as the Bible has it, after our expulsion from the Garden of Eden—when women had been turned into mere male-controlled technologies of reproduction, as insurance of a sort that conception had not occurred before the bride was handed over to her husband?

"The new knowledge about our true human heritage is still meeting enormous resistance."

We may never have complete answers to such questions, since archeology only provides some of the data and ancient writings, such as the Old Testament, were rewritten so many times, each time to more firmly establish, and sanctify, male control. But what we do have is far more critical in this time when the old patriarchal system is leading us ever closer to global holocaust. This is the knowledge that it was not always this way: there are viable alternatives that may not only offer us survival but also a far, far better world.

Riane Eisler is codirector of the Institute for Futures Forecasting, and author of many books, including The Blade and the Chalice: Beyond War, Sexual Politics, and Fear.

"The myths of Eve's apple, Pandora's box . . . have been replaced by the myth of Former Matriarchal Greatness and the Overthrow of the Mother Goddess."

viewpoint 8

Prehistoric Matriarchies Are Mythological

Sally R. Binford

Once upon a time, about 4,000 or 6,000 years ago, women were powerful, free and in control of their lives. Society was organized along matriarchal lines, and political decisions were made according to female principles that, as we all know, are sensitive, just and loving. In the context of this culture, women invented ceramics, agriculture and weaving. Women also knew how to control their fertility; there were means of contraception available that were nontoxic and completely reliable. Since we wanted the babies we had, our relationships with our children were relaxed and loving. We worshiped the Goddess in temples of great beauty, and priestesses conducted rites celebrating our sexuality. The world was at peace.

Soon, however, this blissful life was disrupted by patriarchal males who were bent on negative uses of power and who harbored a predeliction for warfare. They destroyed our temples and suppressed our rites. The Goddess was replaced by a vengeful male god, and in order to assure his dominance and assuage his jealousy, all records of matriarchal rule and goddess worship were destroyed. Since this takeover, women have been oppressed. The patriarchs took away our knowledge of contraception and forced us into motherhood; they taught us to be ashamed of our sexuality. They denied our inventions and claimed them as their own.

For centuries, males controlled access to historical records and wrote of the past in ways that denied our former greatness. This conspiracy has been carried on by anthropologists who have consistently denied the existence of a state of prepatriarchal matriarchy. Their very denial of a matriarchal stage in the human past is suspect; indeed, it is one more striking example of suppression of the truth. If only we can reclaim our past, we can once again be strong and free. We can

rediscover herbal methods of birth control and healing and reassert control over our lives. There is an abundance of mythic material that confirms the existence of formerly powerful matriarchies; and art objects—from the Venus figurines of the Paleolithic through Indian temple engravings—reveal the long-suppressed existence of Goddess worship. The strength we gain from the knowledge of our past will help us to reclaim our former greatness.

New Myths

Feminist anthropologists are faced with a formidable task. Not only have we had to deal with the macho interpretations of prehistory offered by Robert Ardrey, Desmond Morris and Lionel Tiger, who attempt to rationalize male supremacy, but we also have to cope with the flip side of the myth-as-history coin currently in vogue in some feminist circles. The myths of Eve's apple, Pandora's box and Freud's penis envy have been replaced by the myth of Former Matriarchal Greatness and the Overthrow of the Mother Goddess. The tenacity with which many women cling to this belief is enormous. As an anthropologist, I am fascinated and can explain it only as a religious phenomenon.

Indeed, in some places, belief in former matriarchies has taken an explicitly religious form. In Los Angeles, for example, a group of Mother Goddess worshipers have formally organized themselves into a church, complete with temple, priestesses and rituals.

In the many discussions I have had with partisans of this myth over the past several years, I am persuaded that logic, reason and arguments based on knowledge of the data cut no ice at all. The only experience I have had as an anthropologist that is analogous in its lack of susceptibility to reason is trying to argue the evidence for biological evolution with hardcore fundamentalists, whose faith also renders them impervious to information.

These beliefs are not limited to a lunatic fringe of the Women's Movement. Academic institutions have recently become involved in the Mother Goddess/Matriarchy madness. A recent conclave at the Santa Cruz campus of the University of California was organized for the very purpose of resisting the interpretations of professional archeologists. Amid charges of a conspiracy by the anthropological establishment, author Merlin Stone—a leading proponent of the faith—urged untrained women to march through Europe and the Middle East on their own excavation expeditions in order to discover long-suppressed truths.

A less inflammatory conference was held at the University of Washington to discuss whether or not ancient matriarchies and powerful female religions really existed.

"Academic institutions have recently become involved in the Mother Goddess/Matriarchy madness."

Since faith is dictated by a need to believe that is stronger than reason, I entertain no hope of persuading the true believers. What follows is an attempt to restate the major articles of faith of the New Feminist Fundamentalism and to weigh these against current anthropological understandings of the evolution of culture so that those still uncommitted may have a basis for evaluating the claims of the new faith.

Matriarchy

Matriarchy (rule by women) preceded patriarchy (rule by men) in the evolution of cultures.

This is one of the fundamental cornerstones of the faith and is supported largely by mythic material collected by Johann J. Bachofen and other early armchair anthropologists. The resurrection of the misguided thinking of the opening decades of the 19th century by the propagators of the faith has done little to enhance the reputation of feminist thought. According to early armchair anthropologists, human society went through the stages of savagery, barbarism and then (at last) civilization, by which they meant Western European society.

Living non-Western cultures were seen as cultural fossils surviving from an earlier stage. Each stage was characterized by a mating pattern; promiscuity was rampant among the savages, while the slightly more advanced barbarians were polygamous. The civilized pattern was, of course, monogamy. According to this formulation, inheritance and tracing ancestry varied with cultural level also: savages scrambled for what they could get, barbarians inherited rights and goods from their mothers, while Western civilization was sublimely patrilineal. Political power, it was assumed, was distributed randomly, if at all, among savages; often to women, among matrilineal barbarians; and with the appearance of civilization, patriarchy took its rightful place in the world.

This neat tripartite scheme was demolished when anthropologists began doing serious field research. Fieldworkers learned that rules of residence, ways of reckoning kin, methods of manufacturing and distributing goods and services (technology and economy) and patterns of assigning political power varied in much more complex ways than early theorists could have imagined. As prehistoric archeologists and cultural anthropologists gathered more and more data, the simplistic notion of a matriarchal stage in the human past had to be discarded.

Suppressed Knowledge?

In recent years, several women authors such as Elizabeth Gould Davis in *The First Sex* and Merlin Stone in *When God Was a Woman* have revived the notion that humanity experienced a golden age of matriarchy in the past. This belief has been combined with the assertion that there is a conspiracy against its acceptance, making those who question the faith subject to suspicion of being coconspirators. I am the last to deny that anthropology—perhaps even more than other academic enterprises—is dominated by sexist males. I am, however, equally persuaded that if a male anthropologist discovered evidence of past matriarchies, he would publish his findings rather than suppress them. The existence of a past stage of matriarchy would lend support to the thesis that patriarchy is the more advanced cultural form in evolution; it would also support the notion that matriarchies had inherent weaknesses that allowed them to be replaced by patriarchies. Further, the unique discovery of matriarchal cultural systems would also guarantee research grants, and I cannot believe that any academic male social scientist would suppress his findings on principle, thereby denying himself funding.

One of the basic objections to the mythic matriarchal past—apart from the lack of evidence to support it and the consistent body of data that argues against it—is the use of myth as history by the propagators of the faith. We do not attempt to reconstruct biological evolution or the history of the universe by recourse to myth, and the data of cultural evolution are no more amenable to this kind of methodology than are these other attempts to understand evolutionary processes. Myths are not appropriate primary data for reconstructing the past. The Persephone myth, for example, elucidates little about either Greek history or the causes of seasonal variations in temperate zones. The story of Noah's

Ark tells us nothing of past geological processes.

Matrilineal inheritance and kinship systems are evidence of former matriarchal societies.

The confusion of matrilineality (reckoning inheritance and descent through the female line) with matriarchy (the rule of women) is an almost essential component of the New Fundamentalist faith. In fact, matrilineal institutions tend to be associated with certain patterns of male warfare rather than with female political authority. The Iroquois, for example, were warlike and strongly matrilineal. Their principle investigator, Lewis H. Morgan, wrote that Iroquois men "regarded woman as the inferior, the dependent, the servant of man, and from nurture and habit, she actually considered herself to be so."

In most matrilineal societies, the authority figure is the mother's brother rather than her husband. This may make for decisions that favor the woman's family rather than her husband's, but decision-making still rests with males. The presence of matrilineal institutions may have modifying effects on male dominance for individual women, but matrilineal kinship and inheritance in no way confer political authority on women. In *Sexual Politics,* Kate Millett points out: "Matrilineality does not constitute an exception to patriarchal rule, it simply channels the power held by males through female descent.". . .

The Mother Goddess

Prehistoric art reveals the existence of the worship of the Mother Goddess and documents the former power of women.

To assume that the representation of the female figure in art signifies matriarchal power is so fraught with fallacy that I find it difficult to take it seriously as an argument. Does *Playboy*'s artwork imply that it represents a matriarchal cultural system? The Venus figures of the Upper Paleolithic appear to be the earliest example of a common human fascination with the female form. There exists, by the way, a great deal of cave art from the same period that is not discussed either by male art historians or by women seeking to document the existence of the Mother Goddess—representations of female genitalia that would be right at home in any contemporary men's room.

Art always exists as an integral part of a cultural system, and it bears systemic relations to that culture's mode of production, to its political system, to its ideology. The method of assigning one's own meaning to certain symbols and then tracing them over broad geographic areas and through tens of thousands of years of cultural change is, to put it mildly, not a reliable means of reconstructing the past. It would be possible to take any artistic representation—cattle, for example—and construct a theory about a religion based on the worship of livestock. Enough cattle exist in prehistoric art and

in all later periods for a plausible argument to be made that humanity once worshiped cattle but that the history of such worship has been suppressed. What sounds plausible, using such methods, is not necessarily true.

Unsupported Assumptions

In summary, the New Feminist Fundamentalism is based on assumptions that cannot be supported; these include the notion of matriarchy as a stage in cultural evolution, the equating of matrilineality with matriarchy . . . and the assigning of unitary significance to art forms that appear in widely differing contexts.

I can find no valid reason for the need to believe in a golden age of matriarchy. Certainly, if we did once live in matriarchal societies, we blew it by letting the patriarchs take over. How did this happen? One of the most intriguing "explanations" is offered by Elizabeth Gould Davis: because of their carnivorous diet, men grew enormous penises, and women were so turned on that they voluntarily surrendered their power. I cannot accept this as a serious piece of history—only as a thoroughgoing putdown of women.

The overwhelming body of evidence from anthropology and from history argues against a universal stage of matriarchy. There are those who will contend that this statement simply indicates how brainwashed I have been by my male colleagues. This must mean that my female colleagues have also been intellectually victimized. Another putdown of women!

"Myths are not appropriate primary data for reconstructing the past."

It is often argued that the reality or truth of a former matriarchal stage is irrelevant, that the idea is a useful one around which women can rally. I take strong exception to this. In order to cope intelligently with the present and the future, we must understand the past. We must come to terms with the cultural processes that have caused male dominance to be so widespread and long-lived. Anthropologist Joan Bamberger argues this point cogently in a contribution to *Women, Culture and Society:*

> Myth and rituals have been misinterpreted as persistent reminders that women once had, and then lost, the seat of power. This loss accrued to them through inappropriate conduct. . . . The myths constantly reiterate that women did not know how to handle power when they had it. The loss is thereby justified so long as women choose to accept the myth.
>
> The final version of woman that emerges from these myths is that [woman] represents chaos and misrule

through trickery and unbridled sexuality. . . . The myth of matriarchy is but the tool used to keep woman bound to her place. To free her, we need to destroy the myth. . . .

The true believers in the fundamentalist faith of the Fall from Matriarchy and the Overthrow of the Mother Goddess contribute nothing but confusion and misinformation, and their insistence that those who question their assertions are part of a sexist conspiracy does little to enlighten us. In this period of backlash and antifeminism, an investigation of the relationship between women's control over their own reproduction and the forces that seek to keep women "in their place" might be of much greater utility. It is no accident that women's oppression is most often expressed as a "right to life." The historical and cultural antecedents of such thinking need to be explored and understood.

"Does Playboy's artwork imply that it represents a matriarchal cultural system?"

It is hoped that efforts to understand the evolution of women's culture will continue and that these efforts will be based on current information and sound methodology. The assertion of a mythic past as history and questioning the goodwill of those who doubt its validity constitute an attitude that has much in common with the orthodoxy of Freudian psychology, fundamentalist Christianity and other religions based on blind faith.

Sally R. Binford is an anthropologist and sex researcher living in San Francisco.

"[The '80s man] has combined aspects of Neanderthal Man and the painfully introspective 'New Man' of the '70s in a way that works."

viewpoint 9

Men Have Successfully Adapted to Changing Sex Roles

Karen Heller

This may seem unfashionable to state, perhaps even imprudent, but it is true: Men have changed. For the better. Some of them are finally, actually, getting it right. Well, not right—that would be absurd—but *almost* right.

The '80s man has evolved into what you might call the New New Man. This is a man who is too smart to be blatantly macho in the Clint Eastwood mode, too cool to be sensitive in the moist-eyed manner of Phil Donahue. He is beyond chauvinism, beyond earnest empathy. He has combined aspects of Neanderthal man and the painfully introspective "New Man" of the '70s in a way that works.

For the New New Man, some of the archaic has become au courant (like courtship, like pride), yet some of the new has prevailed. Now it is possible to know a secure, confident man who cooks (and from a repertoire vaster than McDonald's), who gardens (harvesting a crop more varied than marijuana), who dresses (somewhere between Brooks Brothers and Beau Brummell) and who can care for his apartment (not in an anal-retentive fashion, but certainly so it doesn't resemble Dresden after the fire). Mostly, this New New Man is an adult.

There's a problem, though. These New New Men, these guys who have melded the old with the modern, are so damned pleased with themselves. They hawk themselves like laundry products: cleaner, brighter, new and improved. And remember, their egos were pretty impressive to begin with. Alas, there is more. They've been told by too many people (Who were they? Let's shoot them) that there aren't a lot of single, successful, heterosexual guys out there. This was stupid. This has gone straight to their already swelled heads. So let's be clear: These New New Men aren't perfect. It's just that,

compared to what they once were, the macho and then the mush, they're not all that bad.

You know this New New Man. He may even be close at hand. You may even be going out with him. Popular culture, too, offers ample evidence of these heroes of progress: Look at Bruce Springsteen, he of the taut body and tender heart. This guy is clearly dominant, clearly in control, but he sings so hard and feels so deeply his gut shakes, his hair sweats, his throat rusts, his pecs quiver. Or Aidan Quinn in *Desperately Seeking Susan,* hip and strong but slightly confused, an artist lost on the street. Or Bruce Willis in *Moonlighting,* a cool jerk with a fast mouth. He wears his heart so openly it isn't just on his sleeve, it's all over his suit—but he still knows how to keep Cybill guessing. Think of Bryant Gumbel: a natty know-it-all who can talk tersely with bureaucrats and sweetly with children. Or Ted Danson's Sam: a smooth-talking jock, but a true lover of women.

A Product of Social Darwinism

This New New Man is the product of Social Darwinism when it works, when man actually improves over time. That men waded through the '70s like swine through the mire was not feminism's fault; it was history's. Revolutions, after all, do a notoriously poor job of educating the authorities on proper behavior. Did the populace invite Louis XVI and Marie Antoinette over for cake during the storming of the Bastille? Did the Bolsheviks inform the Romanoffs as to how to conduct themselves during the autumn of 1917? Of course not. When radical change occurs, surprise is the order of the day and chaos rules supreme.

That is, to some extent, what happened in the '70s when women finally woke up, smelled the coffee and wondered why they were always the ones who had to make it. A man was left with two choices, both of them miserable. He could continue being an old-fashioned, oppressive bastard, or he could ooze

Karen Heller, "Meet Mr. Almost-Right: The *New* New Man," *Mademoiselle*, August 1986. Courtesy Mademoiselle. Copyright © 1986 by The Condé Nast Publications Inc.

unctuous empathy, pretending he was the lone male who realized that women had long been treated as the unfairer sex. What, pray tell, was a poor boy to do?

He did nothing. He was just confused. He didn't know if he was supposed to call; if he did, was he to make the plans, the meals, the first move? A woman learned that she could call a man and then realized, *very quickly*, that now it was her turn to face constant rejection. If this was liberty, perhaps death was better.

The New Man

And then sensitivity seeped into men's souls. Along came Alan Alda and Phil Donahue and Jimmy Carter to weep the way. This was the New Man, a guy so earnest he wasn't just willing to have your baby, he was willing to have your period, too. Most men couldn't stand this new breed, but men are nothing if not politically smart. (Politically, in fact, they are brilliant. That is why they continue to rule the world.)

Men understood that women liked the new, sensitive fellow with the rumpled smile, the dewy eyes, the moth-eaten cardigan. So they became that fellow. They cared, honest they did. They knew women were swell. They knew women deserved better. They knew women appreciated a nice home-cooked meal. But they overdid it. They had heart, but lacked vertebrae. The wimp was born. And, like moths too close to a flame, these new softies got burned. Tough gals took advantage of their tender hearts.

"We don't want wimps."

Some confessions. Women like men who like sports, even though it may drive them crazy. And most women don't mind a man who enjoys a boys' night out, provided that the boys are men and the nights aren't nightly. Women like men who look nice, but not *too* nice. (We all know men are vain; we just don't want them to broadcast it so loudly that they could start a new network.) And about working out, that's great—up to a point. Men with chests that are better-developed than ours make us nervous.

We don't want wimps. And we don't want men who are just like women, only male. We want men who are warm but not weak, tender but not limp. After a period of time, we have calmed down, the dust has settled. A man needn't offer us a seat on the bus. On the other hand, a door opened makes a woman feel like that rarest of species, a lady. I don't mind preparing a meal at all, but fixing a car, well, if a man wants to change a tire or the oil, I may be

inclined toward love. I like to cook; I do not like fixing cars. Cooking does not make me feel enslaved, and changing the oil will not make me a better person—it will just make me a dirtier one.

Men, as I say, are clever. They smelled change in the air; they knew it was time to reassert their manhood. But much was gleaned from those oh-so-sensitive times. Now there's a difference.

New and Improved

What is new and improved? During the Alda-Donahue Reign of Tears, men learned that women are fun to talk to, that they make the best of friends. Nothing is more attractive than a man who has platonic women friends; it means the man is truly comfortable with women. It means that he does not rely, as in the past, on his romantic interest of the moment as his sole source of female companionship other than Mom. That men and women can be friends may be the single most important social development of the last 20 years.

On the romantic front, they seek your opinion—not just on restaurants and clothes but on business and family and even (get this) sports. Men ask women's opinions on wines, instead of insisting they know more when often they do not. In addition, men now open doors again. They let you walk out of elevators first. On first dates, there's no more check splitting, a gesture that can put an end to romance as quickly as head lice. Now men pay first, or women pay first if they have done the inviting; what follows is a balance of gifts, a trading off of treating each other.

Of all these New New Men, I know of few more amazing cases than that of my baby brother. (He will always be my baby brother although he is 26 and so ardently adult that he owns Manhattan real estate.) I grew up believing he was more jerk than saint; now he lists decidedly towards the latter. He cares, he calls, he cleans, my God, he even cooks. This lover of Rambo, of rugby, of rock and roll, prepares meals with a vengeance. And at Thanksgiving my brother, who idolizes Clint Eastwood as others do Olivier, comes bearing two magnificent apple pies baked from scratch. My brother is exceptionally proud of those apple pies.

My brother's wife, who is a traditionalist in most respects, does not cook; she does not care to learn. He does the cooking. She does the laundry. They share the cleaning. And they are happy.

A Few Problems

Sometimes, the man and woman equally dislike cleaning. In these cases, there are only two solutions: Either the woman does it, or a housekeeper is hired. A woman who does not understand this is a fool.

Not everything with the New New Man is going smoothly, of course. Men, having learned that they're hot commodities now, have sometimes been allowed to act like jerks. Jerks believe in double-dating—that is, in seeing two wonderful women at the same time. (It used to be that they'd see a bimbo on the side; now they see someone you'd actually like.) Jerks believe in using charm like bait, something to hook a woman on before they bone, fry and devour her. It would be nice to report that jerks aren't getting anywhere with women these days, but that is simply not the case.

On the whole though, as a rule, in general, men are getting better. Reports are that all this progress has helped in the bedroom. Fewer men seem interested in amassing countless casualties. And even the most old-fashioned ones have proven generous, learning that half the fun is in the giving. They also have learned that the happy are usually willing to return the favor.

Cagey Men

It bears repeating, however, that men are smart. They're downright cagey. They pretty much know that if they give us what we want, we're going to give it right back to them twofold. They're not affected so much by fashion as by realism. When we wanted swine, or expected swine, we got them. And when we desired caring, confessional types, they delivered. Now the happy medium has arrived, and we're happy—well, we'll never be *completely* happy—and men are positively ecstatic about what magnificent mortals they've become.

"During the Alda-Donahue Reign of Tears, men learned that women are fun to talk to."

How do we know this? Because men will tell us. They will rattle on for days with reports of their glory, their progress, their brilliance. They will clean the bathroom for five minutes and talk about it for hours. Men, it should be noted, are not subtle in victory.

Of course, they will never get it entirely right. Or if they do, it will be wrong. We will change the rules. We will make up a new game plan. While they are asleep. In the middle of the night. Then they will cry out, again, with great exasperation and for the zillionth time, *"What do women want?"* We'll look pretty and smile and shake our heads. We won't say a thing. To any of them. Won't that be fun?

And then it will begin all over. Again.

Karen Heller is a staff writer for the Philadelphia Inquirer.

"The vast majority of American men today are confused, angry, stressed, and downright uncertain about the direction in which things are going for them."

viewpoint 10

Men Have Not Successfully Adapted to Changing Sex Roles

Morton H. Shaevitz

Adam was a lonely guy, but he would never let on to anybody, particularly not to Eve. Men have always, from the beginning, felt lonely and dependent on women. But men certainly were not going to tell them about it. Better to stand strong, to look cool, to stay in deep disguise, the quintessential silent man, or so the thinking usually goes.

This is not the rare man I describe. This is *most* men, the men that most women are having or trying to have relationships with today. Adam is merely the figurative forefather. When it comes to the opposite sex, the American male has had a long history of being the Great Pretender.

The Great Pretender, our late-twentieth-century Adam, is the guy who now finds himself thrust into the storm of the sex-role revolution. He's found himself taking on an even more complex disguise in response. Most men today present a calm public face, even to lovers and partners, that hides their more turbulent feelings about the shake-up in role relations with the other gender.

Women, of course, have been way out in front in all of this. Over the last several decades, much has changed for women. These changes have been explored and applauded exhaustively in the popular media and continue to be. We have learned a great deal about who women are, what they want, where they're going, and how they are or aren't balancing their complicated lives. Far less is known about what's happened to men during this time. Compared with the avalanche of reporting on women, there's not been much on men to speak of, and what exists may be more distortion and exaggeration than fact.

The public image of men today would lead us all to believe that men have changed right alongside women. Feature films and made-for-TV movies

showcase the house husband. Men's consciousness-raising groups make the news (in women's magazines or the women's pages of the paper, of course). Surely, untold thousands have swollen the ranks of a men's liberation movement, and thousands more are waiting for the next weekend of self-exploration to begin. That, more or less, is the popular perception.

Nonsense!

The *un*popular reality is decidedly otherwise.

If the truth be known, in spite of all the transformations in the lives of women, the hearts and minds of men have changed very little. House husbands, in fact, are scarce. A relative handful of men have gone to have their consciousness raised (and even fewer ever followed through).

And the vast majority of American men today are confused, angry, stressed, and downright uncertain about the direction in which things are going for them. They are also unhappy about the many apologetic portrayals of men that float about these days. Men tell me they are fed up with images of the wimp, the workaholic, the insensitive guy.

The Reality Gap

So why the reality gap?

Part of this may be due to men themselves. Men as a group are not very revealing about feelings. But they're talking even less on this particular subject because the contemporary social climate makes it difficult to acknowledge (to women or in mixed company) anything but positive feelings about women and the changes they're promulgating. They say that questioning the "revolution" or expressing negative feelings about it is often met with a barrage of criticism. Men are accused of being reactionary, chauvinistic, Neanderthal.

So, in public men's comments are supportive, but in a bland, vanillalike way. And I might add that these comments are often what gets reported, giving the impression that most men are pleased by everything that's happening.

However, when men are just with one another, when there are no women present, they have a lot of things to say. After a few minutes of discussion, the true feelings emerge. "Pressured," "resentful," and even "exasperated" are the words I hear.

Because weakness is not acceptable to men, what often don't get expressed are other feelings such as "deserted," "isolated," "ignored," "vulnerable," "uncared for," or "upset." Women often have to deal with the consequences of men's anger. However, they almost never hear men expressing these deeper needs.

Saying the Right Things

What is most confusing is that many men are *saying* all the "right things" (often with seeming conviction), but inside they are *feeling* very different. And men (and women) usually behave as they feel rather than as they say.

"What is most confusing is that many men . . . are saying *all the 'right things' . . . but inside they are* feeling *very different."*

In the actual, day-to-day relations between the sexes, this benign male deception is only partially successful. Feelings have a way of making themselves known, one way or another. A man may consistently "say" all the "right" things, for instance. But you know the phrase "actions speak louder than words"?

Consider Steve and Laura.

Laura: Sometimes I can't understand what's happening. Here I am, living with this thirty-one-year-old man who openly professes a deep commitment to women's equality. He tells me how proud he is that I am advancing in my career. He talks about how much my salary helps "our" budget. All his words to me say *go for it, do it, I support you!*

But then there's that unmistakable look on his face when I tell him I have to work on the weekend or that I'm meeting a friend for lunch. And, in spite of all that I'm doing, he still expects home-cooked dinners, our social life planned, innovative sex, me to join him jogging, and God knows what else.

I feel totally frustrated.

Steve: Laura keeps telling me that her work is important to her. She also has a lot of friends she's close to. I think it's great she's so involved. But where am I on her priority list? I'd like to be back toward the top like I was before. As things stand now, I feel closer to the bottom.

She keeps talking about balancing her life and organizing her time better. But if you look at what actually happens, there doesn't ever seem to be any time for *us.* Whenever I ask her to do anything—spend time by ourselves, make love, talk about what's going on in our respective lives, or, God forbid, cook dinner once in a while—she seems to resent it. And when she does agree, she's not really there. It's like she's doing me a favor.

Everything has become such a big deal. So more and more I'm just not asking. And that seems to suit her just fine. Frankly, I'm getting worn out by our hassles and by her constant anger. She's a wonderful woman. But I'm beginning to wonder if she's the wonderful woman for me.

Sound familiar?

Millions of men and women are wrestling at this very moment with just these kinds of issues, and these are men and women across the board—professional or working class, in two-career or traditional arrangements. Laura is typical of women who are out forging new paths for themselves. Steve is typical of the men who are of two minds about this.

The New Male Myth

To put it plainly, the New Male is a myth. (If you're a woman who has been looking for him, you may want to reconsider that particular search.) Pieces of the New Male exist, sure. (You're more likely to spot him in the early stages of courtship.) But the idea that there are lots of "whole" New Men out there, consistently, is wishful fiction. It's also way off the mark to think that there are lots of men out there today wishing and wanting to *become* New Men.

All of this is not to say that men aren't changing at all, or that there's a major backlash going on. There are some men who wonder if "things have gone too far." But, in my view, there is no going back. The revolution has happened, so to speak, and it's moving forward. It's just not finished yet. And it's just that men reside more in the backwaters of this massive revolutionary wave.

Men are moving far more slowly, quietly, and reluctantly than women. They're lagging behind. They're being pushed, pulled, and pressured every which way into a new future.

Remember, women are the active agents of change in all this. Men find themselves, perhaps for the first time in history, in the position of having to adapt. That responding position is a less than comfortable one for most men, accustomed as they are to initiating and being in charge. It's the rare individual who relinquishes privilege without resistance, however attractive the reasons for doing so might be.

The implications of men's having to divest themselves of power, or to redistribute it, to be exact, are enormous. Mostly, this rearrangement opens up far deeper issues for men today, issues seldom discussed, emotional issues that have to do with men's deep, long-standing, and largely *hidden* dependence upon the opposite sex. The American male's reluctance in the face of all the changes unfolding is intimately related to his ancient, largely unspoken need for the presence of women.

"If the major issue for women today is overload . . . the crisis for men today is loss—the loss of women."

Imagine our Adam, the first man, alone in the Garden of Eden, and you have a glimpse of how men are really feeling these days. If the major issue for women today is *overload* (balancing relationships, career, and if she's married, household, children, and all the rest), the crisis for men today is *loss*—the loss of women. At least, to men it feels like loss.

Women aren't available in the same ways as before, so men, in their hearts of hearts, are feeling let down, deserted, and keenly vulnerable to women's absence, whatever form that may take. Women remain mostly in the dark on this, because men aren't talking.

The other sex has pretty much always been duped into thinking that men need them *less* than they need men. That the reverse is more true is one of men's best-kept secrets. Men are much more dependent on women than women have even begun to realize. This is probably the most important thing for women to get through their heads about men, all seeming evidence to the contrary.

Men and Women Are Different

The next most important thing for women to understand and to accept is the many ways in which men are deeply different from them, for both biological and cultural reasons. Time and again, in trying to penetrate beneath that male inscrutability, women will mistakenly assume that men respond and feel as *they* do about many things. There is even more of a tendency now, in this "age of equality," to do this. Sameness between the sexes is emphasized as though differences have to mean problems. Well, differences *can* mean problems, but only when they are not properly understood. In fact, it's pretty much guaranteed they will be when that's the case. Assuming sameness when it doesn't exist, failing to recognize differences, is sure to lead to what I have come to call Perfect Misunderstandings between the sexes.

Our present-day Adams come to the sex-role revolution with an emotional landscape similar to women's, of course, but far from identical. Most men have few close bonds with anyone other than their lovers or partners (and perhaps their children). They value nurturing tremendously but usually have less skill than women in giving it. They are also less masterful than women at expressing their feelings and even at knowing them. . . .

Virtually all the men I see and talk with are either *in* a relationship or *looking* to be in one. So while this is . . . about changes and differences, the need for intimate relationships with women has remained inviolate. We just somehow, together, have to weather the storm of shifting rules and expectations.

There has probably never been a harder time for relations between the sexes, and I expect that things won't settle down for some time to come.

Morton H. Shaevitz is a psychiatry professor at the University of California, San Diego Medical School, and directs the Institute for Family and Work Relationships in California.

"As a result of a man's training to take care of himself, millions of women have been freer to look at their own values."

viewpoint 11

The Traditional Male Role Should Be Embraced

Warren Farrell

Every virtue, taken to the extreme, becomes a vice. For the past twenty years I have critiqued traditional masculinity because masculinity has been taken to the extreme. And taken to the extreme it creates anxiety, homicide, rape, war, and suicide; not taken to the extreme it has many virtues not to be tossed out with the bathwater.

Praise of men is an endangered species. But the good about men is not. And when something good is being endangered it needs special attention. And so, for a rare moment in recent history, here is special attention to what's good about male socialization. . . .

Giving/Generosity—Why do we think of women as giving of themselves and men as giving gifts? Because women's socialization teaches direct giving—as listening nurturers, cooks of men's meals, and doing more of his wash than he does of hers. He may give by working in a coal mine and contracting black lung so his child can attend college as he never could, but his giving is done at the mine—where we don't see it. The result of his giving is a check. With women's giving we appreciate more than the result, we appreciate the process: we see her cook the meal, serve it, and usually clean it up. We don't see him wading through water in a dark and damp mine shaft, or driving a truck at 2 A.M. on his fourth cup of coffee, behind schedule in traffic and with no time to nap. We see him at home withdrawing from the coffee.

He may spend much of his life earning money to finance a home his wife fell in love with, but we don't think of him as giving when he's away from home nearly as much as we think of her as giving when she cleans up his dishes.

Sometimes a man's giving is reflexive and role-based, such as when he reflexively picks up a tab at a restaurant. We forget this is also giving: fifty dollars for dinner and drinks may represent a day's work in after-tax income. Theater tickets, gas, and babysitters are another day's work. We don't think of his picking up these tabs as being as giving as when a woman spends two days preparing a special meal for him. Both forms of giving are role-based; hers are just more direct. . . .

Fairness—The best thing emerging from sports, games, work rules, winning, and losing is fairness. Not necessarily honesty—fairness. In Little League, when I trapped a ball in my glove just after a bounce, the umpire credited me with catching a fly. I volunteered to the umpire that I hadn't. The umpire, embarrassed, changed the decision. The angry coach bawled me out. The other coach bawled out my coach for bawling me out. They disagreed on honesty. But neither would have disagreed with the fairness of a neutral umpire making the decision.

Male socialization teaches the value of a careful system of rules, within which anyone can work to gain advantage, and some of which can be gotten around (with possible consequences). Once mastered, the rules give everyone a much more equal chance than they would have had without the rules. To men, mastering these rules feels like survival—survival of themselves and their family. A lifetime of practicing these rules gives many men a sixth sense for fairness. Groups of men and women who have disregarded these rules as "too male" or "too establishment," as did the Students for a Democratic Society in the sixties and seventies, soon evolve into backstabbing elites which self-destruct.

Male Action

Nurturing—Carl wasn't great at expressing feelings. And he didn't understand fully that sometimes Cindy just needed a listening ear. His way of supporting her was to volunteer to help Cindy with the problem that was making her upset. For Carl,

Warren Farrell, *Why Men Are the Way They Are*. New York: McGraw-Hill Book Company, 1986. Reprinted by permission.

male / female roles   51

taking Cindy seriously meant taking Cindy's problem seriously, and taking Cindy's problem seriously meant trying to find a solution. To him this was an act of love. Anything less, like just standing around when she was hurting, was an act of cruelty. "If Cindy's bleeding," he'd say, "find a solution. . . . Don't just stand there with that sickening supportive smile on your face while the woman I love is bleeding to death!" *Solutions are male nurturance. . . .*

Leadership—Accusations that "men have the power" have appeared more frequently in the past decade and a half than appreciation for the billions of hours sacrificed by men to give themselves the leadership training to get that power. Or the benefits of the leadership itself. For example, few articles explain how male socialization has trained millions of leaders to lead thousands of businesses that are now providing millions of women with opportunities for leadership that might not exist were it not for male leadership.

"Male socialization teaches the value of a careful system of rules."

Outrageousness—While women are socialized to get male attention by being "good girls" or not offending male egos, men are being socialized to get female attention by standing out. One way a man can stand out is to be outrageous. The best part of outrageousness is the barriers it breaks to allow all of us more freedom to experiment with discovering more of ourselves. The Beatles' hair, considered outrageous at the time, permitted a generation to experiment with their hair; Elvis the Pelvis allowed a generation to experiment with their sexual selves; the Wright Brothers were told it was scientifically impossible to fly—and suicidal to try; and Salvador Dali, Picasso, and Copernicus looked at the world in ways considered outrageous in their time; in retrospect, we can see that they freed us to live in it in a way we could not have dreamed of before.

Male Psychology

To Keep Emotions Under Control—Although in relationships, this tight lid leads to a "male volcano" after months of repressed emotions, the flip side is our dependence on this male trait in crisis situations. Dirk recalls a head-on collision. "Five cars crashed. There was glass and blood everywhere. Four of us guys ran from car to car, following the screams and preparing tourniquets. We stopped two cars to recruit passengers to redirect traffic, called the police, and removed a woman and her son from a car that burst into flames a minute later."

The newspapers reported the accident. But no

headlines read "Men Control Their Emotions in Order to Save Lives of Women and Children." They ran a picture—not of four men standing next to the women and children they saved, but of the five *cars* that collided.

Ego Strength—When women reevaluate what goes wrong in a relationship the unspoken assumption is that this takes ego strength. When men compete fiercely to be number one, we see it as a reflection of their fragile egos (which it can be) and call it strategizing, *rather than recognizing the ego strength required to conduct a self-reevaluation immediately after a loss.* A man needs to ask, "What did *I* do wrong?" And then, when he finds the answer, rather than credit himself with his introspection, he must focus immediately on correcting it before the next game. . . .

To Express Anger—"One minute we were shouting and calling each other names. A minute later we were concentrating on the next play." The male tendency to take sports seriously combined with the willingness to express feelings intensely leads many adult men to say, "I lose my temper for a minute, then it's done with." The positive side of male anger is the quick, intense release of emotions, with the subsequent calm that follows the storm. If the intensity is understood, and not exacerbated, grudges are rarely held. The intensity, like all powerful energy, can be harnessed—and channeled into powerful lovemaking. . . .

Male Strength

To Save Her Life at the Risk of His Own—I described in the introduction [of my book] how my younger brother Wayne died in an avalanche as he ventured ahead to check out a dangerous area alone rather than have his woman friend share the risk or do it herself. No news account of his death discussed this as an example of men's willingness to forfeit their lives for the women they love. We read of accounts of women lifting automobiles to save the life of a child, but not to save the life of a husband. Frequently, a woman who hears about this difference gets defensive even though she says she wants to appreciate men more.

There is nothing to be defensive about. It is not a statement that men are better. Members of each sex do what they are socialized to do both to give themselves the feeling of being part of a whole and to deviate a bit to feel like an individual. This makes both sexes equal—with different programming. A man's dying for a woman he loves doesn't make him better at all, but part of his socialization leaves him vulnerable. My brother was quite vulnerable.

To Give Up His Life for His Beliefs . . . —Some men give up their lives at war because they believe in their country; others do it because if they cannot be a hero they'd rather not live; others do it to support families. Others risk their lives in war so that if they live, they will earn enough money and status to "earn" a wife. Men with different class or ethnic backgrounds do the same in the CIA, FBI, State Department, and Mafia: their beliefs or their willingness to support their families are as important as their entire existence.

For these men, these are not empty words. While the worst part of this is an extraordinary statement of male insecurity and compensation for powerlessness, the best part is the extraordinary conviction men have for their beliefs and their families. It is a statement (within their value system) of the importance of values, responsibility, and quality of life: theirs and their family's. . . .

Male Responsibilities

Self-Sufficiency—We don't call men "career men," because the word *career* is built into the word *man*. Self-sufficiency is built into masculinity. . . .

Male socialization is an overdose in self-sufficiency. There are no fairy tales of a princess on a white horse finding a male Sleeping Beauty and sweeping him off to a castle; no fairy tales glorifying a man who is not self-sufficient. When the going gets tough, he doesn't talk it through, he gets going.

How do these fairy tales translate into reality? Liberation has been defined as *giving* women the "right to choose": to choose the option of being at home or being at work. *Men do not learn they have the right to choose to be at home. That would imply someone else would have to take care of him at home.* A man doesn't learn to expect that. He learns, instead, "The world doesn't owe you a living." Self-sufficiency implies *earning* rights. The right to choose, he learns, comes from choosing, for example, to take a job that pays a lot so he has more choices when he is away from the job. As a result of a man's training to take care of himself, millions of women have been freer to look at their own values—and to criticize men—than they would be if they had to support them. . . .

"Self-sufficiency is built into masculinity."

Risk Taking—The male socialization to take risks on the playing field prepares a man to take risks investing in stocks, businesses, and conglomerates. To invest in his career with years of training, and then extra training. A plastic surgeon may have risked from age five to thirty-five as a student or part-time student, underpaid and overworked, in order, during the second half of his life, to be able to earn a half million dollars a year. . . .

On numerous levels, male socialization teaches men to risk a lot and be willing to fail a lot—and all

for the hope of being rewarded a lot. (Conversely, if he doesn't risk, he doesn't expect the rewards.) If he survives, he will then be able to provide a security for his wife and children that he never had for himself. . . .

To Develop Identity—The pressure on men to be more than self-sufficient, which forced them to take risks and self-start, to sort out their values quickly, to learn how and when to challenge authority, and to invent, resulted, at best, in the development of *identity*. Identity arises out of seeing both how we fit in and how we don't fit in—but especially how we don't fit in. The foundation of society is here before we arrive and after we pass. Identity is discovering our uniqueness in that continuity. As we take risks, and challenge what exists, the friction between ourselves and society makes all the boundaries clearer. Which is how we develop identity, and why the best parts of male socialization are helpful in developing identity. Of course, most men sell a good portion of their identity out to institutions just as most women sell out to a man. But the part of a man true to the values he has sorted out still challenges, still takes risks, still benefits from the development of identity. . . .

Responsibility—Male socialization is a recipe book of taking responsibility. From the responsibility of getting a job at age fourteen so he can pay for his first date's food and tickets, to performing adequately within view of the girl he wants to ask out to increase his chances of acceptance, to actually asking his first date out, to arranging for his parents to drive, then, in later years, to borrowing the car, then driving himself, then taking initiatives—all of these are responsibility. . . .

My study of male-female language-pattern differences reflects the male training to take responsibility. Men are much less likely to use phrases like "This happened to me," and much more likely to use phrases like "I did this."

What Males Can Do

Sense of Efficacy—In the process of learning to take risks, men get especially strong training in learning what is and what is not effective—a sense of efficacy. In the process of trying a wide variety of jobs, we learn what we are effective at. We are socialized with a different attitude toward lost investments—as experiences that fine-tune us to the questions we must ask to prevent the next loss. We see the loss as an investment in investing. Tinkering for hours under a hood teaches him by trial and error how to be effective with a car (I said teaches him—it hasn't taught me!).

Once again, this is reflected in male-female language differences. Men are much less likely to say, "Maybe we can get Bill to do that," and much more likely to say, "Maybe if I try . . . "

Doing Rather than Complaining—To become

effective, men learn to make the unarticulated distinction between two types of complaining: "I'm helpless" versus "This is the complaint, now here's the solution." Men are not tolerant enough of other men complaining, "I'm helpless." But the best part of this intolerance is the pressure it exerts on a man to get rid of the problem that created the complaint.

Pushing the Limits of One's Talents—Doing may be better than complaining, but doing is not enough. A man's pressure to earn as much as he can with his talents means a constant pushing of the limits of each and every talent to discover which one can support him best. When people hear "pushing the limits of one's talents" they think of talents as raw capability; they feel that job advancement involves an expansion of talents and an application of talents toward an appropriate job and frequent promotions. Successful people learn that pushing the limits of one's talents also means balancing the politics of everyone else's egos while making themselves shine; balancing facade with personal integrity; and selling themselves repeatedly without appearing as if they're selling. The struggle to master the complex politics of advancement is the real pushing of the limits of one's talents.

The recent focus on discrimination has made us feel that the formula for success is qualifications plus lack of discrimination. That one-two approach has limited our appreciation of the extraordinary subtlety and range of talents required for advancement. . . .

Male Flexibility

Sense of Humor—Whether it's Woody Allen's ability to laugh at the schlemiel in himself or George Carlin's ability to laugh at masculinity itself, one of the best things that emerges from men's training to see life as a game is the ability to laugh both at our own roles in the game and at the game itself. Even the most traditional and serious of male systems are mocked, such as Bill Murray in *Stripes* mocking the military. It is difficult to find movies similarly mocking the traditional female role—for example, a movie mocking motherhood. . . .

"Although men have made fewer changes than women, what changes they have made . . . have occurred without movements that blamed women."

Change Without Blame—Although men have made fewer changes than women, what changes they have made—as in fathering—have occurred without movements that blamed women. Fifteen years ago, few men were sensitive to orgasms or clitorises. Few had heard of the ERA. Few fathers-to-be joined their wives in the delivery room, in the preparation for the birth of their child. But soon, men had changed in all these ways.

The changes that occurred happened without attacking women with equal-but-opposite rhetoric, such as "Women hold a monopoly of power over the child," or "Women have a fragile mothering ego perpetuated by a quiet matriarchy that sends men into the field to die while women conspire to sleep in warm beds at home." Nor did men respond to blame by labeling it psychological abuse.

When we hear the phrase "the battle between the sexes," there is an unspoken assumption that both sexes have been blaming equally. The battle, though, could easily be called "the female attack on men," not "the male attack on women." There is a distinction between responding to blame and initiating it. Men have changed less, but they have also blamed less.

Warren Farrell is an author whose books include The Liberated Man *and* Why Men Are the Way They Are. *He has been called "the Gloria Steinem of Men's Liberation."*

The Traditional Male Role Should Be Rejected

Cooper Thompson

I was once asked by a teacher in a suburban high school to give a guest presentation on male roles. She hoped that I might help her deal with four boys who exercised extraordinary control over the other boys in the class. Using ridicule and their status as physically imposing athletes, these four wrestlers had succeeded in stifling the participation of the other boys, who were reluctant to make comments in class discussions.

As a class we talked about the ways in which boys got status in that school and how they got put down by others. I was told that the most humiliating put-down was being called a "fag." The list of behaviors which could elicit ridicule filled two large chalkboards, and it was detailed and comprehensive; I got the sense that a boy in this school had to conform to rigid, narrow standards of masculinity to avoid being called a fag. I, too, felt this pressure and became very conscious of my mannerisms in front of the group. Partly from exasperation, I decided to test the seriousness of these assertions. Since one of the four boys had some streaks of pink in his shirt, and since he had told me that wearing pink was grounds for being called a fag, I told him that I thought he was a fag. Instead of laughing, he said, "I'm going to kill you."

Such is the stereotypic definition of strength that is associated with masculinity. But it is a very limited definition of strength, one based on dominance and control and acquired through the humiliation and degradation of others.

A New Image of Strength

Contrast this with a view of strength offered by Pam McAllister in her introduction to *Reweaving the Web of Life:*

The 'Strength' card in my Tarot deck depicts, not a warrior going off to battle with his armor and his mighty sword, but a woman stroking a lion. The woman has not slain the lion nor maced it, not netted it, nor has she put on it a muzzle or a leash. And though the lion clearly has teeth and long sharp claws, the woman is not hiding, nor has she sought a protector, nor has she grown muscles. She doesn't appear to be talking to the lion, nor flattering it, nor tossing it fresh meat to distract its hungry jaws.

The woman on the 'Strength' card wears a flowing white dress and a garland of flowers. With one hand she cups the lion's jaws, with the other she caresses its nose. The lion on the card has big yellow eyes and a long red tongue curling out of its mouth. One paw is lifted and the mane falls in thick red curls across its broad torso. The woman. The lion. Together they depict strength.

This image of strength stands in direct contrast to the strength embodied in the actions of the four wrestlers. The collective strength of the woman and the lion is a strength unknown in a system of traditional male values. Other human qualities are equally foreign to a traditional conception of masculinity. In workshops I've offered on the male role stereotype, teachers and other school personnel easily generate lists of attitudes and behaviors which boys typically seem to not learn. Included in this list are being supportive and nurturant, accepting one's vulnerability and being able to ask for help, valuing women and "women's work," understanding and expressing emotions (except for anger), the ability to empathize with and empower other people, and learning to resolve conflict in non-aggressive, non-competitive ways.

Learning Violence

All of this should come as no surprise. Traditional definitions of masculinity include attributes such as independence, pride, resiliency, self-control, and physical strength. This is precisely the image of the Marlboro man, and to some extent, these are desirable attributes for boys and girls. But

Cooper Thompson, "A New View of Masculinity," *Educational Leadership*, December 1985. Reprinted with permission of the Association for Supervision and Curriculum Development. Copyright © by ASCD. All rights reserved.

masculinity goes beyond these qualities to stress competitiveness, toughness, aggressiveness, and power. In this context, threats to one's status, however small, cannot be avoided or taken lightly. If a boy is called a fag, it means that he is perceived as weak or timid—and therefore not masculine enough for his peers. There is enormous pressure for him to fight back. Not being tough at these moments only proves the allegation. . . .

Ultimately, violence is the tool which maintains what I believe are the two most critical socializing forces in a boy's life: *homophobia*, the hatred of gay men (who are stereotyped as feminine) or those men believed to be gay, as well as the fear of being perceived as gay; and *misogyny*, the hatred of women. The two forces are targeted at different classes of victims, but they are really just the flip sides of the same coin. Homophobia is the hatred of feminine qualities in men while misogyny is the hatred of feminine qualities in women. The boy who is called a fag is the target of other boys' homophobia as well as the victim of his own homophobia. While the overt message is the absolute need to avoid being feminized, the implication is that females—and all that they traditionally represent—are contemptible. The United States Marines have a philosophy which conveniently combines homophobia and misogyny in the belief that "When you want to create a group of male killers, you kill 'the woman' in them."

The pressures of homophobia and misogyny in boys' lives have been poignantly demonstrated to me each time that I have repeated a simple yet provocative activity with students. I ask them to answer the question, "If you woke up tomorrow and discovered that you were the opposite sex from the one you are now, how would you and your life be different?" Girls consistently indicate that there are clear advantages to being a boy—from increased independence and career opportunities to decreased risks of physical and sexual assault—and eagerly answer the question. But boys often express disgust at this possibility and even refuse sometimes to answer the question. In her reports of a broad-based survey using this question, Alice Baumgartner reports the following responses as typical of boys: "If I were a girl, I'd be stupid and weak as a string;" "I would have to wear makeup, cook, be a mother, and yucky stuff like that;" "I would have to hate snakes. Everything would be miserable;" "If I were a girl, I'd kill myself."

The Costs of Masculinity

The costs associated with a traditional view of masculinity are enormous, and the damage occurs at both personal and societal levels. The belief that a boy should be tough (aggressive, competitive, and daring) can create emotional pain for him. While a few boys experience short-term success for their

toughness, there is little security in the long run. Instead, it leads to a series of challenges which few, if any, boys ultimately win. There is no security in being at the top when so many other boys are competing for the same status. Toughness also leads to increased chances of stress, physical injury, and even early death. It is considered manly to take extreme physical risks and voluntarily engage in combative, hostile activities.

"Traditional masculinity is life threatening."

The flip side of toughness—nurturance—is not a quality perceived as masculine and thus not valued. Because of this boys and men experience a greater emotional distance from other people and few opportunities to participate in meaningful interpersonal relationships. Studies consistently show that fathers spend very small amounts of time interacting with their children. In addition, men report that they seldom have intimate relationships with other men, reflecting their homophobia. They are afraid of getting too close and don't know how to take down the walls that they have built between themselves.

As boys grow older and accept adult roles, the larger social costs of masculinity clearly emerge. Most women experience male resistance to an expansion of women's roles; one of the assumptions of traditional masculinity is the belief that women should be subordinate to men. The consequence is that men are often not willing to accept females as equal, competent partners in personal and professional settings. Whether the setting is a sexual relationship, the family, the streets, or the battlefield, men are continuously engaged in efforts to dominate. Statistics on child abuse consistently indicate that the vast majority of abusers are men, and that there is no "typical" abuser. Rape may be the fastest growing crime in the United States. And it is men, regardless of nationality, who provoke and sustain war. In short, traditional masculinity is life threatening.

New Socialization for Boys

Masculinity, like many other human traits, is determined by both biological and environmental factors. While some believe that biological factors are significant in shaping some masculine behavior, there is undeniable evidence that cultural and environmental factors are strong enough to override biological impulses. What is it, then, that we should be teaching boys about being a man in a modern world?

- Boys must learn to accept their vulnerability, learn to express a range of emotions such as fear and sadness, and learn to ask for help and support in appropriate situations.

- Boys must learn to be gentle, nurturant, cooperative and communicative, and in particular, learn non-violent means of resolving conflicts.
- Boys must learn to accept those attitudes and behaviors which have traditionally been labeled feminine as necessary for full human development—thereby reducing homophobia and misogyny. This is tantamount to teaching boys to love other boys and girls.

Certain qualities like courage, physical strength, and independence, which are traditionally associated with masculinity, are indeed positive qualities for males, provided that they are not manifested in obsessive ways nor used to exploit or dominate others. It is not necessary to completely disregard or unlearn what is traditionally called masculine. I believe, however, that the three areas above are crucial for developing a broader view of masculinity, one which is healthier for all life.

These three areas are equally crucial for reducing aggressive, violent behavior among boys and men. Males must learn to cherish life for the sake of their *own* wholeness as human beings, not just *for* their children, friends, and lovers. If males were more nurturant, they would be less likely to hurt those they love. . . .

Schools and Athletics

Where will this change in socialization occur? In his first few years, most of a boy's learning about masculinity comes from the influences of parents, siblings and images of masculinity such as those found on television. Massive efforts will be needed to make changes here. But at older ages, school curriculum and the school environment provide powerful reinforcing images of traditional masculinity. This reinforcement occurs through a variety of channels, including curriculum content, role modeling, and extracurricular activities, especially competitive sports.

School athletics are a microcosm of the socialization of male values. While participation in competitive activities can be enjoyable and healthy, it too easily become a lesson in the need for toughness, invulnerability, and dominance. Athletes learn to ignore their own injuries and pain and instead try to injure and inflict pain on others in their attempts to win, regardless of the cost to themselves or their opponents. Yet the lessons learned in athletics are believed to be vital for full and complete masculine development, and as a model for problem-solving in other areas of life.

In addition to encouraging traditional male values, schools provide too few experiences in nurturance, cooperation, negotiation, non-violent conflict resolution, and strategies for empathizing with and empowering others. Schools should become places where boys have the opportunity to learn these skills; clearly, they won't learn them on the street, from peers, or on television.

Despite the pressures on men to display their masculinity in traditional ways, there are examples of men and boys who are changing. "Fathering" is one example of a positive change. In recent years, there has been a popular emphasis on child-care activities, with men becoming more involved in providing care to children, both professionally and as fathers. This is a clear shift from the more traditional view that child rearing should be delegated to women and is not an appropriate activity for men.

"Males must learn to cherish life for the sake of their own *wholeness as human beings."*

For all of the male resistance it has generated, the Women's Liberation Movement has at least provided a stimulus for some men to accept women as equal partners in most areas of life. These are the men who have chosen to learn and grow from women's experiences and together with women are creating new norms for relationships. Popular literature and research on male sex roles is expanding, reflecting a wider interest in masculinity. Weekly news magazines such as *Time* and *Newsweek* have run major stories on the "new masculinity," suggesting that positive changes are taking place in the home and in the workplace. Small groups of men scattered around the country have organized against pornography, battering and sexual assault. Finally there is the National Organization for Changing Men which has a pro-feminist, pro-gay, pro-"new man" agenda, and its ranks are slowly growing. . . .

Boys Will Be Boys

I think back to the four wrestlers and the stifling culture of masculinity in which they live. If schools were to radically alter this culture and substitute for it a new vision of masculinity, what would that look like? In this environment, boys would express a full range of behaviors and emotions without fear of being chastized. They would be permitted and encouraged to cry, to be afraid, to show joy, and to express love in a gentle fashion. Extreme concern for career goals would be replaced by a consideration of one's need for recreation, health, and meaningful work. Older boys would be encouraged to tutor and play with younger students. Moreover, boys would receive as much recognition for artistic talents as they do for athletics, and, in general, they would value leisure-time, recreational activities as highly as competitive sports.

In a system where maleness and femaleness were equally valued, boys might no longer feel that they have to "prove" themselves to other boys; they would simply accept the worth of each person and value those differences. Boys would realize that it is permissable to admit failure. In addition, they would seek out opportunities to learn from girls and women. Emotional support would be commonplace, and it would no longer be seen as just the role of the female to provide the support. Relationships between boys and girls would no longer be based on limited roles, but instead would become expressions of two individuals learning from and supporting one another. Relationships between boys would reflect their care for one another rather than their mutual fear and distrust.

"In a system where maleness and femaleness were equally valued, boys might no longer feel that they have to 'prove' themselves to other boys."

Aggressive styles of resolving conflicts would be the exception rather than the norm. Girls would feel welcome in activities dominated by boys, knowing that they were safe from the threat of being sexually harassed. Boys would no longer boast of beating up another boy or of how much they "got off" of a girl the night before. In fact, the boys would be as outraged as the girls at rape or other violent crimes in the community. Finally, boys would become active in efforts to stop nuclear proliferation and all other forms of military violence, following the examples set by activist women.

The development of a new conception of masculinity based on this vision is an ambitious task, but one which is essential for the health and safety of both men and women. The survival of our society may rest on the degree to which we are able to teach men to cherish life.

Cooper Thompson is the director of Resources for Change, a Massachusetts organization providing training on masculinity, sex roles, and homophobia.

> *"The deep, nourishing and spiritually radiant energy in the male lies not in the feminine side, but in the deep masculine."*

The Traditional Male Role Should Be Redefined

Robert Bly, interviewed by Keith Thompson

[KT]: After exploring the way of the goddess and the matriarchs for many years, lately you've turned your attention to the pathways of male energy—the bond between fathers and sons, for example, and the initiation of young males. You're also writing a book relating some of the old classic fairy tales to men's growth. What has your investigation turned up? What's going on with men these days?

[RB]: No one knows! Historically, the male has changed considerably in the past thirty years. Back then there was a person we could call the '50s male, who was hard-working, responsible, fairly well disciplined; he didn't see women's souls very well, though he looked at their bodies a lot. Reagan still has this personality. The '50s male was vulnerable to collective opinion: if you were a man, you were supposed to like football games, be aggressive, stick up for the United States, never cry, and always provide. But this image of the male lacked feminine space. It lacked some sense of flow, it lacked compassion, in a way that led directly to the unbalanced pursuit of the Vietnam War, just as the lack of feminine space inside Reagan's head now has led to his callousness and brutality toward the poor in El Salvador, toward old people here, the unemployed, schoolchildren, and poor people in general. The '50s male had a clear vision of what a man is, but the vision involved massive inadequacies and flaws.

Then, during the '60s, another sort of male appeared. The waste and anguish of the Vietnam War made men question what an adult male really is. And the women's movement encouraged men to actually look at women, forcing them to become conscious of certain things that the '50s male tended to avoid. As men began to look at women and at

Keith Thompson, "What Men Really Want: an interview with Robert Bly" from *New Men, New Minds*. Freedom, CA: The Crossing Press, 1987. Copyright 1982 Keith Thompson. Reprinted with permission.

their concerns, some men began to see their own feminine side and pay attention to it. That process continues to this day, and I would say that most young males are now involved in it to some extent.

Now there's something wonderful about all this—the step of the male bringing forth his own feminine consciousness is an important one—and yet I have the sense there is something wrong. The male in the past twenty years has become more thoughtful, more gentle. But by this process he has not become more free. He's a nice boy who now not only pleases his mother but also the young woman he is living with.

The Soft Male

I see the phenomenon of what I would call the "soft male" all over the country today.

Sometimes when I look out at my audiences, perhaps half the young males are what I'd call soft. They're lovely, valuable people—I like them—and they're not interested in harming the earth, or starting wars or working for corporations. There is something favorable toward life in their whole general mood and style of living.

But something's wrong. Many of these men are unhappy. There's not much energy in them. They are life-preserving but not exactly life-giving. And why is it you often see these men with strong women who positively radiate energy? Here we have a finely tuned young man, ecologically superior to his father, sympathetic to the whole harmony of the universe, yet he himself has no energy to offer. . . .

In every relationship, something fierce is needed once in a while; both the man and the woman need to have it.

At the point when it was needed, often the young man didn't have it. He was nurturing, but something else was required—for the relationship, for his life. The male was able to say, "I can feel your pain, and I consider your life as important as mine, and I will take care of you and comfort you." But he could not say what he wanted, and stick by it; that was a different matter.

In The Odyssey, Hermes instructs Odysseus, when he is approaching a kind of matriarchal figure, that he is to lift or show Circe his sword. It was difficult for many of the younger males to distinguish between showing the sword and hurting someone. Do you understand me? They had learned so well not to hurt anyone that they couldn't lift the sword, even to catch the light of the sun on it! Showing a sword doesn't mean fighting; there's something joyful in it.

Iron John

KT: You seem to be suggesting that uniting with their feminine side has been an important stage for men on their path toward wholeness, but it's not the final one. What is required? What's the next step?

RB: One of the fairy tales I'm working on for my *Fairy Tales for Men* collection is a story called "Iron John." Though it was first set down by the Grimm Brothers around 1820, this story could be ten or twenty thousand years old. It talks about a different development for men, a further stage than we've seen so far in the United States.

As the story starts, something strange has been happening in a remote area of the forest near the king's castle; when hunters go into this area, they disappear and never come back. Three hunters have gone out and disappeared. People are getting the feeling that there's something kind of weird about the part of the forest, and they don't go there anymore. Then one day an unknown hunter shows up at the castle and says, "What can I do around here? I need something to do." And he is told, "Well, there's a problem in the forest. People go out there and they don't come back. We've sent groups of men to see about it and they disappear. Can you do something about it?"

"Every modern male has, lying at the bottom of his psyche, a large primitive man covered with hair down to his feet."

Interestingly, this young man does not ask for a group to go with him—he goes into the forest alone, taking only his dog. And they wander about in the forest, they come across a pond. Suddenly a hand reaches up from the pond, grabs the dog and drags it down. The hunter is fond of the dog and he's not willing to abandon it, in this way. His response is neither to become hysterical, nor to abandon his dog. Instead, he does something sensible, he goes back to the castle, rounds up some men with buckets and then they bucket out the pond.

Lying at the bottom of the pond is a large man covered with hair all the way down to his feet. He's kind of reddish—he looks a little like rusty iron. So they capture him and bring him back to the castle, where the king puts him in an iron cage in the courtyard.

Now, let's stop the story here a second. The implication is that when the male looks into his psyche, not being instructed what to look for, he may see beyond his feminine side, to the other side of the "deep pool." What he finds at the bottom of his psyche—in this area that no one has visited in a long time—is an ancient male covered with hair. Now, in all of the mythologies, hair is heavily connected with the instinctive, the sexual, the primitive. What I'm proposing is that every modern male has, lying at the bottom of his psyche, a large primitive man covered with hair down to his feet. Making contact with this wildman is the step the '70s male has not yet taken, this is the process that still hasn't taken place in contemporary culture.

As the story suggests very delicately, there's a little fear around this ancient man. After a man gets over his initial skittishness about expressing his feminine side, he finds it to be pretty wonderful, he gets to write poetry and go out and sit by the ocean, he doesn't have to be on top all the time in sex anymore, he becomes empathetic. It's a beautiful new world. But Iron John, the man at the bottom of the lake, is quite a different matter. This figure is even more frightening than the interior female, who is scary enough. When a man succeeds in becoming conscious of his interior woman, he often feels warmer, more alive. But when he approaches what I'll call the "deep male," that's a totally different situation! . . .

The Golden Ball

Now, let's go back to the story. One day the king's eight-year-old son is playing in the courtyard and he loses his beloved golden ball. It rolls into the cage, and the wildman grabs it. If the prince wants his ball back, he's going to have to go to this rusty, hairy man who's been dying at the bottom of the pond for a very long time and ask for it. The plot begins to thicken.

KT: The golden ball, of course, is a recurrent image in many fairy stories. What does it symbolize in general, and what is its significance here?

RB: The golden ball suggests the unity of personality that we have as children—a kind of radiance, a sense of unity with the universe. The ball is golden, representing light, and round, representing wholeness, like the sun, it gives off a radiant energy from inside.

Notice that in this story, the boy is eight. We all lose something around the age of eight, whether we are girl or boy, male or female. We lose the golden ball in grade school if not before; high school finishes it. We may spend the rest of our lives trying to get the golden ball back. The first stage of that process I guess would be accepting—firmly, definitely—that the ball has been lost. Remember Freud's words? "What a distressing contrast there is between the radiant intelligence of the child and the feeble mentality of the average adult."

Where the Ball Is

So who's got the golden ball? In the '60s, males were told that the golden ball was the feminine, in their own feminine side. They found the feminine, and still did not find the golden ball. That step that both Freud and Jung urged on males and the step that men are beginning to undertake now, is the realization that you cannot look to your own feminine side, because that's not where the ball was lost. . . .

"The ancient societies believed that a boy becomes a man only through ritual and effort . . . it doesn't happen just because he eats Wheaties."

After looking for the golden ball in women and not finding it, then looking into his own feminine side, the young male is called upon to consider the possibility that the golden ball lies within the magnetic field of the wildman. Now, that's a very hard thing for us to conceive the possibility that the deep nourishing and spiritually radiant energy in the male lies not in the feminine side, but in the deep masculine. Not the shallow masculine, the macho masculine, the snowmobile masculine, but the deep masculine, the instinctive one who's underwater and who has been there we don't know how long. . . .

And I think that today's males are just about ready to take that step, to go to the cage and ask for the golden ball back. Some are ready to do that, others haven't gotten the water out of the pond yet, they haven't yet left the collective male identity and gone out into the wilderness alone, into the unconscious. You've got to take a bucket, several buckets. You can't wait for a giant to come along and suck out all the water for you; all that magic stuff isn't going to help you. A weekend at Esalen won't do it either! You have to do it bucket by bucket. This resembles the slow discipline of art; it's the work that Rembrandt did, that Picasso and Yeats and Rilke and Bach all did. Bucket work implies much more discipline than many males have right now.

KT: And of course, it's going to take some persistence and discipline, not only to uncover the deep male, but to get the golden ball back. It seems unlikely that this "un-nice" wildman would just hand it over.

RB: You're right; what kind of story would it be if the wildman answered: "Well, OK, here's your ball—go have fun." . . .

So in "Iron John," a deal is made, the wildman agrees to give the golden ball back if the boy opens the cage.

At first, the boy is frightened and runs off. Finally, the third time the wildman offers the same deal, the boy says, "I couldn't open it even if I wanted to because I don't know where the key is." The wildman now says something magnificent, he says, "The key is under your mother's pillow."

Did you get that shot? The key to let the wildman out is lying not in the toolshed, not in the attic, not in the cellar—it's under his mother's pillow! What do you make of that?

KT: It seems to suggest that the young male has to take back the power he has given to his mother and get away from the force field of her bed. He must direct his energies away from pleasing Mommy and toward the search for his own instinctive roots. . . .

RB: Obviously, you've got to wait until your mother and father have gone away. This represents not being so dependent on the collective, on the approval of the community, on being a nice person, or essentially being dependent on your own mother because if you went up to your mother and said "I want the key so I can let the wildman out," she'd say, "Oh no, you just get a job" or "Come over here and give Mommy a kiss." There are very few mothers in the world who would release that key from under the pillow because they are intuitively aware of what would happen next—namely, they would lose their nice boys. The possessiveness that some mothers exercise on sons—not to mention the possessiveness that fathers exercise toward their daughters—cannot be overestimated.

Freeing the Wildman

And then, we have a lovely scene in which the boy succeeds in opening the cage and setting the wildman free. At this point, one could imagine a number of things happening.

The wildman could go back to his pond, so that the split happens over again: by the time the parents come back, the wildman is gone and the boy has replaced the key. He could become a corporate executive, an ordained minister, a professor, he might be a typical 20th century male.

But in this case, what happens is that the wildman comes out of the cage and starts toward the forest and the boy shouts after him, "Don't run away! My parents are going to be very angry when they come back." And Iron John says, "I guess you're right; you'd better come with me." He hoists the boy up on his shoulders and off they go.

KT: What does this mean, that they take off together?

RB: There are several possible arrangements in

life that a male can make with the wildman. The male can be separated from the wildman in his unconscious by thousands of miles and never see him. Or the male and the wildman can exist together in a civilized place, like a courtyard, with the wildman in a cage, and they can carry on a conversation with one another, which can go on for a long time. But apparently the two can never be united in the courtyard, the boy cannot bring the wildman with him into his home. When the wildman is freed a little, when the young man feels a little more trust in his instinctive part after going through some discipline, then he can let the wildman out of the cage. And since the wildman can't stay with him in civilization, he must go off with the wildman.

This is where the break with the parents finally comes. As they go off together the wildman says, "You'll never see your mother and father again," and the boy has to accept that the collective thing is over. He must leave his parents' force field.

KT: In the ancient Greek tradition a young man would leave his family to study with an older man the energies of Zeus, Apollo, or Dionysius. We seem to have lost the rite of initiation, and yet young males have a great need to be introduced to the male mysteries.

RB: This is what has been missing in our culture. Among the Hopis and other Native Americans of the Southwest, a boy is taken away at age twelve and led down into a kiva (down!): he stays down there for six weeks, and a year and half passes before he sees his mother. He enters completely into the instinctive male world, which means a sharp break with both parents. You see, the fault of the nuclear family isn't so much that it's crazy and full of double binds (that's true in communes too—it's the human condition), the issue is that the son has a difficult time breaking away from the parents' field of energy, especially the mother's field, and our culture simply has made no provision for this initiation.

The ancient societies believed that a boy becomes a man only through ritual and effort—that he must be initiated into the world of men. It doesn't happen by itself, it doesn't happen just because he eats Wheaties. And only men can do this work. . . .

Father-Son Separation

KT: Underneath most of the issues we've talked about is the father or the absence of the father. I was moved by a statement you made in *News of the Universe* that the love-unit most damaged by the Industrial Revolution has been the father-son bond.

RB: I think it's important that we not idealize past times and yet the Industrial Revolution does present a new situation because as far as we know, in ancient times the boy and his father lived closely with each other, at least in the work world, after age

twelve. . . .

In the world of offices this breaks down. With the father only home in the evening, and women's values so strong in the house, the father loses the son five minutes after birth. It's as if he had amnesia and can't remember who his children are. The father is remote, he's not in the house where we are, he's somewhere else. He might as well be in Australia.

"In the ancient tradition, the male who grows is one who is able to contact the energy coming from older males."

And the father is a little ashamed of his work, despite the "prestige" of working in an office. Even if he brings his son there, what can he show him? How he moves papers? Children take things physically, not mentally. If you work in an office, how can you explain how what you're doing is important, or how it differs from what the other males are doing? The German psychologist Alexander Mitscherich writes about this situation in a fine book called *Society Without The Father*. His main idea is that if the son does not understand clearly, physically what his father is doing during the year and during the day, a hole will appear in the son's perception of his father, and into the hole will rush demons. That's a law of nature; demons rush in because nature hates a vacuum. The son's mind then fills with suspicion, doubt, and a nagging fear that the father is doing evil things. . . .

KT: Once the father becomes a demonic figure in the son's eyes, it would seem that the son is prevented from forming a fruitful association with *any* male energy, even positive male energy. Since the father serves as the son's earliest role model for male ways, the son's doubts will likely translate into doubts toward the masculine in general.

Positive Male Energy

RB: It's true, the idea that male energy, when in authority, could be good has come to be considered impossible. Yet the Greeks understood and praised that energy. They called it Zeus energy which encompasses intelligence, robust health, compassionate authority, intelligent, physical, healthy authority, good will, leadership—in sum, positive power accepted by the male in the service of the community.

The Native American understood this too—that this power only becomes positive when exercised for the sake of the community, not for personal aggrandizement. All the great cultures since have lived with images of this energy except ours.

Zeus energy has been disintegrating steadily in

America. Popular culture has destroyed it mostly, beginning with the ''Maggie and Jiggs'' and ''Dagwood'' comics of the 1920s in which the male is always foolish. From there the stereotype went into animated cartoons, and now it shows up in TV situation comedies. . . .

This kind of attack is particularly insidious because it's a way of destroying not only all the energy that the father lives on but the energy that he has tried to pass on. In the ancient tradition, the male who grows is one who is able to contact the energy coming from older males—and from women as well, but especially male spiritual teachers who transmit positive male energy. . . .

KT: What can men do to get in touch with their male energy—their instinctive male side? What kind of work is involved?

RB: I think the next step for us is learning to visualize the wildman. And to help the visualization, I feel we need to return to the mythologies that today we only teach children. If you go back to ancient mythology, you find that people in ancient times have already done some work in helping us to visualize the wildman. I think we're just coming to the place where we can understand what the ancients were talking about.

"The ability of a male to shout and to be fierce is not the same as treating people as objects."

In the Greek myths, for example, Apollo is visualized as a golden man standing on an enormous accumulation of dark, dangerous energy called Dionysius. The Bhutanese bird man with dog's teeth is another possible visualization. Another is the Chinese tomb guardian, a figure with enormous power in the muscle and the will, and a couple of fangs sticking out of his mouth. In the Hindu tradition this fanged aspect of the Shiva is called the Bhairava. In his Bhairava aspect, Shiva is not a nice boy. There's a hint of this energy with Christ going wild in the temple and whipping everybody. The Celtic tradition gives us Cuchulain—smoke comes out of the top of his head when he gets hot.

These are all powerful energies lying in ponds we haven't found yet. All these traditions give us models to help us sense what it would be like for a young male to grow up in a culture in which the divine is associated not only with the Virgin Mary and the blissful Jesus, but with the wildman covered with hair. We need to tap into these images.

KT: These mythological images are strong, almost frightening. How would you distinguish them from the strong but destructive male chauvinistic personality that we've been trying to get away from? . . .

RB: The ability of a male to shout and to be fierce is not the same as treating people like objects, demanding land or empire, expressing aggression—the whole model of the '50s male. Getting in touch with the wildman means religious life for a man in the broadest sense of the phrase, the '50s male was almost wholly secular so we are not talking in any way of a movement back.

KT: How would you envision a movement forward?

RB: Just as women in the '70s needed to develop what is known in the Indian tradition as Kali energy—the ability to really say what they want, to dance with skulls around their necks, to cut relationships when they need to—what males need now is an energy that can face this energy in women, and meet it. They need to make a similar connection in their psyches to their Kali energy—which is just another way to describe the wildman at the bottom of the pond. If they don't they won't survive.

Robert Bly is a major American poet and translator. Keith Thompson is a California writer.

Men and Women Can Share Role Responsibilities

David Hellerstein

"It's impossible," my adviser told me. "You can't possibly combine the two. You'll have to decide—it's either one or the other."

I must have heard that a hundred times—when I entered college, during medical school, and through the four long years of residency training as a psychiatrist—from my premed adviser, my writing teachers, my medical school professors, various relatives and friends and supervisors. "It's just *not possible*," they told me, "to be both a doctor and a writer." Both careers were demanding of total commitment, of the entire force of one's energies. Any compromise would be deadly.

For the better part of a decade, I was in constant turmoil, trying to force a decision that would not come. All I could do was keep on going as I was, writing, getting my medical training, juggling my time.

A Common Dilemma

The reason I'm going on about my dilemma is this: it was strikingly similar to the dilemma that many women I knew were also facing. Women in my college organic chemistry class, or in my medical school anatomy classes, were also torn. They too had legions of advisers who told them they could only do one thing, that they *had* to decide. For many, the dilemma was between a medical career and having a marriage and family. "You can't be a doctor and a mother," they would be told by experienced, senior doctors. "You'll shortchange your patients *and* your children." They too had no choice but to keep going day by day, week by week—and hope that things would work out.

Never mind the fact that nobody ever questioned whether *I* could be a doctor and a father; or suggested—before Perri Klass—that a woman could

be a doctor *and* a writer *and* a mother. The similarity was this: we were trying to play multiple roles, to satisfy multiple personal and professional needs, and as such, we were accused of trying the impossible.

At a certain point, after I finished medical training and had two books accepted for publication, I began to be able to look back at that dilemma without a rising sense of panic. I had discovered that what seemed impossible was not impossible at all, just very difficult. And even better, that having multiple identities could lead not to unending frustrations but to multiple satisfactions; the rewards from doctoring could balance the frustrations of writing, and vice versa. Similarly, my women friends who had agonized so much in medical school were thriving—practicing medicine *and* raising children. Their lives might be complicated, even wearing at times, but clearly they were rich and rewarding.

Then my wife and I decided to have a baby, and the old questions came up with a new urgency. How could I possibly fulfill my responsibilities in my various career roles while being a husband and a father as well? How could we work out things so my wife could continue her thriving career in hospital finance? Especially since—like so many men of our generation—I wanted to be more involved in child-rearing than our fathers had been. What would have to give? According to received wisdom, my wife and I would no doubt soon be going crazy.

A Quiet Revolution

One of the quieter aspects of the feminist revolution, and one whose repercussions are just beginning to be explored, is this issue of multiple roles and how they affect our mental health. Research is showing (and the experience of millions of two-career couples is confirming) that, in contrast to traditional thinking, adults of *both* sexes *can* have multiple roles, and that rather than being invariably

David Hellerstein, "Multiplying Roles: The Next Step," *Ms.*, October 1987. Reprinted with the author's permission.

destructive, multiplicity can often be a positive influence on our lives.

It's amazing how much things have changed in this regard. Not too long ago it was assumed that a man would take a "male role," a woman would take a "female role." He would work, she would stay home. The family had a clear hierarchy, with a straightforward division of labor from the moment one got up in the morning until the moment one went to sleep. Simplicity could easily become rigidity; roles could become prisons; but there was a clear order to life—an order for which *unity* of identity was essential.

"There are no 'roles,' but instead just jobs or responsibilities to be divided."

Now, in little more than a decade, everything has changed. For one thing, an entire generation is going through a natural experiment of multiplicity. For instance, in 1970, only 24 percent of married women with children less than one year old worked; by 1985, 49 percent did. At the same time, men have begun to do more in the home—their household work has gone from 20 percent of the couple's total work in 1965 to over 30 percent by 1981, according to a study by psychologist and Wheaton College Professor Joseph Pleck. Put another way, men used to do one fourth as much in the home as women; now they do half as much. But I see a positive trend buried in this statistic. While it includes older men, who presumably haven't changed much, their numbers are offset by the younger men, among whom it is now the norm to do their share of shopping, cooking, laundry, and so on—a change that I believe is here to stay.

Another change, and one for which it is difficult to find statistics, is in the number of people with dual or multiple careers. It's no longer a surprise, for instance, to hear of doctor-writers or businessmen-poets not to mention actor-restaurateurs and accountant-rock musicians. These changes are partly a result of economic forces, partly a result of feminism, and partly a result of the "having it all" yuppie ethos—and the consequences are major.

Roles vs. Jobs

In this new world of dual (or triple or quadruple) career families, there is no prescribed order to family life. Hierarchies have been dissolved or realigned; often there are no "roles," but instead just jobs or responsibilities to be divided: parent, spouse, worker, homemaker. Flexibility and tolerance for uncertainty are essential, as is the ability to balance many often conflicting demands. The rewards, at best, are that we find life offers many more satisfactions than we ever dreamed possible. The risks, though, are that we will succumb to chaos and overload.

Why would multiple roles, despite the time crunch and conflicting obligations, often lead to more happiness? Smith College psychologist Faye Crosby, who has done several studies of multiple roles, says there are several reasons: "For one thing, there's *buffering*—if something negative happens in one role, it can be buffered by something positive in the other. Also, if something positive happens, you can take your accomplishments from one role and can share them in the other. If you publish a book, your colleagues at work may feel jealous; if you go home, you can tell your friends, husband, kids, relatives—and unless they're in your line of work, they won't feel competitive." There's also a point raised by sociologist Cynthia Fuchs Epstein, author of *Women in Law*, that too much of any one thing is exhausting, that if you have more than one role, when you finish one thing, you can begin work on another; if you finish the main course, you can go to dessert.

Applications for Men

How do these conclusions (by now familiar to many women) apply to men? To even begin thinking about this, it's important to realize, as Joseph Pleck puts it, that "men are starting from very different places as far as multiple roles are concerned." For women, it frequently means adding paid work to household responsibilities; for men it is vice versa. Despite cultural expectations of "one person, one role," men have long known instinctively that having a job or career with the authority that allows for multiple roles is more stimulating than having only one type of responsibility—it's better to be a foreman than an assembly line worker, or to be head of a department rather than a "number-cruncher" tied to a computer. Multiplicity is one of the perks of professional advancement.

But the hard fact is that for a man to make the commitment to increase the number of roles in his life may mean a sacrifice of status in his profession. Not only that, but a man's commitment to his partner's right to have multiple roles in *her* life may add stresses to his life. For instance, in one of Grace Baruch and Rosalind Barnett's studies for the Wellesley Center for Research on Women, men who participated more in child care often felt increasingly anxious, experiencing conflict between career goals and family responsibilities; they were also more dissatisfied with their wives' child care (adding stress to the women's lives too).

Long-Term Benefits

Does this mean that the increasing amount of housework and child care done by men is going to make things *worse*, not better, after all? Not necessarily. "It's important," Faye Crosby says, "to think about what age in the family cycle you're talking about. The hardest, the most stressful, is for families with young children. Also, it can be hard to see *long-term* benefits of fathers' increased involvement when you're involved in the day-to-day battles. Equality may be much more beneficial to have in the long run, but possibly more stressful in the short run." For families with *older* children, the stresses of dual career and dual caretaker may be much less.

Pleck believes that even in the short run men benefit from their increased participation in the home. In one of his national studies, in two-earner families, the more housework and child care a man did, the higher he scored on measures of "overall well-being" and "marital contentment." Why this might be so is not entirely clear—Pleck speculates that it is because more actively participating men have increased communication and more positive shared experiences with their spouses, which counteract the increased stresses of the two-career family.

Theorists of male development, from Erik Erikson to George Vaillant to Daniel Levinson, have focused almost exclusively on male identity as formed in the workplace. But recently, a number of studies have shown that for the vast majority of men overall happiness has far more to do with satisfaction in family roles than on the job. Consequently, entire new frontiers in research have opened up.

Everyday Reality

But getting back to basics, how can these emerging understandings of multiplicity be applied to everyday life? How does it help a man to know multiple roles are good when you're arguing with your wife about who cleans the bathroom?

"For the vast majority of men overall happiness has far more to do with satisfaction in family roles than on the job."

For one thing, it can help get through the kneejerk cognitive barriers we encounter, the automatic sense of "I can't" or "It's impossible." The fact is, most people *can* handle multiple roles. For men, an active response to increased demands at home can decrease stress—whereas, as Pleck points out, a passive response can lead to feelings of increased helplessness and depression. In addition, as Cynthia Fuchs Epstein discovered in her study of women lawyers, certain strategies, though not ones all of us can afford, can help people thrive from multiplicity:

being able to delegate duties, being organized, having good child-care help, having a supportive spouse and family. Given such ideal conditions, multiplicity can actually reduce stress.

On the other hand, at times of extreme overload, something may have to give. For my wife and me, for instance, our daughter's birth meant cutting back on other things—trimming back work schedules, cutting out nonessentials as we adjusted to our new role as parents. I used up my vacation time to help with the baby, and for about six months put my writing career and other outside activities on hold. My wife took four months off work, and recently has returned to her job three days a week. Not exactly fifty-fifty, I suppose, but an arrangement in keeping with what we both wanted, accommodating realities like the lack of paternity leave policies and my wife's desire to breast-feed the baby. As our daughter has begun to sleep through the night, we have started picking up on other activities, and to negotiate various issues (for instance, each watching the baby certain nights so the other person can have some time off).

It's important to note that my wife and I are lucky, in that we could afford to drop certain roles for a time—and could survive on less than two full salaries. One obvious risk these days is of *forced* multiplicity—of needing to take on more roles than one can handle at a particular time because of economic or other demands. It used to be that both men and women were confined to one role apiece—a tyranny of society. Now economic and social realities often *require* both men and women to have several roles. That can be liberating—or it can, in its own way, be tyrannical.

An Improvement

On the whole, though, I think most people would agree that multiplicity is for the best. Certainly it leads to more complicated lives, to lives of improvisation, to balancing acts. But, on the other hand, it leads us to question our limitations, to apply experience and insights from one area to another—a lesson women, who have always known how to do several things at once, have taught us. It gives us a larger view of life. To give up multiplicity would mean going backward to less complex, more impoverished days—in which we'd be forced once again to make impossible decisions.

David Hellerstein is a doctor and novelist.

"The vast majority of instances in which wives work do not result in equality in the home or . . . the workplace."

viewpoint **15**

Sharing Role Responsibilities Is Difficult

Rosanna Hertz

The dual-career couple has been hailed in the 1980s as the new ideal middle-class marital relationship. The popular press has highlighted this phenomenon, filling lifestyle or social issues sections with tales of such couples: She's a doctor and he's a lawyer, or he's a diplomat and she's a corporate consultant. They went to graduate school together, and after completing school, both went on to pursue their chosen careers. Each morning they awake, jog together, eat breakfast, and are off to their respective jobs. She flies off on Monday for a three-day business trip, and he leaves on Wednesday for a two-day business trip. Candlelight dinners, cultural events, and shared sports activities fill weekends. The same zeal and energy couples bring to their work, they also bring to their relationships. The message: the dual-career couple is glamorous. . . .

Stories of "America's New Elite," as *Time* magazine dubbed them, have captured the imagination and interest of the American population. For years we've read such sagas, which are perhaps rivaled only by stories of the rich and famous. Earlier generations of young girls grew up on Cinderella and Snow White, dreaming of princes to carry them off so they too could live happily ever after. Young girls today dream a different plot. There is still the prince, but happily-ever-after now includes a career. The dreams of young men are not so easily characterized. For earlier generations, a man's success was envisioned in occupational and financial terms; boys dreamed of being rich, strong, and independent. Wives, for many, were beautiful, faithful, and supportive, important symbols of success, as were bright, cheerful children and a comfortable home. The dreams of young men today (willingly or unwillingly) often include a wife who also works, as

well as a vision of building family, house, and future together.

There are seemingly no barriers to fulfilling this new dream. Many young women believe not only that sex discrimination in the workplace is dead but also that the new 1980s man is looking for a wife who has an exciting, rewarding career just like his. The media offer an endless supply of stories about the successful female corporate executive and the happy dual-career couple. She knows how to dress, how to act in the board room, how to compete, and also how to be a team player with her colleagues. Not only is she accomplished in her chosen field, but she is also the perfect wife and mother. In her home dinner is served on time every night, the house is clean, her children receive "quality time," and she and her husband are mutually supportive of their respective careers. He remains aggressive in pursuit of career success, but his aggressiveness is now tempered by a "soft" side. He is an active participant in the broad range of family chores: he takes his turn at cooking, doing the laundry, cleaning the house, caring for the children, shopping, transporting the children and their friends, and participating in the P.T.A. and neighborhood groups. He takes parenting seriously—from prenatal care to birthing, nocturnal feedings, and beyond. In short, the traditional job of the wife becomes a shared career.

Wanting It All

In this vision of shared careers and responsibilities, there are few, if any, conflicts and even fewer obstacles to happiness. It seems eminently feasible from these accounts that both a husband and wife should be able to devote themselves to their respective careers, find self-expression in their work, and also pursue a stable, intimate, and enriching family life. Therefore, young men and women not only assume that they can have

Rosanna Hertz, *More Equal Than Others*. Berkeley, CA: University of California Press. © 1987 The Regents of the University of California.

it all—spouse, children, and career—but they also are encouraged to want it all. A full, well-integrated life is easy to come by, and it can be had at no personal cost. . . .

The attention paid to those situations in which career and family are successfully combined overshadows the fact that there are simply not many dual-career couples. Moreover, the vast majority of instances in which wives work do not result in equality in the home or reflect lessening inequality in the workplace. Married women who work are often expected to do double duty as wage earners and domestic laborers (homemakers). Their employment is viewed as secondary, even when their income is not supplementary or targeted for a specific purpose (such as purchasing a household appliance, a new home, or a vacation). The money they bring in does not count for as much as their husbands' salaries. Many more married women work because the ravages of inflation (especially in the 1970s) and debt have made two incomes necessary to support a family. . . .

> *"Male career success has been predicated on the existence of a nonworking wife."*

A major distinction must be made between "careers" and "jobs." Most women do not have careers; they have jobs. Careers involve employment in which some realistic expectation of upward occupational and financial mobility is expected and available. Careers most commonly begin within the salaried ranks of an organization (although they need not always do so) and provide a clear path for advancement from lower to higher levels of responsibility, authority, and reward. In contrast, jobs offer limited opportunities for advancement, responsibility, and authority, are paid by the hour, and promise little significant increase in financial reward for achievement or for longevity of employment. Despite the rapid increase in women's (especially married women's) participation in the labor force over the last twenty years, women still find, accept, or are relegated to jobs, not careers. The oft-cited statistics on women's over-representation in dead-end, low-paying work have been well documented. Women generally receive lower pay, work shorter hours (often part-time), and have less protection in employment than do men. Since far more women are likely to hold jobs than to have careers, the focus on married women with careers hardly reflects a typical circumstance.

Finally, the dual-career couple is a *contingent* phenomenon. This description is a major theoretical argument of this study and as such deserves a brief explanation here. Dual-career marriage assumes that the right combination of resources makes the integration of personal and professional lives easy. What is lacking in this facile analysis is an appreciation of the privileges status of those who have careers to begin with. One-half of a dual-career couple—the woman—who was interviewed for this study said it best:

> Not everyone can afford to live the way we do. You really need a six-figure income. I feel that the popular magazines like *Redbook* do women and marriages a disservice. Some of the articles sound like everybody can have a dual-career marriage. A lot of people read these articles and use the dual-career couple as the ideal marriage, but most marriages will by definition fall short of this ideal because of the money aspect. What I mean is, my secretary gets paid about the same amount of money as my housekeeper. Can my secretary afford to have the type of dual-career family we have—a full-time housekeeper who also cares for the children? The answer is no.

Not only do this woman's observations emphasize an important precondition for the dual-career family—a high income—but they also challenge another representation of these families: their self-sufficiency. In fact, the couple's capacity to sustain two careers (and to acquire them in the first place) often depends on the availability of someone else to perform, for a wage, the duties necessary to maintain the household. The dual-career couple can prosper professionally in part because there are other couples or individuals who do not. . . .

Replacing the Wife

The division of labor in the home is an important influence on individual career success. In the past particularly, male career success has been predicated on the existence of a nonworking wife. The "invisible work" of women . . . was a major contributing factor to men's careers. Women's role was more than simply taking care of the hearth; the unpaid work wives did for their husbands' organizations also facilitated the husbands' career advancement. But most important, men were released from domestic responsibilities—both childcare and housework—so that they could concentrate their energies on meeting work-related goals. And wives provided two crucial services that complemented their husbands' work demands: they provided the stability of home life, and they were flexible and adapted to the special needs of the children's and husbands' respective worlds.

When both husbands and wives work, there is no one person whose primary responsibility is homemaking, a fact that the addition of children only emphasizes. From the corporate employer's point of view and, increasingly, from the couple's point of view, career success depends on a home life that does not preoccupy the worker. If *both* husbands and wives are to be released from domestic responsibilities, who will undertake these tasks? Perhaps more important, are the steps taken by these dual-career couples altering the traditional gender-based division of labor in the home?

"The problems of turnover and the unstable nature of housekeepers are regarded as wives' problems."

I will argue that, at least among the couples interviewed, a shift in household responsibilities has indeed taken place. The traditional duties of the wife are changing; but the change represents not so much a transformation of responsibilities as a shift in who assumes them. Yet another shift involves the more general question of gender roles in the family. Wives have, to some extent, been released from the direct physical demands of childcare; but dual-career demands have not resulted in a shared process of recruitment and supervision of hired childcare or housecleaning labor. Rather, wives have assumed principal responsibility for these tasks.

Wives and Housekeepers

Housekeepers and sitters are expected to provide the home with the stability that *should* relieve the couple from worry about family matters during workday hours. But because home duties remain, even for these couples, the domain of the wife, it is mainly wives who express such relief. This woman explains how her daytime sitter helps to stabilize her work concentration:

> The ideal is to have someone in your home—the ideal for the person working, because then you work harder. You are not worried about what is going on at home. People are not calling you to tell you about your kids, which happens frequently at daycare. I know because I work with people in that situation. You don't have to run and pick them up if they are throwing up, or whatever. All that kind of stuff relieves you to do a good job, and that is what I think you pay for. . . .

Cloistering wives in the home is unthinkable for dual-career couples. Instead, both husbands and wives spend their days working outside the home, and the housekeeper/sitter is a paid replacement for the wife. She is now the person who keeps daily watch over the home. Even when parents feel their children are old enough for nursery school, full-time, day, or live-in housekeepers still offer an advantage, especially when women have erratic work hours or when their work cycle includes a busy season. Housekeepers can adapt to these needs, and more important, there is always someone at home. One woman illustrated this point:

> I'm starting my son in nursery school in the mornings, and in the afternoon he's in a play group. I'd like to keep him one-on-one with someone in the house as long as I can. I'm not so afraid now of what would happen if my housekeeper quit, because he's under the supervision of other options during the day. I like the fact that she's at home all day long, though. But I need her at night. There are nights when I wouldn't be home till twelve o'clock, and there are nights when it might be better not to come home at all—during my busy season, it's easier for me to stay downtown. . . .

Housekeepers and sitters are not simply performing the traditional role of wife and mother. If this were the case, both spouses would be equally freed by hired labor to pursue careers, and both would be equally responsive to and responsible for their workers. In this regard, a gender-based division of labor, at least for dual-career spouses, would not exist. Instead, what appears to be a symmetrical relationship between a childless husband and wife may be deceptive; and a division of labor allegedly not based on gender is definitely challenged when the couple decides to have children. For example, when these couples had no children and the cleaning person failed to show up, the house could remain uncleaned. But such neglect is not possible when the sitter fails to show up; children need continuous care. Incorporating children into the family's structure entails a reorganization of the couple's joint and separate lives that results in the resurrection of an asymmetrical relationship—that is, housekeepers and sitters become primarily the wife's responsibility. Normally, it is the wife who finds the help, indoctrinates the help, worries about losing the help, and daily converses with the help. As one woman angrily complained:

> My husband has never lost a day's work or a night's sleep over insecurities about help. It has never entered my husband's head that this would have any effect on his career. He has never interviewed a housekeeper. He's never had this affect his life in any way, shape, or form.

Wives are the ones who rearrange work schedules and normally report having more flexible careers. They are either more willing to figure out flexible work arrangements, or they are more apt to change jobs to regularize their work hours. They are, as one woman explained, charged with relieving the housekeeper from her duties:

> Since my schedule is the much more predictable one, it's my schedule that I coordinate. So I stay. Generally, I stay in the morning till she comes, and then when I come in the evening—I'm usually the first person home—she leaves then.

Wives, therefore, are the ones who really provide their husbands with continuous flexibility. And, in turn, the housekeeper provides the wife with flexibility.

The problems of turnover and the unstable nature of housekeepers are regarded as wives' problems.

Wives thus express more insecurity about losing this help because such a loss would immediately and directly disrupt their work lives. For example, each new childcare worker must be initiated into her responsibilities, and it is the wife who must take time off from work, staying home during this period of sitter adjustment. In an effort to avoid penalizing their careers, wives may take vacation time for this training period. One woman explained why she has not taken a "real" vacation since her child was born three years ago:

> Every time I get a new housekeeper, I will spend a period of time at home to stay with her while she gets to know my son, while she gets to know my house and everything else. So, for every new housekeeper, I have to count a vacation week out of work, which results in my never taking vacation time because it doesn't accumulate.

Furthermore, when the housekeeper or sitter fails to meet her daily responsibilities, the husband's work life is rarely disrupted. If the sitter arrives late in the morning, the wife is the one who will have to answer to clients and bosses and rearrange her work schedule. One woman has live-in help mainly to avoid this potential problem in the winter.

> I wanted live-in help because I didn't want the fear of—for example—on a snowy winter day at eight-thirty in the morning not having my help come in to take care of the baby when I have to be in the office. We very rarely go out at night during the week. First of all I'm tired, and I haven't seen my daughter all day, and I like to be with her. So there isn't a need to have live-in help to babysit. I could get around having live-in help if it weren't for the fact that I need to know someone is there in the mornings.

Emergencies and Legwork

Couples prenegotiate these structural arrangements, and although wives are the ones expected to take time off from work when housekeepers or children are sick, husbands may help out for short periods in an emergency or when other back-up systems are unavailable. One man described the arrangement he and his wife had negotiated.

> We have worked it out that when it comes to the kids, she's on the line first. If it is really touch-and-go, like the kids are sick, Sally will stay home. If she were out of town or something, which occasionally she will be, and they were sick, I would just stay home if it was required. Anyone in this firm can take a day off for personal reasons without being docked or having it charged to vacation time. But it hasn't happened, because we have two healthy kids.

Another man's responsibility when childcare arrangements fail is to "help my wife think of somebody she can call."

Sometimes, husbands and wives will jointly interview a potential sitter or housekeeper. But it is the wives who have already done the "leg work," made the connections, and weeded out unsuitable

individuals. In terms of who makes decisions about hiring childcare providers, one husband said, "I would say that it's more her decision—80 percent her decision and 20 percent my decision. I would just have a little input. She would make the ultimate decision."

Building Trust

These comments further underscore the fact that hiring childcare labor is a female responsibility. Women are no longer doing the actual housework or caring for the child all day long; instead, they are now one step removed, overseeing the work their mothers did in the past. "Replacing the wife," therefore, is not simply a metaphor for describing the role of hired labor, but it also indicates the tenuous position of the dual-career female—at any time the wife can be recalled to the home to reassume homemaking activities.

"Another man's responsibility when childcare arrangements fail is to 'help my wife think of somebody she can call.'"

Working women need to trust and feel secure about their hired labor in order to feel that they exert some control over the childcare situation. Without this trust, they cannot effectively replace themselves with a housekeeper; and if they cannot, then the whole point of having an independent career is undermined. But despite the critical elements of trust, these wives do rely on what is generally an unpredictable and unregulated labor market. They build trust based on systems of hiring and payment that have few if any guarantees of performance. For this reason, housekeepers and sitters are often given quasi-family membership and a relationship of reciprocal loyalty and trust is developed. To encourage the childcare worker to assume part of the mother's traditional responsibility and to maximize the stability and continuity of the parent-worker-child relationship, the relationship between employer and employee must be something more than the exchange of a wage for a service. . . .

The Importance of Low Wage Labor

On the surface, dual-career couples *appear* to be able to operate as a self-sufficient nuclear family. Nonetheless, they are dependent as a group and as individuals on a category of people external to the family. Couples view their ability to purchase this service as another indication of their self-sufficiency (or "making it"). Yet appearances are deceptive, because the self-sufficiency of the dual-career couple depends on a system external to the family. What appears to be self-sufficiency for one category of workers relies on the existence of a category of less advantaged workers. What appears to be progress for women is really the progress of some women at the expense of equal progress for other women.

Rosanna Hertz is a sociology professor at Wellesley College.

> *"What appears to be progress for women is really the progress of some women at the expense of equal progress for other women."*

[Daniel] Fusfeld argues that the low-wage economy of urban ghettos plays a significant role in the overall economy of the larger metropolitan area. In analyzing the position of middle-income groups, he states:

> If wages are raised in the low-wage industries, the cost of living will rise and their standard of living will fall. Many people are aware of this relationship, although it is usually expressed in some phrase such as, "someone has to wash the dishes," or "who will collect the trash?"

The relationship between housekeepers and these dual-career couples is analogous. Two incomes are necessary for these couples to maintain their lifestyle, but even with the cost of hiring domestic labor, the lifestyle of the dual-career couple is more affluent than that of their one-income family counterparts. Hiring domestic labor is not an equal exchange of one spouse's salary in return for work in the home. Dual-career couples have an indirect but material interest in maintaining an unstable, low-wage pool of labor, in part because the couples place a high value on affordable, private childcare. For women to replace themselves with domestic help, their income must be large enough to make their work outside the home financially worthwhile. If the wages of domestic help were raised to accord with the value placed on childcare, the question of why this work was being farmed out would arise, even if higher wages produced a more stable and more skilled labor supply. Paying more would not only result in a decline in the standard of living for these couples but would also call into question the value of women's working outside the home. Thus, the relation between domestic labor and dual-career couples represents one aspect of the more generalized and structured relationship of inequality between low-wage labor in the urban ghettos and high-wage labor in the middle- and upper-class neighborhoods and suburbs. This relationship, though often obscured by a focus on individual or group characteristics, is nonetheless important in understanding how such phenomena as dual-career couples with children are possible within modern society.

"A woman's enduring fantasy is of marriage to one man, who offers her protection, security, and her choice to work, to stay at home . . . or to combine work and family."

Women Want Traditional Men

Suzanne Fields and Lawrence Wade

Editor's note: The following viewpoint is in two parts. Part I is by Suzanne Fields. Part II is by Lawrence Wade.

I

Does a man who does housework turn a woman on?

Does a man fall in love with a woman because she offers him security and protection?

Does a woman ever fantasize about giving a man a diamond for an engagement present?

The answer to all of the above is obviously no, even though sophisticated, hip, struggling-to-be-nonsexist men and women search for qualifications, exceptions, and contradictions to their instinctual responses.

No one tries harder than Warren Farrell, "the liberated man," who rails against the double messages in women's magazines, television shows, romantic novels, and life itself.

"Many men hear women saying they'd like a man who shares the housework," he writes in his book, *Why Men Are the Way They Are.* "'Is this true?' the men ask. Yes. Women *do* want men who share the housework, but only if it's in *addition* to being successful enough to buy the wardrobe and diamond."

Some Things Don't Change

No one, as far as I know, has packaged a heart throb with a broom except for comic purposes. Househusband is rarely Hero, even to the woman whose house he cleans and keeps. A woman is less than thrilled to tell her best friend that Mr. Wonderful is a part-time whatever who will never be anything more (though a man is often proud of his wife's part-time outside work, since this is proof that she is something approaching a full-time wife.)

Some things don't (and probably won't) change, with or without a sexual revolution. A woman's enduring fantasy is of marriage to one man, who offers her protection, security, and *her* choice to work, to stay at home with the children, or to combine work and family. Most women actually want a man to be more successful than they are.

No matter what statistics say about "nontraditional households," common sense screams that women yearn for men to do the courting with old-fashioned gestures like flowers and perfume. Don Regan was right, diamonds are still a girl's best friend. Not only does she find a 2-carat diamond infinitely more exciting than a cruise missile, she prefers it to a power saw or a lawn mower.

Even the readers of *Ms.* magazine. The difference between a De Beers ad for its diamonds in *Ms.* and an ad in *Time* is that the Miss in *Ms.* gets credit for choosing the jeweler who will offer her fiance his "spending guidelines." In *Time*, the man does it all on his own, naturally.

Money, Power Are Sexy

In the high-powered female self-improvement magazines, women who work, work harder at improving the ways they can attract a man than they do to improve their efficiency in the workplace. Advertisers and editors know this. Cosmetics, not computers, make up the majority of the ads.

Playboy centerfolds and Pets of the Month are rarely women chosen for their wealth or fame, but the 50 "eligible" bachelors in *Good Housekeeping* are eligible on the basis of their money, titles, and power. *Playgirl*'s sexiest men include George Bush and Bob Hope. Jeane Kirkpatrick is a powerful woman and Betty Friedan is one of the most famous women in America, but power does not confer sexiness nor fame confer eligibility.

Only 5 percent of the subscribers to *Forbes* are

Suzanne Fields, "House-Hubby No Hero Makes," *The Washington Times*, August 14, 1986. Reprinted with the author's permission.
Lawrence Wade, "But Who Still Gets the Girl?" *The Washington Times*, October 17, 1986. Reprinted with the author's permission.

women, but 8 million women subscribe to *Better Homes and Gardens*. Brides' magazines are having a resurgence; there is still no magazine called *Bridegrooms*. (The jury is still out on *Fathers*, a magazine aimed at men, if any, who are more interested in layettes, bassinets, and the absorbent qualities of diapers than in fishing rods, stereo components, and automobiles.)

Feminists say women don't have the interests and concerns catered to by the likes of *Forbes* and *Fortune* magazines because so few women have become senior executives in the major corporations. But will they ever? If not, why not?

Choosing Family over Work

According to a new survey in *Fortune*, more than 30 percent of the women MBAs from the top business schools in the country—class of '76—have dropped out of the management force to become self-employed or unemployed, a figure considerably higher than for their male counterparts.

Theories abound for why this is so—prejudice in the workplace, fatigue from the Superwoman Syndrome. But a recurring theme is that women themselves have decided that the trade-offs aren't worth it.

"We have more women than before who are having second thoughts about everything-for-the-career," says Allan Cox, a Chicago executive recruiter. "When the baby comes along, the six-week maternity leave becomes a two-year maternity leave."

Research continues to show that women who have a managerial career are less likely to have a husband and children. This raises the chicken or the egg question: do women who choose to be managers choose to sacrifice family life, or is it because they are less interested in becoming wives and mothers that they choose to become managers in the first place?

Ms.-Interpretations

Many women who were gung ho for careers when they were fresh out of college are surprised by the gratifications they find at home and in part-time work. These women, who sometimes work as hard for themselves as they did for the corporation, find they like the flexibility of scheduling their own hours, often when the children are asleep, without the rigid rules of the corporation to cope with. They're older, their values have changed, and many feel betrayed by unrealistic expectations fostered by feminism.

Modern feminism, like every other modern "ism," strains under the weight of its false promises, its narrow reading of human nature, its ms.-interpretations of sexual differences.

Just as Karl Marx overlooked the positive power of private economic incentives, radical feminists overlooked the gratifications generated by the ancient differences in male and female. But some things have to be learned the hard way, and one of them is that in our rush to liberate women to be what they want to be, we ought not to bend the expectations of the majority of women to serve the ambitions of the minority.

II

Men and women speak different languages.

And to make matters worse, one sex doesn't hear well.

But for too long men have been blamed for the misunderstandings.

Consider yet another of those "what women want" studies. This one says women don't *really* want money, sex, or Don Johnson. "Intimacy" is what they're after, says a psychologist at New York's Columbia University.

In the study, Lois Leiderman Davitz looks at women from their 20s to their 60s, and finds their needs in constant conflict with men's. This is no exercise in man-bashing, says Ms. Leiderman Davitz from her home in Somers, N.Y. "It's not the fault of either sex that their needs are different."

But I feel that some blame can be placed. And regardless of what Bella Abzug or the Cosmo Girl might say, it's not the fault of sexist men.

It's *women* who don't understand what men want. In fact, they often want what men can't provide. And that, not the much-maligned macho man, is what's wrong today between women and men.

Unreasonable Demands

Ms. Leiderman Davitz's study mostly proves my point, though, no doubt, she'd take issue with me. In every decade I see women demanding from men what they're least capable of giving.

Take the 20s. That's when "women want love and romance," says the lively Ms. Leiderman Davitz. But at 20, I had plenty of passion. What the women I knew wanted was *cash*.

"Radical feminists overlooked the gratifications generated by the ancient differences in male and female."

Oh, they'd never *ask* for it. But any guy who has been a college student with just a 10-speed bike and three pairs of jeans to his name knows of what I speak.

The guy with the grades gets to be a friend. The guy with grades and good looks, a friend for life. The gorilla with a red Porsche gets to spend the night.

That was a decade ago, and I thought things had

changed. But lately I've heard the same complaints from male students here in Washington.

Says one guy from Howard University who'd pass for William "The Refrigerator" Perry, efficiency-size, "If you don't have a fancy car, forget it!"

A car—when many male students, just like female students, can barely afford books. That sort of childish demand, I thought, ended years ago in high school.

But even back then, women wanted too much. How often did we frustrated 15-year-olds lose dates at parties as soon as the older guys driving daddy's T-bird came around?

Women at Fault

The 20s are bad, but the 30s are worse. That's when "women want helpmates," Ms. Leiderman Davitz says. And that's when ironing a rug . . . I mean, a shirt . . . is least on most guys' minds.

And that's not because men are insensitive. "This whole thing about insensitivity is being written by mixed-up 30-year-olds and hard-bitten lib women," says the psychologist, who speaks like no one's Marilyn Monroe.

"At 30 a man doesn't [fail to] pick up a vacuum cleaner because he's cruel," explains the psychologist. "His whole culture is directed toward having a job and career."

"We guys spend our best years trying to please women and, in the end, they get it all."

But to judge from countless articles on struggling career women, it's that meanie macho man who's mistreating wives and girlfriends.

"He doesn't do laundry.

"He doesn't 'do' food.

"He doesn't even *know* where the Windex is!"

But it's women who are at fault—not men—in this decade of differences between the sexes. A guy does what guys have always done. A woman today is likely to be changing roles.

By the 40s, things grow even worse. Women want "it" all—cooperation, caring, sex, attention. It's when any guy with ambition greater than GS-12 can provide "it" least.

In their 40s guys are blamed again. So much so that "mature" women are now encouraged to take younger lovers. A man still "robs the cradle." But the hands that rock it can take what they want.

Well, it's just not fair. And is it any wonder that after decades of unceasing demands, by our 50s, when our needs at last become one, guys start to croak?

Don't get me wrong.

I don't hate women.

From my Mom to my second wife—if I could—I'd have loved them all.

I don't hate gays. But, frankly, all a gay guy can do for me—besides be my friend—is lead me fast to some good-looking woman he knows.

But I am mad.

And I'm sure that I speak for millions of angry men grown tired of being told just "what women want."

We guys spend our best years trying to please women and, in the end, they get it all.

It's time now that we consider the wants of men.

Suzanne Fields is a columnist with The Washington Times, *and Lawrence Wade is a syndicated columnist.*

"Women increasingly feel that what's best is that both *man and woman should succeed."*

Women Want Liberated Men

Rose DeWolf

My friends and I do not agree on exactly what constitutes a new style man. We agree in principle, but not on the specifics. Not at all.

A lot has already been written, of course, about the difference between traditional and modern men and women, but unfortunately a lot of that has been hostile, unhelpful, and wrong.

For one thing, there is a notion that we have to be clearly modern or unmistakably traditional, when in fact, on a scale of one to ten, most of us fall somewhere in between.

Some people seem to think that new style can be determined by whether or not a woman works or whether a man does needlepoint and is willing to cry. But those are choices anyone can make. The real thing goes much deeper than that.

There are those who would dismiss the matter by saying that a new style woman is one of those angry ladies who are unfeminine, anti-family, and unreasonable. They claim that any man who is attracted to this kind of woman would have to be a wimp. But, let's face it, often the opposite point of view is equally uncharitable. An old style woman is defined as an object to be pitied, a doormat that breathes, submissive to a terrible man who is tyrannical at worst and merely selfish at best.

"The Best"

A more realistic and certainly less antagonistic description of how to tell old style from new is provided by sociologists John Scanzoni and Maximiliane Szinovacz. They give both groups full credit for wanting the best for both themselves and their families. The difference is in how each group defines what it means by "the best."

Scanzoni and Szinovacz point out that for generations—at least since the Industrial Revolution—what "the best" meant to *most* men and women was "making sure the man succeeds." The credo of the traditional woman goes something like this: "If he does well, we both do well; the whole family does well." Or put another way: "If I iron his shirts and he looks good, that's good enough for me."

What has changed, of course, is that women increasingly feel that what's best is that *both* man and woman should succeed. The credo of the modern woman is more like this: "He should do well, and I should do well, too." She is not saying that he, or the family as a whole, isn't important, but merely that she is an important part of the family.

As Scanzoni and Szinovacz describe her, a traditional woman who is offered a great job—but one that would interfere with her ability to get her husband's dinner on the table at 6:00 P.M., when he wants it—would turn the job down without a second thought. Why? Because she would *rather* have dinner on the table at six. She doesn't feel deprived, and she doesn't feel coerced. If taking that job means inconveniencing the man in her life, then it's too high a price to pay—like being offered a free week in Europe as long as you are willing to swim there. Thanks, but no thanks.

A traditional woman who is just a smidgen less cheerfully self-sacrificing might go so far as to broach the matter at home. Would he mind if she took the job? Would he allow her to? Would he be willing to eat at seven instead of six? However, if he says no, that just as surely ends the idea. The old style woman believes not only that the man is the boss, but also that he *should* be. She couldn't enjoy doing anything he disapproved of. And, of course, because she wouldn't think of him as Attila the Hun for being unwilling to delay his dinner hour in her behalf, he, quite naturally, wouldn't think of himself that way either.

The new style woman has a different outlook on life. She backs her man's goals, but not to the point of submerging herself in them. Thus, she would feel it is her right to consider this job. That doesn't mean she would automatically take it any more than it means she would automatically turn it down. But she would definitely expect to discuss the matter at home, and she would not so willingly take no for an answer. She would press her own position. If he objected, she would want to know why. She might even decide to take the job over his objections. But of course, since the new style woman values mutual trust, mutual respect, cooperation, and partnership, she would much prefer to reach some sort of compromise. And that could be anything. Maybe they would have dinner a little later. Maybe he could cook it, too.

"Even though the majority of Americans still claim the man is the head of house, that phrase no longer means quite what it used to."

It's pretty obvious, then, that if both halves of a couple are old style, a lot of matters that call for debate in other marriages don't even come up between them. Most "choices" are decided by custom or tradition. In the matter of household chores, for example, he is Mr. Outside (lawn mowing and car washing) and she is Mrs. Inside (dishes, diapers). Those choices still remaining (except for such homey matters as the color of the furniture) are decided by him. He takes for granted that any goals she has are secondary to his, and *she takes it for granted, too.* Thus, perfectly matched, they wonder why all others aren't as contented as *they* are.

Equally obvious, of course, is that when the new style woman is matched with a new style man, the combination works just as well, and they would say even better. He is proud of her for getting a job offer. He *wants* to do something to help. He, as well as she, assumes they can work something out. Under their roof, everything is fifty-fifty, nifty, nifty.

Alas, we are rarely so cleverly aligned.

Giving Up on Traditional Men

And so we hear all the sad stories. There's the one about the new style man who left his old style woman behind. It turned out he didn't appreciate her willingness to live her life through him. Even though she cooked like Julia Child and wore her neckline down to here, he felt something was missing. She never understood his attitude. "But I did *everything* for him," she said.

More common are the tales of the determined modern woman who decides to give up on, rather than put up with, her rigidly traditional spouse. She doesn't appreciate his willingness to take total responsibility for her. She feels hemmed in. Though he looks like a movie star and bought her a mink, it isn't enough. He simply cannot understand it. "But I gave her *everything,*" he moans.

Some years ago a man using the pen name Albert Martin wrote a piece for the *New York Times* that provides a typical example. Albert's marriage had broken up, and he was miserable about it. "I don't want to be [divorced]," he wrote. "I am horrified by the prospect. I think it is the most devastating thing that could happen to my family, but it is going to happen. My wife wants it." He went on to assure *Times* readers that he and his wife had led a wonderful life with "everything to live for." Their comfortable house, set on two acres with a woods, a ball field, and a toboggan slope, had been perfect for raising four boys. He had been happy, and he thought his wife was happy, too—until she told him she wanted a divorce.

"I am one man, hurt," he wrote, and predicted that many more men would be hurt—victimized by women whose concern for themselves was greater than their regard for "the needs of the family" or "of the other partner."

No doubt Albert thought his anguished words would bring sympathy for him and scorn for his ungrateful spouse. But no, most of the letters (from men as well as women) to the editor of the *Times* heaped the scorn on Albert for being an insensitive clod, a man so wrapped up in his own satisfactions that he neither knew nor cared what his wife thought. Letter after letter claimed to have have Albert's number, all right, and it was zero.

Just recently, a similar appeal appeared in the *Philadelphia Inquirer:* "My marriage was splendid before my wife went to work. I could count on the meals being on time, the house clean and the children well taken care of. Now everything has changed. My wife says she's happy, but we're all going hungry, the house is a mess and the kids forever ask, 'Whatever happened to Mommy?' I don't know what's going to happen. What is a reasonable price for a family to pay for the wife's happiness?" Son of Albert. Albert Part Two. Everything used to be splendid. For him, yes. For her, obviously not.

Conflict

So many questions leap to mind. How frustrating to have only a few paragraphs and no way to get at the really juicy details. Has she truly abandoned her home and loved ones? We picture her out dancing until dawn—Margaret Trudeau at Studio 54 while hubby Pierre takes care of Canada and the kids. We picture her moving up in the corporation. "Just a second, B.G., while I tell my secretary to call my husband and tell him I'll be working late. Now, about our meeting next week in Cairo . . ." Could she be having an affair with B.G., too?

But also: Why is this family going hungry? Can they not open a can? Could it be they put down their forks rather than eat anything less than gourmet fare? Do they likewise refuse to eat if the meal is not "on time"? Why is the house such a mess? Can't *he* dust? Has he suggested hiring somebody to straighten up one afternoon a week?

Only one thing seems clear. Old style and new style are in conflict . . . again. What a mess.

What saves most of us, as I mentioned before, is that we are neither *totally* old style nor totally new but scattered erratically along a scale. Usually, she is closer to one, he closer to the other. Usually one is racing ahead while the other lags behind, yelling, "What's the hurry?"

Researchers have found that those who are younger and better educated are more likely to be new style, although it's hardly a guarantee. Better-educated men, in fact, seem to prefer the superwoman system: she has a career but cares for the house, too. Research also shows that the possibility for compromising between the old and the new increases the closer the partners are in job status, personal income, education, and self-esteem.

But they also found that, across the cultural and income spectrum, the gap between old and new is narrowing. More men are saying, for example, that they would be *willing* to do some household chores, even when they admit they are not doing them.

Small Changes

And it seems that even though the majority of Americans still claim the man is the head of house, that phrase no longer means quite what it used to. A guy may say, as a friend of mine did, "I've been pleading with my wife to take her hands out of the dishpan and do something she'd find more interesting, but she won't." If his wife were truly an old style wife, she would do what he says, even if what he says is new style. But, further, one could argue that she is being very new style by insisting on doing her own (old style) thing.

A woman may say, as a friend of mine did, "I used to wait on Walter hand and foot. But then, one Saturday morning, we were eating breakfast—which I had cooked and I had served—and he said, 'I don't have any jam.' And I said, 'It's on the second shelf of the refrigerator, on the left.' I think I was as surprised as he was that I didn't just jump up and get it. But when he saw that I wasn't moving, *he* got it. Heh. Heh. Heh."

She would claim that Walter is still head of the house, of course, but . . .

Small changes occur and are accepted—with puzzlement, perhaps, but with no great fuss. I

interviewed a woman named Lila who recalled that shortly after she and her Jerry had returned from their honeymoon, they were sitting together in the living room and he said, "I'd like a glass of water." Whereupon she said, "So would I. Would you bring one for me when you get yours, hon?"

Well, that certainly was never what his mother said, so he said, "Can't you get it?" And she replied, "No more easily than you can. And it was your idea." At which point he got up, got two glasses of water, and said, "Here's yours."

Lila now ranks "Here's yours" in the same momentous league as Alexander Graham Bell's "Mr. Watson, come here; I want you" and Samuel F.B. Morse's "What hath God wrought?" All three sentences, she says, ushered in new eras of communication.

You might think that's no big deal. But Lila is right: what is today a minor change in a man-woman relationship would have been as unlikely as space flight for most women twenty-five years ago. . . .

Recognizing Women's Needs

When I asked my women friends what would indicate to them that a man was new style, they all agreed he would have to show some recognition of their needs. Yet no two cries for simple justice were alike. One woman said that her husband ("just like a man") doesn't clean the bathroom until it's totally covered with mold and she herself is turning green. If he were new style, she said, he wouldn't wait around to be told. But another woman found that kind of goal downright unbelievable: "You know a man who would actually consent to clean a bathroom and you're *complaining*?"

"We aren't asking that men approve of where women are going, just that they accept us as we accept them."

Mona says she'd call it even if her husband just showed a little appreciation, but Nan says she wants more than appreciation; she wants cooperation.

Rita asks, "How come *he* can announce he's going on a fishing trip and expect me to go along with the idea though not on the trip, but if I were to announce that I was going off for a week and he could look after the kids and wait for the electrician, he'd go into shock?" And Sandy flatly states that, since they have now moved four times so that he can get a promotion, it's his turn to move now so that she can get ahead.

In short, what you want, what would satisfy you, and whether you get it depend on where you and your man are on the old style-new style continuum—more specifically, how far apart you are from each other.

It's terrible to admit this, but even those of us who believe in change can have mixed emotions about it. On the one hand, when I tell Bernie I have a meeting to go to and I won't be home for dinner, I know I wouldn't like it at all if he put his foot down and told me that my job is to cook. On the other hand, I'm not as thrilled as I might be at how wonderfully he manages without me. "You *could* look just a little more desolate," I have told him. "A brief speech about indigestion wouldn't go amiss."

Sometimes when the men decide to enlist in our new style ways, we'd just as soon they did not. I don't want Bernie to learn to cook, for example, because I like to cook and I like things in the kitchen done my way. If that makes me a throwback, so be it.

Miriam says Milton volunteered, without being asked, to accompany her to the supermarket, to push the cart, and to help make selections. But after a few trips in which he compared products in one aisle when she wanted to move ahead, and she compared prices in another aisle while he grew impatient, she decided she'd rather he stayed home to carry in the bags when she got there.

What rapidly becomes clear is that in this business of how two lovers become friends there is no right or wrong way. It is, as lawyers would put it, whatever pleases the parties at any given time.

Moving to Where Women Are

I don't think I could ever have imagined in advance the kinds of choices that have come up. There was the time that Bernie thought we should buy a new sofa, and I wanted to spend the money on a copying machine. I thought that showed how modern we had become. Wouldn't you think the woman would want the sofa, the man would want the machine? Apparently, we hadn't changed that much because we got the sofa first. We weren't exactly old style either, because it was understood that the very next big purchase would be my copier—which he uses more than I do, as it happens. But, then, I sit on his couch.

It seems to me that all we are asking of men is that they move closer to where we are. She doesn't have to prove that his way is inferior or accept that hers is. If he says Mother Nature intended males to be in charge and then brings up birds, she can bring up bees. There is more than one way of doing things, that's all.

We aren't asking that men approve of where women are going, just that they accept us as we accept them. This is a kind of variation on the golden rule: do unto others as they would like done unto them, even if you think it's nuts.

Rose DeWolf is a columnist with the Philadelphia Daily News.

> *"A man really wants a woman he can respect. He is looking for a friend as well as a lover."*

Men Want Intelligent, Understanding Women

C.D.B. Bryan and Jim Sanderson

Editor's note: The following viewpoint is in two parts. Part I is by C.D.B. Bryan. Part II is by Jim Sanderson.

I

I have never felt comfortable speaking or writing about the "typical woman" or the "typical man." I don't know why that is. I keep feeling I should have learned *something* in the course of my travails in life—enough at least to come up with a strongly worded opinion or two. But generalities make me uneasy. I am only now beginning, with confidence in my accuracy, to be able to talk about myself.

Therefore, let me make some suggestions: I would think that if you really want to find out what a man needs, you might first ask the man yourself. Even if he is not able to articulate those needs, he will not be untouched by your question.

Next, ask yourself what *you* need from a man. The stand-up comedienne Elayne Boosler was not referring to gender confusion when she said, "I am a human being *trapped* in a woman's body." We Homo sapiens have more in common than we have at odds. You and I are both fragile creatures on a fragile planet; we both need love and sanctuary, respect and loyalty, nurturing and companionship, someone or something worth living for, peace and laughter, kissing and touching, sleep, potable water, a bit of privacy, an occasional hot meal and honesty from those we live with—honesty, that is, tempered by *tact*.

Honesty not tempered by tact becomes criticism. Criticism causes defensiveness. Defensiveness leads to withdrawal. Withdrawal promotes anger. Anger generates hostility. Hostility is an antiaphrodisiac. Lack of satisfying sexual relations produces

resentment. Resentment leads to betrayal. Betrayal provokes choas. Chaos invites violence. Violence ends up in court. Ending up in court is big trouble.

Here is what I need from a woman: I need to be hugged. My heart effervesces when my woman squeezes me for no apparent reason or sidles up and plants a wet one smack on my lips. I don't like being plucked at, but I do like to be touched.

I need friendship from the woman I love, a bond of intimacy which, depending on the circumstances and needs, permits me to be her lover, her husband, her coconspirator, her brother, her warrior, her teacher, her pupil, her sanctuary, her father—and even her mother during those moments of illness, stress or fatigue when she is too harried to properly take care of herself—but I do not want to be trapped in the role of parent. I do not want a woman to be a child. I want to take care of her when she needs it, just as I want her to take care of me when I need it. I want a relationship of equals.

I need moments of peace—time to unwind, reflect, to appreciate and dream.

I need to *waste time*, to escape into a *Magnum P.I.* or a Mets game. Do not underestimate the beneficial effects of an alpha-wave rinse gained from an occasional evening of mindless TV.

I need to be apart from my woman so that I can have the opportunity to miss her. I do not want separate vacations, but I do need the sometime business trip that takes me to a lonely hotel bedroom and reminds me of what I have left behind.

I need a woman with a sense of humor, someone able to laugh with me, about me, about herself, about life, about garter belts and PMS, the disappointing hotel room we ended up with in the Caribbean, the ex-wife who keeps cruising by our house to see what we're doing. Laughter diffuses crises; it prevents us from losing sight of what is really important: us.

I need a woman who tries to *understand* me, who is aware of my quirks and rhythms, who senses when to let me talk about what's bothering me and when to let me work it out by myself. I need a woman willing to listen to what I am trying to say without telling me, "What you really mean is . . . ," when really that is not what I meant at all. I need a woman to realize that if I *disagree* with her, it does not mean that I *dislike* her; that if I think she is *wrong*, it does not mean I think she is *bad*. I need her to be patient when she explains her feelings to me and not assume that if I do not immediately understand, I am being bullheaded and stupid, rather than simply unable to yet comprehend her point of view.

We all know by now that even Mr. Right has his flaws. And so it is helpful if a woman keeps a man's imperfections in perspective. He, I, *we* men need and like being told every now and then what we do right. I do not need to be constantly reminded of the stupid way I behaved six years ago. (There should be a statute of limitations on past noncritical transgressions.) I do not need to hear sentences beginning, "You always . . . " or "You never. . . ," nor to be told things for my own good which, in fact, are not for my own good, but do hurt me a great deal.

Wisdom and Experience

I do not need being compared unfavorably to "X," who is smarter, richer, kinder, stronger, and "Y," who is more thoughtful, successful, admired, ambitious, and "Z," who is a better lover, provider, driver, cook, gardener, joke teller and—on those rare occasions when his first serve gets in—tennis player, too. And yes, I am aware that the reason the woman one loves might say such cruel and awful things is because one has failed to respect and take care of *her* needs. Still, a woman, like a man, should know when to button her lip.

That's why I need a woman to give me her wisdom and experience and, when appropriate, the benefit of the doubt. I need a woman who argues and ends it cleanly rather than harboring resentments for days; a woman who is willing to compromise from time to time.

Most of all, I need what, thank God, I have: a woman who says she needs me.

II

In the dentist's waiting room the other day I was sitting opposite a women reading Cosmopolitan magazine. Attractive and wearing a well-cut businesswoman's suit, she might have been a lawyer. I must have made her self-conscious. Slowly she moved one hand to cover the top headline on the magazine cover, which read something like "Thirty-six and aching for sex: What's a good girl to do?"

I was tempted to tell her to relax because I'd already read that issue and the article didn't have much to do with sex at all. It merely pointed out that while "girls" in their 30s didn't have as many men available to them as before, they were now better at culling the losers.

Misleading headline? Always tempting, I suppose, when you're trying to sell at the supermarket checkout counter next to the National Enquirer.

Women, Not Girls

A more serious complaint, it seems to me, is the way Cosmo persists in treating adult women as "girls." How come no feminist ever picketed editor Helen Gurley Brown? They certainly gave Hugh Hefner, publisher of Playboy, a hard time.

Both magazines pander to the underdeveloped teen-ager, which hangs on in a portion of everybody's psyche. Playboy's photos of young naked females are nothing more than prettied-up porno—no question about it. Yet when this magazine, in its Playboy Advisor column, sets out to help readers it does so with responsible, mature authority. No smirking allowed.

I wish I could say the same for Cosmo. Some of its articles are becoming less sexist, but consider the advice in a feature titled "Foxy Suggestions for a Girl in Love";
—"If he thinks a Big Mac is the ultimate in dining pleasure, so do YOU."
—"Ask him to tell his favorite joke at a party. (Laugh.)"
—"A fishing holiday off the coast of Newfoundland? You'd adore it!"
—"Praise his indifferent backhand."
—"Put it down to 'sheer luck' that you've beat him at Trivial Pursuit six times running."
—"Let him set up your stereo, even though you've moved so many times you can do so yourself in five minutes flat." Etc., etc.

"When it comes right down to it, men don't like helpless women. They get to be a bore."

Advice like this seems too flip and fluffy to be taken seriously, and yet cumulatively it reinforces a stereotype that is devastating to the kind of relationship men and women want today.

Market research shows millions of young women (not all of them single) believe in Cosmo as a kind of bible as to how they should look, act and, above all, deal with that strange jungle animal, the male.

Cosmo teaches readers to be cute, helpless, childishly sexy, flattering, manipulative, obsessed with surface appearance. If you're still a "girl" at age 36 how can you possibly be expected to take charge of your own life? It's as if the women's movement had never happened.

Many males are initially attracted to these adorable little doll-women because they seem so eager to please. But the relationship soon falls apart. What if he actually takes her on that distant fishing trip?

When it comes right down to it, men don't like helpless women.

They get to be a bore. Males also aren't quite as dumb as Cosmo suggests; when a woman starts falling over herself ''to protect his ego'' we start to distrust her generally. A typical response is to turn her into a sex object.

A Woman To Respect

A man really wants a woman he can respect. He is looking for a friend as well as a lover. The more competence she displays in her life the more interesting she becomes; and the higher her self-esteem (if she has a sense of humor about it), the more valuable the prize to be won.

Yes, good looks and sex appeal still attract us, but only in the initial encounters. Since we really aren't as powerful and sure of ourselves as we pretend, we are consciously or unconsciously looking for a woman who can add strength to the relationship.

Traditional female games are a turn-off because they smack of the weakness and dependency inherent in manipulation. Dear Faithful Cosmo Reader, I have to tell you about real love today. It means you never have to say you're sorry—if you don't like Big Macs.

C.D.B. Bryan is an author and novelist from Connecticut. Jim Sanderson is a retired syndicated columnist on men's issues.

viewpoint 19

Men Want Passive, Unintelligent Women

Roberta Anne Grant

When Gary Hart's presidential campaign came to an abrupt halt after press reports linked him with Donna Rice, a voluptuous blond model who was not his wife, all of America asked "Why?" Why would a smart, successful politician, married to an attractive, supportive and politically astute helpmeet, Lee Hart, bring ruin upon himself by associating with a curvaceous young woman who seems to be rather naive despite her Phi Beta Kappa key from the University of South Carolina? It's only fair to point out that Hart appears to be just one example—certainly the most publicized—in a long line of political philanderers. Presidents from Jefferson to Roosevelt were known to have had mistresses. John Kennedy, it has been reported, was unfaithful to Jackie almost from the moment they became engaged. Ted Kennedy's womanizing became public after he drove off a bridge at Chappaquiddick in 1969, which resulted in the death by drowning of Mary Jo Kopechne and the end of his presidential aspirations.

Women as Playthings

Throughout history, in fact, men of power and wealth, even men of God, have broken their marital bonds to enjoy illicit fun with women they saw merely as playthings.

Since the women's movement, however, relations between the sexes are supposed to be different. And to some degree they are. Yet many of the men moving in the corridors of power, whether in Washington, on Wall Street or in Hollywood, are still giving women a very mixed message. On one hand, successful men say they want an intelligent, independent mate. But ironically, many of them also seem to want an old-fashioned girl on the side: someone pretty yet passive whom they can conquer sexually and dominate intellectually. Why the ambivalence? And why do some women still feel obliged to play dumb?

One simple explanation is that men who have reached prominence often feel entitled to the time-honored symbol of achievement—the affection of beautiful women. Traditionally, a glamorous girl on the arm of a powerful man has been a trophy he could show off to other men.

It's the ideal of feminine beauty that men seek, says Warren Farrell, Ph.D., author of *Why Men Are the Way They Are.* "Men get exposed to approximately twenty million advertisements featuring beautiful women every year. By the time we enter high school, we're addicted to the idea of the beautiful woman. But she's paying attention to the seniors, not to us. Then society tells us there *is* one way to fulfill our dreams—by becoming successful. For men in some professions, like politics, getting married and living a traditional lifestyle is almost a necessity. Yet it limits their access (or at least it should) to what they may feel is a reward of achievement—the adoration of a beautiful companion."

"My husband and I see it all the time," says a prominent Washington hostess. "Married senators and congressmen are constantly having affairs. When they hit this town, they know they've finally made it. And they're not about to miss out on the goodies."

A Form of Relaxation

If sex and status are the most obvious reasons smart men seek decorative women, there is also another explanation. "A lot of driven professional men really want to 'veg out' when they're not working," explains business psychologist Srully Blotnick, Ph.D., author of *Otherwise Engaged: The Private Lives of Successful Career Women* (Penguin, 1986). "Spending time with a beautiful girl who makes few demands gives them a sense of release and relief. All too often," adds Blotnick, "it is only the man's perception that these women aren't bright."

One surgeon, married with a month-old daughter, was late to work one evening. When a colleague asked why, he replied, "I've been with my girlfriend." Then he went on to complain how exhausted the hospital routine was making him and how guilty he felt about his young wife, who kept asking for more of his time. "So why don't you give it to her?" the colleague asked. "I'd like to," he replied, "but I'm burnt out." "With the girlfriend," the colleague theorized, "he'd found someone who made no demands—someone with whom he could really relax and forget all his cares."

"Equality, apparently, is still an unwelcome idea to many men."

Some men are aware of the contradictions implicit in their thinking. Bruce, a thirty-nine-year-old single doctor, confided that when he marries, he will choose a strong, independent woman, one with her own career and interests, "because otherwise it would be boring." But then he admitted that just the other night, he'd canceled plans for dinner and a movie with an intelligent, successful woman. "I'd worked so hard all day, I didn't have the energy for serious conversation. I just wanted someone to take care of me," he said.

But a smart woman can be caring. Men who claim they just want to relax with a woman may have another motive as well. "My gut feeling," says noted writer Isaac Asimov, author of more than three hundred books and the husband of a psychoanalyst, "is that an intelligent man will socialize with a not particularly bright woman because she's not a threat. If a woman is able to outthink a man, it can really hurt his ego."

Equality, apparently, is still an unwelcome idea to many men. One well-known film director, currently single, described how he carried on several relationships with women who were not as bright as he was. "I guess I get some kind of gratification," he says, "because I can run the show in a way I couldn't with a woman who was more of an equal partner." So it is not so much what a playmate has, like beauty or charm, that attracts certain men to her. It is rather what a "bimbo" lacks, what makes her a joke, that most appeals to the outwardly successful yet inwardly insecure man.

An intelligent woman clearly expects admiration and respect to flow in both directions. The man who cannot reciprocate is often afflicted with a deep, narcissistic hunger for adulation, say psychologists.

"Most of us get a sense of self-worth in childhood. We don't need to rely on constant praise from others," said Robert Michels, M.D., chairman of the department of psychiatry at Cornell University Medical College, in New York City. "But if as a child you had a sense of being unloved, then you can go through life forever seeking love and approval; you need praise simply to feel adequate."

Such men often enter high-visibility professions, such as politics, medicine and show business, to gain adulation and respect. Clinical psychologist Ann Watson, M.A., refers to this type of man as the hero. "The hero's job is to conquer," she says, "and the woman's role for such a man is to be always adoring and understanding."

Unfortunately, reality is often disappointing. "A hero type needs a hero's welcome," Watson continues, "and his wife can't always provide it. She knows his weaknesses and flaws, and she may not want to have sex as often as he does."

Thus the hero will turn to political groupies, to secretaries in the office, to someone younger, naive or simply not too bright. A new girlfriend will see only the man's carefully constructed facade. She'll stroke his ego and be eager to have sex. She won't offer any complications or make demands—at least initially.

"A lot of men here in Washington need to have their egos constantly fed," says one senior government official. "A smart girl wouldn't let herself be used this way. But some passive women are quite willing to go along."

Fear of Closeness

Dallying with "bimbos" can also be a man's way of distancing himself from his wife, says psychoanalyst Richard Robertiello, M.D. "When some men sense real intimacy developing with their wives, they experience an unconscious fear of losing their masculinity.

"Little boys have to tear themselves away from Mom and develop psychological defenses in order to become men," Robertiello explains. "Little girls don't have to go through that violent wrenching to reinforce their gender identity. And the more domineering or controlling his mother, the more a man may have to put up barriers.

"That's why," continues Robertiello, "even if a man has rapport with his wife, he may have to prove he's a conquering male. He may love his wife and still find her sexually attractive, but he can't really *conquer* her. She'd resent it. So he has to go outside marriage to vent this masculine urge."

Watson agrees. "Men often fear closeness within the marital relationship," she says. "By having an affair, he's got a secret, a part of himself his wife knows nothing about. In his own eyes, he's a real man."

However logical the explanations, this kind of

behavior shows immaturity. In fact, most womanizers are not men who love women or sex but men who simply haven't grown up. And as they acquire power, they can also acquire a dangerous and blinding arrogance, a feeling that they are above the rules that govern ordinary people. This, say experts, was one of Gary Hart's characteristics.

Adds David Spiegel, M.D., a psychiatrist at Stanford University Medical School, in California, "Such men do not consider the cost of their actions to their wives or families."

What can a woman do if she has the misfortune to be married to a compulsive womanizer? "He's unlikely to change," says Robertiello. "Not unless he feels deep remorse and wants to mend his ways, and most don't."

Is there any hope? Robertiello says that in rare cases, a wife may be so confident of her husband's love and sexual affection for her that she can tolerate his infidelities—although today the threat of AIDS would probably modify her attitude. For most women, however, the pain of a husband's philandering is not sufficiently offset by his positive qualities. In such a situation, advises Robertiello, the woman would be wise to leave.

Why Women Still Play Dumb

But what about the other women? Why do they still choose to become sex objects, status symbols or toys? "Some women love to be involved with men of power; it's a mutual seduction," says Judd Marmor, a psychoanalyst in Los Angeles. In addition, there may be some not-so-dumb calculations. Some women believe that association with power and status is a shortcut up the career ladder. And sometimes they are right.

"Women who let themselves be used are either coldly cynical or so insecure that they expect nothing more."

In fact, shrewd "bimbos" frequently collect in centers of power. They are not the soft headed, passive females their lovers and bosses think them to be. Indeed, many are street-smart and manipulative. They often end up with great jobs, great husbands and great fortunes. "It happens on *Dallas*," said one society columnist, "so why shouldn't it in real life? Where do you think they get their story ideas, anyway?"

Power Plays

In most cases, psychologists agree, men who womanize have little respect for women as human beings. And women who let themselves be used are either coldly cynical or so insecure that they expect

nothing more.

One woman whom John Kennedy courted but never captured said, "The whole thing with him was pursuit. I think he was secretly disappointed when a woman gave in. It meant that the low esteem in which he held women was once again validated. It meant also that he'd have to start chasing someone else.

"I once asked him why he was doing it," continues the woman, "why he was taking a chance of scandal while trying to make his career take off. He took a while to answer. Finally he shrugged and said, 'I don't know. I guess I just can't help it.' He had this sad expression on his face. He looked like a little boy about to cry."

Roberta Anne Grant is a senior editor with Ladies' Home Journal.

"Women have too many good reasons to turn us down."

Dating:
A Man's View

Steve Carter

Now that self-sufficiency has freed women from the traditional constraints of male dependency, women can take their time, be selective, and resist settling for anything less than what they want. In terms of dating, this means that the new woman is not interested and not pressured to date any half-decent prospect who comes along. Instead, she may only be willing to date the handful of men who immediately meet her standards. But even these men cannot let themselves be lulled into a false sense of security, for the screening process has just begun. These days, few women view dating as a pleasant way of getting to know someone. Instead, dating has become a vehicle for conducting a series of highly critical evaluations of compatibility, where one disappointing evening in the beginning stages of a relationship can be grounds for termination.

This hardly seems fair, especially since we are all aware of how people's feelings and perceptions can change dramatically once they have the chance to get to know someone better. But today, women seem unwilling to give men that chance. Why have women become so difficult? Because the dating process is no longer a source of pleasure for these women, but instead, a never-ending source of pressures and problems.

The Dating Timetable

Many of women's confusing, seemingly unpredictable reactions to the dating game become easier to understand, and perhaps, not so unpredictable, when viewed as different reactions to the same problem: sex. Dating has become an unending source of sexual pressure, and at the heart of this problem lies the "dating timetable"—the concept that sex is expected to become an integral part of the dating process after only one or two

dates.

Why is this timetable a problem? Because a woman's decision to sleep with a man is a very personal, emotionally complex decision that has little or nothing to do with the number of times she has dated him. Granted, some women may be ready to sleep with a man after knowing him for only a few days, but others may not be ready for weeks or months. Yet the dating timetable does not account for this. Ready or not, the pressure starts, and a woman quickly finds herself forced to make an unpleasant decision: Does she reject a man's advances and spend an unpleasant evening arguing about it, or does she give in and spend another depressing night in the arms of a stranger? The choices are not pleasant.

In light of this, it should come as no surprise that many women, sick of the pressures of this timetable, are creating a third option for themselves: they are opting out. Women are turning off—if they are not ready to sleep with a man after one or two dates, the next date never comes, and the sexual confrontation is avoided. In the words of Ruth K., a magazine editor from Florida, "I'm good for about two dates. After that, the pressure starts to build, so I make myself scarce."

What is particularly unfortunate about this is that many relationships with tremendous potential never get a chance to develop. As Barbara B., a hospital administrator from New York, put it, "In a way I regret it, but if a guy doesn't impress me as being Mr. Right on the first date, I usually won't go out with him again. Maybe I could have had a few good relationships . . . or a brief fling or two . . . even a good friendship would be better than nothing. But it's too much trouble—this sexual-liberation thing makes everything too complicated."

At this point you may be thinking, "But I'm not like most men—I never pressure women into bed. Why do they stop dating *me*?" Unfortunately, it

Steve Carter, *What Every Man Should Know About the "New Woman."* New York: McGraw-Hill Book Company, 1984. Reprinted by permission.

doesn't matter what you are like—women have become so sensitive to the dating timetable that they don't want to stick around long enough to find out your particular views on the subject. If you can't quickly convince a woman that you are very different from most of the men she has met (a difficult task, since she won't be giving you much time to do so), she will automatically assume that you expect to be sleeping with her after one or two dates, and she will react accordingly.

"If your true personality does not show through and a woman doesn't get the chance to discover your best qualities, then you become just another boring dinner date."

Of course, in this era of progressive sexuality, every woman isn't worried about the consequences of the dating timetable—some women have willingly integrated it into their lifestyles, and have no objection to sleeping with a man on the first date. But there is a catch—although these women may sleep with every man they date, they don't date every man who asks. In fact, these women won't give most men the time of day—they are extraordinarily particular about the men they date (far more particular than the many women troubled by the dating timetable). Therefore, although women's feelings about the dating timetable may vary, for men it is always a no-win situation.

The Dating Equation

Another concept which has made dating less appealing to women is the dating equation:

$$\$\$\$ \text{ Invested } ♂ = \text{Sex Owed } ♀$$

This equation implies that the more money a man spends on a woman, the more that woman is obligated to sleep with him. Now you may be saying to yourself, "That's ludicrous" (I *hope* you're saying this), but many men accept the validity of this equation without question.

If you find this hard to believe, you would be interested to hear about an experience I had recently while being interviewed on a talk show in Connecticut. To get the audience involved in the show, the host decided to ask them their opinion of the dating equation. By a show of hands (and a few cheers), *half* the audience indicated that they agreed with the principles of this equation. Even I was a little bit surprised to see how many people felt this way.

How has the dating equation affected women's behavior? For one thing, more and more women are now insisting they pay their own way on dates.

True, some of these women are only asserting their independence, but many more are clearly demonstrating that they don't want to be sexually obligated. And rightfully so! A woman is not some sort of glorified vending machine—an object a man pumps money into expecting something in return (and wants to kick when nothing comes out)—a woman is a complex human being who wants to be treated as such. . . . DON'T FORGET IT!

The dating equation has also made women more wary of men who shower them with gifts after only one or two dates, and men who insist upon taking them on high-priced, whirlwind evenings (unless, of course, the man asks the women to pay half the bill at the end, but that can create other problems). Some women won't even go out with men who are known to spend excessive amounts of money on the first few dates. "After all," one woman remarked, "who knows what they'll want in return?"

Don't misunderstand me, I am not implying that women are attracted to cheap guys—they're not. But spending a lot of money does not always make the kind of impression you would like it to make.

Other Concerns

In addition to the dating timetable and dating equation, there are several other factors which are having a considerable influence on women's dating behavior:

Commitment Pressure: Many women terminate the dating process very quickly when they are subjected to premature commitment pressure. (Is there such a thing as mature commitment pressure? Yes, but it doesn't come until a relationship has been well-developed.) Anna G., a real-estate broker from New York told me, "Most men *don't give you the chance* to get to know them. After a couple of dates, they start telling you how they don't want you to see any other people, how you're the most wonderful woman they've ever met, how they want you to meet their family . . . this is too much to handle after only one or two dates. I can't imagine what they would say after three or four." This woman, like many others I've spoken with, told me she is constantly cutting off relationships because she can't handle the pressure men put on her to make a commitment. She also emphasized that, "Men have to learn that a woman's desire to make a serious commitment doesn't develop overnight. If a man doesn't have any patience, he'll never have a successful relationship . . . at least not with any of the women I know." I couldn't have said it any better myself.

Superficiality: "Sometimes you can go out with a guy five or six times and still know nothing about him—that's what I hate about dating," complained Catherine B., a nurse from Texas. We all know how dating tends to be extremely superficial. Everyone puts on their best face for the evening and acts out the role of "winer and diner" or "winee and dinee."

Yet because we are trapped in these rigid roles, often our best, most natural qualities don't surface—even if we want them to.

But if your true personality does not show through and a woman doesn't get the chance to discover your best qualities, then you become just another boring dinner date. Once this happens, the likelihood of rejection increases dramatically, as illustrated by this comment from Mary L., a high-school math teacher from New York: "If a guy isn't comfortable enough with himself to just *be* himself, I get turned-off. Maybe some women like stiff, formal dates, but to me, there's nothing worse."

A Woman's Fears

Personal Safety: Women's fears and concerns do not magically disappear once they are outside the bar scene. Most women will admit that they often worry about their personal safety when they are considering whether or not to go on a date with a man (especially one they don't know very much about). As Sherri V., a computer saleswoman from California, explained, "It's amazing how insensitive most guys are to a woman's fears. They expect you to think nothing of getting into a car with a guy you hardly know and spending the entire evening at his mercy. Dating new guys used to scare me to death—I would smoke half a pack of cigarettes just waiting for my dates to arrive . . . and the other half during the date. Thank God I got married when I did. If I hadn't, my lungs would have been black by the time I was thirty."

Although you may find such fears to be totally irrational (you know you would never hurt a fly), to a woman, they are very real. The less a woman knows about you, the more these fears are apt to affect her decision to accept or not accept a date with you.

"Even a man who passes the initial screening process can easily become a rejection statistic after one or two dates."

The Limitations of Time and Energy: For the working woman, the lack of free time has made dating even less appealing. Shauna C., a department store executive from Massachusetts, admitted, "My job gives me so little free time, the last thing I want to do is spend an entire evening on a date with some strange guy." Many women share this feeling. What could be worse than spending your precious free time worrying about things like sexual pressure and personal safety?

In addition, many working women find dating more exhausting than their jobs. Janice P., a lawyer from New Jersey, told me, "I can't date all the time—it takes too much energy. I have to worry about what I'm going to wear . . . I have to clean my apartment just in case he comes in . . . I like to relax when I'm not working—dating is *not* relaxing."

The Decline of Dating

Now you know why men are having so much trouble dating: women have too many good reasons to turn us down. Even if a woman is attracted to you, think of everything else she has to consider before accepting a date—the pressures, the problems, the fears. It's overwhelming. Therefore, it is not surprising that women are finding more pleasant, less pressured things to do with their valuable free time. More and more, I hear women say things such as, "I hardly date anymore," and, "I'm taking a break from dating." Some women have given up on dating entirely, including Cathy J., a free-lance writer from New York, who told me, "I don't care if I never have another date—dating is a pain in the ass."

Considering all the problems dating can bring, you may find it surprising that *any* women are still willing to date. But most see no alternative—they feel that to have a relationship, they must play the dating game. Unfortunately, few of these women continue to have an easygoing attitude toward dating. Not only have they become incredibly particular about selecting dating prospects, but most remain extremely sensitive to the slightest sign of pressure or any other problems, ready to end everything at a moment's notice. As a result, even a man who passes the initial screening process can easily become a rejection statistic after one or two dates.

What is even more disconcerting is that men's problems with dating are likely to get much worse before they get better. As more and more women turn away from promiscuity in an effort to put meaning back into their relationships, dating—which is so hopelessly intertwined with sex—is becoming less and less appealing. Indeed, it may only be a matter of time before it is impossible for any man to develop a relationship by proceeding on a date-to-date basis.

What can men do? Is there any way to cultivate relationships without encountering all of these unpleasant pressures and problems? Yes there is, if you're willing to stop dating. But how can a man have a productive social life if he doesn't date? The truth is that any man can lay the foundation for a successful relationship *without ever going on a single date*—it all begins with two simple steps:

A New Vocabulary

Every time I hear a man use the word "date," I cringe. Like "pick-up" and "score," the word date brings too many negative images to a woman's mind—eliminate it from your vocabulary (regardless of whether or not you're in the company of women). From now on you will be "spending time" with women, "getting together" with them, "meeting" them, "seeing" them—anything but dating them.

A new vocabulary is not enough. If you treat today's woman the same way you always treated your dates, she will react to you accordingly, no matter what words you use. If you want to develop a successful relationship with women, you must also change your attitude. As I have said before, relationships do not develop on a fixed schedule. Each proceeds at a different rate, determined by circumstances unique to that relationship. Any attempt to push this natural developmental process forward will only discourage a woman's interest.

From now on, instead of forcing a woman to reject you before she knows anything about you (a decision brought on by the pressures of dating), you must give a woman plenty to time to get to know you without making her feel pressured to make any decisions. This means *you must establish friendship and trust first*, and leave romance for later. If you do, you will open the door to unlimited possibilities.

Steve Carter is a former professional tennis player. He conducts seminars for men who have problems relating to women.

"Why it is that if a date doesn't work out we assume it's because we talked too much or talked too little or had flabby thighs or overwhelmed the poor guy with our assertiveness?"

Dating: A Woman's View

Dalma Heyn

The following is a true story.

The woman arrived at the restaurant at 7 P.M. sharp. Her date had arrived just moments before, so together they picked a corner table. Then they spent three and a half hours drinking, eating, laughing. They left the restaurant, arm in arm, and (please guess the evening's conclusion). . .

A) went to her apartment, got undressed and made love. He took her face in his hands and explained to her carefully how deeply he loved her. Then he told her that he also loved Fred.

B) found a charming café where they had Irish coffees. She looked at him with a grateful smile. He looked suddenly sad. "I'm getting married Saturday," he said, reaching for her hand, which he then kissed.

C) kissed passionately all the way to her place. They decided not to sleep together yet, but he whispered that he'd call her in the morning. He didn't—that morning or ever again.

D) walked back to her apartment, and ended the evening as happily as they began it.

The actual conclusion to the evening was D. If that makes you howl with laughter, you could be suffering from a new and common affliction of young unmarried females: dating paranoia.

Dating Paranoia

Dating Paranoia is an insidious ailment, a slow virus that attacks when your resistance is low: that is, after maybe two or three experiences with endings like A, B, and C. The fever starts when, instead of assuming you might have a nice time with a man on a date, you feel a deep, obscure sense of pain. You predict the worst possible outcome: He'll say you're right for him, but he's not ready for you; he'll fall in love with you, but his pattern is to destroy the person he loves; you'll try to act warm and interested, but you'll come across instead as anxious, too breezy, nervous.

You are in the throes of dating paranoia when you can no longer face this kind of endeavor with equanimity, when the thought of a nice evening with a friendly man is incomprehensible. There are no friendly men, no nice evenings. All you know is this: If you go out with a male who is not "just a friend," something terrible is going to happen. "Dating is like volunteering to be one of those counselors in the movie *Friday the 13th*," says my friend Sara. "You are a willing participant in a horror show."

One 25-year-old woman who lives in San Francisco disconnects her answering machine after midnight because she can no longer bear hearing her friends' hysterical reports of their evenings. "My own dates are tough enough," she says. "I don't need to hear other hair-raising war stories. These are not cute little tales of nerds who talked about software, or funny, mildly embarrassing sex scenes," she adds miserably. "These stories keep me up all night." Like the one about her friend who found out after eight passionate dates that her beloved was married. Why didn't he tell her? "Because," he answered, "I knew if I did you wouldn't go to bed with me anymore."

Dating Not Fun

Dating was probably never fun. But it wasn't navigating shark-infested waters, either. At least, it used to be clear that a man was looking for the same thing a woman was: a mate. If you wanted sex, you got married; society required it—it was not optional. Men pursued women ardently and openly; women pursued men ardently and covertly. The game was clear to all players. It was clear, too, that a terrific woman was highly regarded and a smart young man made an effort to win her heart. What man that your mother dated bored her into a coma with the news that he'd never get close to a woman again because of the miserable relationship he'd just gone through? Or that he sure hoped she liked pizza because his alimony payments put him on a tight budget? Or—and this is actually being said these days—that although she was beautiful and terrific, the city they lived in was "a candy store," and why should he settle for just one sweet when he could taste them all?

The game has clearly changed. Men are doing very little pursuing, not only because they're not required by society to marry in order to have sex (or even to have children), but also because of the surfeit of women that is so endlessly publicized.

"Single men and women have been polarized into caricatures: You're the voracious, marriage-crazed she-devil; he's an ego-crazed commitment-phobe."

Then there's the newest anxiety-provoker: mathematical data hell-bent on calculating why you won't find a man to marry you if you're a career woman over some age or other. Now we have science feeding the perception that finding a husband is extraordinarily difficult. Young women are responding to this perception with an odd mixture of hysterical self-improvement, dashed hopes, frustration, desperation and severe disappointment—a combination that adds up to raging ambivalence about meeting "eligible" men.

"The feeling women have that a man could make them happy has diminished a great deal," says Judith Sills, Ph.D., a psychologist in private practice in Philadelphia and author of *How to Stop Looking for Someone Perfect and Find Someone to Love* and a forthcoming book on romance. "They're trying lots of strategies to avoid disappointment, defend against it, pretend it doesn't matter, but underlying their paranoia is the belief that 'ultimately something bad is going to happen here—it's just a question of when.' Whereas I think when our mothers were dating they thought, 'Oh, one of these men is going to be it and he'll make me very happy and it's all very exciting.' That men were a disappointment—you only heard that conversation among women who had already been married for ten or fifteen years."

Chilling Men Out

Plenty of men are disappointing, but it doesn't stop you from working out on Nautilus machines three times a week to land one. Disappointment doesn't hold a candle to desperation, and, by God, you're going to win one of these hearts, even if it takes the world's tautest thighs to get one. Trouble is, when some sweaty guy with great pecs and lats

does come over to you while you're doing stomach crunches, you suddenly become overwhelmed by the absurdity of your maniacal drive to get his attention, and you chill him out the minute he says hello.

The worst part is how you act once you go out with a guy. Single men and women have been polarized into caricatures: You're the voracious, marriage-crazed she-devil; he's an ego-crazed commitment-phobe. Any women who wants a permanent relationship finds herself playing out this idiotic stereotype, and then defending herself against looking so hungry. "The result," says Beth, an adorable and smart woman of 29, "is that you get so scared of what you want from a man that you come out with the exact opposite in words and actions. I hear myself telling men that I don't want to make a commitment when that's exactly what I *do* want."

And God forbid you find a straight, eligible man you just happen not to want to kiss. You've *got* to want to. He walks, doesn't he? Talks? He's got a good job? What's the matter with you? As Joan Rivers's mother shouted at her, "He's a lawyer. So what if he has pimples. Marry him and his pimples will go away."

But if you *do* like him, the anxiety is horrendous. You become mute with over-interest. Says Beth, "I'm afraid to ask normal questions because they sound like *leading* questions. I'm positive that 'Do you have any sisters?' will be interpreted as 'Will we have in-laws?'"

The Underlying Goal

All this anxiety isn't really about *dating*; it's about finding a permanent lover, which is the underlying *goal of dating*. "And even if that goal is far in the distance," says Judith Sills, "it's your feelings about that goal—how needy you are, how anxious you are and how angry you are—that very much colors your feelings about dating."

Obviously, the reality of dating offers plenty to be panicky about, but real hardcore dating paranoia is a blend of maybe a third what's going on out there—and two thirds what's going on inside your head. According to Sills, the internal component is made up of two separate sets of expectations. One is: *There really are no good men, anyway.* "It's a thought that a woman doesn't admit out loud—that most men she's going to date will be jerks, losers and not be good enough for her."

The other expectation is: *If I ever find anyone who interests me in the least, I'll blow it.* So you combine the feeling that the guy's going to be a jerk with a certainty that if by some miracle you like him, you're in far worse trouble because for sure he's going to reject you. Sometimes these two separate, miserable anxiety attacks occur sequentially over the same man, because it's not about him, but about you. Says Sills: "For four dates, 'He's a jerk, he's stupid'—then, when the woman begins to drop some of that defense and *like* him, it's 'I'm going to fall apart, he's not going to call, I can't leave the house.' She almost wants the rejection, just to get it over with.''

Says Janet Wolfe, Ph.D., a psychologist at New York City's Institute for Rational-Emotive Therapy: ''Women are in a bunch of double binds. When they're too assertive, they think they're going to put the guy off. Just when women were getting comfortable with the idea of calling a guy three or four days after a date, they've now become terrified that if they call it's going to drive the guy away. What's more, they're afraid that if they're not assertive and don't take the initiative, they'll lose out because of the female/male ratio we keep getting drummed into our heads.''

Curing Paranoia

Admittedly, these are big problems. But wouldn't you think that by now we would be sick to death of our low self-esteem? Why is it that if a date doesn't work out we assume it's because we talked too much or talked too little or had flabby thighs or overwhelmed the poor guy with our assertiveness? What's dangerous here is our tendency to ascribe to men the power to determine our worth. ''It's not that women don't make mistakes,'' says Wolfe, ''but they exaggerate them and deify the man—as if he can do no wrong. Women need to understand that being rejected has nothing to do with their worth.'' She adds, ''There are so many wonderful women just turning themselves inside out to be pleasing to these schlemiels. It's so degrading.''

Maybe it is degrading, but it's not hopeless. You can cure dating paranoia—without pretending you don't want a relationship with a man and without giving up entirely after too many hysterical fits. But you do have to do four simple things.

"You must . . . stop selling yourself. You are not a package to be perfected, marketed and sold to any bidder who's male and single."

One is to make up your mind, both about whom to spend time with and also about what a good time *is*. Just because a man has a list of qualities that crown him king of the great catches doesn't mean you should want him. Look at all men, not just the ones that happen to be in favor at this moment, the men you could call ''bionic yuppies,'' indestructible go-for-it types who are forever renovating their lofts and buying new scuba equipment. Go for what pleases *you*.

You must also stop selling yourself. You are not a package to be perfected, marketed and sold to any bidder who's male and single. It is too much work and ultimately a time-consuming process that has little to do with involvement, love, commitment, marriage and happiness. In other words, two perfect packages do not make a couple.

Readiness

The third part of the cure is subtler. You'll find a partner in life when you've developed what psychologists call ''readiness,'' according to Judith Sills. ''Readiness is not about going to the right place, finding a better bar, having a fabulous line. It's not having your body in top shape, and it is not waiting at home until you lose those last ten pounds,'' says Sills emphatically. ''It is a sense of being comfortable enough with yourself, restless enough so you are ready and open to change—and it is reflected in how you're living, not how you're dating. People who are ready to connect lose a lot of dating paranoia—because they're ready to connect with a *person* and they're not in a frenzy for the *goal*.''

These people don't win each man they go out with. They don't look perfect. They don't act perfectly. They don't starve themselves to please and they don't go on an eating binge if they don't please.

The fourth way to lose your dating paranoia is to realize that the prognosis is good, despite boring statistics that say your chances of finding a husband are terrible. Unmarried men do not fare well in the long run, emotionally or physically. Statistics actually show that women handle being without a partner better than men do. There are even statistics that show that men are happier *being* married than women are. Sooner or later, these guys are going to commit.

It just depends on which statistics you choose to believe. I say, believe the ones that tell you that you will meet someone nice and dating will be fun. My Aunt Edie, a widow, fell in love again when she was 79 and Carl was 81. They've been dating for six wonderful years.

There are probably statisticians busy at this very moment disproving the chances that two people of that age could meet, date and be exciting to each other. But Edie doesn't know from numbers; she is on vacation at this moment, in the Caribbean, with Carl.

Dalma Heyn is a free-lance writer in New York.

*"White, college-educated women . . .
who are still single at 30 have only a
20 percent chance of marrying."*

Women Over Thirty Are Not Likely To Get Married

Eloise Salholz

Her sister had heard about it from a friend who had heard about it on "Phil Donahue" that morning. Her mother got the bad news via a radio talk show later that afternoon. So by the time Harvard graduate Carol Owens, 23, sat down to a family dinner in Boston, the discussion of the man shortage had reached a feverish pitch. With six unmarried daughters, Carol's mother was sounding an alarm. "You've got to get out of the house and meet someone," she insisted. "Now."

It was Valentine's Day when Sharon Makover learned of it on the news, and the irony did not elude her. "I thought, 'This is not what I want to be hearing today.'" Having recently split up with one boyfriend, Makover was at a crossroads: should she throw herself into her career or commit to a new boyfriend living in another country? "It got me thinking about what I wanted to do with my life," says Makover, 26, a curatorial assistant at the Jewish Museum in New York. A month later she was engaged.

All things being equal, Los Angeles screenwriter Nancy Rigg would prefer having a husband. Nevertheless, the news infuriated her. "It reinforces an old myth that once you hit 30, you're over the hill," says Rigg, 36. "I imagine that women who are buying into this are pretty depressed right now. It was like Moses came down the mountain and said, 'Boo on you women.'"

Not Now Means Never

The traumatic news came buried in an arid demographic study titled, innocently enough, "Marriage Patterns in the United States." But the dire statistics confirmed what everybody suspected all along: that many women who seem to have it all—good looks and good jobs, advanced degrees and

high salaries—will never have mates. According to the report, white, college-educated women born in the mid-'50s who are still single at 30 have only a 20 percent chance of marrying. By the age of 35 the odds drop to 5 percent. Forty-year-olds are more likely to be killed by a terrorist: they have a minuscule 2.6 percent probability of tying the knot.

Within days, *that* study, as it came to be known, set off a profound crisis of confidence among America's growing ranks of single women. For years bright young women single-mindedly pursued their careers, assuming that when it was time for a husband they could pencil one in. They were wrong. "Everybody was talking about it and everybody was hysterical," says Bonnie Maslin, a New York therapist. "One patient told me, 'I feel like my mother's finger is wagging at me, telling me I shouldn't have waited.'" Those who weren't sad got mad. The study infuriated the contentedly single, who thought they were being told their lives were worthless without a man. "I'm not a little spinster who sits home Friday night and cries," says Boston contractor Lauren Aronson, 29. "I'm not married, but I still have a meaningful life with meaningful relationships."

In fact, the study doesn't say that women should get married or even speculate about how many would like to do so. It merely points out that for those who wait, "not now" probably means "never"—and it pertains mainly to the huge cohort of baby-boomer women, victims of what demographers call the "marriage squeeze." Between 1946 and 1956 each year's new crop of births was greater than the one before. Since most women marry men several years their senior, baby boomers looking to pair up with even slightly older men far outnumber the available pool. "If we tried to match each women born in 1950 with a man three years older, we would come out with millions of women left over," reports "The Feminization of Loneliness," a study out of the University of California, Berkeley.

Black women face an even larger gap, since there are far fewer black, college-educated males than females. And the older a woman gets, the worse her chances of finding a suitable partner. One reason is that divorced men remarry women four to seven years younger. Factor in a gay-male population estimated to be 13 percent—three times that of lesbians—and you have a numbers game women can't win.

Even more unsettling than the statistics, however, are the long-term social implications. The study reflects a time of transition for millions of women and for the institution of marriage itself. Many career women no longer need husbands for economic security. Nor, thanks to the sexual revolution, do they need to marry for sex. Indeed, as the marriage rate has declined, the number of people cohabiting has been rising sharply, quadrupling since 1970. But while couples continue to get together, they seem to have trouble connecting. The reason is that the rules of the marriage game have changed. "This talk of intimacy rather than security is a relatively new phenomenon," says Berkeley psychologist Lillian Rubin, author of the book "Intimate Strangers." Men and women are struggling to reach a new accommodation. Even though men say they respect women's career aspirations, many openly long for full-time wives and mothers. For professional women, the challenge is to remain independent without sacrificing companionship.

Many women in their 30s facing biology's ticking clock are setting about the task of finding a mate with the same efficiency they have brought to managing investment portfolios. There, at least, they are not alone. A booming singles industry has emerged to cater to a more upscale clientele, and people are playing mating games they never would have considered a few years earlier. And many women have frankly come to terms with staying single—perhaps even preferring it to settling for Mr. Wrong. Some are creating surrogate families made up of fellow singles; others are having or adopting children on their own. Clearly, women are no longer putting their lives on hold.

"Select Group"

Perhaps no one was more stunned by the reaction to the study than the authors—Yale sociologists Neil G. Bennett and Patricia H. Craig, and Harvard economist David E. Bloom—who disclosed their findings in an interview with a small Connecticut paper. . . . For one thing, 8 out of 10 female college graduates *will* marry, so the researchers are admittedly "talking about a select group of women." (The reason they didn't study male marriage patterns is because no reliable census data were available for men.) They also acknowledge that "as with any demographic prediction there is no certainty." It's

conceivable, for example, that large numbers of women will suddenly begin to marry much later than the mean age of 24, or to marry younger men—but they would have to do so in unprecedented numbers to statistically change the trend line.

The authors are careful to note that their predictions represent statistical averages, not individual odds. They also point out that women born after 1957, when the baby boom peaked, should face a rosier statistical picture: the ever-smaller cohort of women will be drawing on a larger pool of somewhat older men. . . .

"Women are no longer putting their lives on hold."

The study's main message—that delaying marriage may ultimately mean forgoing it—clearly came as a slap in the face to this generation's best and brightest women. "When you look at men who don't marry, you're often looking at the bottom of the barrel," says Berkeley sociologist Nancy Chodorow. "When you look at the women who don't marry, you're looking at the cream of the crop." Career patterns are mainly to blame. Up and comers are expected to work hardest in their 30s; that those are also the years a career woman would wed and have children is her tough luck. . . .

Cynicism and Romanticism

Many of today's singles bring a curious mixture of rank cynicism and starry-eyed romanticism to their quest for a mate—as though it were not worth giving up space in their closets for anything less than Mr. Perfect. Two years ago Andrea Quattrocchi broke off an engagement. Her fiancé was "very loving, very old-fashioned, but I felt like I was settling for second best." Now 28, the Boston sales manager says she is eager for someone "who likes all the things I like. Like if they hate sailing, that's really a deterrent. I like to experience everything in life. So if they hate sushi, I can't stand that." Still, Quattrocchi's desire to have a family is so strong, she may have to settle for a meat-only man the next time around.

Susan Cohen wishes she had been able to see her way clear to the altar. "Not being of sound mind," she refused several marriage proposals when she was younger. Looking back, she concludes that she was immature too long. "I had a long run of being 22," she says. "I think I was 22 until I was 38." Now 40, the New York fashion consultant is finally ready for a man, if not necessarily a husband. "I would really like to meet somebody."

Most men would like to meet somebody and marry, too, but their feelings of self-worth come primarily from work. For women, however, marriage seems to be far more central to their basic identities. Even now, many singles, including those without any husband prospects in sight, cannot imagine never marrying and in their most private moments they testify to the anguish of being single. "You have a great day at work and you want to celebrate, but you don't have anyone to call. Or you have a bad day at work and all you want is for someone to put his arms around you," says Cathy Porter, 32, a real-estate appraiser in Los Angeles. "Men have become an obsession with me. Even if he's not for me, I want him anyway, so it's hard to let go."

The pain may be most acute for singles in their 30s who still can have children but are running out of time. Even though a growing number of women can and do have kids on their own, "very often what a woman wants is not the actual child," explains UC Berkeley psychologist Karen Paige. "She wants the closeness and intimacy of a whole family." "All my friends are having kids," says Penny Stohn, 33, a director for the New Jersey Department of Higher Education. "They tell me how glamorous my life is but I just sit there and envy them their kids."

Men Taunting Women

Men, of course, do not feel that pressure. As Chicago accountant Tim Bussey, 27, puts it: "Women are under the big time crunch. They don't have forever the way a man does." With biology and demographics on their side, many men can exercise what Laurel Richardson, author of "The New Other Woman," calls "ultimate power": there is little impetus to stick out a difficult relationship or to meet an older woman's child-bearing schedule. "If you have a fight with one woman, it isn't so traumatic," says Murray Manus, 32, a lawyer in Chicago. "You think, so what—there are others out there." One date taunted Christine Stroebel with the new study, making a special point of telling the 30-year-old Chicagoan about her diminishing chances.

Despite what women tell one another, not all men are jerks. When Chicago Tribune writers Cheryl Lavin and Laura Kavesh began their syndicated singles column, "Tales From the Front," one year ago, they were amazed by the volume of mail from men with legitimate complaints. One frequent cavil: women don't really appreciate nice guys. Another is that super-achieving women set impossibly high standards. Bill Amatneek, a good-looking 40-year-old computer consultant from Mill Valley, Calif., who says he wants a wife and child, has encountered both problems. He blames the women's movement for "making women have a critical attitude toward men: 'Men are too macho. Men aren't emotional enough.' It's not fun having a woman always tell you what's wrong with you." Worse, says Amatneek, the demographic numbers don't tell the whole story.

"It's not a buyer's market if you're shy. It's ironic that women say they want sensitive men, but end up marrying aggressive men.". . .

Women Not Waiting for Men

Some women simply aren't waiting around for men. Nowhere is the determination to make a life for oneself clearer than among women having children on their own. The fastest growing rate of single mothers is for white women between the ages of 30 and 34. To be sure, most say they would prefer having a conventional family, but many financially secure singles say they will not give up having children just because they do not have husbands.

For some, actually giving birth is an important part of the experience; others are happy to adopt. After many years on her own, Lillian Brown, an associate dean at the City College of New York, is about to adopt a 10-year-old girl. At 50, Brown has "come to terms with being a single woman and being quite comfortable in that role." Like most women, Brown grew up assuming she would one day marry, but it wasn't till her 30s that she realized she truly preferred being single. Shelling out $52,000 for a brownstone was a big step. "I said to myself, 'Why am I sitting around waiting for some knight in shining armor to get me a house?'"

Making a major purchase can be a powerfully symbolic act. Single women have emerged as the fastest growing group of new-home buyers. In some cases they are treating themselves to the sorts of luxuries that traditionally came as wedding gifts. A number of department stores have introduced the "Self Registry," for singles to list their china and crystal choices. Jill Roland, a New York publicist, signed up at Bloomingdale's for a toaster, clock and coffee maker and got them all. "They're from clients and family members who wanted to give me a housewarming gift or something for my birthday," says Roland, 25.

"Many singles, including those without any husband prospects in sight, cannot imagine never marrying."

Still, what singles crave most is companionship. "It's a challenge to be single today. I have relatives in Colorado and on the East coast, so I don't have family to have dinner with on Sunday," says screenwriter Rigg. Some singles band together for "orphans" dinners at holidays and take comfort in surrogate families. Many women speak of female friends as permanent parts of their lives, the men as transient. Indeed, experts say that one of the positive side effects of the man shortage has been the re-emergence of the value of community.

For better or worse, for richer or poorer. Today the poetry of the marriage vow has come to represent a practical choice. For many economically independent women, the consequences of their actions have begun to set in; even though they say they want to marry, they may not want it enough. Ultimately, of course, whether to wed is the most personal of decisions, based on individual dreams, neuroses and priorities as much as on demographic conditions. Those numbers will improve for future cohorts. But the social realities underlying them probably will not change. Younger women will continue to face difficult choices about whether to marry and when. Chastened by the news that delaying equals forgoing, they just may want to give thought to the question sooner than later.

Eloise Salholz is a general editor with Newsweek.

Women Over Thirty Are Likely To Get Married

Susan Faludi

Time was when Emory University instructor Janet Page would look out over a barely filled classroom and wonder if there really was call for her $40 three-night course, "Before the Year Is Over, I Will Be Married." Then came word of That Study, the Harvard-Yale marriage report auguring a shadowy life of Campbell's Soup for One cans for unwed women passing 30. Soon the joint was jumping.

The women came in droves, bearing well-thumbed copies of *Smart Women, Foolish Choices*, the tome that tells how to settle for less in a man. During class breaks, they spoke darkly of That Study's findings: 30-year-old single, college-educated women would have only a 20 percent shot at marriage; 35-year-olds only a 5 percent chance. By the new year, Page, a psychotherapist, had 120 students sign up for one class, triple her usual number. Nearly all were women. (She had to recruit the men by announcing on a local television show that she guaranteed all male applicants a date with one of her female students.) "That study certainly has helped the course bloom," says Page cheerily. "It's all that depression." She promised her pupils quick pick-me-ups with tips on "how to get out of the house and how to develop approachability, superlevel courtesy, and people skills." In class, they charted their "love résumés." Page had an even larger turnout.

Media Hype

We might like to believe we are too smart for all this media hype, that no one wants to marry some lug who thinks the little woman ought to be grateful to him forever after. But something about this study has wormed its way into the hearts of American women, gnawing away at still-precarious self-confidence. Many have reacted with anger to That

Study. But, it seems, at least as many of us are buying the books and periodicals for rejected maidens that are lining the shelves. Who would have thought 15 years ago that among the hot best-sellers of 1987 would be *How To Get Married: A Proven Plan* and *How To Get Married and Stay That Way*? Interest is brimming as well in Tracy Cabot's latest book, *How To Make a Man Fall in Love with You*. Cabot also teaches a "Mini Love Seminar," in which she reveals the secrets of the "Man Plan." Her publicists at Dell Books find it helpful to cite the marriage study in press releases. "Do you know that 40-year-olds are more likely to be killed by a terrorist than find a husband?" one reads. The study "only confirmed what everybody suspected all along: that many women who seem to have it all will never have mates."

For the record, the study actually predicts that 1.3 percent of all college-educated women in America who will turn 40 in the 1990s are likely to marry, which no matter how you count 'em is a sight more female bodies than have been getting bumped off by terrorists lately. But let's not blame Dell Books. It only cribbed that tidbit from *Newsweek's* June 2, 1986, cover story, the article that launched the year-long campaign of hysteria.

Now, a few things have come to light since the *Newsweek* article on the Harvard-Yale study was published. Stuff like:

• The U.S. Bureau of the Census marriage study, which found that college-educated women are *more* likely to marry than women with a high school diploma, and that single women at age 30 have *not* a 20 percent but a 58 to 66 percent chance at nuptials.

• A University of Illinois statistical study that found the much-blamed "man shortage" among Baby Boomers was mostly fiction and had only "a small effect" on the number of women marrying, because the tendency of women to marry older men has been overestimated.

Susan Faludi, "The Marriage Trap," *Ms.*, July/August 1987. Reprinted with the author's permission.

• A 1986 *Women's Day* study that found 50 percent of those lucky wedded women surveyed said if they had to do it again, they would not have married their husbands.

But feeling bad still reigns.

"Did you tell your students about the U.S. Census Bureau study?" I ask how-to-marry-in-a-year specialist Janet Page.

"What Census Bureau study?"

"The one that offers a much brighter picture than the Harvard-Yale study."

"Oh, really? I've never heard of it."

Does she ask for more details? Does she ask where to get a copy? Well, no.

Anxiety about the Family

Jeanne Moorman, author of the Census Bureau marriage study, says that since her findings were officially unveiled in January [1987] and shipped off to media across the country, she has received perhaps a few dozen inquiries and four or five requests to appear on radio talk shows. "We certainly didn't make the cover of anything."

The Harvard-Yale study, on the other hand, grabbed top billing wherever it went. "It may just be a matter of man bites dog being seen as more newsworthy than dog bites man," Moorman says. Maybe, but I think a case could be made for just the opposite: the media seized on the Harvard-Yale study precisely because it only confirmed, as the Dell Books publicists said, "what everybody suspected all along."

"Unwillingly, we women today, for all our sophistication, have fallen victim to an old trick. To emotional manipulation."

The press, though commonly seen as some grotesque alien force by its readers, is nothing more after all than the reflected mind of the public. And the public is increasingly anxiety-ridden these days about the decline in the American family, the increase in both childlessness and single mothers, the discourteous tendency of uppity educated women to do as they please. The articles on the marriage report—like the hostility toward women in the work force, the reluctance to provide decent day care, and the general talk of a backlash against feminism—all serve a pent-up desire to censure women for messing with the traditional order of things. 'There's a political line that is beginning to emerge," says Judith Wallerstein, a California psychologist who recently completed a 10-year longitudinal study on divorced women. "Every week

there's another book on women saying, 'Oh, my God, what have we wrought?'"

The handwringing is not limited to the bookshelves. I attended a pool party of mostly single professional men and women one weekend to take my own unscientific attitudes survey. Here's what they had to say about the Harvard-Yale study.

"If a woman devotes herself to her career and lets herself go," said one male criminal lawyer, "then yes, she deserves it." Another man warned, "Look, none of us are going to say it's retribution, but it's there on a subconscious level."

The women at the party mostly gazed demurely at the pool and said nothing. One said she found the study "very depressing."

Emotional Manipulation

For women who remember the late 1940s, this national alarm might also jog memories of another effort in American history to squeeze women out of the workplace. "This is much less coordinated and official than the post-World War II campaign to get women back in the home," says Judith Stacey, a sociologist specializing in gender at the University of California at Davis, "but the attitudes expressed reflect a feeling that women have gone too far."

Modern-day career women won't be deserting their jobs as a consequence—the economy won't allow it. But what's disturbingly reminiscent of the earlier era is how, unwillingly, we women today, for all our sophistication, have fallen victim to an old trick. To emotional manipulation. To what even Neil Bennett, coauthor of the Harvard-Yale study, calls "hyped-up twaddle," referring to the articles written about his study.

Here's how it happened—and how we let ourselves get duped.

On Valentine's Day of 1986 a reporter at the Stanford *Advocate* was grinding out the usual hearts-and-flowers fare and called the Yale sociology department for comment. He got Bennett on the phone, who let slip that he and Harvard economist David Bloom were tinkering with some figures on college-educated women's chances of marriage, and they looked pretty bleak. The *Advocate* ran the story, the Associated Press picked it up the next day, and by evening Bennett was fielding calls from as far away as Australia. Like an international game of telephone, the story got increasing muddled as it made the rounds. Speculation became fact. Predictions were transmogrified into conclusions. And some information passed along was just plain wrong. For instance, news spread that 25-year-olds had only a 50 percent likelihood of marrying. In fact, Bennett says they never made projections for women that young; the study was restricted to women born from the mid-1930s through the 1950s.

It was also widely reported that women in the bulging Baby Boom generation would suffer from the "marriage squeeze" because they would insist on drawing from the smaller pool of older men. Women *used* to marry men two to four years their senior. But now, those who are remarrying choose men slightly younger, and first-timers are marrying up by only one and a half years.

The story of the spinsters went unchallenged by the press and the public. Like tales of rat hairs in McDonald's hamburgers, it felt good to believe.

No one asked the obvious:

(1) Is the study right?

(2) So what if it is?

(3) And what of the chances of men, who do after all represent the larger population of "spinsters"?

Is the Study Right?

Any report issuing from both Harvard and Yale must be true, the Ivy League-awed press murmured as it genuflected. End of analysis.

In fact, to reach their conclusions, the study's authors used a parametric model designed to look back at the marriage patterns of women in 19th-century Europe. "In principle, the model may be applicable to women who haven't completed their marital history," its inventor, Princeton University Professor Emeritus Ansley Coale, says, "but it is risky to apply it to a subcategory such as college graduates."

The study also used what many statisticians consider an unrepresentative sample. It drew on the Census Bureau's 1982 Current Population Survey of only 60,000 households, which, when shrunk down to college-educated women in certain age brackets, shakes out to about 1,500 women.

In contrast, the Census Bureau study used a large representative sample—the 1980 Census, which polls one in six households, or a total of 13.4 million.

The Harvard-Yale authors also claimed that the marriage rate for college-educated women in their twenties and thirties was falling. In fact, according to the Census Bureau, between 1970 and 1980 the marriage rate actually rose for only one group: college-educated women between 27 and 39 years of age.

Bennett and Bloom also believe that women are forsaking marriage, not just putting it off to a later date. They claim that the age of women at first marriage has remained "quite stable" over the past 20 years. Wrong again. The median age of women at first marriage has risen from 20.5 to 23 in the last 20 years, says the Census Bureau. In fact, it climbed a full year from 1980 to 1984.

The increase suggests that "women are postponing marriage, not forgoing it," says Kathy London, a marriage analyst for the U.S. National Center for Health Statistics.

The Harvard-Yale men made another mistake. As Jeanne Moorman recently pointed out, they presumed that all women marry over a similar range

of years. In fact, the more educated women tend to spread their marriages over a wider period. Now this may sound like a big so-what, but the difference is essential. After correcting for this error, the Census Bureau ran the Harvard-Yale figures through the parametric model again. "This time," says Moorman, "the results came out looking much the same as ours."

How do the Harvard-Yale professors respond to all this?

Believe it or not, Bennett and Bloom want to collaborate with the Census Bureau on yet *another* marriage study.

"Women who live the longest and report the most peace of mind are unmarried."

Say that, horror of horrors, fewer college-educated women do in fact get married.

Well, first off, it won't be that many fewer women. The study concludes that eight out of 10 women will ultimately wind up married. In earlier generations, it was nine out of 10. Calculate into that the number of women cohabitating—a fourfold increase since 1970—and you are not looking at major demographic shifts.

But let's just take at face value the study's message: college-educated women are less likely to get married than their high school graduate counterparts. That doesn't mean women with less education have more fun. Poorly educated women just have fewer options for financial support outside the framework of marriage. Bennett himself says, "The fact that many women no longer are marrying out of economic necessity is good. A lot of people got in touch with me and said that their loneliest times have been in bad marriages."

There are other reasons besides wealth for remaining in an unwed state. Nearly every sociological study on health and happiness as they relate to marital status reaches the same finding: women who live the longest and report the most peace of mind are unmarried. In a 1975 study of college-educated women, sociologist Judith Birnbaum found that homemakers had the lowest self-esteem, felt the least attractive, reported the most loneliness, and believed themselves to be the most incompetent—even at child care.

What about Men?

"For women," the *Newsweek* story asserted, "marriage seems to be far more central to their basic identities" than it is for men.

Nope.

On national surveys, it is men who say that their families are far more important and provide more satisfaction than their work. Married men live the longest and are the happiest. Single men are more likely to commit suicide. "One of the reasons men do so well in marriage is that women still provide the emotional caretaking," says sociologist Terry Arendell at the University of California at Berkeley.

Men may even be more desperate than women. Look at video dating services. Nationally, many more men than women sign up.

If so much seems wrong with their research, why indeed did Bennett and Bloom conduct That Study at all? They say it was just academic curiosity, and maybe that's all it was. "The bottom line is we really don't know what will happen in the future," admits Bennett—and Moorman at the Census Bureau agrees: "Most likely we're both wrong," she says.

> "Men may even be more desperate [to find a spouse] than women."

But if you still want to believe in studies, here's one more. About the time angst over That Study peaked, ad agency D'Arcy Masius Benton and Bowles released a national survey of 1,550 men and women. The agency asked these people, "Which of the following items gives you a great deal of pleasure and satisfaction?" The list included marriage, religion, friendships, sexual relationships, sports, and so on. Guess what rated tops?

Television.

While 68 percent said TV was a high point of their lives, only 45 percent said marriage actually was a source of pleasure. These men and women chose over marriage, not only the tube but hobbies, vacations, and reading. Reading. This from a society that barely checks a book out from the library anymore.

Now what we really need is another study—one that measures a college-educated woman's chances of owning a wide-screen Zenith.

Good news, ladies. Your ability to purchase large electronics components increases with age.

Susan Faludi is a staff writer for the Sunday magazine section of the San Jose, California, Mercury News.

"Family refers to that social unit constituted of a married father and mother and their children."

viewpoint **24**

The Family Should Be Defined Traditionally

Bryce J. Christensen

In recent decades, the family in America has found itself under unprecedented ideological attack. Feminists like Germaine Greer and Kate Millett rejected the family as "the prison of domesticity" and "patriarchy's chief institution." New Left thinkers like R.D. Laing and Peter Irons denounced the family for its "repressive functions" in enforcing monogamy, sexual restraint, and the capitalist work ethic. Now, however, many leading feminists proclaim themselves "pro-family," while the political heirs of the New Left declaim passionately on the need for a "national family policy."

What's going on here? In a few instances, the feminists and radicals of the 1960's and 1970's have outgrown their former passions and have accepted the traditional responsibilities of marriage and childrearing. However, a careful examination of the new "family policy" forces reveals that most of its leaders still carry deep grudges against the traditional family but find it politically useful to cloak their agenda in pro-family rhetoric. In adopting the "family" label as their own, many feminists and politicians hope to play a semantic shell game with the American people, capturing the widespread popular sentiments that attach to the word *family* while quietly emptying the word of all its historical, moral, and paternal content. In this ideological redefinition of *family*, we are witnessing what C.S. Lewis aptly describes as "verbicide, the murder of a word."

The Definition of "Family"

For most people, *family* refers to that social unit constituted of a married father and mother and their children. In extension, the term is often applied to grandparents, aunts, uncles, cousins, and other relatives. Modern redefiners of *family* propose a

Bryce J. Christensen, "War Over a Word: Redefining 'Family'." Reprinted with permission from *The Family in America*, September 1987, published by The Rockford Institute.

quite different set of meanings. In a typical redefinition of *family*, the American Home Economic Association cheerfully disposes of centuries of semantic and moral tradition:

> AHEA defines the family unit as two or more persons who share resources, share responsibility for decisions, share values and goals, and have commitment to one another over time. The family is that climate that one "comes home to" and it is this network of sharing and commitments that most accurately describes the family unit, regardless of blood, legal ties, adoption, or marriage.

Only slightly less radical than the AHEA redefinition of *family* is the functional definition of the term provided by the leading sociologist Ira L. Reiss. "The family institution," Reiss declares, "is a small kinship-structured group with the key function of nurturant socialization of the newborn." The virtue of this definition, in Reiss's view, is that it can apply to "any type of family structure" that provides care for an infant: "The structure of a kinship group, like the family, can vary tremendously. The biological mother can be alone with her child or she may not be present at all. . . . Whoever performs the major share of the nurturant function for the newborn comprises the heart of the family unit." In Reiss's definition of *family*, references to "father" or "marriage" are about as important as references to "sunroof" or "bucket seats" in definitions of *automobile*.

Some scholars are quite candid about their motives for redefining *family*. In a critique of "the definition of family," David G. Allen, professor of women's studies at the University of Wisconsin, argued that "an overly rigid definition of the family and its responsibilities can contribute to limiting women's participation in the work force, perpetuating constrictive gender identities, and sustaining a sense of entrapment." To advance "emancipatory interests," Allen argues that he and his colleagues must go about "opening up a plurality of definitions" for the term.

Trying to create such semantic plurality, feminist writer Letty Cottin Pogrebin attacks the application of *family* to any "particular living unit" or to any social grouping that is "concrete, secure, and orderly." Pogrebin complains that when *family* is "used prescriptively" the word serves to "coerce people into roles" and "to create a national ethos out of a myth of domestic bliss." Better in her view to acknowledge the confusion in "current varieties of usage" of the word. "*What* is family is a contradictory mess," she declares in a sentence laden with more passion than grace. *Family*, Pogrebin informs her readers, carries "different meanings and produces different results in different contexts." Consequently, Pogrebin argues that it is time to discard terms like "broken family" and "single-parent family." Broadcasting on the same feminist wavelength, Joan Walsh has recently urged feminist leaders to curry political advantage by declaring themselves "pro-family" while they "generously define the family to include women and the people they care for."

"The ambitious redefiners of family *turn the word into a mere echo chamber for amplifying current passions."*

Joining in the ideological redefinition of *family*, Bob Frishman of People for the American Way rejects any attempts to define *family* normatively, maintaining that "the family in America always has had a changing and changeable form." "At any time in our history," Frishman writes, "one could find many kinds of people living in many kinds of households." In defending a pluralistic vision of "families of many types," Frishman takes particular pains to erase the family significance of marriage: "Unmarried and married couples are alike in most respects. There are the same ups and downs, the same strong emotions, and an equal emphasis on monogamy." It is within the context of this radical redefinition of family that Frishman contends that "nobody deserves to be called 'antifamily' for rejecting the simplistic, unrealistic, and incomplete assessments and solutions of the 'pro-family' movement."

Even more daring is Karen Lindsey of Emerson College, who argues that unless it is "recognized that the family, historically, *was* a prison," then "the family becomes . . . a creation of false naming." In challenging "the oppressive definitions of family," Lindsey proposes that "for people who have shared

history, who have loved each other and lived through major parts of each other's lives together, the concept of 'family' should apply." The time has come, she announces, for people to "reclaim for themselves the power of naming" by declaring their circle of friends to be a "consciously chosen family" or an "intentional family." Such intentional "families" may be made up of those who share professional interests, economic needs, political views, or sexual preference. "We can all translate our ideals of deeper, freer family structures into reality. We can name, and we can create."

Family vs. Families

Popular journalists naturally bend to such tides of opinion. *Ladies' Home Journal* suggested that "we are witnessing a renaissance of the family," while informing readers that "the family of the mid-eighties is very different from the one most Americans were reared in. In fact *family* in the singular is somewhat of a misnomer. Better: the plural *families*. . . . The family is flourishing in a multiplicity of forms—single parent family, stepfamily, extended family." "At bottom, the basic American concept of family is being transformed," concluded a trendy article in *Woman's World*. Redefiners of *family* are scoring points in the public schools as well. In a recent survey of the social studies texts most commonly used in grade schools, psychologist Paul Vitz found "no explicit, objective definition of family." Instead, he found such "vague and inaccurate" notions as "a family is a group of people" or "a family is defined as 'the people you live with.'" . . .

While President Reagan has shown himself sympathetic to the traditional family, many prominent congressmen now repudiate any normative definition of *family*, even as they push for a "National Family Policy." In his recent book *Family and Nation* (1986), Senator Moynihan dismisses the very notion of "*the* American family, for there is yet no such thing, but rather [a] great range of American family modes." Representative Pat Schroeder likewise wants federal "family" policies that will acknowledge "the changing reality of parenthood in this country," especially the increasing number of "single-parent households." Representative Don Bonker strikes a harmonious note when he reasons that because "new concepts in living arrangements . . . are gaining acceptance," the federal government "needs to be more creative to support these new arrangements."

Family Rhetoric

But while some are busy blurring over the old definition of *family*, others are reappropriating the word for more sweeping ends. This reappropriation of *family* may perhaps best be seen in the "family" rhetoric used by New York Governor Mario Cuomo in his highly successful speech at the 1984

Democratic National Convention. In that oft-quoted address, Cuomo declared: "We believe in a government strong enough to use the words 'love' and 'compassion.'... We must *be* the family of America, recognizing that at the heart of the matter we are bound to one another." "Those who made our history," Cuomo declaimed, "taught us above all things the idea of family." "No family that favored its strong children—or that, in the name of evenhandedness, failed to help its vulnerable ones—would be worthy of the name."

Cuomo even fused his "family" references with the rhetoric of the American frontier:

> We . . . believe that we can make it all the way, with the whole family intact. . . . Wagon train after wagon train . . . to new frontiers of education, housing, peace, with the whole family aboard. Constantly reaching out to extend and enlarge that family. Lifting them up into the wagon on the way.

Political activist Jesse Jackson has likewise publicly equated the family and the government, insisting that government must be "unusually committed and caring as we seek to expand our family to include new members."

The semantic blurring of the boundary between state and family appears especially dubious at a time when an increasing number of unwed mothers are turning to the state for support. As Professor Randal Day of Washington State University has pointed out, the emergence of the "mother-state-child family" has imposed tremendous financial burdens on traditional families, forcing breadwinning fathers to support their own children directly and to support the chldren of unwed mothers indirectly through taxes. The result, Day believes, is that more and more young men reject the responsibilities of family life altogether.

"Semantic 'cues' that point to marriage, fidelity, and parental responsibility all vanish when family *is redefined to include cohabiting couples, unwed mothers, and every other social grouping."*

But when people start redefining words simply for political advantage, both language and society suffer. As the distinguished scholar of rhetoric Richard Weaver once observed, "One of the most important revelations about a period comes in its theory of language, for that informs us whether language is viewed as a bridge to the noumenal [i.e., the transcendent] or as a body of fictions convenient for grappling with transitory phenomena."

Instead of listening to the voices of our ancestors as they speak to us through our inherited tongue, the ambitious redefiners of *family* turn the word into a mere echo chamber for amplifying current passions. . . .

A Traditional View of Language

In the traditional view, words are representative, that is, words *re*-present patterns, concepts, or truths found in the past, in nature, or even in the Mind of God. In this view, possible meanings of words are fixed, abiding, and shared. The universe of semantic significance is received as a treasured inheritance, not as mere raw material for partisan reinvention. With astonishing insouciance, those now redefining *family* repudiate the traditional view of language. Instead of a representative understanding, an *instrumental* view of language dictates the new definitions of *family*. Recognizing no past or transcendent concept of family as worthy of being re-presented, the redefiners of *family* take up the word as an available and useful tool for shaping an entirely unprecedented social order. It does not disturb most contemporary advocates of a statist "family policy" that they are repudiating a semantic heritage traceable all the way to our Indo-European forebears. For many, any redefinition of *family* that secures political advantage is justified.

In a[n] article in *Commonweal*, historian Laura Gellott lays out the reasons that she liked Mario Cuomo's 1984 "We Are Family" speech. Such familistic rhetoric is necessary, she argues, in order for "liberals to reappropriate 'family' as their issue, wresting it away from . . . groups on the political right." Gellott believes that "liberal politicians and political thinkers" can respond to the "political and social needs of the present generation" if they are successful in "challenging the state and society to envision itself anew as family." Similarly, Robert S. McElvaine, former speech writer for Walter Mondale, praises Cuomo for his shrewd use of "family" rhetoric. "Family is a fitting way to summarize the New Progressive objective. . . . The vision of society as a family also allows Mario Cuomo to present his views in a way that voters find most attractive." This kind of language, McElvaine believes, "will win majority support" while a more straightforward call for expanding the welfare state would not. Those reading this kind of justification for redefining *family* would do well to remember the words of C.S. Lewis: "Men often commit verbicide because they want to snatch a word as a party banner, to appropriate its 'selling quality.'"

Gellott acknowledges but brushes aside the fear that "in defining *family* so broadly, even to the point of using it interchangeably with society itself . . . liberals . . . run the risk of emptying the term of its meaning and evocative power." She believes that "liberals need to appropriate the ideal of family . . . by putting it at the service, not of nostalgia for the past, but anticipation of the future. It is the sense of family as a commitment to the future that is essential." Through "intellectual commitment and financial sacrifice," the redefiners of *family* can give the term new semantic substance. In any case, the semantic intent is not fidelity to any past meaning of *family* but rather political control over future public policy. . . .

Code-Switching

In his *Theory of Semiotics* (1976), the Italian scholar Umberto Eco offers an analysis of "code-switching" that helps to explain the sudden popularity of *family* among people who have never much cared for the word before. As Eco describes it, "code-switching" occurs whenever ad-men, propagandists, politicians, and others engaged in "rhetorical discourse" choose to "switch from one code to another without making the process evident." In this switching, words with a favorable "emotional connotation" are invoked to camouflage denotative "incompatibilities." Eco notes, for example, how advertisers change their catch phrases every time the public mood changes. In the "code-switching" now being performed by many advocates of a "national family policy," the favorable connotations of *family* are being used to dispel concerns about growing government paternalism and to quell fears about declining personal morality. Big Brother knows the value of good slogans. Eco observes, however, that code-switching may fail in the long run because "denotative incompatibilities" eventually poke through, causing the "explosion" of the contrived system of meaning.

"A normative definition of family *must be vigorously affirmed in the nation's courts, legislative chambers, churches, editorial offices, and broadcast studios."*

In the short run, the advocates of a national family policy may succeed in winning political support for their programs. But in the long run, these code-switchers will probably trigger the kind of cultural "explosion" described by Eco. For far from reinforcing the moral, emotional, and spiritual commitments that make family life possible, the political reappropriation of *family* can only weaken those bonds. Legal theorist Christopher Stone notes correctly that "the way we employ morally significant words embeds cues to right conduct." Semantic "cues" that point to marriage, fidelity, and parental responsibility all vanish when *family* is redefined to include cohabiting couples, unwed mothers, and every other social grouping.

Government initiatives—subsidized day care, generous welfare benefits for unwed mothers, guaranteed maternal leave—can make the decline of the family less visible and (temporarily) less painful. But people will eventually notice that nothing government does in the name of *family* aptly compensates for the disappearance of intact marriages and parental care for children. None of the deep and reassuring feelings found in the traditional family will easily transfer to the day-care administrator, the social worker, or the child-support officer. . . .

But for all of the rhetorical dishonesty now swirling about "family" questions, some people do still remember what the word really means, and not all of them are traditionalists. It is almost refreshing that Eleanor Smeal, former president of the National Organization for Women, reaffirmed her dislike for the word *family*: "I happen to think the word *family* is very exclusive, very controlling." Smeal has even denounced the current efforts by some liberals and leftists "to out-family the Right," calling it a form of "hypocrisy." Smeal, in turn, has been criticized by Joan Walsh in *The Progressive* for squandering political advantages for the sake of mere "semantic purity" in her use of the word *family*. Hypocrisy comes from a good, old Greek word referring to "play acting." Even that good, old Greek Socrates would applaud the purity of Smeal's use of it.

"Tongues, like governments, have a natural tendency to degeneration," observed Samuel Johnson, who yet challenged his fellow English-speakers to "make some struggles for our language." The time is now to fight for the word *family*, to prevent it from losing its historical, moral, and descriptive content. The fight for this particular piece of our linguistic heritage will not be without serious cultural and political consequences. Inaccurate words are dangerous, George Orwell warned, because "the slovenliness of our language makes its easier for us to have foolish thoughts." Foolish thoughts quickly translate into ruinous policies. A normative definition of *family* must be vigorously affirmed in the nation's courts, legislative chambers, churches, editorial offices, and broadcast studios. The word *family* can retain the meaning acquired through centuries of moral effort only if those in our cultural centers insist that it not be applied indiscriminately to cohabiting couples, unwed mothers, or the federal government. It would be terrible indeed if the wonderful thing our ancestors called *family* were to become unspeakable.

Bryce J. Christensen is editor of The Family in America, *published by The Rockford Institute Center on* The Family in America, *a conservative research organization on family issues.*

The Traditional Family Is a Myth

Sara B. Taubin and Emily H. Mudd

The terms "traditional marriage" and "traditional family" have no clear, generally accepted meaning and elicit a wide range of emotional reactions. They are sometimes used derogatorily to denote a way of life that is seen as passé, limits human growth and potential, and inhibits individual expression. Using selected census figures to document their case, supporters of this view argue that what was traditional is now vestigial, finished, and representative of only a small percentage of today's households. At the other extreme are those who deplore the changes that have occurred and argue that human survival depends on unquestioning adherence to the established way.

In between these extremes are the great numbers of persons who respect and practice those conventions, customs, and ideals that seem relevant and functional to their present well-being, while adapting those that no longer seem to fit. Politically, economically, and socially they live in the present, while attempting to preserve the accumulated experience and wisdom of the past. "Contemporary traditional" is the term that will be used . . . to describe this group, the clear majority of American adults.

Many of the current family forms in this country fall under the broad category of "contemporary traditional." [D.] Mace and [T.] Mace are talking about "contemporary traditional" when they describe "companionate marriages," where the emphasis is on equality and a sharing of responsibilities and intimacy within a context of commitment and exclusivity. Most modern couples, struggling to make the necessary accommodation to the demands of a changing time, reject a marriage

based on male dominance and female submission, concepts that the Maces relegate to "the ancient world." Those, in their view, were the "old traditional" patterns, no longer functional for most in today's society. "Contemporary traditional" also characterizes the two-paycheck family, in which the wife typically takes time out for child rearing and then reenters the labor market—below where she might have been had she continued without a break, but still making a significant contribution to the family income and to her own sense of self.

[M.J.] Bane documents the existence of contemporary traditional families when she states that census data "provide convincing evidence that family commitments are likely to persist in our society." It seems clear to her that family ties are not "archaic remnants of a disappearing traditionalism," and that human needs for stability, continuity, and unconditional affection remain unchanged. [E.D.] Macklin reiterates the point when, after a review of research on nontraditional family forms, she concludes that the dominant pattern continues to be very traditional. The great majority continue to marry, have children, and desire a permanent, heterosexual, exclusive relationship in a home of their own. Although the divorce rate is increasing, most divorcees remarry, still hoping for a happy, permanent relationship. Although increasing numbers of women are in the labor force, the great majority of households are still organized around traditional family roles. Macklin states:

> The 1970s have brought an increased awareness of the stresses associated with complex relationship systems and a healthy respect for human limits. . . . It is now clear that most, at least at this stage of our societal development, find complex relationship systems, such as multilateral marriage, sexually-open marriage, and communal life, too stressful to allow for long-term participation.

This continuation of themes from the past must be borne in mind as one reads the research on the

Sara B. Taubin and Emily H. Mudd, "Contemporary Traditional Families: The Undefined Majority" in *Contemporary Families and Alternative Lifestyles: Handbook on Research and Theory*, edited by Eleanor Macklin. Copyright © 1983 by Sage Publications. Reprinted by permission of Sage Publications, Inc.

many variants of the common pattern. . . .

Misconceptions about the past, and about transitions from past to present, are prevalent in family study. [J.R.] Gusfield has identified a number of such fallacies that serve to distort our view of societal change:

> Fallacy 1: Traditional culture and society were consistent and homogeneous.
> Fallacy 2: Values and customs are inevitably displaced by social change.
> Fallacy 3: Existing beliefs and behaviors are antagonistic to and in conflict with changing beliefs and practices.
> Fallacy 4: Tradition and change are mutually exclusive.
> Fallacy 5: Contemporary values and behaviors undermine traditions.

Gusfield suggests that viewing past and present as discontinuous entities—setting up polarities of traditional and nontraditional—wastes the accumulated worth of the past, thus undermining the supporting base for current enterprises. The reality is that traditions persist, in varying forms, and permeate and influence the direction of change. Their very strength lies in their pragmatic malleability.

"Americans hold onto a nostalgic ideal of traditional family . . . that is often far from actuality."

Additional confusion arises from the tendency to equate traditional with ideal. [G.] Masnick and Bane note that Americans hold onto a nostalgic ideal of traditional family, of how families were and ought to be, that is often far from actuality, either past or future. Ideal is in fact, by definition, a mirage or fantasy that rarely conforms to past, present, or future reality. Moreover, this rigid conceptualization of the "ideal" family often results in "either/or" labels (good/bad, success/failure, whole/broken) that serve only to distort and alienate.

Yet ideal images do express human striving for perfectability, and an ideal family type does provide a hypothetical model toward which humans can aspire. For example, a bronze sculpture of a family group of heroic proportions was recently placed on a busy business street corner in Philadelphia. A local art critic describes the work by Timothy Duffield as "a rather ecstatic scene of a nude mother and father with a nude son and daughter standing above them on the parents' outstretched arms." He continues, "Because the bronze will endure, the sculpture does stand as a moral statement, a celebration of the family." However, [T.] Hine sees a "disquieting element" in "this conservative message." By celebrating this particular configuration, there may

be an implicit and perhaps unfortunate message that others are less than ideal and, hence, less acceptable. . . .

Today's Average Family

By what criteria should we define traditional? How far back in time should we look for our model? Macklin has suggested that the most recent traditional family pattern in this society is that of "legal, lifelong, sexually exclusive marriage between one man and one woman, with children, where the male is primary provider and ultimate authority." How different is the average family today from this criterion?

Census data document continuing conventional choices and a surprising stability in family patterns. Permanent marriage is still, for most, both the ideal and the reality. Although persons may be marrying somewhat later than in the recent past, over 95 percent of the adult population still marry at some point in their life, and more than 60 percent of all married couples remain married. Although the divorce rate has been steadily rising, the great majority of divorced men and women remarry, with the rate depending somewhat on their age at divorce.

Lifelong mutual sexual fidelity has been and is still preferred, although evidence suggests that clandestine affairs and occasional indulgence in sexual opportunities are common and apparently nondisruptive of many marriages. What is new is that wives are increasingly as likely as husbands to have had such an "outside" relationship. Sexually open marriages designed for personal growth continue to be far more rare and few couples find it a lifestyle that they prefer to continue over time.

Families and Children

Over 90 percent of all married couples have children, although the number of children per couple has declined. Moreover, more than three-quarters of all children under 18 (excluding those who are maintaining their own households) are living at any given time in a household with two parents, at least one of whom is their natural or adoptive parent. Even when children live in a single-parent household, they often have a very significant relationship with the nonresidential parent. The biggest difference for children may be in the number of children living in stepfamilies and the nature of that experience. Unlike earlier years when stepfamilies usually resulted from remarriage after the death of a spouse, most stepfamilies today result from divorce. The result is that the children are often part of two households and have more than one set of functional parents.

An increasing percentage of households consist of a married couple without children present, or a single adult living alone, but it would be misleading to conceive of them all as nontraditional families. Because of increased longevity and smaller families, couples who are in every other way quite traditional are likely to spend more time living together without children. It is true that more persons are living as never-married singles or as unmarried couples, but these numbers still remain a small percentage of the whole, and most of them eventually move into a more traditional family form. Although large numbers of mothers work, many dual-worker families go through an "employed father, mother at home with young children" stage, and at any given time, about one-fifth of all families are in this situation.

Marriage, child rearing, loss of a spouse, remarriage, and finally the death of that spouse—this is the customary sequence of life stages for large numbers of people and it has been for some time, although more of initial loss today is due to divorce than to death. Legal, heterosexual marriage in separate households with children is the way most of us still live, at least at some point in our lives. However, there is no reason to either idealize this form or to label it pejoratively as prototypically traditional. . . .

Healthy Families

An important development in the field of marriage and family studies is the research attention being devoted to identifying those factors associated with successful family functioning.

After a review of the family therapy literature, [L.R.] Barnhill identified eight dimensions of healthy family functioning: individuation versus enmeshment, mutuality versus isolation, flexibility versus rigidity, stability versus disorganization, clear versus unclear or distorted perception, clear versus unclear or distorted communication, role reciprocity versus unclear roles or role conflict, and clear versus diffuse or breached generational boundaries. Concerted efforts must now be made to operationalize and measure these variables if research on well-functioning families is to progress.

"Family histories are marked by pragmatic, flexible adaptation."

In the late 1950s, the Division of Family Studies of the Department of Psychiatry, School of Medicine, University of Pennsylvania, initiated a study of a carefully selected national sample of 100 middle-income families who were perceived to be functioning well. In 1979, 59 of these families completed the latest set of follow-up questionnaires. By then, their average length of marriage was 37 years and the majority of their grown children were married with children of their own. Approximately half of the wives had been gainfully employed outside of the home, in the various patterns characteristic of contemporary women who work. Many of the husbands had had periods of illness and unemployment, gone back to school, and changed careers.

Keys to Success

The responses are exceptionally detailed, candid, and revealing. Consistency over the two decades is a dominant theme of the family profiles. [E.H.] Mudd and [S.B.] Taubin summarized some of the major findings:

> Family histories are marked by pragmatic, flexible adaptation. Family dynamics are equalitarian in the marital dyad, democratic with regard to the sons and daughters. Relations with adult children are frequent, reinforced by a thriving transfer economy. Close friendships and active community involvement are cited as important sources of strength. While severely troubling situational events affecting family members are enumerated, few are defined as problems. Perceived problems are most often resolved within the family or in lesser degree with appropriate professionals. Husbands and wives express continuing satisfaction with marriage and family. They are optimistic about the future and through careful planning anticipate positive later-year development.
>
> The work history of the wives is confused by the interruptions in childbearing and job, and by persistent ambivalence. Some women worked steadily as teachers, in a family business, as self-employed artists or writers. By today's standards, most had jobs not careers. The wives say they worked "most" of their married lives for "personal satisfaction," for "necessities," and to "improve the standard of living." The husbands' responses are fewer in number and less certain why wives work. Yet the voluntary comments of the husbands express pride in accomplished wives and appreciation of the efforts behind the family benefits. More men than women admitted the wife as an equal or major wage earner at times. These families struggled with the issues of the incipient women's movement but were not ideological leaders. They adapted pragmatically to changing individual and family needs, and maintained their marriages. . . .

Findings from the above study suggest that the crucial factors leading to cohesive, durable, high-quality contemporary family life include at least the following: low-keyed adaptation (as opposed to rigid adherence to ideology); cooperation and mutual support (as opposed to competition); belief in marriage and a willingness to work at maintaining the marital relationship; commitment to and pleasure in family and in helping the children to grow as individuals; a democratic approach to family interaction; a lifestyle characterized by planning, work, and education; and a sense of being embedded within the community.

Variations Encouraged

What can be predicted for the decade to come? It is obvious that family units—parents and children—

will continue. They seem to be compatible with ingrained human inclinations and with prevailing social structures. Utilitarian in nature, they are bolstered by millenia of ethical and religious traditions. Variations on this norm—alternative lifestyles and individual experiments—will also continue, are to be expected, even welcomed, and cautiously encouraged. Homoerotic liaisons, polygamy, and communal living have existed in the past as well as in the present, appeal to, and are functional for some. Archaic family structures will also continue to flourish in small ideological enclaves where personal growth is deemed secondary to family and group cohesion.

"Variations on this norm . . . are to be expected, even welcomed, and cautiously encouraged."

What changes are foreseen? Will new demands be placed on marriage and family? Will lifelong sexual satisfaction and unlimited personal gratification be seen as the new entitlements? To a degree, yes. But the major factors determining the direction of change will be the realities of economics and demographics. Masnick and Bane have observed the following trends in family patterns:

(1) Far from being abnormal, the low marriage, high divorce, and low fertility rates of today's generation of young adults are consistent with long-term trends, though inconsistent with the pattern established by their parents' generation.
(2) Between now and 1990, households made up of married couples will increase dramatically.
(3) Fewer and fewer households will have children present.
(4) Although more wives are working, their contribution to family income is small and has not changed.
(5) A revolution in the impact of women's work is on the horizon.

The above trends demonstrate the evolutionary nature of the changing American family and the large role played by economics and demography. Increased longevity and a higher proportion of older adults in the population has already accounted for much of the dramatic increase in single-person and child-free households. The increasing number of women employed outside the home will continue to have an impact on the pattern of child care and care for the elderly, the spousal relationship, and the division of labor within the home. . . .

Pluralism best describes families today in this land of regional, racial, ethnic, and religious diversity. To seek to categorize contemporary families into traditional or nontraditional is far too simplistic and fosters an undesirable and unrealistic polarity. It does an injustice to the enormous complexity of the modern American family.

The human family has been in slow evolution since the beginning of time, changing its structure and norms to fit with the realities of its environment, the basic needs of its members, and its inherited past. So too, today, contemporary families are evolving and adapting old traditions to fit with modern realities and, in the process, creating new traditions. Because other structures are changing more rapidly than has been true in the past, the family, as a subsystem within the larger system, is also changing more rapidly. Hence, the change can appear more dramatic and more alarming than might previously have been the case. But the process is essentially the same as has existed for centuries.

Choices

Individuals and collections of individuals called families, when they can, choose a way of life that best meets their needs. They choose, experience, reconsider, and choose again, as they seek some integration of the learnings from their past, the pragmatics of their present, and their dreams for the future. Contemporary families are no different. They refer to the past but they refuse to be left behind. Their choices are based on a core of common needs that unites all humans and all human families. Their resulting actions are their best response to the present, and the future will build on the lessons learned from their experience. It has ever been thus.

Sara B. Taubin is associate professor in the department of human behavior and development at Drexel University in Philadelphia. Emily H. Mudd is professor emeritus of family study in psychiatry at the University of Pennsylvania.

"Many of the things that have gone wrong with this country stem from the disintegration of the nuclear family."

The Decline of Traditional Nuclear Families Is Harmful

William Tucker

The 1980s are shaping up as the "Decade of the Family." It is finally beginning to dawn on Americans that many of the things that have gone wrong with this country stem from the disintegration of the nuclear family.

The statistics are astounding. "By 1990 half of all American families may be headed by only one adult," announced *Newsweek* in a cover story entitled "The Single Parent." More than 25 percent of all children are now being raised in "single-parent homes"—up from 12.5 percent in 1970. In over 90 percent of all cases, this parent is the mother.

Single-parent homes quickly veer toward poverty. A staggering 54 percent of all single-parent families are below the poverty line, compared to 18 percent of two-parent families. Over 60 percent of black children are now living in single-parent homes, and 70 percent of these are officially classified as "poor."

Faced with this overwhelming evidence that something remarkable is happening, the really important competition has already begun—the race to define the problem.

Defining the Problem

As usual, liberals are first out of the starting gate, riding high on a horse called "The Feminization of Poverty." They have taken their usual early lead.

According to their interpretation, family breakups mainly victimize women. Since women are the victims, then the feminist agenda must be the solution. Raise women's salaries, legislate "comparable worth," eliminate "sex discrimination," and these truncated families of women-and-their-children will be able to take their rightful place in society.

I was up at Harvard when Senator Daniel Patrick Moynihan presented his own somewhat similar

William Tucker, "Why We Have Families," *The American Spectator*, December 1985. Reprinted with permission.

analysis in a widely reported lecture series on the "Crisis in the Family." Senator Moynihan is an odd source for such idea. His classic 1965 report, "The Negro Family: A Cause for National Action," which traced increasing black poverty to female-headed households, is more relevant today than it was twenty years ago. Unfortunately, Moynihan received so much criticism for being a "racist" that he now shies away from the issue.

Senator Moynihan's present interpretation is that *children* are the "new poor." "In the 1930s, everyone feared getting old because it meant falling into poverty," he said. "But government intervention, through social security, solved the problem. Today we face a situation where *children* are becoming an impoverished group," he argued. The solution—unfortunately—is increased welfare payments to female-headed households.

Moynihan casually brushed aside Charles Murray's argument that welfare is actually aggravating black poverty. "He hasn't been able to prove his case to me," Moynihan said grandly. Therefore the perverse incentives in the welfare system can be casually dismissed.

A Human Institution

What was remarkable about Moynihan's performance—and about the entire liberal approach to the problem—is its incredibly shallow perception of the family as a human institution. Through the entire three days at Harvard, Moynihan made only one reference to the origins of the nuclear family. This was a vague suggestion that the nuclear family emerged "somewhere around the seventeenth or eighteenth century in Europe." Although I'm sure Senator Moynihan doesn't realize it, this notion is taken straight out of Friedrich Engels's portrait of the family as an "oppressive institution" invented by capitalism. The implication, of course, is that since we are now headed into a post-industrial welfare state, we can safely lay the nuclear family aside in favor of single-parent homes, "group" families, and whatever other kinds of "alternative" institutions catch people's fancies.

Even more remarkable is that all this ill-formed discussion is taking place at the precise moment when anthropologists have been revising evolutionary theory to put the nuclear family at the center of human culture. Not only is the nuclear family now believed to be as old as mankind itself. It also appears that the family may have been the primary social invention that turned us into human beings in the first place.

Since 1979, the anthropological view of the human family has changed rapidly. In that year, Owen Lovejoy, an associate of Donald Johansen (discoverer of the "Lucy" skeleton), proposed that the nuclear family was the first evolutionary step that lifted us above the apes and put us on the road to becoming human beings. The theory has since been elaborated in many ways, but the major premise still stands and most anthropologists now agree with it.

Prehistoric Family

Thrilling confirmation of Lovejoy's thesis came in 1981 when anthropologist Mary Leakey discovered the "first human footprints" in a fossil lava bed in East Africa. Made more than 3.5 million years ago, they clearly indicate two creatures about four-and-a-half feet tall, walking upright.

What is most astonishing is the "family constellation" that can be inferred from the discovery. The fossil impressions show two different-sized creatures—probably a male and female—walking side by side. Mary Leakey thinks they were holding hands.

But there is also a third set of footprints, made by a smaller creature. They are within the larger footprints. It appears that a young child followed one of the adults across the newly fallen lava ash the same way a boy would follow his father's footsteps across a field of freshly fallen snow.

The nuclear family was not invented in Europe in the eighteenth century nor in Europe of the eighth century, nor even Ancient Egypt of the eighteenth century B.C. When the first diminutive human-like creatures walked on the planet 3.5 million years ago, they had already formed the nuclear family.

The Crisis

"The crisis in the family" is very much an American phenomenon. It is not occurring to the same degree in any other country.

There are really two things going on. First, divorce, for many reasons, has become easier. This has produced single-parent homes across the entire population. But something else is happening as well. Among American blacks in particular, families are no longer *forming*. Women are simply having children without bothering to acquire husbands—a practice that is the rule in nature, but has been almost unknown in human cultures.

How have we entered what can accurately be called "an evolutionary retrogression"? To answer this, we should review what biologists and anthropologists have discovered in the past ten years about why the human family formed in the first place. And we can start by asking a simple question that doesn't seem to require an answer: "Why do we have mothers?"

"The family may have been the primary social invention that turned us into human beings in the first place."

About ten years ago, biologists developed the concept of the "selfish gene." This theory essentially confirms Samuel Butler's aphorism, "A chicken is just the egg's way of making another egg." According to selfish-gene theory, the *gene* is the fundamental unit of evolution, with every living creature operating under an imperative to "spread its genes." One of the most immediate payoffs of selfish-gene theory has been an explanation of "motherhood."

Both male and female reproductive cells—the sperm and egg—carry half an offspring. As carriers of genetic material they are identical. Where they differ is in their *post*-conception reproductive strategy. "Sperm strategy" is built around the tactic of producing many offspring and hoping that a few will survive. "Egg strategy" is built around producing a few offspring and taking good care of them to ensure their survival.

Thus, there is a certain inherent promiscuity built into male reproductive strategy. The male's advantage lies in spreading as many sperm cells as possible as widely as possible. Eggs, on the other hand, are usually fewer and larger. They often come packaged with nurturing material for post-conception survival. Egg strategy is based on using resources wisely.

Choosing the Mother

Once an egg has been fertilized, both male and female have an interest in seeing that it survives. But the job can often be handled tolerably well by only one parent. How is it decided which parent does the "mothering"? Selfish gene theory has provided an answer. It may not be very pretty, but it is a good thing to have in mind while designing social policies.

The answer appears to lie in the "first chance to abandon." After coitus, each parent knows that if he or she abandons the fertilized egg, the other parent will still be there to take care of it. Thus, the abandoning parent will have the opportunity to go out and mate with other partners, and increase his or her chance of "spreading its genes."

The parent who is abandoned, on the other hand, has a more difficult choice. If he or she now abandons the fertilized eggs, no one will be there to protect them. The abandoned parent may be able to go out and find other mating partners, but it will only face the same dilemma as before. Therefore, once the first parent has abandoned, the second parent's best bet is to stay and nurture the fertilized egg to viability.

This is how "motherhood" comes into being. Of course, individual animals don't go through this reasoning process; such behavior has been selected through evolutionary history until it has become "instinctive."

In almost all species, the male deposits its sperm in such a way that the female is left "holding the egg." The female may carry the egg, or lay it, or nurture it within her body. In any case, the female is almost always left with the "last chance to abandon," while the male can be long gone. Thus, in the great majority of species, the female becomes the "mother."

There are a few exceptions, however, and they very nicely prove the rule. With many fish, for example, males care for the young. This is because, when fish mate, the female first releases her eggs into the water. Only then can the male fertilize them. By the time he is finished, the *female* can be long gone. Therefore, the male is left "holding the egg" and must assume the task of nurturing the young.

Motherhood Among Mammals

The pattern of female motherhood has become particularly well established among mammals, where females carry the fertilized eggs within their bodies over a long period of time. Moreover, because this extended period of gestation is more time-consuming, females have an incentive to nurture their young following birth as well. Mammals have extended post-natal "motherhood" far beyond that of most other animals. Chimp mothers, for example, nurture their babies for five years.

Thus, nearly all mammals form "families," but they are very different from the human family. Mammalian families almost always involve only the mother and her children. Males will often collect "harems" or "prides," but only to have a group of fertile females available for reproductivity. In many species, males and females live entirely apart, coming together only briefly during the mating season.

The mammalian family of mother-and-her-children became so common as to be almost a universal "law of nature." Yet once it became firmly established, evolution suddenly took another unexpected turn. It

created the human family—the mother, her children, and that peculiar human invention, the "father.". . .

What was the key behavior mechanism that triggered family formation? Writing from a mildly feminist viewpoint, [Helen] Fisher suggested "the human female's increased capacity for sexual enjoyment." The female orgasm is unknown to other species, she pointed out, and females can theoretically exhaust several males in non-stop sexual encounters. It was this increased sexual capacity, argued Fisher, that tied a single male to his female partner, and bound him to child-rearing.

A Flawed Theory

This is an attractive theory, but it has a serious flaw. Human females do indeed have an increased capacity for sexual activity, but that does not necessarily create a pair-bond. If only one women possessed it, she could use it to attract and hold onto a male of her choice. But once every woman has it, we are back where we started. Males still retain an evolutionary advantage in promiscuity, while females have to worry about getting pregnant. The permanent sexual availability of every female does not automatically create a male-female bond. It only increased the opportunities for male philandering.

"What does a woman want?" was a question that puzzled Freud. The answer turns out to be very complicated. While it is true that human females have evolved into highly sexed creatures, with a capacity for sexual enjoyment greater than that of other mammals, this isn't the end of the story. Their evolution has only left them more vulnerable to the inherently more promiscuous males.

"We have 'liberated' ourselves by shifting the system to work in favor of both individual men and women, but against stable families."

In short, once the human female developed this capacity for year-round sexual enjoyment, she had to turn around and repress it again, in order to attend to the age-old concern of binding the male to the task to raising children.

The evolutionary task assigned to the human female is indeed one of the most complex in nature. Human females obviously have a highly developed sexuality, yet most cultures have been built around courtship, chastity, and the "myth" of the female's lower sexual capacity. In almost every culture, women withhold sex in order to obtain marriage. This pattern predominated in our own culture up until less than twenty-five years ago. (When I was in college in the 1960s, I knew men who would sleep with every girl they met until they ran into one who refused them. Then they would marry that one.)

Yet these patterns have now been changed radically, if not entirely shattered. What has happened to undermine them? And what has it meant for family formation?

Sexual Freedom and the Family

The most obvious new element is the sexual revolution. Birth control and abortion have erased the need for females to act coyly and to refrain from premarital sex in order to avoid getting pregnant.

A recent study among blue-collar families in Chicago, for example, shows that premarital sex is actually quite common. Couples often live together for more than a year without getting married. At some point, however, they "make a mistake" and the woman gets pregnant. At this point, they "have to" get married. To the researchers, it seems obvious that this "mistake" is actually a mutual consent between the couple that they are willing to make a long-term commitment. The possibility of abortion, however, has considerably disrupted this folk custom.

Like it or not, the new sexual freedom is now a technical possibility. Still, the sexual revolution is probably overrated as a cause of family breakups. Whatever havoc it may have caused originally is now largely over. Social custom is adjusting. Of probably much more lasting impact have been long-term changes in the divorce laws.

Traditional divorce laws were built around the principle that the *father* got custody of the children. Our immediate reaction may be to say this was determined by "male chauvinism." In fact the underlying principles were much different.

"The disintegration of the family . . . is bound to create poverty."

Consider again the biological impulses of males and females. The fundamental inclination of male sexuality leads to abandoning children and going on to produce others. The inclination is intensified in human males who can reproduce often well beyond the age of 50. It is always easier for a man to pick up his stakes and start a new family.

Female biology, on the other hand, argues for keeping the children. Women usually feel they have made a larger biological investment in their offspring. There is more physical pain involved, and it is much more difficult for a woman to begin reproducing anew after 40.

Thus, traditional divorce laws—awarding custody of children to the father—worked against the biological interests of both men and women, but in favor of the family and a family-oriented society. If men wanted to divorce, they couldn't just dance off care-free. They had to take the children with them. On the other hand, if women wanted to divorce, they couldn't just "take the children and run." They had to give up their children in the process. By working against the biological impulses of both men and women, paternal custody made divorce much more painful for both parties.

We, of course, have quickly and effortlessly dismantled this convention. Since the 1920s we have "liberated" ourselves by shifting the system to work in favor of both *individual* men and women, but *against* stable families. Women now routinely get custody of the children in most cases.

As a result, it is the easiest thing in the world for men to run off and leave the responsibility of child-rearing to the mother. Alimony payments once restricted this freedom, but lax enforcement and "no-fault" divorce have weakened the deterrent. It is also the easiest thing in the world for a woman to walk out on her husband (or ask him to leave), knowing that the courts will award her custody. As for the long-term social costs, everyone else pays the bill.

The male tendency to wander is well documented in history. What has been less recognized, however, has been the female desire to have children without going through the trouble of securing a husband. Women do not automatically desire to share their children. Jane Goodall noted that chimp mothers are very possessive and usually reluctant to allow their children to play with friendly males, even when the children themselves obviously desire it.

In truth, the family is really a carefully constructed compromise. The female exchanges sexual availability for male companionship. The male is assured of paternity by the promise of female chastity (as the saying goes, only women really know when they are raising their own children). The female gives up her claim to be the sole creator of life in order to secure male cooperation.

Yet this delicately created social institution cannot suffer too much disruption—particularly the kind of social mayhem that we have created over the past twenty-five years. The evidence of this can be seen in what has happened to the American black family.

The Breakup of Black Families

The breakup of the family among blacks is a phenomenon that is almost unique. This is often overlooked in statistics that lump together black and white single-parent homes. Although 25 percent of the nation's families are now headed by single women, fully one-third of these are concentrated in the 12 percent of the population that is black.

Divorce rates among whites have soared in recent years. What is rarely observed, however, is that black divorce rates were always about double the white rate, and have *remained* almost twice as high as white rates have soared. Over half of black marriages now result in divorce—and this doesn't include the shifting common-law marriages that have become characteristic of lower-class black culture.

More important, however, is the rate at which blacks are completely failing to form families. Although 17 percent of white children are in single-parent homes, all but 2 percent of these are the result of divorce or death of a parent. But 28 percent of black single-parent homes are headed by a mother who has *never* married. One-half of all black females now have a baby before they turn 20, and one-quarter have two. A small percentage of these teenage mother are married.

Marvin Harris, perhaps the country's most widely published popular anthropologist, examined the disintegration of the black family in his 1981 book, *America Now.* Not surprisingly, he traced the disintegration of black families to America's ill-conceived "family allowance"—Aid to Families with Dependent Children (AFDC).

The Damage of AFDC

The AFDC grant, Harris pointed out, serves as a kind of dowry—a "nest egg" a woman inherits when she becomes pregnant. "In a world without stability or assets," he wrote, "AFDC [becomes] a vital resource that puts women and motherhood at the center of things. Inner-city men respect women who have this resource; they vie with each other for their favors. And by having children with them the men establish a claim on the shelter which women control."

As Harris pointed out, the welfare matriarchy has not entailed a *complete* disintegration of the black family. Instead, it only shifted its center of gravity to a new female-dominated structure built around a woman who has a string of children with various men. For a woman, this can be a very positive strategy. She no longer has to share all her children with a single father. The family becomes "matrilocal" and "matrilinear." "At sixteen [welfare daughters] can get pregnant and apply for AFDC on their own, adding their own child's stipend to the family's income and perpetuating the female-centered dynasty of their mothers and grandmothers."

In addition, the various paternities give welfare mothers a wide net of potential economic support. "As . . . shown in [one] study of a black Midwestern ghetto neighborhood, AFDC women have a surprisingly large circle of relatives based on ties built up by their sequential liaisons," wrote Harris. "These kinship ties give AFDC women additional security and influence and people to turn to in case of emergencies."

What AFDC has accomplished, then, is to free lower-class women from the age-old female problem of having to find a husband before she can have children. It has also freed black men of the age-old problem of having to take on the responsibility of a family in order to produce offspring.

And so, as Marvin Harris concluded: "Despite all the crafty scheming that has gone into the design of AFDC, the program has succeeded best in achieving exactly what it was designed to prevent: the formation of mother-centered families living on the dole."

"Although the family has been with us since the beginning of human evolution, it remains a relatively fragile biological institution."

The first thing to be recognized about the disintegration of the family, then, is that it is bound to create poverty. The great contribution of the nuclear family has been its efficiency in yoking men and women together to the task of raising children. Family disintegration undoes the original compromise on which the evolution of our species has been built. Thus, to say that people are becoming "impoverished" because they have broken up their families (or are failing to form them) is about as profound as saying that people have trouble picking things up after they have cut off their thumbs.

What can be done to stem the tide of family disintegration? Changing the divorce laws to favor paternal custody is a first priority. As long as both men and women can run off from their responsibilities without sacrificing anything, high divorce rates will continue. As for the failure in family formation—particularly among blacks—the welfare system is the obvious target. It cannot be said often enough that reforming welfare would be the single most positive way to begin lifting black Americans out of poverty.

Although the family has been with us since the beginning of human evolution, it remains a relatively fragile biological institution. The desires of individual men and women do not "naturally" work in its favor. Without cultural reinforcement—or with wrong-headed social intervention—our biological drives can quickly carry us back to the earlier mother-and-her-children mammalian family. The pain we feel in witnessing this retrogression is only a measure of the degree to which we have become human.

William Tucker is The American Spectator's New York *correspondent and author of the book,* Vigilante: The Backlash Against Crime.

"Those who bemoan the decline of 'the family' . . . are wrong . . . to assume that the traditional patriarchal family is essential for a healthy society."

The Decline of Traditional Nuclear Families Is Not Harmful

Jane Flax

Is "the family" declining? Social commentators and political activists from the left and the right seem to agree that it is. On the left, Marxists bemoan transformations in the economy that have made it more difficult for the family to function as a unit of resistance against capitalist exploitation. Social theorists . . . perceive a decline in patriarchal authority within the family that deeply affects children's psychological development. According to their analysis, social authority is replacing paternal power as the primary socializing force in the child's life. Consequently, the child develops a weak ego and for that reason is less able to exercise autonomy and resist social or political control.

On the right, influential writers like [George] Gilder also discuss a loss of paternal power, which they treat as both symptom and cause of the family's decay. The villain for Gilder is the state; he believes the state is displacing the individual father as provider, thereby making it possible for women to achieve a measure of economic and social independence from individual men. Women are no longer compelled by economic or social pressure to perform their traditional civilizing task—to tame men, to persuade them to sublimate their aggressive energy into a competitive struggle for the economic survival of themselves and their families. Lacking such pressure, men become demoralized, engage in antisocial acts, or both. Divorce increases; worker productivity declines; unmarried women have children; women (married or unmarried) receive welfare or jobs secured through affirmative action programs; and men become more discouraged, eventually abandoning their traditional familial responsibilities (and economic risk taking) altogether.

In this essay I treat as problematic what

Jane Flax, "Contemporary American Families: Decline or Transformation?" From FAMILIES, POLITICS AND PUBLIC POLICY by Irene Diamond. Copyright © 1983 by Longman Inc. All rights reserved.

these and similar accounts of the "decline" of the family take for granted: that "the family" as a simple unit exists, that "the family" as such is declining, and that this decline threatens to destroy the very possibility of civilized life. Also implicit in all these accounts is the claim that the family is/was/can be a private realm, a retreat from the power- and interest-motivated activities of the "public" world. Here, it is alleged, the individual can be herself or himself. The individual's moral development and capacity for autonomy is said to be rooted in experiences within this realm. It follows, therefore, that any state or other public interference in the family must be an attack on the individual's freedom and integrity and on the essential civilizing force within society.

Decoding the Family

Contrary to this cluster of ideas, I argue that "the family" does not exist and that although one form of the family *is* declining, this development presents the possibility of an emancipatory transformation in social relations. Those who bemoan the decline of "the family" are not wrong in assuming that the social relations that constitute it are essential to civilization. They are wrong, however, to assume that the traditional patriarchal family is essential for a healthy society. On the contrary, these social relations are destructive to individuals of both genders and to social and political life as a whole. This conclusion is supported by a four-part argument that (1) decodes "the family" to reveal its constituent social relations, (2) analyzes data on the present composition and trends in the organization of households, (3) presents a psychoanalytic account of human development within patriarchal family organization, and (4) discusses some of the social and political consequences of that account.

In order to evaluate the claim that the family is declining, we must first clarify what the family is. In doing so, it soon becomes evident that the family does not exist. Rather, what we call "the family" is a series of social relations that crystallize into apparently concrete social structures. These structures become reified into an abstract entity, which is then called "the family."

Reification arises in part from the intense (and often unconscious) emotional investment in particular notions of the family developed precisely because we all grow up in families. We project wishes on to this abstract entity, and the intensity of those wishes infuses the abstraction with a false concreteness, making distortions difficult to recognize and overcome.

Three kinds of social relations constitute the family: production, reproduction, and psychodynamics. These relations in turn reflect the family's embeddedness in other social structures, which are also constituted by similar social relations. Analysis is further complicated by the fact that the family is internally constituted by very different sorts of persons and their interrelationships. There are adults and children (but the adults are also partly children since their childhood lives on in the unconscious). There are males and females, both children and adult. There may be a variety of relations governed by kinship and gender rules, and each of these persons engages in a variety of social relations with persons "external" to the family. . . .

The Changing Family

Families are the intersection of the three primary forms of social relations. Given its social location, it is clearly impossible for the family or familial experience to assume one unchanging form. The social location of the family makes possible *both* a moment of autonomy ("privacy") from other institutions and renders it particularly sensitive to them. Whether its resistance or its vulnerability is more evident depends upon the particular character of each form of social relation at the moment of their conjunction.

In any case it is unlikely that change, even in only one form of social relation, will have strictly localized effects. In a period of major change in productive relations, for example, it is likely that a family may be forced to alter its internal relations. A wife may take a paying job to counter inflation, and this in turn may bring unexpected tensions within the psychodynamic balance of the family as a whole. Fewer women available for volunteer work and who require instead more social services for themselves and their families (e.g., day care) puts increased demands on the state and other institutions within the relations of reproduction. These demands then arouse both psychodynamic and political resistance to changes in women's "traditional" role. Counter pressure is put on the state, and cuts in social services result in additional work for families,

especially women. New tensions are created within the family, and the process of adjustment and resistance continues.

Currently, or so many social commentators and politicians claim, the family's vulnerability is most evident. Leaving aside the already discussed problems of identifying "the family," what is meant by its decline? This is not always clear. Phenomena as diverse as the availability of abortion, teenage pregnancy, drug abuse, sex education, violence in the schools, the juvenile crime rate, the inability of high school graduates to read, the divorce rate, the entrance of women into the labor market, and especially the demands of the feminist movement are offered as evidence for and examples of causes of this decline.

Celebrating the Decline

Demographic information on family structure necessitates a more complex diagnosis. There *are* important changes occuring in the behavior of family members, especially women. Whether these changes constitute or will cause a decline of the family depends, in part, on a *political* judgment as to the desirability of one traditional family form, the patriarchal nuclear family. The traditional form is both remarkably stable and experiencing stress. . . .

"It is clearly impossible for the family or familial experience to assume one unchanging form."

Do[es] . . . the increase in the divorce rate, in female-headed households, in female labor market participation, and in the number of unmarried people living together mean that the family is declining? One definite consequence is that the family of four, with two children cared for by the mother at home while the father is working for a wage is no longer the norm. However, it is certainly an error to equate this particular family structure with "the family" and then to assume that therefore "the family" is declining. As research in anthropology and history has shown, family and kinship systems have varied widely over time; there has never been a single entity called "the family," even within one culture or at one time. Furthermore, rather than bemoan the decline of the patriarchal form of the family, perhaps celebration is a more appropriate response. Although its current stress and potential disappearance is threatening to every aspect of our existence (psychodynamic, economic, and reproductive), the patriarchal nuclear family is itself the source of, or a contributor to, many of our most fundamental social and psychological difficulties. . . .

Writers on both the left and the right are not wrong to blame some of our social and individual unhappiness on the social relations of the family. They are wrong to look to the past for a model of the healthy family or to assume that it can exist in isolation from other forms of social relations. . . . The only adequate ground for human emancipation is a radical transformation in all forms of social relations (productive, reproductive, and psychodynamic). This emancipation can only occur through a long struggle with our own demons as well as externalized forms of power. New forms of political activity for which both consciousness raising and "speaking bitterness" can serve as partial models must be developed.

> "Rather than bemoan the decline of the patriarchal form of the family, perhaps celebration is a more appropriate response."

The task of political transformation is thus infinitely more complex than conservatism, liberalism, or orthodox Marxism generally comprehend. What is at stake, as Aristotle understood so long ago, is the very possibility of genuine, full human development for both the individual and the social whole. For, as Hanna Pitkin states:

> Accurate self-knowledge and responsible self-government, autonomy rightly understood, have been the dual aspects of human maturity, at least since the Greeks. To be grown up means to understand who you are and what you are doing, and to take competent responsibility for it. Since we are all in fact members of one another, connected to others through the conditions and consequences of our actions in countless ways, being grown up means knowing those connections and taking responsibility for the consequences. Only in interaction with many and diverse other[s], only in relation to the "we," can we gain that knowledge in a determinate way or make that assumption of responsibility effective. I cannot fully discover who I am, learn public judgment, in exclusively private relationships. And I am not yet fully taking charge of my life and of what I do until I join with my fellow citizens in political action.

It is time to grow up, to discard our fantasies of the all-powerful mother. As long as we unconsciously believe that we can go home to her (or to nature) and she will make everything all right (or that it is all her fault when things go wrong), we can never reach maturity either as individuals or as a (potential) polity. We'll be paralyzed in the state of unhappy consciousness in which "actions and its (the self, the species) *own* concrete action remain something miserable and insignificant, its enjoyment pain and the sublation of these positively considered, remains a mere 'beyond.'"

These fantasies grow out of and are nourished by a particular form of the family, which is in turn reinforced by and reinforces other forms of social relations. To transform a set of social relations so deeply rooted within us is a dangerous enterprise that is certain to arouse deep resentment in men and women. Yet an examination of some of the psychological, political, and economic consequences of the patriarchal family provides compelling reasons for celebrating, even working to hasten, its decline.

Transforming the Past

As women leave home, it is important that they learn to take responsibility for public acts, to confront and transform power relationships. Men need to take responsibility for knowing their own feelings and being responsive to the feelings of others. Domination and submission can be replaced by reciprocity as the governing principle of all social relations. Can two genders—bent and distorted, weighted with conscious and unconscious history—transform and redeem the past, in the name of a future nobody can clearly see? On this question rests not only the future of feminism and the family but perhaps human life itself.

Jane Flax is an associate professor of political science at Howard University and a practicing therapist in Washington, DC.

"Members of traditional families, dual-career families, and single-parent families were found to be strikingly similar."

viewpoint 28

Nontraditional Families Are Healthy

Research & Forecasts, Inc.

No one doubts that family structure today is changing. A rising divorce rate and the increasing number of working mothers are just two of the most notable sociological changes affecting the family today. In 1950, for example, less than one in five marriages ended in divorce. By 1980 there was one divorce for every two marriages.

Statistics show that the decade of the 1970s was a crucial time. According to the Bureau of the Census, only 2.1% of the total population in 1950 was divorced. By 1965, the number had risen only slightly, to 2.9%, but in 1982, 7% of the population was divorced.

One result has been the increase in female-headed families. During the last decade alone the number of children living in one-parent families increased by 60%. In 1970, 10.2% of all families with children were female-headed households. By 1982, that number had nearly doubled to 18.9%.

The number of women in the work force also shows a marked increase over the last decade. In 1970, 42.7% of all married women between the ages of 25 and 44 were working. In 1982, 62.6% of married women in this age group were working. Another indication of changing households is the rise in the number of Americans living with people outside of their family. The number of nonfamily households has markedly increased from roughly 5 million in 1950 to over 22 million today.

The Impact of Change

Reports on these radical shifts have long since ceased to be the exclusive concern of demographers and urban planners and have become matters of interest and concern to the general reading public, and new statistics are often featured as front-page news. The impact of these changes on parental roles,

Research & Forecasts, Inc., *The Ethan Allen Report: The Status and Future of the American Family.* Danbury, CT: Ethan Allen, Inc., 1986.

eating and shopping patterns, and even corporate culture, among many other things, has also been studied and widely discussed, while the public policy implications have entered a new era of public debate.

Less clear, however, is the impact of these structural changes on the actual *fabric* of the family itself. Despite many claims to the contrary, there has not been proof that the family as a living institution is in decline, or is any weaker today than a generation ago. Nor is there any substantive indication that people place less value on their own family relationships, or on the role of the family within society at large, than they once did.

Much of the public outcry on the perceived crisis in the American family is based on two unproven suppositions:

1) That change in family structure, especially the rise in households other than those consisting of two parents with children and the increased flexibility of male and female roles, is a definite indication of a decline in the family;

2) That this change is responsible for many of the problems experienced within the contemporary family and even within society itself.

Buried within the first supposition is also an assumption that the two-parent nuclear family is somehow the only well-established "traditional" norm, from which recent departures constitute an aberration. Historically, however, this is inaccurate. In fact, there has *always* been considerable variation in family structure. Single-parent families, three-generational families, the commune, and the "nuclear family" have long existed side by side.

Myth of the Ideal Family

In their book *Family in Transition*, Arlene and Jerome Skolnick argue that family conditions have been evolving for centuries in response to changing sociological and economic circumstances. Today, in

America, there are fewer three-generation families and more single-parent families than perhaps at any time in the past. And the ideal of the American "traditional" family consisting of a working father, housewife mother, and one or more children, was only really enshrined in the first half of the twentieth century. Today, that is also disappearing. Only 45% of all American families now correspond to the nuclear family model of a father, mother, and their own children, and out of the 83.5 million U.S. households, only 5.7% consist of a working father, a homemaker mother, and two or more children. Yet the myth persists that this is the dominant household type.

"There has always been considerable variation in family structure. Single-parent families, three-generational families, the commune, and the 'nuclear family' have long existed side by side."

Clearly, the structure of the American family is not what it was 30 years ago, and granted, there are far more single-parent and dual-career families today than ever before, but how do these families really differ from the two-parent model? Do the differences merely apply to superficial patterns of daily routines, or do they extend to more fundamental aspects such as basic commitment to and involvement in family life? This is one of the key questions explored in this report.

In order to determine the impact of family structure (e.g., membership and roles) members of families including children at home were divided into three categories, depending on the type and number of parents and wage earners:
• *Traditional*—Consisting of a working father, homemaker (or part-time employed) mother, and children at home: (19% of our sample)
• *Dual-career families*—Both parents work full-time, with children at home: (14%)
• *Single-parent households*—One parent with children at home: (7%)
When the responses of these three groups to each of the questions asked in the questionnaire were compared, however, surprisingly *few* truly significant differences emerged. Members of traditional families, dual-career families, and single-parent families were found to be strikingly similar in terms of their basic attitudes toward family life and family values. For example, members of all three types appeared equally confident about the way they are raising their children, and equally likely to believe in the importance of fathers spending as much time with their children as mothers do.

Where differences did emerge, they generally deal with practical matters, such as lack of sufficient time to spend together. And in most cases other factors play a far greater role.

In other words, family structure was proven *not* to be the key determinant in most of the fundamental aspects of family life and family values.

What Makes a Family Close?

What, then, *does* determine the level of family involvement, internal conflict, and the basic attitudes toward family matters which different people hold? If they are not a result of structure, are they simply a function of age, gender, education, economic position, or some other *demographic* factors? Or are they the result of deeper, more complex factors that have yet to be identified?

Intensive analysis of the results of the survey reveal that *Household Family Orientation* and *Family Satisfaction* are the two most powerful forces shaping an individual's day-to-day involvement in family activities and the likelihood of his family suffering from a wide range of problems and conflicts. *Family Satisfaction* is also a key determinant for many basic attitudes toward family-related issues.

How important is family in the lives of Americans today, and where does it stand in the hierarchy of personal loyalties? Half of (52%) the respondents surveyed consider their family *the most important* aspect of their lives, and an additional 37% describe it as *one of the most important aspects.* Only 11% assign it a lesser role. (See Table)

From one perspective, this would appear to reflect an overwhelming endorsement of the central importance of the family in contemporary life. On the other hand, it also indicates that nearly half the population (48%) does *not* assign the family unquestioned primacy over all other aspects of their lives.

Nontraditional Families Are Close

Age, marital status, education, and gender all affect the importance of family in one's life. The importance of family increases as people grow older, with people over 50 being significantly more inclined than others to feel that family is the most important element in their life.

Married people are also significantly more inclined than separated or single people to assign family a role of supreme importance. Women and people with little formal education are similarly inclined to rate the value of family higher than men or those with more education. But family structure accounts for only a slight difference. Traditional families are only marginally more inclined than dual-career or single-parent families to feel their family is the most important element in their life.

A large majority of Americans also claim their household family is very close. Eight out of ten

52%

37%

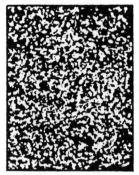

9%

2%

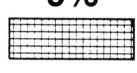

| The most important element | One of the most important elements | A fairly important element | A fairly/very unimportant element |

Number of respondents: 1881

(79%) Americans living with other family members perceive their family unit to be very close, and one in five (20%) perceive it to be moderately close.

Interestingly, the sense of family closeness is *not* affected by most demographic factors. Men and women, rich and poor, blacks and whites, liberals and conservatives, and the better and less educated show few differences when it comes to the degree of closeness they experience at home. The only distinctions worth noting are those relating to marital status, family structure and age.

A Surprising Result

As might be expected, single and widowed respondents are the least likely to report a very close household. But separated and divorced respondents are even slightly *more* likely than those who are currently married to say their household family is very close. This startling result indicates that divorce in and of itself does not necessarily destroy the strength of the family bond connecting those remaining in the household.

Another somewhat unexpected finding is that members of traditional families are only slightly more likely than single parents or dual-career parents to consider their families very close. This, too, argues against the notion that the traditional family is the only true repository of a close family environment.

Finally, age appears to raise the perception of family closeness at two distinct times of life—among those 25 to 34 (those most likely to have young

children) and 65 and over.

Not only is the family perceived as important, and family life as close by a large majority of people, but *spending time* with household family members is also perceived as critical. Four out of five (84%) people who live with family say that spending time together is very important, and 14% say it is moderately important.

Not unexpectedly, people under 25 years old are somewhat less inclined than others to feel it is very important to spend time with their household family. This may be due to the fact that fewer of these people are married or have children. They are also the most likely to still be living with a parent, and so spending time with household family takes on a different perspective. But after this age there is practically no change in attitude toward the importance of spending time together.

People who describe themselves as religious or spiritual are also more inclined than those who do not do so to feel that spending time with the family is very important.

Family structure, on the other hand, has *no* bearing on this issue. Dual-career parents, single parents, and traditional family parents agree equally on the importance of spending time together as a family.

Research & Forecasts, Inc., a public opinion and marketing research organization, was commissioned by Ethan Allen, Inc., to conduct a study on the status and future of the American family.

"If you are a single parent . . . then that is the reality of your life. But . . . yours is not the best of all possible worlds."

Nontraditional Families Are Not Healthy

Paul Kroll

In the United States—the divorce center of the world—6,500 other Americans join . . . each day in the ranks of the divorced.

Nearly six out of every ten married women now in their 30s in the United States will probably experience a divorce at some time. (Nearly one third of all women aged 35 to 39 have already been divorced.) Not a very encouraging statistic. But it gets worse.

About *half* of all marriages in America end in divorce. The peak year for divorces was 1981.

Since then the divorce rate has slightly declined and has leveled out. But this really means the nation is adding *well over one million* couples each year to the divorce statistics.

A mere leveling off in the divorce rate is not particularly encouraging. We're still piling up divorces at an astonishing rate. In fact, in 1985, the divorce rate in the United States temporarily headed up again after a brief decline.

Of course, these are only numbers. We are dealing with human lives here—men, women, children, grandparents.

Divorce is only part of the tragic story. We have the problem of illegitimate children, the burden of the single-parent home, poverty, hurt and traumatized children and adults.

The Single-Parent Family

Consider, for a moment, the epidemic number of families headed by divorced or single females. Approximately one quarter of all families with children under 18 have only one parent in the home.

The U.S. Census Bureau, which reported this latest data for 1984, found that 59 percent of all black families with children were one-parent homes. One study shows that 28 percent of all black females in the United States who have at least one child and head one-parent households have never been married.

Some estimates tell us that by 1990 *half* of U.S. families could be headed by only a single parent or adult. Those aren't very good odds if you're planning to start a family.

But there is further bad news. More than half of the nation's mothers work outside the home. Neither father nor mother is at home during the day—even in a large percentage of *unbroken* families.

The single-parent family and one in which both parents work have created a new social category. It is called the "latchkey kid." He or she is the young child (or teenager) who is alone and unsupervised during the day—with a personal key to the house or apartment.

While a latchkey child is only one problem that both the single-parent and two-parent family must face, a single-parent family also is likely to face a relentless march toward a state of nagging poverty.

The Poverty Cycle

Ideally, the home should be the center of increasing economic productivity and well-being. But in modern society the home has too often become a maelstrom of poverty and want. In part, this is due to having children out of wedlock.

The link between economic difficulties in later years and a pregnancy before or apart from marriage should be obvious. A study of *couples* in which the woman was pregnant before marriage showed they suffered across the board economic problems throughout life.

Meanwhile, the single-family home headed by a female has become a metaphor for want and deprivation. This is especially so among lower income families and those where the former husband does not contribute to the child or the children's upkeep.

One congressional report in 1983 claimed that 79 percent of divorced fathers in the United States did not support their children.

There is more. *Half* of the men in a nationwide study in the United States admitted cheating on their wives. In response to the study, one psychologist pointed out the painfully obvious: "Cheating is a symptom of a relationship in need of improvement."

But the womenfolk are not that faithful either. Recent surveys show that between 21 and 43 percent of married women in America have had an extramarital affair.

Can the Family Survive?

Can the family survive these and other assaults? Some claim the family is doing quite well. They point to a stabilizing of the divorce rate. But can anyone seriously accept well over one million divorces annually—even if the rate never rises by a single divorce—as evidence of improvement in the state of the family?

Can we casually dismiss the plight of the single-parent family—with thousands of new households being added to this group daily? Can we simply paper over these obvious cracks in the social structure?

Most people, of course, are still pro-family. They recognize that the family should be the provider of those things that we humans count dear. It would include economic stability, love, proper instruction, a sense of security, of belonging—and even pure, unadulterated joy.

That any given family (whether intact or not) fails to provide for all the above does not mean the institution is at fault. The fault is in ourselves.

But the ideal is not the reality! Millions of people are not truly family oriented—they have been traumatized off that natural course.

The divorce numbers continue to be chalked up. We abandon the home for careers, for other sexual partners.

We continue to produce illegitimate children in prodigious proportions. We continue to have wife beating, runaway children, parent beating, child molestation, unhappy marriages.

Yearning for the Ideal Family

Why is it that so often the real-life family is painfully different from the ideal family we yearn for?

If there is any one ailment that constantly hammers at civilized Western man it is plain social *confusion*. We are not even sure what the family should be like. We question whether marriage can ever be happy under any circumstances.

It is one of the paradoxes of our time. We want the family to remain strong but we unravel it. We want the family to remain a part of society, but we aren't even sure what society should look like.

It might come as a surprise to most people that very little remains of the ideal or typical family today, particularly in America. As *Ladies' Home Journal* magazine put it: "The 1950s dream of breadwinner father, stay-at-home mom and two kids accounts for only 6.1 percent of all American families today" ("The American Family Today," December 1985, page 64).

Bring Back Which Family?

A tremendous amount of material is available that explains *how* to have a happy marriage and keep the family together. And, yet, in spite of all this helpful information, we see the continual erosion of family life.

Why?

We want to "bring back the family" but seemingly, have no power to do so. We may go into a relationship hoping for the best but end up a victim of the worst.

Part of the problem is we can't even define the word *family* to everyone's satisfaction.

"The single-family home headed by a female has become a metaphor for want and deprivation."

When former U.S. President Jimmy Carter wanted to have a "White House Conference on the Family" it ended up becoming the "Conference on Famil*ies*."

It seems the delegates could not agree on what was meant by a "family." Was it just the traditional nuclear family? What about single-parent families? The homosexual family? The unmarried mother? Was that unit a family?

If we cannot agree on what a family is, how can we know what to "save" and whether we should even want to rescue it?

What the Ideal Family Is Not

What would be the ideal family? First, let's see what common sense would say it's *not*.

We certainly would not consider that a young unmarried or divorced woman struggling to raise a family *alone* to be the ideal. Nor could we consider a divorced father, with custody, struggling to work and care for his children a viable alternative.

Now, of course, it is possible for either of them to muddle through the job. But it is not the ideal. Just ask those who have tried it.

How, then, shall we go about defining the word *family*?

Must we define a family by any form of human cohabitation, to put it bluntly, that any two individuals may desire to engage in? Is an unmarried couple living together sexually a "family"? Or is a homosexual "family," really a family, for example? Do we have the right to have a divorce and still call the separated parts a family?

Suppose we want a child out of wedlock? Does that entitle us to call ourselves a family?

It seems that society no longer allows us to define a true family as a husband and wife—in a permanent relationship—*together* sharing responsibility for the care and upbringing of children.

Causes of the Broken Family

Let's honestly take a look at the two major *causes* of the broken family. And by causes, we do not mean effects. Divorce, for example, is an effect of a more deep cause. The reality of the "working mother" is also an effect.

One of the two major causes for the breakup of the family in the Western world is something you or I have little control over. It is simply the way in which our advanced industrial society has developed.

It used to be that the home was the center of all important economic and social activity. Women, of course, have always worked. They simply worked at home *with* their husbands. This is not well understood.

But wives worked in a cooperative venture with their husbands on the farm or in the local cottage industry or business. As well, children took on an increasingly greater economic role and responsibility in the common household.

Economically, all the members of the household were turned *inward* to the family unit. This is no longer true. What can a young child, for example, contribute when he lives in a tiny apartment in the big city?

In the past, family members depended on each other economically. At the same time they all derived a sense of worth in that husband, wife and children all realized they were *vital* to the well-being of the family unit.

The Hub of Activity

The family unit was the center of all social activities. It took care of the aged, provided much of the entertainment as well as a measure of education. The family at home rather than the child's peers at the school had the opportunity—and duty—to instill values and goals.

The nuclear family reached out first to the rest of the members of the clan, usually living in close proximity. The network then embraced the people in the village or town.

Today, we often deal with complete or partial strangers in our work. Our entertainment comes from individuals we have not met, for the most part.

In past ages, there was no talk of "career." The very idea would have been meaningless to most

people. The *home* was the career.

The home was also the center of life. Mom and Dad were generally present as well as several brothers and sisters. Grandparents and other relatives were close by. There was even animal and plant life (crops) on the homestead or certainly in the immediate area of shop or store.

Home was a living, thriving, pulsating core of human existence. "Home," indeed, was not the house structure—it was the *people*—the family members. We often confuse the two. For example, when we think of a church, we visualize the building. In reality, the church is the *congregation*—the people.

This is not to say that all homes were happy. It does not say children were necessarily happy—nor unhappy. It does not say that life was easy or idyllic. Wars and diseases brought great misery. (Alas, they do so today!) Those are, in part, separate issues altogether.

Society Against the Family

The point is that the *very fabric of society* provided the direction for the family. And the direction was toward a living, cohesive and thriving unit.

That all began to drastically change with the Industrial Revolution. Western civilization itself became hazardous to the health of the family.

The United States has been particularly hard hit. However, this same principle applies to every other nation that is undergoing or has undergone its own technological revolution.

Family problems cannot be legislated out of existence while society goes on its merry way. Moralizing, by itself, will do little good either.

Today, the very structure of our society militates against the ideal home. In fact, from the vantage point of what our society *is*, the very idea of an "ideal home" often seems absurd.

"We certainly would not consider that a young unmarried or divorced woman struggling to raise a family alone to be the ideal. Nor could we consider a divorced father, with custody . . . a viable alternative."

Today, we all too often have houses and not homes. Even within the intact home, there is something vital missing. It is, simply, *life*.

Usually, the husband and father is gone from home much of the time. The wife and mother may have her own job or even career in a nearby city.

Little or nothing of economic importance happens at home. The home is not as it used to be—an earning center; it is only a spending hub. During the day, the home is an empty, lifeless, hollow shell. The only sound is the hum of the refrigerator or hiss of the hot water heater. Socially speaking, it is dead.

What Can Be Done?

All the forces of society are pulling the individual members *away* from the unity of the home, not toward it. So, what can be done?

Even in the home, the basic entertainment medium—the television—arrests the minds of the family members by way of the strangers who perform for them in some distant place.

Who are these intruders? What are their values? Why are they taking up the family's time? Do we let our children and their friends sit there watching in silence? Do we discuss the programming?

Instead of uniting the family, too often the television set hacks the household into discrete little viewing packages sitting in darkened rooms. They become so much fodder for the ratings chart.

"Society no longer allows us to define a true family as a husband and wife—in a permanent relationship—together sharing responsibility for the care and upbringing of children."

As an individual, you cannot change the direction of society. It marches relentlessly on. But if you seek to change your life and that of your family, you will have to recognize what is happening to you and take whatever steps you can to go in the other direction.

It will not be easy. Society has made us like so many drug addicts. Even after we realize what the drug is doing to us, our minds and bodies crave more—in this case, of what society has to offer.

Rejecting Personal Rights

We are sold on the merits of *personal rights* above all else. Indeed, we are made—by society—to feel inadequate if we do not relentlessly pursue our personal interests above those of concern for others.

The mother at home who might not *want* an independent career flailing away in a boardroom or over a typewriter, is subtly informed that she is failing to develop her full potential. After all, doesn't anyone who is anyone strive to make her mark?

The man may actually come to believe he is missing out on all the wonderful thrills that his single and unmarried friends are having. After all, there it is in the magazine, or at the movies, or on the television set.

A major obstacle to strong families then becomes society itself, but it is only one of two faces of our modern Janus.

There is also Public Enemy Number Two. What is it? In the words of a cartoon character: We have met the enemy and he is *us*.

Today, it is fashionable to blame our parents for our sins. Or society. If only things were different in our lives.

Claiming Responsibility

But are parents and society solely responsible for wife beating? For the actions of those who cheat on husbands or wives? For all the other human problems that seem to drive apart and destroy families?

We might like to think so. But the only real authority on morals—the Bible—says we cannot escape the responsibility for our own actions. It is we—*people*—who do all these things. Whatever we do, we have had our part in it.

We cannot excuse ourselves by saying, "The devil made me do it." He and society do have an influence over us. But you and I make the final decision to act or refrain from acting.

What it the point? First of all, we cannot clean up the whole of society. We cannot change the world, nor even another single person, necessarily.

But with the right help we each can change ourselves. If we are not spending enough time with our family, only we can decide to change. If someone is a wife beater or if a woman doesn't respect her husband, only that person can change. If someone is cheating on a spouse, only that person can quit.

If you are a single parent, a divorced person, then that is the reality of your life. But it must at least carry with it the admission that yours is not the best of all possible worlds.

The Final Authority

Yet, without a basis for one's belief, how *are* we to decide what is a family? How are we to decide what social actions are appropriate for us? Perhaps it is quite all right to have "something going on the side," as they say. After all, who is the authority to say no?

It is ultimately, then, a question of authority. Who has the right and the wisdom to make judgments in such matters?

There is only one bona fide authority. Quite simply, he is the messenger of the true marriage covenant: He is the Creator of the human family—the one we call Jesus Christ. Almost 2,000 years ago, he spelled out God's *original intent*: that humans should form unbreakable families.

Paul Kroll is a senior writer for The Plain Truth, *a conservative magazine published monthly by the Worldwide Church of God.*

"The central position of the woman in the home parallels her central position in all civilized society."

Traditional Sex Roles in Marriage Are Best

George Gilder

Nearly a century ago, Karl Marx and Frederick Engels first anticipated and revealed to the world the secret dream of the sexual liberal. "In communist society," they wrote, "where nobody has one exclusive sphere of activity but each can become accomplished in any branch he wishes, *society* regulates the general production and thus makes it possible for me to do one thing today and another tomorrow, to hunt in the morning, fish in the afternoon, rear cattle in the evening, criticise after dinner, just as I have a mind, without ever becoming hunter, fisherman, shepherd or critic."

The contemporary liberal would wish to banish male bias from the dream. Assigning to "society" the duties not only of "general production" but also of reproduction, the new dreamers would extend to women as well as men the life of a British country squire. Liberating both sexes from restrictive roles and moral codes, the dream would bring a new spirit of sharing—of jobs, bodies, vocations, and pleasures. People would be full "human beings" rather than oppressed men and women.

There are two serious problems with this arrangement, and unfortunately both are fatal. The first problem is that except in an abstract sense there is no such thing as "society." Both production and reproduction, therefore, will be left to particular human beings. The second problem is that there are no "human beings," just men and women. Since the nature of things assures that men will do most of the production and women most of the reproduction, we are back where we started before Marx and his modern followers began their reveries.

The communal dream always fed on the vast ignorance of intellectuals like Marx about the production of wealth, and their aristocratic disdain

for the lives of ordinary men and women. To Marx and Engels, the role of men seemed so simple that it could in due course be passed on to a few bureaucrats managing the machines of mass production. To the average sexual liberal, the role of women seems so routine that it can be assumed by a few bureaucrats managing child-development centers. To the current advocates of shared sex roles, both the work of the world and the duties of the home are so undemanding that they can be accomplished with part-time effort.

Importance of Mothers

The truth is, however, that even beyond full-time duties nurturing infants, the mother's role imposes continual challenges. Raising several children is a project that exacts a constant alertness and attention that none of the sexual liberals remotely understand when they urge that "society" do it. With fewer children, kept longer within the household, the focus on each child is even more intense than it was in the past. The near-demise of extended families, though it was crucial to the industrial revolution, also increased the burdens of the mother alone.

As Midge Decter has observed, previously motherhood was regarded as inevitable: one didn't choose it; one accepted it. Without any sense of other options, the responsibility for numerous children may even have seemed less onerous than the responsibility for a few today. In the past, sickness, mortality, slow-learning, and other childhood afflictions were taken for granted as a part of life. Today the mother is expected to control them. To the difficult tasks of caring are now added burdens of medical attention, psychological analysis, and early education. It is not a role that, in its continual and varied demands, men show any serious inclination to perform. Indeed most of the divorced men who gain custody of their children immediately surrender it again to new wives, girlfriends, day-care centers, or female servants.

The dimensions of the new mother's role are evident in the activities that go on in that center of American child care, the single-family dwelling in the suburbs. Ever since Betty Friedan's *cri de coeur* [cry of the heart] from Westchester County—then perhaps the richest spot on the face of the earth—feminists have shed public tears for the women doing this crucial labor in the American suburbs. Isolated, unstimulated, sexually deprived, trapped by babies, frittering away their talents in boredom and drudgery, these women were seen as victims of male oppression in an exploitative capitalist culture. This description caught on widely, particularly among intellectuals in American universities.

"The role of the housewife provides her a base for building a many-faceted life, an opportunity few other vocational roles allow, because they are tied down to single organizational structures and goals."

Two sociologists, however, have actually taken the trouble to investigate in great detail the condition of these housewives. Herbert J. Gans examined Levittown, which was widely regarded as the most alienating of all suburban environments, and Helen Znaniecki Lopata conducted 573 close and specific personal interviews around Chicago. They concluded, like many subsequent observers, that people, particularly women, deeply enjoy suburban living, and that suburbanites tend to be among the happiest and least isolated Americans.

Quality of the Home

In general, Lopata and Gans both depict a panorama of social engagement, community concern, cooperative activity, and even, in many cases, cultural and intellectual animation: a realm of options that substantially exceeds those of either men or working women. Mrs. Lopata, for instance, found that suburban housewives, by a significant margin, were more likely than working women to be using their education in their lives, to be reading widely and curiously, to be maintaining close and varied friendships, and to be involved in community affairs. "The role of the housewife provides her a base for building a many-faceted life, an opportunity few other vocational roles allow, because they are tied down to single organizational structures and goals." Working women normally looked forward to leaving their jobs. Gans found that only 10 percent of suburban women reported frequent loneliness or boredom.

Women's activities are far richer in intellectual and social challenges than most academic writers comprehend. It is foolish to imagine that these complex roles and relationships can be abolished or assumed by outside agencies. The woman's role is nothing less than the hub of the human community. All the other work—the business and politics and entertainment and service performed in the society—finds its ultimate test in the quality of the home. The home is where we finally and privately live, where we express our individuality, where we display our aesthetic choices, where we make and enjoy love, and where we cultivate our children as individuals.

The central position of the woman in the home parallels her central position in all civilized society. Both derive from her necessary role in procreation and from the most primary and inviolable of human ties, the one between mother and child. In those extraordinary circumstances when this tie is broken—as with some disintegrating tribes—the group tends to sink to a totally bestial and amoral chaos.

Most of the characteristics we define as humane and individual originate in the mother's love for her children. Men have no ties to the long-term human community so deep or tenacious as the mother's to her child. Originating in this love are the other civilizing concerns of maternity: the desire for male protection and support, the hope for a stable community life, and the aspiration toward a better long-term future. The success or failure of civilized society depends on how well the women can transmit these values to the men.

Woman's Role Is Personal

This essential female role has become much more sophisticated and refined in the modern world. But its essence is the same. The woman assumes charge of what may be described as the domestic values of the community—its moral, aesthetic, religious, nurturant, social, and sexual concerns. In these values consist the ultimate goals of human life—all those matters that we consider of such supreme importance that we do not ascribe a financial worth to them. Paramount is the worth of the human individual life, enshrined in the home, and in the connection between a woman and child. These values transcend the marketplace. In fact to enter them in commercial traffic is considered a major evil in civilized society. Whether proposing to sell a baby or a body or a religious blessing one commits a major moral offense.

This woman's role is deeply individual. Only a specific woman can bear a specific child, and her tie to it is personal and unbreakable. When she raises the child she imparts in privacy her own individual values. She can create children who transcend consensus and prefigure the future: children of private singularity rather than "child-development policy." She is the vessel of the ultimate values of the nation. The community is largely what she is and what she demands in men. She does her work because it is of primary rather than instrumental value. The woman in the home with her child is the last bastion against the amorality of the technocratic marketplace when it strays from the moral foundations of capitalism.

In recent years, the existence of a distinctive feminine role in ethics has been discovered by feminists. Seeking to answer male psychologists who regard masculine defense of justice and equality as the highest level of moral development, female scholars have offered a contrary case for the moral perceptions of women. The leading work in this field is *In a Different Voice*, by Carol Gilligan of Harvard. She postulates a uniquely feminine moral sense rooted in webs of relationship and responsibility, in intimacy and caring, rather than in rules and abstractions.

Gilligan's point is valuable and true and her book is full of interesting evidence for it. But contrary to her egalitarian vision, women's moral sense is not merely an equal counterpoint to masculine ideals. Stemming from her umbilical link to new life itself and from a passionate sense of the value and potential of that life, the woman's morality is the ultimate basis of all morality. The man's recognition of the preciousness and equality of individuals is learned from women and originates with the feminine concern for relationships, beginning in the womb and at the breast. This concern contrasts sharply with his own experience of hierarchy and preference, aggression and lust, and the sense of sexual and personal dispensability he experiences as a single man. Just as outside male activity is regarded in all societies as most important in instrumental terms, women's concerns are morally paramount, by the very fact that they are female, part of the unimpeachable realm of life's creation and protection.

"Society" Can't Raise Children

What is true for individual moral issues is also true for the practical needs of a nation: the maternal role remains paramount. There is no way to shunt off child care to the "society" or to substantially reduce its burdens. If children lack the close attention of mothers and the disciplines and guidance of fathers, they tend to become barbarians or wastrels who burden or threaten society rather than do its work. Raising children to be productive and responsible citizens takes persistent and unrelenting effort. The prisons, reformatories, foster homes, mental institutions, and welfare rolls of America already groan under the burden of children relinquished to "society" to raise and support. In the sense of becoming self-sufficient, all too many of

these children never grow up at all. To reproduce the true means of production—men and women who can uphold civilization rather than subvert it—the diligent love of mothers is indispensable. In fact, the only remedy for the "overpopulation" in female-headed families is the creation of a larger population of children brought up by two active and attentive parents.

Crucial to the sexual liberals' dream of escape from family burdens is zero population growth. Because each individual no longer depends on his children to support him in old age, many observers seem to imagine that children are less important than they were in the past. But substantially fewer offspring are a possibility only for a while in modern welfare states. No less than in the past, the new generations will have to support the old. The only difference is that now the medium is coercive taxation and social security rather than filial duty.

With some 15 percent of couples infertile and others child-free by choice, in order to raise enough workers to support the social programs of retirees, each fertile woman must still bear more than two children. In order to prevent a substantial decline in the quality of children—their willingness to work hard and contribute to society in the face of high taxes and a generous dole—women must devote long hours to raising and disciplining the new generation. The decline in the quantity of children demands a rise in the quality of their contributions to society—a rise in their diligence and productivity.

"[Men] endure their submission to the marketplace chiefly in order to make enough money to sustain a home, to earn a place in the household, to be needed by women."

This female responsibility, as Gilligan observes, entails difficult sacrifices of freedom and autonomy. Other researchers, notably Jessie Bernard, have noted that these sacrifices produce a significantly elevated incidence of emotional stress and neurosis among full-time housewives, particularly when their children are young. Some of this anxiety clearly reflects the sharp rise in expenses and tax burdens incurred by families raising children. Some of the problem is simply hard and grueling work. Part of the distress, though, may derive from the media's widespread disparagement of traditional women. Margaret Mead found that women are most contented not when they are granted "influence, power, and wealth," but when "the female role of wife and mother is exalted." A devaluing of "the sensuous creative significance" of woman's role, she wrote, makes women become unhappy in the home. But regardless of the source of this stress, Gilligan's point is correct. Women do make great sacrifices, and these sacrifices are essential to society.

Some theorists list sexual restraint high among these sacrifices. But women's sexual restraint is necessary for the fulfillment of their larger sexuality in families, which cannot normally survive the birth of children by men other than the family provider. In general, a man will not support a woman while she philanders.

Men also Sacrifice

Contrary to the assumption of most analysts, it is men who make the major sexual sacrifice. The man renounces his dream of short-term sexual freedom and self-fulfillment—his male sexuality and self-expression—in order to serve a woman and family for a lifetime. It is a traumatic act of giving up his most profound yearning, his bent for the hunt and the chase, the motorbike and the open road, the male group escape to a primal mode of predatory and immediate excitements. His most powerful impulse—the theme of every male song and story—this combination of lust and wanderlust is the very life force that drives him through his youth. He surrenders it only with pain. This male sacrifice, no less than the woman's work in the home, is essential to civilization.

Just as the female role cannot be shared or relinquished, the male role also remains vital to social survival. For centuries to come, men will have to make heroic efforts. On forty-hour weeks, most men cannot even support a family of four. They must train at night and on weekends; they must save as they can for future ventures of entrepreneurship; they must often perform more than one job. They must make time as best they can to see and guide their children. They must shun the consolations of alcohol and leisure, sexual indulgence and flight. They must live for the perennial demands of the provider role.

"The self-sacrifice of women finds a perfect complement in the self-sacrifice of men."

Unlike the woman's role, the man's tends to be relatively fungible and derivative. He does not give himself to a web of unique personal relationships so much as to a set of functions and technologies. Just as any particular hunter might kill an animal, so within obvious bounds any workman can be trained to do most jobs. The man makes himself replaceable. For most of his early years at the job site, individuality is an obstacle to earnings. He must

sacrifice it to support his wife and children. He must eschew his desire to be an athlete or poet, a death-defying ranger or mountaineer, a cocksman and Casanova, and settle down to become a functionary defined by a single job, and a father whose children are earned by his work. Not his own moral vision but the marketplace defines the values of that work. . . .

Among men, the term *dilettante* is a pejorative. Yet, because the range of human knowledge and experience is so broad, the best that most people can ever achieve, if they respond as whole persons to their lives, is the curiosity, openness, and eclectic knowledge of the dilettante. Most men have to deny themselves this form of individual fulfillment. They have to limit themselves, at great psychological cost, in order to fit the functions of the economic division of labor. Most of them endure their submission to the marketplace chiefly in order to make enough money to sustain a home, to earn a place in the household, to be needed by women. This effort most of the time means a lifetime of hard labor.

As with the woman's role, what is true in most specific cases is still more true on the level of general rules and expectations across the entire society. On forty-hour weeks the world dissolves into chaos and decay, famine and war. All the major accomplishments of civilization spring from the obsessions of men whom the sociologists would now disdain as "workaholics." To overcome the Malthusian trap of rising populations, or to escape the closing circle of ecological decline, or to control the threat of nuclear holocaust, or to halt the plagues and famines that still afflict the globe, men must give their lives to unrelenting effort, day in and day out, focused on goals in the distant future. They must create new technologies faster than the world creates new challenges. They must struggle against scarcity, entropy, and natural disaster. They must overcome the sabotage of socialists who would steal and redistribute their product. They must resist disease and temptation. All too often they must die without achieving their ends. But their sacrifices bring others closer to the goal.

Feminism Destroying Society

Nothing that has been written in the annals of feminism gives the slightest indication that this is a role that women want or are prepared to perform. The feminists demand liberation. The male role means bondage to the demands of the workplace and the needs of the family. Most of the research of sociologists complains that men's work is already too hard, too dangerous, too destructive of mental health and wholeness. It all too often leads to sickness and "worlds of pain," demoralization and relatively early death. The men's role that feminists seek is not the real role of men but the male role of the Marxist dream in which "society" does the work.

"Women's liberation" entails a profound dislocation. Women, uniquely in charge of the central activities of human life, are exalting instead the peripheral values—values that have meaning only in relation to the role they would disparage or abandon. In addition, sexual liberals ask society to give up most of the devices and conventions by which it has ensured that women perform their indispensable work and by which men have been induced to support it. As a result, in many of the world's welfare states that have accepted the feminist vision, the two sexes are no longer making the necessary sacrifices to sustain society.

Shunning the responsibilities of family support, men are rejecting available jobs and doing sporadic work off the books and stints on unemployment insurance. Shunning the role of wife and mother, many women are forgoing marriage. Consequently many Western nations are far overshooting the mark of zero population growth. With the average couple bearing scarcely more than one child, most of Northern Europe now shows a fertility rate about 60 percent of the replacement level. If this rate continues, dictated by the pressures of excessive welfare programs, it would mean near-extinction of the genetic stock within four generations. To a less but still dangerous degree, the same pattern is evident in America. The U.S. also is under the replacement level of reproduction.

A nation may gain the illusion of a rising standard of living by raising and supporting fewer children. To paraphrase Allan Carlson, a society may consume for a while the ghosts of the unborn. More specifically, we may eat the meals that would have gone to our prevented or aborted babies. But these gains are rapidly lost. In a vicious circle well known in Europe, smaller generations of workers find themselves devoting ever larger portions of their pay to supporting the child-free aged. Soon the young workers begin reducing their efforts in the face of rising tax rates and their wives themselves begin bearing still fewer children. This is the final contradiction of the welfare state. To the extent that it deters work and childbearing, it ultimately self-destructs. . . .

Woman's Place Is in the Home

Sexual liberalism is the cause, not the solution, of the problem of the West. But the error of the liberals comes not only in their fantasies of flight from work and children—not only in their illusion that full-time work and child care have declined in importance to modern society. They also deeply misunderstand what makes people happy. The pursuit of promiscuous sexual pleasures which many of them offer as an alternative to the duties of family leads chiefly to misery and despair. It is procreation that ultimately makes sex gratifying and important and it is home and family that gives resonance and meaning to life.

The woman's place is in the home, and she does her best when she can get the man there too, inducing him to submit most human activity to the domestic values of civilization. Thus in a sense she also brings the home into the society. The radiance of the values of home can give meaning and illumination to male enterprises. Male work is most valuable when it is imbued with the long-term love and communal concerns of femininity, when it is brought back to the home. Otherwise masculine activity is apt to degenerate quickly to the level of a game; and, unless closely regulated, games have a way of deteriorating into the vain pursuit of power.

"It is the judgment of women that tames the aggressive pursuits of men."

It is the judgment of women that tames the aggressive pursuits of men. Men come to learn that their activity will be best received if it partakes of the values of the home. If they think the work itself is unworthy, they try to conceal it and bring home the money anyway. Like the legendary Mafiosi, they try to please their women by elaborate submission to domestic values in the household, while scrupulously keeping the women out of the male realm of work. But in almost every instance, even by hypocrisy, they pay tribute to the moral superiority of women.

In rediscovering for the secular world this feminine morality, rooted in "webs of relationship," Gilligan has written an important book. What she and the male moralists she criticizes do not see is that the self-sacrifice of women finds a perfect complement in the self-sacrifice of men. On this mutual immolation is founded the fulfillment of human civilization and happiness. For just as it is the sacrifice of early career ambitions and sexual freedom that makes possible the true fulfillment of women, it is the subordination of male sexuality to women's maternity that allows the achievement of male career goals, that spurs the attainment of the highest male purposes. In his vaunted freedom and sexual power, the young single man may dream of glory. But it is overwhelmingly the married men who achieve it in the modern world. They achieve it, as scripture dictates and women's experience insists, by self-denial and sacrifice.

George Gilder is a former speechwriter for President Reagan and the author of several books on social and economic subjects, including Wealth and Poverty *and* The Spirit of Enterprise.

"Equitable relationships are more satisfying than traditional relationships, because each spouse has access to two worlds rather than one and the children have access to two parents."

Egalitarian Sex Roles in Marriage Are Best

Gayle Kimball

"We are the head geese breaking the path: there are more behind us."
—*A Delaware husband*

"We're at the cutting edge of change."
—*A California husband*

A Wisconsin man who is part of an equal marriage reports that "men with feminist wives who have left them have come to me and said, 'What do you do?' I try to talk to them and tell them books to read, but there is nothing about how to make an egalitarian marriage work." The experience of 150 couples who live in thirty-three states and three Canadian provinces provide examples of equal marriages. Their knowledge is gained from daily efforts to share decision making, housework, child care, and moneymaking, as they described in interviews. . . .

These couples are not typical. They are in the vanguard of a movement for equality between the sexes, spurred on by women's entry into the paid work force and by the women's and men's liberation movements. *Perhaps for the first time in human history the worlds of men and of women are beginning to merge.* Couples who share equally the burdens and joys of being breadwinners, bread bakers, and nurturers of children are pioneers. The couples interviewed are unusual because most families, including dual-career couples, maintain a traditional division of labor, with the man's career primary and the woman responsible for family work. Despite being highly educated and well paid, the interviewees find role-sharing difficult. They are going against the mainstream of a society that is still geared toward the male worker with a wife who takes care of domestic tasks. One couple, co-owners of their own business, think that "our situation is probably the easiest you can get, but even then we find it difficult. We can't find adequate child care,

for example."

Learning about the struggles and rewards these role-sharing couples face can be of use to other couples who wish to be equal, including young adults who are unaware of the enormous difficulties involved in balancing careers, marriages, and children. Many men and women want to participate equally in careers and family life but have no examples of how to do so. Because we have so few models and because society neglects the needs of working parents, the experiences of couples who successfully share working and parenting are valuable.

The egalitarian couples' accounts of how their marriages work are also significant because, in an era of high divorce rates, most consider themselves happily married. The fact that the number of divorces in the 1970s was twice the number of the 1960s, so that at current rates half of recent marriages will end in divorce, indicates the stress put on marriage by changing expectations. . . .

Defining an Equal Marriage

One role-sharing couple, both of whom are psychologists, define an equal marriage as one in which neither partner has priority over the other or more authority or power—even if one makes more or all the money, has a higher-status job, or is bigger or older. Equal marriage requires that "there should be no monopolies for either sex in any sphere." An egalitarian relationship is one in which tasks, responsibilities, and privileges are shared. Assignment of tasks is flexible, based on practical considerations of proper male and female behavior. If a man likes to cook and his wife does not, he cooks. Since they both use the toilet, she is not the only one to clean it. Power is fluid, not based on a rigid hierarchy of dominance and deference.

Egalitarian marriage contrasts with traditional, patriarchal marriage in which the husband is head of the household and his paid job is most important, while the wife is responsible for nurturing the family. An example of a traditional relationship is the marriage of President Ronald and Nancy Reagan. She states, "In marriage it's the woman who has to do an awful lot of the adjusting. Men think they're making adjustments, too, but they're really not. That's what makes them both happy." Her view is that a wife finds fulfillment in pleasing her husband. A *Ladies' Home Journal* survey of 30,000 readers, however, found that traditionally feminine women who sought their identity in husband and children were the most unhappy respondents and suffered most from symptoms of stress. The more independent respondents, "the changing women," were happier and felt closer to their husbands. Traditional roles are stressful for men as well: A physician reports that 90 percent of the leading causes of death in males are specifically associated with the masculine role.

"Traditionally feminine women who sought their identity in husband and children were the most unhappy . . . and suffered most from symptoms of stress."

The underlying assumption in egalitarian relationships is that women's and men's time is of equal value, that a man is not demeaned by washing dishes or caring for children, and that a woman deserves as much leisure time as her husband. Most fair people would agree that men and women are of equal worth, but few act on that assumption, as evidenced by the fact that women earn only 59 percent of what men earn and men generally have higher status in society. Most wives do more housework and child care to compensate for their lower earnings and lower self-esteem or to carve out an area in which they feel in charge, even if they work outside the home for the same number of hours as their husbands. Many middle-class couples say they believe in equality between spouses, but their belief is rarely translated into practice. A study conducted by the Catalyst Career and Family Center of 815 dual-career couples found that couples considered their careers of equal importance but acted traditionally, as in moving for his career rather than for hers and in the wife's assuming more household responsibilities. The same pattern was found in a study of 200 married couples, all psychologists. A 1980 Harris poll of 1,503 U.S. adult family members found that 90 percent thought child-care responsibility should be shared by both parents, but only 36 percent reported sharing it equally in practice.

The benefits for couples who share marriage roles are especially recognized by spouses who began their marriage with the burden of economic support solely on the husband and the burden of domestic tasks solely on the wife. Annie and Jack own a small record business; when their sons were three and six, they decided to share its management, switching from traditional roles. As a result, Jack explains,

> We communicate better. I think we have stronger feelings for each other, because we share so much now that we didn't share when we were playing the male-female roles. Plus our sex life went to hell when I was working the long hours. Since we have shared the business, the problems are not so large, because there are two of us working at it and we both know what is going on. We both come up with ideas. There is nothing that has to be kept inside anymore, that one person is brewing on, not wanting to tell the other person.

Men Feel Less Pressure

Many husbands appreciate the freedom they gain with two wage earners in the family: freedom to escape the pressure to earn more money, to quit an unpleasant job, or to study. Another benefit for husbands is having a partner who feels she is living up to her capabilities and therefore does not look to him to shape her identity. As a Colorado husband, Charlie, puts it:

> To me, being egalitarian is the ultimate meaningful relationship, the coming together of equals to nurture each other and form a partnership. To be totally caught up in the male career means no sharing can go on. The other rewards are even greater than the prestige of affluence—a balanced life in which you participate with your children and have a lot of time with your loved ones.

Studies concur that equitable relationships are more satisfying than traditional relationships, because each spouse has access to two worlds rather than one and the children have access to two parents. A study that followed married couples from the late 1930s to the early 1950s found that marriages with the greatest role differentiation were unsatisfying "empty shells." Couples who perceive equal benefits from their relationship are the happiest, and the more housework and child care a husband performs the less likely his wife is to divorce him.

One woman, Lisa, a personnel director in Illinois, reports:

> I work with over 100 women; what some of them put up with is unbelievable, and it makes me appreciate what I've got. If I had to walk in every day and my husband sat there and watched the news while I fixed dinner and tried to get my son fed and bathed, if I had to do everything that 98 percent of the wives do—we would have a lot more problems.

Despite the backlash by reactionary religious and political groups, the reality is that a minority of American families fit the nineteenth-century definition of the family: husband as sole breadwinner, wife as full-time mother. In the majority of marriages today, both spouses are wage earners and 54 percent of the children under eighteen (including almost half of the children under six) have working mothers. The number of working mothers has increased tenfold since World War II. Women's ability to earn income influences their roles as wives, because their financial resources often result in more decision-making power. Economic necessity generated by inflation is an impetus for women to assume more equality.

Women in the Workforce

Equality is also made possible because women are earning more university degrees than in the past—for the first time there are as many female college students as males. Women are marrying at a later age (22 is the average) and having fewer babies (1.8 per mother). Also, the number of women giving birth after age thirty almost doubled between 1973 and 1981. The movement of women into the work force is described as the most significant social change in the twentieth century, leading to the major change in men's role—their increasing involvement in the family. . . .

Two important factors in preparing for egalitarian marriage are living alone for some years to establish an autonomous career and identity and knowing one's mate well before marriage. One Colorado couple, a teacher and an attorney, lived alone for five years after college graduation and were married eight years before they had children. Their pattern is typical of egalitarian couples in their thirties. As one such woman stated, "If you have some living under your belt you know that nothing is uncomplicated and just because you believe in equality doesn't make it easy to be equal."

"The unequal roles of traditional mothers and fathers are not conducive to marital happiness."

Many egalitarian couples believe that maturity leads to fewer illusions and false expectations about marriage and that they have an advantage over inexperienced, younger people who expect their partner to change. A Michigan woman feels that waiting until she was twenty-nine to marry was critical; if she had married at twenty-one, which is what she originally wanted, she would have been very traditional. The women's movement and living on her own entirely changed her perceptions. Other women agreed that if they had married in their early twenties, they would have fallen into the usual roles, stayed home to mother their babies, and probably gotten divorced. They needed time to mature, to

establish a career, and to practice independence and self-sufficiency. As a Connecticut woman, Joanna, explains:

> My growing feminist awareness meant that I didn't feel any rush to get into a relationship. When I did I was twenty-five years old and able to make real decisions about what I wanted. I didn't feel pulled by a domineering man, or feel entrapped, unlike many women who have so many years wasted and then are angry when they realize their error in judgment.

Delaying Parenthood

Women who did not wait and entered into an early first marriage as a result of college-senior panic found that they were children playing house. They knew neither themselves nor their spouses very well. The early marriages that survived most harmoniously are those in which the partners knew each other many years before the wedding and both continued their education and career. Generally, however, a New Jersey man, William, notes,

> There is a pattern [of marriage] we are aware of that leads to a nonegalitarian type. If a woman goes from her father's house to her husband's house without any period of independence, that's almost guaranteed to reproduce a hierarchical relationship. The husband in some ways becomes the new father.

Waiting to have children is also beneficial to achieving a nonhierarchical marriage. Many couples who did not wait wish they had, but most egalitarian couples waited many years before having children. A father from Pennsylvania, Ben, relates:

> We were married for six years before our daughter was born. During those six years we really got into an egalitarian living situation, although I don't think we had any role models. As a matter of fact, we've looked very hard to find some and felt frustrated because not only can't we find any role models but we have some difficulty in finding professional couples with children who manage to stay together. When the woman gets pregnant and the baby arrives, the woman stays home and gets a lot of pressure to do so from her husband.

Studies indicate that young couples often function equally until the birth of the first child causes the woman to drop out of the work force. The presence of children under twelve makes role-sharing more difficult. It has been repeatedly shown that the curve of marital satisfaction drops when children enter the family and it climbs when they leave. The unequal roles of traditional mothers and fathers are not conducive to marital happiness. In reaction, younger egalitarian couples delay childbirth and often opt for an only child. . . .

Men as Equal Partners

If it is difficult for men to be equal partners in family work, the backgrounds of men who have equal marriages are worth examining. One husband feels thousands of women could step into his wife's shoes but very few men could replace him. His wife, a teacher, agrees, "The key is not me; it's Don."

Other men ask him how he manages to do most of the cooking, share in the care of their daughter, and attend law school. It is difficult to replicate what he does, he believes, since other men "need to see it on TV or read about it and there is nowhere to do that." Another wife agrees that men are less willing than women to be in an egalitarian marriage. Because we live in a society where men have more power, they have more to give up; men have to be willing to put their privilege on the line. She feels it is a rare man who will try equality for a while and not quit when it "gets hard.". . .

Numerous role-sharing husbands state that the reason for their lifestyle is its logic and fairness. They define themselves as rational, a stereotyped male attribute that can be put to good use in breaking out of rigid roles. A young technical writer with one child gives an example of this orientation:

> I looked around at what my relatives and people around me were doing in terms of traditional roles and I didn't think that it made any sense, or that what they were doing was based on any sort of logic or reason. I've always been a big person for having everything around me make sense and be explainable. My family tended to think that the woman should be at home and I could never see a reason for that.

Currently he and his wife are moving from Ohio, despite his well-paying job there, so that his wife can complete her college education. His relatives think that is an unwise reason to move, but the couple is doing it nevertheless.

"Role-sharers do not have an image to defend because they are content with who they are."

Some wives who struggled to get their husbands to do more housework successfully used the argument that fairness was the principle at stake. Since the men prided themselves on being fair, they conceded. Ron, a Washington co-owner of a business, explains that his marriage began with very traditional roles; even though his wife was the wage earner putting him through graduate school, she did most of the housework and all the cooking. She finally pointed out that her workload was ridiculous. He recalls:

> I had a lot of respect for my mate and the argument made so much sense that I couldn't say anything but "okay." I had a nice deal going; it was a little painful at first to come home from a day of work and actually organize and prepare a meal and do the dishes. That was quite a change, but it made so much sense that I didn't have any argument against it.

They now manage their business together as well as share the care of their three children.

A sense of fair play also made the president of a company, married to an IBM saleswoman, realize that "if she was going to be beating her brains out all day to earn money, it was only fair" that he contribute at home. He enjoys the income she earns and wants to make it comfortable for her to keep on working. The thought that some women put up with coming home from work to do all the housework makes one husband, Victor, feel sick to his stomach. He and his wife are physicians, and his wife's equal education and earnings give her status. Also, as professionals they could afford to take several months off from work when their young son was born. Their having a housekeeper also relieves tension. . . .

Appealing to a man's sense of logic and fairness is one of the best tactics a woman can use to point out the rationale for shared roles, since men are usually trained to rely on their reason rather than their emotions. . . .

The Egalitarian Male

A woman seeking a role-sharing husband should avoid men who are constantly proving their manhood to an invisible jury that never lets them relax except when they are numbed by television or drinking. Role-sharers do not have an image to defend because they are content with who they are. Several men spoke of the social pressure to maintain a masculine image and recalled how they rejected it; a man who is insecure about his image will likely stay away from cooking, sewing, and changing diapers, according to a New York television engineer. . . .

If a man does not need his wife to make him feel superior, he can appreciate a partner who will challenge him. "One of the worst things in the world is to spend your life with a half person, a woman who will only reflect you without any aspirations of her own and be dependent," states David, a Louisiana writer. His wife is an administrator and a feminist, and she is active in politics. A man who is comfortable with himself will not need his wife to diminish herself to make him feel important.

Gayle Kimball is a sociology professor at California State University, Chico.

"We have learned that men and women can mother together."

Mothers and Fathers Can Parent Together

Diane Ehrensaft

The unforgettable images on these pages are *Ladies' Home Journal*'s salute to today's fathers— loving dads who truly nurture their children.
Ladies Home Journal, June, 1986

The times they are a'changin'. The article in the *Ladies Home Journal*, entitled "A New Kind of Father," goes on to tell us that . . . the percentage of fathers present in the delivery room has made a phenomenal jump, from 27% [in 1974] to 80% [in 1986]. Furthermore, a survey of their readers in 1985 showed that 84.2% of their readers under forty believe that men are just as good with children as women. This is no radical magazine with a left-wing readership. The *Journal* is genuinely tapping a remarkable shift in the attitudes of the American public. Part of that public, shared parenting families, not only bring Father in the delivery room; they make sure he continues his involvement after returning home.

Is parenting together a revolution or an evolution? Probably both. Years ago, when I and other feminists were demanding equality of the sexes in the home, the idea of a man doing half of the parenting was an outlandish proposition. Then the idea was a threatening and disturbing one, not readily welcomed by the world around us. Now the *Ladies Home Journal* prints in boldface that "what has taken place is not so much a revolution as an evolution— from rigid roles to today's fluid parenting styles." No longer a feminist demand, but now a mainstream idea, the shift is understood as an erosion, over the last generation, of the norms that kept women primarily in the home and men primarily in the workforce.

The erosion is no more clearly evidenced than in the reports of older fathers with second families or

with a latecomer amongst their first flock of children. And so one father reports, in the *Journal*, about his second marriage, "I never read *The Cat and The Hat* the first time around. I never diapered or bathed the babies. I just came home after my wife had them all fed and in their pajamas, and I kissed them good night. It wasn't macho to really mother them. Now the rules have changed. Real men take care of the kids. I like that."

There has been a media splash of men hugging, kissing, or gazing in the eyes of their young children: pictures plastered all over magazines, newspapers, even billboards. Kodak shows us bigger than life a "real" man, muscle-bound and stripped to the waist, lovingly cradling a tiny infant in his strong arms. Second-time-around fathers also see these photographs, and are obviously proud to be one of these "new" men. They are immensely relieved that they made it just under the wire by getting to do in the mid-1980s what they would not have even dreamed of ten years before—mothering a child. Fathers of grown children who never had that opportunity express remorse and sadness that they themselves did not grow up in a generation that would have allowed or encouraged them to have greater contact with their children.

A Drastic Transformation

This is a drastic transformation. The underlying forces that have allowed this new family form to unfold, such as changes in the economy or a shift from physical to technological forms of labor, may have been evolutionary, slowly gathering force over time. But the actual acknowledgment of and acclamation given to men and women parenting together is much more sudden.

Those of us who were the pioneers are thrown off-balance: We do not know whether to feel victorious or co-opted. For we know full well that with all the recognition given to babies on men's laps and the visibility of fathers and children on Sunday strolls, the percentage of men and women who genuinely share the tasks of parenting is quite small. But the fact that such a practice is increasingly lauded rather than condemned *is* a large victory, one that will make it decidedly easier to receive social support for this new family style.

Mothering Together

Although it is easier said than done, we have learned that men and women *can* mother together. The stories we have heard document the possibility of a loving, fruitful, and happy life outside the confines of the traditional nuclear family, a model our society until recently took for granted as the benchmark of health. The success of the sharing couples and their children proves that we can stretch the form of the family very far without stretching the people in it out of shape. Further testimony is that the parents themselves end up feeling that shared parenting is not simply a choice, but an imperative. They may have "chosen" it in the beginning, but now they cannot do without it.

Nonetheless it is a slow process. Even with the remarkable shift in public consciousness about gender roles and men's involvement in parenting, the emotional scripts deep within us are not easily discarded. It still makes some people squeamish to imagine a man changing a diaper, even though they would like to admit that wasn't so, and the sharing parents themselves confess that deeply internalized feelings within them sometimes make the experience of parenting together a difficult one.

"The parents themselves end up feeling that shared parenting is not simply a choice, but an imperative. . . . Now they cannot do without it."

Along with the emotional resistances, the economic and social realities of the surrounding culture are not changing as rapidly as the culture's new openness toward fathering. Rather than supporting the experiment, the structure of the economy and the workplace has put up barriers to the success of men and women mothering together.

When a sharing arrangement fails or never gets off the ground, financial necessity is often the cause. A man's retreat to the primary breadwinning role is often forced upon the family by the sobering reality that on the whole, working women still earn less than two-thirds as much as working men. If that doesn't make things hard enough, the lack of flexibility in the workplace and the great risks to an individual's advancement if one works less than full time and full steam make it hard to find an

arrangement that simultaneously satisfies a family's child care needs and the realities of the parents' work life.

Lack of community support can have a further dampening effect. Just as a little boy might have to hide some of his "girl" toys or activities in order to survive in the neighborhood, fathers may have to leave some of their "mothering" activities underground—as with the man who never took his family's turn as secretary of his children's babysitting co-op because it would be so shocking to the other co-op mothers in his conservative community. . . .

A Strong Commitment

To parent together, then, takes an exceptionally strong commitment. Not just these external impediments but internal psychological tensions about work and family pull at the parents, tugging the woman toward the mothering end of the balance and the father toward the primary breadwinner end. With the added pressures of intricate scheduling, struggles over gender disparities, and work overload that come with shared parenting, it can be tempting to throw in the towel.

Yet these couples overwhelmingly do not do so. They look over the fence at families in which mothers carry the backbreaking load of both a full-time job and full-time responsibility for the children. That does not seem like an enticing alternative, although it is one faced by more and more women today as over 60% of mothers with children enter the workforce.

They think of a life in which Dad would be denied the intimate relationship with the children that has grown so central to his life. They imagine their sons and daughters denied that daily access to Dad which the children so take for granted. The feelings of loss and sorrow which accompany that fantasy are one of the strongest safeguards of the sharing arrangement. So, in the words of one father, "Would I go back to a traditional parenting situation? Not if I can help it!"

Parenting together can work and does work, and once chosen it is tenaciously held on to by most. But it also has some problems that should not be overlooked in planning for the future. Some worry that one untoward consequence of shared parenting is that the child actually ends up with two *fathers* rather than two *mothers*.

Fathering and Mothering

Just as mothering does not reside in a person but rather consists of a set of socially constructed tasks and obligations, so fathering, in traditional terms, consists of primary breadwinning, being at the helm of the family, and providing *secondary* love to the children. A mother whose career is vitally important to her, as is her husband's, explains to me that she and her husband are not doing anything like the mothering she had known as a child. "We're both mothering, but we're also both fathering. Actually, you could say our little boy has two fathers." Because she and her husband both work long hours and have their small son in full-time child care, she imagines her son's parenting to be provided by two fathers—except that a father would not be the one to have arranged that child care or to pick up baby, bring him home, and give him a bath.

More realistically, in social terms children in such families have two working mothers: parents who go out during the day to earn a living and, equally, devote their evening and weekend time to their child. But this mother's point, that the child with *no* parent who is primarily responsible runs the risk of being a child with two secondary parents, is well taken. Traditional fathers were not intended to bring up children on a daily basis. So *two* of them will never do when it comes to raising a child.

To avoid this potential risk of diluted parenting, some sharing families with heavy work schedules opt for the split-shift arrangement. When one parent is on, the other is off. But this solution generates another set of risks. A parent from a sharing family told me this funny story. When he and his wife sat down together for a meal one day, their three-year-old daughter let out a gleeful shriek. "Oh, is this a holiday?"

The point of shared parenting, obviously, was not to make family meals a rare occasion. But with two parents overloaded and strapped for time, the children and adults alike can be deprived of a familial communal experience. The times with everyone together become few and far between. Better social and economic supports for the sharing family, such as flextime jobs and job sharing, could alleviate those stresses, and must be worked toward as we plan for the future of the family. . . .

Reports from the Frontier

When the first sharing couples embarked on their journey, they were looked at with either trepidation or excitement, as is true of any pioneering venture. The old ways of raising a family, in which Mom stayed home and Dad earned a living, may have been crumbling, but people were left with no clear vision of where to go next.

A decade or more later, we now have reports back from the frontier. We find that there are few of the feared harmful consequences to either parents or children when mothers and fathers share the care of the children—that it is safe out there. We can even invite others to follow. They may not choose to move out all the way into the new terrain, doing a full 50-50 arrangement; but the benefits of any shift toward having men more involved in childrearing and women freer to develop identities outside motherhood far outweigh any of the drawbacks—for

the parents, the children, and the marriage.

As in any pioneer movement, as time goes on the settlers are no longer mavericks, but become part of the mainstream. So it is that men and women who parent together ushered in a new arrangement that has now been, at least in part, absorbed into the culture: not necessarily egalitarian parenting, but the expectation that fathers be more involved in family life while their wives combine work and mothering.

The shared parenting family is also truly a social laboratory, teaching us much about the interface of culture, gender, and personality. If given the opportunity, men can mother. Gender roles are not immutable categories. Theories that say that only women can mother are merely culture-bound, a product of their time, rather than objective scientific fact. But at the same time, the inner experience that is so different for the man and for the woman who parent together alerts us to the reality that gender shifts involve more than an alteration of roles or changes in behavior. It involves a restructuring of personalities, a shift in the balance of the masculine and feminine components of our psyches.

The Children of Sharing Parents

What we are as men or as women is deeply embedded within us, not because of biology but because of our very earliest experiences in our own families and the internalization of the beliefs, mores, and practices of the culture we grew up in. We can chip away at the personality differences between men and women that make both parenting and female-male relationships such a disjunctive affair, but the personalities we came with will in many respects be the ones we leave with. It is the *children* of sharing parents, entering adulthood with a different family history and in the context of a changing set of cultural beliefs, mores, and practices, who will show the personality integration most conducive to women and men mothering together.

It is not, then, simply a one-generation transformation. Things are drastically different, yet something of the old still remains. The male-female personality differences that make parenting a lopsided affair will fade with each new generation, but will take at least one or two to really disappear. The sons and daughters will exhibit a better balance of doing and being than their parents. And their children, if they are also offspring of sharing parents, will show an even better one. That balance, in two parents, is the harbinger of a man and a woman truly parenting together.

Diane Ehrensaft is a practicing psychotherapist, professor of psychology at The Wright Institute in Berkeley, California, and author of Parenting Together.

"Sharing is fine in theory. Sharing in practice means spending a lot of time doing uninspiring household slog that his father never did."

Parenting Cannot Be Truly Shared

Beppie Harrison

"God knows I was nervous about handling him," Reva said about their first days with their son, "but I have to admit that poor Elliott was even more nervous than I was. At least I'd held a baby before: I don't think he ever had."

Elliott is hardly alone. Everything is still set up so that girls and women are expected to be interested in babies and small children; a man has to go out of his way to be initiated into the routines of child care before he's a father. Not that most of it is particularly mysterious: learning how to take care of a baby is, after all, in many ways a business of acquiring confidence and some basic skills. You learn how to pick her up so that she doesn't flop all over the place, how to wrap her snugly so she'll feel secure, how to feed her, how to burp her—and all of it gets more matter-of-fact each time you do it. By the time mother and baby come home from the hospital, mother has had a chance to begin to find that out. She has a few days' experience of coping under the watchful eyes of the maternity ward staff. Father has been a visitor. He may have held the baby a few times, but he's unlikely to be quite as confident as his wife is getting to be that the baby really won't come apart in his hands.

But there is more than that. For a lot of us, the intensity of the bond between a mother and her baby is dazzling in the beginning, especially for a bystander trying to work out how to love them both. David Osborne is a father who has had to take over a lot of nurturing responsibilities from his wife, a doctor in her residency working the standard 100-hour work weeks of that grueling traditional ordeal. But he wrote about the first three weeks of their son Nick's life, when his wife was on maternity leave at home with the baby, "Rose had

carried Nick for nine months; Rose had been through labor; and Rose was nursing him. For nine months he had listened to her heartbeat, felt her pulse, been a part of her being. Now he hunted her scent and drank from her body, and the bond between them was awesome. I was like some voyeur, peeking through the window at an ancient and sacred rite." Faced at the very beginning with such an elemental need, a father may well feel that sharing is not so much impractical as irrelevant....

A Cute Puppy

Whether it's because of this nearly inescapable early mother/child exclusivity, or whether it's one thing that, intentionally or not, we arrange out of memories of how our own parents handled things, or whether there is some fundamental difference—hormonal, maybe?—between the nurturing of males and females, the fact does seem to be that most fathers find it very hard to relate to their young babies in the same intense way mothers generally do. "Marty didn't seem to know what to do with her at first," as one mother described a very typical situation. "He *liked* her all right, but it was sort of like liking a cute puppy. He changed her, and he carried her around some, and he kind of poked at her, playing, but he didn't act as if she was a real person until I guess she was crawling—she must have been eight or nine months old by then. That was when he started really talking to her and looking for her when he came home."...

When all is said and done, however, there are a lot more fathers sharing parenting these days than there used to be.

Undoubtedly much of this arises from sheer desperation. Our cities and suburbs are full of young mothers who feel totally isolated from all the traditional sources of support. Their mothers live three states away or have gone back to work and are not available for baby-sitting or long leisurely counsel and comfort. The neighbors are distant or gone all day. The pediatrician is kind but hurried and always visibly waiting for them to get to the point. A lot of them have jobs themselves and just plain run out of hours in the day. So they turn to their husbands, not only for the emotional support that women have always looked for from the men they love, but for practical help with the children and the house.

"Most fathers find it very hard to relate to their young babies in the same intense way mothers generally do."

John and Angela, who came straight home from the hospital with their brand-new daughter and sat down with a couple of beers to contemplate her with appalled awe, wondering what on earth they'd gotten into, are not at all untypical. The month before Joanie was born, they had moved to another city 800 miles away from where they'd both grown up, and they didn't know anybody yet. John had to pitch in because Angela felt completely at sea and there wasn't anyone else to call on. Anyhow, Joanie was his baby, too. They started out learning together. Angela had to learn faster, because the economic facts of life were that John could earn a better salary than she could—they had made the move in the first place because of a job opportunity for him. So he was the one who went out to work, and she stayed home with Joanie. Now, two years later, they still share a lot of the job. Angela has Joanie all day, but they alternate evenings. On her nights off, Angela is free to walk out and let John cope on his own. She does. It isn't completely equal co-parenting: John, for example, doesn't give Joanie a bath on his nights to put her to bed—it apparently doesn't strike him as necessary. Angela lets that go. Crabbing about details guarantees a squabble, and she needs that time too much to waste it arguing. Joanie will get her bath the next night, when Angela's the one coping. It hasn't been roses all the way as it is. "It's taken a long time," Angela said musingly. "I didn't like the way John parented in the beginning. I thought he was too flip with Joanie. Even when she was three months old, he was whipping her around, turning her upside down. I didn't like that, and I would have to sit there and bite my tongue, because he enjoyed it and she enjoyed it and I was the only one who wasn't enjoying it. Only over the last year have I finally been able to totally leave the house, body and soul, and not worry about what was going on. Somehow we've made the transition."

Even so, Angela still carries the psychological responsibility. John is a knowledgeable relief worker.

Psychological responsibility implies much more than changing equal numbers of diapers, or alternating nights of putting the kids to bed. Sharing the psychological responsibility means that both of you remember that Toby says the blue pajamas are itchy and it's important to make sure the red ones get brought up from the laundry. It means both of you know that children have to have baths. It means that both of you are subconsciously alert to the baby's cries during the night. However willing he might be to get up at 1:30 to see what's wrong, if you have to wake him up to tell him the baby's crying, you're the one with the psychological responsibility. (My own husband slept peacefully through the nights of our oldest daughter's infancy until I had to be out of town for a week, when he astonished himself—and me—by rousing whenever she whimpered. Obviously he had been hearing her all along, but before then it wasn't his problem.) It means he can take care of the children for a day, or a week, without your having to leave him a long list of what has to be done when. He doesn't baby-sit for you— he's the father. It means he knows as well as you do about allergies and favorite blankets and where they are likely to be when they are mislaid, and when the next booster shots are due. Sharing the psychological responsibility means that neither of you acts as an intermediary with your children for the other. You don't have to interpret to him what Toddy's gibberish means (unless he is equally capable of interpreting it for you), and both of you see his contribution to the child-related jobs around the house not as helping you out, but as the things he does because Toddy is his son. The other side of it is that Toddy is equally comfortable being taken care of by either one of you.

Theory and Practice

In theory it sounds terrific. In everyday experience, there are a few hurdles to having it all unfold this way. The biggest is that when it comes right down to it, a lot of fathers really don't want to. Sharing is fine in theory. Sharing in practice means spending a lot of time doing uninspiring household slog that his father never did and a considerable percentage of his friends still don't. Women have been complaining loudly for the past twenty years about the confining aspects of housework and child care. It is hardly surprising that the average man doesn't take up the same burden with glad cries of delight. Unfortunately, while he is probably measuring his contribution of household effort against those of his friends who do less, his wife is almost certainly comparing him to her friends' husbands who do more, and each can accuse the other of beastly unfairness with complete sincerity and conviction.

Many fathers are still convinced that child care is basically a mother's job. They may help out now and then. In fact, they probably do considerably more than their fathers ever thought of doing. But it is always done as a favor to their wives, and they usually need to be told what to do. For many wives, this is enough. They prefer to be captains of their own ships. Other husbands pitch in when there is a genuine crisis and their wives can't do it alone, often discovering that the special closeness and warmth that mothers have with their children grows out of spending time with and doing things for the kids. "Alan left Victoria up to me until I suddenly collapsed with appendicitis and was carted off to the hospital," Barbara said. "Neither my mother nor his mother could come to take over, so he took a week off and took care of Victoria himself. She was thirteen months old, and it was like learning from scratch for him—it must have been awful. I'm glad I wasn't around to have to watch. But by the time he brought me home, he and Victoria had worked things out amazingly well, and he thought she was the greatest thing in the world. I think he talked solidly the first half hour I was home about what had happened each day and what she could do and what she was trying to say, and when she woke up from her nap and wanted to sit in his lap instead of mine I felt like something dropped out of my middle. But he was so obviously relieved that she still wanted him, even with me there, that I didn't have the heart to say anything. I think he was really afraid that all their closeness would just evaporate once I came home. From that time on Victoria belonged to both of us, and when Benjy was born, Alan was right there from the start. He's turned into a fantastic father."

"Many fathers are still convinced that child care is basically a mother's job."

The unfortunate part is that even when a man is genuinely motivated to share the parenting responsibilities, our society doesn't make it easy. The hard fact is that job demands on an ambitious, successful man allow little space for him to share child care with his wife. Building a relationship with a child—not to mention sharing the mundane details of feeding and dressing and teaching acceptable manners—can't be crammed into a spare half hour here or fifteen minutes there, and it can't be done in the middle of the night if Daddy has stayed late at the office. Inevitably, choices have to be made. Ours is an intensely competitive society. Career patterns for the ambitious are based on the overachiever. There are a lot of men—and some women—out there working seventy hours and more a week. They aren't seeing much of their children, if they have any, but those are the men and women with whom the men and women who want to be active parents are competing in their careers. You have to be extraordinarily good at what you do to stay ahead of the competition if your colleagues are working half again as many hours as you can give. We read a lot of glossy profiles of hard-driving, achieving couples where both husband and wife are holding down demanding jobs and rearing their children in their spare time, but most of us lack their energy or can't afford the delicate balance of support personnel they have to make it all possible. Children do take up a lot of hours, particularly when they are young. What happens with most of us is that during the early years, it's the mother who—even if she is working— makes the necessary compromises and finds herself with the primary responsibility. It is still usually the man's paycheck that the family relies upon most heavily and whose current work demands are therefore most immediately important. . . .

Shifting Roles

Our generation is working out how to parent at a time when the whole question of what roles women and men should take in the wider society is being vigorously debated. At least our parents had a less controversial notion of what they expected of each other. We've all been influenced by the propaganda that declares that determining role by sex alone is unfair. What we choose to do about that in our own lives is up to us. At the moment we can almost certainly find theoretical backing for any division of labor we choose to try. Deciding what is going to happen in our individual families is a fertile field for disagreement, and working out what actually does happen can turn our homes into a battlefield. On the one hand is the comfort of defined, traditional family roles; on the other, the freedom of working out what suits us best. For some couples, the traditional roles work out fine. He has his job and isn't fighting upstream all the time about work versus home expectations; she really relishes being the special person to their children and doesn't mind the heavier child care load that secures the position for her. Another father and mother both want to share the good parts of being close to their children and are willing to negotiate the equal division of the chores, from picking up the toys to doing escort duty to the pediatrician's office. Given good will and mutual forebearance, it's certainly possible to weave a way down the middle—but nobody should be too surprised and dismayed to find themselves crashing into the wall every now and again.

Beppie Harrison is the author of The Shock of Motherhood *and co-author of* Giving Time a Chance.

"The catastrophe of the inner-city black family is the catastrophe of the whole concept of the family in America."

The Black Family Is Falling Apart

John A. Howard

On April 29, [1986,] a radioactive cloud drifting over Scandinavia brought news of a catastrophe that had occurred in Soviet Russia. The meltdown of the power plant at Chernobyl spelled a frightful and devastating end to a system that was intended to bring light and fruitfulness to the Russian people.

Three months earlier, on January 25, the airwaves over North America brought news of a catastrophe in the United States, a catastrophe which, in the loss of lives and destruction of property, makes the Chernobyl casualties seem paltry and insignificant. For Americans, too, there was a moment of truth as it became clear that miscalculations about a system intended to bring enlightenment and fulfillment had resulted in vast destruction. The Russian calamity was technological. It involved a single incident at one location. The American calamity is cultural. It pervades the nation and the damaging impact is a continuing process, not a passing event.

The revelation of America's troubles occurred on a CBS two-hour television special hosted by Bill Moyers. The title of the program was, "The Vanishing Family—Crisis in Black America." It revealed the way of life and the attitudes of young blacks in Newark, New Jersey, who are trapped in a sub-civilization that degrades and trivializes human beings. The importance, the abiding importance, of that television program was that it established the fact that what has rotted the fabric of inner-city life over the last twenty years is the collapse of America's primary value system.

A Twilight Zone

The transcript of the television show identifies fixed patterns of harmful behavior. The inner-city young person tends to live according to impulse without any rational system of constraint or

obligation, and expects other individuals to do the same. Drug-dealing, crime, and homicide are accepted as part of life's routines. The young men have little inclination to accept responsibilities for a wife, a home, or any children they may sire. They are caught in an institutionalized adolescence. The young women seem to accept their fate as sex partners and single-parent child-rearers, without complaint or self-pity. As was borne out in the TV interviews, this way of life is made possible and perpetuated by the programs of government support. The work disincentives of government welfare subsidies, combined with the failure of cultural systems to impart any understanding of or commitment to emotionally mature behavior, fixes these people in an endless cycle of generations living in a twilight zone of sub-human existence. It is of interest that recent studies by Charles Murray reveal that the same causes have produced a permanent white underclass in small cities as well as large ones.

There are, it seems to me, two important lessons to be learned from the Moyers' TV program. The first is that we have made a profound mistake in abandoning the moral and ethical values which sustained a remarkable level of civic virtue in the American colonies and which continued to give character and vitality to the American nation through its first century and a half. In the inner-city today where no social institutions exert a civilizing and restraining influence, and where concentrated poverty aggravates all the most destructive consequences of the rejection of a cooperative value system, there has been a cultural meltdown. The damage is inflicted not only upon the residents and the property and the institutions of the inner-city, but it also radiates poisons into the surrounding areas: crime, drugs, prostitution, and mistrust of all strangers.

The second large lesson is that, contrary to what

John A. Howard, "Civic Virtue and the Modern City," *The St. Croix Review,* August 1986. Reprinted with permission.

has been supposed, there cannot be any special strategies and programs that will alleviate the problems of inner-city populations. Their problems are not unique. The plight of the inner-city is nothing but the plight of the entire society in its most aggravated and concentrated form. Any successful remedial action will have to address the problems, generically, for the whole society. To the extent that a nationwide program brings relief, the inner-city people will benefit proportionately more than other people.

Little Hope for the Black Family

The point deserves illustration. For a long time, there has been a growing chorus of black columnists and black sociologists, black clergy and black civic leaders, all crying out that America must not tolerate the further destruction of the black family. They insist that we must move swiftly to help blacks rebuild a respect for marriage, a commitment to the traditional family. Those who join in this appeal include liberals and conservatives and progressives and people with no labels at all. They are simply black leaders who have eyes to see and hearts to care about the ever-worsening circumstances of inner-city life.

Are there ways to reestablish among inner-city blacks a new allegiance to the family norm while the rest of society keeps marching further away from that norm into the realms of sexual liberation and sexual aberration? Not likely. Listen to this interchange between Bill Moyers and Detective Shahid Jackson of the Newark police force.

Det. Jackson: You're born into a dead end, you know. And you're in that rut. If you're born into that cycle situation, how do you escape?

Moyers: Why do they have kids so early? Why do these children have children? This is a dead end; that's a perfect description for it.

Det. Jackson: Well, when I was growin' up, sex was almost a dirty word. Now, sex is what's happening. You know, they see sex on TV, sex in the movies, sex everywhere. And some girls think it's cute walking down the streets pregnant.

There is no way the family can be restored to a position of high respect among inner-city blacks while the national culture aggressively celebrates the sex-is-what's-happening laidback lifestyle. The catastrophe of the inner-city black family is the catastrophe of the whole concept of the family in America. The one cannot be repaired unless the other is.

The Family's Role

It is not just black leaders who have come to recognize the pivotal role played by the family in determining the productive or destructive life course for the children. In [a] major study of street and youth gangs . . . the first item cited among the

probable causes which lead to youth involvement in gangs and delinquent activity is the ravaged condition of the family.

> The family has always been the basic institution of society. . . . It is there the child learns to love, to be loved, to work, to play, and to worship. It is a place where the child is cared for and taught the value of getting along with people of all ages. However, the family has undergone a dramatic change. For all practical purposes, the nuclear family no longer exists. . . . Traditional values, attitudes, and skills are not being taught to many of our children in their homes.

Here is one other brief quotation from that same report.

> What do street/youth gangs do? Gangs pass on values, develop attitudes and skills required to achieve their primary purpose. They provide their members with the same advantages as do other normal groups. The major difference between joining a gang or a scout troop is one of values, attitudes, and activities. Both groups meet the same basic human needs of belonging, acceptance, security and being somebody. The scout troop will concentrate on developing constructive values, attitudes and skills, while the gang may shoplift, sell drugs, assault, and engage in numerous other criminal activities that relate to their purposes.

Values and attitudes, values and attitudes—the recurrent theme of the Moyers' documentary and the Rockford gang study, and the chorus favoring a strong black family. It would take a long time to list and describe all the headaches and the heartaches that bedevil the mayor of a modern city, but I think it a safe conjecture that a large majority of the most difficult and the most costly problems with which a mayor must deal have their roots in this matter of destructive values and attitudes.

"The plight of the inner-city is nothing but the plight of the entire society in its most aggravated and concentrated form."

In times gone by there was a consensus of support among American citizens for a set of principles that defined civic virtue. Those principles specified what was right and what was wrong, and how a good citizen should behave. Patrick Henry, for example, wrote that he was guided through his life by a credo instilled in him by his uncle. It was, "To be true and just in all my dealings. To bear no malice or hatred in my heart. To keep my hands from picking and stealing. Not to covet other mens' goods, but to learn and labor to get my own living, and to do my duty in that state of life into which it shall please God to call me."

I think that says it all rather nicely, but if you or

I . . . were to take to the streets and the air waves to urge that the Patrick Henry credo be taught to all our young people in the schools and colleges, you know what would happen. First, many folks finding the vocabulary a little heavy, would suppose some character actor had escaped from a Shakespearean tragedy. But the big reaction would come from those who do understand, and who will be outraged that anyone should try to impose a single concept of right behavior on anyone else, much less on all our young people.

"Are there ways to reestablish among inner-city blacks a new allegiance to the family norm while the rest of society keeps marching further away from that norm . . . ? Not likely."

Here we are at the crux of the whole thing. Here we are, as I see it, at the fulcrum on which will balance the chance for building hope and civility and productiveness and dignity among inner-city residents or relegating them permanently to dismal, marginal living. Will the American culture permit the reestablishment of societal ideals of virtuous conduct and societal standards of right conduct and wrong conduct? At the present time, any suggestion that our nation should embrace a specific set of ideals and standards will provoke fear, anger, and scorn rather than praise from the news media, the universities and, sad to say, even a number of religious bodies. Value-neutrality, or non-judgmentalism as it is called, sits in the heart of power in America's opinion-making activities.

If that seems an overstatement, I invite you to try to enumerate the non-black columnists, non-black sociologists, non-black clergy and non-black civic leaders who have even acknowledged, much less endorsed, the pervasive appeals of prominent black spokesmen to rescue and reinvigorate the black family.

This is not the occasion to review our progression from a society in which civic virtue had specific meaning and was embraced by a solid majority of Americans to a society wherein the very term "civic virtue" is regarded as an anachronism in the dominant culture. There is, however, one category of participants who have been so influential in bringing about the change and are so powerful in resisting a reversal that we need to understand their role.

Defending a Free Society

There are professional groups which are the natural guardians and defenders of the political principles of the free society. Journalists of every

political persuasion close ranks to prevent any narrowing of the interpretation of the First Amendment. So, too, do college and university professors when academic freedom is at issue. Any question bearing on the right to privacy will also bring a phalanx of defenders of that principle.

There are, however, occasions when the free exercise of one of those political principles causes a genuine problem for society. When such a conflict does occur, it turns out to be a lopsided encounter and an almost instantaneous victory. There is no effort to find a workable accommodation between two worthy and important concerns that have clashed. The defenders of the political principle rise in such numbers and with such indignation, that the people charged with safeguarding the community usually back way off and are reduced to nibbling at the edges of the problem.

For example, a number of state legislatures have tried to do something about pornography. The professional guardians of freedom of speech and freedom of the press so forcefully opposed any restrictions on what may be printed that the pornography laws usually end up with only a tiny fragment of substance forbidding the enlistment of children under a stated age, perhaps 14 or 15, in the production of pornographic materials. The implication of such a restriction is that as soon as the child has reached the specified age, he's fair game for pornographers. The legislators don't mean that, of course, but an endangered child is about the only thing that can withstand the impassioned lobby for freedom of speech and freedom of the press, and so the legislators hide behind the bibs of the little children.

You will recognize that any effort to reestablish the traditional family as the desirable pattern for life in our society is going to encounter more extensive and aggressive organized opposition than did the pornography laws. Even so, I am convinced that the family must be restored as the societal norm before we can realistically hope for progress in reconstituting standards of civic virtue. If within the family, as the most fundamental of human relationships, there is no pattern of commitment, cooperation, and willing sacrifice, then it is naive to suppose that self-disciplined civility and cooperation can be made the acceptable norm for strangers living together as fellow citizens. The family is where we must begin to reweave the fabric of a civilized, sensitive, helpful, and amicable community.

A Difficult Task

The restoration of the family norm and of the moral code that sustains the family may seem too difficult a task. It did to Bill Moyers. He was talking to a Mrs. Wallace who, with her husband, runs a community center which serves the troubled people in downtown Newark. Listen to that conversation. I will conclude my remarks with it, because Mrs. Wallace says most eloquently what needs to be said.

Moyers: You're worried about the black family. You think it's precarious.

Mrs. Wallace: . . . It's gonna be an endangered species.

Moyers: Even though the messages that kids are getting from the society seem to say, "Do anything you want to," the United States Government, the government of New Jersey, a whiteman like Moyers can't step in and say to young black kids, "It's not right to have children out of wedlock; welfare needs to be changed; you've got to take responsibility." Who's going to say these things to these kids?

Mrs. Wallace: Why can't you say it?

Moyers: They won't listen to me.

Mrs. Wallace: It doesn't make any difference; you gotta say it anyway. They may not listen to me, either. But I'm saying if you say it in your corner and I say it in my corner, and everybody is saying it, it's going to be like a drumbeat. But it's not just for me to talk about, it's for us all to talk about. And it's going to surpass [people's] color. And you're not going to be safe, and I'm not going to be safe unless we send out this drumbeat. Let's deal with it. Let's deal with the problem.

John A. Howard is president of the Rockford Institute, a conservative research organization located in Rockford, Illinois.

The Black Family Is Alive and Well

James Lyke

Two years have passed since my black brother bishops and I addressed you in our first pastoral. "What We Have Seen and Heard" announced our coming of age as it shared our enduring gifts within the family of our Catholic Church.

"What We Have Seen and Heard" dealt with many issues. However, many black Catholics in our diocese and many across the country felt that the section on black family should be addressed in a special way. Therefore, I am directing these thoughts to you, the black Catholics of the Diocese of Cleveland. This pastoral reflection also offers me the opportunity to follow up on Bishop Pilla's inspiring pastoral, "The Christian Family: The Church of the Home," a document he prepared for the entire diocesan family.

My friends, we are all in search of family, "the heart of the Christian community," built on the common ground where our right to belong is never questioned and our claim to dignity and to love are unassailable. This is what we black bishops said in "What We Have Seen and Heard." Though this pastoral letter commented on many issues, all were, in a sense, "issues of the family." Thus, in this pastoral reflection I now address to you, I build upon the ideas of "What We Have Seen and Heard."

The need has been made abundantly clear. Programs and conferences like "The Vanishing Black Family" and "The Summit Conference on the Black Family" have served only to heighten the importance of the subject. Some would say that only a total effort of the African-American community can save the traditional black family from destruction. . . .

For us the family has always meant "the extended family"—parents, grandparents, uncles, aunts, godparents, all those related by kinship or strong friendship. In practice, the extended family often goes beyond kinship and marital relationship to include persons who, having no family of their own, have been accepted into the wider family circle. These family members feel a deep responsibility for one another in both ordinary times of daily life and in the extraordinary moments of need or crises.

There are those who believe that the extended family continues to exist only among blacks in the rural South. However, one social worker wrote:

"Even today, the extended family still plays a dominant role in the survival of black people in rural and urban areas. Without the black extended family, the prisons, nursing homes, foster homes, soup kitchens and shelters for the poor in urban areas would be more crowded with blacks than they are now. The extended family assures thousands of jobless urban blacks the basic amenities of life. It informally adopts thousands of children whose parents cannot properly take care of them. It keeps thousands of elderly people from being unwanted and alone in the cities. And in countless other ways, black kin aid one another in urban areas." . . .

We Have Survived

I know that the "demise" of the black family is a cyclical theme in American mythology, perhaps arising from the unconscious desire that we might disappear. However, for black people there has always been the conscious realization that, through the grace of God, we have survived every test of evil and oppressive systems.

At the same time, my brothers and sisters, we must not avoid reality. To do so would be naive. We are dealing with crises within the black family. We must respond as free people in controlling our destinies, even when we cannot control all forces that intrude upon the sanctity of our lives as families.

James Lyke, "The Family in the Black Community," *Origins*, December 25, 1986.

When I think how the circumstances of our society make survival of black family life difficult, the words of Henry Highland Garnet echo in my mind:

"The forlorn condition in which you are placed does not destroy your moral obligation to God. You are not certain of heaven, because you suffer yourselves to remain in a state of slavery, where you cannot obey the commandments of the sovereign of the universe. If the ignorance of slavery is a passport to heaven, then it is a blessing, and no curse, and you should rather desire its perpetuity than its abolition. God will not receive slavery, nor ignorance, nor any other state of mind, for love and obedience to him."

Henry Highland Garnet addressed his black sisters and brothers trapped in slavery, one of the most sinful arrangements any society has every conceived. Nonetheless, the message is clear for us as well: We must with all our strength resist any system that saps our moral values, robs us of our spiritual life and degrades our humanity.

"In slavery and freedom, black people have used all of the resources at their disposal to ensure the endurance of the family."

As John Blassingame and Herbert Gutman attest, marriage and family were of overwhelming importance to African-Americans in slavery and freedom. They fought to maintain their families despite the persistence of the malevolent forces that strove to destroy them. In slavery and freedom, black people have used all of the resources at their disposal to ensure the endurance of the family.

Black families must continue to think "free." We must not permit economic or social arrangements to enslave us individually or as families. While we cannot control all the ways in which society chooses to define our portion, we must control the ways in which our family values are formulated and lived. *Family is survival.*

In Search of Common Ground

If I am to speak of family to you, friends, we must have a common ground on which we stand as Catholic and as black. I am reminded of a passage from one of the last books of Howard Thurman, the great black man of religion, a mystic and a teacher. He wrote:

"At this moment, there is vast urgency . . . for isolating the black experience . . . and establishing on that basis a grand windbreak behind which the black community can define and articulate its unique identity as a self-conscious participant in

American and, indeed, world society."

Our common ground, sisters and brothers, must be the "value ground" of our religion and our culture. It is the shared definitions, the shared assumptions, the deep unspoken reasons why we do what we do. We must learn to articulate the unspoken values. We must state the shared truths ourselves. We must define ourselves.

Still, it is impossible to speak of African-American people and their condition without speaking of racism. Racism, even today, is most violently and destructively alive when its victims see their world through its prism and can only see themselves as powerless.

One of the most dangerous traits of black people is our tendency to absorb, sometimes uncritically, negative images of ourselves. The outpouring of articles and the innumerable comments on subjects ranging from the black underclass, black-on-black crime, pregnancy among black teen-agers, etc., have often been the work and utterances of black people. While we have no intention of denying the existence of these problems, we must not degenerate into a "blaming the victim" mentality. We must recognize the strengths in black families, which function in spite of the vicissitudes of life as communities in which common meaning exists.

Let us, then, look at the institution that the Lord used to deliver us to this place, the traditional black family, the institution that we must consecrate anew.

The Black Family

The black family is the heart of our culture. It is the link between private pain and public joy, between the glorious expression of the demands of godliness and the earthly canons of issues and ideas.

The black family teaches black people values, a philosophy, a view of the world rooted in ancient tradition and a theology learned on the other side of the Jordan, a theology that begins and ends with God's calling and coming "for to carry us home."

The black family teaches us the notion of sacrifice for kin, reverence for the aged and the child, and belief in the natural sequence of cause and effect.

The black family is the place of our life; the place in which we move; the mirror through which we discover our being. The black family is the "domestic church" in which we learn who we are and whose we are and how we are to live.

The black family is our school, where we have learned in the work and the worries and the wonder of every day how to venerate the "natural human" over the sounding brass of machines with all their magic, how to hold the deed in esteem above the wish, where we learn that God sees the mind and knows the heart and—"everybody talkin' 'bout heaven ain't goin' there."

The black family is where we have learned to love life. The black family is the prophet who foretold the coming of an age of justice, love and peace. It produced the Sojourners and the Harriets, the Martins and the Malcolms, that old train of men and women who knew and taught their children freedom, who knew their lives would be transformed into the immortal freedom that the Lord would grant their posterity.

The black family is the sanctuary in which black men and women loved and were loved when nobody knew their troubles except Jesus and the blood.

The black family is the institution that has endured in spite of the insistence down through history that it, like the people who made it, was a flaw on the face of the earth, requiring no respect and commanding no care.

For black people in America, family is a value. In the African culture of our foreparents, the *I* and the *me* found meaning in the *us* and the *we*. It was the sense that family and community gave identity to the person.

Because family was a value, so too was marriage. Marriage and its permanence were critical. It was in this context that children would be born and grow and survive. Children would be taught as were their parents. Rare is the black family without its proverbial charter for principled survival in the infinity of tight places occasioned by racist oppression. In short, holding fast to values was a family value: the soul-bound belief that if we kept our values, they would keep us as a people. . . .

Faith

A Raisin in the Sun is a classic play about the Younger family. They are poor. They are black. They are crowded—grandmother, her daughter, her son, his wife and child. The daughter, Beneatha, plans to go to medical school. She and her mother, Lena, are discussing Beneatha's future:

Beneatha: Listen, I'm going to be a doctor. I'm not worried about who I'm going to marry yet—if I ever get married. . .

Mama: (Kindly) 'Course you going to be a doctor, honey, God willing.

Beneatha: (Drily) God hasn't got a thing to do with it.

Mama: Beneatha—that wasn't necessary.

Beneatha: Well—neither is God. I get sick of hearing about God.

Mama: Beneatha!

Beneatha: I mean it! I'm just tired of hearing about God all the time. What has he got to do with anything? Does he pay tuition?

Mama: You 'bout to get your fresh little jaw slapped!

Ruth: That's just what she needs, all right!

Beneatha: Why? Why can't I say what I want to around here, like everyone else?

Mama: It don't sound nice for a young girl to say

things like that—you wasn't brought up that way. Me and your father went to trouble to get you and Brother to church every Sunday.

Beneatha: Mama, you don't understand. It's all a matter of ideas, and God is just one idea I don't accept. It's not important. I am not going out and be immoral or commit crimes because I don't believe in God. I don't even think about it. It's just that I get tired of him getting credit for all the things the human race achieves through its own stubborn effort. There simply is no blasted God—there is only man, and it is he who makes miracles!

(Mama absorbs this speech, studies her daughter and rises slowly and crosses to Beneatha and slaps her powerfully across the face. After, there is only silence and the daughter drops her eyes from her mother's face, and Mama is very tall before her.)

> *"The black family is the institution that has endured in spite of the insistence down through history that it . . . was a flaw on the face of the earth."*

Mama: Now—you say after me, in my mother's house there is still God. (There is a long pause and Beneatha stares at the floor wordlessly. Mama repeats the phrase with precision and cool emotion.) In my mother's house there is still God.

Beneatha: In my mother's house there is still God. (A long pause)

Mama: (Walking away from Beneatha, too disturbed for triumphant posture. Stopping and turning back to her daughter.) There are some ideas we ain't going to have in this house. Not long as I am at the head of this family.

Beneatha: Yes, ma'am.

In the house of the black Christian family there must be God. Faithful, we must be, with the faith that is the "confident assurance concerning what we hope for, and conviction about things we do not see."

This faith—that in the domain of our forebears there was always God, that in our house there is still God, that everything in our life as a people is a revelation of the Lord, is the context in which our strength is to be understood. It is this faith that grounds our memory. It is in this memory that our values preside. The healthy black family is a family that cooperates because of its common memory and values.

James Lyke is auxiliary bishop of Cleveland.

"It is crucial to remedy neglect of the family by the state taking an active role in promoting and supporting strong family life."

Government Programs Strengthen the Family

Lela B. Costin

Concern is expressed in many quarters about the ability of "the family" to care for its children. This is not surprising in troubled times. To contemplate the ubiquitous accounts of divorce, single-parent families, teenage pregnancies, child abuse, domestic violence, school failures, drug use, and lack of marketable skills among many parents and their adolescent children is to be drawn into a disturbing anxiety about the status of the family with respect to its childrearing functions.

To assume that denial of parental duty has increased, reflecting a new inherent weakness in the family as an institution, may be unjustified. It is an assumption that overlooks the not always steady but significant gains that have been made in the care of the nation's children, physically, intellectually, emotionally, and socially. These improvements in the state of the child have required the cooperation of parents. In many instances, parents themselves have played a critical role in major social policy changes affecting parental duties. A notable example is the passage of the Education for All Handicapped Children Act in 1975 which prohibited the exclusion of handicapped children from school and insured a free and appropriate education for the handicapped child. In doing so, the act strengthened family life by making obsolete the necessity to send handicapped children out of the family into institutions for some uncertain level of both education and childrearing. Other examples of the gains in good parenting include the trend toward a more active role of fathers in child care, the growing instances of successful joint parenting through shared custody following divorce, and a more informed understanding on the part of many parents of the concepts of childhood and child development.

Many of the problems that hold the spotlight in today's ahistorical era are very old problems. Rather than signifying some new breakdown of parental care and responsibility, we might take the position that it is a mark of maturity that the public, including millions of parents, is now willing to confront openly some of these centuries old, previously concealed phenomena, for example wife-mother battering and sexual abuse of children. The sale of cocaine on school grounds, an important concern today, was documented in the child-protection literature as early as the 1920s. Pregnancy among teenagers has occurred through generations with common remedies being (1) adoptive placement, which served a social purpose for childless couples or (2) early marriage, which legitimized the child and weakened public censure. Leaving aside the question of the extent to which the incidence of these old problems has increased, the ominous factor today is that they occur in a vastly changed world from that of a few decades ago. Today's disturbing social problems stem from causes different from those of the past; today's remedies must be different as well.

Pressures on Parents

High population mobility with the concomitant loss of family and neighborhood support groups, disintegrating patterns of community, soaring housing and medical costs, widespread unemployment among both adults and older adolescents in a new technological labor market, the growing necessity for both parents to provide income for the family, the frustrations that arise from attempts to arrange stable and nurturing child care during working hours, schools that may provide neither essential learning nor physical safety—these are some of the conditions that often place intolerable pressures on parents struggling to bring their children into healthy and productive adulthood.

Published by permission from Transaction Publishers, "Is the Family Neglectful or Neglected?" by Lela B. Costin, SOCIETY, Volume 24, No. 3, March/April 1987. Copyright © 1987 by Transaction Publishers.

In a society that provides insufficient and unreliable social supports for the family, the result is erosion of valuable family strengths.

Parents with sufficient personal resources and supports usually function very well. Many others could do better with access to preventive and supportive services. Undeniably, some parents are hazardous to their children and will require society's protective intervention under legal sanctions. In any case, the family is the only reliable and continuing institution that we have for the rearing and nurturing of children. Our best substitutes for the family are only substitutes. It is crucial to remedy neglect of the family by the state taking an active role in promoting and supporting strong family life.

The old value of the sanctity of the family and the right of parents, within limits, to rear their children without outside intervention is still valid. As has been true for generations, this value is too often called upon to justify ignoring the need for protection of children and the lack of social services. Acknowledging the problems in our society that bear upon parents so heavily raises the question of the right of parents to essential and tested societal supports.

Crises and Cutbacks

The power of parents to maintain a decent and reliable standard of living is an essential component of children's well-being. This relationship was recognized in 1909 when the participants of the first White House Conference on the Care of Dependent Children stated the often quoted principle that a child's own home should not be broken up for reasons of poverty. The conference urged that financial aid be given to maintain suitable homes for the rearing of children. In the decades that followed, poverty in America has been rediscovered, awakening the conscience of citizens and prompting legislation to interrupt the cycle of poverty. Unfortunately, these attempts at reform have tended to be unsustained or, at best, continued at a level that leaves recipient families still in poverty. Distractions among policymakers as other major social and economic problems press forward, coupled with outmoded attitudes of much of the public toward the poor, have defeated progress in ending poverty. Widespread restrictive beliefs hold that it is the nature of the poor to be poor and that they have particular characteristics that predispose them to poverty, thus precluding effective societal remedies. Such a frame of reference ignores the poverty inducing impact on a set of environmental forces over which an individual has little or no control.

The damaging effects of poverty upon children's growth and development begin early and too often continue throughout their lives. Poor mothers lack adequate prenatal care and proper nutrition. Their babies are at risk of prematurity and low birth weight with all the attendant risks. Low birth weight is clearly associated with poverty, which denies mothers and their children adequate nutrition, health care, and housing. Poor parents endure debilitating stress in their efforts to provide material necessities, stress that erodes their potential to attend to their children's developmental needs. Poor people live among other poor people in neighborhoods that are often dangerous and lack the quality of public services of higher income neighborhoods. Despite the movement in the 1960s to establish neighborhood-based services, clinics and social agencies still are usually located outside of poor neighborhoods. Mothers have no safe place to leave their children while they seek help or go to their jobs. Their children are subject to gross inequality of opportunity at school and in the working world. Their mothers almost inevitably become involved with the dominant society's agents who scrutinize and judge their behavior. Coping with crises such as lack of money or food, homelessness that is not solved by shelter programs, family violence, serious illness, demands to assist in the care of peripheral family members—all these constraints on well-being and effective parenting are almost routine for poor families.

> *"The old value of the sanctity of the family . . . is too often called upon to justify ignoring the need for protection of children and the lack of social services."*

In the last decade, poverty in America has increased dramatically. This loss in the population's well-being has been compounded in the 1980s by a severe recession and heavy cutbacks in hard-won social programs: Aid to Families with Dependent Children, food stamps, day care, Medicaid, training, employment, and more. In the slack economy, the safety net of social services and forms of cash assistance has become virtually nonexistent for many poor and near poor families. The burden of poverty has fallen disproportionately on women who head families and upon their children. Recent statistics show that one child in five is classified as poor. Minority children in female-headed families fare the worst: two out of every three of these children live in poverty.

Women on Welfare

The relationship of indigent men to welfare policy has been conditioned largely by the work ethic and historical concerns about the effect of relief on the ablebodied male. For women who are dependent upon the state for support, a variant of this ethic plays a more central and controlling role. Mimi Abramowitz, in the 1985 *Journal of Social Work Education*, defined this variant as the "family ethic," a familiar and well-worn social norm that defines a woman's proper status as married, at home, bearing and rearing children, and supported by a male breadwinner whose needs come before her own. In the labor-short, agricultural economy of colonial America, women, although at home, were expected to be, and were rewarded for being, economically productive. A facet of the work ethic was thus incorporated into the family ethic. Poor women who moved out of their prescribed role and family form were subject to punishments in the administration of relief policies, including the denial of relief in their own homes, the loss of their children on charges of unfitness, being contracted-out to exchange their labor for support, and other forms of control. In her examination of the family ethic in relation to the female indigent, Abramowitz showed how these punishments were intensified with industrialization. With transformation of an agricultural economy to an industrial pattern, men moved out of the home for work. Women found themselves denied a productive economic role at home, and their relationship to family and home intensified. At the same time this cult of domesticity excluded respectability from increasing numbers of immigrant female workers who were recruited into the postcivil war industrial expansion at meager wages, leaving them vulnerable to the status of pauper and dependent upon harsh relief policies. Public relief and "welfare" policy began to focus more directly on the female heads of households.

Keeping the Family Strong

Conflicting attitudes toward the role of women at home and in the workplace reflected an ambivalence in beliefs as to the best way to keep the family system strong as an essential ingredient of social order. A major policy issue was how to use public assistance to protect the "suitable home" and enable worthy dependent mothers to care for their children in that home, and at the same time protect the children of "unworthy" mothers who had moved farthest from the female role of the family ethic. As a result, conflicting tendencies were built into mothers' pension programs of the early twentieth century. To protect their new programs and secure public support, reformers applied a policy of financial aid for the dependent children of mothers who came closest to the role prescribed by the family ethic—usually those who were white, widowed, or separated—if no fault attached to the mother. Those who failed to fit this mode were deemed unsuitable, forced to seek work outside their homes, and placed at risk of losing their children to

the care of foster homes or institutions.

The Aid to Families with Dependent Children (AFDC) program began with commitment to the family ethic. Large numbers of families had been disrupted by the Great Depression. The new program was to provide public assistance rather than an innovative child welfare service. Needed income was to be made available to mothers so that they could be restored to carrying out their own normal adult responsibilities to children. During the early years of AFDC, minimum concern was expressed about the program, largely because it fit the acceptable model carried over from the mothers' pension movement. A conflict in the underlying philosophy of the program did not yet have to be faced, but its outlines could be found in the combination of new and old values on which the AFDC program was being built.

"In the slack economy, the safety net of social services and forms of cash assistance has become virtually nonexistent for many poor and near poor families."

New emphasis was being given to the value of the child's own family and the importance of a mother's being able to maintain a home in which she could continue to rear her children in her own way. Social workers who helped to develop and administer the new depression-born programs believed that relief should be given in ways that preserved the dignity and sense of self-worth of the recipients. The family's right to economic security was emphasized. There was also the old allegiance to moralistic evaluation of good and bad homes, with strong undertones of stigma attached to poverty, especially when mothers and children were not only poor but also did not fit the expectations of the family ethic.

Major changes in social and economic conditions after 1950 escalated the numbers of families on AFDC and its costs. Reasons for dependency were more and more related to desertion, separation, divorce, and unmarried parenthood—all suspect as unacceptable departures from the family ethic. In an attempt to reduce case loads, new work requirements, benign and coercive, were used to move "unsuitable" mothers into the low-paid jobs for which poor, immigrant, minority women could qualify.

Current public assistance policy presents an AFDC mother with a dilemma: a grant that leaves her and her children well below the official poverty level; probable loss of the grant if she works regularly even at the low-wage employment she can secure, plus probable loss of essential benefits such as food stamps and Medicaid. President Reagan's proposal to simplify the public assistance system by supplying one direct grant to a family and to substitute cash for other forms of aid such as food stamps, housing subsidies, and day care is deceptive. If adopted it may well complicate the lives of poor mothers further. Welfare recipients live in poverty all the time. Any extra cash is subject to use for any one of a demanding list of pressing needs. Intensive counseling, which is not presently available, would become essential to assist many families in managing their money. The proposal also ignores the insufficient number of varied social services at a place and cost that public-aid recipients can manage.

Directions for Reform

In seeking policy changes to improve the lives of poor families, the traditional role assigned to women must be readdressed. Many of the hardships and inequities endured by mothers on public assistance flow from the prejudices, expectations, and constraints embedded in the family ethic as it has been applied to these women, holding them answerable for all their families' problems. A higher level of support is essential in those states that leave AFDC mothers deepest in poverty. Equally needed throughout is an expanded job market for women and effective job training programs, particularly ones that enable young mothers to gain work experience, earnings, and self-respect. The range of penalties that all women and especially poor women experience as a price for working requires attention and correction in public aid policy. Given the disadvantages and deprivation that poor children endure, provision of day care to keep young children safe while their mothers work and to give these children the proven benefits of planned preschool experience is basic to improving their well-being. For purposes of revising public aid policy, new studies are needed that will reveal more sensitively the daily lives of public aid families. Especially important is a clearer understanding of the characteristics and coping patterns of those mothers who move off the welfare rolls, how they achieved that move, at what risks and price, and what specific problems they experience in becoming independent.

Basic for effective welfare reform is an understanding of the career line of public aid recipients after they begin to receive payments. For some time, policymakers have accepted findings that said at least half of AFDC recipients leave the program within two years. A more cautious view has been that welfare recipients do leave the rolls within a relatively short period but are unable to sustain this gain and are forced back upon welfare payments again and again. From his current study of over five thousand welfare families, Charles A. Murray reports, in *Losing Ground: American Social Policy,*

1950-1980, that among the youngest entrants into AFDC, long-term involvement is the norm and that a large majority of new entrants under twenty-five years of age stay on the rolls for at least five years.

These new findings are not completely surprising. Applicants to AFDC are now more often older teenagers who have probably dropped out of school, who lack marketable skills that can command a living wage, and who are in a state of uncertainty about their future relationship to the baby's father. That these welfare mothers require five years or more to search for and possibly find a way to escape a life of welfare dependency is not unlike the time required by middle-class mothers who, for the sake of rearing children, set aside their uncompleted career preparation and eventually require time to successfully reenter the labor market.

"That these welfare mothers require five years or more to . . . escape a life of welfare dependency is not unlike the time required by middle-class mothers who . . . successfully reenter the labor market."

What seems clear is something that many critics of public welfare have advocated for some years: the proposition that welfare recipients and other poor people are not all alike. They fit into different categories. To be effective, policy changes must reflect an understanding of these differences with provisions for more flexible programs and expectations. . . .

The report of the Reagan administration's inter-departmental Working Group on the Family illustrates a persisting ideology which holds that liberal approaches to reducing poverty and to other social supports for families are destructive of family life. Disagreement and struggle over the basic tenets of welfare reform are to be expected. More objective and dispassionate study will be required to achieve effective social welfare policy for strengthening family life.

Lela B. Costin is professor emerita at the University of Illinois, Urbana-Champaign. She has taught and written extensively on policy issues related to social services for families, children, and school-age youth.

Government Programs Harm the Family

Allan C. Carlson

"Privatization" is a relatively new political word. It describes the process whereby modern welfare states divest themselves of the ownership of goods and resources or of the detailed regulation of private activities. Usually, state economic activity is the focus.

There may be merit, though, in transferring the concept to the social policy realm and in raising a call to "privatize" the family. It is certainly true that the private/public distinction lies at the heart of America's current family problem. Most recent historians of the family, for example, have made the argument that the traditional American view of family life as "private" is historically peculiar, bound only to the "abnormal" system of bourgeois capitalism. They argue that extensive public intrusion into family life is the normal pattern of human existence, and they would like to see much more of it in this country.

It would be foolish, of course, to misuse the privatization paradigm and to force an analysis of the family into an inappropriate economic framework. For many Americans, family life is primarily a question of private values—or even metaphysics—with no apparent connection to demand curves and measures of marginal utility. Nonetheless, a focus on the public intrusion into private family life and the identification of strategies to free the family from the public yoke are the central tasks for a modern family policy agenda.

The Family and the State

We might begin by exploring the true history of the family and the state. An honest look at the development of the Western Christian philosophical tradition reveals that, for most of our civilization's history, the autonomy of the family relative to

government was virtually unchallenged. This understanding was born with Aristotle, who, in rejecting Plato's utopian vision of a shared community of wives and children, argued that all human society began through "a union of those who cannot exist without each other; namely, of male and female, that the race may continue." This marital bond, expanding into the household, served as "the first" social institution.

When several of these households united, Aristotle said, the village was born, and as several villages came together, the state sprang into existence. The foundation of social order, though, clearly lay in the natural society of the home.

The Christian theological tradition carried forward this understanding. Augustine, the fifth-century Bishop of Hippo, saw the union of man, woman, and their children as the sole "natural bond of human society," the place where humans learned the power of love and friendship. In contrast, his opinion of the state was low. "What are kingdoms but great robberies?" he wrote. "For what are robberies themselves, but little kingdoms? The band itself is made up of men; it is ruled by the authority of a prince; it is knit together by the pact of confederacy; the booty is divided by the law agreed on." It is true that Medieval theologian Thomas Aquinas saw the human as "a social animal" and understood the state to be an institution complementing familial bonds. Newborns depended on the family group for their birth and early nurture, while the state also "provide[d] public services beyond the means of one household, and for moral advantage." Aquinas was clear, though, that the state's role was one of service to and support of the family. The 16th-century reformer Martin Luther stressed that marriage was the first and primary social bond, a natural community instituted by God for the bearing and raising of children and for the renewal of society. As he wrote: "There is no higher office, estate,

Allan C. Carlson, "Privatizing the Family," *Persuasion at Work*, November 1986. Reprinted with permission.

condition, or work than the estate of marriage." Luther saw government as an imperfect human device instituted by God to maintain order by preventing vice and by punishing those who offended society, so protecting the natural society of the family.

A Traditional Vision

This traditional vision carried into modern times. In his 1891 encyclical *Rerum Novarum*, Pope Leo XIII declared: "Behold, therefore, the family, a very small society indeed, but a true one, and older than any polity! . . . For that reason it must have certain rights and duties of its own entirely independent of the state." Leo denounced the temptations of the state to displace the family, to weaken marriage, or to undermine parental authority, and called on governments to permit maximum freedom of action for families.

Recent centuries, though, have witnessed the eclipse of this religiously grounded defense of family autonomy. Instead, the family has increasingly found itself under siege, an attack that one commentator has labeled "sweeping and unremitting." In light of the privatization model, it is instructive to note that this intervention of the state into family life and the progressive restriction of family autonomy has occurred for reasons identical to those long used to justify state intervention into the economy and state ownership of resources and industry. . . .

Those Unintended Consequences

Studies of state regulation of the economy over the last decade have revealed that government ownership and regulation of resources produces a vast array of distortions, inefficiencies, and unintended consequences, a perverse warping of intended outcomes. Not surprisingly, state regulation of the family has had similar consequences.

In his comprehensive history of American efforts to control juvenile delinquency, for instance, Robert Mennel discovered a system of almost unredeemed "drudgery and debasement," where "institutions and juvenile courts smothered decent instincts and encouraged further crime and deviance." Turn-of-the-century reform schools, geared to turning out farmhands for a declining rural sector, were primarily characterized by "a fair amount of deviant sexual activity." Methods of control within the institutions varied from jack-booted systems of physical punishment to "reform-school self-government," allowing "boy captains" to win their positions by physically terrorizing other children or by spying on fellow inmates. From 1825 to the present, Mennel shows, the juvenile justice system has been characterized primarily by intense competition between "reform schools," "parental schools," "industrial schools," the juvenile courts, the foster system, and "private" philanthropies for

shares of the lucrative "child-saving" business. He notes that even the middle class, which spawned the "child-savers" as a means of social control, now finds itself at risk, as "affluent parents . . . come to realize that they can no longer guarantee their children's immunity from the system of juvenile justice so long reserved for the children of the less favored."

Campaigns against child abuse have had similar unintended results. Under existing reporting laws, and given the "appropriations" appeal of the "stop child abuse cry," state welfare authorities have a strong interest in maximizing the number of reports of abuse and the number of families dragged into the system. Accordingly, in 1985 alone, at least 500,000 *innocent* American families were falsely accused of child abuse and dragged to varying degrees through the indignities and subtle terrors of a state investigation into their character. There is growing evidence, moreover, that the very act of state intervention into the family, even "for the best motives," commonly worsens an already negative situation. The psychological relationship of the child to his parents requires the privacy of family life, under the guardianship of parents who are seen as autonomous. When the state intervenes and family integrity is broken, the young child's needs are denied and his belief in his parents as omniscient is prematurely shaken. As three eminent scholars have concluded, "The law does not have the capacity to supervise the fragile, complex interpersonal bonds between child and parent. As *parens patriae* the state is too crude an instrument to become an adequate substitute for flesh and blood parents."

> "There may be merit . . . in raising a call to 'privatize' the family."

Research in Britain supports this contention, showing that visits by social workers to families actually *increase* the battering of children. Among families supervised by the state, the incidence of "rebattering" was found to be 60 percent; among families without supervision, the "rebattering" rate was estimated to be only 30 percent. It is also striking how little attention is given to the children who are abused or die in state institutions, "shelters," or foster care, perhaps the most widespread of officially covered-up crimes. Moreover, there is mounting evidence that social welfare professionals know no limits in identifying children at risk. An influential current theory sees abuse in any cultural setting where a stratified relationship exists or where the "victim" is treated as an inferior. As one sociologist frankly concedes, "If this interpretation is right (and it must be at least part of the explanation), then *all children* are at risk of abuse and [state] registers should contain the names of the whole child population.''

Third, family allowances have proven more attractive in theory than in practice. In France, government officials have found the enrollment of a newborn in the program to be a valuable way of bringing families further into the web of state control. The mother's mandatory visit to the state family allowance office allows officials to open a file on the family and to record information on family structure, income, and history. In addition, the state's concession of an allowance gives social service agents the legal right to intervene in families without warrant or other authorization. All that is necessary for intervention is a judgment that a given child may be ''at risk.'' In Sweden, the provision of child allowances has similarly been used as a crowbar for other purposes, as in the decision to funnel all checks through the child's mother. Following the logic of feminist ideology, state planners took this step purposefully to enhance women's and to reduce men's influence within each family.

Liberating the Family

So what's to be done? We can begin by noting that the legal battle over parent's rights in America is far from over. While the courts have generally supported the *parens patriae* doctrine and the projection of state authority into the family, there has been a notable line of dissent. For instance, in its 1944 decision in the case of *Prince* v. *Massachusetts,* the U.S. Supreme Court did say that ''the state's authority over children's activities is broader than over like actions of adults.'' Yet the majority opinion also affirmed that ''it is cardinal with us that the custody, care and nurture of the child reside first in the parents, whose primary function and freedom include preparation for obligations the state can neither supply nor hinder. And it is in recognition of this that [our] decisions have respected the private realm of family life, which the state cannot enter.'' Chief Justice Warren Burger, in his 1979 decision in *Parham* v. *J.R.,* made a related point with even firmer words, arguing that ''the statist notion that governmental power should supercede parental authority in *all* cases because *some* parents abuse and neglect children is repugnant.''

Nonetheless, the institutions of the therapeutic state follow their own bureaucratic logic and continue to grow. Retreat in one sphere (*e.g.,* among the juvenile courts in the wake of *in re Gault* [1965]) is more than compensated for by expansion in another sphere (*e.g.,* child abuse). Given this reality, it is clear that the family can be reprivatized only by direct and real cuts in the size, funding, and power of the specific therapeutic agencies. Such tasks cannot be undertaken lightly, for two centuries of entrenched growth lie behind the vested interests which dominate the state's governance of families. Budget reductions in the areas of ''child protection'' and ''family services'' will predictably bring howls of protest and charges that legislators are abandoning children to the inhuman monsters which are or might be their parents. Such cries are best countered by investigations, legislature- or media-led, into specific cases of state abuse of children and families, and by the knowledge that most (although not all) children would be better served if state intervention did not exist.

''There is growing evidence . . . that the very act of state intervention into the family . . . commonly worsens an already negative situation.''

More generally, the neglect and abuse laws in all 50 states need to be reformed, in recognition of the perverse incentives which now reward those welfare authorities who increase the number of innocent families charged with neglect and abuse. The ancient legal protections of parents, including the common law presumption in favor of the reasonableness of their actions, also need to be restored.

A second strategy for privatizing the family is to substitute vouchers, whenever possible; for direct state welfare services. Such devices, which give benefit recipients the equivalent of cash to spend among a range of public and private service providers, would be most applicable to areas such as care of the severely handicapped and means-tested day care. The importance of vouchers derives from their ability to reverse existing power relationships between welfare official and client. This encourages personal independence among recipients as well as innovation and true service among providers.

Third, the ''family wage'' problem posed by a market system can find a nonstatist resolution. Instead of state-paid family or child allowances, tax deductions and credits keyed to family size can be used to allow families with children to keep more of their earned income. Immediate steps would include an increase in the tax exemption, for dependent children only, to $4,000 per child. Since this change would primarily benefit middle- and upper-income families, this reform should be accompanied by an expansion in the existing Earned Income Tax Credit (EITC), which allows the working poor with at least one child in the family to recover a portion of their payroll or FICA tax. Modifications could include raising the income ceiling for eligibility for the EITC (for example, to $27,000) and keying its size within income levels to number of children (the more children, the larger the credit). In the long run, Congress could merge the EITC and the existing Child Care Tax Credit into a universal, refundable Dependent Child Credit, available to all families at a set level (*e.g.*, $500 per child) up to the total value of the taxpayers and employers payroll tax. Such proposals have the advantages of a family allowance plan (families with children have more disposable income while the efficient functioning of a competitive economy is not compromised) while avoiding an allowance scheme's weaknesses (higher general tax rates to pay for the system, the transformation of families into a state-dependent class, and the use of the allowance as a lever for social engineering).

In the end, the sole alternative to privatization policies such as these can be starkly drawn: the continued socialization of families and child-rearing, and the ongoing destabilization of a free and responsible people.

Allan C. Carlson is the director of The Rockford Institute Center on the Family in America, a conservative, nonprofit organization in Rockford, Illinois.

"Successful women decry the frequently asserted notion that . . . they cannot have it all—a fulfilling career, children and a happy marriage."

viewpoint **38**

Women Can Have Both Work and Family

Sharon Nelton and Karen Berney

In the 1950s, Dad worked and Mom kept house. As the day drew to a close, middle-class American families gathered for a sacred rite—the evening meal.

So it was in Claudia Marshall's childhood home. She might have been expected to carry on the tradition. After all, "It's what I was taught," she says.

But Marshall came of age in the '70s, when women were scrutinizing their roles in society and joining the work force in record numbers. Marshall had a liberal arts degree and wanted to use it. So, after the birth of her first son, Marshall hired a baby-sitter and got a job as a marketing representative for IBM in New York. Still, "I wanted to do some things the way my mother used to," she says. As she envisioned it, she would rush home from work to recreate the home of her youth.

Yet as her eight-hour workday stretched to 10 and sometimes 12 hours, her commitment to the cozy family dinner began to waver. "I took a close look at the ritual and decided that it had to go," she says. Rather than cook, she would have the baby-sitter feed her son before she got home, and she prepared light, late night suppers for herself and her husband James.

Letting go of a time-honored practice is one of many trade-offs Marshall says she has willingly made. Today she has a master's degree in business administration and directs 130 employees as vice president of the marketing and communications services division at the Travelers Corporation in Hartford. She is rearing a 5-year-old and a 9-year-old, has a marriage partner of 13 years and aspires to higher level management. She is convinced that she is a better manager because of motherhood and that her work experiences enrich her family life. When

Marshall reviews her decision to trade a life of domesticity for a full-time career, she feels no remorse: "I can't imagine having done it any other way."

Embracing Work and Family

Marshall's attitude is increasingly common among managerial women. That attitude embraces work and family with equal enthusiasm because it sees the two as mutually reinforcing. Successful women decry the frequently asserted notion that, as much as they try, they cannot have it all—a fulfilling career, children and a happy marriage.

Such talk infuriates them, reports Ellen Van Velsor, a researcher at the Center for Creative Leadership in Greensboro, N.C., who interviewed 76 senior executives in the nation's 100 largest companies for *Breaking the Glass Ceiling* (Addison-Wesley Publishing Company). She says they resent the assumption that to reach the top, they must have made decisions to the detriment of their families. They want to know why it is business as usual for a man to stay late at the office, but a sacrifice for a woman.

Like Marshall, the women in Van Velsor's study speak not of sacrifice, but of trade-offs: less personal time, reliance on baby-sitters, working vacations. They are not trying to be supermoms, perfect wives and ideal employees. Says Van Velsor: "They made their choices, and they are not looking back."

Some women are bailing out of corporate life. They are taking less demanding jobs in small companies, staying home or launching their own businesses. The greatest number, however, are shaping careers in companies they do not own. But whether they are entrepreneurs, CEOs or managers, these women are finding ways to reconcile conflicts between work and family.

Bonnie Sevellon's struggle was to confront and conquer the superwoman myth. Currently director of advertising at Potter, Hazlehurst, Inc., a

Sharon Nelton & Karen Berney, "Women: The Second Wave." Reprinted by permission, *Nation's Business*, May 1987. Copyright 1987, U.S. Chamber of Commerce.

male / female roles 167

Greenwich, R.I., public relations agency, she got her first break a few years ago when she was a single mother of two and was offered a sales manager's position requiring her to travel 50 percent of the time. For months she wrestled with this question: Would she be a bad and neglectful mother if she left her kids in someone else's care?

Sevellon took the job and hired live-in help. But before she could set foot on a plane, she had to accept that she couldn't have it both ways—be a perfect mother and a traveling executive. "I couldn't let myself fall into that trap," she says.

As women let go and turn duties over to others, says Mary Murphree, regional administrator of the New York Labor Department's Women's Bureau, they are creating a demand that is fueling the growth of the services economy. "Today's working parents are more dependent than ever on purchasing services," she says. This raises a new issue for employer and employees: What to do when the day care center unexpectedly goes out of business or the baby-sitter walks out? "The family of the 1980s," she says, "is undergoing a shakeout. No longer is it invisible in the workplace."

Women, who are learning how to maximize their time at the office, must do the same at home, says Linda Albert, a Tampa, Fla.-based consultant and syndicated columnist who also leads a seminar on balancing career and family for the Business Women's Forum of Clifton, N.J.

After a hard day's work, you want to "hang loose," she says, but in reality, organization and discipline give you the freedom to do the things you want. And mismanagement at home spills over into the office. Women who do not get their kids up, fed and out the door efficiently and pleasantly feel drained and exhausted 15 minutes after arriving at work, she says.

Business Skills and Motherhood

Marion Fredman, co-owner of Such A Business, a children's retail outlet in Oakland, Calif., says she runs her home "with the same formality and rigidity I use to run my business." She pencils in time when the entire family can be together and plans activities in advance.

But, Fredman says, motherhood also has taught her a thing or two about operating a business. At her store, she is as adept at juggling her responsibilities as she was when she had a household of four active toddlers to manage.

Claudia Marshall makes a point of setting aside time for the family equivalent of staff meetings. And she uses her professional skills in community service. Because she cannot participate in her sons' school day, she contributes in the evening "in the best way I know how," conducting management development seminars for local school principals.

Good managers listen to the concerns of staff members and offer constructive feedback. This skill works equally well with spouses and children, says Lulu Wang, married with a son and senior vice president of the Equitable Capital Management Group in New York. "Raising children is like managing subordinates," she maintains. "You have to be caring, but also make the hard decisions that earn their respect and trust."

Wang also refuses to separate business from home life, because trying to do so increases stress. At the age of 12, Wang's son could read the stock pages of the *Wall Street Journal* and join in a lively discussion about a merger at the dinner table. Why not? As a pension fund portfolio manager, his mom controls over $1 billion in assets.

"I've always made it a point to integrate my professional and family lives," says Wang. Keeping the two lives separate produces stress and anxiety. "Your family sees your job as something which strings you out and competes with them for your time." But if you let them share in your highs and lows, "they can't help but be supportive partners," she says.

Involving the Family

Marion Fredman agrees wholeheartedly, noting that her family is "emotionally involved in every aspect of my business." This eased the strain on them when she relocated her store, decided to paint it herself and "did not show up at home for months." They are flexible—not balking when dinner is pizza three nights in a row—because "they feel part of what I do," she says.

Husbands who shoulder the weight in child rearing and housecleaning help working mothers balance the demands on their time. But the kind of support that helps a woman succeed, rather than just cope, runs a lot deeper.

Judith Campbell, the manager for accounts for administrative operations at Xerox Corporation, Rochester, N.Y., was on a business trip in California when her young son developed blood poisoning in his elbow. Her husband did not leak a word of it until she got home. Campbell was enraged. "Why didn't you tell me?" she implored. "Because," said her husband quite calmly, "you couldn't have done anything, and it would have interfered with your business." In retrospect, Campbell says he was right.

"Women are finding ways to reconcile conflicts between work and family."

Wang says the most powerful support a husband can give is honest respect. Lots of men encourage their wives, she says, but when something goes wrong, they retreat to habit and offer such comforting words as "Don't worry, dear, I'll take care of you."

There is no principal breadwinner in Lulu Wang's family. Her husband Anthony, president of Computer Associates International in Garden City, N.Y., says her job is as important as his own. That respect, says Wang, "has given me the confidence to take on any challenge."

"Women . . . are devising their own strategies to ensure that they have a fair shot at getting it all."

Yet it is not easy for men to overcome the predominant pattern of men leading and women following. When Claudia Marshall was recruited by a headhunter to join the Travelers, her husband James gave up a 13-year career at Chase Manhattan Bank, moved to Hartford and searched for months to land his current position of senior vice president at Connecticut Bank & Trust. "I had to get off my white charger," he says. "There were many ego things to deal with." But husband and wife agreed that the move would benefit the family as a whole. Though it was a personal loss for him, "it was a win for the partnership," he says.

A Fair Shot at Having It All

The question is no longer whether women prefer motherhood to a career. According to the Department of Labor, 65 percent of new mothers return to the work force within a year of childbirth. Studies of female college graduates indicate that a majority of young women are training for a career they plan to pursue the rest of their lives.

While the issue of work and family will continue to reverberate beyond the home into corporations and legislatures, women are not waiting for their employers or the government to act: As this report shows, they are devising their own strategies to ensure that they have a fair shot at getting it all.

Sharon Nelton and Karen Berney are senior editors with Nation's Business, *a monthly magazine published in Washington, DC.*

Women Cannot Have Both Work and Family

Amy Gage

Every time the phone rings at nine o'clock on a Saturday morning, I know it's my mother, calling long-distance from Denver. She calls me like clockwork, twice a month, and we always cover familiar ground, with a few topical updates. She tells me what's up with my sister and brother in Colorado, complains about how much she misses Minnesota ("But it's cold here, Mom!"), repeats for the millionth time her advice that I should never leave the Twin Cities, and kvetches about her job. Then she recounts the latest exploits of whichever of the four grandkids is her current favorite—the perfect prologue to The Question.

It's always the same. "So when are you and David going to have kids?" she asks. She feigns a nonchalance that she can never quite carry off.

I've learned to wait a few beats before I answer. Maybe, this time, hesitation will derail her. "Well, Mom, we haven't decided on that yet. He's not too keen about it, and I don't want to quit working, you know."

"Why couldn't you work at home?"

"I can't edit copy at home, Mom, and I can't drag a kid along with me while I work on a story."

"There's always day care, Amy." Her breezy air buckles. She becomes motherly and stern. She talks about women she knows who juggle family and career, and she reminds me of the important role that grandparents can play in a young child's life. I know she's right on that score at least, because I've seen her with my two sisters' kids. She's patient, and funny, and accommodating. They adore her. She is everything she almost never had time to be with her own five kids.

I can write this about my mother—knowing full well that she'll read it—because we're a lot alike. She

Amy Gage, "The Baby Question: Should We?" *Minnesota Monthly,* December 1987. Reprinted with permission.

exasperates the hell out of me at times, and she knows it, and I exasperate the hell out of her at times, and I know it, but the power of the basic bond never fails to draw us back together. It's still important to me to please her. I want her approval. Besides, she is never more charming than when she is getting her way.

When it comes to having children, though, I can't take my mother's happiness into account. It's not stubbornness, or pride, or rebelliousness, or leftover resentment. I simply don't know the answer to The Question. I can't decide.

A few years ago, I started noticing children. Really seeing them. I used to scoff whenever I heard about "maternal instinct," but I think that's what it was. I stared at kids in supermarkets, in clothing stores, on the street. My heart would contract, and a lump would rise in my throat. I'd look for opportunities to talk to them, to reassure them that some strangers are O.K. I discovered that I like children, and they seem to like me. Kids feel secure with an adult who treats them with interest and respect.

The intensity of my kid-watching has subsided lately. I'm not really sure why. I know that I've been busy, at home and at work. But The Question lingers: Should I have kids, or shouldn't I? What will I give up if I do it, and what will I miss if I don't?

Ambivalent About Children

I wish, sometimes, that my husband were more romantic about it. I wish he could find the soft spot inside him that sees the wonder in children. To say that David doesn't care about kids is to make him sound callous, which he is not. What he is—what we both are—is ambivalent about having our own. I swore throughout my teens and early twenties that I would never be a mother. David once talked about going under the knife and being done with it all. He's mellowed a bit, as I have, but he holds fast to his conviction that the decision is more mine than his. He's right, of course, but it still makes me feel lonely sometimes.

I've talked to friends and learned that my urge to parent, to shape a life, is not at all unusual. Nor is it the exclusive province of women. A man came up to me at a party last summer and asked if I had ever had "baby hunger." I thought I had heard every line in the book, but procreation wasn't what he was after. He wanted to talk about his kids. He told me how he, too, had yearned to have a child. How he had helped his wife through three pregnancies and been at her side throughout the deliveries. "It hurts," he said, with authority. "Having a baby is hard on a woman." He talked about the magic of children, the joy they can bring to your life. And I found myself thinking again that I like a lot of the young fathers I see. I like men who spend time with their kids.

My own husband would be a wonderful father. I can just sense it. In many ways, he'd be a better parent than I would be. He's more patient, less prone to snap judgments, less susceptible to roller-coaster rides of emotion. He would teach a child how to read and how to skip a stone; he would point out Cygnus and Lyra at night in the summer sky. He would take a child to basketball games and parks and the Science Museum.

I, on the other hand, would expect something from a baby. I don't want just any child. I want a certain kind of child. A made-to-order child.

The Perfect Child

In the thick of my baby hunger several years ago, I often envisioned the child that David and I would have. Occasionally, I would even dream about his birth—always *his* birth. Our son's name would be Samuel David Studer. We would call him Sam, and one day we'd all laugh about the joke we'd played with his initials. He would have the brown eyes of both of his parents, the energy and idealism of his mother, the calmness and tolerance of his father. He would lead a good life. No adolescent trauma. No drug problems. Good grades. A great skier. Witty and handsome, but not enough to make him vain. He'd never turn against us. He'd be wowed by our taste in music and applaud our political views. He would be a reader, a smart child. A curious, compassionate young man.

The thought of my husband's laughter interrupts my reverie. I hear him warning me of my high expectations and reminding me of my own adolescence, when the failings of my parents seemed so painful and so great. If we do have a child, says David—and he is warming to the idea—I must destroy my image of Samuel, before I destroy Samuel himself.

A girlfriend and I discussed The Question over breakfast the other day. We drank Viennese coffee with two-percent milk and watched it storm outside

while we munched on our muffins. I've known this woman for nine years, and she is very dear to me. I value her opinion on almost everything. I value it especially on The Question, because—unlike so many of the women I know—she has answered it.

Kitty and her husband will not be having kids.

It helps, of course, that her husband had a vasectomy when he was with wife number one. That fact "makes the discussion more academic," Kitty says with a laugh. But vasectomies can be reversed, I say, or else you two could adopt. Those aren't the issues. Kitty doesn't want to have children any more than her husband does. She says that she would be too demanding a parent, that she has no patience with kids. Then she ticks off a list of other reasons, with a briskness that startles me. She obviously has given this a great deal of thought—enough that her gut-felt ragings have been banished by the cool voice of reason.

"Deep down, I know that despite his good intentions and my hip Eighties lingo, [my husband] can simply never assume the biological burden."

"Neither of us had demonstrative, loving parents, so we don't have many parental feelings," she says. "It sounds cold-blooded, but it's very expensive to have a child. We wouldn't be able to give a child a lot of material things. Also, we both like what we do for a living, and the thought of giving it up for even three years, which seems to be the minimum requirement, is very depressing to me. So practically, it's a problem."

A Narrow Life

I ask Kitty how she thinks a child would affect her marriage. She and her husband spend a lot of time together. Intellectually and creatively, they are the most compatible couple I know. I wonder if she fears losing him—if not in body, then in mind. "I would never want a narrow life," she says, "and when you're home all the time, your world becomes your four walls."

I'm surprised to hear Kitty speak with the assumption that she would stay home with her kids—if she were to have any, that is. She and her husband share all of the household tasks and generally seem to operate as equals. He is as likely to iron clothes or buy groceries as she is to change the oil in their car. Both of their jobs are important to them and net them about the same income. Why couldn't he raise the kid? Why should she have to give up her work?

Kitty has to leave for an appointment before I get the chance to ask her. As she said, the issue is academic for them, anyway. But the question dogs me. Why do I assume, like Kitty, that I will pay the price for having children? Why do I think that only my career will suffer? That only I, and not my husband, will atrophy inside those dreaded four walls? I'm married to a decent man. His consciousness has been raised. He's enlightened.

Maybe, deep down, I know that despite his good intentions and my hip Eighties lingo, David can simply never assume the biological burden. He cannot carry our child, or bear him, or give him milk. Those are facts that a woman, and a woman alone, must come to terms with.

Lost Dreams

I was raised by a woman who wanted more out of life than housework and motherhood. "Don't get married, and don't have kids," she instructed me when I was a little girl. She wasn't being unkind, at least not intentionally. I think she just wanted to spare me the unhappiness she felt. So she channeled her ambitions into me: her youngest daughter, her favorite.

My mother had wanted to be a journalist herself. Instead she dropped out of college and supported her new husband while he went to law school. She lacked the drive to buck the postwar ethos, which told women that their highest calling was to make a home and raise a family. It was 1949.

Audrie was an astonishingly pretty young woman, with thick auburn hair and an hourglass figure. I love to look at pictures of her when she and Dad were newly married—before disillusionment set in, long before the divorce. My sisters and I used to joke that Mother's beauty was divided among us. Debbie got the big bust, the small waist, and the tiny ankles. Penny got the high cheekbones and the photogenic face. And I got what was left over: the eyes, perhaps, and the smile, and the unerring eye for clothes.

"In the end, something gives: the marriage, the children's happiness, the father's temper, the mother's career."

Were I more gorgeous, I might be less ambitious. I don't know. What I do know is that I never thought I would land a rich man with my looks. I have always wanted to work, to learn a skill, to earn my own keep. I learned that lesson at my mother's knee (before she discovered that being Grandma is a whole lot more fun than being Mom) and had it reinforced in college, during the height of the women's movement. To change course now and step off the track—have a baby or two, stay home for awhile—strikes me as a betrayal of what I've

struggled for all these years.

I'm not fooled by any woman who says she can "have it all." That may be possible at isolated moments, but, in the end, something gives: the marriage, the children's happiness, the father's temper, the mother's career. What gave in my sisters' lives was their ability to pull in a good paycheck and, to some extent, their ability to realize their dreams. Each of them has two children, and each believes strongly in staying home with her kids. They're lucky to be married to men whose salaries make that possible. One of my sisters has not had her own income for seven years, and the other has held a job only sporadically since her children were born.

I don't know if I could make that sacrifice. I couldn't afford it. I have too much to do. And so The Question becomes not "Do I *want* to have children?" but "Should I take the risk?" If other women can't have it all, why do I think that I can?

My eldest sister, Debbie, was a radio reporter for several years. After she married her second husband, they each decided to change professions. He would go to law school at Berkeley, and she would start taking the undergraduate science courses that med schools require. Two children and a decade later, he is close to making partner in a San Jose firm. She is waiting for her kids to be old enough so she can get on with those college classes.

Relief and Longing

Debbie is an excellent mother. Her children talked and read early. They seem confident and well adjusted. Debbie is convinced that her around-the-clock presence has a lot to do with how well they're turning out, and I don't doubt it. She writes to me often about the joys and struggles of being home with two kids. Reading her letters, I alternate between relief, because her life isn't mine, and longing, because I wish it were. "Christmas morning was a little overwhelming for Kate," Deb wrote last December. "She was too distracted to open all her presents, and at about 8:45 she screamed, 'I'm hungry! I haven't had breakfast!' and burst into tears. We rushed into the kitchen and got her a muffin so she wouldn't pass out."

My other sister, Penny, has never shared Debbie's and my penchant for an all-consuming career. She, too, is an excellent mother—a career homemaker, really. Her suburban house is spotless. Her children are well behaved and well groomed. Her yard could qualify for the cover of *Better Homes and Gardens*. Lately, though, Penny has seemed restless, ready to return to work. She is 34. Her kids are nine and 11. They no longer need her undivided attention. Penny is not the first woman—just the most recent—to tell me this: It's hard to feel that your work has real worth unless you earn money for it. Penny says it's time she got paid for some of her labor. Her sagging self-esteem could use the boost right about now.

And so this is what it come down to: choices. I can work. I can have children. I can try to do both, if I'm really ambitious. I belong to the first generation of women who have truly been free to decide. My mother had three unplanned pregnancies (I was "a diaphragm baby"), and my friend Kitty's mother had at least one. My late mother-in-law was pregnant 13 times, from which six children survived.

Modern birth-control methods have spared me such surprises. Yet I'm no less fascinated by children than my mother was, or her mother before her. I think about children a lot: the things I would do with them, how they would look.

Lately, since I've turned 30, I've been thinking about the consequences of not having kids. It's a tug-of-war with myself. My emotions pull at my intellect. I don't want David and me to split up because we can't agree on whether we want children. I don't want to end up at 45 with just me and my lonely career. Nor do I want to make the necessary sacrifices now to have kids. We have a lot of freedom, David and I do, and both of us are reluctant to lose it. A childless marriage can be a good way to live. Dinners out, friends over, spur-of-the-moment movies, Sunday drives.

"This is what it comes down to: choices. I can work. I can have children."

When I want some perspective, I think back to a time when I visited Debbie in Oakland. Her first daughter, Emma, was five months old. I slept on a mattress on the floor of Emma's room in their cramped apartment. Every morning, about six o'clock, Emma's head would spring up like a jack-in-the box. She slept on her stomach, and from the floor I could just barely see her eyes over the padding in the crib. I would entertain her as long as I could, until she got hungry and we had to call Debbie. Then the three of us would move out into the living room, where Emma would nurse.

Choices

I was 23 years old, and the sight of my oldest sister holding a baby to her breast was the most touching, tender moment I had ever seen. It made me feel warm and happy, so at peace. Deb and her husband were both in school. They were tired all the time, and broke. I remember asking her then how she did it, how she kept on day after day.

"You do what you have to do," she said, and that has always stuck with me. My sister is right: You make choices in life. You give up one thing to get another. I guess that's the most of any philosophy I shall ever want, or need.

Amy Gage is managing editor of Minnesota Monthly, *a regional magazine published for the Upper Midwest.*

Children Benefit from Working Mothers

Anita Shreve

Katherine was three. It was four o'clock in the afternoon. I was carrying a bundle of laundry from my bedroom to her closet when I saw her in the hallway between our room and hers. She was sitting at a small wooden drafting board that my husband and I had set up for her under a window some weeks earlier. It had a stool that allowed her to reach the surface comfortably, and we had thought she might use it to scribble in her coloring books or to draw pictures. A winter sun poured in over the drafting board and illuminated in red-gold light her tiny body bent over her task. Arrested by the scene and also by her frown of concentration, I stood there and watched. She was cutting up pieces of paper with a pair of child's scissors and was pasting some of these bits onto other larger pieces of paper with Scotch tape. The leftover scraps were periodically dispatched with a gesture that made me smile since it was a part of my own repertoire, a luxurious sweep of the arm that caused the debris—rough drafts, junk mail—to rain onto the floor, to be picked up all at once at day's end. When she had the larger papers as she wanted them, she began "writing" on them, occasionally stopping to consult her "computer"—a Speak and Spell game she had received for her birthday. Beside her on the "desk" was a light blue telephone that a year earlier had been on its way to the dump before my husband rescued it and gave it to her.

"What are you doing?" I asked quietly behind her.

She looked up, startled. "I can't talk to you right now," she said in a voice full of authority and purpose. "But as soon as I'm finished my working, I can. I have a lot of hard working to do. I have to write a article and I am going to have important phone calls, and you can't talk to me while I'm

having them."

My eyes widened in amusement and surprise. I turned away quickly before she could see. But for a few changes in grammar, she had it right. The words were my words, I realized with some chagrin, the work was my work. As I had done countless times, she was writing an article and she was announcing that this was a moment when she could not be disturbed.

Like Mommy

After that afternoon, there were many incidents that struck me with the same incompatible mix of feelings—a kind of giddy delight at her earnestness and her sense of importance, a smile at the charm of a three-year-old trying to imitate her parent, some mild embarrassment when expressions I had used in a crisis or on deadline to buy time or silence came back to haunt me, a puzzlement as to how she perceived me and my endeavors in the world, and the first stirrings of curiosity as to what it all meant. She had the persistent belief, for example, that whenever I left the house, even if I was going to a movie, I was going to my "work." She said often that she was going to grow up to be a writer ("like Mommy") and use a "typo-writer," and this occupation for many months was rivaled only by that of Supergirl. She understood that work generated income and once asked me when my husband and I were going out to dinner, "When you go get the monies, can I stay home with Daddy?" (this in lieu of a babysitter).

Presently she began to ask for an "office," which her father built for her as part of a loft-bed arrangement, and to go to it with the same frequency as she played house with Cheer Bear or went out to her swing in the backyard. She would often say, "I'm working at my office [or "my computer"] just like Mommy," and would "write" and make things while there. It wasn't so much the fact that she aped me that I found intriguing (all children imitate their parents—pretending to be "shaving" in the mirror, scolding their dolls in borrowed tones of voice); it was the nature of the activity. "Mommy works; therefore, if I want to be like Mommy, I work, too," she seemed to be saying. I found it especially interesting that although she saw me "working" at other tasks—and surely carrying heavy bags of groceries or digging up a garden might appear to be more arduous than writing an article—she never referred to these chores as "work." Work was something you did when you went to your office and wrote things and had phone calls.

One day a friend of mine came to dinner. She was the mother of an eight-year-old boy who, although exceptionally bright and engaging, had never been particularly adept at entertaining himself. And so it did not escape her notice when Katherine, seeing that we mothers were momentarily involved in meal preparation and with news of each other, went off to her "office" and began cutting and pasting and writing and drawing—or as Katherine was fond of putting it, doing her "working."

"Do you think," asked my friend, returning from a visit to my daughter's room, "that Katherine's ability to play by herself at her desk stems from seeing you creating 'work' out of unstructured time?"

I didn't know the answer, but I liked the question. . . .

Mothers as Role Models

The term "role model" is a difficult and awkward phrase—one of those unlovable combinations of words that gets the job done, in that it accurately conveys the thing meant, but smacks of laboratories, experimental trials and sociological constructs. As a concept, it defines a relationship between what might loosely be called a superior and an inferior, or a teacher and an apprentice; but where it fails is in its ability to convey any warmth or passion—the underpinnings of the mother-child bond. The term, for example, doesn't even begin to suggest the idiosyncratic love, playfulness or even exasperation that passes between one individual mother and her child, and by which the child comes to define her mother. Nevertheless, it is a term with which we are stuck, both because of its legitimacy in the various fields of scientific research that employ it and because it does accurately describe an important aspect of the parent-child relationship. It's not so much that the term is incorrect that tends to grate; it's that it falls short of conveying the rich panoply of passions that make this bond such a powerful one.

Long before there were researchers and sociological terms, however, mothers knew that they were role models. For centuries, others before us have accepted as a given the fact that a mother

teaches a child, influences that child's behavior, and helps to shape that child's beliefs and values. How that is done, however, is a matter of controversy.

Regardless of whether one believes that a child acquires his or her sex-role identity through imitation, biologically internalized motivations or cognitive researches, the various theories agree that most of this effort takes place in early childhood and that the mother first, followed by the father (if one is present), is the most important "shaper" and "influencer." The work the child does during his or her early years is part of a socialization process to fit the child for the adult world in which he lives. In the past . . . this process has tended to prepare girls for nurturing roles as wives and mothers and boys for active roles as breadwinners. Today, however, that sexual division of labor is changing. Mothers (and fathers) are socializing children of both sexes to possess characteristics that will help them in the work force as well as in parenting. . . .

The Power of Modeling

That the mother is an influential role model for her child is believed by most researchers to be true, and some have set out to examine the power of this modeling. In a study conducted in 1981, researchers found that daughters mirrored their mothers' attitudes about work in every respect, except that 98 percent of them expected that they would always work with minimal time off in order to raise children.

"'Mommy works; therefore, if I want to be like Mommy, I work, too,' she seemed to be saying."

Dr. J. Brooks-Gunn of the Educational Testing Service recently conducted a study which also demonstrates the power of modeling. She evaluated 132 mothers as being either "masculine," "feminine" or "androgynous," according to a list of sex-role characteristics developed by Sandra Bem of Cornell University. "Androgynous" mothers, who, according to Dr. Brooks-Gunn, share personality characteristics with working women, scored high in both masculine and feminine traits. For example, they were self-reliant as well as tender, affectionate as well as assertive. "Feminine" mothers scored high only in feminine traits. Dr. Brooks-Gunn then watched the androgynous and feminine mothers at play with their own children. (The masculine sample was judged to be too small to be significant.) She discovered that feminine mothers promoted feminine behavior in their girls, and that androgynous mothers promoted self-reliance and independent behavior in their daughters.

The power of modeling was also demonstrated during a study conducted at Yale University's Child Study Center. Researchers there found a relationship between the quality of interaction between the mother and child and a child's personality. Researchers observed both mothers and children in play situations. Children who had mothers who were "in charge" and prohibitive were aggressive and assertive in play situations. Children with flexible mothers were somewhat more sociable and tended to watch one another more carefully.

The Working Mother's Impact

That the mother is a powerful role model is clear, but some critics of the working mother have suggested that her influence as a role model wanes in direct proportion to the number of hours she is absent from the home. Is the impact of a working mother on a child diluted by the presence of a surrogate caretaker (or multiple caretakers, as in the case of a day-care center)? Is it possible that a mother who has only three or four hours a day to spend with her child can be as potent a model for her child as the at-home mother who is with the child all of his or her waking hours?

Lois Hoffman, in her review of the literature on the effects of maternal employment on the young child, published in 1984 in *The Minnesota Symposia on Child Psychology,* offered some interesting findings: "Employed mothers spend less time with their preschool children, but the time spent with them is more likely to be direct or intense interaction." She also discovered that "either because of intrinsic motivation or conscious effort, employed mothers, and particularly the more educated, compensate to some extent for their absence." In conclusion, she found that "there is no evidence for diminished quality of interaction between employed mothers and their young children and some evidence for the opposite pattern."

Sandra Scarr, in a review of maternal time-use studies in her book *Mother Care, Other Care* also had some intriguing observations: "It is popularly assumed that mothers at home spend a great deal of time in direct interaction with their children, playing educational games and improving their children's minds. . . . [But] in middle- and working-class families, the child of a mother at home full-time spends only five percent of her waking hours in direct interaction with her mother. . . .

"Time-use studies . . . show that employed women spend as much time as nonworking women in *direct* interaction with their children. Employed mothers spend as much time as those at home reading to and playing with their young children, although they do not, of course, spend as much time simply in the same room or house with the children."

The amount of time a working mother spends with her child seems to me to be at the very heart of the maelstrom of feelings that surround the issue of working mothers and children. A recent *Redbook* survey of one thousand respondents (40 percent of whom worked outside the home) highlighted the anxieties that many working mothers feel simply because they don't have enough hours in the day with their children. Although 66 percent of the working mothers felt that "quality time" could compensate for a mother's absence, others wrote of "missing something by being gone from seven in the morning until six at night," and of being "haunted" by their children's faces.

"There is no evidence for diminished quality of interaction between employed mothers and their young children and some evidence for the opposite pattern."

I'm not sure that "quality time" is a very useful phrase to employ when assessing what happens when a mother and child spend time together. By referring to it, one assumes that all *direct* hours are "better" than all *indirect* hours. While it is almost certainly true that reading to a child or teaching that child how to paint a fence is a better way to interact with a son or daughter than putting him or her in front of a TV while you vacuum the rug, there are many moments of indirect interaction that seem to me to have just as much "quality" as those spent one-on-one.

I know, from my own experience, that I like being in the same room with my child, even if I am cooking or paying bills. When the atmosphere is relaxed, my daughter goes about her business in tandem with mine, and I think she feels a sense of comfort at having me nearby to help her find a Lego piece or set up a paintbox should the urge to paint strike her. Yet it is also true that she has the same sense of comfort if it is her father in the room, or her grandmother or a neighbor she has gotten to know well. This sense of nurturing or comfort—of having a loving adult nearby to *take care of you*—is at least as important, I believe, as being read to or taught something and should not be devalued by not coming under the umbrella of "quality time."

Mother or Others?

The question that remains to be answered, however, is how important is it that it be the mother who provides those long hours of nurturing and comfort—that indirect interaction that nevertheless give a child a sense of security? The question is a particularly difficult one to answer because the solution seems to rely heavily on the personality and needs of each individual child and mother, and on the culture in which these mothers and children live. I know one at-home mother of a seven-year-old boy, to give one unusual example, who recently discovered, via a child psychologist, that her son was emotionally "at risk" because he needed *more* time and attention from his mother. The mother had certainly been giving her child more hours per day than any working mother; but the child's own personality, different from the norm, required exceptional amounts of maternal maintenance.

Some working mothers speak of terrible anxieties at being away from their children, and the need to intensify their mothering when they are at home. Elaine, the dentist, for example, said that because she is with her daughter for only a few hours a day, she feels a special responsibility to "have an impact on my daughter."

Doing Fine

Yet Carol, the waitress, felt that her children were better off for having three primary nurturers—herself, her mother and her husband. She believed her children were getting the best of each adult, and that they were doing "fine" because of this. In other cultures I have observed—the Kikuyu society in Kenya, for instance—children learn early on that nurturing comes from a variety of female adults and semi-adults (older girl children). In that society, the "working" mothers often form a kind of informal collective within their villages and settlements, whereby all adult females are responsible for all children, and these responsibilities vary according to the schedules and tasks of the individual mothers.

"Time-use studies . . . show that employed women spend as much time as nonworking women in direct *interaction with their children."*

What is missing in our culture is a feeling of comfort at allowing children to have multiple nurturers, stemming not only from the traditional upbringing, with its rigid set of expectations, in which most mothers today were raised, but also from a lack of suitable surrogate nurturers and an inflexibility in the workplace. Good quality childcare . . . is difficult to obtain for many working mothers and has become something of a national scandal. The workplace, in large part, remains inflexible, denying part-time work, job-sharing, flextime schedules or at-home work to most working mothers. Without adequate childcare or the opportunity to discover for oneself the optimum number of hours per day a child needs with the mother, anxiety, guilt and discomfort may take precedence over any good feelings the mother has about her role.

A mother who is deeply troubled may not be an effective role model, but for those families in which the mother is not so distraught, an argument can be made that children today see the working mother as a kind of super role model with enhanced powers. The concept of power is extremely important to a young child. "One of the most significant forces for the child in the early years is the notion of power," says Dr. Sylvia Feinberg, chairman of the Eliot Pearson Department of Child Study at Tufts University. "Who's got it, and in what circumstances?"

In the past, the mother had the power in the home, and the father had the power in the world outside. It was common, in fact, for girls in previous generations to take their fathers for role models if they planned to become achievers outside the home. Today, in the homes of working mothers, children perceive mothers as having power in both arenas. Mothers are often perceived, in fact, as having more power than fathers.

Working mothers still perform work that deeply affects the child's well-being: cooking, feeding the family, bathing the child, nurturing other children. For a very young child, ultimate power resides in the home. But as that child matures and gains a clearer understanding of what the mother does outside the home, becoming intrigued by the "coming and going" nature of the mother's work, he or she will associate this work with power in the same way that previous generations of children assigned power to their fathers. The child may understand that the mother gets money outside the home (economic power), makes things happen in the outside world (produces goods or services) and may even have an important position in the workplace. This mother may then be perceived as having more cumulative power (power both inside and outside the home), and perhaps being a more powerful influence than either the at-home mother or the father. In an important study of over ninety teenagers in two-career families, conducted by Patricia Knaub at the University of Nebraska, she asked the following question: "Thinking back to your childhood and up through your teenage years, which of your parents seems to have been the more influential, on the whole, in shaping your attitudes and your general outlook on life? Decide between your mother and father, even if the difference was slight." The mother was indicated by 72.7 percent of the sample (80 percent of the females and 63.1 percent of the males), whereas 27.6 percent (20 percent of females and 36.9 percent of the males) said it was their father who was more influential. . . .

Conveying a Sense of Fulfillment

It is extremely important to point out, however, that the way in which a mother perceives that power is more important than the power itself. The attitude of the working mother toward her own work life and sexual role may be the single most important factor in shaping the child's perceptions. If a mother is oppressed in the home by her husband or by her economic situation, and in the workplace by the nature of her job or by her supervisors, the ideas that she will convey to her child about the value of working—*and the effects of that mother's employment on her child*—will be considerably different from the mother who is happy and comfortable in her home life, who is proud of her accomplishments in the workplace and who is pleased with the way she is combining the two. Mothers who feel ambivalent about working and mothering may convey negative messages to their children. Job satisfaction, self-esteem in the workplace, self-definition as a worker, her husband's attitude toward her employment as well as the extent to which he shares household and child-rearing tasks, her confidence in her childcare arrangements, and her economic situation will all affect a working mother's attitudes toward her employment. *It is not the working itself that has such a powerful effect on the child, but what the mother conveys to that child about her own satisfaction or dissatisfaction with her life as a working mother.*

"In other cultures I have observed . . . children learn early on that nurturing comes from a variety of female adults."

As noted earlier, jobs that inspire alienation rather than some measure of fulfillment are not a fertile environment for the development of self-esteem—a crucial prerequisite for extolling the value of work, whether in words or by actions. In an ideal society all jobs would be filled by people who enjoyed them, or they would have built-in incentives, variation and opportunities for advancement that made them at least tolerable. In reality, however, many jobs in America, both corporate and noncorporate, are demoralizing, if not actually demeaning. There are certainly women (and men) who leave their homes daily to perform tasks in which they can find no value (other than to their employer), and they return home disgruntled and feeling in some way abused by their day's work. Nightly complaints about work assignments, workload, work environment, fellow workers, employees, or even commuting are commonplace in many homes; and when both parents are employed, the chance of children experiencing such dissatisfaction is obviously twice as great. Given the case that most women who find themselves in jobs or careers that depress them must continue to work out of necessity, it is clear that the mere fact of a mother working does not

automatically result in her children growing up with an appetite for success or self-expression in the workplace. As hard as a mother might try to hide her frustrations, it is inevitably impossible to lie to a child about something as primary as work.

The Benefits of Meaningful Work

This . . . is in no way a call to women to adjust their lives and aspirations so as to feel at home in jobs with which they can make no personal connection or in which they can find no meaning. On the contrary, it is an affirmation of the benefits to children as well as to their mothers of *meaningful* work—work that results in a feeling of accomplishment. Without reference to any studies or statistics, common sense dictates that a mother who conveys a sense of self-esteem and accomplishment to her children functions as a better barometer of life's possibilities than a mother filled with nostalgia for what she might have been or what she might have done.

Anita Shreve is the author of Remaking Motherhood: How Working Mothers Are Shaping Our Children's Future *and a former editor and writer for* Us, Newsweek, New York, *and* Redbook.

"My purpose in being with them was to teach them how to live successfully."

Children Benefit from Mothers Who Stay Home

Linda Burton, Janet Dittmer, and Cheri Loveless

As much as we would like to deny it, women are in truth discovering that children rarely need their mothers at their mothers' convenience. Those of us who have tried—and tried and tried and tried—to make the "quality time" theory work have, quite simply, come up empty-handed. A working mother from Virginia, whose current employer allows a seven-to-four workday so she can be home when her daughter returns from school, remembers a time circumstances weren't so favorable: "I would be tense during the entire drive home from work, thinking 'I must relate with Emma, I must relate with Emma.' But when I arrived home, Emma wouldn't want to relate. Emma would want to watch television."

A former working mother from Michigan remarks: "When I got home at night, I read to my son and played with him. I gave him lots of undivided attention. But you know, it wasn't 'quality time.' I think it's a myth to say you can give quality time to a child after eight hours of work. I was tired and washed out. Many nights we ate TV dinners because I was too tired to cook. Although I read to Danny and played with him, I forced myself to do it. In spite of how dearly I loved my son, I really didn't enjoy him. I was too tired."

"Quality Time"

Trying to make a success out of "quality time" has also disappointed many at-home mothers, for parenting "experts" have made them just as conscious of the importance of one-on-one interaction. It seems that no matter how thoughtfully we plan or present a special mother-child activity, it rarely equals the exultation of those uncapturable moments that seem to fall in and out of our hands like dandelion dust, without benefit of plan or

Linda Burton, Janet Dittmer, and Cheri Loveless, *What's a Smart Woman Like You Doing at Home?* Reprinted by permission of Acropolis Books, 2400 17th St. NW, Washington, DC.

appointment.

"I recall a moment one day [last] fall," writes Joanne Bruun of Ellicott City, Maryland. "It was a beautiful September morning, a day that offered the promise of fall but retained the fullness of summer. The sky was brilliant. The air was warm and held September's special stillness, yet the trees hung lush and ripe with not a leaf lost. My baby awoke from her nap and she was warm with sleep. I carried her downstairs and as I did, Billy Joel's 'Leave a Tender Moment Alone' came on the radio. The song sang to me, the day spoke to me, and the baby warmed to me. I began to dance with her, just my little miracle and I dancing on a perfect fall day. One of the joys of being at home is being open to just such a moment."

But when we are at home full-time, we find ourselves open to other kinds of moments as well—the moments when we wonder if we are really doing right by our children; the times we wonder if someone else might not do a better job of raising our children than we could. In the following essay, Linda Burton considers these times.

Unquality Time

When I was twenty-two and gorgeous, I saw this woman in the parking lot at the supermarket. She was driving a large station wagon, and she was yelling loudly at three disheveled children who had fudgesicle dripping all over their faces and onto their clothes. Groceries were spilling out of bags onto the back seat and floor. The woman's hair was uncombed and her clothes looked as if she had slept in them. With complete disgust, I pointed her out to a friend. "Ugh," I said. "I will never let *that* happen to me!" This unhappy woman in the station wagon represented everything I never wanted to be.

At the time, I remember discussing with my friend how this obviously miserable woman would be a lot happier in an office. Her children drove her crazy, I suspected, and what she needed was a lot more mental stimulation. What her children needed, I thought was a calm, loving mother. There was no question in my mind that she should "get a job and leave her kids with a sitter or something."

I forgot the incident until quite recently while in the car (a station wagon, as it happens) with my own children. I had had a sleepless night, dealing with the latest progression of flus and viruses which seem to adopt my children whenever the temperature dips below fifty-two degrees, and I was not in a good mood. In my rush to get out and pick up a new prescription at the drugstore, I had thrown on some soiled khakis and a T-shirt and had ignored my hair entirely, hoping I could just "shake" it into shape along the way. My thoughts were focused on the approaching evening.

A Smart Move?

Several months earlier, I had agreed to teach a few one-night classes for the county's Continuing Education Department. It seemed like a smart move. I thought teaching these classes would be a good way to keep up my professional resumé—put on "hold" for the years I was raising my family—and get me out in the world of adult stimulation. Best of all, the classes carried the extra bonus of requiring only a very small investment of my time. The day of the first class had arrived. Despite considerable advance notice, I was still not completely prepared. As I stuffed my overcoated children into their carseats, fussing with securing the various latches and locks, my mind was racing furiously ahead, trying to mentally tie up the loose ends of my class outline. Why did I ever agree to teach these classes?

"I made the firm decision to remain at home with my children. I knew no one could have taught them as much as I did."

Fear gripped me for a minute as I pictured myself standing dumbstruck in front of twenty-eight students, without an organized idea to call my own. These thoughts consumed all my attention as I wearily came to a stop at the traffic light signaling the edge of our community. Just at this moment, the eighteen-month-old decided to throw his bottle on the floor, jarring the top loose and allowing apple juice to flood the floor and creep under the passenger seat. He screamed loudly for me to pick up the bottle. My three-year-old began to whine at a grating decibel level, and his brother screamed louder. The light turned green.

Angrily, I jerked the car over to the side of the

road and lit into both children in a very unpleasant way. I had had it. My nerves were raw, my mind was flaccid from being pulled in spokelike directions; I looked terrible. I wasn't prepared for my class that evening. And at that moment, it felt like my predicament was all their fault. For what must have been a full minute, I screamed uncontrollable vituperation at my children. As I slumped against the car seat in exhaustion, I noticed that the traffic light had turned red again, and there was a girl—about twenty-two—in an MG directly opposite me. Beautifully dressed and looking terrific, she was staring at the picture I presented in horror and disgust. Our eyes met only for an instant before the light turned again and she went on her way, but it was a moment of complete insight.

Better To Work?

I had become the woman I never wanted to be. I was the living caricature of everything that could go wrong with motherhood. I felt like there was only one place to turn. If being a mother was this exhausting, this draining—if it meant that my frustrations would make me turn on my children so cruelly—then I should go back to work. The mounting tensions in my life had caused me to be grossly unjust to my children, and nothing was worth that. Knowing that I had frightened them in the bargain made me feel even worse.

Maybe it would be better, I thought, if I were to go to work and hand my children over to someone kinder than I was, someone who was "better" with children than I was. Surely there were people who were "made" for the job of mothering; it's just that I wasn't one of them. Perhaps if I were away from my children for much of the day, I would appreciate them more at day's end. I wanted to feel good about myself as a mother, and it seemed at that moment as if the only way I was going to feel good was to turn over most of the job to somebody else.

But for the time being, the three of us were stuck together in a very small space, and we couldn't really walk away from the problem. Somehow, I had to disentangle us all from the frenzy of the last several minutes.

I apologized.

It was not easy, because I was feeling as victimized as they were.

"Look guys," I said. "I'm really sorry I yelled at you. It wasn't right. I wasn't fair to you. I shouldn't have done it. Do you know why I was yelling?"

The three-year-old solemnly nodded his head. "You were mad," he said.

"Honey," I explained, "I wasn't mad at you."

"Then who were you mad at?"

"I don't think I was really mad at all; I was tired, and sometimes just being tired makes you feel mad. Isn't that silly?" He didn't say anything. "But you know what else, honey?" I added. "There's something I have to do that's kind of scaring me, and that made me act mad. Sometimes we act mad when really what we are is scared." He seemed to absorb the complex logic easier than I would have thought. "Did I scare you, honey?" I asked. He nodded. "I'll bet I did," I said.

We discussed it a bit longer and we all seemed to feel much better as we continued our drive to the store.

Staying at Home

At that unlikely moment, I made the firm decision to remain at home with my children. I knew no one could have taught them as much as I did in that car. I also knew that there was no job that could teach me as much as I had learned from them during that one incident.

What had they learned? First of all, they learned that it is okay to be mad. If my children saw me only during my "good" times and not during my bad, how might they feel about themselves when *they* got mad? Second, they learned that when we don't do the right thing, there is usually something that can be done about it. We do not allow ourselves to continue repeating an unkind behavior. We can apologize, and we can try to amend our behavior. Finally, they learned that sometimes when we feel angry, something else may really be going on, such as fear or lack of sleep. I hope this episode taught my children to occasionally look beneath their own anger to see what else might really be bothering them.

From this very bad time—this supremely "unquality" time—I learned why it is crucial for me to be at home with my children. My purpose in being with them was to teach them how to live successfully, how to get through the vicissitudes of life as well and as happily as possible. I suddenly realized that I could not possibly teach them those important lessons if they did not see me go through some dismal times. I knew that my children would be carefully examining how I handled my own inadequacies to use as a model for overcoming their own.

So much of our success in life, after all, is measured by how well we are able to get through the times that aren't so good—the times when we are too tired; when we're frightened; when we fail. If we are not around to serve as examples for our children for how to get through those times and emerge victorious, then how will they learn the lessons?

I'll Never Quit

Few of us, I learned, are really "born" for the job of mothering. Rather, being a good mother is a privilege earned through hard work and a continual, daily recommitment to the importance of that work. It means being willing enough to confront the very

worst in ourselves, and brave enough not to run away from it when the going gets rough. In point of fact, mothering is rough and scary work. I understand fully how great the temptation is to hand the job over to somebody else—somebody "born" to do it.

Since that day at the stoplight, I have wanted to quit with great regularity. But then I have never begun a new job that I didn't periodically want to quit—especially when I was afraid that I was not going to do well. I would come home and say, "This job isn't for me; I'm no good at it. I'll never learn to do it." A real terror at the idea of failure has always made the idea of "giving up the ship" especially attractive to me. Unfortunately, however, whenever I have chosen to "give up the ship," I have also chosen never to experience the sea.

> "Mothering is rough and scary work. I understand fully how great the temptation is to hand the job over to somebody else."

Sometimes I think that when we feel our most inadequate, we are presented with our greatest opportunity for self-revelation and growth. We are presented with an opportunity to take a chance on ourselves and come out on top—to build a confidence-reinforcing chain of success.

So I do not, at bottom, believe that mothers are either "born" for the job or not. We may be frightened of mothering. We may not feel up to it, we may run from its challenges, and we may call our fear a simple inborn ineptitude for the job. But then we will never experience the sea, and we will never see the view from the mountaintop.

Teaching a Child Independence

One of the greatest joys of motherhood is watching our children become independent of us. To share in those moments when a child first begins to realize that he might amount to something in this world, to urge him to try his wings more and more, and to applaud his victories as he becomes an independent, self-confident little human are among the most gloriously satisfying experiences a mother can have.

But there are different ways to teach a child to become independent. Someone can take us to a swimming pool when we are small, throw us in the water and shout, "SWIM!" Or they can gently bounce us in the water when we are babies, play with us in the water when we're a little bigger, and then, eventually, teach us how to float, do the crawl, sidestroke, backstroke, and breaststroke, and then say, "SWIM!"

Doubtless either method would produce an adept swimmer—and a child taught by the first may indeed become an independent swimmer long before the second. But to what avail?

If a mother simply wanted her children to learn independence, she could look out for them much less, spend less time with them, think about them less. But most mothers want their children to learn more than that. It is the quality of a child's independence that concerns most mothers: Was it born of necessity or of self-confidence? Do their children know they can make it on their own because they are rich in resources? Or do they know they can make it on their own because, by golly, they had to? Can they help other people along the way because somebody took the time to help them? Or do they ignore the needs of other people because no one was there when they had a need? Will they be able to combat any potential challenges to their independence because they feel nurtured, secure in themselves and their abilities? Or will they be able to combat any potential challenges to their independence because they had to fight to get it, and they'll fight to keep it?

In their quiet moments of reckoning—of measuring humanity against detached textbooks, and intuition against edict—most mothers come to terms with what they truly believe is best for their children.

They Never Stop Needing You

It is ironic that a nation that has developed a veritable fetish of "bonding" with an infant at birth advises us of the wisdom of leaving them as early as a tender six weeks of age. As child-care "experts" conduct studies and draft papers and haggle over pinpointing the time at which a child no longer needs our full-time attention, mothers themselves have long known the answer.

"If a mother simply wanted her children to learn independence, she could look out for them much less. . . . But most mothers want their children to learn more than that."

Mary Molegraaf, a mother of three school-age children from Grandville, Michigan observes, "I was so anxious for this time to come so that I could get out of the house and go to work. Now that it's here, I feel that it's more important than ever for me to be home to get [the children] off to school in the morning and be here when they get home." . . .

Dee Cosola of Leona Valley, California, did go back to work briefly. "I am forty-seven and have three grown children, all married and doing fine. I was home with them until the youngest was sixteen; then I listened to the world and sought a career so I could be *fulfilled*. My sixteen-year-old daughter became very depressed and I knew something was wrong. She needed me as much at sixteen years as she did at sixteen months."

"Sure we have outgrown the 'first tooth' and 'first steps,'" says Donna Harper of St. Louis, Missouri, "but somehow Rob's grand slam home run, or Tim's 'most valuable player' in the holiday soccer tournament can be just as great an accomplishment, and I'm lucky to be home to share it. My girls are grown, one at college and one on the way, but they have their needs, too. Whether it's a sympathetic ear to steer Missy through 'puppy love,' or listening to the long-distance tears when Christa decides to be 'strung out' about her exams, I'm still glad to be here for them."

Not many of us realized, when we first set out on this obscure road, the impact children would have on our lives. Yet for all the uncertainty, and the sometimes frightening challenges we see on the horizon, most of us still find ourselves surprisingly eager to complete the journey.

Linda Burton, Janet Dittmer, and Cheri Loveless are the authors of What's a Smart Woman Like You Doing at Home? *and founders of Mothers At Home, an organization for women who choose not to work outside their homes.*

"When you're drawing up your list of life's miracles, you might place near the top the first moment your baby smiles at you."

Fatherhood: A Traditional View

Bob Greene

Editor's note: This viewpoint is taken from a diary Bob Greene wrote during the first year of his daughter's life. It was later published as the book Good Morning, Merry Sunshine.

June 11

People talk about the emotions that come when a baby is born; exuberance, relief, giddiness, pure ecstasy. The thought that you have seen a miracle in front of your eyes.

I knew I was supposed to be feeling all of those things, and of course I did. But the dominant emotion inside me was a more basic one. I was scared—scared of what I knew was sure to come, and more scared about what I didn't know. I am of a generation that has made self-indulgence a kind of secular religion. I looked down at that baby, and suddenly I felt that a whole part of my life had just ended, been cut off, and I was beginning something for which I had no preparation.

A Changing Scene

June 12

She had microscopic fingernails and a scrawny, funny ducktail hairdo and tiny replicas of a wizened old man's hands. She lay in a see-through hospital bassinet in Room 808 of Michael Reese [Hospital].

Susan was in bed next to the bassinet. A document had arrived with Amanda's vital statistics. The piece of paper said that she had weighed 6 pounds, 15 ounces at birth, and was 20½ inches long. . . .

Susan held our baby as if she had been doing it all her life. When she handed Amanda to me, I felt as if I was trying to balance 20 crystal goblets on my forearms. Every time the baby moved I thought I was going to drop her. I don't see how anyone ever gets used to this. . . .

June 13

I have been wondering what this is going to do to my ambition. I have always been a pathologically ambitious person; it is probably the one quality that defines me most clearly. All my life I have been running off on stories. It is what I do, and there has never been any question that I was ready to go anywhere on a moment's notice.

I am under contract to ABC News "Nightline." In March and April I went out on nine stories for the show. In the year previous to that—my first year working for the broadcast—I did 32 pieces. This is in addition to my newspaper and *Esquire* columns.

In the month before the baby was due, however, I had asked not to travel for the show. I know that I am in no emotional condition to leave Susan and Amanda Sue alone in the immediate future, but how long can this feeling last? What's going to happen the first time the phone rings and it's "Nightline" telling me to meet a camera crew at the airport?

If I'm going to be the same person I've always been, I have to live on the run—but in the last 48 hours I haven't been able to sit next to a silent phone for more than 15 minutes without checking the hospital and seeing how Susan and Amanda are doing.

I'm sure this is a dilemma that new fathers have faced over the ages. But that doesn't make it any less new to me. I will hate myself if I give up any of the professional drive that has always consumed me. But already I feel myself changing. This is going to be very difficult.

My first triumph. Amanda had been nursing, and she apparently had some gas. She started to cry, hard, and Susan couldn't make her stop.

I leaned over and started whispering to her and stroking her head. She looked up at me, and I kept whispering. And she stayed silent. . . .

June 15

It doesn't matter how many books you read before

your baby arrives. Nothing gets you ready for that first night when you're out of the hospital and alone, and she's crying and won't stop, and you're holding her against you while her screams rock your chest.

Tonight Amanda Sue was howling from midnight to dawn. In a cartoon it's funny to see an open-mouthed baby bawling wildly; when it's happening to you for the first time, though, you simply don't know what to do. Intellectually you have always known that babies cry a lot. But when you're holding your own in your arms, all you can think about is that she's in some kind of pain and that you're impotent to do anything about it.

When dawn came after her first night at home, we were still awake, red-eyed and exhausted, rocking her and wondering what all of us had gotten into.

Grandparents and Burps

Susan's mother arrived from Ohio. It's peculiar how you never notice things about people until those matters affect you directly. From the moment Mrs. Koebel walked into the apartment, things calmed down. She picked the baby up and started walking around with her and talking to her. Amanda Sue was crying just as hard, but watching Mrs. Koebel holding her made me less nervous. I have no idea how to handle a baby, and Susan, although she's better than I, is still brand-new at it.

I may not have learned anything else useful from this situation, but I know this: if you're having your first baby, make sure you get a grandmother there as soon as possible. . . .

June 17

The littlest things take on importance. Babies have to be burped; everyone knows that. Yet Amanda has trouble bringing up gas after nursing—and if she can't bring up gas, the pains start. I just can't stand the sight of her doubling up and screaming.

"If a week ago you had warned me that the failure of a baby to burp would be a crisis in my life, I would have thought you were joking."

So after each feeding, Susan, Mrs. Koebel and I take turns holding Amanda and trying to get her to burp. No one told me this was going to be a problem. If a week ago you had warned me that the failure of a baby to burp would be a crisis in my life, I would have thought you were joking. Now it is starting to consume me.

June 26

Susan's father arrived today. He will be driving her mother home tomorrow. This is the first time he has seen Amanda.

The thoughts I've been having about the difference between men and women when it comes to babies were reaffirmed with Mr. Koebel. He looked at Amanda, and he was clearly moved to see her, but he didn't know quite what to do.

Men and Women

When she started crying, he looked around for someone else to do something. While Susan and her mother took turns carrying Amanda around the living room, he sat in a chair and watched. I knew exactly how he felt. When Amanda is crying and won't stop, I do what I can to help—but I know, in the end, that it is Susan's responsibility. That may sound pretty archaic, but there's no getting around it.

When Susan or her mother holds Amanda, it seems right; when Mr. Koebel or I hold Amanda, it seems unwieldy. When she cries and Susan or her mother sits for a few minutes without reacting, it seems as if they are neglecting her; when she cries and Mr. Koebel or I just sit there, it seems as if we merely don't know what to do.

I am aware this is contradictory to what we are being told the world is becoming. Women and men, we read, need to take equal roles in the care of a baby. And I'm not saying that the differences are genetic—not exactly. But when the four of us are in the room, and Amanda cries from the nursery for attention, it is clearly Mrs. Koebel and Susan who instinctively know what to do. It is not an inherent lack of capability on the part of the men. Mr. Koebel landed fighter planes on aircraft carriers during World War II, and he can take care of himself. But when it comes to a two-week-old baby, there's something that has been passed down through the ages, culturally, that makes women think they can handle it, and men doubt that they can. At least this is what I'm coming to believe. . . .

July 1

When you're drawing up your list of life's miracles, you might place near the top the first moment your baby smiles at you. . . .

Amanda was on her back in a carriage in the living room. As I have every day, I leaned over and looked at her. I tickled her stomach and scratched her foot.

Every day since she was born she has reacted by gurgling or shifting her body. Today, though, she looked right at me. And she smiled.

Her toothless mouth opened, and she scrunched her face up, and it really was a grin. It went away momentarily, and then she did it again—looked me in the eye and smiled at my face.

The sleepless nights, the worries, the crying—suddenly it was all worth it. I called to Susan, and she came running from the bathroom, thinking something was wrong. Amanda was still smiling when she got there, and we looked down together, smiling back. She is no longer just something we are nursing and carrying—somewhere inside, part of her knows what's going on, and that part of her is telling us that she's with us. She will never remember any of this, of course. And I will never forget.

July 11

I went into Amanda's room this morning and, as I have every morning, I looked down into her crib and said, "Good morning, Merry Sunshine." She smiled back.

Today Susan asked me why I was saying it.

"I don't know," I said.

But I started thinking about it, and I figured it out. "Good morning, Merry Sunshine" is what my mother used to say to me every morning when I was a child. I hadn't heard the words since I was five years old—30 years ago. But without being reminded, here I was saying the same thing every day. I would tell my mother about it, but I think I'm too embarrassed.

Future Plans

July 13

In the middle of the night, between feedings, when Susan has drifted off into exhausted sleep and so has Amanda, I will wake up and wonder if everything is all right.

I will walk into Amanda's room. She will be up in the left-hand corner of the crib, and her head will be jammed between the padded bumpers, and she will be still.

Carefully, I will slip my finger under her nose, just to make sure I can feel her breath. Amanda, asleep, doesn't know I'm doing it. I haven't told Susan, either. But I fall back to sleep better, having checked.

"One of the gifts of having Amanda is this: we notice things we never took the time to notice before."

July 14

My work world is getting back to normal. My thoughts are still filled with Amanda, but just looking at the columns I have written since I returned to the paper tells me that I have other things on my mind too.

When I get home every night, I learn anew that Susan and Amanda have been preoccupied only with each other.

Tonight I walked into the apartment and heard the sounds of the television. I called hello, but there was no answer. I walked into the living room, and Susan, looking tired beyond tired, was asleep on the couch. In the carriage a few feet away, Amanda slept too.

When they awakened I could tell that this is getting to Susan. She is beginning to feel the difference—the confining difference—that the baby has brought to her world. She can tell that even though my world has changed, too, at least I have the discipline of my work to remind me of the way things used to be.

She feels that she and Amanda will inevitably be closer than Amanda and I. After they woke up, the baby started hiccuping, as she often does. I said, "Amanda, you get the hiccups all the time."

Susan picked her up to burp her and said to her, "He doesn't know that you used to hiccup all the time in my tummy, does he, Amanda?" Just a little reminder that they have a history together that I was never part of.

July 15

Amanda makes bicycling motions. Yesterday she wasn't yet doing it; today she is. As she lies on her back, she raise her arms, and it's almost as if she's trying to swim. At the same time her legs are pumping. Sort of like she's running in a race—but she's not strong enough yet to roll over, so the whole race is run on her back.

And now there are noises. Not just the crying sounds, but noises she makes when she sees something and is curious. I don't know whether this counts as the very first stages of trying to talk. But to sit there and see her look at something and come forth with a quizzical sound—it's something. . . .

Walking Through a Dream

August 18

The kitchen counter used to be where I would put soda-pop bottles after I had finished using them, where I would make myself peanut-butter sandwiches. No more.

Now the kitchen is where Amanda takes her baths. Susan fills a yellow-plastic tub with lukewarm water, and then puts a sponge lining into it. When the sponge is soaked through, Amanda goes on top of the sponge. She pretty much hates it.

But it is always a shock for me to go into the kitchen and find Amanda, naked and dripping wet, where my pop bottles used to be. If you ask me, a baby shouldn't take her bath in the kitchen. No one has asked me. . . .

September 17

One of the gifts of having Amanda is this: we notice things we never took the time to notice before.

We were in the living room holding her; it was a gray afternoon. Suddenly the sun broke through the clouds, and the streets below were flooded with light.

Susan held her up to the window. "Look, Amanda!" she said. "The sun's coming out! Look at it!"

The three of us looked together. I can't remember the last time, before Amanda, that we paid any attention to the sun and the clouds.

October 6

I came home late last night in a foul mood. I had been called in to the ABC Chicago bureau to do a "Nightline" commentary. The piece had read well, and I had delivered it well, and the videotape had looked good. I was anticipating the show with even more enthusiasm than usual.

But when the show had aired, I wasn't on it.

Everyone was quite complimentary about the piece, but I have learned that in television, if it doesn't make the broadcast, it doesn't exist. So I was silent and angry when I got home, and I climbed into bed and stared at the ceiling until 3 A.M. I woke up still fretting about the show.

And then I heard Susan saying, "Things didn't go so well for your daddy last night, so you be nice to him." She was carrying Amanda. She put her down on the bed next to me, and Amanda grinned at me and started to gurgle.

Despite myself I had to smile back and put my finger in her fist and hug her. This delighted her, and she started to kick against me; in a moment we were playing and, for that precise slice of time, the troubles went away. . . .

"Eight months ago she didn't exist. And now I find that, without her at home, there is a huge void in my life."

November 17

She's getting really good at scooting around on her back. She will be on her vinyl cloth on the living-room floor, and in a matter of seconds she will propel herself all the way across it. I'll pick her up and put her in the middle. She will squeal and start kicking her legs again, and there she'll go.

I hadn't been expecting this. I thought all babies learned to move by crawling on their stomachs first. Still none of that; it's as if she thinks zipping along on her back is the most natural thing in the world.

December 25

On her first Christmas the relatives all called. We held the telephone up to Amanda's ear and they talked to her. She knew something was going on; a quizzical expression came to her face, and she looked at Susan and me as if we could somehow explain it to her.

We gave her presents, including her d-o-g, which she seemed to enjoy. We made certain that we gave her something special: cloth books.

They're just what they sound like: short books printed on cloth. She has no idea what they are, of course. The only reason she likes them is that they feel soft in her hands, and they're colorful.

Our theory is that they probably are good for her.

If she can learn—even subliminally—that it's a positive thing to have books in the house, it's a start. So many factors these days fight against a child's having any respect or reverence for reading; we figure that if we can signal to her, at this young age, that books are equated with pleasure, maybe she'll continue to turn to them when she's old enough to read.

It was great to see her playing with her d-o-g on Christmas Day. But it was even better to see her holding and examining her cloth books—even though she did decide, after the examination, to try to eat them.

The First Crawl

January 1

Well. My. Today is the first day she was officially able to crawl.

We had some friends over to say Happy New Year. They were holding Amanda, passing her back and forth. She was more amenable to this than she usually is with strangers, but I could tell that she wanted to get back to Susan.

One of our friends handed her to me, and I put her down on the floor to see if she wanted to play. And . . . there she went. She saw Susan sitting on the floor about ten yards away, and she decided she was going to go to her.

Mainly she pulled herself with her arms. Her knees were getting into the act, too, but the strength was coming from her shoulders and arms. Susan started to come forward to get her.

"Don't," I said.

Amanda kept inching forward. It took her a few minutes, but she made it to Susan's lap.

Our friends didn't seem to think it was all that amazing—they don't have kids, and I'm sure they assume that babies crawl all the time. So we tried to contain our enthusiasm until they left.

And then Amanda really went to town. I moved to the kitchen and turned on a radio. She heard it and crawled all the way from the living room. In the space of a day, she seems much older.

An Empty Home

January 17

Susan has been saying for months that she needs a break. She said that with all my traveling I get regular diversions, a luxury she doesn't have. She has no desire to take a vacation with me and leave Amanda with a baby-sitter or a relative; she would be missing Amanda every second.

What she did want to do, she said, was to go to Ohio and stay with her parents for two or three weeks. Her mother could help her take care of Amanda, and she wouldn't have to worry about cooking or cleaning.

There was no way I could get that much time off from work. But I agreed with her that it would do her a lot of good. I said I would feel much better if I flew to Columbus with them and then flew back.

We went tonight. My own parents greeted us at Port Columbus International Airport. My father was crouched just inside the terminal with his camera, like a paparazzo who feared his subject might bolt before he captured the scene on film. So as we walked in, a flashbulb popped, and then my parents drove us to Susan's parents' house.

January 18-February 13

I suppose I was prepared to miss Susan and Amanda; I knew that the apartment would seem empty without them. But I wasn't all that concerned about it. Because I have traveled so frequently myself during the months she has been with us, I assumed that going home every night to the apartment would feel pretty much the way it feels when I am on the road in some strange hotel room.

I was wrong.

When I'm on the road I always know, in the back of my mind, that Amanda and Susan are at home waiting for me. In an airport or in bed at a hotel, I can envision the apartment, with them there. When I pick up the phone and call, it's not just their voices I respond to—it's my visual image of our home, and what it's like with Amanda there.

It's not like that now. I've been coming home after work, and there's no one around. But the artifacts are all there, and that's what gets to me. Her Christmas toy dog sitting in the living room. Her carriage in the hallway. Her box of toys on the floor. Her crib in her room.

I really had no conception of how much she has come to mean in my life. Eight months ago she didn't exist. And now I find that, without her at home, there is a huge void in my life. I almost ache for not seeing her.

She and Susan seem to be doing fine in Columbus. I've been calling every day—several times a day, as a matter of fact. Susan says that Amanda's top front teeth are coming in. It's not that major a development, but I want to be there for it. . . .

First Steps

February 24

I came home and walked into the living room. Amanda was standing there looking at me.

That's so strange. She's begun to do it all the time now. She pulls herself up into a standing position, and she stays up. Susan or I don't have to help her; she does it all on her own. Without support she couldn't stay upright. Tonight, for example, she was standing by one of the bookcases, grasping a shelf so that she didn't fall.

It gives everything such a different perspective. As ready as I am for her to grow older, it's shocking to walk into the apartment and to see Susan sitting—and Amanda standing. It just doesn't fit in with any of the attitudes I have built up about her.

As great as it is to watch her physical development, if we pay close enough attention we can see signs that her mind is developing too.

In the last few days, when she has dropped something, she has looked down to the floor to see where it went. There was a first long stage when she didn't pick up anything at all, and everything had to be handed to her. Then there was the stage when she gladly picked up anything within reach, but discarded it without paying any more attention.

Now it's different. If she is playing with a toy and it slips out of her hand, she will follow it with her eyes; we can see her wondering what has become of it. A month ago it would have stayed on the floor, no longer a part of her consciousness. Now, most of the time, she will return and pick it up. She understands that even though it's momentarily out of her hand it's still a part of her world. . . .

"She stepped forward one more time with her right leg, and then fell into my arms. We just stayed there hugging each other."

April 6

I got home from work a little late tonight. In the front hallway, toys were scattered all over the carpeting. In the living room, magazines were spread everywhere. In the bathroom, the toilet paper had been unrolled and left on the floor. Near the stereo, all of the albums had been pulled out and discarded. "Hi," I said to Susan. "I'd ask you what she's been doing all day, but I guess I know." . . .

May 29

She walked.

I was supporting her in an upright, standing position. She was clutching my hands. She was balanced on her feet.

Slowly I uncurled her fingers so that she wasn't connected to my hands anymore. She was standing on her own. I moved backward.

She bent her knees, as though she wanted to get down on the floor and crawl.

"No, Amanda," I said. "Come here. Come to me."

I was perhaps five feet away. She looked me right in the eye.

"Come to me," I said.

She lifted her right leg and moved it forward. She still didn't fall.

"That's great," I said. "Now the other one."

She lifted her left leg—really lifted it, higher than she needed to—and brought it level with the right.

"A little bit more," I said.

She brought the right leg forward again. Then—much quicker this time—the left.

There was fear and excitement in her eyes. She stepped forward one more time with her right leg, and then fell into my arms. We just stayed there hugging each other. . . .

A Year of Change

June 7

She was drinking milk from her bottle this morning. I was holding her in my lap. She was holding the bottle all by herself.

Suddenly she took the bottle from her mouth and offered it to me. I laughed and handed it back to her. But she shoved it toward me again. It was clear that she wanted me to take a drink.

I pretended to put the bottle in my mouth, and to drink. She smiled broadly. She took the bottle back and took a swig herself. Then she gave it to me again.

She wouldn't drink any more until I had some—or, more correctly, pretended to have some. And so it went for ten minutes—Amanda taking a drink, insisting that I have a drink, and then drinking some more herself. I don't know what gave her the idea to do this, but it made me feel very good about life in general.

June 9

Of all the things she might learn to identify and say this early in her life, I wouldn't have predicted that the human navel would be one of the first.

She's always pulling up my shirt, sticking her finger in my navel and saying "belly button." She doesn't say it that clearly, of course; it usually comes out more like "beww bumm." But she knows what it is. It seems to fascinate her. "Beww bumm," she will say, poking me. Then she'll look at me for confirmation.

"I am a different person than I was a year ago."

"That's right," I'll say. "That's Daddy's belly button."

And she'll shriek with laughter, and lurch away, arms spread for balance.

June 11

It's five o'clock in the morning. I'm in the living room. Amanda and Susan are asleep.

Today my parents and Susan's parents arrive for Amanda's first-birthday party. Susan has hung crepe paper and balloons. There will be gifts and picture-taking.

I don't know why I couldn't sleep, but here I am—looking out the windows and trying to sort out my thoughts. I suppose it's a futile task; maybe someday, years from now, I'll be able to delineate what this year has meant to me. But not now.

All I know is that, here in my home, I have a completely different feeling than I ever expected I'd have. Everything has changed. I guess I knew that was bound to happen, but I couldn't have predicted in precisely what ways. Quite simply, I am a different person than I was a year ago.

I just went into Amanda's room and looked down at her. She never knew me as the man I was before. She may never be aware that, just by living, she has changed another life so much. Someday I can try to explain it to her, and she can try to understand. But she will be attempting to understand the words of a person she knows only as her father—and it will be too much to expect her to decipher who that person was before he became her father.

I should be getting back to bed—it's going to be a long day. But something in me wants to stay here alone, in the darkness, and let the unfocused thoughts drift over me.

When I hear the first sound from my daughter's bedroom I will go in and lift her to me, as I have on so many mornings, as I hope to on so many mornings to come. There will be one candle on a cake today. I will accept that as marking the end of this particular story. But the story goes on. It is unlike any I have ever been a part of, and it goes on.

Bob Greene is a writer and television journalist.

viewpoint 43

Fatherhood: A Nontraditional View

David Osborne

"Friends who visit me nowadays probably think I'm crazy, the way I rush compulsively to get dinner ready or mow the lawn or finish the laundry."

If I ever finish this article, it will be a miracle. Nicholas woke up this morning with an earache and a temperature, and I spent half the day at the doctor's office and pharmacy. Another ear infection.

Nicholas is my son. Twenty months old, a stout little bundle of energy and affection.

I will never forget the moment when I realized how completely Nick would change my life. My wife is a resident in obstetrics and gynecology, which means, among other things, that she works 100 hours a week, leaves the house every day by six and works all night several times a week, and often all weekend too. I'm not a househusband; I take Nick to day care five days a week. But I come about as close to house-husbandry as I care to. I am what you might call a "nontraditional" father.

Bottles

Nick was three weeks old when I learned what that actually meant. Rose had just gone back to work, and Nick and I were learning about bottles. I don't remember if it was Rose's first night back or her second, but she wasn't home.

I stayed up too late; I had not yet learned that, with a baby in the house, you grab sleep whenever you can—even if it means going to bed at nine. Just as I drifted off, about 11:30, Nick woke up. I fed him and rocked him and put him back to sleep. About 2 A.M. he woke again, crying, and I rocked him for 45 minutes before he quieted down.

When he started screaming at four, I was in the kitchen by the time I woke up. As every parent knows, the sound of an infant—your infant—screaming sends lightning bolts up the spine. Bells ring in the head; nerves jangle. Racing against my son's hunger, I boiled water, poured it into the little plastic sack, slipped the sack into the plastic bottle,

put on the top, and plunged the bottle into a bowl of cold water to cool it. I had not yet learned that in Connecticut, where I lived, the water need not be sterilized. (Fathers are the last to know.) It takes a long time to boil water and cool it back to body temperature, and I was dead on my feet even before the screams rearranged my vertebrae. By the time the water had cooled, I was half-crazed, my motions rapid and jerky. I mixed in the powdered formula and slopped the nipple back on. I ran toward Nick's room, shaking the bottle as hard as I could to make sure it was thoroughly mixed. As I reached his crib, the top flew off—and the contents sprayed all over the room.

At that point, I lost it. I swore at the top of my lungs, I stomped around the room, I slammed the changing table, and I swore some more. That was when I realized what I had gotten myself into—and how much I had to learn.

Journals Ring False

With baby boomers well ensconced in the nation's newsrooms, fatherhood is sweeping American journalism. You pick up the *New York Times Magazine*, or *Esquire*, or Bob Greene's best-seller, *Good Morning, Merry Sunshine: A Father's Journal of His Child's First Year* (Penguin), and read all about the wonders of being a father.

By all accounts, today's fathers are more involved and more sensitive than their own fathers were. But as warm and tender as their writing may be, it rings false. Rosalie Ziomek, a mother in Evanston, Illinois, said it perfectly in a letter to the *New Republic*, after it printed a scathing review of Bob Greene's book. "I was enraged by Greene's book," Ziomek wrote. "Anyone taking care of a newborn infant doesn't have time to write about it. Greene was cashing in on the experiences that most women have quietly and painfully lived without the glorification of fame and money. Meanwhile, because of the structure of

David Osborne, "Beyond the Cult of Fatherhood," *Ms.*, September 1985. © 1985 David Osborne. Reprinted with the author's permission.

his work/social life, which he is unwilling to alter, he avoids the thing that is the hardest part of new motherhood: the moment-to-moment dependency of a tiny, helpless, and demanding human being. I have more to say on the subject, but I have three children to take care of and writing is a luxury I can't afford right now."

Ziomek is right. I've been trying to keep a journal, as Greene did, and it's impossible. There's no time. And how do you capture the essence of an exhausting, never-ending 24-hour day in a few paragraphs? Snapshots work if you spend an hour or two with a child, but if you spend days, everything dissolves in a blur.

My experience is different from that of the fathers I read about. Certainly I am not fulfilling the role of a traditional mother, and certainly no child could ask for a more loving mother than Nick has. But I do fix most of the meals and do most of the laundry and change a lot of the diapers and get Nick up and dressed in the morning and shuttle him back and forth to day care and cart him to the grocery store and sing him to sleep and clean up his toys and wipe his nose and deal with his tantrums and cuddle with him and tickle him and all the other wonderful and exhausting things mothers do. If you ask me what it all means, I can't say. After 20 months, I'm still dizzy, still desperate for a free hour or two, and still hopelessly in love with my little boy. All I have to offer are fragments; profound thoughts are for people who have more time. But if you want to go beyond the cult of fatherhood, I think I've been there.

Starting the Day

My day starts about 6:30 or 7 A.M., when Nick stands up in his crib and calls out for me. I stumble into his room, pick him up, give him a kiss and a "Good morning, Pumpkin," and carry him back to bed. I lay him down on his mother's empty pillow, lie down beside him, and sometimes I drowse again before it's really time to get up. But most mornings Nick is ready to start his day, and he gradually drags me up toward consciousness. He smiles at me, climbs up on me, and rests his head against my cheek—even kisses me if I'm really lucky, or sits on my bladder and bounces, if I'm not. I tickle him, and he laughs and squirms and shrieks for more.

Sometimes he lies there for a few minutes, thinking his little boy thoughts, before sliding himself backward off the bed and going in search of something to do. Often he arrives back with a toy or two and asks to be picked "Up! Up!" Then he plays for a few minutes, making sure to keep an eye on my progress toward wakefulness. When he has waited long enough, he hands me my glasses, takes my hand, and pulls me out of bed.

While I shower, Nick plays in the bathroom, sitting on the floor with his toys. By the time I'm

dressed, the kettle is whistling, and he's ready for breakfast. We always eat together; he has hot cereal, I have cold cereal, and often we share a bagel. I wish you could hear him say "cream cheese."

Weekends

The rough times come on weekends. After 24 hours, I'm ready to be hung out on the line to dry. After 48 hours, I'm ready to pin medals on women who stay home every day with their kids. For single mothers, I'm ready to build monuments.

Don't let anyone tell you otherwise: traditional mothers work harder than anyone else can even imagine. They are on duty 24 hours a day, 365 days a year. I remember wondering, as a youth, why my own mother always rushed around with such urgency when she was cooking or cleaning. To me, she was like a woman possessed. Now I do the same thing. When you have a young child (or two, or three), you have very little time to get the dishes done, or cook dinner, or vacuum, or do the laundry. So when you get a moment, you proceed with all possible haste. If your children are asleep, they might wake up. If they're playing, they might get bored and demand your attention.

"Don't let anyone tell you otherwise: traditional mothers work harder than anyone else can even imagine."

Friends who visit me nowadays probably think I'm crazy, the way I rush compulsively to get dinner ready or mow the lawn or finish the laundry. I do feel somewhat self-conscious about it. But the fact is, if I'm cooking, Nick is going to start demanding his meal soon, and if it's not ready, he's going to get very cranky. And with all the chores that pile up on a weekend—the lawn, the laundry, the groceries, and so on—I have to seize every possible instant. If he naps, that may give me an hour and a half. If he wakes up before I'm done, whatever I'm doing will never get finished.

One Small Crisis

In any case, it is on weekends alone with Nick that I feel the full brunt of child-rearing. Consider a typical weekend: Nick wakes at 7:00, and we lie in bed and play for half an hour before getting up. But this morning he feels feverish, so I take his temperature. It is 101.6—not high for a young child, but a fever nonetheless.

The first thing I do is call Maureen, who takes care of him during the week. Both of her kids have a bug, and I want to find out what the symptoms are, to see if Nick has the same thing. From what we can tell, he does. On that basis, I decide to give him Tylenol for the fever, rather than taking him to the pediatrician to see if he's got an ear infection. Besides, he wants to lie down for a nap at 10:00, before I have decided, and doesn't wake until 1:00. By then the office is closed.

After lunch he feels much better—cool, happy, and bubbling. We play with his lock-blocks for a while, then watch a basketball game. He's very cuddly, because he's not feeling well. After the game it's off to the bank and grocery store. He falls asleep on the way home, at 5:45. It's an awkward time for a nap, but he only sleeps until 6:30. He wakes up crying, with a high fever, feeling miserable.

To get him to swallow more Tylenol, which he hates, I promise him ice cream. I give him half an ice-cream sandwich while I rush around the kitchen cooking dinner, and when he finishes it, he cries for the other half. I tell him he can have it after he eats his dinner. But when dinner is ready, he won't eat; he just sits there pointing at the freezer, where the ice cream is, and wailing. This is a major tantrum— hot tears, red face. I can't help but sympathize, though, because it's born of feeling absolutely wretched. How should I respond? I don't want to give in and teach him he can get his way by screaming. I try to comfort him by holding him in my lap, but he just sobs. Finally I take him into his room and rock him, holding him close. Gradually the sobs subside, and after 10 minutes I take him back into the kitchen, hold him on my lap, and feed him myself. He doesn't eat much, but enough to deserve his ice cream.

See the Doctor?

Though Nick gets over the incident in no time, I am traumatized. The fever is frightening—it has hit 102 by dinnertime, and it only drops to 101.4 by 8 P.M. Should I have taken him to the doctor? Will he spike a really high fever tonight? Am I being too relaxed? And what will Rose say? I cannot stop worrying; I feel heartsick as I read him his bedtime stories, though he cools down as he drifts off to sleep in my arms. Would a mother feel so uncertain, I wonder? Do mothers feel adequate at moments like this? Or am I in a father's territory here?

Sunday morning Nick wakes at 6:30 and devours his breakfast, but pretty soon his temperature begins to rise. I call our pediatrician, who reassures me that it doesn't sound like an ear infection, and that I'm doing the right thing. Still, Nick isn't feeling well, and it makes him more demanding. He want to be held; he wants me with him constantly; he insists that I do what he wants me to do and cries if I balk. It is a wearing day. He naps late, and when I wake him at seven, he is again miserable—temperature at 102.4, crying, refusing to let me change his diaper. But after more Tylenol and a good dinner he feels better.

I haven't heard from Rose all weekend, so I decide to call her at the hospital. She is furious that I haven't taken Nick to the doctor. A child who gets ear infections as often as he does has to be checked, she yells at me. He could blow out an eardrum! And why haven't I called her—she's his mother, for God's sake! I'm exhausted, I've been busting my hump all weekend, alone, doing the best I can, and now I'm being abused. I don't like it. My first impulse is to hang up on her, but instead I hand the phone to Nicholas, who has a long talk with her. He says "Mommy!" she says "Nicholas!" and he laughs and laughs.

"Rose has felt guilty since the day she went back to work. . . . I feel guilty only occasionally."

Rose may be right, I know, but that doesn't help my anger. We part tersely, and I promise to take him to the pediatrician the next morning before I leave for California on an article assignment. After that's out of the way, Nick and I have a good evening. We read books, and several times he leads me into his room to get another handful. A short bath, more books, then off to bed. He wants to take two of his trucks to bed with him—a new wrinkle—but I finally convince him to say "night-night" to his trucks and turn out the lights.

I have several hours of work to do before I leave, so I don't get to bed until after midnight. I'm absolutely shot. When the alarm rings at 6:00, I haul myself out of bed, shower, get dressed, and get Nick up and fed and dressed. We speed down to the library to return several books, then to the doctor's office. No ear infection; it's just a bug, says the doc, and he should be over it by nightfall. I drop Nick off at Maureen's by 9:30, race home, and spend the next hour packing, vacuuming, cleaning up the dishes and defrosting something for Rose and Nick's dinner. When I get to the airport, I realize I've misread my ticket and I'm half an hour early. I'm exhausted, and the trip has yet to begin.

Comparing Guilt

Two nights later I call Rose. When I ask how she is, she bursts into tears. Nicholas has fallen at Maureen's and cut his forehead on a metal toy. Rose was caught in an ice storm between the hospital and home, so Maureen had to take her own kids to a neighbor's and rush Nick to the pediatrician's office for stitches. They gave him a local anesthetic, but he screamed the whole time.

"I feel so awful," Rose sobs, over and over. "I should have been there. I just feel awful!" Guilt floods in, but it is nothing to match Rose's guilt. This is one of the differences I have discovered between mothers and fathers.

Rose has felt guilty since the day she went back to work—the hardest single thing I've ever watched her do. Deep inside her psyche lies a powerful message that she belongs at home, that if she is not with her child she is terribly irresponsible.

I feel guilty only occasionally. When I dropped Nick off at day care the first day after returning from California, and he sobbed because he thought I was leaving him again, the guilt just about killed me. I turned into a classic mother: as soon as I got home, I called to see if he was still crying. (He was.) Two guilt-ridden hours later I called again, desperate to hear that everything was fine. (It was.)

Belong at Work

Deep within my psyche, however, the most powerful message is that I belong at work, that if I am not out making my mark on the world I am worth nothing.

The contradiction between family and career is nothing new; it is perhaps the central unresolved conflict in the lives of American women today. What I did not expect was the force with which that conflict would erupt in my life.

"How many women would be content with men who stayed home with the kids? Not many, I'll wager."

Like an addict, I now find myself squeezing in every last minute of work that I can. I wait until the last possible instant before rushing out the door to pick Nick up in the afternoon. I dart out to my studio while he naps on weekends, using a portable intercom to listen for his cries. At night I compulsively page through old newspapers that pile up because I can no longer read them over breakfast, afraid I've missed something important. As I hit deadline time, I pray that Nicholas doesn't get sick. I have even tried writing on a Saturday afternoon, with Nick playing in my studio. That experiment lasted half an hour, at which point he hit the reset button on the back of my computer and my prose was lost to the ages.

This frantic effort to keep up is clearly not good for me, but I cannot seem to abandon it. I constantly feel as if I live in a pressure cooker. I long for a free day, even a free hour. But my career has taken off just as my responsibilities as a father have hit their peak, and I cannot seem to scale down my commitment to either.

When Nick was four months old, I took him to a Christmas party, one Saturday when Rose was working. After an hour or so he got cranky, so I took him upstairs with a bottle. A little girl followed, and soon her brother and sister—equally bored by the goings-on downstairs—had joined us. It wasn't long before Dad came looking for them.

We introduced ourselves and talked for a bit. His wife, it turned out, was also a doctor. The curious part came when I asked what he did. First he told me all the things he had done in the past; carpentry, business, you name it. Then he said he'd done enough—he was about 40—and felt no need to prove himself anymore. Finally he told me he stayed at home with the kids. And frankly, he pulled it off with far more dignity and less stammering than I would have, had our places been reversed.

I don't think I could do what he does. If I were to stay home full-time with Nick, I would quickly lose my self-esteem, and within months I would be deep into an identity crisis. Part of the reason I love my role as a father is that I am secure in my role as a writer. Without that, I would not feel good enough about myself to be the kind of father I am.

This is not simply a problem inside male heads. How many women would be content with men who stayed home with the kids? Not many, I'll wager. And not my wife, I know. From my experience, modern women want a man who will share the responsibilities at home but still be John Wayne in the outside world. They don't want any wimps wearing aprons. And men know it.

Who's in Charge?

We are in a Burger King, in Fall River, Massachusetts. We are not having a good day. We drove two hours to shop in the factory outlets here, and all but a handful are closed because it's Sunday.

Nick likes Burger King, but he's not having a great day either. He has recently learned about tantrums, and as we get ready to leave, he decides to throw one. He doesn't want to leave; he doesn't want to put on his coat; he just doesn't want to be hauled around any more. So he stands up and wails.

Rose is mortified; she takes any misbehavior in public as an advertisement of her failings as a mother. It triggers all her guilt about working. This time, the timing couldn't be worse, because she is already on edge.

Our tantrum strategy is generally to let him yell, to ignore him, and thus to teach him that it does no good. But in a public restaurant, I don't have the stamina to ignore him, so I cross the room to pick him up.

Rose orders me away from him in no uncertain terms. There are no negotiations, no consultations. We are going to do this her way or no way.

That lights my fuse, of course, and after simmering for 10 minutes, I bring it up. "Let it go," she tells me, almost in tears over Nicholas. "It's not important."

It's not important.

Ah, the double bind. You're in charge one day, playing mother and father all wrapped into one, depended upon to feed him and clothe him and change him and bathe him and rock him and meet his every need. And the next day you're a third wheel, because Mom is around. You are expected to put in the long hours, but to pretend in public that you don't, for fear of undercutting your wife's sense of self-worth as a mother. How could she be doing her job, her psyche seems to whisper, if she's letting someone else make half the decisions and give half the care? There are many double binds in modern relationships, and this is the one I like the least.

I didn't let it drop that day, of course. At home, when Rose asserts the traditional mother's prerogative to make decisions and handle problems alone, on her terms, I often let it go. But when it happens in public, or in front of family, it is too much. It is as if my entire contribution to raising Nicholas is being denied, as if the world is being told that I am nothing more than a spectator. Luckily, as Nick grows older, and it becomes clear to Rose that she will always be number one in his heart, she has begun to relax her public vigilance, and this problem seems to have abated.

Yanked Into the Women's World

This is the first time I've ever been part of a woman's world. I'm not really a part of it, of course; the chasm between the sexes is too wide to step across so lightly. But when it comes to children, I have instant rapport with most mothers. We talk about the same things, think about the same things, joke about the same things. With men, it is almost never that way, even when the men are fathers and the subject is kids. We can share enthusiasms, but the sense of being there, on the inside—the unspoken understanding that comes out of shared experience—that is missing.

"Most men don't have the slightest idea what my life with Nick is like."

In fact, most men don't have the slightest idea what my life with Nick is like. When I tell colleagues—even those with children—that I have no time to read, or to watch television, I get blank stares. (I never tell mothers that; they already know. Who has time to read?) One friend, also a writer, stopped in the middle of a recent conversation and said, "You have Nick at home while you're working, don't you? What do you do with him?" No such thought could pass a mother's lips.

None of this would have been possible had I not been forced into taking care of Nick on my own much of the time. In fact, my entire relationship with Nick would have been different had I not been forced off the sidelines. I am convinced that in our society, when Mom is home with the kids, it is almost impossible for Dad to be an equal partner in their upbringing, even if he wants to be.

I believe this because for three weeks, while Rose was home after Nick's birth, it felt impossible to me. Rose had carried Nick for nine months; Rose had been through labor; and Rose was nursing him. For nine months he had listened to her heartbeat, felt her pulse, been a part of her being. Now he hunted her scent and drank from her body, and the bond between them was awesome. I was like some voyeur, peeking through the window at an ancient and sacred rite.

Then Rose went back to work, and I had no choice but to get off the sidelines. I *had* to get Nick dressed in the morning. I *had* to feed him. I *had* to burp him and rock him and change him and get up with him in the night. He may have wanted his mother, but she wasn't there.

Gradually, it all began to come naturally. I learned to carry him on my (nonexistent) hip and do anything—or any combination of things—with one hand. I learned to whip up a bottle in no time, to change a diaper and treat diaper rash and calm his tears.

Even on vacation, it is remarkably easy to slip back into a traditional role—for both Rose and me. But the day Rose goes back to work, I am always yanked back to reality. I complain a lot, but in truth, this is my great good fortune.

Rewards

Last night Nick asked to go to the beach—"Go? Beach? Go? Beach?" I walked him the two blocks down, one of his hands firmly in mine, the other proudly holding the leash for Sam, our dog. We played on the swings for a long time, then strolled along the beach while Sam went swimming. It was that very still hour before dark, when the world slows to a hush, and little boys and girls slowly wind down. It was almost dark when we returned. Nick asked his daddy to give him his bath, then his mommy to put him to bed.

This morning when I woke he was lying beside me, on his mother's empty pillow. I looked over and he gave me a big smile, his eyes shining with that special, undiluted joy one sees only in children. Then he propped himself up on his elbows, leaned over and kissed me. If there are any better moments in life, I've never found them.

David Osborne is a free-lance writer.

"Many young fathers . . . are pushing aside stereotypes to become more involved in the everyday care of their children."

Men Are Becoming More Active Fathers

Marilyn Sherman

As Dan pushes his laughing 15-month-old son on the swing in the bright sunshine, he muses about the canvas he'll start painting during Steven's nap.

Rick picks up his two children, ages 6 and 9, at school every day. The owner of a trucking firm, he schedules his work hours so he can spend time with his children.

Last year, John worked as a reporter for a local newspaper while Lisa stayed at home to take care of their infant. This year, Lisa teaches fifth grade, and John is on duty at home in the nursery.

Shared Parenting

What do you think would be the ideal marriage? For 76 percent of the young Americans polled, the answer was a marriage in which the spouses share child-rearing, housework, and breadwinning.

Many young fathers, like John, Rick, and Dan, are pushing aside stereotypes to become more involved in the everyday care of their children. None of them wants to be just the guy who brings home the paycheck or the man with his nose buried in the newspaper.

Years ago, most fathers didn't consider the option of child-rearing. But today, a growing number of men are making room in their lives for the important job of fathering. In fact, says Andy Lidgus, a primary caregiver for his 4-year-old, "There is no choice. The child is yours, and you should be involved. . . . I can't see it any other way."

Ways To Be an Involved Father

Fathers who are highly involved as caregivers usually have taken one of these routes:

• *Part-time employment*—Although part-time work is hard to find, some men have sought out job sharing, half-time appointments, home-based jobs, or running a family business in order to make more time for their children. Part-timers are fathers who know they'll lose out unless they get involved. They rank child-rearing over their jobs, but don't want to abandon their careers completely, explains James A. Levine in *Who'll Raise the Children? The Options for Fathers.* According to a study in Norway by researcher Erik Gronseth, this compromise has rewards for the mothers, fathers, and children—as well as for the marriage.

• *Househusbanding*—The rare real life "Mr. Moms" are independent thinkers who value flexibility and openness, notes Levine. They are committed to rearing young children full-time, and they respect their wives' careers. Sometimes the decision to househusband is a financial one, if the wife has more earning power. As the economic picture brightens for women, more men may be able to choose this option.

• *Child custody*—In the film *Kramer vs. Kramer,* a single father, played by Dustin Hoffman, becomes an expert at making French toast and running carpools. Like many single fathers, he discovers he is capable of—and gets satisfaction from—caring for his child. The movie also shows the strain on the single parent juggling a job and a family.

According to the latest census figures, over 1 million children live with 893,000 fathers in single-parent homes. Traditionally, divorce courts have routinely awarded custody to the mother; less than 8 percent of divorced fathers presently have custody. But fathers'-rights groups are active across the country, and the prospects for divorced dads are improving.

• *Adoption*—There is still prejudice against single men who want to be adoptive fathers, but a rare few beat the odds and are able to adopt children. These fathers are men who feel a deep-seated desire to care for children and are often in child-related occupations.

Marilyn Sherman, "A New Look at Fathering," © January 1986, *Current Consumer & Lifestudies.* Reprinted by permission of the publisher, General Learning Corporation, Northbrook, IL.

- *Paternity leaves*—In Sweden, either the mother or the father may take up to seven months' leave with pay after the birth of a baby. In the United States, however, only a small fraction of companies offer males the opportunity to stay home with a newborn. Even when paternity leave is offered, few men accept it. The reasons they give for turning it down are economic need, the mother's desire to stay home and breastfeed, and disapproval from co-workers.

- *Flextime*—Innovative, flexible work schedules may allow men more time for fathering. For example, with flextime a father might start work later in the day so he can give the children breakfast and get them off to school. A shortened workweek is another progressive plan that can give fathering a boost. Researcher David Maklan's study of men working for 10-hour days found that these fathers spent more time than average caring for their children.

Participative Fathers

Fathers who choose to spend their time in the world of fingerpaints and tricycles have some traits in common:
1. flexible beliefs about parenting roles
2. available time at home
3. good role models of involved fathers
4. adequate family finances

Today, nearly 60 percent of women with children ages 6 or under are employed outside the home, and fathers in dual-career marriages are more likely to be involved in caring for their children.

In traditional families, psychologists have found that mothers do more of the nitty-gritty child-care tasks, while fathers spend their time with their children in play. In role-sharing families, fathers begin to do the same things with their children that mothers do. Both serve up similar doses of hugs, nutritious meals, ballgames, baths, and discipline. And compared with traditional families, role-sharing families are found to play more.

When fathers share in child-rearing, the biggest bonus is a better father-child relationship, research shows. Fathers report feeling more sensitive and attuned to their children, and the child has two very close relationships instead of the one-and-a-half that the workday-father plan often provides. Lidgus says of his relationship with his daughter Annie, "I've gained just as much as Annie has. I am as important to Annie as she is to me."

Advantages of Fatherhood

Right after a baby is born, involved fathers are less likely to feel "blue," found Martha Zaslow of the National Institute of Child Health and Human Development. In addition, surveys have shown that fathers who share as primary caregivers tend to have happy marriages. Fathers learn the joys and rewards of watching their children develop. And, finally, nurturing fathers gain self-esteem from knowing that they are competent at child care.

In *Daddy's Home,* Mike Clary, a househusband for the first two years of his baby's life, summarizes his satisfactions: "Annie makes me vulnerable—to longing, to daydreams, to fears, to pain. She has also made me capable of a love that seems boundless. . . . Annie has, finally, by making me a father, made me more of a man. As a househusband, I was forced to take stock of what I am, and what I think and believe, and what I want to do. While mixing my emotions, she has ordered my priorities and irrevocably changed my life. She makes me proud."

"Studies overwhelmingly show that men are just as capable of child care as women are."

Incidentally, mothers pick up some pluses in role-sharing arrangements too. Most feel less stress. They also benefit from boosts in self-esteem because of the equality they have in their careers. . . .

Changing Attitudes

Role-sharing gets a straight-A report card from researchers and involved parents. Will it catch on with your generation? Right now, according to a Wellesley College study, the average father spends little time alone with his children—about 30 minutes a day. And of the couples who try role-sharing, few continue more than a few years.

Attitudes are changing, though, and many experts say behavior changes are not far behind. Eighty percent of fathers are present during the births of their babies, compared with 27 percent 10 years ago. And according to a recent Gallup Poll, 25 percent expect to be primary caregivers when their wives return to employment outside the home. "A growing minority of men are experiencing new highs in nurturing children and new roles in families," says Robert A. Lewis, professor of child development at Purdue University.

Studies overwhelmingly show that men are just as capable of child care as women are, if they accept that challenge. In the future, boys your age will probably be part of a new fathering trend. And the person pushing the baby carriage may just as likely be a dad as a mom.

Marilyn Sherman is a contributing writer for Current Consumer & Lifestudies, *a magazine distributed to junior and senior high schools nationwide.*

"For many new men fathering is largely a verbal accomplishment. . . . When push comes to shove, they are often missing."

viewpoint 45

Men Are Not Becoming More Active Fathers

Sylvia Ann Hewlett

Looking after a home and a family is still an enormously time-consuming activity. According to one study, a good home life for a family of four takes about sixty hours of nurturing work per week. That work may have been more physically strenuous in the past but never more complex. Homemaking in our modern industrial society includes the management of extensive relationships with stores, banks, schools, hospitals, and government offices as well as housekeeping and child care. It involves seeing that thousands of personal needs are met. The five-year-old needs a booster shot or a costume for the school play, camp applications have to be filled out for the seven-year-old and name tapes need to be ordered, an appointment must be set up with the kindergarten teacher to explain Johnny's stammering problem, and 300 family snapshots are waiting to be put into albums. Sometimes relationships with stores, schools, or government offices are fraught with problems. If the new car is a lemon, if the grade-school teacher can't discipline the children, if the Social Security benefit is late, or if a credit card is lost or stolen, "then the stressful nature of the homemaker's brokering work between home, market and state is exacerbated."

A Fathering Boom?

Over the last fifteen years there has been a great deal of talk about men taking on more household responsibility. Magazines have discovered a "fathering boom," and films such as *Kramer vs. Kramer* and *Mr. Mom* have tried to convince us that modern men develop intimate nurturing relationships with their children. And it is true, some men have taken on considerably more housework and child care. I have interviewed men who take care of their children by day and work

factory shifts at night, and my own husband takes 50 percent of the responsibility for our children. But in the aggregate this increased participation by men does not add up to very much. Recent studies show that American men still do less than a quarter of all household tasks, and that married men's average time in family work has increased by only 6 percent in twenty years despite the massive shift of women into paid employment. One survey finds that the work week of American women is twenty-one hours longer than that of men. Indeed, economist Heidi Hartmann claims that men actually demand eight hours more service per week than they contribute.

Philip Blumstein and Pepper Schwartz sum up the contemporary situation in their 1984 book *American Couples:*

> Working wives do less housework than homemakers but they still do the vast bulk of what needs to be done . . . even if a husband is unemployed he does much less housework than a wife who puts in a 40 hour week. . . . This is the case even among couples who profess egalitarian social ideals. . . . While husbands might say they should share responsibility, when they break it down to time actually spent and chores actually done, the idea of shared responsibility turns out to be a myth.

Joseph Pleck hits the nail on the head when he describes "men's characteristically low level of family work" as one of the key problems of contemporary life. . . .

Economic Pressures

The division of household labor between men and women seems stubbornly resistant to change, and part of the problem is that women earn so much less than men. Married women when working full time earn less than half the wages earned by married men, and when you weigh in part-time workers, employed wives contribute only 26 percent of the family budget. In view of this asymmetry it is hardly surprising that men have picked up so little domestic responsibility. It still makes economic sense for a family to put the husband's job first. When a parent has to leave the work force in order to take care of a child, it usually costs the family less for the mother to stay at home than for the father. But this is a vicious circle. As we have seen, by "interrupting" her career, the mother permanently lowers her earnings potential.

"It is Mom who gets to make the school lunches. . . wipe up the vomit, and stay home with the sick kid."

A raised consciousness on the part of a man is not enough. Many husbands have the best of intentions when embarking on family life. Over the long haul goodwill is often defeated by the economic facts of life. As French feminist Simone de Beauvoir put it some thirty years ago, "Many young households give the impression of being on a basis of perfect equality. But as long as the man retains economic responsibility for the couple, this is only an illusion." You cannot expect to change behavior without first changing the economic logic on which this behavior is based. In *American Couples* Blumstein and Schwartz demonstrate that "money establishes the balance of power in relationships," and according to them, this shows up most crudely in who does what in the household.

Catch-22

For women the wage gap sets up an infuriating Catch-22 situation. They do the housework because they earn less, and they earn less because they do housework. The only way to break this vicious circle is to develop public policies that support women in their domestic roles so that they can do better in the labor market. Doing better in the labor market has to include limiting those interruptions that so severely depress women's earnings. High-quality, subsidized child care would enable many women to take fewer years out of the labor force when they have children and thus pay a smaller penalty in terms of a lower wage when they reenter (remember a two- to four-year break in employment lowers average earnings by 13 percent while a five-year break in employment lowers average earnings by 19 percent). Indeed, generous maternity leaves with rigorous job-back guarantees would enable many women to bear children without paying any penalty at all in terms of earning power or seniority. In short, public policies that support women in their efforts to bear and rear children would go a long way toward narrowing the wage gap. And once the gap between male and female earnings narrows significantly, the household division of labor may

well shift. It seems that an equal sharing of housework and child rearing between men and women will await the day when a woman's job is as important to the household economy as a man's. . . .

When Push Comes To Shove

A few modern fathers have gotten into nurturing. Like Dustin Hoffman in *Kramer vs. Kramer*, they deal with nightmares, meet the kids from school, cook dinner, and sometimes even put parenting ahead of career. I am married to such a man, so I know that they exist. However, for many new men fathering is largely a verbal accomplishment. They take natural childbirth classes; talk with great eloquence at dinner parties about bonding, separation anxiety, and role models; and quite convince themselves that they are great fathers. When push comes to shove, they are often missing. Only a third will come through with child support in the event of divorce, and on a daily basis the division of labor remains the traditional one. It is Mom who gets to make the school lunches, buy the gift for the birthday party, wipe up the vomit, and stay home with the sick kid. Parenting mostly involves hard, relentless work and the willingness to be there when needed. Most upscale new men do not arrange their priorities that way. As Donald Bell puts it in *Being a Man*, "for many adult males there persists a gnawing sense that we have more important things to accomplish than to be stuck changing diapers, feeding a drooling infant, or arranging for playmates or babysitters . . . childcare tends to turn the adult mind to mush [and] since contemporary middle-class men work mainly with their minds, we can ill afford to allow our minds to become mushy." What of women? I guess it's all right if their minds turn to mush!

Sylvia Ann Hewlett is vice president for economic studies at the United Nations Association.

"Divorce is a financial catastrophe for most women."

Divorce Devastates Women's Standard of Living

Lenore J. Weitzman

Divorce has radically different economic consequences for men and women. While most divorced men find that their standard of living improves after divorce, most divorced women and the minor children in their households find that their standard of living plummets. This [viewpoint] shows that when income is compared to needs, divorced men experience an average 42 percent rise in their standard of living in the first year after the divorce, while divorced women (and their children) experience a 73 percent decline.

Precipitous Downward Mobility

These apparently simple statistics have far-reaching social and economic consequences. For most women and children, divorce means precipitous downward mobility—both economically and socially. The reduction in income brings residential moves and inferior housing, drastically diminished or nonexistent funds for recreation and leisure, and intense pressures due to inadequate time and money. Financial hardships in turn cause social dislocation and a loss of familiar networks for emotional support and social services, and intensify the psychological stress for women and children alike. On a societal level, divorce increases female and child poverty and creates an ever-widening gap between the economic well-being of divorced men, on the one hand, and their children and former wives on the other. . . .

The income disparity between men and women after divorce profoundly affects their relative standards of living.

To examine this effect we rely on an index of economic well-being developed by the U.S. government. The model for our analysis was constructed by Michigan researchers who followed a

sample of 5,000 American families, weighted to be representative of the U.S. population. Economists Saul Hoffman and John Holmes compared the incomes of men and women who stayed in intact families with the incomes of divorced men and divorced women over a seven-year period.

A comparison of the married and divorced couples yielded two major findings. First, as might be expected, the dollar income of both divorced men and divorced women declined, while the income of married couples rose. Divorced men lost 19 percent in income while divorced women lost 29 percent. In contrast, married men and women experienced a 22 percent rise in income. These data confirm our commonsense belief that both parties suffer after a divorce. They also confirm that women experience a greater loss than their former husbands.

The second finding of the Michigan research is surprising. To see what the income loss meant in terms of family purchasing power, Hoffman and Holmes constructed an index of family income in relation to family needs. Since this income/need comparison is adjusted for family size, as well as for each member's age and sex, it provides an individually tailored measure of a family's economic well-being in the context of marital status changes.

The Michigan researchers found that the experiences of divorced men and women were strikingly different when this measure was used. Over the seven-year period, the economic position of divorced men actually improved by 17 percent. In contrast, over the same period divorced women experienced a 29 percent decline in terms of what their income could provide in relation to their needs.

To compare the experiences of divorced men and women in California to those in Michigan, we devised a similar procedure to calculate the basic needs of each of the families in our interview sample. This procedure used the living standards for urban families constructed by the Bureau of Labor

Statistics of the U.S. Department of Labor. First, the standard budget level for each family in the interview sample was calculated in three different ways: once for the predivorce family, once for the wife's postdivorce family, and once for the husband's postdivorce family. Then the income in relation to needs was computed for each family. (Membership in postdivorce families of husbands and wives included any new spouse or cohabitor and any children whose custody was assigned to that spouse.) These data are presented in Figure 1.

Figure 1 reveals the radical change in the standards of living to which we alluded earlier. Just one year after legal divorce, *men experience a 42 percent improvement in their postdivorce standard of living, while women experience a 73 percent decline.*

Severe Deprivation

These data indicate that *divorce is a financial catastrophe for most women:* in just one year they experience a dramatic decline in income and a calamitous drop in their standard of living. It is hard to imagine how they deal with such severe deprivation: every single expenditure that one takes for granted—clothing, food, housing, heat—must be cut to one-half or one-third of what one is accustomed to.

Figure 1

Change in Standards of Living*
of Divorced Men and Women
(Approximately one year after divorce)

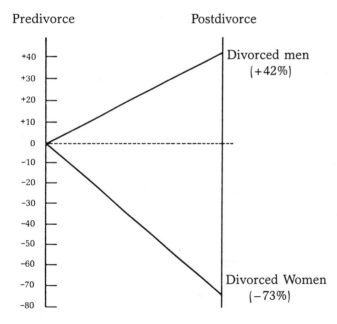

*Income in relation to needs with needs based on U.S. Department of Agriculture's low standard budget.

Based on weighted sample of interviews with divorced persons, Los Angeles County, California, 1978

It is difficult to absorb the full implications of these statistics. What does it mean to have a 73 percent decline in one's standard of living? When asked how they coped with this drastic decline in income, many of the divorced women said that they themselves were not sure. It meant "living on the edge" and "living without." As some of them described it:

> We ate macaroni and cheese five nights a week. There was a Safeway special for 39 cents a box. We could eat seven dinners for $3.00 a week. . . . I think that's all we ate for months.
>
> I applied for welfare. . . . It was the worst experience of my life. . . . I never dreamed that I, a middle class housewife, would ever be in a position like that. It was humiliating . . . they make you feel it. . . . But we were desperate, and I *had* to feed my kids.
>
> You name it, I tried it—food stamps, soup kitchens, shelters. It just about killed me to have the kids live like that. . . . I finally called my parents and said we were coming . . . we couldn't have survived without them.

Even those who had relatively affluent life-styles before the divorce experienced a sharp reduction in their standard of living and faced hardships they had not anticipated. For example, the wife of a dentist sold her car "because I had no cash at all, and we lived on that money—barely—for close to a year." And an engineer's wife:

> I didn't buy my daughter any clothes for a year— even when she graduated from high school we sewed together two old dresses to make an outfit.

The wife of a policeman told an especially poignant story about "not being able to buy my twelve-year-old son Adidas sneakers." The boy's father had been ordered to pay $100 a month child support but had not been paying. To make up that gap in her already bare-bone budget, she had been using credit cards to buy food and other household necessities. She had exceeded all her credit limits and felt the family just could not afford to pay $25 for a new pair of Adidas sneakers. But, as she said a year later,

> Sometimes when you are so tense about money you go crazy . . . and you forget what it's like to be twelve years old and to think you can't live without Adidas sneakers . . . and to feel the whole world has deserted you along with your father.

Others spoke of cutting out all the nonessentials. For one woman it meant "no movies, no ice cream cones for the kids." For another it meant not replacing tires on her son's bike "because there just wasn't the money." For another woman it meant not using her car—a real handicap in Los Angeles—and waiting for two buses in order to save the money she would have had to spend for gas. In addition to scaled-down budgets for food ("We learned to love chicken backs") and clothing ("At Christmas I splurged at the Salvation Army—the only 'new' clothes they got all year"), many spoke of cutting down on their children's school lunches ("I used to plan a nourishing lunch with fruit and juice; now she's lucky if we have a slice of ham for a sandwich") and school supplies and after-school activities ("He had to quit the Little League and get a job as a delivery boy").

Still, some of the women were not able to "make it." Fourteen percent of them moved onto the welfare rolls during the first year after the divorce, and a number of others moved back into their parents' homes when they had "no money left and nowhere to go and three children to feed."

Explaining the Disparity

How can we explain the strikingly different economic consequences of divorce for men and women? How could a law that aimed at fairness create such disparities between divorced men and their former wives and children?

The explanation lies first in the inadequacy of the court's awards, second in the expanded demands on the wife's resources after divorce, and third in the husband's greater earning capacity and ability to supplement his income.

Consider first the court awards for child support (and in rarer cases, alimony). Since judges do not require men to support either their children or their former wives as they did during marriage, they allow the husband to keep most of his income for himself. Since only a few wives are awarded alimony, the only supplementary income they are awarded is child support and the average child support award covers less than half of the cost of raising a child. Thus, the average support award is simply inadequate: even if the husband pays it, it often leaves the wife and children in relative poverty. The custodial mother is expected to somehow make up the deficit alone even though she typically earns much less than her former husband.

In this regard, it is also important to note the role that property awards play in contributing to—rather than alleviating—the financial disparities between divorced women and men. Under the old law, when the wife with minor children was typically awarded the family home, she started her postdivorce life on a more equal footing because the home provided some stability and security and reduced the impact of the income loss suffered at divorce. Today, when the family home is more commonly sold to allow an "equal" division of property, there is no cushion to soften the financial devastations that low support awards create for women and children. Rather, the disruptive costs of moving and establishing a new household further strain their limited income—often to the breaking point.

Wives Face Greater Financial Demands

The second explanation for the disparity between former husbands and wives lies in the greater demands on the wife's household after divorce, and

the diminished demands on the husband's. Since the wife typically assumes the responsibility for raising the couple's children, her need for help and services increases as a direct result of her becoming a single parent. Yet at the very time that her need for more income and more financial support is greatest, the courts have drastically reduced her income. Thus the gap between her income and her needs is wider after divorce.

"Men experience a 42 percent improvement in their postdivorce standard of living, while women experience a 73 percent decline."

In contrast, the gap between the husband's income and needs narrows. Although he now has fewer absolute dollars, the demands on his income have diminished: he often lives alone and he is no longer financially responsible for the needs of his ex-wife and children. While he loses the benefits of economies of scale, and while he may have to purchase some services (such as laundry and cooking) that he did not have to buy during marriage, he is nevertheless much better off because he has so much money to spend on himself. Since he has been allowed to retain most of his income for himself, he can afford these extra expenses and still have more surplus income than he enjoyed during marriage.

The final explanation for the large income discrepancy between former husbands and wives lies in the different earning capacities and starting points of the two adults at the time of the divorce. Not only do men in our society command higher salaries to begin with, they also benefit from the common marital pattern that gives priority to their careers. Marriage gives men the opportunity, support, and time to invest in their own careers. Thus marriage itself builds and enhances the husband's earning capacity. For women, in contrast, marriage is more likely to act as a career liability. Even though family roles are changing, and even though married women are increasingly working for pay during marriage, most of them nevertheless subordinate their careers to their husbands' and to their family responsibilities. This is especially true if they have children. Thus women are often doubly disadvantaged at the point of divorce. Not only do they face the "normal" 60 percent male/female income gap that affects all working women, they also suffer from the toll the marital years have taken on their earning capacity.

Thus marriage—and then divorce—impose a differential disadvantage on women's employment prospects, and this is especially severe for women who have custody of minor children. The responsibility for children inevitably restricts the mother's job opportunities by limiting her work schedule and location, her availability for overtime, and her freedom to take advantage of special training, travel assignments, and other opportunities for career advancement.

Although the combined income of the former spouses typically increases after divorce, most of the rise is a result of the husband's increased income. Even though women who have not been employed during marriage seek jobs after divorce, and part-time workers take full-time jobs, neither of these factors accounts for as much as the rise in male wages in the first year after divorce.

"The average support award is simply inadequate: even if the husband pays it, it often leaves the wife and children in relative poverty."

It is, in fact, surprising to see how many divorced men receive salary increases (and bonuses) immediately after divorce. While some of these are probably routine raises, and others may be the result of more intense work efforts or overtime work, it is also evident that some men manage to delay a bonus or commission or raise until after the divorce is final. This allows them to minimize the income they have to report to the court when child support (or alimony) awards are being made.

While the courts have long been aware of the control that self-employed men can exercise over the amount and timing of the income they receive, our data suggest that many salaried employees may exercise similar control over their income since many of them manage to obtain salary increases soon after their divorces become final. Whether or not this is coincidence, the fact remains that the income of divorced men often increases substantially in the first year after the divorce.

During the same period, the obligations that these men have for alimony and child support typically remain fixed or diminish: some support obligations have been reduced or terminated by terms of the divorce settlement (and others have been reduced or stopped without the court's permission). The result, once again, is that divorced men have more "surplus income" for themselves. . . .

Feminization of Poverty

The rise in divorce has been the major cause of the increase in female-headed families, and that increase has been the major cause of the

feminization of poverty. Sociologist Diana Pearce, who coined the phrase "feminization of poverty," was one of the first to point to the critical link between poverty and divorce for women. It was, she said, the mother's burden for the economic and emotional responsibility for child-rearing that often impoverished her family.

Contrary to popular perception, most female-headed single parent families in the United States are *not* the result of unwed parenthood: they are the result of marital dissolution. Only 18 percent of the nearly ten million female-headed families in the United States are headed by an unwed mother: over 50 percent are headed by divorced mothers and the remaining 31 percent by separated mothers.

When a couple with children divorces, it is probable that the man will become single but the woman will become a single parent. And poverty, for many women, begins with single parenthood. More than half of the poor families in the United States are headed by a single mother.

The National Advisory Council on Economic Opportunity estimates that if current trends continue, the poverty population of the United States will be composed solely of women and children by the year 2000. The Council declares that the "feminization of poverty has become one of the most compelling social facts of the decade."

Consequences of Divorce

The economic consequences of the present system of divorce reverberate throughout our society. Divorce awards not only contribute heavily to the well-documented income disparity between men and women, they also lead to the widespread impoverishment of children and enlarge the ever-widening gap between the economic well-being of men and women in the larger society. Indeed, if current conditions continue unabated we may well arrive at a two-tier society with an underclass of women and children.

Thrust into a spiral of downward mobility by the present system of divorce, a multitude of middle-class women and the children in their charge are increasingly cut off from sharing the income and wealth of former husbands and fathers. Hampered by restricted employment opportunities and sharply diminished income, these divorced women are increasingly expected to shoulder alone the burden of providing for both themselves and their children. . . .

The result is that the economic gulf between the sexes in the larger society is increasing.

Lenore J. Weitzman is an associate professor of sociology at Harvard University in Cambridge, Massachusetts.

"Women and children rarely get enough to live on but fathers . . . are 'pinned to the wall.'"

Divorce Devastates Men's Standard of Living

Susan Anderson-Khleif

The financial difficulties of fathers without custody, and the impact of these difficulties on relationships with their children, have not received much attention. Interest and sympathy have been focused on mothers and their children who are trying to make ends meet in their single-parent households. Let us hear the fathers' concerns about housing and money after divorce.

Fathers without custody of their children almost always move out of the marital home or apartment and seek a different place to live. The first move is usually just the beginning step in a series of moves—divorced fathers move around a lot. It is common for fathers without custody to make from three to five moves within the first five years after separation and divorce.

Losing the House

If a man owns a home during marriage, he loses it. This is almost always the case. Even if he retains joint ownership with his ex-wife, for all practical purposes he loses it because he moves out. His investment is literally tied up; it will be years before he will reap the profits—if at all. Owning a house makes the overall settlement much more expensive and much more difficult. And a man who would like to end an unhappy marriage usually has "no choice" about the house. For instance, one man left a long marriage when he was in his late 40s. He struggled for years to reach a decision about the divorce because he could not bear the idea of living apart from his children, then in their teens. He moved out and returned three times before moving out for good. In the end, his ex-wife kept the house; he moved to a one bedroom apartment. He has this to say:

My divorce wasn't very fair. My wife didn't want a divorce, she said it was against her religion. The only way she'd give me the divorce was if I'd give her the house. It was all paid for except $1,000 on the mortgage. So I did. (upper-middle-class father, sons 18, 20, 22)

This is a side of the story that one rarely hears from women—that part of the price of leaving unhappy marriages for men who own homes is often "signing over" the house and, perhaps, the equity too.

Oddly enough, the father often "gives up" the house even in cases where it is actually the woman who wants out of the marriage, or when there is a "mutual agreement" to end the marriage. A man may find his wife has a "lover" or "wants her freedom" and yet finds he must concede the house as part of the settlement because she is the custodial parent. These fathers are left wondering: "How? Why did she come out way ahead on the deal?"

Another factor in the dynamics of housing settlements is the father's concern for the well-being of his children. Especially at the time of divorce, before the long-term inequities of extended periods of time—or to end up "sleeping on a friend's couch" or "sleeping in the truck" while they try to figure out what to do and where to go.

Making Support Payments

From the fathers' point of view, the amount of support set by the court is decided without much thought to how fathers can actually pay and still "survive" themselves—that is, still cover their own basic living expenses. The court is usually faced with dividing up an income that is not adequate for supporting two separate households. Women and children rarely get enough to live on but fathers, as they put it, are "pinned to the wall." Fathers have their own horror stories to tell—many end up trying to live on a couple of hundred dollars a month, a feat just as impossible these days for men as it is for women.

Susan Anderson-Khleif, *Divorced But Not Disastrous*. Englewood Cliffs, NJ: Prentice-Hall, 1982. Reprinted with the author's permission.

If we are concerned about relations between fathers and children and about understanding the reasons for nonpayment of support by fathers, then *we need to take a closer look at the financial squeeze faced by fathers during the first months of separation and the first couple of years after the divorce.* It is during this period that the fathers face desperate financial problems, just as single-parent mothers do, and many fathers withdraw at this early stage, setting precedents for nonpayment and sporadic visitation that are hard to correct in the future.

Proportion of Income

Most fathers go to court with evidence demonstrating the limits of their ability to support, and they come out puzzled and shocked over the settlements. Many are left "almost without the means for a dignified existence" or "robbed of self-respect" after the "settlements" are made. As this father says,

> I really felt they were cutting off your nose to spite your face. They were assessing the breadwinner to a point where he could have very easily thrown up his hands. I felt they relegated the breadwinner to a point where he couldn't live a dignified life. (middle-class father, sons 18 and 21)

The majority of men I interviewed were ordered to pay from 25 to 50 percent of their net incomes in child support or alimony to their ex-wives. (Those with higher incomes and more children were ordered to pay the highest proportions of their incomes in support.) At first these may sound like reasonably fair settlements. However, if we think of the many fathers with only average or below-average incomes, we can see their side of the predicament more clearly. Some are left with near-poverty level incomes. It is not just the amount or proportion of income that is important—it is what is left over.

"[Divorced fathers] are left 'almost without the means for a dignified existence' or 'robbed of self-respect' after the 'settlements' are made."

If a man is established professionally at the time of divorce and if he owns a home, he probably can count on a very stiff settlement. Typically, his ex-wife gets the house, the furniture, a car, a proportion of the savings, and about 30 to 50 percent of his net salary until all the children are 18. Added to that there may be obligations to cover medical insurance, dental bills, or other expenses. A man with a professional salary usually can pay this support and still cover his own basic expenses, but he cannot hope to live as his peers do. His living and housing standards are immediately reduced well

below those of others at his educational and occupational level.

Just as single-parent mothers face extra expenses associated with divorce, so do fathers. There are the direct costs of the divorce itself, moving costs, perhaps another car, deposit on an apartment, telephone installation, and the costs of furnishing the new apartment (even modestly). If divorce comes at a time of economic instability—unemployment, a layoff, a change to a new job—their difficulties are compounded. Many fathers assume the debts built up during the marriage *in addition* to other support responsibilities, and these debts often make their overall financial situations quite impossible for the first few years after the divorce.

Divorced fathers go through a process of "digging out" financially after divorce. It may take a period of two to four years for middle-income men. Even professional fathers find that it takes a couple of years to get their finances "above water." Many working-class men never make it—their financial situations get worse as the arrears on their support payments pile up. Some are set back for good.

Where Does the Money Go?

Fathers have a number of concerns about child support that we do not hear about when talking with divorced mothers. One issue foremost in the minds of the fathers is whether or not the child support is actually being used for the benefit of the children. Some have cause to wonder about this. Many fathers who pay regular child support have had experiences where their children come to visit for the weekend or for a vacation with only one pair of socks or no jacket, or otherwise inadequate clothing. Very often the first act of the "vacation" is a trip to the local department store to buy the basic necessities—underwear, pajamas, a bathing suit. There are many incidents that feed fathers' doubts about whether or not their support is actually spent on the children. They discover that birthday money was spent on a luxury item for "the apartment." They call to say "Hi" and find their 7-year-old "babysitting" for himself or herself. Fathers hope their support checks are being used for clothing, food, childcare—items of direct benefit for the children. They hope that "the apartment" would go without luxury items or that expensive trips would be forgone before their children go without babysitters, school meal tickets, busfare, basic clothing, and other personal items.

Some fathers end up working two jobs to cover the expenses of child support plus their own living costs, especially in the first five years after the divorce. They work weekends, teach extra courses, work overtime, or "moonlight" at a second job after their usual day's work is done. One father who pays regular support for four children and has a good steady income explains his feelings about the situation:

> My ex-wife, she takes ballet lessons, she takes college courses, she's not working. I'm working two jobs. Some may say, well, I'm supplying their expenses and she's supplying her time in caring for them. She's not the most attentive mother. For example, last Saturday she wasn't there when I picked them up and wasn't there at 8:00 p.m. when we dropped them off. They can take care of themselves but here they were, 8:00 p.m., no dinner. They had to take care of themselves. It irks me, it burns me. (working-class father, daughters 10 and 13, sons 14 and 16)

Liberated Ex-Wives?

In this age of changing sex roles and women's greater freedom, men are wondering about the justice of situations in which child-support decisions are based on traditional sex roles. One man who signed over both home and equity to his ex-wife, and who has always paid a good portion of his moderate income in child support, puts it this way:

> I don't think the courts really looked into the total situation. I don't have anything against women, but with all the talk from women these days about equal rights, they should have to bear part of the cost. I really think the men get fleeced, but the woman never thinks she gets enough. At first, it took almost 50 percent of my net income.
>
> All I can say, if they made the support payment reasonable, they would eliminate part of the problems. That's where they should take the wife into consideration, even if she's never worked a day in her life. (middle-class father, sons 18 and 21)

And if the ex-wife has an education for a career or profession of her own, large support or alimony payments just do not seem justified. This father feels there should at least be some "cut-off" date:

> I don't think I should support a woman forever who's going to law school. A woman who insists on being called Ms. and who is liberated. I don't say that with acrimony and bitterness. If I have a wife who's going to be an attorney, why should I be supporting her all her life? I can pay, I'm perfectly capable of paying forever, but why should I be expected to? (upper-middle-class father, son 7, daughter 11)

Supporting Boyfriends?

Another issue distressing to some fathers is that their ex-wives have boyfriends who are "living-in" or seem to be there "most of the time." For instance,

> She has her boyfriend over on weekends and they spend the night and the kids know it. But she does have just that one boyfriend. I don't know if he lives there. I strongly suspect he does, but she claims he doesn't.
>
> She's had that boyfriend for, ever since the day the divorce was final. I drove in and there he was. I've seen his car in the driveway ever since. (middle-class father, daughter 2, sons 9 and 11)

A father may pay his support notwithstanding, but the boyfriend's presence leaves the father feeling as if his money is being used to support this new union instead of the children. In some cases where the father does not pay regular child support, he

mentions the boyfriend living with his ex-wife as one factor which weakens his willingness to pay:

> I would be more willing to pay if she was living alone. But as it is, her boyfriend's getting all the benefits. (working-class father, daughter 6)

Threats and Hassles

Most fathers who have had disputes with their ex-wives over child support—concerning amount, regularity, or increases—have also been limited by their ex-wives in visitation with the children. The problems of exchanging visitation for support is an ever-present threat. As one father says, "The hassle just reared its ugly head this week. She said, 'In view of the fact that you're only paying $60.00, you can only have one child on Sunday.'"

"Some fathers end up working two jobs to cover the expenses of child support plus their own living costs."

In some cases, threats are tossed back and forth even though the father pays regularly and neither party has yet acted on their "threats." For instance, one father discovered that his ex-wife was considering a move to a distant state—a move that would make it almost impossible for him to see his children:

> I told her if she moved out of state, it will go down to $50.00 per week. She said, you can't do that. I said, I don't care, I will. I don't want some guy living on easy street [reference to her new partner in the distant state]. She didn't move.
>
> I was told if I ever fell short of the $75.00 she'd take me to court. With these new laws, I'd like to see females paying alimony! Women's Lib, but when it comes to the courts, the poor little defenseless thing. Even though she's making $16,000. The guy's getting pinned to the wall. These are the hassles I did not want. I walked away with my clothes. I may just do it sometime [fall short of the support payment] to see if she really would [take me to court]. (working-class father, daughters 4 and 6)

There are often "hassles" from ex-wives even in the "best" situations—where mothers and children are "well off" and fathers are paying support and visiting regularly. One professional father who has always been in regular contact with his children just cannot understand this. His children spend lots of time with him, and yet his young son said to him one day, "What does 'abandon' mean? Mommy said you've abandoned us."

The Cost of Visitation

Mothers place great importance on fathers giving time and affection to their children instead of gifts and special treats. If we listen to mothers, we hear about the need for fathers simply to make themselves available, show their love, and stay involved in their children's lives. Mothers, in fact, stress that it is not important to do "expensive things" with the children. From the fathers' perspective, however, it is clear that money is a crucial element in visitation. In a very real sense, *visitation is expensive*. In addition to the payment of support, fathers find that maintaining relationships with children involves spending money.

"Divorced fathers routinely find their meager resources are totally gone after weekends, holiday visits, vacations, and summers with the kids."

Divorced fathers who keep in touch with their children, the Regular Visitors, end up with many of the same expenses that live-in fathers have. They pay for many "extras" that have nothing to do with their legal child-support obligations:

> You end up giving a lot more than what is decreed in the long run. You can't forget your obligations to your children. If your son asks you for $20, you give it to him. (middle-class father, sons 18 and 21)

Even trips to zoos, parks, beaches, fishing, and so forth cost money. Many fathers take their children on vacations and camping trips, buy them special clothes, hockey skates, books for school, and other items. Movies, stops at the hamburger stand, birthday presents and cakes, gifts at holiday times (those "second" celebrations), miniature golf, carnivals, and concert tickets all add up:

> It's very expensive, even to do things with children. They don't want to sit in the apartment all weekend either. Taking them bowling. A trip to a museum. It costs money. (middle-class father, daughters 7 and 11)

Divorced fathers routinely find their meager resources are totally gone after weekends, holiday visits, vacations, and summers with the kids. There are many costs that go unrecognized. As we have seen, fathers need a place to bring their children during visitation. They need housing with extra space for the children, and that means higher housing expenses—an extra bedroom, a decent neighborhood, a yard or recreation facilities. Fathers must also stock up on "snacks" and extra food for the kids. They must have toys and paints and books around for rainy days. Divorced fathers who stay in contact with their children soon find the expenses simply do not stop with the support check.

The Price Tag of Fathering

Being a father has many costs whether the father lives with his children or not. In his book, *What Money Buys,* [Lee] Rainwater discusses the importance of money and other economic resources

for social participation and for feelings of well-being in our kind of society. There is a "price of admission" which must be paid to engage in most activities which are considered meaningful, appropriate, and rewarding in our society. Lack of sufficient resources damages the ability to participate in meaningful social roles and activities. This perspective is very useful in understanding the situation of divorced fathers. A close look at the costs of father-child contact after divorce certainly reveals the "price tag" of fathering and the link between economic resources and the ability to fulfill the role of father after divorce.

Often fathers cannot pay their support, cannot afford activities with the children, and certainly cannot provide "extras." These financial difficulties have a strong impact on patterns of father-child visitation. Some fathers can get along—they manage to pay their support and can afford to do things with the children—but many cannot. As this father explains,

> In my case, I'm not too bad off. I have been able to give the children extra money and take them places. But the settlement that the father gets is often something he can't handle.
>
> I've heard many fathers say, I'm ashamed to go get my children; I don't have a decent place to bring them. I can't afford to take them places. I don't see my children as often as I'd like to, but I just don't feel I have a place to bring them. (middle-class father, daughter 12, sons 14, 17, and 21)

If the divorced father is "cleaned out" entirely—if he is ordered to pay an amount of support that makes it impossible to meet his own living expenses and to pay for visitation activities—he probably will not see much of his children. He must be able to keep enough resources in his own hands to allow him to lay claim to the social role of father. . . .

Fathers Grants for Children

A society concerned about its children is concerned about relationships between children and *both* of their parents—mothers and fathers. After divorce, a child usually remains living with the mother, in her custody; most fathers live apart from their children. . . . After divorce, many fathers end up being excluded because they cannot pay regular child support—the reports of divorced parents demonstrate the disruptive effects of irregular support on father-child visitation. Such disruption does not help women, men, or children. *Let us direct our money toward supporting family relations, even after divorce. Make it more possible for fathers to pay regular child support and for mothers to feel good about father-child visitation. Make it more possible for mothers to get supplemental support from fathers instead of going without or receiving AFDC, foodstamps, and other "welfare."*

For many years, low-income, single-parent mothers have been able to receive welfare through AFDC to help support their families. Many researchers, policy experts, and family-life professionals have pointed out that AFDC, for which eligibility is determined through the mother, effectively excludes fathers from the family group. It weakens bonds between fathers and children. We could take a totally different approach: we could initiate Fathers Grants for Children and channel societal support to children through the fathers.

"[The divorced father] must be able to keep enough resources in his own hands to allow him to lay claim to the social role of father."

Fathers Grants for Children could be designed as time-limited support (cash transfers) that would be available to separated and divorced fathers who are otherwise unable to pay regular child support during the period of peak economic stress following separation and divorce. Fathers could make their child-support payments through the courts or present some proof of payment—then, say within a week or ten days, they would receive a reimbursement grant (check). The amount would be based on the severity of their financial difficulties. This would be an income supplement for children, not fathers; it would allow fathers in financial difficulty to put their children first, demonstrate their responsibility to paying regular support, and still be able to "get by" financially themselves. Once the father starts "digging out" financially, the grants would cease and he would reassume full responsibility both for making his regular support payments and providing for his own living expenses. Under the Fathers Grants for Children, the father would also assume responsibility for filling out forms, dealing with officials to process these forms, and establishing eligibility—instead of placing these tasks on mothers.

Safeguards for Women

Obviously there would have to be some safeguards built into the system for women so that they would not experience increased dependency on their ex-husbands for support. That is, there would still have to be an option for alternative support, channeled through mothers themselves, for women whose ex-husbands do not utilize the Fathers Grants for Children. But most women who receive regular child support from their ex-husbands do not need "welfare." The child support provides the needed steady income supplement to the mothers' own wages.

Regular income directed to children through their fathers could break the cycle of sporadic visitation or exclusion for many divorced fathers. *Fathers would be drawn within the resource network of the single-parent family.* A father who wants to be in contact with his children could become an integral part of the financial support system and, thus, be in a greatly improved position for maintaining regular visitation with his children. *Fathers Grants for Children could be developed as a major alternative to AFDC,* and one with many more potential benefits for mothers, fathers, and children. The benefits would appear not only in economic well-being, but in improved family relations. Fathers Grants for Children would be one way to minimize the problem of "exchanging" support for visitation. These grants would be an investment in promoting fathers' self-esteem and enhancing fathers' responsibility for their children. This seems a much more fruitful approach than giving mothers AFDC money, and then attempting to collect from fathers who do not have the means to pay anyway. The father must be allowed to retain enough income and resources to fulfill his fathering role. The development of Fathers Grants for Children could be one step in that direction. It could improve the overall situation for all three parties: mothers, fathers, and children.

Susan Anderson-Khleif is the manager of education and training for Digital Equipment Corporation's Storage Systems division. She has done extensive research on divorce in the United States and abroad.

"Although two-thirds of their lives have been spent in the divorced or remarried family, [the children] spoke sorrowfully of their loss of the intact family."

viewpoint **48**

Divorce Harms Children

Judith S. Wallerstein

This is a report from a ten-year longitudinal study of responses of parents and their children to separation and divorce. The study, which began in 1971, was designed to explore the experiences of 60 Northern California families whose 131 children were between 2 1/2 and 18 years of age at the time of the decisive separation. This paper provides the first overview of the early latency age children from that sample, as they appeared a decade later. . . .

The Enduring Effects of Divorce

Focus here is on the psychological and social functioning of 38 young people, 16 girls and 22 boys, most of whom were between 6 and 8 years old at the decisive parental separation. At the ten-year follow-up, these children were between 16 and 18 years old and in the last two years of their high school careers, or just beginning college. During these late adolescent years, they confront the critical developmental tasks of separation from their families and the consolidation of the internal psychological structures and identifications that will enable them to undertake the last stretch on their road to young adulthood. Their attitudes toward themselves and their parents, their views on how their lives have been shaped by the divorce and its many-year aftermath in the postdivorce or remarried family, their aspirations and achievements, the extent to which they look ahead with courage and reasonable self-confidence, and the extent to which their present relationships and their hopes for future intimacy, love, and marriage are dimmed by foreboding—all fall within this present inquiry. The relevance of such broad-based questions has been demonstrated by recent research on the enduring effects of psychic trauma, findings that showed that effects which may not be visible immediately, or

Judith S. Wallerstein, "Children of Divorce: Report on a Ten-Year Follow-Up of Early Latency-Age Children," *American Journal of Orthopsychiatry*, April 1987. Copyright © 1987 the American Orthopsychiatric Association, Inc. Reproduced by permission.

even in later specific behavior or symptoms, may, in fact, profoundly influence an individual's subsequent guiding conceptions and personal expectations of the world. . . .

There were few differences between boys and girls in their attitudes towards the divorce or their anxieties regarding their present and future relationships. Significant differences emerged, however, in the capacity to seek out and make use of a range of relationships and resources within the environment. Girls were much more likely to reach out to peers, to develop and rely on their friendships, to engage in extracurricular activities, to pursue a range of interests, to become more quickly involved in dating and sexual relationships. Girls were significantly more likely, as well, to draw psychological support from their mothers. By contrast, a majority of the boys showed considerable caution and holding back from heterosexual relationships and a reserve in their feelings that shaded into emotional constriction, rigidity, and severe loneliness for a significant subgroup.

Memories of the Marital Rupture

Unlike the preschool children, now in early adolescence, who had largely repressed their experiences from that time, only a few youngsters (14%) in the original latency group claimed at the ten-year mark to have no memory of the separation. They did not suffer from the intrusive, sometimes overwhelming images from the past that the older group reported. However, more than half of the group retained vivid, if somewhat fragmented memories, usually painfully recalled scenes of physical violence between the parents. Often, after recounting a violent scene, the youngster described with sadness the subsequent departure of the father from the home, as if these events formed the tragic, inexorable sequence of divorce: the origin was marital conflict; the outcome was loss of the father, not relief from conflict. Harry told us:

> Fighting is what I remember. I tried to get between them but Dad would throw me down. I just remember Dad leaving home. It hurt me not to see Dad except a couple of times a week.

Sarah said:

> I remember being sad because they fought. I would wake up and hear glasses being thrown. I was scared at night, but I did not want Dad to go. I wanted him to be around for us.

Youngsters who were doing well in the present were likely to have dimmer, more limited memories. Their statements often reflected conscious efforts at suppression and emotional distancing. Betty told us: "About the divorce. I have blocked it out. I have no idea what caused it and I do not like to think about it." Nora, who was also doing well, said: "All I remember is that my dad moved to a hotel."

Longing for the Intact Family

In their unhappiness, their loneliness, their sense of neediness and deprivation, the youngsters now 16 to 18 years old suffered more than the other age groups in the study. The divorce was regarded as the central experience in their lives by over half of these young people, who spoke longingly of their lives in the intact, predivorce family. Some volunteered that their difficulties had escalated through the years, indicating that they had been more protected from parental quarrels when they were younger. An overwhelming majority, boys and girls alike, spoke wistfully of their longing for an ideal intact family. These feelings were unrelated to their judgment of the wisdom of their parents' decision to divorce. The majority, in fact, regarded their parents as incompatible, the divorce as irreversible, and the relationship between the parents as beyond repair. . . .

"The longing for the father may reflect . . . the feeling so many of these young people had of being rejected by a busy, working mother who was not available to them."

The recurring theme was loss of the father, even though there seemed to be almost no link between the father for whom they yearned and the actual father, to whom access was entirely open and who in many instances lived nearby. When asked if she had gained anything from the divorce, Olga said empathatically, "Absolutely no." Asked what she had lost, the girl responded, "My father. Being close to my dad. I wish it were different, but it is not going to change. It is too late." Olga's father lived nearby

and she saw him monthly. He paid little attention to her at these meetings, preferring his son.

Larry's father also lived close by. The boy and his mother had asked the father to take Larry into his home, but the father had refused. Larry told us:

> Life has been worse for me than for other kids because I was a divorced kid. Most of my friends had two parents and those kids got the things that they wanted. Not having a dad is tough for me. I wanted to live with him but he would not take me. He never told me why.

Karl, who lived with his mother and stepfather and two older sisters, said, "I needed a father, not because I like him more, but because there was no one in the home like me. That's my true feeling." We were interested that Karl did not include his stepfather in his perspective of someone who would be like him within the home.

Perhaps one clue to the distress expressed by so many youngsters was their sense of the unavailablity of the working mother. It was not unusual for the youngster to equate the mother's unavailability with uninterest or rejection. Chuck said that his mother did not care for him. She was busy working all the time. "She does not pay any attention to me. I want her to be a mom with an interest in what I am doing with my life, not just a machine that shells out money." It would appear that the longing for the father may reflect not only feelings about the father, but also the feeling so many of these young people had of being rejected by a busy, working mother who was not available to them, and the overall sense that so many shared of not having been provided with the close support that they wished for and needed from their family during their childhood and adolescent years. It is possible that, in the same way that the youngest group of children at the ten-year mark were preoccupied with the idealized family of their fantasies, these youngsters are preoccupied with the lost father as the symbolic equation of the divorce. Their preoccupation with the father, unrelated to the actual quality of their father-child relationships, repeats their responses of ten years earlier. . . .

Attitudes Toward Relationships

Most of these young people believe in romantic love. With few exceptions, they expect to fall in love, marry, and have children of their own. Like most of the other young people in this study, their values are conservative. They do not regard the divorced family as a new social norm. They consider divorce a solution that reflects marital failure, one that should be used only as a last resort when there are children. They agree on divorce when there is physical violence in the family. They believe, on balance, that divorce helps parents, not children. Their values include fidelity and life-long commitment. It is painful for them to acknowledge what many of them know, that one of their parents had been unfaithful during the marriage. Anger at a parent whom they know to have been promiscuous can be very bitter. Describing her father's many affairs, Betty said tartly,

> Some day he won't be able to cultivate all those 21-year-old girls and life will catch up with him. He is going to be an old man and he will be punished.

Close to two thirds of these young people were apprehensive about the possibility of disruption in their own future marriages. Girls were especially fearful that their marriages would not endure. A recurrent theme was a sense of vulnerability and fear of being hurt by romantic relationships. Talking about the future, Brenda said,

> It is hard to make a commitment. All the work and all the trust that is involved. I don't want to get married and do what my mom did. I don't know if marriage will last or not. How can you be sure that marriage will last? I hate to think of what will happen. I am afraid. I am afraid of being hurt. That's why I am a loner.

One half of the boys and girls were fearful of being betrayed, not only in their future, but in their present relationships as well. Of all the age groups, these youngsters were most worried about repeating their parents' relationship patterns and mistakes. Nancy said, "I always find myself attracted to guys who treat you bad." Maureen said, "A problem I have is not being able to show my feelings. I am afraid that they might get stepped on. Once in a relationship, I feel that I will be afraid of losing it if I get attached." Teresa said, "There is a lonely, shaky part of me. I am afraid of what happened to my parents happening to me."

A repeated fear among the boys, somewhat different from the fear of betrayal that the girls emphasized, was their fear of being unloved. Zachary said, "The divorce made me cautious of my relationships. Whenever I meet a girl, I have the unconscious feeling that when she gets to know me she will not love me." . . .

Playing in Pain

The forthcoming move toward independence created a great deal of anxiety in these young people. Although many . . . spoke proudly of their independence as a positive outcome of their parents' divorce, their behavior was often discrepant with their pronouncements. Mary told us: "Nobody helped me. Just my own determination and my friends." She had learned from a soccer accident that, "If you want to play, you play in pain." Diana said, "The outcome of the divorce was that to survive I had to be independent." Others told us how they had learned to solve problems on their own. Yet, although most of them were employed at least part-time and taking responsibility for themselves to a high degree, few spoke of *wanting* to

establish themselves independently, and only three of these young people had left home to live on their own. Several of the youngsters who spoke bravely of their independence had suffered intensely during their freshman year at college and sought to return home.

A dream of Katherine's which occurred during her freshman year at an out-of-town college, reveals some of the difficulties faced by these young people who were attempting to establish independence at a time when their own insecurities and need for parenting dominated their thoughts. Katherine told us,

> I had a dream at mid-term. In real life, I told a friend that the first thing I would do when I would get home was that I would hug my dad, and that would be proof that he loved me, and that I loved him. In the dream, I came home and my dad wasn't there. The person who met me said, "Haven't you forgotten that your dad is dead?"

Katherine said that what disturbed her most was not that her dad was dead, but that there was no one to hug her, and she had worried so much about getting home for a hug.

"Poor overall adjustment at the ten-year mark in boys was significantly associated with . . . feelings of rejection by the father."

It appears that independent behavior, and the pride young people feel in it, can mask an intense hunger for further nurturance and powerful feelings of not being sufficiently nurtured to make it on one's own without "playing in pain."

Quality of Father-Child Relationships

Whether they visited regularly or sporadically, whether they lived nearby or in a distant state, fathers remained a significant psychological presence in the lives of these young people. This was so despite the fact that well over half of their growing up years had been spent in the divorced family, mostly in the custody of the mother, and despite the fact that almost half had lived for many years with a stepfather. Furthermore, there is evidence in our findings that the need for the father as a benign image, if not a real presence, increased during the adolescent years. Donna, aged 16, said, "I never felt that I needed a dad until this year."

It is important, however, not to confuse the yearning that so many of these young people expressed for a closer relationship with the father with the actual quality of these father-child relationships at the ten-year mark. At that time, visiting patterns were mostly disappointing and had been so for many years. Even among that minority of the youngsters who were visited regularly, some had fathers who showed so little interest or initiative during the visits that these contacts were experienced as rejections. Only a minority, 25% of the girls and 30% of the boys, enjoyed adequate or good relationships with their fathers. Over half of the group suffered intense feelings of rejection. Yet, with all of this disappointment, most of these youngsters expressed a great deal of affection for their fathers, along with compassion for their failings as parents.

"Where the father failed, in reality, to meet the boy's needs for a benign and virtuous figure for identification, it was not uncommon for the boy to invent the father image that he needed."

We were interested to find significant links between the relationship with the father and the overall psychological adjustment of boys. Frequency of visiting was unrelated to the level of psychological functioning in boys or girls. But the quality of the father-child relationship was significantly related to good or poor psychological outcome among boys, though not among girls. Poor overall adjustment at the ten-year mark in boys was significantly associated with low self-esteem, poor academic achievement, weak aspirations, and feelings of rejection by the father. At the other end of the spectrum, good psychological functioning was significantly connnected with feeling accepted by the father and with an adequate, or better than adequate, father-son relationship. Thus, a boy's perceptions of his father's feelings toward him, and his need for affirmation and encouragement from his father, appeared to be of critical significance at this time.

Devastating Effects of Rejection

Several subgroups particularly gravitated toward the father during adolescence. Their overtures were often undertaken with great trepidation and their vulnerability to rejection at these times was striking and often not recognized by either parent.

Disappointment often led to bitterness and great sorrow. One girl became preoccupied with thoughts of suicide following her return from a visit with her indifferent father.

One subgroup among the boys suffered repeated rejections by their fathers, often rejections alternating with invitations. The consequences for this group were tragic. There was only limited evidence of a son's ability to disengage from a capricious relationship with the parent. Paradoxically, the more capricious and rejecting the father, the more intense was the admiration of the child and the more powerful the child's efforts at identification. In fact, identification with the rejecting father, especially one who had been neglectful, abusive and demeaning to the mother, was an all-too-common solution that repeated the phenomenon we had observed at early latency when the same youngsters, as despairing little boys, donned articles of clothing that belonged to the absent father and, in full identification with his role, hurled insults at their distressed mothers.

The Abusive Father

Unfortunately, the rejection by the father at adolescence had even more devastating effects on the development of these boys, who felt trapped, hurt, and humiliated by their fathers. Dora captured this theme in her family when she confided, "My brothers are just like my father—the anger, the violence, the loss of control." The boys fully identified with the father's demeaning view of women. They were fearful of regressing into the mother's orbit, and they seemed unable to find within themselves suffcent resourcefulness to generate goals and move ahead on their own. Larry was a gifted 17-year-old, who appeared to be drifting aimlessly. Speaking as if the divorce had happened only yesterday, he told us,

> My mom *is* responsible for pushing my dad out of the house and out of my life. I have never forgiven her for this. She is good at getting on my nerves, just the way she got on Dad's nerves.

Larry described his increasingly infrequent contact with his father. On one occasion, he told us, his father telephoned when Larry had been "really drunk" and threatened to "come over and kick [my] rear end off." Larry smiled at this prospect and continued,

> I have a drinking problem. I worry about that. I drink more than my dad did when he was a kid. I drink because it helps me solve my problems. Last week, I broke up with my girlfriend and I got thoroughly bombed. I think I am probably going to live my life a lot like my dad.

Asked if there were any other parts of his father that he saw in himself, he replied,

> Yes, in my relationships with girls. I get angry with them and I want to slap them, or hit them. Once, I hit my girlfriend in the face.

His bitterness about his father's erratic attentions to him often played itself out in aggression toward the women in his family. Once, during Larry's adolescence when his father failed to show up, as promised, at an important school function in which Larry was a participant, the boy became extremely agitated and physically attacked his sister.

For Larry, as well as for other boys who were

caught up in an identification with the disturbed parent, the divorce had failed. Though the divorce may indeed have benefited one or both parents by providing the legal and geographical separation that enabled them to restructure their own lives, it failed to separate boys like Larry from their internal need to identify with the abusive father. These identifications have, in fact, been newly infused at adolescence by the boys' developmentally governed needs to consolidate their masculine identity. They have also been strengthened by the unfortunate vicissitudes of the postdivorce father-son relationship and by the intense anxiety felt by these boys at being left with the "demeaned woman." The entire psychological constellation at the close of adolescence appears to repeat the boys' experiences at the marital rupture, ten years earlier, but with more grave and lasting consequences.

Psychological Significance of the Father

A range of complex motivations led these young people to turn to their fathers at this developmental stage. Another subgroup consisted of boys whose ties to their mothers had been close and protective over many years. They now sought a closer relationship and identification with their fathers to facilitate the psychological separation from the mother and the transition to manhood. The relationship with the father has an enormous potential value for the boy at this time: it can provide an identification figure and a relationship that can encourage the boy to undertake the first slippery steps towards independence. Where the father failed, in reality, to meet the boy's needs for a benign and virtuous figure for identification, it was not uncommon for the boy to invent the father image that he needed.

Jim's father had sought divorce after many years of infidelity and frequent absences from the family. The mother had opposed the divorce out of her intense love for her husband and her anxiety at being left with three children to care for. Jim had been very close to his mother for many years and treated her with unfailing love and kindness. He told us when he was twelve years old, "I stuck with Mom and tried to help her because Dad left her all alone." At age 17, the boy startled us with an entirely new version of his history. He said,

> I never could understand how Dad could marry Mom, after she forced him to leave the East Coast and move out here. I still have not figured it out. Maybe Mom does not like men, I worried about whether Mom is gay, because she did not like my Dad, or me. My Dad and I have become very good friends. He is like me, and he is honest with me and tells me both sides of the story.

A third subgroup of youngsters who gravitated towards the father included those who were living with a psychologically deteriorating mother, or who were experiencing serious conflicts in their relationships. Some went in search of a more permissive household. Those who left the mother's home often ran the gauntlet of her anger and humiliation; the move was rarely easy, for parent or child. . . .

The Legacy of Divorce

This is the fourth report from a ten-year longitudinal study of 131 children from 60 divorcing families in Northern California. Findings have been presented regarding 38 young people, 16 boys and 22 girls, who were 16-18 years old at the ten-year follow-up and who had experienced marital rupture during their early latency years. Most of these young people are in school full-time, live at home, hold part-time jobs, and are law-abiding. Most have remained in the legal and physical custody of their mothers. The one quarter who now reside with their fathers made the changeover during their adolescent years.

"A significant number [of young men] . . . will suffer psychological conflicts that will impair their capacity for the love and intimacy for which they long."

Feelings of sadness, of neediness, of a sense of their own vulnerability, were expressed by the majority of these young people. Although two thirds of their lives have been spent in the divorced or remarried family, they spoke sorrowfully of their loss of the intact family and the consequent lack of opportunity for a close relationship with the father. They spoke wistfully of the more nurturing, protective environment that they envision in intact families. Anxieties about relationships with the opposite sex, marriage, and personal commitments ran very high. A central concern was fear of betrayal in relationships, both present and future, and of being hurt and abandoned. Although few differences were noted between boys and girls in attitudes toward the divorce and anxieties about the future, the girls seemed more able at this developmental stage to draw sustenance from their social relationships and from their relationships with their custodial mothers. Girls were more likely to become involved in dating and sexual relationships. Boys were far more likely to be lonely and to hold back in their relationships with girls. They showed more reserve, even constriction, in their capacity to feel or to express affection and anger. Half of the boys and one fourth of the girls were considered poorly adjusted and at high risk at the time of the ten-year follow-up.

Although, for the majority, relationships with the father were poor, the psychological significance of the father had persisted and appeared to have gained importance during the adolescent years for both sexes, but especially for the boys. . . .

Separation from the divorced family and transition into young adulthood is especially painful for these young people. They are burdened by intense worries about failure in their present and future relationships, by their sense of having been insufficiently nurtured and encouraged during their years of growing up, and by an overall sense of their own powerlessness. They have realistic concerns about their college years. In the process of negotiating their important steps away from the custodial mother and the regressive pull of early relationships, the boys are haunted by their earlier separation from the father at a critical time; they experience a renewed, intense need for his reassuring presence, encouragement and protection. Although it is likely that many of these young men will make the transition to psychological independence successfully, the evidence in these findings is that a significant number will enter adulthood with lowered expectations of themselves and others and that they will suffer psychological conflicts that will impair their capacities for the love and intimacy for which they long. Many will need psychological treatment.

Judith S. Wallerstein is executive director of the Center for the Family in Transition in Corte Madera, California. Since 1971, she has been principal investigator of the California Children of Divorce Project, the longest continuous study of divorced families in the nation.

viewpoint **49**

Divorce's Impact on Children Is Exaggerated

Laurie Dixon

Editor's note: The following viewpoint is excerpted from Laurie Dixon's testimony before the Select Committee on Children, Youth, and Families in Washington, DC on June 19, 1986.

I am a child of divorce. My parents separated when I was two years old and divorced two years later. I live with my mother and older brother and sister and see my father on Sundays.

I interviewed many Bethesda area high school students whose parents are divorced for an article in my school newspaper. Since then, I've talked with more high school students with divorced parents, many of whom feel insulted by the image and treatment of children of divorce as pitiful products of a "broken home" or as trouble-making "latchkey waifs."

Thankful for the Divorce

My own experience with divorce was not very negative. The main difficulty I had in dealing with my parents' divorce was that I didn't understand what was happening at the time, and my parents never really explained it to me when I was older. Consequently, there was a time when I really longed for my parents to remarry. I loved both my parents, and I didn't understand why they couldn't love each other. However, when I became a little older, I easily recognized my parents' inherent differences. I am now thankful that my parents *did* divorce.

If my parents were together, I would have a terrible home situation. I have few memories of my parents before the divorce, but one is particularly striking. I think it was after their separation, and my father had taken us kids out for dinner. He was now leaving, and he and my mother were yelling at each other. I'm not sure about what they were arguing. It

may have been that my father had kept us out too late. But I do remember that I was trying to say good-bye to my father and that he didn't hear me. This is probably the type of situation that would exist today if my parents were together. They would probably be so caught up in their own problems that they would forget their children.

If my home situation were strained and tense or outwardly hostile, as I'm sure it would have to be if my parents lived together, I know that I would try my best to stay out of the house as much as possible. If avoiding my parents became my first objective, a much worse situation could result. I would like to say with conviction that I would never have been stupid enough to abuse illegal drugs or alcohol, but with me trying to escape such a rotten reality, I don't think it is entirely out of the question. Drugs appear to be a very good way to escape and forget.

I firmly believe that it is the quality not the quantity of parents that is important. My mother is wonderful; trusting, understanding, fair, sympathetic and helpful are just a few of the adjectives that come to mind. She knows what I need in a parent and she does that job very well. Of course, we sometimes argue. Of course there are times that you could throw my above testimony at me, and I would have a hard time believing that I even said it. But all in all, we get along really well. How many parents, divorced or not, can say that of their teenaged kids?

I am not so close with my father. We have very different values and opposite stances on almost every major political issue. If I lived with him in a joint-custody arrangement or saw him more often, we would have a much more difficult time staying friendly. As it is, I see him once a week at most, and we generally avoid certain topics of conservation.

When I interviewed other children of divorce, I was surprised at how well they all seemed to have taken it. They were all very willing to talk to me

Laurie Dixon, *Divorce: The Impact on Children and Families*, hearing on June 19, 1986 before the Select Committee on Children, Youth, and Families. Washington, DC: U.S. Government Printing Office, 1987.

about their experiences. I think they were excited to have a chance to change the media's image of divorce as having such horrible effects on children. Many even cited positive effects, such as growth, greater self-reliance, closer relationships with one or both parents and a greater sense of responsibility. In general, problems, if there were any, were worked out early on. None of the students I talked with regret their parents' divorce, even those who lost contact with or rarely see one of their parents.

When I recontacted many of the students to ask them if there was anything specific they wanted me to say at this hearing, the response I got was, "Just show them that we are not any different from other kids."

Divorce itself is not the true problem for kids today. Bad marriages which continue or end and lack of communication pose much more substantial threats to the healthy upbringing of a child. If we are to combat effectively the problems between parents and their children, we must teach both children and adults responsibility, sensitivity, and the art of communication.

I would also like to direct your attention to the article which I included in the record.

[The article, "Questions that Follow Divorce," follows:]

Other Children of Divorce

"Even if it's a rough divorce, I think the kids make out pretty well," says Freshman Ken Holloway, whose parents separated when he was nine.

Researchers and psychiatrists debate this point, arguing whether, in the long run, divorce hurts, doesn't affect, or even benefits a child. With nearly half of marriages ending in divorce, more and more children are experiencing divorce. Mental-health experts are finding it crucial to study the effects of divorce on children in order to help other children undergoing divorce.

Dr. Richard Gross, a [Bethesda] child psychiatrist, discusses some of the more immediate effects of divorce on children:

"They often feel caught between parents," he says. They feel they have to take sides; they feel that one person must be right and one person must be wrong.

"Sometimes," Gross continues, "they feel guilty that they may have caused their parents to break up. . . . They worry that if one parent can leave them, the other could also leave them. They worry that they'll be abandoned, deserted. . . . Sometimes," he adds, "children think they'll be put in an orphanage because their parents divorced."

"In the beginning, I felt terribly responsible," says Bethesda-Chevy Chase (B-CC) Sophomore Erika McConnell, who was about seven at her parents' separation. "I felt it was all my fault, all (my sister) Rachel's fault. As kids, we took a lot of blame—

which was ridiculous. . . . One reason I think I blamed myself was because the one thing they argued most about was raising kids."

Joyce Winston, a local social worker who works in a family counseling agency, describes divorce as "often a mourning process."

"The initial separation, rather than the divorce per se, brings a sense of loss," she explains. "There's the loss of a parent, the loss of the family as a whole, sometimes the loss of a home or school."

"(The divorce) affected my life in a lot of ways," Junior David Fernades, whose parents separated when he was nine and divorced a year later, remembers. "I had to live in a different house, deal with a different school—different everything. . . . But I'm not a changed man because of it."

A Normal Part of Life

What do children of divorce themselves think about their experiences?

"You learn to grow up with it," explains Senior Chris Harriot, whose parents separated when he was five and finally divorced when he was eleven. "It just becomes a normal part of life."

"I don't think anyone's thrilled when their parents get divorced," says Senior Duward McDonell, who was five when his parents divorced, "but nobody I know seems incredibly devastated or anything."

"My parents were separated two or three years before they were divorced," Winston's daughter Rachel, a senior, recalls. "I was seven when they separated. My dad got custody of my brother, and my mom got custody of my sister and me. At the same time, it was not a whole barrel of fun in any sense. It *sucked*—but it was about ten years ago. Things have worked out pretty well. I think (my parents) are a lot better off apart than together.

"Right now, it seems a long time ago," Winston's daughter adds, "a tremendously long time. I was old enough to understand they were fighting. It was obvious why my mother was leaving.

"Divorce itself is not the true problem for kids today. Bad marriages . . . and lack of communication pose much more substantial threats to the healthy upbringing of a child."

"Consciously," she continues, "I understood. I *knew* why; it was most evident why. But I still wanted to get them back together. Subconsciously, I thought it could get better the next time. I think *all* children whose parents divorce don't want all these changes in their lives. They can't handle the disruption in their life and all the bad feelings that can accompany divorce."

Senior Jennifer Jones was six when her parents separated. Her father remarried the next year but soon divorced a second time.

"I remember vividly the moment my dad told me in a phone call that he and his second wife were splitting up," Jones recalls. "As soon as we hung up, I started jumping around my bedroom! I was *so* glad *"she"* wasn't part of the family anymore.

"Then my mom and dad were able to be more civil to each other," she continues. "I guess at that point I still really wanted them to get back together. I love both of them so much, and I thought it would be good to have all of us under one roof.

"It didn't happen that way," Jones explains, "and now I'm glad. Their individual happiness is greater than their mutual happiness ever could be. It's been said before, but it's *so* true: I'd rather have them apart and happy than together and unhappy."

All of these above children stayed in contact with both parents, under various arrangements. McConnell, however, encountered a more difficult situation.

"I've always missed not having a father," she says. "It's weird not growing up with a male in the household. I never had a father to brag about when people started talking about their fathers."

McConnell's parents at first attempted to have joint custody of their two daughters. McConnell's father lived two blocks away. However, says McConnell, switching houses every week was "too much moving." Also, the parents "had very different ideas about how to raise kids.

"I haven't seen him (my father) at all in five years now," McConnell says. "It's really tough. . . . Oh, we might see him if he's working in the yard as we go by, or at the neighborhood pool—but I'm afraid to reopen communication. I don't know how he'll react."

Despite her sense of loss, McConnell believes it "would have been a mistake" for her parents to stay together. "What they did was best for us," she contends.

A Positive Experience

Some children of divorced parents see the divorce as a positive experience.

"It's made me a little more self-reliant," Senior Pippa Holloway, eleven at her parents' divorce, explains. "I can manage difficult situations because of it. You have to be strong enough to know that, even though there's turmoil (between your parents), you're okay. I think I rely more on myself more than I would have."

Holloway recalls her feelings when her parents informed her and her brother of their decision to separate.

"It was pretty nice," she says. "We all sat down in the living room—it was in the evening—and both

(our parents) talked; it wasn't one-sided. Then we all went out to dinner. It was really peaceful. We all felt good about the decision."

Holloway's brother shares her positive feeling. "I think it's a good thing they got divorced," he says, "because now I have to deal with my parents as individuals. It's helped me sort of understand how marriages can go wrong and what mistakes they made."

"There are a lot of negatives out of a divorce," Winston's daughter believes, "but it's a great deal more positive in the long run. I grew a lot.

"Right around the divorce, we were living well," she continues, "but at the separation our standard of living went down. What we took for granted was out—vacations and trips were out. I had to leave my private school, we had no TV. We had to start from scratch—with a lot of help from friends.

"I don't think anyone's thrilled when their parents get divorced, . . . but nobody I know seems incredibly devastated or anything."

"The divorce forced us to adjust. We had to deal with the way we were living before." Winston's daughter adds, "Around the divorce, we were 'latchkey' children. We took care of ourselves. We would make dinner and find our own entertainment. There are so many areas where we grew!"

"It's been good for me and my (older) brother," Harriot says, "living with just our father. He was not around a lot, so we learned to take care of ourselves. We became totally independent. We had no curfews, no limits. We were basically free—we learned to manage our own time, money, etc.

"We've been living in the outside world all the time," Harriot continues. "I kinda like it this way, except for the fact that Mom's not living with us now. But I think it turned out pretty well. I have no regrets."

"I'm a much different person because of the divorce," Jones believes. "My pre-teen years I spent in my mom's single-parent household. I think that gave me a greater sense of responsibility and independence.

"At fourteen," she continues, "I came to Bethesda to live with my dad; and he's really drawn me out, in terms of understanding and improving my personality. We have the *neatest* conversations.

"I doubt that my relationships with both my parents would be as strong as they are now if they were still married; so it has all turned out for the best," she concludes.

B-CC Sophomore Daniel Shapiro, who was about

eleven when his parents separated, feels that his parents' divorce made his life "more diverse, more independent."

"I think I might be less independent for having a stronger, more unified home situation," he explains.

Shapiro's parents opted for joint-custody, which Shapiro sees as "probably the best arrangement." He now lives about three weeks with his mother, then the next three weeks or so with his father.

"It wouldn't be right to stay in one house all the time," he believes. "I mean, it's a pain to move back and forth all the time, but I think everyone benefits."

"I think it's a good thing they got divorced. . . . It's helped me sort of understand how marriages can go wrong and what mistakes they made."

Harriot says his parents "despise each other" and haven't seen each other for six years, except at his brother's graduation.

"Mom and Dad are *totally* two different people," he says. "They do *not* accompany each other in the right way. It'd be total hell if my parents hadn't divorced."

"My parents are so different it's strange to think they married anyway," McDonell comments. "I couldn't imagine them together. They're so different. I couldn't imagine them getting along.

"If parents yell all the time, are unhappy all the time, it seems it can't be any better than one parent," McDonell reasons. "All those horrible 'latchkey waif' stories and broken home stories are probably written by people who grew up in two-parent homes, are happily married, and want others to look bad."

Healthier Atmosphere in the Home

"I think it's in the kid's interest to divorce if the parents can't get along," Winston's daughter states. "There would be too much tension and stress, perhaps fighting and violence if parents stayed together ('for the sake of the children'). That would be unfair to the children.

"I think the divorce was definitely necessary," she concludes.

Fernades describes his family's predivorce atmosphere as "boring."

"There wasn't the kind of affection my parents have now (for my stepparents)," he explains, "but it wasn't stormy." He believes there would have been a lot of tension if his parents had stayed together.

"It would have been miserable," he theorizes. "There was very low-key tension before the divorce.

I think there would have had to be high-key tension. I hate, hate, *hate* it when people fight—I just leave. My parents never fought openly; I never had to live with that. I'm grateful for that."

"As time passes, it could be worked through," Winston declares. "It helps mightily if the non-custodial parent *stays* in the picture, but that's not always the case. How kids do depends on how stable the custodial parent is, how they adjust, and the other biggie is the importance of the other parent staying in the picture.

"There's not anything inevitable over the long run," Winston believes. "I don't believe that kids come out any different from it. It greatly depends on how the parents do."

The Least Negative Effects

Gross agrees. "Often, if it's a divorce which is upsetting to the custodial parent, at a time when children most need reassurance from the remaining parent, the parent can't give.

"A child who's better adjusted before separation is more likely to adjust after," he continues. If there's already a problem, it's likely to get worse. If the parents continue to fight even after the separation, often it's worse for the child. Often the child becomes the battle ground. "If there's been a lot of fighting in the home prior to the breakup of the marriage, it's usually troubling to the child and there's more trouble when the breakup occurs.

"In the most ideal of circumstances of divorce, with all the right things being said, it's still traumatizing for the child," Gross concludes. "There's just a better way of doing it, with the least negative effects."

Laurie Dixon was a student and managing editor of The Pitch *at Walter Johnson High School in Bethesda, Maryland, when she testified in 1986 before a congressional hearing on children and divorce.*

"Mothers have no enforceable right . . . to initiate a divorce unilaterally, pursue a 'career,' move away, . . . without risking a custodial challenge."

viewpoint 50

Custody Battles Victimize Divorced Women

Phyllis Chesler

Editor's note: The following viewpoint is excerpted from Phyllis Chesler's seven-year study of women and custody of children.

An ideal mother is very different from an ideal father. A real mother is also different from a real father.

Traditionally, an ideal mother is expected to choose married motherhood for her future at a very young age. She is expected to become pregnant, give birth, psychologically "bond" with, and assume bottom-line responsibility for her children's physical and emotional needs.

She is also expected to behave in physically non-violent and psychologically self-sacrificing ways. This female socialization into and practice of motherhood is devalued and taken for granted.

Anti-Mother Biases

We experience the same parental abuse as "worse" when a mother performs it. We condemn mothers more than fathers for failing the parental ideal, for performing parental work inadequately, for being psychologically imperfect, and for being physically abusive.

What with such double standards and anti-mother biases, what kind of custodially challenged mother would automatically be viewed as a "good enough" mother? ("There must be something wrong with her. Why else would her husband or the state challenge her?")

Do judges, priests, politicians, psychiatrists, or social workers view unwed, imprisoned, or "career" mothers as maternally fit? Would they view their custodial victimization as unjust? Do white married mothers or white social workers view non-white or welfare mothers as maternally fit? . . .

Phyllis Chesler, *Mothers on Trial*. New York: McGraw-Hill Book Company, 1986. Reprinted by permission.

I decided to study sixty custodially challenged, predominantly white mothers, who had internalized the Western ideals of motherhood and who were demographically similar to the majority of divorced white mothers in America. These sixty mothers were custodially challenged in every geographical region of the United States and Canada between 1960 and 1981.

I interviewed fifty mothers who were black, brown, yellow, and red. Some, but not all, are part of this study. They are very much a part of this [viewpoint].

In general, these mothers had married as virgins—or had married the first men they slept with. They had married and given birth at relatively young ages. They had assumed the bottom-line domestic, emotional, and primary child-care responsibilities of traditional marriages. In general, these mothers had stayed at home until their youngest children were of grade-school age. Both psychologically and physically they had put "work" or a "career" second to motherhood.

During our interviews together, these mothers casually and matter-of-factly described performing at least twenty-five very specific maternal domestic and child-related chores—quite separate from domestic chores that are husband-related.

I was exploring a "worst case" scenario. Could a "good enough" mother ever lose custody? Could she lose custody to a relatively uninvolved or abusive father? Could this happen more than once? Could this happen often? . . .

Paternal Kidnapping

How many fathers currently have custody of their children? No one really knows. Do more fathers have custody of their children in 1985 than had it in 1885 or 1785? No one knows.

Researchers have estimated that from 1965 to 1972 the number of households headed by divorced or separated fathers increased by 71 percent; that as of 1976, 500,000 fathers had sole legal custody of their children; that as of 1981, between 25,000 and 100,000 formal custody disputes were occurring annually; and that 40,000 fathers have won judicial custody *each year* since 1977.

Such estimates never include the number of fathers who won "kidnapping" custody of their children. Nor do they include the number of fathers who privately coerced mothers into "agreeing" to paternal custody, nor the number of fathers who obtained custody because mothers became ill, were hospitalized for long periods, died, or were genuinely unfit.

American mothers have probably lost more children during the 1970s and early 1980s to paternal kidnapping than to judicial decision. *Parental* child kidnapping is an almost all-male crime. Conservative estimates from the mid-1970s range from 100,000 to 125,000 child snatchings a year. More recently, Dr. Richard Gelles estimated that 459,000 to 751,000 parental "child snatchings" have occurred each year.

I would estimate that from 1975 to 1985, at least 2 million fathers won "kidnapping" custody, and that 400,000 won judicial or courtroom custody. In a single decade, nearly 2.5 million fathers probably won custody of their children in *quantifiable* ways. . . .

Such a statistical estimate not only is partial and conservative, but also respresents only the tip of the American custodial iceberg. Each *publicized* custody battle terrorizes married, divorced, and unwed mothers in non-measurable and unknown ways. . . .

Mothers Are Custodially Vulnerable

We do not know if mothers were custodially challenged or victimized more frequently between 1960 and 1981 than between 1860 and 1881. It is almost impossible to confirm a statistical increase in a previously uncharted area.

This study can and does confirm the custodial vulnerability of "good enough" mothers; and the ease with which a domestically violent father or one with no previous involvement in child care can win custody.

This study can and does confirm that "good enough" mothers have no enforceable right to freedom from male domestic violence; no enforceable right to alimony or child support; and no right to initiate a divorce unilaterally, pursue a "career," move away, engage in nonmarital sexual activities, or hold any opinions opposed by their husbands—without risking a custodial challenge. . . .

"Respectable" mothers were unprepared for the consequences of divorce. They were stunned when their unchosen poverty, their need to work, their career achievements, and their sexual independence were viewed as maternal crimes. "Respectable"

mothers were also surprised when policemen, lawyers, judges, neighbors, and relatives did little to protect them from male violence—including that of a custody battle. . . .

Sixty-two percent of the custodially challenged mothers were perceived as "uppity." "Uppity" behavior included: exercising freedom of thought or speech, especially if a "minority" opinion was involved; exercising civic duties, such as exposing government corruption; having a "career"; having to work; wanting to move away in order to find or accept employment; and daring to initiate a divorce.

"A statistical estimate . . . represents only the tip of the American custodial iceberg. Each publicized *custody battle terrorizes married, divorced, and unwed mothers in non-measurable and unknown ways."*

Nearly half the mothers (47 percent), and nearly a third of the fathers (27 percent) initiated the divorce. Some fathers behaved as if they "owned" both their wives and children and "allowed" their wives to take care of their children—as long as they took care of their husbands too. Once these husbands became convinced that their wives were about to "steal" paternal property (her domestic services, "his" children), the divorce escalated into a custody battle. . . .

The Crime of "Uppity" Behavior

What if a mother not only initiates a divorce, but dares to become a successful artist? Ella Mae is a painter and sculptor. In the early 1960s, she married a lawyer. From the beginning, Donald resented and opposed Ella Mae's work—even though she worked at home; even though dinner was always ready, and the house always clean. Ella Mae was devoted to their infant daughter, Mary. She said:

> During the day I would feel very happy, very whole, very satisfied with my work in my attic studio. Mary gurgled or slept right beside me. It was blissful. Donald was becoming more and more unhappy. He hated his job. He had no friends. Here I was, this happy person. When he'd come home, he'd just have to knock me down.
>
> After I sold my first painting, he demanded that I pay for my own oils and canvases. I did. As I became more successful, he demanded household money. As long as I could actually sell one of those damn paintings—he wanted me to pay for Mary's clothes. I was like some dog he could kick. After a year and a half I decided I deserved a better life than this.

Donald wouldn't move out. He wouldn't let Ella Mae take "anything he'd paid for": the iron, the first-aid kit, her sewing machine. He wouldn't give her any child support. Ella Mae outraged him by managing to survive that first winter without heat or hot water. By spring, she had sold a painting. She made new friends. Within a year, she was under the "protection" of another man, whom she eventually married. Ella Mae said:

> There was nothing Donald could do to hurt me. He was very frustrated by my successful escape. He couldn't forgive me for my strength. He thought I was a monster with no feelings. He thought I should be destroyed.
>
> For seven years I mothered Mary. I grew as an artist. I forgot that Donald had a score to settle with me. He sent twenty dollars a week for her. He thought this was a lordly sum. He thought he was a good father. This amount didn't increase in seven years.

Ella Mae divorced her second husband. Her reputation as an artist and her feminist awareness grew. She began living with an emotionally supportive younger man. When Mary was nine years old, three things happened: Ella Mae was asked to coordinate a national show of women's paintings; Mary developed a learning disorder that required special medical and educational attention; and Ella Mae decided to request an increase in child support. "At Donald's request," said Ella Mae,

> Mary was with him for one month every summer. I was working on the art show. Donald hired a detective who posed as a magazine photographer. He took pictures of my home and interviewed me about the art show. After Donald thought he had a good enough case, he refused to return Mary. He accused me of being a "bohemian" and of "having orgies."

Donald was a local lawyer with a substantial and respectable practice. Donald was remarried, and had two other children. Despite Ella Mae's unblemished record as a full-time mother, a judge ordered Mary into her father's permanent custody. He allowed maternal visitation only at "Donald's discretion." Ella Mae said:

> Seven years after I left him, Donald began to exact his revenge. First, he got custody. He didn't let me see Mary for a year. Then he let me see her, now and then, for a day at a time—if I was very grateful, and never demanded her back.
>
> After a year, Mary was no longer the child I knew. She wore tiny pearls and an expensive little suit. She wouldn't look me in the eye. She talked about her swimming pool and her ballet classes. My Mary! So quiet, so ladylike. What had Donald done to her? How could he punish a child in order to get at me? How could he do to her what he wanted to do to me?
>
> You know, I've painted women as heroines and goddesses. I'm Demeter, and Mary is my Persephone. But I couldn't force Donald to return Mary to me—not for a single summer. I lived with Mary for three thousand days. Since I lost custody nine years ago, I've spent about forty days with her.
>
> Donald is my most powerful teacher. Whenever I think my success has moved me out of the female ghetto, I remember: I am without Mary.

What if a mother has no artistic "calling," no "bohemian" sexual lifestyle—but needs to move away in order to pursue a livelihood, a "career," or a chance at a new life?

Nearly a third (31 percent) of the fathers who *won* custody moved away afterward. Half these fathers obtained court approval to do so; a third moved away without entering the court system or without "mentioning" their intended move in court. One-fifth of the fathers moved away by permanently kidnapping their children.

Nearly a third (32 percent) of the mothers wanted to move away. With one exception, they all were prevented from doing so—with their children. Judges (and others) all viewed children as their fathers' "landed property," not as part of a moveable maternal unit. Judges also viewed the paternal right of visitation as more important than the maternal right to survive economically and psychologically.

"Judges viewed the paternal right of visitation as more important than the maternal right to survive economically and psychologically."

For example, Beth was privately forced into a joint custody arrangement. She received no alimony and no child support. Her children lived with her for half the week. When Beth found employment in a nearby city, she petitioned the court to have the childen with her for fewer days—but on weekends. She said:

> This was 1974. The judge told me to live on welfare. He said I couldn't just move these kids or change their established living pattern. I moved away. I had to in order to survive. Then I had to beg, whine, and wheddle weekend visitation on my own as a favor from my husband. I had to pay their fare down or my fare up. The court wouldn't order my ex-husband to share travel costs with me. After all, I was the one who decided to move.

The belief that working, career, or remarried mothers will neglect their children is very great. The belief that such mothers will neglect children more than their working, career, or remarried fathers will—or that divorced career mothers in large cities will abuse their children more than divorced career fathers in small towns—remains virtually unshakable.

Move to a Big City

Miki is tall and very elegant. She moves swiftly, like a samurai, across the room, her eyes masked in pain. She starts speaking abruptly:

"Ten years ago, I married a white student. Together, we organized radical demonstrations. Pretty soon, Alvin became cynical and contemptuous. He began to criticize the masses—and me.

"We were living in Alvin's two-bit hometown. I was a trapped animal, far from home; a full-time mother, with a minimum-wage factory job. I couldn't pursue politics or music. I had no child care and no encouragement. When the kids turned five and seven, I moved out. Three weeks later, Alvin moved a girlfriend in.

"When I got a lawyer, Alvin stole my car. He refused to sell our house and divide up the proceeds. He threatened a custody battle if I demanded anything. He scared me. I gave up all my economic demands.

"Over the next year I began to yearn for San Francisco. I put out feelers. My parents said I could live with them or with my brother, who had young children. I could study the piano again. The kids could spend summers and vacations with Alvin. What difference would our moving to San Francisco make? Alvin traveled four months every year. *He* wasn't stuck in the Midwest. *I* was.

"Alvin got an order restraining me from leaving the state with the kids. By this time, my daughter Suzi was hostile to the idea of San Francisco. She screamed that she would be mugged there. She cried a lot. 'It's all your fault,' she said. 'The divorce and the custody battle. You're a bad mother.' Sam, my son, kept totally quiet.

"I feel a little like a slave whose master owns my children. I'm not supposed to be free. But if I manage to escape, I'm supposed to leave my children behind as my master's property."

"My lawyer told me there was no way I could lose custody. I believed him. Five days before the trial, Alvin married his live-in girlfriend. He began talking about how this white stepmother would be a very stable influence.

"Alvin's lawyer mocked the idea of my having a career as a concert pianist. He accused me of wanting to go to San Francisco to have 'boyfriends.' He accused me of feeding my kids un-American (Japanese) food.

"Didn't anyone notice that my children looked Japanese? Didn't anyone care about their mother's ethnic heritage? One of Alvin's witnesses was a neighbor who had once told me to 'go back to China.' I always wondered what they called me and my kids behind our backs.

"My lawyer called me two weeks after the trial. He said: 'I've got bad news for you. The judge gave Alvin custody of both children.' Alvin pulled the kids out of bed in the middle of the night and drove away with them.

"I fell apart. I begged a close friend to persuade him to let me see the children that evening. He refused. I drove by the house alone. I sat outside in the car, crying. His new wife finally sent Suzi out. She was like a zombie, straight-faced, arms at her side. Alvin followed her out. He sat down on my fender, watching everything. I tried to hug Suzi, but she held herself very stiffly. Sam hugged me, but very carefully. I could feel how scared he was.

"Alvin finally had ultimate control over me. It's as if he had the atom bomb.

Racist and Sexist Decision

"I immediately appealed the decision. I wrote and called organizations everywhere to join me in protesting this racist and sexist decision. No Japanese or civil rights or feminist organization wanted to get involved. My only support came from a group of black women social workers. They wrote a group letter to the judge on my behalf. It only infuriated him.

"Does the state have the right to force me to remain hobbled to my ex-husband's definitions of home? Do my determined and effective steps toward independence mean I am unstable? Does wanting to live with my Japanese-American family in San Francisco define me as 'rootless'? Are white married males the only people with 'roots'?

"I feel a little like a slave whose master owns my children. I'm not supposed to be free. But if I manage to escape, I'm supposed to leave my children behind as my master's property."

Jessie's Story

What if a mother exercises her conscience and her civil responsibilities by exposing government corruption? Can an exercise in public virtue result in her private custodial punishment? Jessie is such a mother. She said:

"The Civil Air Patrol shaped my personality. I was trained to survive in the desert and to participate in rescue missions for downed planes. My mentors are American patriots, soldiers, idealists.

"Mark and I married when we were both eighteen. I became a mother at twenty, and again at twenty-three. While Mark was in Vietnam, I took care of the kids, finished college, taught Sunday school, ran our house—and still had time for political campaign work.

"Mark came back a changed man. He drank. He beat me and the kids. He refused to look for work or to go for counseling. After two years, Mark drifted off. He rarely visited or even called the kids.

"I was offered a job in the Census Bureau based on my volunteer campaign work. I was very excited until I realized that Wade, my boss, was running his own political three-ring circus. He provided girls, booze, and pot for the party regulars. My job was recruiting the 'girls'—and manipulating the census findings.

"I went to my immediate superior in tears. He calmed me down. Then Wade called me in. 'If you persist in talking against me, I'll destroy you politically. I'll spread rumors about *your* sex life.' Within hours, my office was moved. I'd come into work and find my files missing, my phones dead. I'd be ordered to travel fifty miles to a meeting. When I'd arrive, there wouldn't be any meeting. People stopped talking to me.

"Then Wade fired me. Within three weeks, I found another government job in another state. I was there when the bureau scandal hit the newspapers. Apparently, another employee had called the papers. Wade thought I was behind it. He went on a drunken rampage. He found Mark and took him into court. Wade told the judge: 'This is Mark Morehouse—you know, the guy married to the one who's causing all that trouble. She's up and left the state.' That was it. The judge gave Mark custody. Mark went into hiding with the kids.

"Four months later, my appeal of the custody decision came to trial. Mark admitted he had a bad temper and an unstable work history. He admitted hitting me and the kids. He admitted not seeing the kids for more than a year. Mark's lawyers grilled me for two hours on whether I supported the Equal Rights Amendment."

Judicial Opinion: The father can provide a more stable home environment. That doesn't mean that the mother cannot in the future provide a stable home environment, but we do have a problem with her. She's moved. She has a new job. She had other problems. She is going to have to show this court that she has become stable enough to take these two children out of their home state and provide for their needs. There has been a substantial change in conditions. Based upon that finding, and in the best interests of the children, I am remanding the children to the custody of the father.

"Mark dropped out of sight again. The judge didn't order any maternal visitation. Whenever I wasn't at work, I was interviewing lawyers and meeting with the Justice Department. After eight months, my lawyer was finally able to arrange visitation for me.

"Lea had lost a lost of weight. Devon was withdrawn. He kept picking at himself. He was covered with sores. My lawyer convinced a judge to order temporary custody on medical and psychiatric grounds. He ordered a new custody trial in my new state.

A Painful Good-Bye

"Mark flew right up with *his* custody order. He and the local police removed the kids from school. The school called me at work. I ran over, crying. The kids were crying behind a locked door. When the police took them away, they wouldn't even let me say good-bye.

"I went into the church across the street. I threw myself on the floor before the cross and cried my heart out. I couldn't stop crying. That night I sat on the children's beds all night. I left their half-eaten breakfasts in the refrigerator for months. It was worse than if they were dead.

"A week later, my doorbell rang. It was the sheriff's department with a warrant for my arrest for having 'kidnapped' the children. I was arrested as a fugitive from justice.

"If women fear they'll lose their children, we'll all just move one step backwards away from careers, and into deeper servitude."

"I hired two criminal lawyers: one in each state. I already had two custody lawyers: one in each state. There were three civil lawyers working in D.C. to build the criminal case against Wade.

"One of my lawyers finally convinced the U.S. attorney general's office to get beyond 'this is a family argument' and look at the custody case itself as an obstruction of justice. I was extradited one month later. I was terrified that I'd be killed in prison. Wade could easily make it look like suicide. 'Depressed mother kills herself.' I had visions of me swinging from my Sheer Energy panty hose in my cell.

"They allowed me one visit with my children— under armed guard. I had to pay a hundred dollars for the armed guard. Wade was indicted one day before my trial. Mark didn't press any kidnapping charges. He just turned the kids back to me.

"If you're going to take women's children away, none of the rest matters. If women fear they'll lose their children, we'll all just move one step backwards away from careers, and into deeper servitude. I would have done anything to get my kids back.

"Women: whatever you do, don't quit fighting for your kids."

Phyllis Chesler is a psychologist and writer. Her major works include Women and Madness; Women, Money and Power; About Man; *and* With Child.

"Many men . . . find themselves frozen out of their children's lives—for an angry ex-wife determined to keep a father away from his children can do just that."

Custody Battles Victimize Divorced Men

Jane Young

The neglectful, irresponsible father who "runs away from his family" while his ex-wife and children live in penury has become a staple of contemporary American folklore. But while the media continue to dramatize the grievous financial and psychological plight of single mothers and their children, some men are fighting hard to stay in their children's lives after divorce. It's a tough fight—society and the courts put serious obstacles in their way. These men run up against such suspicion and mistrust, in fact, that all across the country they've formed fathers'-rights groups to lobby for custody laws that are fair to them, and for overall divorce reform. . . .

Denial of Visitation

One issue that infuriates many men is the fact that they find themselves frozen out of their children's lives—for an angry ex-wife determined to keep a father away from his children can do just that. This problem (it's called "denial of visitation") has been increasing since the advent of no-fault divorce in many states. "We don't call it visitation, we call it *parenting time*," says [John] Rossler[vice-president of the Fathers Rights Association of New York State]. "Fathers are not cousins once removed or casual friends of the family; they don't *visit* their own children.". . .

Some form of visitation is routinely awarded in all divorces. "New York law states that the custodial parent has an obligation not only to *permit* visitation but to actively *encourage* a relationship with the non-custodial parent," says Joel Brandes, a Garden City lawyer. But unless the custodial parent abides by a court order for visitation, a separated or divorced father may never see his kids at all. "Enforcing a father's visitation rights when a mother won't give

him access to his children is often more difficult then winning sole custody for him," says New York lawyer Carol Zimmerman. . . .

The ultimate remedy is a switch of custody, which some judges are now threatening, and, in a few cases, actually ordering. But for most men, switching custody is a pipe dream. "My kids have been so turned against me that if the judge gave me custody, they'd probably run away the minute I shut my eyes," says one bitter "ex-father," whose son and daughter have refused to see him for several years. "When children have been brainwashed, there's not much you can do."

Classic Brainwashing

Experts believe that classic brainwashing—intensive, systematic indoctrination over a certain period—occurs in only 10 to 15 percent of divorces. When it is effective, the children form what [Judith S.] Wallerstein and [Joan Berlin] Kelly called "a pathological and often enduring alliance with the embittered custodial parent" that entirely shuts out the non-custodial parent. In cases of brainwashing, even if the court supports the noncustodial parent's efforts to sustain a relationship with his or her children, legal intervention is of no help.

Twenty-three million viewers watched a taped segment of ABC's *20/20* on November 22, 1984, in which hidden cameras followed 42-year-old Bob Raggi, a New York City cop, as he tried "for the umpteenth time in four years" to pick up three of his five children for a court-ordered Sunday outing on Long Island. "They're over at their friend's house," said his ex-wife, whom he'd met when he was seventeen and been married to for eighteen years. Summoned, the children hung their heads. Playing listlessly with a football, Raggi's twelve-year-old son, Shawn, refused to look up. "Guys, come on—you want to come in?" she said, coolly ushering them into the house.

Jane Young, "The Fathers Also Rise," *New York*, November 18, 1985. Reprinted with the author's permission.

Raggi was finally ready to quit. Only his oldest daughter, Laurie Ann, seventeen, had kept in touch. "She was punished whenever she spent time with me," he says. A few weeks after the *20/20* program aired, he withdrew petitions asking for enforcement of his visitation rights. It was his twenty-third court appearance.

"How many times must a father be told by his own offspring to stay out of their lives before he begins to take it to heart?" he asked Nassau Family Court judge Aaron Cohen. "Abiding by the rules, I expected that my rights as a father would be equally respected and supported. It was an assumption that I finally came to discover was entirely false. . . . Something terribly *wrong* has taken place here."

People Assume

Raggi finds it difficult to explain how—and why—four of his children came to reject him. "Most people assume—I always did—that when children refuse to visit with their father he must have done something awful to them or to their mother," he says. "In my case, it seems to have little to do with anything I've ever done. I never hit my wife or kids, never fooled around, never gambled. My ex-wife has never accused me of any sort of physical abuse. The worst thing anyone can say is that I worked long, irregular hours and wasn't home as much as I would have liked to be."

> "Abiding by the rules, I expected that my rights as a father would be equally respected and supported. It was an assumption that . . . was entirely false."

A devout Roman Catholic, Raggi describes himself and his ex-wife, Jan, as "the Dale Evans and Roy Rogers of the born-again charismatic movement." They both gave marriage encounters, attended church regularly, and were active in the community. "When Jan informed me that she no longer loved me, had not loved me for years, and asked me to leave immediately, I was stunned," recalls Raggi. "Everyone assumes that when a marriage ends, the man 'runs away' and 'abandons his wife and kids.' What nobody sees is the man getting pushed, unwillingly, right out of the door."

After the breakup, Raggi moved to a furnished room in the home of an elderly couple nearby. "There were times when I gave my wife my entire paycheck, supporting myself on part-time jobs," he says. During one six-month period after the separation, Raggi was allowed to see his children only six times. Then, he says, his estranged wife informed him that he should not see the children at all, "because I was not a good example for them. Once, when my three-year-old daughter got into my car, she blessed herself because, she said, Mommy had told her I was the devil," he recalls.

When he visited his kids, Raggi says, his ex-wife always had an excuse as to why they couldn't meet with him. "She told me the kids were sick, they had other plans, and, finally, that they just didn't want to see me; they went along with it." Jan enrolled two of the children in a therapy program at Hofstra University. "I called the therapist five times and asked if she would see *me*," says Raggi. "'We don't do it that way,' she told me."

The Raggis were divorced in 1982. Five months after the final decree came through, Jan Raggi got a religious annulment of the eighteen-year marriage. In January 1983, after a Family Court Probation Department investigation, Raggi won a court order stating that his ex-wife had "done nothing to encourage visitation between the children and their father, and has, in fact, interfered with and refused visitation on various occasions." The order recommended specific times and days for visitation, and declared that if Raggi's ex-wife persisted in this conduct, "it may be sufficient grounds to change custody of the children and the Court would entertain an application to suspend support payments." "There was no change in her behavior after this decision," says Raggi. "My ex-wife acted as if it didn't exist. Still, I couldn't stop paying. I knew it wouldn't do any good.". . .

When Ex-Wives Move Away

Normal visitation becomes almost impossible when a parent takes the children far away. Anywhere from 25,000 to 100,000 children each year are said to be kidnapped, the majority by non-custodial parents. But there are no statistics on children removed by divorced custodial parents. When ex-wives with sole custody move away, men without a geographical-limitation clause in their divorce decrees have no legal recourse. Even decrees specifying that the custodial parent must not move out of state or beyond a 50-mile radius, and including such penalties as loss of support, do not keep many custodial parents from leaving. Once the parent moves, support may be withdrawn or assigned to the parent who has moved, but enforcement of visitation rights must be sought through the courts in the new location—an expensive, sometimes futile procedure.

Sandy Slomowitz, a knowledgeable advocate of fathers' rights and co-chairman, with her husband, Leon, of the Long Island Association of Divorced Fathers, is stepmother to a boy and a girl, neither of whom she and her husband were allowed to see for six years. Leon's children are in Florida, where they were taken by his ex-wife, who disappeared a few months after their divorce (there was no geographical clause in his divorce agreement). "For years, we had no idea where she'd gone. Leon's support checks were going to her through an enforcement agency that refused to give him her address," Sandy says. Finally, the Slomowitzes were able to obtain the Florida address of the ex-wife's parents.

Combing all the schools in the area of the address, Sandy finally found the one in which the children were registered. The Slomowitzes sent the school Leon's divorce decree and a copy of the federal law requiring public schools to release records to the non-custodial parent. In May 1984, the principal of the school arranged a surprise visit with their long-lost father. "They were naturally shocked," says Sandy. "We didn't stay long. We just wanted to let the children know their father had been searching for them." Through a Florida attorney, the Slomowitzes brought an action for enforcement of visitation, and the children were ordered to begin counseling. "The social worker told us the children had been alienated too long for them to want a relationship with their father," says Sandy sadly. "It's been seven years now."

Discrimination in the Courts

Male judges, the fathers'-rights groups say, are often career-oriented traditionalists who have left child-rearing to their wives and think other men should do the same—before and after divorce. Judge Richard Huttner takes a dim view of fathers who push for more than the usual amount of visitation. "You have never seen a bigger pain in the ass than the father who wants to get involved; he can be repulsive," he says. "He wants to meet the kid after school at three o'clock, take the kid out to dinner during the week, have the kid on his own birthday, talk to the kid on the phone every evening, go to every open-school night, take the kid away for a whole weekend so they can be alone together. This type of involved father is pathological." Says Gus De Marco, former president of Westchester Equal Rights for Fathers, "If a man aggressively pursues visitation, he's harassing; if he doesn't, he's indifferent. It's a Catch-22 situation.". . .

In 1985, only 10 percent of the 12 million children of divorce are in the custody of their fathers. It wasn't always so. Until just before the turn of the century, fathers routinely got custody. Mothers weren't regularly awarded custody until the late 1880s, when the concept of "maternal preference" took hold; that idea, coupled with the "tender-years doctrine," which claimed that children under seven belong with their mothers, changed things: Giving custody to the mother was presumed to be "in the best interests of the child." In New York State, Section 240 of the Domestic Relations Law gives neither parent a prima facie presumption of preference in custody disputes. In practice, it's another story.

"Men are definitely discriminated against in the courts when it comes to awarding custody," says Joel Brandes. "New York State has has a maternal preference for years, and most judges will still favor the mother, especially in the more traditional counties." Says Manhattan lawyer Raoul Felder, "A woman can be psychotic, a prostitute, or an alcoholic and still keep custody. I had a case in which the mother kept custody even though she had been hospitalized for depression thirteen times."

"When ex-wives with sole custody move away, men without a geographical-limitation clause in their divorce decrees have no legal recourse."

[In 1981] when his wife boycotted their divorce trial, Charles Suntzenich, a 26-year-old Long Island aircraft mechanic, was awarded sole custody of his six-year-old daughter, Julia. Some weeks before, his ex-wife had disappeared with the child. Suntzenich filed a felony complaint for abduction. By the time he saw his daughter again, he had spent two years and $50,000, for detectives as well as for legal fees. "Julia was filthy, dressed in old clothes three sizes too big for her; her hair was matted, and she was suspicious and hyper-alert," says Suntzenich. "She hadn't been allowed to have friends, and she'd been kept out of school the whole time."

At a second trial, a Nassau County judge gave custody of the child back to her mother. "He didn't seem to be concerned about the things that had happened to Julia. He obviously believed children belong with their mothers, period," Suntzenich says. Learning that his ex-wife planned to move to Maine, Suntzenich's lawyer brought a "show cause" order and won a new trial. "This time, the judge listened and probed," he says. Suntzenich got his daughter back. His ex-wife hasn't been heard from since. . . .

Women Activists

Although 90 percent of all children of divorce are in the custody of their mothers, women activists, who favor custody decisions based on who is the "primary caretaker," are alarmed at what they see as a trend toward granting custody to men in half of contested cases. According to Nancy Polikoff, staff attorney for the Women's Legal Defense Fund in Washington, D.C., custody is increasingly being given to fathers on discriminatory grounds—"because they have more economic resources, remarry more quickly than women, and because divorced women must work, which now makes both parents equally fit in the eyes of the courts." But, family-law experts say, the overwhelming majority of men get sole custody only because their wives agree to it or because their wives are demonstrably unfit parents.

Because the concept of joint custody symbolizes both the right and the responsibility of men to remain actively involved in the upbringing of their children after divorce, it has become a major goal of the fathers'-rights movement. "Once you are a non-custodial parent, you fall into the category of a non-parent," says Michael Diehl, an advocate of divorce-law reform. "Non-custodial parents simply have no *enforceable* rights."...

"Men are definitely discriminated against in the courts when it comes to awarding custody."

Despite setbacks, fathers'-rights advocates in New York State remain hopeful that the Legislature and the courts will eventually see the light. "The feminist movement has made a superb case for the victimization of divorced women," says John Rossler. "But divorced men feel victimized, too. We're fighting to change a system that hurts both us and our children. All the evidence points to the fact that the sole-custody arrangement is not really working. We'd like to see *some* form of shared parenthood after divorce—call it joint custody, liberal visitation, or co-parenting—as a realistic option for all divorcing parents, not just the fortunate few."

Jane Young is a free-lance writer. This viewpoint is excerpted from the weekly New York *magazine.*

"Cooperative custody arrangements are in the best interests of the majority of children and should be so presumed under law."

Divorced Parents Should Negotiate Shared Custody of Children

Ciji Ware

There are periods in the lives of normal people when they are crazy—certifiably, verifiably wacko. Times when characteristic good sense and judgment depart, and all that is left is bizarre behavior—and pain. Divorce is one of those times. With all its attendant disruptions, the dissolution of a marriage can cause a kind of temporary insanity, a diminished capacity to cope with problems at the very moment parents are asked to make decisions that will affect them and their children for years to come.

The Notion of Cooperating

At a time when it is agonizing even to talk rationally to each other, a divorcing couple is asked to sit down, feeling totally disoriented, to try to negotiate solutions for issues that run from high finance to who gets the wedding silver, the pet goldfish, the family photos, and the most precious products of any marriage: the children. The notion of *cooperating* with the one person who represents the source of all that pain is almost unthinkable. "You expect me to do *anything* for that bitch/bastard?" is a typical attitude. "You must be out of your mind!" Perhaps the only "solution" most divorcing parents seek during the initial upheaval of separation is an end to its accompanying torture. They want the divorce to be over, done with, put in the past. "If only someone or something would swoop down and take this awful burden off my back, maybe I could get on with my life!"

Usually that "someone" is an attorney, a person trained as a legal warrior with sparring skills honed in the adversarial arena of the court system of the United States. "We're trained to be tigers," chuckled one family-law specialist when asked how he saw his role as a top child custody attorney. Robert Mnookin, a professor of law at Stanford University,

is deeply concerned that "the behavior of lawyers can *create* disputes" that often escalate and prolong the very misery they've been hired to abate. There is a desperate need, Mnookin believes, to examine the role lawyers play in the settlement of marital disputes, especially those involving children. "Some lawyers make things worse and heat up the battle," he notes. And the battle can have grave consequences with which the parents and children will have to contend long after the lawyers have collected their fees.

The adversary legal system itself, through which custody fights are supposedly settled, attempts to apply a legal solution to what is essentially a highly charged emotional problem: Who gets the kids? And emotions are felt by *people*. Waging a custody fight in court may satisfy a need to retaliate. But for most parents the exhilaration of fighting and "winning" a custody battle is short-lived—and often disastrous for the entire family, as it was for Don and Sarah Gilbert, pseudonyms for a couple I have come to know very well.

Don and Sarah

Don is a professor of history at a California college. Sarah, a former high-school teacher, is now a computer consultant. Don is thirteen years older, and they began dating when Sarah was an undergraduate and Don was studying for his doctorate. They married in 1967. Their son, Ronnie, was born in 1969 and their daughter, Penny, in 1970. When they divorced in 1975, these highly motivated, middle-income parents fought a two-and-a-half-year custody war that resulted in attorneys' fees amounting to $38,000 and the kind of heartache no family should endure.

In the beginning, Don had not asked for sole custody. "I felt that the children needed both parents. I just didn't want to lose my position as a parent." For a while Don and Sarah were able to work out a time-sharing plan under which both of them took care of the children on an alternating basis. "I was willing to let Don have the children physically half the time," says Sarah, "but I wanted legal custody to be mine. I felt then that the children needed one home base." Don, on the other hand, was concerned that Sarah would leave the state, as she had threatened to do, taking the children with her.

Sarah also acknowledges now that she was feeling rejected and abandoned at the time of the divorce. "The divorce was Don's idea. I felt devastated. I had lost my husband to another woman and I was leaving my home as well. I couldn't bear the thought of losing custody of my children, too. I needed the respect given a mother with custody." Don, for his part, felt there had been basic problems with their relationship for years and maintained that the issue of custody should be kept separate from the failure of the marriage. He insisted he wanted to share the children on a legal as well as physical basis and wanted them for the same number of school days as Sarah. Sarah refused to agree to that and, through her lawyer, filed for sole custody; so Don and his own lawyer, a well-known Beverly Hills family-law attorney, countersued for sole custody. . . .

The thirty-two-month battle left them and the children in emotional collapse. Don's second wife, Lucy, still chokes up when recalling what the children suffered during the fight in and out of court. "Besides the hostile way they acted toward us and each other, they had headaches, stomachaches, and a fear of going to sleep at night." Ronnie, who was very close to his father, became "manipulative," all the adults now agree. "I was afraid to discipline the children when they were with me," Sarah says, "because I was afraid if I yelled or punished them, someone would hear me and report it to Don. I even felt like the kinds were spies and I was walking on eggs all the time. I had to be the 'perfect parent' every moment, and I was afraid that if I did anything the children didn't like, they'd report it to Don and it would be brought up in court." Don's fear was that, in spite of his close relationship with his two children, "because of the tradition of the court that the mother always gets custody of the kids" he would lose access to his children. The fear that motivated each parent was "I might lose custody."

The Legal Game

And that was the name of the legal game: Who would receive custody? As the Gilberts entered their third year of psychiatic evaluations, frantic phone calls to attorneys, financial declarations, escalating lawyers' fees, interrogations by attorneys and social welfare workers, a very fortunate thing happened: the court-appointed investigator, after interviewing both parents and the children, refused to make a recommendation to the judge in Superior Court as to which parent should prevail, saying that both Sarah and Don were good parents. The judge looked up from the bench in suprise as the investigator suggested the couple be referred to Conciliation Court, a division of Los Angeles Superior Court, for a process known as mediation. The judge agreed.

"When I walked into the first session," Sarah remembers, "I had no intention of coming to an agreement with Don." Sarah saw Conciliation Court as one more delay before the custody trial. "For the first three sessions," she recalls, "our counselor, Hugh McIsaac, provided a place where we could express our hostility and get out the hatred that had been building up for all those years." By this time, the two parents absolutely despised each other. "The whole legal system, in terms of family law," Don insists now, "is designed to bring out the worst in parents, not the best. Before I realized it, I had gotten myself entrapped into saying awful things about my former wife and her family," he says, "things which I absolutely didn't believe."

When the Gilberts began the mediation process, both were emotionally exhausted. "We were broke; we'd gone through one trying experience after another," recalls Sarah. "I, especially, did a lot of attacking, finally getting my feelings out." At the time of the third session she began to feel better when Don acknowledged that he understood Sarah's feelings of rage concerning his own attempts to prove that he was the better parent. However, Don added softly, he still didn't want to be a weekend parent.

"I felt that the children needed both parents. I just didn't want to lose my position as a parent."

"I had been hearing him say that for two and a half years," says Sarah, "but when he said it that day, I *felt* it. I didn't just hear it, I felt it. I realized that I didn't want to be a weekend parent, either." It was at this crucial point, with a neutral third party helping them focus on the issues they had in common, that the Gilberts could conceive of coming to some sort of agreement. "For the next seven sessions we started talking about things we would want to put in an agreement *if* we could make an agreement." Through the process of mediation, the former couple had agreed to agree to try being parents together—separately. They had agreed to give cooperative custody another try. . . .

Ultimately the Gilberts agreed to joint legal and physical custody. They agreed to share equal rights and responsibilities regarding the welfare of Ronnie and Penny, who by then were eight and six years old. For two successive Mondays, the children were picked up after school by Sarah, and they stayed with her through the week. On the following two Fridays, Don picked them up after school and they spent the weekend with him and his second wife, Lucy. Then Don brought them back to school on Monday. Every two weeks, the schedule was reversed, so that each parent had two full school weeks and two full weekends a month with the children. The children could call either parent on the telephone any time. . . .

"We found the agreement worked out beautifully. . . . No more stomachaches, no more nightmares."

"We found the agreement worked out beautifully," says Don. "The kids are tops in their classes; socially, the other kids love them, and they love themselves." No more stomachaches, no more nightmares. All the adults and the Gilbert children meet once a month for breakfast to discuss any problems. Sarah insists that "before, it was impossible to be a parent to the children. Now that we're cooperating, I think we're both doing a really good job with the kids." Don agrees.

In the beginning, implementing the plan wasn't easy, even though the agreement was in writing. "I could finally communicate with Don," Sarah says, "but I really didn't like him after all we'd been through, and he didn't have good feelings toward me, either. It was only after we started to put the agreement into practice that our relationship with each other began to change." The couple at first managed to take only baby steps in the slow process of building up trust in each other as parents. Sarah told Don of one or two problems she'd had disciplining Ronnie, and Don acknowledged he'd encountered similar snags. The couple began to work on presenting a united front, which not only produced improvement in their son's behavior but also gave them confidence they could trust each other on specific issues. In time the results were dramatic. "Before," says Sarah, "the children were miserable with us fighting over them; now they know we love them and we're all involved in their lives. I'm positive they are happier now."

But even a war that ends with a signed peace treaty is bound to leave scars. The Gilberts still owed several thousand dollars in past-due attorneys' fees three years after their final divorce decree. And tensions still surface occasionally between Don and his former in-laws, between the children and their grandparents, and even among Don, Lucy, and Sarah. When a problem becomes too severe, they return to their Conciliation Court counselor to talk

things over. "Mediated shared custody may not work in every case," admits Sarah, "but for us it's right." . . .

The American Cultural Tradition

Criticism of shared custody is based on the American cultural tradition, which has held for decades that women are the proper custodians of underage children. Because of this tradition, sole custody is granted to the mother in more than 90 percent of cases. Yet the courts did not begin to exalt women as the crucial influence in the upbringing of children until the Industrial Revolution left Mother in the house to raise the kids so Dad could work in the factories and in commerce.

Up to the turn of the century, American *fathers* had always been granted sole custody, regardless of the circumstances, in the nation's infrequent divorce cases. After all, women and children were chattels, owned and controlled by men. But in post-industrial society, when Father was no longer around the farm, and therefore unavailable to baby-sit occasionally while Mama fed the chickens, it was good-bye Daddy, and men began to buy the notion that they were inept as parents. They rarely practiced their skills as parents anymore, at least not before Junior was old enough to throw a baseball on a Saturday afternoon or to go swimming during summer vacation.

Particularly from the 1920s onward, male judges and lawyers began to condemn their divorcing brethren to absentee parenting. Fathers were allowed to "visit" their children at the convenience of the mother. In a stunning evolutionary reversal, fathers had lost the knack of nurturing youngsters into adulthood. It became a psychological truism that *mothers* bonded more meaningfully with their offspring.

The next major development in courtroom philosophy came with the publication in 1973 of *Beyond the Best Interests of the Child*, which became the Bible for most experts in family law. Written by three academic heavyweights—Joseph Goldstein, a law professor at Yale; Anna Freud, a renowned child psychoanalyst; and Albert Solnit, a child psychiatrist and the director of the Yale University Child Study Center—the book strongly recommends that *one* parent, mother *or* father, have total management and control of custody. The other parent, say the authors, should have no legally enforceable right to see the child unless so allowed by the custodial "psychological" parent. This, they say, is to provide consistency and stability in the child's life. For these authors, what was beneficial for children when their parents were living together—that is, two parents acting as positive role models—is no longer good for them psychologically once the parents have ended their marriage because, according to the authors, divorced couples are too angry to cooperate with regard to their children's needs. Therefore, a child having equal access to both parents will automatically be faced with conflicting loyalties, guaranteed to produce devastating consequences over time.

Substantial Evidence to the Contrary

Goldstein, Solnit, and Freud cite no scientific studies on family interaction to prove that parents are constitutionally unable to put the needs of their children above their anger at each other. In fact, the authors ignore substantial evidence to the contrary. Nor do these experts offer much more than opinion to support their thesis that sole custody is, de facto, the best solution for most children of divorce. However, the prestige of the authors effectively silenced any dissenters until recently.

Long-term studies, completed in the 1970s and early 1980s, began to reveal the problems of children who have been deprived of, or abandoned by, one of their parents. One such five-year study was completed in 1979 by Dr. Judith Wallerstein, lecturer at the School of Social Welfare of the University of California, Berkeley, and her colleague, Dr. Joan Kelly. The authors concluded that "the children [131 in the study] who were not visited by the absent parent frequently showed diminished self-esteem, except where the relationship with that parent was psychologically destructive to the child." Dr. Wallerstein voices alarm for these children, whom she considers to be emotionally "at risk." Although she does not believe that joint custody will work in every case, she says, "What makes for a good adjustment after a divorce is an arrangement in which the child maintains contact with both parents."

Wallerstein and Kelly's findings are in agreement with other new studies that refute many of the assumptions upon which custody decisions were based during the last century. In a paper presented at the 1978 meeting of the American Orthopsychiatric Association, Judith Brown Greif, chief social worker of the Division of Child/Adolescent Psychiatry at New York's Albert Einstein College of Medicine, wrote that research has made it "abundantly clear that with few exceptions, the trauma of divorce can be minimized by the child's continuous open and easy access to both parents." Greif believes that standards for what is in their "best interests" are the same for children of divorce as for children from intact families. "Rather than support the imposition of legal visitation restrictions," she says, "we should do everything in our power to maximize contact between the child and both parents. One clear way is through joint custody arrangements."

Perhaps the most public challenge to Goldstein et al has come from Dr. Mel Roman, director of family studies at Bronx Municipal Hospital Center and professor of psychiatry at the Albert Einstein College of Medicine. In *The Disposable Parent: The Case for Joint Custody*, Dr. Roman concludes from his study of forty joint custody families that cooperative custody arrangements are in the best interests of the majority of children and should be so presumed under law unless there are compelling reasons to the contrary. "Our evidence suggests that [joint custody] should be increasingly the pragmatic, and hence American choice.". . .

"Before [shared custody], . . . the children were miserable with us fighting over them; now they know we love them and we're all involved in their lives."

In the long run, American parents themselves will bring about the most meaningful changes. There are some eighty-five militant fathers' rights groups around the country whose members refuse to accept any longer society's notion that fathers are "disposable." The present system of sole custody, usually granted to the mother, doesn't work for them. It's lonely, it's depressing, and it's unfair, they say, that they and their children should be deprived of their basic civil right of access to one another. . . . The burdens of being mother, breadwinner, plus chief cook, bottle-washer, chauffeur, homework adviser, and psychological cheerleader, are clearly beginning to take their toll in mental and physical stress among these women. . . .

Clearly the arguments in favor of mediated joint custody are growing stronger. Nevertheless, there is still a great deal of deep resistance to shifting our thinking from *competitive* to *cooperative* solutions. The very terms "joint custody," "alternating custody," "divided custody," "split custody," "shared custody," and "coparenting" are controversial and, like most phrases that have become code words, hold different meanings for different people. Among judges, lawyers, child specialists, and many parents who have never bothered to learn the definitions of such terms, they set off alarm bells and anxiety. In order for parents to begin to understand their options, they must know the definitions.

Defining the Options

Joint (or *shared*) *custody*. There are three kinds of joint custody: joint *legal* custody, joint *physical* custody, and joint *legal and physical* custody. Joint legal custody means both parents retain and share the legal responsibility and authority for the management and control of the child. If Johnny becomes a juvenile delinquent and robs the five-and-dime, both parents are responsible. If Allison runs up debts at the record shop, both parents have to pay. Theoretically, parents with joint legal custody share equally in all decisions concerning the child's welfare: what school he or she attends; what religious training he or she has or doesn't have; where he or she spends Christmas or Hanukkah. But in America, *possession* is nine tenths of the law. So if the parents have joint legal custody but one has sole physical custody, the other can end up legally responsible for a child and yet be prevented from actually guiding or influencing the child. Sharing legal custody with an ''uncooperative'' parent who has sole physical custody is the worst of both worlds. Joint legal custody is more meaningful if the physical custody is shared by the parents in such a way as to assure the child frequent and continuing contact with both parents.

There are also thousands of joint custody arrangements in which a couple shares the *physical* care of a child on a fairly even basis, but not the legal custody. One parent, usually the mother, retains the legal rights over the child according to the legal order filed originally with the court at the time of divorce.

In the best of all possible worlds, cooperative custody means joint legal *and* physical custody with a time-sharing formula devised to benefit and accommodate both the children and the parents. Joint legal and physical custody is also referred to as *shared custody, cocustody,* or *coparenting after the divorce.*

Divided or *alternating custody* may sound like joint custody but is actually sole custody for each parent part of a year or in alternating years. For example, Susie is with Mom in California for the school year and spends the summers with Dad in upstate New York. When Susie is with her, Mom has the sole legal and physical responsibility for the girl. When Susie is with him, Dad has sole responsibility. Unless the parents also agree to make all major decisions about the child together, regardless of which parent she happens to reside with at the time, this arrangement is not joint custody.

''Evidence suggests that [joint custody] should be increasingly the pragmatic, and hence American choice.''

Split custody is an arrangement whereby one child lives permanently with Mom while the brother or sister lives permanently with Dad. Under most split custody agreements, each child ''visits'' the parent and sibling he or she does not live with. Again, unless the parents agree to make all important decisions regarding the children together and accept jointly all responsibility for the children's actions, split custody is not joint custody.

Sole custody is an award of custody to one parent with the other maintaining rights to see the child from time to time. The sole custodial parent is legally responsible for the child's activities, conduct, and well-being. She or he is also the administrator of the custody and therefore, in reality, controls the child's access to the parent with whom the youngster does not live. The final court document may state that Dad has the right to see his children on alternating weekends and every Wednesday night for supper, but if Mom moves from Chicago to Colorado, as she is free under many orders to do, she effectively negates whatever theoretical rights Dad thought he had under the law. Also, there is nothing in a sole custody agreement which guarantees that the parent without custody will exercise his or her right to spend time with the children. The custodial parent may (and frequently does) find that an uninvolved parent will simply bow out, leaving the ''winner'' with the entire financial, physical, and emotional burden of rearing the children.

Genuine shared custody is any time-sharing formula that has, as an *operating premise,* the commitment of both parents to continue to be involved in all important decision-making regarding the children, and to maintain as much frequent and continuing physical contact as circumstances and geography allow.

Ciji Ware has been reporting on behavior, psychology, and economic news for more than twenty years on ABC radio.

"The children should go with the parent who will care for them best, with due regard to how strong their bond is with that parent."

One Parent Should Have Custody of Children

Richard Neely

When I was first practicing law, I avoided starvation by handling divorce cases. In rural areas a lawyer either tries divorce cases or searches land titles; since I find real estate practice consummately dull, I opted for divorce cases to pay my rent. Although I represented men and women about equally in the three years that I applied myself to the divorce court trade, I never represented a father who wanted custody of his children. I do not infer from this experience a total absence of men willing to risk death to keep their children, but I do infer that such men are rare. Through the years I have consulted practicing lawyers around the country on this subject, and they confirm my experience. It is an extraordinary man who wants to take care of a two-year-old from morning till night. In my experience, fathers who are awarded custody of young children delegate actual child care to a female, often their own mothers.

My faith in mothers as more dedicated parents is not just outdated and uninformed homespun wisdom. In 1977 Sharon Araji of Washington State University published a study entitled "Husbands' and Wives' Attitude-Behavior Congruence on Family Roles." In plain English, she asked her subjects what they believed the proper division of family labor should be and then asked how, in fact, such work was divided. More than two-thirds of those asked how child care *should* be divided responded that the division should be equal. When asked about actual performance, however, those same individuals overwhelmingly responded that it was the woman who bore the brunt of child care duties. Sharing responsibility for child care would seem to be more a cosmopolitan pretension than a common practice.

Another study, done at the University of Nevada

that same year—"The Division of Labor Among Cohabiting and Married Couples," by Rebecca Stafford, Elaine Bachman, and Pamela Dibona—found that division of labor within the household remained resistant to change. Furthermore, responsibility for the maintenance of children was among the duties least often shared. To the extent that husbands participated in child care at all, they were more likely to be involved in playing, baby-sitting, and disciplining rather than in such day-to-day tasks as feeding, changing, and bathing. . . .

Finally, "Problems of Professional Couples" by Norma Heckman, Rebecca Bryson, and Jeff Bryson, a study of professional couples done at San Diego State University, found that even among highly career-oriented women it was taken as a given by both spouses that the woman had the primary child care responsibilities. The role of mother was seen as far more limiting than that of wife. One of the study's crucial findings was that the decision to take primary responsibility for children was frequently a voluntary one for women who saw parenting as a fundamental part of a successful female life.

The Individual Approach

The fact that women as a group are either more enthusiastic about parenting or simply do more of it because that is how labor is divided in their homes does not mean, of course, that in every case the mother is the better parent. Fathers who want to retain the companionship of their children and who believe that under single-parent conditions they would be better parents than their wives expect the judicial system to operate on more refined principles than simple statistical discrimination.

Fathers are now demanding that courts award custody based on an individualized inquiry into the specific parent-child relationships in their particular families. All this appears reasonable until we understand just how much sinister bargaining is

Richard Neely, *The Divorce Decision*. New York: McGraw-Hill Book Company, 1984. Reprinted by permission.

carried on in the shadow of this unpredictable, individual-oriented system.

The individual approach, in fact, would be unexceptionable if courts actually considered the relative merits of the parents in each case. Very few divorce cases, however, ever get to court. Nationwide, about 92 percent of all divorces are settled without a courtroom encounter. Divorce decrees are typically drafted by the lawyers for the parties after private compromise, and these compromises are then approved by a judge. Mothers routinely sacrifice necessary financial support in order to get custody of their children without a fight. This distasteful form of barter is one of the reasons that single women with dependent children are becoming a new class of the poverty-stricken.

Trading Support for Custody

My first experience with the use of the divorce laws' unpredictability to terrorize women into trading away their support occurred soon after I began my career as a small-town lawyer. My client was a railroad brakeman who had fallen out of love with his wife and in love with motorcycles. Along the way he had met a woman who was as taken with motorcycles as he. After about a year my client's wife filed for divorce. My client had two children at home—one about nine and the other about twelve. Unfortunately for him, the judge in the county where his wife had filed her suit was notorious for giving high alimony and child support awards. The last thing that I wanted to do was go to trial. The wife had a strong case of adultery against my client, and the best my client could come up with as a defense was a lame countersuit for "cruel and inhuman treatment"—not a showstopper in a rural domestic court fourteen years ago.

"The everyday occurrence of children being traded for money should . . . invite a reevaluation of a system that puts custody awards up for grabs."

During the initial interview I asked my client about his children, and he told me that he got along well with them. When I asked whether he wanted custody, he emphatically indicated that two children were the last thing he wanted from divorce. Nonetheless, it occurred to me that if my client developed a passionate attachment to his children and told his wife that he would fight for custody all the way to the state supreme court, we might settle the whole divorce fairly cheaply. . . .

My client's wife, as I had hoped, was unwilling to take any chance, no matter how slight, on losing her

children. Consequently, the divorce was settled exactly as I wanted. The wife got the children by agreement, along with very modest alimony and child support. All we had needed to defeat her legitimate claims in the settlement process was a halfway credible threat of a protracted custody battle. As Solomon showed us, the better a mother is as a parent, the less likely she is to allow a destructive fight over her children.

We are led to an inescapable conclusion: a sex-neutral approach has the unintended effect of terrorizing mothers into accepting bad deals. In the end, on statistical average, women come out of divorce settlements under our purportedly sex-neutral system with the worst of all worlds: they get the children but insufficient or no money with which to support them. . . .

Ideally, in a domestic case we want to take a broken-down marriage and sort out emotional and economic problems. The children should go with the parent who will care for them best, with due regard to how strong their bond is with that parent; to his or her ability to provide financially; and to his or her capacity for love, concern, leadership, and emotional support. Similarly, we want to allocate economic benefits—either alimony or property division—to reflect relative degrees of fault in the breakup of the marriage as well as the economic needs of the parties. Central to this latter consideration is whether one party has responsibility for supporting the children.

Overworked Divorce Courts

Although divorce requires a court order, most court orders are entered at the behest of both parties who have agreed to a settlement. The judge merely signs the agreed-to order presented by counsel. On a typical morning a domestic judge will sign as many as thirty divorce decrees. The busier the court and the more harried the judge, the less attention he or she gives to the equity of the settlements. Judges, it must be stressed, do not enjoy extra work any more than do posthole diggers or elevator operators. If a bargain is good enough for the litigants and their lawyers, it is usually good enough for the judge. The judge supposedly supervises the fairness of these settlements, but this rarely occurs in busy courts unless the agreement is so outrageously one-sided that its inequity almost leaps off the page.

The everyday occurrence of children being traded for money should be sufficient in and of itself to invite a reevaluation of a system that puts custody awards up for grabs. Yet there are additional reasons for questioning the wisdom of our apparently fair, sex-neutral system that relate directly to the welfare of children. Those who have studied family relations, such as the famous lawyer/psychoanalyst team of Joseph Goldstein, Anna Freud, and Albert Solnit, after extensive study of children under the strain of divorce, found that custody decisions should be made quickly. Protracted hassles over custody undermine a child's sense of security, and once a child is placed in one environment he or she should not be moved to another. Their research indicates that from the point of view of the child's best interests—supposedly the legal standard—differences in relative parenting ability are less important than both the speed and permanency of custody arrangements. The current system for handling child-related matters, involving as it does years of possible litigation, is calculated to produce results that thoughtful scientists consider contrary to the child's best interest.

> *"Once a child is placed in one environment he or she should not be moved to another."*

All courts are in the business of measuring things. But in domestic litigation the measurements are qualitatively different from other measurements that courts routinely make. Courts are designed to deal with discrete issues and tangible evidence. Did Hatfield shoot McCoy? Did PepsiCo steal Coca-Cola's trade secret? Domestic courts are asked to be moral arbiters of the righteousness of lives. The problem is not that courts are incompetent to make such decisions but rather that the sheer complexity of their task means that the measurement process itself changes the thing that is measured.

Lack of neutrality in measuring things is a recurring problem in many areas of human endeavor. In physics the problem is known as the Heisenberg uncertainty principle—which refers to Werner Heisenberg's discovery that it is impossible to measure both the speed and the location of an electron simultaneously because the measuring devices themselves affect the speed and location being measured. A similar principle applies to divorce cases, and measuring family problems usually makes those problems worse.

The way divorces are handled in practice by underpaid lawyers and overworked courts gives rise to a fundamental proposition: all divorce law must be crafted with a view to voluntary settlements and not to courtroom litigation. A rule that is wondrously fair when it is actually used before a judge can have a distortive effect in out-of-court settlements. In order to make this proposition spring to life, let us take the hypothetical case of Steve and Jane who are about to get divorced in a state like Iowa, where in contested cases children are awarded to the better parent, after exhaustive judicial inquiry into the parenting ability of each.

Steve and Jane are a typical middle-class couple. Steve graduated from a good midwestern university, and Jane married him after completing her second year of college. They have two children, a boy aged seven and a girl aged four. Steve is a salesman with a large company and makes about $27,000 a year; Jane works part time as a buyer in a department store and earns about $10,000 a year. Steve sells office equipment. His territory is his own city, so he is not required to travel or work at night. Steve is a good parent; he spends several hours with the children each evening. On the weekends Steve makes every effort to include the children in chores, like painting, that he does around the house, and he tries to take them on at least one outing a week to a sporting event, the zoo, a park, or the local swimming pool.

Jane, on the other hand, has been the primary caretaker of the children. When their son was born, Jane left work to stay home with the baby, and she did not return to work until their daughter was in nursery school. She arranges her part-time work around the children's schedule so that she is home when they are home, and one of the conditions of her job is that she can stay home if her children are sick. Jane often gets frustrated by the children; she does a lot of yelling and occasionally spanks them without justification, but on balance she is a good parent. She reads with her children, teaches them arithmetic, discourages them from watching television excessively, and spends her time at home in active parenting.

Steve, on his side, is a good provider. Although Steve and Jane bicker in the usual way about money, they agree that the children come first. Neither Steve nor Jane has done anything reprehensible in the marriage; they have just come to thoroughly bore each other. They have nothing in common except for the children and they fantasize that if divorced each could find a more sympathetic, supportive, and amusing mate. Their decision to divorce is mutual, and they contemplate a no-fault proceeding. Jane, who has the closer relationship with the children because she spends more time with them, wants the children and would not give them up under any circumstances. Steve understands that he is unsuited to care for young children day in and day out, and he also understands that his social life after divorce will be circumscribed if he has children to tie him down.

The Ideal Solution

Ideally, Steve and Jane would agree that Jane will keep the children. Steve will have unlimited visitation rights, and the children will stay with him whenever he wants—weekends, summer vacations, and holidays. Since Jane is young and can both earn a salary and remarry, it is not expected that Steve will pay alimony, but he will pay about $500 a month child support so that the children can continue to enjoy their current standard of living. Jane will work more hours to increase her income to $15,000 a year, and some type of day-care arrangement will be made to take care of the children while she is at work.

I have drawn a portrait of an entirely reasonable couple who understand the advantages and disadvantages of divorce. Most important, they have taken into consideration the children's needs and have organized their settlement with the welfare of the children at least partially in mind. Steve and Jane have done their best to accommodate everyone's interest, and if they continue to be reasonable and conciliatory, the judicial process will not distort their divorce arrangements.

"Even in states with a weak maternal presumption, child custody is awarded to the parent who will do the better job of child rearing."

If, however, we change the scenario a little, as it would probably be changed in real life, the Heisenberg uncertainty principle immediately enters the picture. . . .

It should be remembered that at this stage nobody has filed divorce papers in court. Yet the prospect of divorce—with everyone taking the advice of lawyers who are trying to set their clients up for a courtroom drama—has set the Heisenberg uncertainty principle in motion as both parties alter their behavior with an eye toward the upcoming litigation. . . .

The Better Single Parent

Assume that Steve is one of those rare men who wants his children every bit as much as his wife does. Steve is in fact more interested in securing custody than in any other aspect of the divorce. He is a good father and Jane is a good mother; for Steve the problem now is to prove that he would make the better single parent. Jane, of course, must do the same thing, but in most trial courts regardless of what the statutory or common-law rule may be, she has a leg up because she is the "primary caretaker," that is, she has spent more time with the children. . . .

Even in states with a weak maternal presumption, child custody is awarded to the parent who will do the better job of child rearing. This is called the "best interests of the child" standard, and to meet it Steve's lawyer must demonstrate that Steve is the better parent. The maternal presumption is only a tie breaker, at least in theory, and it is theory that dictates the legal *process*, if not the courtroom result.

Since Steve's lawyer cannot show that Steve is better than Jane at everyday parenting responsibilities, Steve's lawyer must explore the deep, dark recesses of psychological theory to prove that in the long run the children will be better off with Steve.

This undertaking inevitably leads to the hiring of "expert witnesses"—psychologists, psychiatrists, social workers, and sociologists. . . .

I am not in favor of expert psychological testimony. My disparagement does not come from any contempt for a science that has contributed much to the quality of our lives. Rather, it comes from my experience that in a courtroom context there is a "Gresham's law of experts": the bad experts drive out the good ones. When we hire an expert witness, we want a person with the lowest possible integrity so that he or she will lie under oath. Expert witnesses are, after all, very much like lawyers: they are paid to take a set of facts from which different inferences may be drawn and to characterize those facts so that a particular conclusion follows. . . .

In the case of Steve and Jane—an accurate composite of cases I handled as a lawyer—once a custody battle is contemplated, the relationship between parents and children changes for the worse. The overriding need to prepare for court will dominate the lives of both parents, and if the opinions of the children are to be polled—either directly through court testimony or indirectly through the probing of experts—each parent is going to attempt to poison the other parent's well. . . .

The Primary Caretaker Parent Rule

Most of the problems of child custody litigation can be avoided by not litigating the issue in the first place. It is at this point that the wisdom of the old maternal preference, or its sex-neutral alternative, the "primary caretaker parent rule," becomes evident. The primary caretaker parent rule severely limits the adverse economic and psychological effects of litigation concerning custody, and we have adopted this rule in West Virginia. Sadly, however, the sex-neutral primary caretaker parent rule is unique to West Virginia law.

In West Virginia we do not permit a maternal preference. But we do accord an explicit and almost absolute preference to the "primary caretaker parent," which is defined as the parent who: (1) prepares the meals; (2) changes the diapers and dresses and bathes the child; (3) chauffeurs the child to school, church, friends' homes, and the like; (4) provides medical attention, monitors the child's health, and is responsible for taking the child to the doctor; and (5) interacts with the child's friends, school authorities, and other parents engaged in activities that involve the child.

This list of criteria usually spells "mother," but such is not necessarily the case. In West Virginia we have women who pursue successful lucrative careers while their husbands take care of the children, and those caretaking fathers receive the benefit of the presumption as strongly as do traditional mothers. Furthermore, where both parents share child-rearing responsibilities equally, our courts hold hearings to determine which parent would be the better single parent. This latter situation is rare, but provision for its occurrence is evidence of the actual sex neutrality of the "primary caretaker presumption.". . .

Under West Virginia's scheme, the question of which parent, if any, is the primary caretaker is proved with lay testimony by the parties themselves and by teachers, relatives, and neighbors. Which parent does the lion's share of the chores can be satisfactorily demonstrated to a court in less than an hour. Once the primary caretaker is established, the only other question is whether that parent is a "fit parent." In this regard the court is not concerned with assessing relative degrees of fitness between parents but only with whether the primary caretaker achieves a passing grade on an objective test. It is very much like a high school examination where sixty points get you a D. All that is required is the passing D; the fact that the parent who is not the primary caretaker gets a C is irrelevant.

A Fit Parent

To be a fit parent a person must: (1) feed and clothe the child appropriately; (2) adequately supervise the child and protect him or her from harm; (3) provide habitable housing; (4) avoid extreme discipline, child abuse, and other similar vices; and (5) refrain from *grossly* immoral behavior under circumstances that would affect the child. In this last regard restrained sexual behavior does not make a parent unfit. We do not attend to traditional immorality in the abstract but only to whether the child is a party to, or is influenced by, such immorality. Whether a primary caretaker parent meets these criteria can also be determined through lay testimony, and the criteria themselves are sufficiently specific that they discourage frivolous disputation.

Furthermore, we divide children into the three age-group categories; [children under six, children between six and fourteen, and children over fourteen]. With regard to children of tender years, our primary caretaker presumption operates absolutely if the primary caretaker is a fit parent. When, however, we come to those children who may be able to formulate an intelligent opinion about their custody, our rule becomes more flexible. When the trial court judge is unsure about the wisdom of awarding the children to the primary caretaker, he or she may ask the children for their preference and accord that preference whatever weight he or she deems appropriate. Thus, the only experts who can rebut the primary caretaker

presumption are the children. The judge is not required to take the testimony of the children, however, and will usually not do so if he or she suspects bribery or other undue influence. Nonetheless, by allowing the children to be the only acceptable experts in our courts, we do provide an escape valve in the very hard cases.

Finally, once a child reaches the age of fourteen, we permit the child to name his or her guardian if both parents are fit. Often, as might be expected, this means that the parent who makes the child's life more comfortable will get custody; but there is little alternative, since children over fourteen who are living where they do not want to live will become unhappy and ungovernable anyway. In all three types of cases, the parent who receives custody is then primarily responsible for making decisions concerning the child and for providing the child's principal home. The other parent, however, is usually accorded liberal visitation rights, including the right to have the child during holidays, part of the summer, and on some weekends.

"The wisdom of the old maternal preference, or its sex-neutral alternative, the 'primary caretaker parent rule',. . . severely limits the adverse . . . effects of litigation concerning custody."

Although West Virginia's method for handling child custody may appear insensitive, we have reduced the volume of domestic litigation over children enormously. Because litigation per se is highly damaging emotionally to children, we consider this in the best interests of our state's children. More to the point, children in West Virginia cannot be used as pawns in fights that are actually about money. Under our system a mother's lawyer can tell her that if she has been the primary caretaker and is a fit parent she has *absolutely no chance* of losing custody of very young children. The result is that questions of alimony and child support are settled on their own merits.

The Joint Custody Fad

At this point, the reader may be desperate to interject that many of these problems could be better solved by using the newest divorce court fad, joint custody. Under joint custody, divorced parents have equal time with the children and equal say in decisions about their schooling, religious training, and lifestyle. But this does not solve the problems of trades in the settlement process because many mothers find sharing custody as terrifying as complete loss of custody.

Joint custody works well when both parents live in the same neighborhood, or at least in the same city, and so long as they can cooperate on child-rearing problems. Divorcing couples often agreed to joint custody themselves in the past, long before court-ordered joint custody became a public issue. When joint custody is by agreement, the same cooperative spirit that permitted the underlying agreement will usually permit the parents to rear a child with no more antagonism than is experienced in most married households.

Voluntary joint custody, however, must be distinguished from court-ordered joint custody. A court can order that custody be shared, but it cannot order that the parents stop bickering, stop disparaging each other, or accommodate each other in child care decisions the way married parents would. And if parents do not live close to each other joint custody can place an insupportable strain on a child's social and academic life. . . .

All Conditions Must Be Favorable

In West Virginia we do not encourage court-ordered joint custody, although parents can agree to such an arrangement. Elsewhere, however, legislatures are being urged to make court consideration of joint custody mandatory in all contested custody cases. In states that already encourage extensive litigation over child custody, the sparing use of joint custody may not cause any more damage than does the existing system. If the geography is right and the parents are mature, there is no reason why joint custody cannot work at least as well as, and sometimes better than, custody in one parent with visitation rights in the other. Joint custody as an option cannot be rejected out of hand, but it should be understood for what it is—a good middle ground that works occasionally when all conditions are peculiarly favorable.

"All the rhetoric about joint custody amounts to a siren song that leads us from our true course."

The nationwide debate on child custody, including the arguments for joint custody and a greater role for fathers, demonstrates just how acutely many men—often men innocent in the breakup of their marriages—feel the loss of their children. But no matter how modern we seek to become, or how liberated we wish to be from the imprisoning hand of traditional institutions, it is not possible to create custody arrangements that satisfactorily duplicate parent-child relationships in married households. Divorce must be understood for what it is: a tragedy

and a disaster.

Regardless of the custody statutes that legislatures pass, or what powers are given to domestic courts, judges are never going to be architects of a brave new world of happy, single-parent households. Courts are just salvage crews. To the extent that husbands and wives engage in their own program of damage control, they can salvage more from the ruins than can courts. In child custody the parents' own damage control amounts to continued cooperation with each other on child-related problems. The goal of such cooperation is enhancement rather than destruction of the other parent's position in the mind of the child: this involves the maturity to submerge feelings of personal animosity when the child visits the other parent or when information about the child must be exchanged.

A Siren Song

Joint custody is, after all, just a bigger and better version of traditional visitation rights with the added dubious advantage that both parents can give legal consent for the child when required. When there is a cooperative arrangement between parents by which visitation is both extensive and smoothly accomplished, calling the scheme joint custody is entirely cosmetic. The term "joint custody" merely serves to emphasize that both parents continue to have a say in the child's future. Inevitably, if both parents are cooperative, this will be the case any way under traditional visitation. Just as inevitably, if the parents are uncooperative, joint custody will only put the child in an impossible position vis-à-vis both parents and paralyze needed action. In short, in my experience all the rhetoric about joint custody amounts to a siren song that leads us from our true course. The true course is that what a court orders is insignificant in comparison to how the parents behave. Mature parents can make a bad court order work superbly; immature parents will render the best court order less than useless.

West Virginia's scheme for handling child custody and the approach that I have offered in this [viewpoint] are little consolation to divorcing couples in New York, Iowa, or any other state that fails to understand the effect of the Heisenberg uncertainty principle in domestic law. But recognition of what actually goes on in a custody battle—that it is not just a sorting out of preexisting rights but rather a destructive process in and of itself—may help rational parents avoid such battles.

Richard Neely is a justice of the West Virginia Supreme Court of Appeals and a professor of economics at the University of Charleston.

"[Divorced fathers are] forced to recognize that there's no substitute for being there constantly."

The Noncustodial Parent: A Father's View

C.W. Smith

Years ago I called a college buddy I hadn't heard from in a while. He had divorced his first wife but had remarried. I asked him how many kids he had now.

"Just the one."

"One? I thought you had two."

"*Aw* hell!" he snorted. "You're thinking of the ones I had with Judy. They don't count."

A silence several seconds wide dropped between us while I pictured those two fatherless children drifting into space without a tether. How could a man discount his children's existence with the indifference of a claims adjuster?

Judging Others

But now that I've lived for the last five years outside the home where my daughter and son are growing up, I don't judge my friend so harshly. Maybe "they don't count" meant that since he had botched that job, he could hope for a better grade on a new project, offer "the one" as evidence of his reformation. If he had stormy struggles over visitation arrangements, or if he wasn't allowed to help decide who would be his children's doctors, barbers, teachers, or playmates, or if his former wife moved them to another city without consulting him, then I can see why he says "they don't count." When we feel our efforts produce only the frustration of impotence, then we cease trying.

That's a comforting thought. But then, as I seem to remember C.S. Lewis once saying, "An explanation of cause is not a justification by reason." I keep thinking about that.

My father is a pipe-smoking Presbyterian who speaks in witty one-liners; he taught me to stand when ladies enter a room and how to handle hammers, and once, when I was twelve, I saw him

rescue a drowning man, a father, from a river and walk away without giving anyone his name. A hero.

That he would have chosen to divorce my mother and walk out of our house to live elsewhere was inconceivable.

Walking out of my own house twenty-seven years later, I knew I had forfeited the right to be so admired by my own twin son and daughter. But because my parents had not divorced, I wasn't aware of how devastating it might be. And I didn't want to know—I could dream the damage to my children would be minimal by watching other fatherless kids go about their daily lives: in the age´ of divorce, this seemed to have become oddly normal; there were thousands of such children, and they wore no bruises I could see.

I saw nothing to stop me from being the good father I had always been. Aside from the months I commuted to another state for work, I had been around the house constantly. With two "first" children, both my wife and I had to keep diapers changed, bottles washed and filled. For the two years that my wife was a television reporter, I stayed home to write, changed vacuum-cleaner bags, separated darks from whites in the wash, shuttled the kids to school, and greeted them all at the door at the end of the day in an apron, a wooden spoon in hand. . . .

The Dogma of Fathering

My lessons began immediately. Gay and I agreed, I thought, to pad the shock to the kids with a spirit of mutual cooperation. The day we decided to announce that we would separate, I presumed that we would sit them down and break the news, over their heads, together. The words would come hard, I knew. . . . But as the parent who had chosen to go, the duty was rightfully mine, and the difficulty would be part payment for my guilt. Facing them would be both manly and fatherly.

C.W. Smith, "Uncle Dad," *Esquire*, March 1985. Reprinted with permission.

But when I pulled into the driveway late that afternoon, they were huddled together on the sidewalk at the curb, looking stricken, two nine-year-olds waiting for the Dachau bus. . . .

Then Gay reported that she had already told them we were going to separate. "I hope you don't mind," she offered politely. "After all, it's our problem now." *So you go on about your merry way and don't bother about us!*

Yes, I *did* mind—it's one thing to confess you're a scumbag and another to have the news precede your appearance. Obviously, part of my punishment would be to be denied any strategy I might devise for my absolution, however meager. My guilt also said I had no right to be angry.

"How'd they take it?"

"Okay," she said, "considering."

"Unlike traveling dads, [Uncle Dads] never will come 'home' to any welcome . . . and our children gnaw on the suspicion that we've rejected them.*"*

I slunk back to my car. My kids were already in it. My daughter sat in the front seat. Gray coils of mud were clinging to the rims of her tennis shoes. I almost told her to get out and wipe her shoes off but didn't, not because it would have seemed petty in juxtaposition with the news but because I had, in one stroke, lost my moral authority.

We went to Burger King. White tile, hard plastic benches, everything colored in the hues of chewable vitamins. I can't remember what was ordered, but it all came in paper cartons and was cold by the time the first of us had decided to bolt from the silence by stuffing his mouth with something handy. . . .

Nobody had an appetite. I couldn't make myself talk about anything important, and that also discouraged talking about anything inconsequential—it would have seemed vulgar. *The* subject sat on the table between us like a Venus's-flytrap the size of a basketball we were each pretending was only a private hallucination. Not knowing what to say, I was unpleasantly surprised by my own relief that Gay had already "explained" it to them. I asked "How was school?" and "Did you do your homework?" knowing that no child in his right mind could perform any productive work after having heard such crushing news.

"How about some ice cream?"

They shook their heads.

"*Aw*, come on, surely you want some ice cream?"

Surely you won't hate me for the rest of your lives?

My friend Elroy sent me an essay he had written.

"I want to be a father again, with children growing up in my house. . ." he wrote. "I want to hear their voices among the voices of their friends on the front porch. . . I want schoolbooks on the living-room couch . . . I want half-eaten crackers-and-cheese on a plate in the kitchen and a package of oboe reeds on the buffet."

Elroy left his job, his friends, and the city where he had lived for twenty years to follow his children to the town they had moved to five hundred miles away. "I refused to become a stranger to these people, my children," he added in a letter, "who mean as much to me as I meant to myself."

The Uncle Dads

Most of the divorced fathers I know still hang on in some way despite the trouble and pain. We form a legion of what novelist Bryan Woolley has termed the Uncle Dads. Unlike traveling dads, we never will come "home" to any welcome or to settle a quarrel or to hear an appeal, and our children gnaw on the suspicion that we've rejected *them*; unlike stepdads, we live in another house, or even in another city, perhaps with other children whom our "real" children suspect are getting the best of our attention.

Some of us pop irregularly into our children's lives, bearing an irrelevant or even inappropriate gift, disrupting routine, asking that our children's plans be changed to suit our brief visitation or hoping to be included in their activities.

We console ourselves with the notion of "quality time," the divorced parent's fondest way of coping with guilt. "I'm a remote kind of person," said one divorced father who takes his sons to a cabin every summer for two weeks, "so if I was living at home with my kids, I'd probably be removed; this way, I tend to pay more attention to them. I think of using this time for them to talk about anything serious that they want to, but so far," he joked, "nothing's come up."

The truth is, though, that children tend to talk seriously only when it's their choice, and that usually comes when the surface of daily routine is glassy, unruffled. They're helping us to bake cookies or to paint a cabinet, and out comes, "Dad, were you ever in love in the eighth grade?" Or "Have you ever had a friend who was homosexual?"

When we're being honest, we admit that quality time is that rare moment when a stretch of ordinary time is interrupted by an unexpected burst of genuine rapport. To say "We will now have quality time" whether anybody feels like it or not is like saying, "We will now have fun, or else." We fear this truth: that the necessary preparation for quality time is quantity time, and that we can't give. Awakened by a nightmare that some disaster has befallen them miles away, or that they may be troubled by something that happened during the day, we're forced to recognize that there's no substitute for being there constantly; or rather, there are only substitutes for it.

So we live with a sadness that is pervasive and continual, like low-level radiation. Larry, a composer, told me: "There's always a slight little pain that's like that continuing E-string at the back of a score. I live across the street from an elementary school, and sometimes I might be writing a salute to mayonnaise or something and I'll hear some of the kids playing on a swing, and it really hits me. Or when I think of how I'm watching my kids grow up on Polaroids. When they're here, I measure them against the doorframe, and when they're gone I look at it and think I've got a yardstick of my kids growing up and I'm not there. Sometimes you just have to lie down until you feel better; then you get up."

Striving for Quality Time

But then there's hope. Dressed in clean jeans and sport shirts, we platoon up at Jetways on Friday evenings, waiting for the stewardesses to lead our mob of children—some wearing name tags like D.P.s—out of the tunnels to where we stand hoping they haven't seen *Gremlins* yet. Upchuck Cheese Pizza is the last place we would ordinarily choose to dine, but the martyrdom of an awful meal is oddly comforting.

We yearn for things to go well. We're anxious. We fear our children's anger because it hurts us; we fear their love because we know it means they hurt. But we're also elated to have forty-eight hours to wedge slivers of ourselves into the chinks of their armor.

I took furnished digs ten minutes away in an old, Mediterranean-style building said to have been the residence of the man who penned "Home on the Range" in the 1930s, the decade from which the dusty wooden blinds, the furniture, and the smelly mattresses doubtless dated. I was not supposed to have children here, my downstairs neighbors constantly reminded me. On overnights, Keith and Nicole slept in a sagging Murphy bed and fought over the covers. Looking out my bedroom window, they had a view onto an alley where the wan, androgynous denizens of a unisex hair boutique met during break-time to compare rainbow-colored hair and to pass a joint, and sometimes each other's tongues, among them; I was cursed with the terror that my folly had led my own pink-cheeked babies out of innocence much too soon. My best hope was that years later they could tell their more sheltered peers about their lives with voices dripping with blasé sophistication; maybe they could wear all this like a badge. . . .

I didn't worry about Nicole. She was gliding through her days on autopilot, so stunned I read her shock as acceptance. To make up for her broken home I got her an intact Barbie Townhouse where Ken and Barbie could all live happily with Francie; they had a working toilet and a pink-and-yellow van

to take lots of fun family trips in. Barbie had a wedding dress and they could stay married as long as Nicole wanted them to.

Meanwhile, Keith was erupting in purple rages. Where before the divorce he had been a model child, he now roamed his neighborhood saying ugly things to adults and pelting people's houses with eggs. In family therapy I'd watch him braid his arms across his chest, clamp his jaws, and pretend he had nothing to say. His grades tumbled; he told his teachers that when he tried to concentrate, all he could think about was the divorce. . . .

Three years after the separation, Gay announced that she was taking a job in Galveston, three hundred miles away. I panicked. I didn't have room to keep both of them, but I invited Keith to live with me. He turned me down, whether from resentment or loyalty to his sister and his mother, I don't know.

For the three weeks that preceded their moving they both stayed in my apartment while their mother looked for a house in Galveston. I remember wanting to give them such a booster shot of myself that they'd never be able to get me out of their systems. I doled out allowances and lunch money just like a real dad, and labored over Sunday dinner so that when we all—my two children and my new wife—would sit down to eat, there'd be some faint reminder that family life was still possible. The Sunday before they left, when they balked at eating at the table (it seemed it was no longer required at home), I complained, hearing my mother's voice coming out of my mouth, that I had slaved in the kitchen for hours so that we could enjoy a Sunday family dinner. Keith retorted, "This isn't our family."

"We fear our children's . . . love because we know it means they hurt."

I signed up for Sprint and wrote to people I knew in Houston, fifty miles from Galveston, about jobs. . . . I helped them pack; then their mother came and took them.

When they were settled, I called them nightly. I kept saying to myself, *It won't be so bad*, but it was. I was tormented by not knowing what the house just off the beach there looked like, how the kids' rooms were decorated. I didn't know anything about their school, and none of their teachers had faces. Their teachers did not know me, either, and so my children were, to them, fatherless. . . .

When I called, Keith was always "fine." Nicole was always "fine," too, even though, unknown to me, a great dark pterodactyl of depression was making a slow bank before gliding in to land on her rib cage. These telephone interrogations were, I suppose, typically fruitless. What did they do in school today? ("Nothing.") Who were their friends? ("Just some kids.") Where did these kids live? ("*Aw*, you know, everywhere.") What did they all do together? ("Just stuff.")

The phone was a crucial link. Sometimes I worked to hear in their voices all the minute aspects of their lives, the way I replay small night sounds in my inner ear to judge them malign or benign; while we talked I would ask them where they were sitting, what they had eaten that day, what they were wearing. (They had clothes I had never seen.)

To them these interrogations were a rip-roaring bore. I called some five times a week, and invariably they were about to watch *CHiPs*, to eat, to get a call from a friend, or had just gotten out of the shower, and answering my survey was as appealing as having a chat with a magazine-subscription peddler. . . .

Gradually I learned telephone technique. I'd check the TV schedule to avoid pulling them away from their "favorite" shows, though these appeared to be almost anything on prime time. Instead of grilling them I would talk about my day or my work or my car or my wife or my friends. . . .

Monthly Weekend Visits

These telephone tricks didn't improve the quality of the information I got, but they did keep my frustration at a minimum and let me think that at least my calls were serving their main purpose—to let my children know I still loved them, still missed them, still thought about them. But my anxiety disappeared only when they were present during their monthly weekend visits to Dallas. High anticipation would make me step lightly, whistling, as I made my way down the halls of Love Field to where I would eagerly await their flight from Houston. How wonderful this will be! I would have made a few plans for "family" fun, but, invariably, no sooner would we hug and start to discuss them than things would begin to unravel. Keith would want to see one movie, Nicole another; Nicole would go roller-skating, but Keith wanted to go to a party. Now they were twelve, going on thirteen; they did not mind using my house as a base of operations (although Keith was usually quick to let me know what offers he had turned down in Galveston), but they weren't enthusiastic about doing anything with Dad. . . .

We Uncle Dads expect so much from these visits. And it's true of the kids too. My friend Jim said about his daughter's visits in the summer that "she's always anxious to get here as soon as possible after her school year is out. She'll start calling us long distance and writing us notes several weeks before she comes. She always sounds so excited about coming, but soon after she arrives a depression sets in."

We want these visits to be more "meaningful," like, say, an episode of *The Waltons*, where maybe a couple of orphans with bruised psyches show up and act pissy for two segments before Grandpa gives 'em what-for, Elizabeth charms them, Mary Ellen hugs them, Maw finds them a fine foster home, and John Boy says, "and so Huey and Louis discovered on Walton's Mountain what a family truly means."

Most of their visits that spring left me feeling depressed—I had frequent colds and viruses, my blood pressure rose. . . .

In the late spring disturbing hints seeped in like a slow water leak: What was that? Somebody found a partly smoked joint on the living-room carpet? When? And whose? "Not mine!" all the kids said. The neighborhood was a little wild. Then Nicole was said to have drunk a large glass of vodka once when she was alone in the house. *I just wanted to know what it was like.*

"I remember wanting to give them such a booster shot of myself that they'd never be able to get me out of their systems."

When Gay had to go out of town on business, I offered to stay in their house to take care of the kids. . . . Keith, I was happy to see, appeared to be doing well here. His friends had been teaching him to fish and to surf, and you could see him speeding off to a sandlot baseball game with his glove hooked over the handlebars of his bike. His friends wore run-down sneakers and T-shirts, and when you saw Keith and them with fishing poles over their shoulders they were a living Norman Rockwell *Post* cover. He seemed happy to see me and to introduce me to his friends. I was proud to be introduced, glad that we could claim kinship before people who mattered to him.

I found Nicole's new Schwinn ten-speed—this year's Christmas present—in the garage with two flat tires, the cables and spokes and gears corroded by salt spray and gummed with sand. Her room was papered with posters of heavy-metal rock groups on which sets of angry young men clad in black leather and spikes leered and postured. Clothes and papers and used tissue littered the floor; notes from friends were wadded or left lying about where even the most casual eye (and mine was not the most casual) could spot the horrific phrasing of minds just discovering how to relish the vulgar. Drawings she had done of hollow-eyed, screaming Medusas filled a sketch pad. Behind the shut and locked door she played Pink Floyd at top volume ("*We don't need no ed-you-kay-shun. . . .*"), and I had to pound on the door and scream to get her attention. . . .

On Friday night I took her to a dance program given by some of her classmates, where I met her friends; they all seemed older than her thirteen and were dressed in tight jeans and tight T-shirts, dangling earrings, and heavy blue eye shadow—the sort of girls a twenty-one-year-old red-neck cruising in his pickup would imagine to be an easy lay. . . .

I'm luckier than most divorced men, I thought. Four months after this upsetting trip, my children moved back to Dallas and began their eighth grade. Whatever happened now, I would be nearby; I could chauffeur them to malls for shopping, skating, or a movie. They could spend parts of weekends at my apartment without feeling I had stolen all of their leisure time, or I could have them over nights during the week.

Not the Same Children

But they were not the same children. They had contracted adolescence. They ran with a pack at shopping malls on Friday nights. They attended a tough urban school where a custom van with an ear-shattering stereo system showed up promptly at lunchtime to dispense the drug du jour to kids, and where small white boys like Keith were regularly threatened with an ass-kicking from gangs of low-riders. . . .

Nicole's friend Alicia lived with her mother except when her mother was on a bender, when she'd go live with her father, a bricklayer, in a trailer park. She was dumb but friendly (rumor had it that she let college boys abuse her sexually). Nicole's friend Angie and her friend Denise dropped acid, stole some credit cards, and took off in a "borrowed" car with some eighteen-year-old boys and were caught two states away, for which Angie spent a month in juvenile detention. Nicole's friend Melissa was always so stoned that her friends had to prop her up in class and walk her down the halls, and she eventually spent several weeks in a drug rehabilitation program. They stole from their mothers' purses; they sniffed paint; they watched X-rated movies on cable. They all had a variety of parents but very little parenting.

They had no innocence of any kind, but they were ignorant. They could recite all the lyrics to any Van Halen album, but they didn't know if El Paso was a city or a state. Three of her teachers were very concerned about Nicole, but she was failing all of her classes. . . .

I could see we had to get Nicole into counseling. She agreed to it, partly out of curiosity and partly because she was a little worried about herself.

It was called "adolescent reactive adjustment syndrome," which means skipping school, flunking out, mouthing off, screwing up, getting drunk, taking drugs. Her psychologist was a pleasant and intelligent middle-aged woman who approached life with a perpetual Happy Face. She gave Nicole a battery of tests about preferences, aptitudes, and attitudes toward parents, self, and peers. . . .

After several sessions, the counselor reported that Nicole suffered from low self-esteem, and we were advised to accentuate the positive. But when you gave Nicole a compliment, she would counter with, "You're just saying that because *she* told you to make me feel good."

She continued to sneak out at night to join her friends; trapped at home, she'd closet herself in her room amid the hurricane winds of the stereo and draw that black-and-white Fury I first saw in Galveston. The figure had wild, electrified hair, a square jaw, a Frankensteinian forehead, large hollow eyes without pupils, and a howling mouth.

What the counselor didn't know was that Nicole was stoned all the time. Her mother and I didn't know it, either. (Keith kept trying to tell us, but he had been caught at so many lies his credibility was low.) Arriving at school each day, she would load up with whatever drugs were available—speed, grass, Valium—and go blotto through her classes; she'd even attend her sessions with her psychologist three quarters under the influence of some chemical moon.

"We want these visits to be more 'meaningful,' like, say, an episode of The Waltons."

Then in April she took a horse tranquilizer (PCP) with the street name of "angel dust." It scrambled her brains. Voices in her head told her to hurt herself; she insisted the voices belonged to real people, characters to whom she gave fablelike names such as Bendikak. They looked like trolls when they popped into the frame of her vision. Some told her to do "good things," and some "bad things."

Her counselor advised hospitalization. While we looked for the right place, she was "sentenced" to stay at my house, out of reach of her friends and where my wife and I could keep close watch over her. She was furious and deadly silent. She kept drawing that face. . . .

Going into the hospital was scary for her. A part of her welcomed it because she needed help and knew it might be an interesting experience, but when she realized that she would be kept behind locked doors, she balked. She could not eat or drink when or what she wanted to! She would not be allowed to take so much as a measly aspirin on her own! We were putting her in jail! . . .

Her mother, her teachers, her brother, her case workers, and I visited constantly, and we had to learn to deal with the personality that had been buried under that avalanche of chemistry. She was being treated for depression by nonchemical therapies; she had been numb for so long that when her feelings were finally allowed to flow, the wildly oscillating emotional upheaval alarmed her. She deeply resented our "help.". . .

I went to the parents' group, where I discovered the obvious, that such groups are composed of people who share the same problems and that you feel better the instant you realize that. We were a motley crew; we had nothing in common but our troubled children. There was an aging biker with tattoos who wore jeans and a Harley-Davidson T-shirt whose six-year-old son was in the ward; he sat in silence for three sessions, then one day he slumped forward and moaned, "I've been such a lousy father!"

"We who have left our children live with the burden of guilt."

Then there were Connie's parents. He wore plaid vested suits and wing tips and had the bland, rabbit-pink face of a mid-western preacher at an upscale Baptist church. His wife might have been a beauty queen at Baylor in the early Fifties. I thought they felt they really shouldn't be there, and I detested them for that. Connie had apparently fallen into bad company.

None of their friends had had problems with *their* children, nor, presumably, had any of their friends' friends. They were clearly concerned that Connie would be associating with problem children here at the hospital, and they were also very worried about what their friends would think should they learn about this. They had no idea where Connie was learning to say things such as "Piss off!" They had done everything right. "She's got everything a kid could want," he said. "We have good values."

I laughed. I relished their discomfort. I hated them for being so innocent; I hated them because they represented what I yearned to be: a guiltless parent. I acted up; I insulted them by telling them that obviously something had gone wrong somewhere. I should have been sympathetic to their complete bewilderment—they could not find a cause to blame. I could, in my daughter's case. And yet, seeing them agonize, it dawned on me that not everyone in the room was divorced, that such things happened to "nice" folks, too.

Perhaps I was not altogether to blame!

The Burden of Guilt

We who have left our children live with the burden of guilt that makes judgment more difficult. When something goes wrong, we immediately go for our own jugular. What I learned in group was that nobody knows for sure why kids go haywire; the causes could be emotional, chemical, spiritual, psychological, genetic, or social. (Or, as it was in Nicole's case, because of depression.) And yet it is obvious that wholesale rejection by a father of his children will most likely leave a lifelong emotional scar, something my old college buddy whose ex-children "don't count" may someday have to face. "Leaving" my children was not a necessary or even sufficient cause for it, but it certainly was a contributory one. My job was to minimize the damage. Whether I was in their home or not, I had better pay as close attention as I possibly could to how they were doing.

Nicole got out of stir with walking papers that pronounced her sound again, for which I am immensely grateful to the staff of that hospital. We kept her and her brother in constant motion over the summer—to camp, to Yosemite, to San Francisco, to Los Angeles, to Disneyland (she loved it!)—and she started ninth grade at a high school for the arts. Her first report card showed a string of B's interrupted only by a C in science. . . .

For a while Nicole kept drawing renditions of that Medusa, though each successive version seemed to represent something like stages of evolution out of the slime. One of the last she did she colored with pastel pencils: the woman has blond hair, high cheekbones with a slight peach flush. Her mouth is closed, and she has feminine lips; she isn't smiling, but the curve of her lips suggests repose. Her jaw has softened, and she had large, pale blue eyes with curving lashes. One brow goes up, the other down, in some faint intimation of melancholy. The old gal seems human now.

She gave that one to me. The inscription reads, "To Dad, a very special person who helped me through a lot of hard times. I love you."

Lifelong Emotional Scar

As proud as I am for having earned those words, and as much as I'd like to end on that upbeat note, the truth is that no trauma is altogether erasable. The other night Nicole and I were talking about her future as an adult; she couldn't decide between being an artist or a psychologist. Well, there's your love life to consider, too, I said. "Oh, I think I'll just live with somebody," she said. "I don't think I'll get married." Why not? "Because then I might have kids and just get divorced."

C.W. Smith, a novelist, is the author of The Vestal Virgin Room, Country Music, *and* Thin Men of Haddam, *and teaches at Southern Methodist University.*

"I am content. . . . I will always be his mother; he will always be my son."

"I am content. . . . I will always be his mother; he will always be my son."

viewpoint **55**

The Noncustodial Parent: A Mother's View

Lisa Rogak

Editor's note: The names of all the mothers and children interviewed for this article have been changed.

Jane Gibson, a librarian in Queens, split up with her husband ten years ago, after sixteen years of marriage. It was an amicable break—so amicable, in fact, that they used the same lawyer for the divorce negotiations. Gibson moved to Queens and her ex-husband stayed in the house in Westchester. So did their six-year-old daughter.

"I thought, When can I see Rochelle the most?" Gibson says, "and I decided it was on the weekends. If I had custody during the week, a housekeeper would take care of my daughter, not me. I didn't feel I was giving up custody, though some people saw it as abandoning my child."

"I like visiting my mother," Rochelle says. "I like living in the suburbs. If I lived with her, she wouldn't be there much. Here there's always somebody around. But it's hard sometimes, because I don't get to see my mom much."

"If I had been real selfish," Gibson says, "I would have said to Rochelle, 'You stay with me.' Not too many people see it that way, though. As it is, my ex-husband's wife has told me that she does my work during the week."

"When they split," Rochelle says, "I was six years old. I didn't understand what was going on. It didn't hit me that my mom was moving out. I thought it was normal. A lot of my friends' parents are divorced, and my friends don't think anything [of the fact] that I don't live with her."

Challenging Tradition

Rarely encountered in everyday life—rarely even written about—are women who, like Jane Gibson, make the wrenching decision to give up custody of

Lisa Rogak, "When Mommy Moves Out," *New York*, January 5, 1987. Reprinted with the author's permission.

their children. To do so is to challenge tradition: These mothers will find few models in history, literature, or life.

According to a 1985 Census Bureau report, 87 percent of divorced or separated mothers are awarded custody of their children. There is no way of knowing what percentage of the remaining mothers gave up custody voluntarily, as opposed to losing it after a court battle.

Through singles groups, psychologists, and the support group Mothers Without Custody, I tracked down seven women who had made this controversial decision and were willing to talk about it. Years later, most of them were still agonizing over the choice they had made.

"I see a tremendous amount of guilt in mothers who leave their kids—but not as much guilt in fathers," says Dr. Allan Stempler, a child and adolescent psychiatrist in private practice in Great Neck. "The idea of a mother willingly *not* having her kid brings up terrible recriminations in all levels of society, and that's where the ambivalence so common among these women comes from."

"A woman who takes a slightly different tack when it comes to her children is automatically labeled an ogre," Jane Gibson says. And yet, contrary to their expectations, the mothers I interviewed here have encountered surprisingly little criticism from their friends and families. This tolerance often goes against their deep sense that they have done something wrong. . . .

Recognized Limitations

Some of the mothers seemed defensive when I asked them why they'd done what they'd done.

"Many of us recognized our limitations. What's wrong with that?" snaps Alison Morrow, a college administrator in Brooklyn who has been living apart from her four sons for four years. She and her husband separated in the spring of 1982 and he moved out, leaving her with the boys, then four, eight, ten, and twelve. After three months, she'd had enough, and Morrow and her ex-husband switched places: She moved into his apartment, and he moved back into the house. "I realized neither I nor the kids were going to make it," she says. "I was very upset and didn't know where the money would be coming from. They were difficult kids all along, and I didn't know how to handle them."

Morrow's son Billy, now eight, says, "I was four years old when she left. She couldn't afford us." Twelve-year-old Michael adds, "I felt sad for a couple of years; then I got over it. I missed her for a long time. I would keep on calling her." But even though he was sad at his mother's departure, he says her leaving wasn't all bad: "After she left, it was pleasant—there was no screaming and yelling anymore [between the parents]."

Morrow did not fight for custody because she was sure she would lose, given her emotional state and her lack of money. "I couldn't handle the emotional stress of single parenthood, taking care of myself and four kids. Money was an additional burden: I was working part-time and making a total of $3,000 a year. I've short-circuited the system and feel I'm ahead of the game by not going to court. I'm also not as angered at the system as the women who've lost custody. Maybe someday some of my boys will come live with me, but now they want to stay together."

Billy remembers, "Once my mother tried to take me away, but all four of us must stay together."

"Maybe when I'm a little older, I'd like to move in with her," Michael says. "She's closer to job opportunities than where we are, and after-school jobs. If we really, really wanted to move, I guess my father would let us."

"I couldn't handle the emotional stress of single parenthood, taking care of myself and four kids."

Morrow sees her children on Sunday afternoons. She admits she doesn't always look forward to their visits. "In some ways, it would be easier if I didn't see them. There's a distance between us. By Sunday evening, we start feeling warm again—especially my youngest. But then I have to leave."

Billy—the youngest—can't make up his mind about his mother. "Sometimes I wish I lived with my mom. I don't see her enough. I wish I could see her on Saturday *and* Sunday, but we tried it already and she couldn't afford one more day. Sometimes I just don't want to come to my mother's house; I don't want to see her. I like my stepmother. She's replacing my mother."

Peter, the fourteen-year-old, concurs. "Sometimes we look forward to seeing her. But I wouldn't want to live with her. My father has more control over us; we behave better around him."

"If I hadn't had *four* children," Morrow says, "and they weren't so difficult, it might have made me lean more favorably toward custody. But I wouldn't fight my ex-husband for custody, unless I thought they were in a bad living situation. Sometimes I think, 'If only I had been able to do more for them,' and because of this I feel a constant conflict and ambivalence. In many ways I've been fortunate to start a new life, but I switch back and forth. I've had a chance to develop my autonomy more and am able to stand on my own two feet, but there isn't a day that goes by that I don't feel sadness and loss. I gave birth to them, but I'm no longer living with them—I've become the traditional visiting parent who sees them once a week."

One advantage of not living with her children, she concedes, is the fact that she can work past five o'clock—"but," she quickly tacks on, "not without grief." She believes that her departure wasn't as traumatic to her children as the breakup itself. "I'm lucky because my kids are thriving and doing well; it's me who has to deal with all the changes. When I see children playing in the street, I'm reminded of everything I'm missing. And my ex-husband assumes most of the control—he influences them to treat me as an intruder, and I feel my older boys are looking at me through their father's eyes, they've turned out so much like him.

"The question 'Do you have kids?' becomes a heavy trip for me. The social isolation is the hardest thing to deal with, because [even] in light conversation I have to be willing to reveal my sensitive secret. After all, you can't just stop at naming the ages of your kids. Look at me—I have to make an appointment to see my own kids! I'll always ask myself, 'Did I do the right thing?' I can't think of anything worse than the last few years."

Morrow feels such a need to talk with other women in her situation that she has started a group for non-custodial mothers. "People don't realize how alone you are," she says. "We're a funny kind of sorority. Society says we're freaks; the group reassures us that we're okay.". . .

Countering Traditionalist Attitudes

Nancy Houston left her husband because of his traditionalist attitudes. She freely admits that feminism had a lot to do with her leaving two years ago. "I wasn't able to be who I wanted to be," she says, and so when her husband told her *he* wasn't going to be the one to leave and that James, their fourteen-year-old son, wasn't going with her, she left.

Houston, a personnel administrator in Manhattan, stayed on for a year in the southern town where she'd been living, in order to be close to her son. He was, she says, very detached from her at the time. ''Basically, it was my son's decision to live where he wanted, and he said that because he was a boy he wanted to live with his father.''

Would she have fought the decision if James had wanted to stay with her? ''I'm never ready to fight,'' she says. ''I'm not a fighter and I don't like confrontation. If I had fought for custody, I think it would have gone on and on and my ex-husband would still be bitter today.'' As it is, she and her ex-husband do get along, ''though he thinks I'm a complete idiot to live in New York.''

She's content with the situation for the time being; there's a chance James might come up to live with her when he goes to college. ''I wish I was there to impart my values and viewpoints to him, but I do that anyway when he's with me.''

''I feel a constant conflict and ambivalence. In many ways I've been fortunate to start a new life, but I switch back and forth.''

When she first moved out, she kept expecting James to call every day or so, and he didn't. ''I was very disappointed,'' she says, ''but James is not a talker, and once I started to feel his unconditional love for me, things got better. But I am constantly reminded of him. I miss him very much, and not a day goes by without me thinking about him several times. Little things trigger it, like a kid on a Big Wheel, or when I walk by a high school. I feel I'm missing out on day-to-day things.''

Houston reassures herself with the old adage that sooner or later all mothers have to let go. ''In my case it was sooner, but I am content,'' she says. ''I will always be his mother; he will always be my son.''. . .

How voluntary *were* these women's decisions to give up custody? ''How voluntary is it,'' asks Alison Morrow, ''when money and society dictate to you? Society set up the women of my generation, who are now in their forties. You counted on your husband to support you and your children, and if you broke up, you weren't in any position to support yourself. Taking care of myself and my four kids would have been impossible; I wasn't equipped with a career to be able to do it.

''We didn't have a judge coerce us into these choices,'' she says, ''but some women are *intimidated* into it. The enormity of the responsibility was what intimidated me the most, but some women are incredibly intimidated by their husbands.

''Also, when I was living with the children for the first three months of our separation, his child-support payments were sporadic, and it was not very nice to deal with him. It wasn't going to be too easy to raise the kids by myself and be dependent on him for money. There is no real choice. You do it as a last resort or as the best solution at the time. Money is the No. 1 issue, with the state of the emotions close behind.''

Ronee Paget Miller, a Manhattan psychotherapist, maintains that she rarely meets a mother whose decision to give up her child is truly voluntary. ''The *Kramer vs. Kramer* image is wrongly perpetuated in society today. No mother gives up custody of her kids without duress.''

Doing What's Best for the Children

Frances Hopkins, a Long Island teacher who is the part-time mother of a thirteen-year-old daughter, stopped going to a support group because she ''couldn't handle the stories. There was just too much pain—you could hear it in their voices. Simply put, the pain is from losing your children. The guilt is enormous, and there's an enormous feeling of loss. And I really hadn't wanted to do this. That's why the word 'voluntary' bothers me—I did it out of love. I couldn't cope with living a lousy home life anymore, and the court's view is that if the mother moves out, even if she comes back two days later, they'll give the father custody.

''Although the mothers in my group did what they thought was best for their kid, everyone was in so much pain, and the pain was so similar to mine, that I wanted to forget about it and didn't want to confront it. I would leave so upset.''

Hopkins had been married for seventeen years when she left, two and half years ago. She left without her daughter because she didn't want to go to court. ''Sarah had told me, 'Don't ever make me tell a judge who I want to live with,' and I agreed with her; people have told me what goes on with custody battles, and I wanted no part of it.

''When I left, I needed to get away not only from my husband but also from my daughter, who's highly emotional. Now she says she wants to live with me, but she also wants to continue going to the same school and living in the same house, because she's terrified of change. She would love it if I could move back to town so she could live with me part of the time. But there are no apartments in the town she lives in, and we both need our privacy. As it is, we're getting along much better. She's getting along better with her father too. Before, he was a 'non-parent'; now he's a parent.

Hopkins lives about a half-hour's drive from her daughter and sees her for 24 hours every weekend. She pays for half her support, all of her clothes, and one month of camp. ''I'm still 70 percent of the parent,'' she maintains.

''I looked for an apartment in a good school district when I first moved out. I never dreamed this would be permanent. I want her back now, but it's not worth the hassle of a custody battle and uprooting her entire life again, and it just eats me up alive.

"I haven't gotten the negative reactions I expected. One woman did get really nasty with me. I told her I thought she was jealous of me, and she agreed. She's a divorced mother *with* custody. You see, it's very hard to do it all, and it's not so terrible to just do part of it.

"Now I usually tell people about the custody situation as soon as I meet them. But I get sick to my stomach when I'm telling them. I still feel there's something wrong with it, though I would do it again."

Weekend Moms

"Even though women adjust to being without their children, they always have to explain themselves," Dr. Stempler points out. "Women from all levels of society feel that granting custody to their husbands is a rejection of their kids. They have a very strong conflict between being parents and being independent, and because of this constant tearing, they feel they must justify both parts of their lives."

"We're a funny kind of sorority. Society says we're freaks; the group [of noncustodial mothers] reassures us that we're okay."

Douglas H. Reiniger, a Manhattan lawyer with a large matrimonial practice, agrees. "In spite of all women's lib has done, most people still feel that mommies stay home and daddies go out to work. So even if the heart says no to custody, many mothers will still go for it because of the guilt."

"'Weekend mom' is a contradiction in terms," Reiniger says. "Society assumes that the only good mothers are those who have their children all week. Non-custodial mothers are considered failures because they're not maternal. That's why you read about supermoms who don't make choices—who burn themselves out."

No Ambivalence

Miriam Prince sacrificed full-time motherhood for her art. She has no ambivalence about her decision; any guilt she feels, she says, derives only from the negative opinions of other people. Her daughter, Lauren, is sixteen.

Four and a half years ago, Prince left Chicago for New York to pursue her acting career. "I've been living on People Express ever since," she says. (She spends about five days in Chicago every three weeks.) She and her husband are not yet divorced.

He is recuperating from a very serious operation. "Visiting there is difficult," she says, "and being away is difficult. When I'm there, my husband resents me enormously; he wants someone to be there to take care of him. But staying there would be taking me away from my daughter, really, because then I'd resent her. I have very mixed emotions about the entire situation. The moment of saying good-bye is never easy for me. But to be honest, I wouldn't be the greatest mother. As an artist you're naturally compulsive, and the people in your life come next on the totem pole. In New York I'm a role model among artists for putting my art above my family; in Chicago I'm a terrible mother."

She decided she wouldn't put up a fight if a custody battle ever came up. Anyway, she says, Lauren isn't a New York kid, and at sixteen she's only a few years away from being on her own.

"I had a choice of who I wanted to live with," Lauren says. "I wanted to stay with my dad. I got along with him better."

The relationship between mother and daughter is strained, and Miriam concedes that when they're together, they need a few days to get used to each other again. Lauren acknowledges that "her moving out was the best thing that could have happened. We were having little mother-daughter fights. I don't want her to move back. We have a very tense relationship. I need my space, but she doesn't understand boundaries and space. She wants to form some kind of relationship with me because she's afraid of losing me, but she's pushing me away by doing that. We'll have a relationship someday, but not now. It's very tense when she visits. When she gets a cold reception from me, she just tries harder. She's tough, she's really tough."

Doing Better

"My daughter finds it difficult to talk to me, and she was clinically depressed for a time last year," Prince says. "She's now in therapy and on antidepressants, and is doing much better."

Lauren says, "She wants to be the mother and assume the role that I took care of and Dad took care of. I didn't resent her leaving—at least not consciously; I resented her more and more when she came to visit. She broke up the routine me and my father had; it didn't feel like she belonged.

"I don't think she had anything to do with my depression, though my father thought I was angry at her because she left. She moved out when I was eleven or twelve, and my depression began at fifteen. She usually has tunnel vision; she doesn't want a divorce, and he does, and I want them to get one. My friends thought it was pretty weird, me living with my father and my mother moving out."

Prince is considering basing herself in Chicago and traveling to New York, using People Express as her second home. "If I had to do it over again, I wouldn't refuse to have children—for my life they're necessary," she says. "But I've found that you can't have everything."

Children Will Thrive

Karen Baylor knows that all too well. Two years ago, she left her son and daughter, then eight and ten, with her ex-husband under a joint-custody arrangement. She believes this was the best thing for her children, but it hasn't worked out the way she had envisioned.

"Before I moved out, the more I thought about it, the more I realized I couldn't pay my whole salary to babysitters; my husband originally was only going to pay $100 a week in child support. He was getting remarried, and I thought the children would benefit in a two-person household. For the first two years, I saw the kids every weekend, but he's playing a power struggle, and now it's down to every other weekend. My ex pulls the strings, and I have to take what crumbs he throws my way."

This past Mother's Day, Baylor says, she called her ex-husband to arrange a time to pick the children up and he told her, "You'd better plan to come at twelve o'clock. We're taking the mother who raises them out for Mother's Day brunch."

She and his new wife get along well, Baylor says, and she acknowledges that the new wife is doing a good job in raising the children. "I think this arrangement has made all of us—me, the children, his new wife—better people, except for my ex-husband, which is strange, because he's the one who initiated the arrangement, and he's the only one that's not happy."

"When I left, I needed to get away not only from my husband but also from my daughter, who's highly emotional."

"The children were very confused when I first left," she says. "They didn't understand, after all the fighting, why I would agree to let them live with their father. They would ask me, 'Why can't we stay with you, and why do you have to work so much?' I agreed to have them live with their father because I thought my son needed a father figure, but I have since determined that that's not necessarily so; as long as a child has one parent he can relate to, he'll thrive. The bond between me and my son is much stronger now," she says.

Baylor believes that her children respect her in a way they wouldn't if they had lived with her. "I got promoted this summer [she's a corporate executive in Manhattan] and my kids were absolutely thrilled for me. I devote 90 percent of my time to my career now, and it gives me a feeling of power I never had

before. I never could have had a career if I'd had to worry about being home at night, and I wouldn't have gotten promoted if I'd had to come home and help with the homework and cook dinner. The promotion made me feel that at least all this wasn't in vain.". . .

Baylor concedes that her children had many adjustment problems at first; the next year, though, everyone was doing much better. Her son, who's twelve now, has had counseling and remedial help with his schoolwork; he has succeeded in losing weight and is now on the honor roll. "They're much more at ease with the situation now, and they're doing better in school," Baylor says.

"I've thought about going back for full custody, but it's so expensive and there's no guarantee, and you can't reverse the agreement so easily. I also didn't want to put my kids through a fight."

An Unselfish Decision

Katherine Levitan, a Mineola lawyer who handles many matrimonial cases, agrees that changing a custody arrangement is extremely effective. "Mothers considering such a move must be sure they know what they're doing, because unless they can show an existing bad situation with the father—especially with joint custody—the judge is not going to change it back. Judges take a dim view of a mother's leaving her children, even for just a day or two in contested cases," she advises.

Seventeen years ago, a woman came to Levitan with an unusual request: She wanted to give custody of her two little girls to her husband. "I was shocked," Levitan says. "I asked her to go to a therapist and sign a waiver. She felt the husband was the better nurturer, and he wanted them and she didn't.

"You know what? I still keep in touch with her, and I've seen more women like her since then. It was not selfish of her to say 'I do not want to keep my children' when, in fact, she did not want to keep them. She did the hardest thing, which was to let go. Although it was very difficult for her to do that, under her circumstances in life it was better for the children to give them to their father. After I finished her case, I decided she was one of the best mothers I had ever met. I still feel that way."

Lisa Rogak is a free-lance writer and a noncustodial mother. This viewpoint is excerpted from her article in the weekly New York *magazine.*

"Female jobs . . . remain undervalued because of their association with unpaid work in the home and because women are not seen as important economic providers."

Discrimination Harms Women Workers

Nancy Barrett

The increase in women's labor force participation over the last 25 years has brought with it questions of equal employment opportunity, pay equity, and family services that were less frequently raised when the paid labor force comprised largely males and single women, and child care and other household duties were managed by full-time homemakers.

The number of women working or looking for work has increased by roughly 28 million over the past 25 years. . . .

Despite advances made in women's educational attainment and employment opportunities, women remain overwhelmingly concentrated in low-paying female occupations.

In 1985, 70 percent of all full-time employed women were working in occupations in which over three-quarters of the employees were females.

Over one-third of all employed women work in clerical jobs.

Women tend to be employed in low-paying jobs with no on-the-job training and little security, and thus they are often among the first fired.

In almost all areas of employment, women are overrepresented at the bottom and underrepresented at the top.

The average female worker is gaining in experience and should be progressing more rapidly up the job ladder than is actually the case.

Wages

Women college graduates who work full time, year round, have earnings roughly on a par with male high school dropouts.

The concentration of women in low-paying occupations, their ghettoization within male-dominated professions, and their lack of upward mobility translates into a lower average wage for women than for men.

The median earnings for women working full time, year round, in 1985 were 68 percent of men's earnings, up from 61 percent in 1978.

The slight improvement in the wage gap is not due to women moving into higher-paying jobs but to a recession that has had a disproportionately negative effect on the high-wage, male-dominated sectors of the economy.

The wage gap between men and women increases with age. Younger workers of both sexes enter the labor force in the lowest pay categories, but men are more likely to advance in earnings while women remain behind. A 45- to 55-year-old woman makes approximately the same wage as a woman of 25.

During the 1970s, adult women experienced higher unemployment rates than adult men: 6.0 percent for women compared to 4.5 percent for men.

In the 1980s, the average unemployment rates for both women and men rose and were virtually identical at 7.2 and 7.1 percent, respectively. Between 1980 and 1985, 6.9 million new jobs were created in the female-dominated sectors of sales and services, while 500,000 jobs were lost in the male-dominated sectors of manufacturing, mining, construction, and transportation.

The decline of full-time homemaking as the predominant occupation for married women has been accompanied by a rapid increase in the number of women seeking part-time jobs. Roughly one-third of the shift out of homemaking has been into part-time employment.

About three-quarters of women working part time are in the low-paying sales, clerical, and service occupations.

Women workers' low part-time pay is accompanied by the virtual absence of fringe benefits or opportunity for advancement.

Female jobs have traditionally been and remain undervalued because of their association with unpaid work in the home and because women are not seen as important economic providers.

Although women, on average, earn less than men, their contributions to the economic resources of families are substantial.

For all families, and especially for black families, a second paycheck makes a significant difference in living standards and substantially reduces the incidence of poverty.

Women with paid jobs still bear most of the responsibility for housework. The shift to paid employment has not meant an offsetting decline in the number of hours most women spend in the household economy. Thus, women now contribute more total hours to the economy (both paid and unpaid) than they did before the shift. . . .

Women's occupations in paid employment have remained remarkably traditional. Despite the attention afforded to a female astronaut or Supreme Court justice, statistics show that women remain overwhelmingly concentrated in female-dominated occupations. And where they have moved into formerly male domains, they remain on the bottom rungs of the job ladder, or are tracked into predominantly female "ghettos"—relatively low-paying subcategories of jobs held by women within higher-paying occupations dominated by men.

Seeking Traditional Jobs

In 1985, 70 percent of all women employed full time were working in occupations in which over three-quarters of the employees were female. Part-time workers are even more heavily concentrated in predominantly female occupations. Admittedly, there has been some change in the occupational profile of women workers since 1970. Women have increased their representation in the managerial and professional categories and decreased it in the sales and service categories. And while both women and men have tended to move from "blue-collar" to "white-collar" occupations as the manufacturing sectors have declined, occupational changes for women have been more dramatic than for men. Nevertheless, over a third of all employed women work in clerical jobs, and the proportion of the female workforce in clerical work has increased since 1970. The dynamic for change in women's labor force activities seems to be much weaker than the forces that propelled so many women into paid employment to begin with.

It is not surprising that a major impact of the household transformation has been in the professions, since the most substantial increase in labor force participation has been among middle-class, well-educated women who formerly would have dropped out of the labor force during their child-bearing years. By 1985, the proportion of

women aged 25 to 34 in the labor force who had attended college actually surpassed that of men. This gain was accomplished by an explosive increase in the labor force participation rate of college-educated women in this age group over the decade 1975 to 1985—from 69 to 83 percent for college graduates and from 58 to 76 percent for those who had completed one to three years of college—combined with an increase in the percent of college graduates and advanced-degree recipients who are women. Between 1970 and 1979, the female proportion of degree recipients increased at all levels, rising from 43 to 48 percent of bachelors' degrees, from 40 to 49 percent of masters' degrees, from 13 to 26 percent of doctoral degrees, and from 5 to 24 of first professional degrees.

"Women academics are located disproportionately in two-year and four-year colleges and state universities with heavy teaching loads not conducive to research."

Seventy percent of married women with college degrees were either employed or looking for work in 1981, compared with 50 percent 10 years earlier. Moreover, the rise in career expectations among this group, aided by Title IX legislation that, among other things, prohibits discrimination against women in higher education, has substantially increased the number of women pursuing advanced professional degrees in fields like law and medicine. From 1970 to 1979, the percentage of graduates earning degrees in law who were women jumped from 5.4 to 28.5, and in medicine from 8.4 to 23.0.

In considering these gains, however, it is important to bear in mind that broad occupational categories mask important segregation patterns within more detailed occupations. A study of nearly 61,000 workers found that only 10 percent were in job titles that had both men and women assigned to them. There is a substantial pay gap between men and women within the broad occupational categories that reflects a concentration of women in relatively low-paying specialties within them. For instance, in medicine, women predominate in specialties like pediatrics and nutrition, both of which pay considerably less than a male-dominated specialty like surgery. And the few women attorneys entering prestigious law firms are often assigned to library research rather than to the courtroom, or to the less prestigious and less lucrative fields of trusts, estates, and domestic relations.

In academic jobs as well, the status of women is below that of men. Women academics are located disproportionately in two-year and four-year colleges and state universities with heavy teaching loads not conducive to research. Nationwide, women on college faculties account for only 10 percent of full professors but 50 percent of instructors and lecturers. Moreover, male faculty members are concentrated in the physical and social sciences and professional schools, while women predominate in the lower-paying arts and humanities. . . .

Gender-typing of jobs within formerly male-dominated fields is not the only reason for the relatively high pay gap within them. Another factor is the way in which men and women move up the job ladders in these fields. From government civil service to university faculties, private corporations, banks, and insurance companies, women are overrepresented at the bottom and underrepresented at the top. Fewer than five percent of federal civil servants at level GS 16 and above are women, compared with 77 percent in grades 1 through 4. Job ladders for many predominantly female jobs such as secretarial are much shorter than for male jobs; that is, opportunities for advancement disappear after a few promotions. This pattern of women's greater representation in the lower echelons of the job hierarchy repeats itself in practically all large business organizations. . . .

Work Experience

One could speculate that the reason women are underrepresented in the higher echelons of the job ladder is that they lack seniority or relevant work experience. Although it is true that many women interrupt their working life at some point when they are raising children, the trend is for women to remain at work longer than they used to. Then too, male workers frequently change jobs and even occupations. This is becoming more common as male workers are increasingly displaced from jobs. According to the Bureau of Labor Statistics, in 1983 the median tenure on the job was 3.3 years for women, compared with 5.1 years for men. There was little or no difference in the length of job tenure between men and women up to the age of 30.

The household transformation has increased women's attachment to the workforce. Because women today are less likely than in the past to drop out of the labor force when they marry and bear children, the average female worker is gaining in experience and should be progressing more rapidly up job ladders than is actually the case. Moreover, the scarcity of opportunities for upward mobility in female-dominated occupations, and in female ghettos within predominantly male occupations, suggests that the problem is not solely intermittency of participation among women workers, but rather a job environment that fails to provide women the same promotional opportunities that male workers enjoy. . . .

Because women are generally located at the bottom of the job hierarchy and men at the top, there is a considerable difference in how the level of their earnings is distributed within the same category of work. In 1982, 16.2 percent of women managers and administrators earned less than $200 per week, compared with only 3.2 percent of men. On the other hand, only 14.9 percent of those women earned more than $500 per week compared with 51.3 percent of the men. Among craft workers, 28.4 percent of the women and only 7.0 percent of the men earned less than $200 per week, while 7.7 percent of the women and 23.9 percent of the men earned more than $500. Similar patterns were also found in the specific occupations within these general categories.

The concentration of women at the bottom of the distribution of earnings results in a wage gap that increases with age. Young workers of both sexes enter the labor market in the lowest pay categories, but the men are more likely to advance in earnings while the women remain behind. This is either because women are in occupations without opportunities for upward mobility, or because they are denied access to the opportunities that are available to men. . . .

Occupational segregation, ghettoization, and lack of upward mobility deserve great emphasis, but other factors contribute to the pay gap as well. For instance, women work fewer hours per week than men, and despite gains among younger women, have slightly less education than men on the average. However, differences in education and hours worked account for a relatively small part of the pay gap. Together, in 1982, they contributed 3.7 percentage points to a pay gap of 35 percentage points.

"The problem is . . . a job environment that fails to provide women the same promotional opportunities that male workers enjoy."

Lack of work experience and intermittent labor force activity of women are sometimes thought to contribute significantly to their lower earnings. However, a recent study by the Bureau of the Census reports that work interruptions explain only a small part of the earnings disparity between women and men. The bureau found that even if women's education, experience, and interruptions were the same as men's, the earnings gap would be reduced by only about five percentage points. . . .

There has been encouraging progress for some women, particularly young, college-educated women who are entering high-paying professions like law, medicine, and business in record numbers. On the other hand, there appears to be considerable sex segregation within those fields, and women are grossly underrepresented in the highest ranks. It remains to be seen whether, as more women move into these elite occupations, their representation might become more uniform across specialties and in the higher ranks.

Other changes seem less positive. The proportion of women who work in relatively low-paying clerical jobs continues to increase, although some clerical workers may have "moved up" from even lower-paying service jobs. The reduction in the male-female wage gap since 1980 is largely the result of the decline in high-wage, male-dominated manufacturing employment, rather than any real progress for women. . . .

pay plans should be encouraged. Better part-time employment opportunities and flexible work-scheduling are needed. And, finally, government statisical agencies should begin collecting data on the household economy to assess the extent to which men's work roles in the home are changing in ways that complement women's new roles in paid employment, and to improve our awareness and assessment of the human capital embodied in our female labor force.

Nancy Barrett is the chairwoman of the economics department at American University. She has also served on the senior staff of the Council of Economic Advisers and worked in the Labor Department during the Carter administration.

"Differences in education and hours worked account for a relatively small part of the pay gap."

No single policy or program can address the needs of all women workers. For professionals in male-dominated occupations, affirmative action may be needed. For women in traditional jobs, comparable worth offers a potential source of higher pay. And for those trapped in the welfare system, job training and public employment programs could serve as a bridge or gateway into secure jobs paying a living wage.

Common Needs

But these women also have many needs in common. Some of these needs arise from the common stereotypes women experience, the devaluation of women's work, the institutional barriers women face, and women's socialization to sex-specific roles. Others are more pragmatic, such as the need for affordable and reliable child care, and the double burden of household and financial responsibilities. . . .

Programs that enhance women's employability have the potential for reducing future budget outlays. And social investments in the well-being of children may also reap long-term benefits.

There are other areas where government support is needed to further women's employment needs in the private sector. People should not be misled by anecdotal success stories into believing that equal employment opportunity goals have been achieved when statistical evidence demonstrates that such is not the case. Enforcement of Title VII should be strengthened, and more widespread use of affirmative action programs and comparable worth

"Anyone who has had his or her eyes open at all has noticed that women have opportunities today that were unheard of in our mothers' time."

Discrimination Is Exaggerated

Jennifer Roback

You may have seen a pin that says simply "59¢.". . . .

It is a pin distributed by the National Organization for Women (NOW), and according to a fundraising letter signed by NOW president Judy Goldsmith, it symbolizes "the plain, frightening fact . . . that most women are paid just over half as much as men for the very same work—to be exact, 59¢ for every $1 earned by a man." She continues, "Today, nothing better illustrates the economic plight of American women than NOW's 59¢ campaign button."

What Goldsmith is keying into is the much-discussed "earnings gap." It is an article of orthodox feminist faith that this earnings gap requires aggressive intervention by the government. The argument runs something like this: Earnings differences between men and women are evidence of discrimination in the free market. The earnings gap widened between 1955, when women's earnings averaged 64 percent of men's, and 1977, when women's earning level dropped to 59 percent. Therefore, it is concluded, discrimination against women has increased. Since this discrimination takes place in the free market, the government needs to intervene to protect women.

A Gap in the Earnings Gap

However, there is a large gap in this earnings-gap argument, as becomes clear if several key questions are considered. Is the earnings gap really due to discrimination? What other factors might account for the earnings gap? And, most important, is it even possible to distinguish discrimination from some of these other factors?

Surely the most striking change concerning women in the labor market since 1955 is that there are so

many more of us now than there were then. The labor force participation rate of women—the percentage of women who are working or seeking work—jumped from 31 percent to 52 percent from 1952 to 1982, which translates into nearly three times as many working women. This huge increase in the number of women working outside the home is important because increases in the supply of something are usually associated with decreases in its price. In this case, the supply of women workers increased in comparison with men, so it should not be surprising to find the wages of women falling in comparison to those of men between 1955 and 1977.

The Supply Increase

Suppose, though, that the labor market doesn't really work like the market for apples or houses, and therefore a supply increase could not cause that large a wage change. It's a fair enough question. But then consider a different example that can't possibly be explained by discrimination. The baby boom created a huge increase in the supply of young workers in comparison with the number of older workers in the late 1960s. Did the earnings of the baby-boom new workers fall in comparison with prime or middle-aged workers? The answer is a resounding yes. The earnings of young workers fell from 63 percent of the earnings of middle-aged workers in 1968 to 54 percent in 1974.

This supply increase actually caused a larger fall in earnings than the one that women have experienced. And the baby boomers' financial bust happened over a shorter period of time. In fact, some economists have been surprised that the earnings gap between men and women didn't widen even more than it did! Probably the reason is that not all the women entering the labor force went into "female" jobs. Many entered jobs and professions formerly closed to women, in which they compete primarily with men and not with other women.

Because they were not increasing the supply of female-job workers, the women who pioneered in the fields of banking, medicine, construction, and law did not lower the average wages of women.

Even so, a disproportionate number of women *did* enter traditionally female jobs such as clerical and service work. Clerical jobs actually account for a larger fraction of jobs held by women now than in 1960. The wages in these occupations have not kept pace with wages in other sectors of the economy, at least in part because of the flood of new women workers entering these fields for the first time. Since these are the jobs in which women are most heavily concentrated, it is not surprising that women's average wages have fallen in comparison with men's.

Less Experience

Another characteristic of the newly working woman is that she is likely to be an older person, either returning to work after child rearing or entering the labor market for the first time. This means that she very likely has limited experience in the job market. In fact, women have 10 to 15 years less labor force experience on average than do men of the same age. Naturally, the wages that inexperienced women can command will usually be lower than those of men or of other women who have worked longer or more continuously. So the average earnings of women have fallen in part because so many women are relatively inexperienced.

This is not to conclude that there is no discrimination against women. That would be silly. But it is equally silly to conclude that discrimination has increased since 1955 *because* the difference in earnings between men and women has increased over that time. There are many plausible explanations for that fact.

Greater Opportunities

Anyone who has had his or her eyes open at all has noticed that women have opportunities today that were unheard of in our mothers' time. Women who would have been afraid to risk the wrath of society and family are venturing into the workplace for the first time. Others of us are breaking into male-dominated fields and finding a degree of success and acceptance that astounds our mothers. (The percentage of lawyers and judges who are female jumped from 4 percent in 1972 to 15 percent in 1982. The percentage of physicians who are women increased from 10 to 15 percent in the same period. And the percentage of women on college and university faculties has risen from 22 to 37 percent just since 1967.) Still others of us are taking even greater risks and starting businesses of our own. We still have some distance to travel in the job market, but it is difficult to take seriously the idea that women face *more* discrimination today than they did

in the 1950s.

Of course, feminists usually don't come right out and claim that women are worse off economically today than they were 30 years ago. That would be too obviously absurd. So NOW president Judy Goldsmith, for example, talks in a fundraising letter of "the economic plight of American women" and urges the 59¢ button on women as "a symbol that vividly demonstrates the intolerable economic discrimination against the status of women in our society."

The insidious thing is that an argument is implied here rather than stated directly. If Goldsmith were to come right out and say, "The earnings gap is *totally* caused by discrimination," she would have to draw the absurd conclusion that women face more discrimination today than they did in the 1950s. More to the point, her readers might draw that conclusion themselves and then question her initial premise.

"Many of the factors that contribute to the earnings gap are the result of personal choices made by women themselves."

On the other hand, it would be an important concession if Goldsmith were to acknowledge that the earnings gap might be caused by something other than male or market malevolence. NOW's symbol, the 59¢ button, would lose some of its point. More importantly, though, the plain fact of the matter is that it is extraordinarily difficult to establish a linkage between discrimination and a difference in wages. The 59¢ logic side-steps that problem by placing the wage differential on the defensive. It presumes that an earnings difference is prima facie evidence of discrimination.

Personal Choices

Actually, many of the factors that contribute to the earnings gap are the result of personal choices made by women themselves, not decisions thrust on them by bosses. The most important example is marriage.

Married women often are unable to relocate to further their careers as much as they would like. Many married women drop out of the labor force to raise children. As a result of both of these factors, married women tend to choose occupations with easily transferable skills that do not deteriorate when unused. This is why many women traditionally have chosen elementary-school teaching more often than college teaching, nursing more often than doctoring, and humanities more often than technical subjects.

These differences between married women and single women (and between married women and men, for that matter) contribute dramatically to reducing the earnings of married women. Thus we find, in a comparison of the earnings of never-married women and those of never-married men, that the women's earnings in 1980 were 89 percent of men's. This figure has been essentially unchanged since the 1960 census. So if one is looking for a "culprit" for the earnings gap, it is far more plausible to pin the blame on *marital status* than on *gender*.

Some people might argue that these figures simply reflect the oppressiveness of marriage and the need for radical changes in this institution. There is some merit in this argument. Nevertheless, it is undeniable that many women do choose to get married. Perhaps a large number believe that the pleasures of intimate companionship and raising children are worth some financial sacrifice. We might wish that marriage did not require that women make this sacrifice, and we might work very hard to promote better options. But it is entirely unfair to blame employer discrimination for earnings differences that are essentially the result of choices made by individual women.

Moreover, while marriage may often mean a disadvantage in the job market, that has been changing for the better. Women are now less likely to drop out of the labor force to raise their children. More women are training themselves in technical fields. And in many households, the wife's career needs are determining the family's next move.

So why don't married women have higher relative earnings now? This is certainly a valid question. But these different lifestyles have become widespread only over the last 10 to 15 years. The earnings gap is based on aggregate data that include women ranging in age from 25 to 64 years, most of whom have not really been affected by these lifestyle changes. Among full-time workers 25 to 34 years old, women's earnings were 70 percent of men's in 1980.

The Gap Is Understandable

So there are a number of differences between men and women in the job market that may account for their earnings differences. Taken altogether, these very reasonable and understandable factors cannot, it is true, account for the entire earnings gap. But when the gap *is* corrected for these factors, it is not 59 percent but more like 66-87 percent, depending on the study.

It is often claimed that the difference that still remains after all the economic factors have been accounted for must be due to discrimination. That is, discrimination is measured as the residual, or leftover, difference, after all other factors have been taken into account. But this attempt to gauge discrimination is dubious.

The residual actually measures our ignorance. It includes everything that has not been directly measured but that influences a person's wage. The residual includes things as diverse as good luck and personality as well as discrimination. Common sense tells us that personality makes a huge difference to a person's career success. Ambition, aggressiveness, willingness to take risks, ability to get along with and motivate others, commitment to the job, willingness to assume responsibility—all of these factors contribute to higher wages. In fact, many career magazines for women advise their readers to develop exactly these traits. But none of these factors can be measured, and the residual earnings difference could just as easily be due to differences in these factors as well as to discrimination. The point is that we cannot distinguish discrimination from these other, unmeasurable factors.

Do we really know that women are on average so much less aggressive and less ambitious that their earnings would be 87 percent of men's? The answer is that we don't know and we can't know. We cannot rule it out as a possibility, though, because our ignorance of what does generate a person's earnings is so great.

Immeasurable Factors

Clearly, neither feminist fund raisers nor the average well-informed citizen knows this stunning fact: only 40 percent of the earnings of white men can be accounted for by measurable factors. That is, if we look at a population of white men, a full *60 percent* of the differences in earnings among them cannot be explained by anything we can measure. Conventional discrimination cannot possibly be an issue in this particular population. Yet the unexplained residual earnings difference within this group swamps the largest difference in male-female earnings that could possibly be due to discrimination.

"The presence of discrimination can be neither proven nor disproven with statistical tests."

This is why we cannot rule out the possibility that the entire earnings gap between men and women is due to real personal productivity differences that cannot be measured. The upshot is that the *presence of discrimination can be neither proven nor disproven with statistical tests.*

Despite these technical problems, which are well known among economists, statistical tests are often introduced as evidence in discrimination lawsuits. An unexplained earnings gap is usually accepted as evidence of discrimination. And if it is accepted as evidence, the plaintiff will almost always win. In effect, this means that there is a presumption of guilt rather than innocence on the part of the employer accused of sex bias. It is true that the earnings difference in a specific employer's work force could be due to the employer's discrimination. But it could instead be the result of something equally unmeasurable. Mere statistics are not enough to tell.

A few years ago, an economist named George Borjas wrote an article in which he examined the salaries at the Department of Health, Education and Welfare (HEW), now Health and Human Services. He subjected HEW's salaries to the same statistical procedure that HEW itself used to demonstrate that universities were discriminating in their employment practices. Lo and behold, he found that HEW discriminated at least as much and sometimes more than the institutions they were charged with regulating. Many people interpreted this study as an attack on HEW salary and promotions policies. Actually, the point was to attack the methodology that HEW used in its attempts to ferret out discrimination in academia. Unfortunately, these procedures are still widely used in court cases.

"Many of the problems that some women face today will best be solved by the individuals themselves and not by government action."

So the 59¢ button is not really a very good symbol of women's economic plight. It is much more a symbol of a flawed method of correcting some very real problems that exist for some women in the workplace. It is a symbol of the misuse of statistics, both to make a dramatic point in the arena of public opinion and to win in court. It is a symbol of the faith that much of the women's movement places in government intervention as a solution to women's problems.

Liberated Without the Law

Unfortunately for that faith, many women are liberating themselves without the help of the law. They are finding their own path through the maze of the world of work and devising their own way to balance all of their financial, personal, and emotional needs. And the movement's loss is the individual's gain; for many of the problems that some women face today will best be solved by the individuals themselves and not by government action.

Jennifer Roback is an economics professor at Yale University.

"If you can make money for the firm, nobody cares if you're black or female or anything else."

viewpoint **58**

Women Have Gained Widespread Acceptance in the Corporate World

Anne B. Fisher

Anyone who doubts that women have come far in corporate America over the past few years need only take a look at the telephone business. In 1973 AT&T settled a long dispute with the Equal Employment Opportunity Commission by agreeing to pay out tens of millions to employees who had been denied promotions and raises because they were female. The settlement was meant to make up for decades of embarrassingly well-documented male chauvinism. As recently as the early Seventies, the official AT&T policy was to promote college-educated women no further than group chief operator, the boss who supervised those ladies asking "Number please."

These days plenty of women have gone way beyond chief operator. A few are even running big chunks of the former empire. Northwestern Bell, a subsidiary of US West, named Janice Stoney, 46, chief executive officer in June [1987]. Peggy Milford, 41, has been head of Northwestern Bell's operations in South Dakota since November [1986]. In 1985 BellSouth, the largest of the post-divestiture operating companies, hired a General Electric manufacturing executive fittingly named Mylle Bell. In her first year Bell started BellSouth International, whose operations now reach to France, Hong Kong, Shanghai, India, Guatemala, and Venezuela. After two years as president of that subsidiary, Bell, 38, stepped up to head all corporate planning and development at BellSouth. "I've never really felt discriminated against," she muses. "Sometimes people do look at you kind of funny. But then, sometimes guys get funny looks too. The same things make women successful that make men successful. The main thing is the desire."

Even in some of the largest U.S. companies, women are rising higher and higher, a few to within striking range of the top job. So what did you expect? The more fascinating questions now are where have women done best, and why? They have flourished in fast-growing industries and in industries where change—deregulation, restructuring—has opened the way to advancement based on nothing more complicated than managerial ability. They have also forged ahead in businesses that used to hire lots of women for low-level jobs but then neglected to promote them.

Women hold roughly 35% of the 12.6 million executive, administrative, and management jobs in the U.S., says the Bureau of Labor Statistics, nearly double their share in 1972. Such figures can be misleading since companies can label whomever they please a "manager." Other studies are more revealing. A survey by the executive search firm Heidrick & Struggles found, for example, that [in 1986] 83% of the female officers in FORTUNE 500 and Service 500 companies held the title of vice president or better. In 1980 only 35% did. In 1980 only 11% of women officers made more than $90,000 a year. In 1986 nearly 60% earned that or more, and their average compensation had climbed to $117,000. . . .

"Cutting-Edge Industries"

To find the real locus of women's success, . . . look for two attributes in the businesses that employ them: growth or chaos. Women are advancing fastest in what Professor Eugene Jennings of Michigan State calls "cutting-edge industries," where the old rules don't apply, either because there was never time to establish them or because the game has changed radically. Jennings has been tracking the career paths of managers in hundreds of large U.S. companies for 30 years and has watched women managers since the mid-Seventies. He observes that in traditional, slow-growing fields such as steel, railroads, and mining, the rigidity of longstanding hierarchies serves to keep women down. In recent years, while many companies have found they can get by with fewer layers of management, General Motors has continued to lumber along with 18. His conclusion: "The psychological distance to the top is greater for anyone in the more traditional manufacturing company, and particularly for women, who often start out with one strike against them."

Many women have figured this out on their own: A 1986 study by the Equal Employment Opportunity Commission found that women at all ranks and salary levels are moving into high-growth businesses, including retailing and banking, in disproportionately large numbers. They are staying away from industries—tobacco, for example—where government growth projections and common sense suggest the glory days are over.

"The opportunities for women have been great. . . . When you're growing at 500% a year, you grab whoever walks in the door who can get the work done."

The best example of an industry where technological change and corporate restructuring have combined to shake up the old order is telecommunications. Marilyn Laurie, 48, an AT&T senior vice president in New York, believes women would have risen in the business even without the government's intervention 15 years ago. Says she: "When a company is rushing into the future as we have been, management uses talent, *any* available talent, much more eagerly."

High-tech companies have proven similarly receptive to female ability. One reason is that many such firms are too new to have fallen prey to sexist notions. "Companies that have formed since the women's movement began don't have so many old habits to get rid of," says Pam Saloky, 42, one of the highest-ranking female engineering managers at Digital Equipment Corp. Saloky oversees 400 technical and professional staffers in the office systems group. She points out that at Digital and other computer companies, managers typically are promoted from within, usually after having managed a factory or introduced at least one major new product. "The system works well for women, because politics are minimal and the criteria for success are so clear. You have to have produced something."

Sandra Gunn, 44, at Lotus Development Corp., is a case in point: She has started two divisions since her arrival at Lotus and managed the introduction of two new software products, Lotus Measure and Lotus Manuscript. "The opportunities for women have been great," she says. "When you're growing at 500% a year, you grab whoever walks in the door who can get the work done."

Women who have made it even higher in high tech agree. Just ask Phyllis Swerskyd, 36, executive vice president and chief financial officer at Artificial Intelligence Corp., a maker of sophisticated software for IBM mainframes. She was senior vice president of finance and administration at Cullinet, another software company. "Both as an employee and an employer, I've found that gender is irrelevant," she says. "Many computer companies don't even bother with affirmative action programs. The attitude is 'Let's just get the best talent. Period.'"

Gender Blind

At Apple Computer, the prototypical young high-tech company, 30% of managers are women, and 40% of professionals. "The number of women doing well here is one of the reason why I came," says Debi Coleman, 34. "Nobody around here cares which washroom you use." She was named a vice president at 32, ran Macintosh manufacturing, was promoted to head of production worldwide, and is now chief financial officer. Her advice to women—or men—who want to succeed in business: "Don't waste time and energy on trying to predict your future. Concentrate on inventing it."

Gender blindness is spreading rapidly in high tech beyond companies started in the Seventies. This is particularly true in jobs where the measure of successful performance is clear, as in sales. At Xerox, where the path to the top most often leads straight through sales and marketing, women occupy a steadily increasing number of district-sales-manager posts. Out of 14 district chiefs in the eastern U.S., five are female. Until June [1987] their boss was a woman too: Patricia Barron, 44, then vice president and regional manager. She has just been promoted to director of corporate information management for all of Xerox.

Women's rush into high-tech companies seems likely to accelerate. The American Association of Engineering Societies, a Washington, D.C., group that keeps an eye on the pool of future talent, says the number of engineering degrees earned by women has increased thirteenfold since 1975. They amounted to 11,264 [in 1986], or 14% of the total. In 1986 women earned nearly 20% of all degrees in computer science and systems engineering, up from virtually none a few years ago.

Wall Street

On Wall Street, as in high tech, dizzying change and take-no-prisoners competition have brought barriers crashing down. Until the mid-Seventies female investment bankers, not to mention female traders, were rare. Then came May Day. On May 1, 1975, the Securities and Exchange Commission put an end to fixed brokerage commissions, kicking off a decade of deregulation in the money business. For the first time, and to their consternation, investment banks found themselves competing for clients and struggling to invent new financial instruments and services. Booming markets and global expansion have seen some big investment banks double, even triple, in size. The result, as one high-ranking female Wall Streeter puts it: "If you can make money for the firm, nobody cares if you're black or female or anything else. You could be *blue*, and the only question anybody would ask is, 'How much business are you bringing in?'"

About one-quarter of all professionals in the Wall Street financial community today are women. Every major investment bank has at least one woman partner, and some boast several. [In 1987] Morgan Stanley belied its reputation as a determinedly stuffy old-line investment bank by naming three women to its top rank, managing director. In all, Morgan has 139 managing directors. Goldman Sachs, the largest U.S. securities firm still clinging to private ownership, now counts Jeanette Loeb, 34, among its 106 partners. In dollar terms, at least, women on Wall Street are arguably the most successful of all: Average pay for a two-year veteran in corporate finance now exceeds $100,000 a year, and 30-year-old MBAs making twice that much are ubiquitous.

Just as significant, if less spectacular, are the gains women have made in such fields as commercial banking, retailing, advertising, and publishing. All four have always hired lots of women. What is new is that they are promoting them too. The women in these industries finally decided that they would not settle for anything less.

"More and more women have finally become account executives, and hence have a shot at the top jobs in [advertising] agencies."

[Since 1977] the number of women in commercial bank management jobs has risen 68%, reports the American Bankers Association. Roughly half of all officers, managers, and professionals in the nation's 50 largest commercial banks now are female. The most important change, though, is in what they are doing. Throughout the Seventies and early Eighties, most female bankers were found in customer service and operations, not in commercial lending, traditionally the surest route to top management. About five years ago [1982] the proportion of women loan officers began to rise sharply. Many large banks' training programs in commercial lending are now about half-filled with women. "The fact that

women are infiltrating lending is really significant, because it means more women are in line for top-level jobs," says Barbara Mastro, 41, a division executive at the Bank of Boston. She broke into lending in 1974 and made it into senior management in 1985. "We are not oddities anymore.". . .

Retailing

Women are also rising in retailing. For decades, the most successful women in the business were buyers, those taste setters and trend spotters who gamble a season or two in advance on what department store shoppers will spend money on. The job demands talent, imagination, and strong nerves. It pays well, too; accomplished buyers for major chains often earn salaries in the six figures. But until recently they seldom, if ever, were promoted to top management. That is changing. A study by BAR Associates, a New York consulting firm that has done extensive research, shows that about 40% of managers in retailing today are women—more than double the percentage in 1975.

Judi Hofer of St. Louis, CEO of Famous Barr Inc., an 18-store, $500-million-a-year division of May Department Stores, says: "Being a buyer is a terrific job in a lot of ways. But women are moving up and out of it. You see a lot more senior vice presidents and divisional vice presidents around." Those more august titles, once reserved for men, are ranks above buyer—the buyers' bosses' bosses.

Hofer, 46, started at 15 as a part-time stock clerk at Meier & Frank, a department store in Portland, Oregon, and used her earnings to pay her way through college. May acquired the company in 1966. By 1981, Hofer had made her way from the stockroom, through the buyer's job, to the boardroom, becoming chief executive at age 39. "The really hard step for women in retailing now," she says, "is from senior vice president to president."

Hard, but not impossible: Allied Stores announced that Michele Fortune, 38, would become president and CEO of its Ann Taylor fashion chain. [In 1985] the Limited, one the the country's biggest and most profitable retailers, named Verna Gibson, now 45, as its president.

Advertising

In advertising agencies the professional equivalent of the department store buyer has long been the copywriter or art director. Both are creative types who may turn out memorable ads but are rarely encouraged to meet clients. For 60 years women have done well on the arty side of the business; in the 1920s they customarily set themselves apart from the secretarial staff by wearing chic hats in the office. Though statistics are unavailable, advertising people say that more and more women have finally become account executives, and hence have a shot at the top jobs in agencies, Says Rena Bartos, a senior vice president at J. Walter Thompson: "There used to be an impression that clients wouldn't want to deal with women. But now, so many of the clients *are* women."

At some agencies, exceptional growth has helped women advance. Shirley Young, 52, started out as a research assistant at Grey Advertising 28 years ago. She sat at a desk in a hallway. Today the agency is 35 times the size it was then, and Young occupies the president's chair at Grey Strategic Marketing, a subsidiary that devises selling strategies for Mars Inc., General Mills, and other clients. . . .

Chipping Away the Glass Ceiling

Ambitious women still face formidable resistance in many industries that have traditonally not welcomed them at any level. But they are chipping away at the so-called glass ceiling—the invisible barrier to female advancement to senior levels—in businesses where not so long ago there were no women at all.

"Women are even beginning to turn up in some of the last places you would expect to find them."

Accounting, for example. Until 1965 Arthur Andersen & Co., long the largest of the Big Eight firms, had not one female accountant among its thousands of professional staffers. That year Susan Butler was hired. Today, she is a senior partner in the firm. Andersen now has 44 other women partners out of a total of 2,125 partners; around 35% of all recruits are female.

That pattern is mirrored throughout the profession. Shirley Cheramy, 39, a Price Waterhouse partner in Los Angeles, has conducted her own survey of women accountants. In 1983 she found 69 women partners in the nine largest firms; by mid-1986, that number had more than doubled, to 151. Still, that is under 2% of all partners. "But things have changed a lot," says Cheramy. "Gradually we are being accepted. When I went to college, you could count the women accounting majors on the fingers of one hand." In 1987 women earned 49% of all accounting degrees. The American Institute of Certified Public Accountants also reports that over 40% of all new accountants hired by accounting firms were female. . . .

Unexpected Gains

Women are even beginning to turn up in some of the last places you would expect to find them. Automotive metal-casting plants, for instance. For its program designed to prepare gifted young engineers

for plant manager posts, Ford Motor Co. has accepted only 15 handpicked candidates since 1984. Of those, six have been women. Denise Graham is a 1985 metallurgical engineering graduate of Western Michigan University. She wrapped up two years of training in planning, manufacturing, and general management and started as a process engineer at Ford's casting plant in Cleveland, overseeing the molding of cylinder blocks for car engines. "I haven't run into any problems at all with the guys in the plant because of being a woman," she says. "But all of us, including the men in the program, have heard some cracks about our ages." Graham and her fellow fast-trackers are in their early 20s.

The smart money is betting that it's just a matter of time until women make it into the highest-ranking jobs. "It takes the average corporate achiever 25 years to reach the rank of president and 30 years to make chairman," says Michigan State's Jennings. "Women have been managers in significant numbers only since the mid-Seventies."

Carla Hills, a big-time lawyer and a former Secretary of Housing and Urban Development who is a director of five FORTUNE 500 companies, envisions the 1990s as "the decade of the female CEO." About fifteen years ago, she points out, there was much impatient squawking about how few law firms had women partners, even though large numbers of women were graduating from law school. "Now it would stun me to find a major law firm that does not have several female partners," she observes. "I believe we'll see the same steady progression in corporate America. The women who have come out of graduate business school in the past decade, and who are now in middle management, will reach the top jobs in the 1990s." The number of women earning graduate business degrees had ballooned by over 300% in the past decade, to 21,000 [in 1986]; meanwhile MBA degrees awarded to men have increased by about 25% to around 46,000.

When will women really have made it? Maybe when their advance in business is so widely taken for granted that it no longer merits a magazine article. Says Ellen Gordon, president since 1978 of Tootsie Roll Industries, the Chicago candy company: "I look forward to the day when we don't think in terms of a 'woman executive' at all, but just an executive." There is still quite a way to go, but that day is closer.

Free-lance writer Anne B. Fisher was formerly an associate editor at Fortune *magazine.*

"The board room is still overwhelmingly dominated by three-piece, pinstriped suits, locker room camaraderie, and an effective good old boy system."

viewpoint **59**

Women Are Still Behind in the Corporate World

Diane Jennings

Editor's note: Diane Jennings interviewed several successful women entrepreneurs. This viewpoint includes comments from Mary Kay Ash of Mary Kay Cosmetics, Debbi Fields of Mrs. Fields' Cookies, Diane Seelye Johnson of Central Pipe and Supply (an oil supply company), Lillian Katz of Lillian Vernon Corporation (a mail-order shopping business), Kay Koplovitz of USA Network (a cable television company), Sandra Kurtzig of ASK Computer Systems, Faith Popcorn of BrainReserve (a consulting business), and Louise Vigoda, a real estate developer.

When a potential buyer researches information on ASK Computer Systems Inc. in the business pages of their local newspaper, "It doesn't say next to it, 'F' for female or 'M' for male," founder and chairman Sandra Kurtzig points out. "They buy our stock based on earnings per share and whether or not we're going to grow."

That's why she took ASK public in 1981, Kurtzig says. "That was one of the reasons—to be judged. That's the ultimate report card on equality."

ASK was nine years old when Kurtzig decided to go public. The business that had begun in the spare bedroom of her California apartment, as a way for the young mother to earn a little extra money and keep busy while her children slept, had grown to amazing proportions. Kurtzig's initial $2,000 investment started a company that, by developing and selling computer software to businesses, had earnings of $1.5 million on sales of $13 million by 1981.

Despite the company's impressive track record, Kurtzig wanted to put ASK to the ultimate test: the open market. The necessary paperwork was drawn up, and an elaborate slide show and presentation was prepared to showcase the offering. Kurtzig was

preparing to leave for Europe to drum up interest through a whirlwind tour of financial capitals when the company's investment banker pulled her aside.

Long, Red Fingernails

The conservative financial executive quietly guided Kurtzig to a private office and closed the door for a one-on-one conversation. He repeated what he'd already said several times: "No one has seen a woman CEO of a high-tech company before. You're a novelty. Half of them are going to show up to see the freak show to begin with."

Kurtzig, accustomed by now to this litany, waited for the unknown bombshell her advisor seemed about to drop.

"It's certainly not going to help," he said finally, "to have those long red fingernails." He solemnly advised her to cut them short and paint them a pale color, which she did.

"I was very surprised," Kurtzig remembers. "I was worrying about the profits the next quarter."

Though she tells the story with a laugh, the debate over Kurtzig's fingernail color and length highlights a very real issue. Like it or not—and most successful entrepreneurial women don't—gender is still a factor in the business world, even when the business is your own. The freedom of working for yourself, and not having to answer to anyone else, is often cited by many people as a prime reason to become an entrepreneur, but a great part of the success of entrepreneurism is an ability to deal with others. They must sell not only their product, but themselves as well. Despite the burgeoning female work force, for some businesspeople, dealing with a woman in a professional capacity is still an awkward encounter. These entrepreneurial women have learned how to make colleagues and coworkers feel more at ease, to cope, undisturbed by the gender factor.

Ideally of course, gender would not be an issue.

Both sexes would be considered not alike, but equally competent, an acknowledgment of the different strengths both men and women bring to the businessworld.

"I don't think of myself as a woman or a man," says Kay Koplovitz. "In business situations, I'm just there like they are. I earned my stripes."

"I have a terrible problem with these interviews," says Lillian Katz. "I would prefer to be interviewed as an entrepreneur, rather than a 'lady' entrepreneur. I find that should be in the past. For me it is."

But for others, Katz admits, it is not.

According to government statistics, in 1950, less than 30 percent of the labor force consisted of women; by 1982, women accounted for 43 percent. More importantly, since the 1960s, women have represented the major share of labor force growth, and in the 1980s women are projected to account for seven out of ten additions to the work force.

Appallingly Few at the Top

As more and more women enter the labor market, they have ceased to be a rarity in business, but while the number of women in the labor force as a whole is large, the number of women at the executive level is still appallingly small. Of the Fortune 500 companies, the 500 largest industrial companies in the U.S., only one woman executive, Katharine Graham of *The Washington Post*, made the 1986 list. (She initially inherited the position through family control of the company.) Later that year, another woman, Linda Wachner, did take over a Fortune 500-sized company, an apparel business called Warneco, bringing the number to two.

It may be trendy to pay lip service to the idea of executive women, but despite the ever increasing number of women in business, only 2 percent of the top executive ranks are occupied by women. In absolute numbers, that translates to twenty-nine women out of 1,362 respondents, according to the Korn/Ferry study.

In short, the board room is still overwhelmingly dominated by three-piece, pinstriped suits, locker room camaraderie, and an effective good old boy system. For many women the board room remains an exclusive club, one they probably won't be invited to join. The outlook for future female executives is not particularly encouraging either. Though a decade ago less than 10 percent of business graduate school degrees were awarded to women, and today's classes boast an enrollment of approximately 30 percent women, there are indications that despite the increased presence of more qualified women, they aren't necessarily taking significant posts in the corporate world. Those women of a decade ago have not climbed the corporate career ladder as successfully as their male counterparts, and in some cases are jumping off the

ladder completely. While it is true that the first class of women MBAs graduated in 1976, and are just now reaching their mid-thirties, and the Korn/Ferry profile says today's typical senior executive is fifty-one years old, a survey conducted by *Fortune* magazine reveals a surprising trend. According to the survey of MBA graduates from the class of 1976, 30 percent of 1,039 women were self-employed or unemployed. But only 21 percent of the 4,255 men surveyed were in the same circumstances.

Evading the Climb

The feminine trend away from the corporate climb is attributable to several factors.

Some women leave the corporate world because they grow impatient with the lengthy climb it takes to get to the top of an established entity, and/or their inability to break the "glass ceiling." Some are leaving not only the corporate world, but dropping out of the work force completely, in favor of staying home and raising their children, finding the struggle of being both a professional and a parent more than they want to handle. The harsh reality of the effort it takes to succeed in the business world and juggle domestic responsibilities simultaneously has left some women disillusioned. "Right now it's a fight," says Mary Kay Ash. "And I think that's why they're going home. It's a tough, every-minute-of-the-day fight." Still others are choosing to start businesses at home in an effort to have at least part of both worlds.

"Despite the increased presence of more qualified women, they aren't necessarily taking significant posts in the corporate world."

The sparsity of women in the established corporate executive suite comes as no surprise to Faith Popcorn. "It's no accident that there's no Fortune 500 company other than Kay Graham, with a female chairman," notes Popcorn. "People say, 'Well the business people [women] haven't come up yet.' That's not true. In the early '70s they all graduated and we're still waiting. It's not happening. Somebody had to be good enough."

Popcorn, whose reputation for predicting trends based on cultural currents is well known, says she foresaw the present trend toward women bailing out of the corporate work force several years ago.

Male Dominance

The businesswomen of the '70s were good enough to climb the corporate ladder, Popcorn theorizes, but today "nobody wants them," particularly the executive men who have dominated the business world for centuries.

"Why should they?" she asks. "People that usually have the power base don't hand it over to be nice. They're comfortable with other men. It's much more comfortable to stay the way they are than to change."

The business world, Popcorn adds, didn't really need women. "It seemed to be rolling along," she says, smiling. But women decided they were tired of being relegated to low quality jobs, and "they weren't going to put up with it anymore. So then they said, 'I can do this.' Of course they can . . . I think men would have been much smarter to make women more proud and equal of their home jobs."

Whether men could have averted the trend to women working outside the home or not is, of course, a moot point. Women have obviously joined the work force for good, and men must accept and adjust to them as equals in the business world. Change in that direction is occurring, but the pace is sometimes agonizingly slow. According to *Inside Corporate America* by Allan Cox, 85 percent of top executives say their companies are eager to promote women to middle management positions, but only 68 percent support moving women into top executive spots. Many men it seems, are willing to work *with* women, but are less than thrilled at the idea of working *for* them. According to the Heidrick & Struggles survey, that continuing discomfort of management with women in executive positions is considered to be the primary reason women go into business for themselves.

Louise Vigoda, who deals with men more often than women in her business as a real estate developer, agrees that the historically empowered are not particularly eager to turn their power base over to newcomers. "Men had a damn good thing going," she notes. "Why should they [want to deal with women] more than they want any other immigrants? Why should they? They've got to deal with competition for their jobs. They've got to deal with strange creatures. They didn't grow up in the locker room with them." . . .

Men and Competition

Though women business owners are obviously more noticeable in a male dominated field, many women say their male coworkers don't seem particularly concerned by their presence. Many men unwittingly give women colleagues an advantage by failing to treat them like competititon. Instead, they note, men often were surprisingly helpful on the way up, partially because they don't feel the same keen sense of competition with women that they do with other men. Kurtzig jokes that being a woman helped her get ASK started because "men always felt like they had to pay for lunch. It helped expenses." Most men are brought up that way, to pick up the check, to open doors, pull out chairs, carry heavy

items, and generally be helpful to the feminine sex. That tendency becomes second nature to them and they may extend it unthinkingly to the business arena. Aiding another man on the other hand, a traditional rival, goes directly against such traditional upbringing, and chances are they would rarely make that mistake. That urge to be helpful to women occasionally blinds male executives to legitimate competition from females, offering women the advantageous element of surprise.

"Men don't think women are a real threat," says Kurtzig. "They're 'inferior.' They can't succeed. They think you're cute and harmless. They don't have to pat you on the head, but deep down they don't see you as real competition. Their real competition is that other male. So men are apt to help you more because, if you're successful, that doesn't take away from their ego."

"Men don't think women are a real threat. . . . They think you're cute and harmless."

Not only do some men not recognize women as competition, they often don't take them seriously at all. Some men, usually those who still think of women as strictly wives and mothers, also make the mistake of assuming the woman behind the business is merely a figurehead, a front for the company being run by her husband. Though Diane Seelye Johnson and her husband started Central Pipe & Supply together, people often assumed her role was as an employee of her spouse. After ten years in business they no longer ask how she likes working for her husband, Johnson notes, but neither do they ever assume the business is hers. Debbi Fields says she no longer expends energy trying to pierce the myth that the company that grew from one store in 1977 to 350 ten years later, and a multi-million dollar volume, was anybody's brainchild but her own. Even company advisors, who know Debbi is the president in action as well as title, sometimes fail to take her seriously. "To this day I have $3 million in life insurance, and she has $250,000," points out Randy Fields.

Many men realize these women run successful businesses, but they often adopt the attitude, particularly if the woman is married, that the business is merely a hobby, and any financial matter is of only passing interest to a woman. Once again the traditional upbringing that pegs men as breadwinners, and women as helpmates, hampers the ability of men to relate to businesswomen. Often the misperception is unintentional, and men are mystified at women's annoyance over it, but no matter how well intended, the attitude still poses problems to women in business for themselves.

When Johnson and her husband both separately purchased stock in a company as an investment several years ago, she was irritated to find he received notices of annual meetings, but she didn't. When she complained to the man in charge he suggested that her notices must have gotten lost in the mail. She insisted they hadn't, until he finally admitted it was assumed she would share her husband's mail, and she had not been sent the material. His wife, he added pointedly, loved the pedestal she was on.

"Well," replied an annoyed Johnson, "the only things that I ever see on pedestals are inanimate objects—and half of them are covered with bird droppings."

"The henpecking order . . . used to be more crudely expressed in 'Thank God I'm a white man.' It means that no matter what a jerk you are, what an idiot you are, you're better."

Vigoda has also noticed the tendency of male business colleagues to take her less than seriously. She went into business in the '60s, when women were still rare in the corporate world. "Men really thought it was cute," she says. "That was my sense of it. They thought it was cute or sociologically hip. It was an attitude more than anything. Very few people are gauche enough to say 'You're cute.'"

Once a successful real estate agent did drop by Vigoda's office to talk about her venture into business. "He happened to be on his fourth wife," Vigoda says. "He wanted to talk to me about what I was doing because he thought it was 'really neat' and his present wife 'needs something to do.' I can't tell you how offended I was. It was like he was going to buy her a knitting machine or give her a week at the Golden Door. I didn't know how to answer that."

Husbands' Attitudes

Even those close to these women, not just colleagues, are occasionally guilty of failing to take their plans seriously. When Johnson announced that she was bored after years as a housewife, her husband suggested she go bowling with friends. When she said she planned to go back to school, he applauded the idea—of taking a course or two. Randy Fields admits that while he encouraged Debbi, he didn't really expect her cookie business to succeed—and neither did their banker who extended the loan. "He even said to Randy, 'This will be a

great experience for Debbi, from a ''learning perspective,''''' Debbie remembers.

Thankfully, there are some signs, however slow or slight, that gender is becoming less of a factor in the businessworld. The attitudes of men change, with age and experience. "If the man you are talking to is forty-five or over, then he adopts the attitude of 'Oh hi, you sweet little thing,'" notes Ash. "'Honey, darling, sweetheart.' Kind of a condescending attitude toward women. Now fortunately, the younger men are being brought up with women sitting beside them in school . . . If you're talking to a younger man, under forty-five, as a general rule he will have a much better idea, respect for women, than his [older] counterpart."

Louise Vigoda's experience has been somewhat different. Whether due to the fact that top spots are held by older men or because business veterans are more experienced, Vigoda says, while she was often underestimated and not considered a threat in the beginning, many older men take her seriously as she rises in the business world. "The higher you go, the harder it is, because you are no longer 'cute.' You really are a direct threat," Vigoda notes.

The Henpecking Order

"It is very difficult to be sitting across the table from someone, who probably will not make in a lifetime of salaried employment as much as you make in a year or two, look at you and not resent it," Vigoda says. "There's still the henpecking order. They've grown up with men and they expect there will always be some man who's a top dog. They don't expect it of women. When they see a woman sitting across the table from them, there is a lot of power playing that goes on. They may not make as much money as you, they may not be as successful as you, but they are going to try to show you that they are better than you are. It's the henpecking order. It used to be more crudely expressed in 'Thank God I'm a white man.' It means that no matter what a jerk you are, what an idiot you are, you're better. . . ."

Vigoda and other successful entrepreneurial women long for the day when gender will not be a factor, when their male colleagues won't feel threatened or feel the need to be condescending. They look forward to the time they won't attract attention because they are a minority, when they won't be identified as the "first this," or "the only that." They hope eventually no one will sit up and take notice because of their presence in the board room, preferably because they will have feminine company.

Author Diane Jennings writes for the Dallas Morning News. *She has also worked for* Women's Wear Daily.

Women and Men Should Use a Similar Management Style

Charlene Mitchell and Thomas Burdick

"Why can't a woman be more like a man?"

When a baffled and desperate Henry Higgins posed this question in *My Fair Lady*, women were quite different from men. A woman's place was in the home; and a man's role was to provide for her. While a woman may have been worldly-wise, she was also wise enough not to let it show. But that was in another century and, in many respects, another world. It is now the end of the twentieth century. For the first time, women are working side by side with men, competing with them for promotions, and casting an eye toward the same top management spots.

We believe that as women's roles in the world have changed, there has also been an inevitable and inexorable movement toward shared values, beliefs, and thoughts on the part of the men and women in business. With the merging of male and female roles, a latter day Henry Higgins would be incorrect to think that today's businesswoman is so very different from her male counterpart.

Leaving Feminine Traits at Home

A recent study has shown that successful women in business are quite similar to successful men. They share many of the same characteristics, and are more alike than they are different. Ellen Fagenson, a researcher at the State University of New York, studied 260 businesswomen from different levels. Her results show that the women who are rising fastest in corporate America simply are not bringing traditional "feminine" traits and values to their positions.

Instead, these successful women (22 percent of them high-level managers, and 35 percent of them middle-level managers) "exhibit attitudes traditionally assigned to men regarding their

careers." Even more to the point, women who have remained at lower levels are more "feminine"—more committed to family and home.

The number of women entering the ranks of business has grown tremendously in the last decade. Consider that in 1973, women were outnumbered twelve to one in the entering class of the Harvard Business School. At that time, a woman at any level in management was unusual. In 1985, however, 30 percent of the Harvard Business School's entering class were women. Clearly, the business environment is changing, and so is the potential for women in business.

Tough Women Managers

In the past, the founder of a family-owned company would hope for a son to someday assume control of the business. But today, the heir apparent may just as easily be a woman. One of the most famous and surprising examples of this was Hugh Hefner's decision to make his daughter president of the *Playboy* empire. If there was ever a man you would expect to dismiss the idea of a woman running a major corporation, you would think it would be Hefner. And yet, the ultimate chauvinist had no reservations about grooming his daughter to take control of a multi-million-dollar conglomerate.

Politics aside, can anyone conclude that Margaret Thatcher is not every bit as savvy and astute as the men in her government? In fact, she is called the "Iron Lady," a term used as a compliment to her political and intellectual strength. Or consider Thatcher's apparent antithesis, Mary Kay, the frothy founder of the cosmetics company of the same name. She has the strategic insights, toughness, and managerial skills to match any of the top auto executives in Detroit. (Maybe more, considering that her company has never operated in the red.) Look beyond the pink Cadillacs and the diamond tiaras and you find a highly profitable and professional organization with an immediately identifiable culture. Mary Kay understood the value to corporate growth of a strong "corporate culture" years before Peters and Waterman even thought of writing *In Search of Excellence.*

It's Time To Get Down to Business

Perhaps one of the most important factors to the success of women in business lies in the understanding that both men and women encounter problems in their careers. In many respects, women face the same work-related problems that men do. Yet, if you peruse many of the magazines and books designed to help women in their careers, you realize as we did that they treat women as if they are completely different from men. Most guides are filled with endless stories of women having difficulty of one type or another in business, but they never make the point that men have many of the same problems. From these readings you receive the erroneous impression that only women are naive, only women make mistakes, and only women are confused by the mechanisms of the business world.

This advice, rather than encourage, often only discourages women. The subtle message is that their male counterparts, unencumbered by their innate inexperience, naiveté, and ignorance, are scrambling easily up the proverbial corporate ladder. While they, burdened by problems, assumptions, and thoughts that are particular only to women, are doomed to failure.

Biology Is Not Destiny

The biggest impediment to your career is the belief that you are different from your male colleagues, or that you are somehow disadvantaged. This type of thinking is not only a hindrance, but it is incorrect. Men are just as naive, just as confused, and encounter basically the same problems in business that women do.

"The biggest impediment to your career is the belief that you are different from your male colleagues, or that you are somehow disadvantaged."

We are not saying that there are no barriers to the advancement of women in business. They exist and will continue to for some time. But most of these real impediments are in the upper levels. You should realize that while some of the rules of business may be stacked against you, these obstacles are offset by definite, positive advantages in the corporate "struggle." Women professionals are in great demand in virtually every industry today, and they carry high visibility within their organizations. Consider that women graduates of the Harvard Business School Class of 1984 received an average of five offers in their chosen career area, compared to three for the men. This is just one of many positive effects resulting from changes in societal and governmental attitudes toward women since the 1960s.

There *are* differences between men and women. But a woman's destiny is more the result of environment, upbringing, and education than her "biology." And the hard, competitive business environment is tough on both sexes. You should realize that a supposedly astute businessman can be misunderstood by his boss just as easily as a woman can. Or that his position can be undermined by a personality conflict with his secretary. . . .

While some may call our insights cynical, we prefer to call them realistic. The business world is a hard place, and its rules for survival and success are demanding. Those who think otherwise should reconsider. But many opportunities exist, and great rewards await you if you master the game.

A Better Chance than Ever Before

As a woman in business today, you have a better chance of getting ahead than ever before. Some barriers still exist but they are constantly being eroded. And while most successful women today are at the middle-management level, they are moving upward rapidly. Each woman who secures a higher management position will, to paraphrase Neil Armstrong, have made "one small step for woman, one giant leap for womankind.". . .

There are probably more myths, preconceptions, and misunderstandings about business and how it works than about any other kind of career, with the possible exception of medicine. We live in an era when business in general, and management in particular, is glorified. The corporate world has taken on an almost mythical facade—where fortunes are made and superstars wage power battles on a larger-than-life scale. While this translates well into movies and fiction, the reality, with occasional notable exceptions, is not nearly as exciting or as grand. . . .

In previous generations, businessmen and women often stayed with one company throughout an entire career. But it is a fact of contemporary corporate life that most people entering business in the last decade or so will change companies at least several times. While many will attribute their job changes to a better title, a bigger salary, or more responsibility, often the real reason is that they are still searching for that Holy Grail, the perfect job.

Many fall victim to this perfect job myth. Others may envelop themselves in their career, hoping naively that extra long work and company loyalty will be rewarded. For others, "mentor" has replaced the knight in shining armor of yesteryear, and networking—the modern day version of the "coffee klatch"—is thought to offer up the key to rapid advancement. . . .

Myth: Networking is a valued success strategy for women.

Networking is a popular success theory based on the "old boy network," an age-old strategy for men.

Networking is supposed to assist participants in acquiring jobs at other companies, provide useful tips and strategies for succeeding, and serve as the basis for functional power and political alliances.

Networks for women are theoretically composed of individuals in different levels of organizations. These women are united by a common bond of being female in business. They meet in some regular fashion to share their experiences and to lend a helping hand to their fellow "networkers."

The Reality

If the "old boy network" works, why doesn't the "old girl network"?

There is a basic element missing from the embryonic old girl network that is intrinsic to the all-male alliance. The men's network has the advantage of power at the top of organizations.

• Contact with senior level people, whether personally or as part of an organization, is a great asset in business. For a network to be successful it must have such people, not just to provide access to specific jobs, but to offer meaningful direction and insight. Most women's networks suffer from a paucity of top echelon women. The result is a group of mostly low level women who are in no position to help someone else get ahead.

• Many networks are havens for women who are insecure about themselves and their jobs, and want the security of a group. Women in these groups end up exchanging emotional support with women who are in identical predicaments. While there is nothing wrong with this, it hardly serves as a positive tool for the ambitious professional.

• Networks are touted as opportunities to get "a foot in the door" of another company. Some middle-management women even cite instances of young networking acquaintances demanding that they set up a job interview for them. No woman executive who meets you on such a casual basis is going to put her credibility on the line by recommending you. There are faster and more reliable ways to secure an interview with a company.

Rarely will these groups result in any real positive advancement for your career. If you wish to join one, you must see the women's network as an innocuous social activity. . . .

Threatened by Other Women

Myth: Women and bonding.

As the "new kids on the block" in the business world, women know they are a minority and that many barriers against their advancement still exist. For that reason, women within the same company will bond together to overcome these obstacles. They will empathize with each other, and help each other.

The Reality

If only wishing would make it true! Often, exactly the opposite occurs. Rather than see each other as allies, many women view other women in their organization as a greater threat to their careers than their male colleagues.

• As surprising at it may seem, there is generally little "bonding" among minorities at a company. Many minority members are convinced that there are a limited number of spots in the organization that are really available to them. They may believe, for example, that for every ten existing middle-manager positions, only two or three will be filled by minorities. As a result, there is a perception of greater competition with other minority members in the organization than with mainstream white males, who represent the preponderance of professionals in the management ranks of American industry.

• Many minority members enjoy their unique status in the white, male-dominated business establishment. They often, justifiably, see their uniqueness as accelerating their upward mobility. Some will feel threatened by another minority of the same group who will dilute that visibility.

"Many networks are havens for women who are insecure about themselves and their jobs, and want the security of a group."

Two women at the same level in an organization are more likely to view one another as direct competitors than to see each other as allies in the "grand feminist struggle." Experience with other minority groups in business seems to uphold this somewhat pessimistic point. On the other hand, it should not be so surprising that such a situation occurs. After all, it is merely human nature to enjoy the spotlight and the attention of others. And it is only natural that one would not wish to lose that visibility. Even brothers and sisters in the same family vie with one another for attention of their parents. Why should we expect that women in business are any different from the rest of humanity?

Myth: Women will humanize business.

Business is often guilty of less than altruistic behavior. Companies may be aloof and sometimes callous to employees, bosses may usurp credit for subordinates' work, and colleagues may engage in vicious back-stabbing. But this will abate with the influx of women into the business world.

With their innate nurturing and caring qualities,

women will "humanize" business as they ascend the corporate hierarchy. They will discard the existing negative male characteristics. Rather than be changed by the business world, women will change it.

The Reality

Even if one lends credence to the so-called natural differences between the sexes, it takes a rather significant leap in logic to assume that women will change the nature of business. And mounting evidence appears to contradict the theory.

• One problem with this idea is that it ignores the rite of passage to the top of a business organization. Since men are still in positions of power, the women who will be successful are those who are able to assimilate that culture. In other words, those women who can closely match the characteristics of those in power. In order to survive and flourish, women must adapt to the pre-existing business world.

• Many of the so-called traditional values of women have been thrust upon them by society. There is simply no precedence to predict what will happen when they are left to choose their own values.

These so-called "nurturing traits" are not being exhibited by successful female managers. A recent study found that women who are progressing in corporate America are not bringing these presumed feminine traits to their positions. Instead, they are exhibiting those attitudes normally attributed to men.

Seeking a Powerful Guide

Myth: Mentoring plays a key role in women's business success.

The mentor myth espouses the idea that women in business need a mentor to succeed in the business world. A mentor is defined as someone with power at least a few levels above the protégé who serves as a "guide" through the complexities of the organization.

The idea is derived from the fact that some men in the businessworld have been helped immensely by mentors. Utilizing the old adage that "what is good for the goose is good for the gander," many books and business articles today tout the positive effects of seeking and cultivating a mentor.

The Reality

There are success stories of younger men who have been mentored by older, more powerful men. But this is not as common an occurrence as is portrayed. More to the point, it doesn't always work, even for men. In reality, mentoring is a double-edged sword.

• A study conducted by the National Science Foundation determined that of 3,000 mentor-protégé pairs, only 34 lasted three years or more without a fight terminating the relationship. Further, more than 1,200, or 40 percent, of the protégés reported being fired by their mentors.

• One pitfall is choosing the wrong person to cultivate as your guide. For a mentor to be of real value, he or she should be fairly high up in management. But it is difficult to access the politics in an organization more than a level or two above your own. You may very easily, through lack of knowledge, select a mentor who is on the way out. And with the mentor's departure, you could find yourself on the losing side of a political conflict.

• Resentment from others is another serious drawback. No one will be thrilled with the idea that you have a powerful mentor. Your colleagues will be jealous, and your boss will be antagonized. And they would all enjoy seeing you knocked down from your protected position.

"Many of the so-called traditional values of women have been thrust upon them by society."

• For women, the situation is fraught with even greater drawbacks. A professional woman can rarely enter into a mentor relationship with a man (and let's face it, most mentors will be male given the scarcity of women in positions of power) without inciting innuendo. At a minimum, you will be the focus of damaging speculative gossip.

• For some, the mentoring relationship does drift toward a sexual relationship. Attribute it up to the natural attraction of the sexes, or to the stimulating effects of power (his) and dependency (yours). As Henry Kissinger once noted, "Power is the greatest aphrodisiac." If you go along with this tendency, you are playing with dynamite; if you resist it, you risk destroying your relationship in short order.

A Doomed Ploy

A final irony is that many lose sight of the proverbial "forest for the trees." Some women get so caught up in looking for an easy way of succeeding (via mentoring) that they lose track of more important success strategies. Others, when they fail to find or keep that powerful ally on whom they have pinned their career hopes, feel doomed to failure.

Writer Charlene Mitchell has been a manager at Proctor & Gamble and Nabisco. Thomas Burdick is a management consultant and was formerly the editor and publisher of the Harvard Business School newspaper.

Women Should Use a Uniquely Feminine Management Style

Marilyn Loden

The concept of feminine leadership has begun to take shape slowly during the past few years. It is an idea born of the experiences of hundreds of thousands of women who today labor in previously all-male management ranks in the real world of competitive, everyday business. It is a notion based on both their successes and their frustrations, not on some ivory tower academic theory.

While the exact parameters of this different style of leadership are still evolving, the evidence is already overwhelming that it exists and can make a much needed contribution to business and society in general. But before its potential can be maximized, it must first be acknowledged and endorsed by American corporations.

A Valid Generalization

The qualities that define feminine leadership are by no means characteristics limited exclusively to women. These traits can certainly be found among men as well. It is also true that there are individual women who are more comfortable with a predominantly masculine style of leadership, just as there are individual men who find a feminine approach more natural. But the key distinction is that as a class, women exhibit these particular leadership attributes to a far greater degree than do men. The fact that feminine leadership is a generalization, and may not apply to each individual, in no way makes it less valid, relevant, or meaningful.

In discussing the roots of feminine leadership, some people have begun to raise the issue of whether this unique management style is a result of innate differences between men and women or simply a function of socialization. While this is certainly an intriguing question, it is essentially a

moot point. Regardless of its origins, this different leadership style is today much more heavily concentrated among women as a group than among men. Therefore, the descriptor "feminine" seems entirely appropriate.

Over the longer term, some of the current distinctions between masculine and feminine leadership may begin to blur as both sexes benefit from exposure to the other's style of management. However, it seems unlikely that basic differences between men and women managers will ever completely disappear. It is difficult to accept the notion of one "visionary" who said recently, "In fifty years, I can see a situation where there will be no differences between men and women as classes within organizations. There will be lots of differences, but they will be individual differences."

On the contrary, just as gender differences persist in virtually every other aspect of life, it seems very likely that a distinctive feminine management style will also persist. And this will be to everyone's benefit because the feminine style of leadership is not a replacement for the traditional style. Both styles have their own strengths that can contribute to the overall success of organizations. Taken together, they represent a holistic approach to management—capable of taking full advantage of the entire spectrum of human talents.

A Complement to Male Style

By viewing feminine leadership as an effective complement to the traditional style of management favored more by men, one begins to see also how women's different style and perspectives can enhance managerial effectiveness and help organizations and our nation prosper and grow. After all, would society really be better off if a female manager behaved in exactly the same manner as her male counterparts? Or if a female justice brought exactly the same perspectives to the courtroom as her male colleagues? Or a female vice-presidential candidate campaigned with exactly the same vision as her masculine opponent? Once business and society become more familiar with the benefits of feminine leadership, I believe the answers to these questions will become more self-evident. But before this can happen, there must be a basic increase in awareness of feminine leadership as an alternate style of management.

In my own case, an awareness of this feminine leadership style began to develop in 1974 while I was working as an internal organization development consultant for the Bell Telephone System. Early that year, I was asked to create and manage an executive development program titled the Male-Female Awareness Workshop. This program was designed to heighten awareness of sexism in the workplace and to aid in the integration of women into management and other nontraditional jobs. To my knowledge, the program was the first of its kind and, to this day, it remains the most ambitious effort of this sort ever undertaken.

"Instead of humanizing the work environment, . . . the majority of successful women had become clones of the traditional male executive."

For seven years, until the fall of 1981, the program attracted participants from across the nation. In time, it was opened up to participants from other corporations. Throughout those years, I had the opportunity to discuss firsthand the pressing issues that changing roles and relationships among men and women were creating within organizations. In all, I spoke with more than 4,000 managers who passed through the program. Split equally between both sexes, this group spanned all ages and races and came from every geographic region of the country. As a result of my discussions, I became acutely aware of the tremendous frustrations women managers were encountering as they tried to find their way and their place in male-dominated institutions. I also began to see an incongruity developing between the advice that was being offered to them and the actual problems they faced. It seemed to me that these solutions understated the complexity of the problems women faced and largely ignored the added value they brought to the managerial function.

During the summer of 1981, after leaving the Bell System to establish my own practice as a management consultant, I resolved to look closely at this developing issue in order to understand it more fully. What was preventing many competent women from succeeding within middle and upper management? Why were so few reaching senior levels in organizations? Why were so many frustrated in their jobs? As I reflected on my experiences working with women managers at all levels and the progress that affirmative action policies had brought for working women in the seventies, it seemed to me that efforts to promote equal opportunity had too often yielded bittersweet results.

Pin-Striped Clones

While there were certainly more women executives than ever before, their impact on the way organizations functioned seemed to be minimal at best. Instead of humanizing the work environment, as many analysts of the late sixties had predicted they would do when their numbers increased, the majority of successful women had become clones of the traditional male executive. Right down to their pin-stripe suits and bow ties, these women were intent on competing with men and succeeding by beating them at their own game. But although this strategy was popular among many highly successful women in organizations, another consciousness was developing among some women managers that was quite different. This consciousness gave me my first real insight into the feminine leadership style they favored.

In discussions with women executives at management development seminars and conferences across the country, it seemed that many were beginning to question the assumptions being made in organizations about how they should operate. Most of these questions were being asked by women who were still forging their careers and shaping their personal style of management. While they had difficulty describing what their preferred style would be, they had no trouble identifying their discomfort with the traditional managerial roles they were expected to play in order to succeed. What's more, they understood that these traditional roles prevented them from using their full range of abilities and forced them to behave in ways that limited their effectiveness as leaders.

After hearing them express concern about "losing their identities," "diminishing their competence," and "becoming male clones," a clear picture of the dilemma these women were facing began to emerge. It seemed to me that their concern was related to the model of effective management they were expected to follow. This model assumed that there was one "right" way to manage based largely on the behavior of those who had managed successfully in the past. In short, it represented the traditional approach to managing and leading. However, since few women had been part of the management picture until the late sixties, the model was based almost exclusively on experiences of successful men.

But was it reasonable to assume that women managers could and should operate along the exact same lines? By and large, most organizations thought so. What's more, most men and many women managers agreed with this assumption—although they often had very different reasons for supporting the idea. In talking with male managers, it was apparent that the majority saw the qualities of effective leadership as being the same for both sexes. Yet, their descriptions were usually based upon a paramilitary model of control and competitive behavior. On the other hand, women who supported the assumption frequently acknowledged that their natural inclinations were somewhat different from the traditional management model. Yet they insisted that they had to operate along traditional lines to prove they were as capable as men.

Out-Macho the Men

Nonetheless, my own observations about what was happening to women after a decade of climbing the managerial ladder led me to a very different conclusion. It seemed to me that the traditional management style was not effective for many women. Although some highly successful women functioned similarly to their male colleagues, and even a few were able to "out-macho" most of the men with whom they worked, the vast majority of women managers did not seem comfortable with the traditional leadership style used within most corporations. More important, this traditional style did not enhance their innate abilities or make the best use of their natural feminine skills and instincts. Instead, it forced many women to operate in a way that felt unnatural and rendered them less effective in their role as managers. . . .

"A growing body of evidence suggests that, as a group, women compared to most men do indeed have a different natural style of management."

Unlike the traditional masculine style favored more by men, feminine leadership is a style of managing that utilizes the full range of women's natural talents and abilities as never before. It is an approach to leading that is linked to gender differences, early socialization, and the unique set of life experiences from early childhood on, which shape women's values, interests, and behavior as adults.

At its core, the feminine leadership style differs most dramatically from the traditional style of management in its reliance on emotional as well as rational data. Feminine leaders see the world through two different lenses concurrently and, as a result, respond to situations on both the thinking and the feeling levels.

By being in tune with the emotional cues and undercurrents that are a part of all human interaction, feminine leaders have additional data to consider when making decisions and are often more inclined to consider their own feelings and the feelings of others when seeking solutions to complex problems. As a result, they are likely to function somewhat differently from their more traditional counterparts in their roles as problem-solvers, decision-makers, and managers of relationships.

In short, feminine leaders are apt to be more concerned with maintaining close personal relationships with others. They are more likely to consider feelings as well as the basic facts in decision-making—to strive for solutions in which everyone is a winner and to avoid situations where someone must lose. They are also more inclined to subordinate short-term, personal advancement to improve the long-term health of the organization that they and their associates mutually depend upon.

Naturally, these qualities aren't equally pronounced in all women managers, nor are they totally absent in all male managers. However, a growing body of evidence suggests that, as a group, women compared to most men do indeed have a different natural style of management and are likely to function somewhat differently, yet effectively, in leadership roles. . . .

The feminine leadership style is composed of many qualities and characteristics that are different from those used more by men. Yet, taken together, these qualities represent a leadership style that seems to work extremely well for many women— better, in fact, than the more traditional approach. Here is an outline of some of the key characteristics of this emerging style:

FEMININE LEADERSHIP MODEL
Operating Style:
Cooperative
Organizational Structure:
Team
Basic Objective:
Quality Output
Problem-Solving Style:
Intuitive/Rational
Key Characteristics:
Lower Control
Empathic
Collaborative
High Performance Standards . . .

If this feminine leadership style is a more effective alternative for many women than the traditional style favored by men, why isn't it recognized and encouraged in most organizations? Very simply, it isn't recognized because to do so requires acceptance of the idea that women, as a group, are different but equal to men. It requires a change in the way most business leaders, including many who consider themselves progressive, view the world.

Recognizing Feminine Leadership

Instead of recognizing the unique styles that men and women bring to their roles as managers, what the vast majority of organizations have been doing for the past decade is trying to prove that men and women are exactly the same. In short, equality has been interpreted to mean that the exact same behavior based upon the same set of masculine standards must apply to all. The result is that women who succeed in management often do so by adapting to male norms, while those who stay themselves rarely receive the recognition or support they need to move ahead. Masculine bias, whether conscious or unconscious, continues to be the major obstacle facing most feminine leaders in corporations. Although these women perform competently, their style is often undervalued by male colleagues and bosses who are unaccustomed to working with this nontraditional approach.

"As more and more women continue to move into management positions . . . , some are starting to question the assumption that success means having to become one of the boys."

A recent conversation with the vice president of marketing at a major health and beauty aids company helps to illustrate this problem. He stated, "A few years ago, I was very concerned about the need for increasing opportunities for women within my division. . . . But now, looking back, I'm not sure I made the right decision when I started pushing to hire more women. Because in spite of their educational credentials and their background, they don't seem to be doing as well as a group. A few have been promoted, but I can't honestly see any of these women moving up to senior management. Even though they do their jobs well, they just don't seem to stand out in the way that men do. They just don't seem to shine."

Unconscious Bias

The problem of unconscious masculine bias, which defines performance standards in most companies, was also discussed by Betty Friedan in a 1983 article in *The New York Times Magazine*. In it, she describes the powerful impact of the masculine culture on women at Harvard University she observed while working as a research fellow at the Institute of Politics.

She states, "During my year there, I was asked to meet with the women at the law school, women medical students and interns, the women's group at the divinity and architecture schools. These women were awesome in their competence, but they made me uneasy. They seemed too neat, somehow, too controlled, constricted, almost subdued and slightly juiceless.

"A dean of one of the professional schools said: 'We take in the most brilliant women, of course. Their record of achievement is breathtaking, as are their scores on the admission tests. But for some reason, they don't do as well as they should when they get here. Can you explain it?'

"'Not without interviewing them,' I said, 'but I have a hunch it's because your structures—your whole ambiance—is so masculine; it alienates them somehow, though they might not be aware of it. Something around here must not elicit the best of female energy. But if that's so, you'd better find it out. Because it's also having an influence on the men that may not be conducive to the kind of leadership needed now.'"

An Alien Culture

Although Friedan's comments describe the climate for women at Harvard, they could just as easily apply to the management culture of most of our nation's corporations. For the majority of women, it is still an alien culture where enormous trade-offs are required to achieve even moderate success. In order to maximize the contributions that both men and women can make in business, a new perspective is needed. The parameters of acceptable management performance must be expanded to include the total range of skills, both masculine and feminine.

The effects of masculinism and the pressures it exerts on women to conform may help explain the results of many recent studies that claim to have found no difference in the management styles of men and women. Since organizations have forced women to behave like men in order to succeed, it's not surprising that many successful women would identify with a more masculine management style in company-sponsored testing. In addition, the promotion process in most organizations has worked against women with a nontraditional style. Because many companies tend to unconsciously select women who fit the traditional mold for advancement, it follows that differences between the masculine and feminine leadership styles might become even less distinct at higher management levels within traditional organizations.

Fortunately, there are signs of positive change in some organizations. As more and more women continue to move into management positions in companies across the nation, some are starting to question the assumption that success means having to become one of the boys. No longer convinced that they must prove their competence by conforming to the masculine style or by playing accommodating roles, these women recognize that another, more effective and more personally satisfying alternative is available to them.

"[Some women] will never be comfortable or fully effective as traditional managers and, therefore, it is time [for them] to start letting their natural style emerge."

As I traveled across the country and spoke with men and women about this idea, I've been encouraged by the amount of support for this feminine leadership style that seems to be developing throughout industry. Everywhere I go, I find people who seem to spark to the idea immediately. Not only does the concept of feminine leadership address many of the productivity problems that managers face today, but it also acknowledges the unspoken, yet obvious fact that men and women are different. In short, it affirms many of the experiences and observations of women managers that were difficult to understand or describe until now.

As one woman supervisor in the banking industry put it, "For the first time in a long time, I understand why I feel so uncomfortable in my job. I've been trying to change my whole approach . . . my style . . . to prove to my boss that I'm as smart and as competent as my male peers. I've been trying to do things the way other men do them . . . by being less emotional, tougher, and more analytical.

Guessing What a Man Would Do

"It's a lot like trying to write with your left hand after you've been using the right one for thirty years. Instead of improving, you become less effective. You walk around asking yourself, 'What would a guy do in this situation?' and since you don't know, you try to guess. Meanwhile, you stop relying on your own instincts and stop trusting yourself."

For some women managers, there is nothing really new about the concept of feminine leadership. It is simply a new term that describes exactly what they have been doing throughout their careers. For others, there is the growing realization that they will never be comfortable or fully effective as traditional managers and, therefore, it is time to start letting their natural style emerge.

Marilyn Loden is the founder of Loden Associates, a New York consulting firm. She has also been an adjunct member of the faculty at American University in Washington, DC.

Inflexible Working Conditions Force Women Out of the Workplace

Liz Roman Gallese

Mary Draper, 31, has a dream job. As senior publicist for a major New York film company, she's responsible for booking celebrities for talk shows and press interviews, and for escorting them as they plug their latest movies. "You take famous people around in a limo," she says in an offhand tone. "There are parties at the Met, receptions at Tavern on the Green. I've met Bette Davis, Alec Guinness, Katharine Hepburn. . . .''

Draper is good at her job; she's received regular promotions since she began her career ten years ago. But she's ready to quit working—for good. "My goal is retirement—marriage, children," she says. "I've been working for a long time. I would like to try something else."

In Boston, 25-year-old Ann Miller landed the type of job that could have been a solid springboard to a career in management: supervisor of seven technicians at a fast-growing maker of telephone equipment. The job sounded, as she puts it, "so glamorous," explaining that she envisioned herself in a high-tech office, wearing beautiful clothes, just like the actresses who play working women on television. Instead, she found herself haggling on the phone with disgruntled customers all day. She resigned after a year and has taken a low-level job with a less stressful company, looking forward to a time when she is married and has stopped working altogether. "My heart just isn't in it," she says of the working world. "It isn't everything it's cracked up to be."

Dropping Out of the Stock Market

And in an affluent suburb of New York City, Lisa Carroll, 29, has taken the step that Draper and Miller can only dream about: She's stopped working. Until two years ago, she was earning $50,000 a year

as a top Eurodollar broker on Wall Street. Shortly after she married and moved to the suburbs, she left her job, and she speaks about it as if it were the most natural thing in the world to do. She had been successful in her career; now she's turned her attention to other interests, the kind of stuff she never had time for back then. She's fixing up her house, taking care of the cooking and cleaning, working out, involving herself in volunteer work, spending mornings with friends at meetings of the local Newcomers club, taking an intermediate course in German at the local college. "Sure, I was sad to leave work," she says calmly. "But there are other things in my life that are important to me."

For the past two decades, women have been fighting for the right to have the kinds of careers that Draper, Miller and Carroll are now rejecting. The image of the "career woman," with her suits, her status and her perks, became the fashionable role model for thousands of young baby-boom women, and they sought that lifestyle eagerly—acquiring expensive educations, working long hours, rising through the ranks in unprecedented numbers.

In the mid-80s, however, small signs are pointing to a new attitude about careers. Several recent studies show middle-management women dropping out of the workforce at a much higher rate than their male counterparts. Women with M.B.A.'s, which provided entreé into the more elite levels of the working world, are dropping out of full-time corporate work a decade after graduation at a rate that appears to be approaching 25 percent, according to studies underway at the graduate business schools at Pace University in New York City and the University of Pittsburgh. In this author's own study of women of the class of 1975 at the Harvard Business School, about 40 percent were either ambivalent about their careers or frankly not ambitious.

But these figures are only the tip of a much larger

iceberg. According to demographics specialist Tom Biracree, the number of women who enter the work force each year is steadily rising. But as their work lives progress, educated women tend to drop out of work at a much greater rate than educated men. A 1983 study by the U.S. Bureau of Labor Statistics tracked the labor-force participation of men and women with four years of college. Among women aged 25 to 35, 74.8 percent were employed either full- or-part-time; for men of the same age, the number was 96.5 percent. Among women aged 35 to 44, 71.4 percent worked; for men, the figure was 98.3 percent.

Women who drop out of the work force will always be in a minority because work, for most women, is not a choice, but a financial necessity.

But the studies are significant for what they say about the workplace.

"Several recent studies show middle-management women dropping out of the work force at a much higher rate than their male counterparts."

The figures reflect external pressures on working women, such as lingering sexism and lack of adequate child care. They also reflect a widespread disillusionment with the nature of work itself. Frustrated by organizational barriers, bored by the routine tasks indigenous to any line of work, more and more women are plagued by the persistent and disturbing thought that they'd really prefer not to work anymore. The malaise shows up in married women who quit because they can, and in exhausted working mothers who quit because they feel they must. For single women who must work to support themselves, the syndrome may show up in underachievement or in stalled careers, or in an exaggerated desire to get married so that they can get away from all this.

Arlene Kagel, Ph.D., a clinical psychologist in private practice in New York City, has observed an increasing disenchantment with work among her female patients. "There's a feeling of, 'I don't know where I am, but it sure isn't Kansas,'" Dr. Kagel says. "These are women who have promising or well-established careers, but they're feeling shortchanged by work—and somewhat suprised to find themselves feeling this way."

And in a reversal of recent social trends, says Dr. Kagel, "women are beginning to view staying home and rearing children as providing the same kind of freedom and release that women twenty years ago saw in careers."

Film publicist Draper, for one, is hoping her boyfriend will propose soon. "I'd choose him over work in a minute," she says. "I guess I just don't want to wake up at age forty without any relationship, without any kids."

But must there be a choice—home and family versus career? Draper thinks so. "My friends all say, 'Your job is so exciting,' and sometimes it is," she says. "But I work until nine o'clock at least three nights a week. I'm up at six to take people to *The Today Show*. On weekends, I have to work press junkets. . . . The hours are so long in this job. It would definitely interfere with raising a family."

Draper illustrates the classic push-pull situation of women who are ambivalent about work: They're bright and talented enough to do well on the job, even, perhaps, to overdo by working a grueling schedule. But they feel genuinely deprived when their high-powered careers preclude them from cultivating their personal lives. "Women can tend toward overperformance in an effort to succeed in business," says Nehama Jacobs, coauthor with Sarah Hardesty of *Success and Betrayal: The Crisis of Women in Corporate America* (Franklin Watts, 1986). "When these women begin to burn out on careers, they also experience feelings of self-betrayal. They question what they've had to give up, whether the rewards of work are enough to satisfy them as women."

Men, of course, can and do burn out on their careers. But in *The Managerial Woman* (Pocket Books, 1983), a study of 25 career-oriented women, authors Margaret Hennig and Anne Jardim argued that women are less likely than men to view careers as full-time, lifelong obligations. Men's egos are more likely to be bound up in their careers, while women view work as part of a larger landscape in which other aspects of life are equally important.

It's those "other aspects"—personal time, outside interests, relationships—that tend to get lost in the career crunch. That's part of the reason Lisa Carroll decided to quite working shortly after she and her husband moved to the suburbs. She says she loved her job trading Eurodollars, but the hours were punishing: in at 7 A.M. and out at 5 P.M. most days; she spent, on the average, three nights a week wining and dining her valued clients. "I did that for a year. I can't believe I did that! I only had my weekends to do things like cook, pay bills, do the laundry. But if you want that kind of job, you have to give it your all."

Trickle-Down Frustration

Suppose a women genuinely wants to give her all to a job? What is she likely to get in return? What she's not likely to get, according to Sarah Hardesty, coauthor of *Success and Betrayal*, is a promotion to the very top ranks of the company. "While both the men and women we interviewed said it is hard to get to the top in management, both said it is harder still for women," she says. Hardesty cites a 1985

Korn Ferry International study that surveyed 1,362 senior executives. Only 2 percent were women. In 1986, the University of Michigan studied 800 promotions to vice-president and above at medium and large corporations and found that only 2.6 percent went to women.

"I'm not suggesting there's a male conspiracy that's keeping women from the top," Hardesty says. "It's just a system that's traditionally male—and women are *still* outsiders. The real barriers usually occur not at middle management, but fifteen or twenty years into a woman's career. But the vision of older women not getting ahead can discourage women in their twenties. It tips them off that the possibilities are limited."

The problem is compounded, Hardesty says, by the fact that women's expectations for work tend to be higher than men's. "They enter the workplace thinking that the sky's the limit," she says, a feeling fostered in part by the media glamorization of careers. "Women didn't have realistic role models when they were growing up," she adds. "Their mothers didn't work and they didn't know what their fathers did when they went off to the office. It was a secret world, the workplace; it was glamorized. Meanwhile, their mothers, feeling themselves excluded and not knowing a lot about their husbands' experiences at work, pushed their daughters to succeed. But they couldn't give them a sense of the reality of what work is like."

Great Expectations

Ann Miller, the former supervisor for the telephone equipment company, is now on her third post-college job. She calls the working world "a rude awakening. I realized I wasn't going to be on top, that it was going to be like kindergarten again, starting at the bottom." She recalls with a shuddder the uncooperativeness of the technicians she supervised, and the constant haranguing by customers on the phone. When she complained to her boss (a woman) that the job wasn't what she'd expected, Miller says she got the shock of her life. "She told me, 'Welcome to the corporate world!'" Miller had expected sympathy. "Toward the end I was dying to leave, I was under such pressure. I was crying in the bathroom."

At her second job, Miller was disappointed again. She signed on as an administrative assistant to the founder of a Boston-based nonprofit group that arranged tours of historical sites. As the third person in a small office controlled by a female founder, who Miller says was "brilliant" but difficult to work for, she found herself doing everything from typing to research. Once, at a luncheon that was part of a tour sponsored by the firm, Miller says she "actually got up and started serving the sandwiches."

As a result of her experiences, Miller says she doesn't have any more illusions. She's working these days as a secretary for a nonprofit charity organization in Boston, and her aspirations go no further than feeding and clothing herself and paying her share of the rent on her apartment. And she has visions of the day when she'll be able to quit, go home, have children and perhaps do a bit of freelance work on the side.

Josephus Long is one professional who thinks women like Miller opt out of work because they can't meet their own "unrealistic expectations" about careers. Long is the director of human resources at The Boston Company, a major financial-services organization that employs a significant number of recent college graduates. "The young women we hire picture themselves as being instantly irreplaceable at whatever they choose to do," he says. "They have been educated to believe that they should have a fulfilling job. But many jobs are drab and commonplace."

Long says that 60 percent of his new female hirees leave within 18 to 24 months, compared with 40 percent of the males. And he has observed that whereas virtually all the departing men say they're leaving to take better jobs elsewhere, about a third of the women say they're leaving "to find out what it is they really want to do," he says, "through travel, going back to school or moving to another city."

Long's theory is that most men expect only jobs that eventually will pay enough to support a family, but that practically all women expect to be "stars" in their careers, an attitude common to only the best of the men, he says. When most women fail to live up to such lofty expectations (as would most men), they reject work altogether. Long thinks the situation reflects a difference in early training. "Men have played on teams where they've sat on the bench," he says. "They've been in environments in which they weren't the stars—and it was okay."

> "More and more women are plagued by the persistent and disturbing thought that they'd really prefer not to work anymore."

There is another, deeper level at which men and women have been trained differently, and it manifests itself in many women's belief that they have a right to be supported in their role as society's childbearers. It's a belief that's used as a justification by women who anticipate having children as well as those who have them already.

Marie Romano, for example, a 26-year-old executive assistant to the chairman of a Boston-based apparel concern, says she expects to quit when she has children. She plans to get married this fall and to start her family a year later. "I really believe in men's and women's roles," she says, adding that she'll deserve to be supported because "I'll have another full-time job—a household."

A 1982 graduate of George Washington University in Washington, D.C., Romano once had big plans for her future. At one point she wanted to be a diplomat, then set her sights on film directing, and finally majored in radio and television broadcasting. She got a masters degree in the field, and then decided to try for a job in advertising.

But when all she turned up were suggestions that she take a research job, the type of position in which she'd be stuck crunching numbers in some basement, she simply gave up. The agencies "treated me like a little kid, like I had no idea what I was talking about," she says.

"The young women we hire . . . have been educated to believe that they should have a fulfilling job. But many jobs are drab and commonplace."

Romano freely admits that she doesn't really have the desire to put in the kind of effort it takes to have a successful career. She says a part of the reason has to go back to the way she was brought up, as the oldest of three girls in an affluent home. Her father put her through school, and even discouraged her from working part-time while in graduate school. "He said, 'Take as long as you want to write your thesis, I'll support you.' So in a way, I know Daddy's there.". . .

[In a study,] Jeanne Stanton, an assistant professor at Simmons College Graduate School of Management in Boston, found that at least two thirds of the 50 women she interviewed weren't able to combine motherhood with a full-time career, especially after the birth of the second child. "It becomes untenable," she says. "So they reduce the amount of energy they give to their job, either by working part-time or stopping altogether."

She adds that two women who still had demanding careers also had full-time household help and husbands who shared the child-rearing burden. "Those husbands are extraordinary," she adds.

Yet in this post-feminist era in which women are expected to work, and in which one out of every two marriages ends in divorce, a woman's right to be supported while rearing children is far from guaranteed. Ann Miller is herself a child of divorce. She saw her mother forced to go back to work after a lifetime of being supported in fine upper-middle-class style. He mother grasped at straws, finally accepting a job as a receptionist because it was all

she could get after so many years at home rearing four daughters. Which is why, Miller says, she doesn't want to be "a typical housewife." She recently took a course in art at the Cambridge Center for Adult Education, and now plans to develop her new talent into "something I can do from my home," such as freelance illustrating—a goal that, at this point, remains little more than wishful thinking.

When asked her feelings about being supported by her husband, suburban housewife Lisa Carroll hardly blinks an eye. "That doesn't bother me at all," she says, dismissing the query with a little wave of her hand. "Bert doesn't give me a hard time, and I don't feel like it's just his money. We have a little joke. I tell him, 'You'll be paying my salary now.'"

But another question brings her up short, the question of what she would do if she got divorced in ten years. "Why, I never thought about that!" she exclaims, clearly bewildered for the first time in the interview. The skills she fought so hard to master will be out of date by that time, she concedes, and many of her contacts could be gone.

Careers cannot be put down and picked up again like hobbies. "Once you even go part-time, you're off the fast track," says one expert. And fulfilling part-time jobs, such as the one Ann Miller says she is planning to get, are rare. Yet women like Draper, Miller and Carroll, and countless others, will continue to wrestle with their very real desire to "have it all": a good job when they want it, a good personal life and time for themselves.

Just a Job

In the long run, perhaps corporations will help solve the problem by providing flexible hours and decent child care. But in the short run, the women will find solutions much harder to come by and much more prosaic. Perhaps it's time for women to begin viewing work as men have always done, as a lifelong endeavor that more likely than not will become "just a job," hardly the superstardom of which fantasies are made. Perhaps it's time they began planning for the realities of the workplace, that until corporations change, one must make child-care arrangements that dovetail with on-the-job schedules. Given the current economic realities, the vast majority of women will continue to have to work throughout their lifetime. They won't be able to "have it all"—but they will have, in the end, only the things they wanted most.

Liz Roman Gallese is the author of Women Like Us, *a study of women who graduated from Harvard Business School.*

Male Domination Forces Women Out of the Workplace

Ann M. Morrison, Randall P. White and Ellen Van Velsor

Women are not making the same progress as men are in the executive ranks. Among Fortune-500 companies, only 1.7 percent of the corporate officers are women, according to a 1986 study by Mary Ann Von Glinow, a professor in the school of business at the University of Southern California.

Methodology

To get a closer look at how women's movement up the corporate ladder compares with men's, we compared female managers from our recent study composed of interviews with 76 women at or near the general management level in Fortune-100 sized companies to male general managers from another study done at the center by Morgan W. McCall Jr., Michael M. Lombardo and Morrison.

We also interviewed 22 "savvy insiders" at 10 of the same companies—16 men and 6 women who are responsible for identifying and selecting executives for top jobs. (The earlier study of male executives also included interviews of savvy insiders.) Both studies looked at the various factors that contribute to success or derailment among executives.

Our criteria for success included reaching one of the top 10 to 20 positions in the corporation and living up to one's full potential in the eyes of the company. Derailment was defined as achieving a very high level in the company but not going as high as the organization had expected. Derailed women may have plateaued, been demoted or fired, accepted early retirement or had their responsibilities reduced.

The savvy insiders were asked to come up with an example of a woman they knew who had made it and an example of one who had derailed. They described the qualities and characteristics that had helped or hurt these women, and we compiled the

most frequently mentioned answers into a list of success factors and fatal flaws. The insiders gave us case histories on 19 women who were considered successful and 16 who had derailed.

The insiders in both studies listed roughly the same number of derailment factors for women and men (4 for women on the average, 3.5 for men), but they listed nearly twice as many success factors for women (10.4 on average versus 5.7 for men). This finding may add to the evidence that to progress in today's corporate world, women must outperform men.

Leaping Through Hoops

The women described to us as successful and as derailed were put through a number of hoops as they progressed up the corporate ladder. They had to show their toughness and independence and at the same time depend on others. It was essential that they contradict the stereotypes that their male bosses and coworkers had about women. They had to be seen as different, "better then women" as a group. But they couldn't go too far and forfeit all traces of femininity because that would make them too alien to their superiors and colleagues. In essence, their mission was to do what wasn't expected of them, while doing enough of what was expected of them as women to gain acceptance.

The hoops held out for women in or aspiring to executive jobs are often paired up, requiring seemingly contradictory types of behavior at the same time. The trick is to pass through only the overlapping portion of each pair of hoops.

This narrow band of acceptable characteristics and actions reflects the multiple expectations of corporate women and the challenge they face of blending very disparate qualities. It is clear that much behavioral territory is off-limits to executive women. Only certain characteristics traditionally accepted as "masculine" and some traditionally thought of as "feminine" are permitted through the narrow band.

The unacceptable area comprises the extremes that would make an executive woman too much like traditional nonprofessional women or too much like women trying too hard to be like men. "Trying to talk and behave like a man can come across as not genuine," one savvy insider said about mistakes some women make.

Male Behavior

Certain "male" kinds of behavior are not only allowed but required. Some savvy insiders wanted to see toughness demonstrated by a woman on an executive track because they believe, as a rule, that women aren't tough enough to handle the job. Sometimes people require executive women to be more "masculine" than men in certain ways to be accepted. One executive said that the chief executive officer told her, "You're tougher than most of the men around here. Can't you go find some more of you?"

We have identified four contradictory sets of expectations that women must reconcile to succeed in corporate life.

Take risks, but be consistently outstanding.

The senior executives put great value on risk taking, and for good reasons. Risk often is the name of the game at the top. Top managers are responsible for huge sums of money and thousands of jobs and must make countless decisions about whether to invest or divest, compete or retreat, change or grow, all with only a fuzzy feel for the years ahead when the results of those decisions will become apparent. Taking risks early in one's career is often necessary preparation to be considered for top jobs.

A big element of risk taking is changing jobs and taking on new assignments. One savvy insider felt that this was a critical career turning point for highly promotable women: "Taking a job in a different part of the business broadens your experience base and shows risk-taking ability."

In 14 of 19 success cases described by savvy insiders, a risky job change was mentioned specifically. Such risky job changes included tough transitions from academia to industry; deliberate attempts to broaden one's perspective and knowledge by moving into such areas as finance, employee relations and information services; and the all-important move from a staff position to a line position—a move that usually involved going from having responsibility for analysis, service or support to having clear responsibility for profit and loss, implementation and bottom-line decision making. Some involved a technical area with which the manager was unfamiliar.

Perhaps risk taking means more to executives when exhibited by a woman than by a man, since women are often seen as averse to taking risks. In

fact, some see women's reluctance to take risks as a barrier to their moving up. Being too "by the book" and cautious were cited by some of the savvy insiders as weaknesses of women.

Taking More Risks

To achieve a breadth of experience in the business, women must take more risks than men do. The career moves that the successful women we studied had made—from staff to line positions, moving away from headquarters and so on—had elements of risk that probably would not have existed to the same extent for men. Moving into line positions, for example, involved not only the challenge of new demands but also a more hostile, less tolerant environment. The risk for a woman sometimes involves giving up a promotion in her staff function, where her presence is less threatening, to enter a new part of the business, perhaps at a lower level, where she may be as welcome as the plague and the possibility of promotion may be slim.

Women are also expected to be extremely competent, often even more competent than men in various arenas, such as starting or turning around a department, handling the media, running a business, managing subordinates and customers and chairing a task force.

More Than Good

In general, any candidate for a top job has to be good, but these women were more than good. Some senior executives acknowledged that successful women were at least as good as the best men available for the job.

"In general, any candidate for a top job has to be good, but these women were more than good."

Because of the visibility of the few women in high management ranks, there is little leeway for mistakes, little allowance for weaknesses. The successful women impressed senior executives with their intelligence and business acumen, their no-nonsense, bottom-line orientation, their strategic perspective and their management prowess. Women who do merely an acceptable job, let alone a less-than-average job, may be pulled off the track.

Women get little compensation for the greater risks they take in advancing their careers. Their performance must be outstanding, whatever the degree of difficulty. If career advancement can be likened to an Olympic diving competition, the dives performed by women would have a higher degree of difficulty than the men's, yet the judges would not follow the customary procedure of factoring the degree of difficulty into their scores.

Be tough, but don't be macho.

Toughness is another characteristic that savvy insiders said they like to see in executive women. They praised the willingness of successful women to make decisions, to call the shots in a fast-moving business and to take a tough stand. The successful women demanded results from their subordinates, fought for a bigger budget or greater visibility for their unit or said what they really thought and did what they needed to do to avoid compromising their personal integrity.

Cool Under Pressure

Being cool under pressure was another characteristic of successful women noted by savvy insiders:

"She doesn't fall apart when things get tough."

"She has great cool under pressure. In 50 corporate meetings, I've only seen her lose her cool two times. Most people would lose it one time out of every five. She's very controlled."

Being tougher and not prone to collapse in crises makes these women seem different, which is necessary for them to be considered for high-level jobs. Doing what it takes to show a profit, taking the initiative and defending one's resources are admirable, even necessary actions of a high-potential executive. Even such superficial characteristics as being tall—which was said to help give one woman personal dominance and a commanding presence—are sometimes admired because they suggest that these are tough individuals.

While many men fear that women aren't tough enough to handle big business, the desire for these woman to act "like women" still lingers. Toughness, for example, is sometimes qualified or limited to "tough, but not offensive" or "demure, yet tough." And when we look at those who derailed, there is more evidence that being too tough is the kiss of death. One 40-year-old woman with an MBA and an excellent track record was recruited from outside one company some years ago into a job that was a step toward moving her into general management, at a salary of $75,000. Despite her potential, problems developed that made her unacceptable for that critical promotion.

She couldn't adapt to the environment she was in—an "old boy" type of business with older workers who were suspicious and judgmental. She was apparently too willing to be tough and too good at it. Her macho style and her push for perks made her seem too hard and demanding. Some of her business decisions contributed to this image. For example, she got three assignments in a row that took her away from headquarters to assess business units that were not performing up to par. In each case, her conclusion was that the business was a loser and should be closed down. "She got

stereotyped," we were told. "There's 'growth,' 'maintenance' and 'close it.' She was a 'close it' person—take a lot of people out of work and reduce costs. It didn't increase her popularity."

Somewhere in between extremes is a relatively safe zone to which some successful women apparently confine themselves, where they are obviously female and easy to be with but also strong-willed and thick-skinned enough to pass muster. As some insiders told us:

"She's quite feminine, but she doesn't use it or let it get in the way."

"Her uniqueness is that she doesn't differ at all from men. . . . She plays it just like the men do, and she's very comfortable doing it. It's not put on, not contrived. It's very natural."

"Some women derailed at least partly because they made an issue of inequality or simply asked for more pay or perks."

Be ambitious, but don't expect equal treatment.

Equal employment opportunity legislation put pressure on corporate executives to find and promote a woman, and the women they chose in their companies often turned out to be ones we interviewed. In most cases, that pressure provided these women with the avenue they needed to fulfill their own drive—the chance to take on challenging assignments, to progress higher in their company, even to experience the satisfaction and the trappings of success within the establishment.

Personal Drive

Those who were given an opportunity to fill a high-level position were expected to put the job first, family second (if at all). Their strong desire to succeed was a crucial factor that senior executives looked for in designating high-potential women.

"The personal drive and determination to succeed, the willingness to persist and work hard to achieve and a total commitment to career as the top priority in life" were some of the necessary qualities one insider shared with us.

The willingness to be mobile and to devote themselves to their company, despite the cultural obligations to marry, have children, run a household and so on, was applauded and noted as a factor in the success of a number of executive women. But their ambition was not so well received when status and benefits were involved; the chance to show their stuff in a nontraditional management role had its price.

According to some we interviewed, being assigned the same responsibilities or the same title as men in the company didn't mean that women received equal treatment in other respects. The salary differential is the most obvious example. Salary surveys done over the past several years consistently show that women are still paid considerably less than men at their level, even in management jobs and despite having a Harvard University MBA. Even when salaries are the same, women are given smaller budgets than men in similar jobs. Inclusion in the bonus system, access to high-status conferences and a host of other benefits may also be skewed toward men.

The women who obtained an executive position often felt that they had to make other concessions, in such areas as pay, perks and their rate of advancement. As newly appointed members of the executive club, they were still treated as if they had lower status. The fact that some women derailed at least partly because they made an issue of inequality or simply asked for more pay or perks corroborates the perception that women were tolerated in the club as junior members with fewer privileges than men had. "Wanting too much" was a flaw attributed to half of the derailed women in our study.

"The hurdles for women in management seem to be bigger and more numerous."

Take responsibility, but follow others' advice.
Accountability for business performance was emphasized repeatedly by savvy insiders as a necessary factor in executive success. Making difficult decisions, being practical, concentrating on meeting bottom-line goals and even accepting the duties of a supervisory role were all mentioned as aspects of taking responsibility. . . .

Others that we spoke to regarded taking advice and criticism as a strong, positive factor in the struggle of women to adapt to the workplace:

"She had a tendency to get visibly upset if something was happening that she didn't like and also to be very defensive. I spoke to her about the first problem, and she changed. One of her great assets is the ability to listen and make changes."

Responding to this particular feedback was probably a good decision by this woman. Not all of the advice that female executives encounter is that clear, however. Several of our female executives said that it is important to trust people but only certain people. Some also said they came to understand that others' motives are not the same as your own; when others offer help, it may or may not be to your advantage to accept it or even to believe they are trying to be helpful.

Although the assistance that women received from senior executives in getting new opportunities was vital to their career, these women also realized that

they had to choose what was best for themselves and not always depend on others to know what that was. They often had to rock the boat—to turn down high-level staff positions for lower-level line positions, to make an issue of opportunities for career advancement or tuition reimbursement to attend an executive program—to get what they needed instead of what was offered to them. . . .

Not for the Faint-Hearted

The hoops that executive women confront are not for the faint-hearted. They represent tough battles to be waged throughout a career, battles that get a great deal of corporate attention. Of course, men who choose to pursue the executive ranks are also tested. They succeed and derail for many of the same reasons women do.

And there are groups of men who experience some of the same biases and pressures as women. Hurdles that keep minority managers out of top jobs, according to the *Wall Street Journal* and other sources, are not unlike those that women face—having to work harder and longer than white men to get the same things, being sidetracked into staff jobs and being isolated. Relatives of company leaders also may be isolated, the target of other workers' hostility and suspected of insufficient abilities.

Despite these similarities, the hurdles for women in management seem to be bigger and more numerous. Men typically do not have responsibility for home and family care, so they have some relief from the time, worry and conflicting expectations that are part of such pressure. One black executive interviewed for the *Wall Street Journal* told the reporter, "I always tell young blacks you need a very good wife who can support you."

Different Environments

Women in management experience the special hoops and hoopla that they do because executive women and men have been perceived as more different from each other than they really are. Mounting evidence indicates that, when careers are matched, women are remarkably similar to men in their characteristics, abilities and motives. Yet stereotypical perceptions have led to unrealistic expectations of executive women, and these expectations are part of the environment in which the women must work and live. This environment is qualitatively different from the environment executive men operate in, and this difference may be the crucial—and the only meaningful—one between male and female executives.

The authors work at the Center for Creative Leadership in San Diego. Ann M. Morrison is the director, Randall P. White manages the Center's Training Division, and Ellen Van Velsor is a sociologist at the Center.

> *"We find successful corporate women asking, 'Why am I doing what I'm doing? What's the point here?' or confiding bleakly that 'something's missing.'"*

Boredom Forces Women Out of the Workplace

Barbara Ehrenreich

Some of us are old enough to recall when the stereotype of a "liberated woman" was a disheveled radical, notoriously braless, and usually hoarse from denouncing the twin evils of capitalism and patriarchy. Today the stereotype is more likely to be a tidy executive who carries an attaché case and is skilled in discussing market shares and leveraged buy-outs. In fact, thanks in no small part to the anger of the earlier, radical feminists, women have gained a real toehold in the corporate world: about 30 percent of managerial employees are women, as are 40 percent of the current MBA graduates. We have come a long way, as the expression goes, though clearly not in the same direction we set out on.

The influx of women in the corporate world has generated its own small industry of advice and inspiration. Magazines like *Savvy* and *Working Woman* offer tips on everything from sex to software, plus the occasional instructive tale about a woman who rises effortlessly from managing a boutique to being the CEO of a multinational corporation. Scores of books published since the mid-1970s have told the aspiring managerial woman what to wear, how to flatter superiors, and when necessary, fire subordinates. Even old-fashioned radicals like myself, for whom "CD" still means civil disobedience rather than an eight percent interest rate, can expect to receive a volume of second-class mail inviting them to join their corporate sisters at a "networking brunch" or to share the privileges available to the female frequent flier.

The Corporate Malaise

But for all the attention lavished on them, all the six-figure promotion possibilities and tiny perks once known only to the men in gray flannel, there is a

malaise in the world of the corporate woman. The continuing boom in the advice industry is in itself an indication of some kind of trouble. To take an example from a related field, there would not be a book published almost weekly on how to run a corporation along newly discovered oriental principles if American business knew how to hold its own against the international competition. Similarly, if women were confident about their role in the corporate world, I do not think they would pay to be told how to comport themselves in such minute detail. ("Enter the bar with a briefcase or some files. . . . Hold your head high, with a pleasant expression on your face. . . . After you have ordered your drink, shuffle through a paper or two, to further establish yourself [as a businesswoman]," advises *Letitia Baldridge's Complete Guide*.)

Nor, if women were not still nervous newcomers, would there be a market for so much overtly conflicting advice: how to be more impersonal and masculine (*The Right Moves*) or more nurturing and intuitive (*Feminine Leadership*); how to assemble the standard skirted suited uniform (de rigueur until approximately 1982) or move beyond it for the softness and individuality of a dress; how to conquer stress or how to transform it into drive; how to repress the least hint of sexuality, or alternatively, how to "focus the increase in energy that derives from sexual excitement so that you are more productive on the job" (*Corporate Romance*). When we find so much contradictory advice, we must assume that much of it is not working.

Making Do on $75,000

There is a more direct sign of trouble. A small but significant number of women are deciding not to have it all after all, and are dropping out of the corporate world to apply their management skills to kitchen decor and baby care. Not surprisingly, these retro women have been providing a feast for a

Barbara Ehrenreich, "Strategies of Corporate Women," *The New Republic*, January 27, 1986. Reprinted by permission of THE NEW REPUBLIC, © 1986, The New Republic, Inc.

certain "I told you so" style of journalism; hardly a month goes by without a story about another couple that decided to make do on his $75,000 a year while she joins the other mommies in the playground. But the trend is real. The editors of the big business-oriented women's magazines are worried about it. So is Liz Roman Gallese, the former *Wall St. Journal* reporter who interviewed the alumnae of Harvard Business School, class of '75, to write *Women Like Us.*

"Not one among the Harvard graduates or the anonymous women quoted in the advice books ever voices a transcendent commitment to, say, producing a better widget."

The women Gallese interviewed are not, for the most part, actual dropouts, but they are not doing as well as might have been expected for the first cohort of women to wield the talismanic Harvard MBA. Certainly they are not doing as well as their male contemporaries, and the gap widens with every year since graduation. Nor do they seem to be a very happy or likable group. Suzanne, the most successful of them, is contemptuous of women who have family obligations. Phoebe, who is perhaps the brightest, has an almost pathological impulse to dominate others. Maureen does not seem to like her infant daughter. Of the 82 women surveyed, 35 had been in therapy since graduation; four had been married to violently abusive men; three had suffered from anorexia or bulimia; and two had become Christian fundamentalists. Perhaps not surprisingly, given the high incidence of personal misery, two-fifths of the group were "ambivalent or frankly not ambitious for their careers."

Business Burnout

What is happening to our corporate women? The obvious anti-feminist answer, that biology is incompatible with business success, is not borne out by Gallese's study. Women with children were no less likely to be ambitious and do well than more mobile, single women (although in 1982, when the interviews were carried out, very few of the women had husbands or children). But the obvious feminist answer—that women are being discouraged or driven out by sexism—does gain considerable support from *Women Like Us.* Many of the women from the class of '75 report having been snubbed, insulted, or passed over for promotions by their male co-workers. Under these circumstances, even the most determined feminist would begin to suffer from what Dr. Herbert J. Freudenberger and Gail North

call "business burnout." For non-feminists—or, precisely, post-feminists—like Gallese and her informants, sexism must be all the more wounding for being so invisible and nameless. What you cannot name, except as apparently random incidents of "discrimination," you cannot hope to do much about.

Gallese suggests another problem, potentially far harder to eradicate than any form of discrimination. There may be a poor fit between the impersonal, bureaucratic culture of the corporation and what is, whether as a result of hormones or history, the female personality. The exception that seems to prove the rule is Suzanne, who is the most successful of the alumnae and who is also a monster of detachment from her fellow human beings. In contrast, Gallese observes that men who rise to the top are often thoroughly dull and "ordinary"—as men go—but perhaps ideally suited to a work world in which interpersonal attachments are shallow and all attention must focus on the famed bottom line.

Corporate Culture

To judge from the advice books, however, the corporate culture is not as impersonal, in a stern Weberian sense, as we have been led to believe. For example, *The Right Moves,* which is a good representative of the "how to be more like the boys" genre of books for corporate women, tells us to "eliminate the notion that the people with whom you work are your friends"—sound advice for anyone who aspires to the bureaucratic personality. But it also insists that it is necessary to cultivate the "illusion of friendship," lest co-workers find you "aloof and arrogant." You must, in other words, dissemble in order to effect the kind of personality—artificially warm but never actually friendly—that suits the corporate culture.

Now, in a task-oriented, meritocratic organization—or, let us just say, a thoroughly capitalist organization dedicated to the maximization of profit—it should not be necessary to cultivate "illusions" of any kind. It should be enough just to get the job done. But as *The Right Moves* explains, and the stories in *Women Like Us* illustrate, it is never enough just to get the job done; if it were, far more women would no doubt be at the top. You have to impress people, win them over, and in general project an aura of success far more potent than any actual accomplishment. The problem may not be that women lack the capacity for business-like detachment, but that, as women, they can never entirely fit into the boyish, glad-handed corporate culture so well described three decades ago in *The Lonely Crowd.*

There may also be a deeper, more existential, reason for the corporate woman's malaise. It is impossible to sample the advice literature without beginning to wonder what, after all, is the point of all this striving. Why not be content to stop at $40,000 or $50,000 a year, some stock options, and an IRA? Perhaps the most striking thing about the literature for and about the corporate woman is how little it has to say about the purposes, other than personal advancement, of the corporate "game." Not one among the Harvard graduates or the anonymous women quoted in the advice books ever voices a transcendent commitment to, say, producing a better widget. And if that is too much to expect from postindustrial corporate America, we might at least hope for some lofty organizational goals—to make X Corp. the biggest damn conglomerate in the Western world, or some such. But no one seems to have a vast and guiding vision of the corporate life, much less a Gilderesque belief in the moral purposefulness of capitalism itself. Instead, we find successful corporate women asking, "Why am I doing what I'm doing? What's the point here?" or confiding bleakly that "something's missing."

The Catsup Problem

In fact, from the occasional glimpses we get, the actual content of an executive's daily labors can be shockingly trivial. Consider Phoebe's moment of glory at Harvard Business School. The class had been confronted with a real-life corporate problem to solve. Recognizing the difficulty of getting catsup out of a bottle, should Smucker and Co. start selling catsup out of a wide-mouth container suitable for inserting a spoon into? No, said Phoebe, taking the floor for a lengthy disquisition, because people like the challenge of pounding catsup out of the bottle; a more accessible catsup would never sell. Now, I am not surprised that this was the right answer, but I am surprised that it was greeted with such apparent awe and amazement by a professor and a roomful of smart young students. Maybe for a corporate man the catsup problem is a daunting intellectual challenge. But a woman must ask herself: Is *this* what we left the kitchen for?

The Counterculture

Many years ago, when America was more innocent but everything else was pretty much the same, Paul Goodman wrote, "There is nearly 'full employment' . . . but there get to be fewer jobs that are necessary or unquestionably useful; that require energy and draw on some of one's best capacities; and that can be done keeping one's honor and dignity." Goodman, a utopian socialist, had unusually strict criteria for what counted as useful enough to be a "man's work," but he spoke for a generation of men who were beginning to question, in less radical ways, the corporate work world described by William H. Whyte, David Riesman, Alan Harrington, and others. Most of the alienated white-collar men of the 1950s withdrew into drink or early coronaries, but a few turned to Zen or jazz,

and thousands of their sons and daughters eventually joined with Goodman to help create the anticorporate and, indeed, anti-careerist counterculture of the 1960s. It was the counterculture, as much as anything else, that nourished the feminist movement of the late 1960s and early 1970s, which is where our story began.

In the early years, feminism was torn between radical and assimilationist tendencies. In fact, our first sense of division was between the "bourgeois" feminists who wanted to scale the occupational hierarchy created by men, and the radical feminists who wanted to level it. Assimilation won out, as it probably must among any economically disadvantaged group. Networks replaced consciousness-raising groups; Michael Korda became a more valuable guide to action than Shulamith Firestone. The old radical, anarchistic vision was replaced by the vague hope (well articulated in *Feminine Leadership*) that, in the process of assimilating, women would somehow "humanize" the cold and ruthless world of men. Today, of course, there are still radical feminists, but the only capitalist institution they seem bent on destroying is the local adult bookstore.

"Men are just as likely as women to grasp the ultimate pointlessness of the corporate game, . . . but only women have a socially acceptable way out."

As feminism loses its critical edge, it becomes, ironically, less capable of interpreting the experience of its pioneer assimilationists, the new corporate women. Contemporary mainstream feminism can understand their malaise insofar as it is caused by sexist obstacles, but has no way of addressing the sad emptiness of "success" itself. Even the well-worn term "alienation," as applied to human labor, rings no bells among the corporate feminists I have talked to recently, although most thought it an arresting notion. So we are in more or less the same epistemological situation Betty Friedan found herself in describing the misery—and, yes, alienation—of middle-class housewives in the early 1960s; better words would be forthcoming, but she had to refer to "the problem without a name."

A Socially Acceptable Excuse

Men are just as likely as women to grasp the ultimate pointlessness of the corporate game and the foolishness of many of the players, but only women have a socially acceptable way out. They can go back to the split-level homes and well-appointed nurseries where Friedan first found them. (That is assuming, of course, they can find a well-heeled husband, and they haven't used up all their child-bearing years in the pursuit of a more masculine model of success.) In fact, this may well be a more personally satisfying option than a work life spent contemplating, say, the fluid dynamics of catsup. As Paul Goodman explained, with as much insight as insensitivity, girls didn't have to worry about "growing up absurd" because they had intrinsically meaningful work cut out for them—motherhood and homemaking.

"[Someday, I believe, women may] invent some sweet new notion like equal pay for . . . meaningful work."

There is no doubt, from the interviews in *Women Like Us* as well as my own anecdotal sources, that some successful women are indeed using babies as a polite excuse for abandoning the rat race. This is too bad from many perspectives, and certainly for the children who will become the sole focus of their mothers' displaced ambitions. The dropouts themselves would do well to take a look at *The Corporate Couple*, which advises executive wives on the classic problems such as: how to adjust to the annual relocation, how to overcome one's jealousy of a husband's svelte and single female co-workers, and how to help a husband survive his own inevitable existential crisis.

Equal Pay for Meaningful Work

Someday, I believe, a brilliantly successful corporate woman will suddenly look down at her desk littered with spread sheets and interoffice memos and exclaim, "Is this really worth my time?" At the very same moment a housewife, casting her eyes around a kitchen befouled by toddlers, will ask herself the identical question. As the corporate woman flees out through the corporate atrium, she will run headlong into a housewife, fleeing into it. The two will talk. And in no time at all they will reunite those two distinctly American strands of radicalism—the utopianism of Goodman and the feminism of Friedan. They may also, if they talk long enough, invent some sweet new notion like equal pay for . . . meaningful work.

A contributing editor to Ms. *magazine, Barbara Ehrenreich is a prolific writer. Her most recent book is* The Hearts of Men.

viewpoint **65**

Flexible Work Schedules Would Help Fathers

Jane Hood and Susan Golden

Editor's note: The following viewpoint is excerpted from a research paper written by Jane Hood and Susan Golden.

Men's work schedules are the revolving doors through which men leave and enter family relationships. Which and how many hours a man works help to determine not only the length and frequency of family interactions, but also their quality. This paper closely examines the impact of two men's work schedules on their family lives. The men were the same age, worked similar hours, and each had young children and earned similar incomes when interviewed. However, one had a working wife and the other did not. Further, their occupations, social class, and orientations to work and family differ. As we trace the effect of each man's work hours through the complex maze of his family situation, we find that for one, working an afternoon shift has unanticipated negative effects on his family relationships, while, for the other, the same shift has an equally unintended positive effect. However, in the latter case, as the man becomes more involved in his family, work scheduling again becomes an issue. . . .

The concepts presented in this paper have been developed in the context of several research projects. Jane Hood, a sociologist, studied the transition to a two-worker family. She used data from extensive taped discussions with sixteen middle and working class couples over a two year period (1975-1976). The wives had returned to work up to five years before the first interview, after having been home full time for from two to twenty years. Susan

Golden, a clinical psychologist, used interviews and methods of naturalistic observation in home, work and school settings to study the work-family interface in families with infants and pre-school children. The initial observational study of two contrasting families from urban and rural settings was extended to include data from short term preventive clinical work with fifteen families in a similar developmental stage in a pediatric setting. The names used in this article are pseudonyms.

John Williams: A Young Professional

This section of the paper explores some of the ways in which the work hours and commitments of a young professional launching his career interact with family needs during the early child-rearing years. When Susan Golden observed the family, John and Deborah Williams were in their early thirties. John was a systems analyst, and Deborah had left her part-time job after the birth of their second child, planning to return in a few years. The children were 5 years and 5 months old at the time of the study.

John's description of his job centers on the theme of "time" and time use. He is disturbed that there is always more work to be done and not enough time. Accomplishments for him are measured in terms of production. At work, John is "beating time, buying time, selling time, losing time, fighting time." The images of aggressive procurement prevail. Time is the currency of management. His credibility and loyalty to the company are established by his willingness to put in more time for the company.

John feels he works between 40 and 60 hours a week for the sake of his family, but since there are only so many hours in the week, time "spent" in work is taken away from the family and vice-versa. When John's work drew him out of the family for prolonged periods of time, Deborah would find herself embroiled in a spiral of increasing conflict

Jane Hood and Susan Golden, "Beating Time/Making Time: The Impact of Work Scheduling on Men's Family Roles," *The Family Coordinator*, October 1979. Copyrighted 1979 by the National Council on Family Relations, 1910 West County Road B, Suite 147, St. Paul, MN 55113. Reprinted by permission.

with 5 year old Seth. Tense and overloaded by the end of the day, she would greet John in an angry and demanding manner. John, in turn, would withdraw from her.

During a particular period of 4 weeks, John was managing a team of workers attempting to meet a difficult deadline. The project had had more problems than anticipated and they were behind schedule, having difficulty obtaining adequate computer time for their project. As a result, the team went onto a schedule of working from noon to past midnight, in effect, moving to the afternoon shift. John also commuted 45 minutes each way to work. Seth was in nursery school and arrived home after his father had left for work so that they kept missing each other. Deborah did not keep Seth home from school because she needed the break for herself, and John would only be able to spend one hour at most with Seth before he returned to work, if he had the energy to relate to him at all. John also worked throughout most of the weekends. John felt that this was difficult but that it was important for him to stay with his co-workers in order to sustain team support, as well as develop his own expertise.

"John's dilemmas are not his alone, and the pressures he experiences in the dual role of worker and committed father are shared by many young fathers."

During this time, Seth became increasingly provocative with his mother; every small issue became a battle, with resulting temper tantrums and tears. His mother's patience was wearing thin. Seth began to sleepwalk at night, carrying piles of paper around, finally falling asleep at the foot of his parents' bed curled up on his "papers." During the day, he would walk around carrying his "papers" and become very upset if anyone interfered with them. To Seth, the papers were the equivalent of the computer print-out his father always carried to and from work. At the same time, Seth also became more and more preoccupied with Spiderman and his special powers. Deborah said, "I feel as if Seth has turned the house into his own fantasy world. Spiderman is in every corner. Traps are everywhere." The living room was indeed strung from corner and corner with web-like string traps.

In an effort to get out of this uncomfortable power struggle with Seth, Deborah decided to ask Seth what was going on. After talking awhile, Seth broke down, crying, "I hate daddy, I hate daddy, where is he?" alternately hitting the pillow and attempting to hit his mother. Things began to make sense. Deborah had not connected Seth's anger at her to

the changes in John's work schedule. The anger Seth felt towards his father for disappearing from the family was being displaced onto Deborah, who was bewildered by Seth's rage and in need of support from her absent husband. This was a crucial time in Seth's development when he needed increased distance from his mother and identification with his father. Seth has been doing well with this separation in nursery school. His attempts to be like his father are reflected in his frantic carrying of the "papers." However, this was not sufficient to help him sustain needed distance from his mother.

Shifts in the family's social network at this time left the family with few outside resources, all of which exacerbated the intensity of the troubled, reactive mother-son alignment. The extent of Seth's rage became more frightening for him the longer his father was gone from the family. Seth's school hours, combined with the availability of computer time at night meant that he did not see the reality of his father to temper his fantasies as this superhero reenacted the anger Seth felt towards his father by filling the house with traps and tricks. Deborah then become preoccupied with her relationship with Seth rather than confront John with her anger.

Greater Distance and Hostility

At the same time, Seth's father was at work, trying to beat a deadline, and planning strategies, traps and tricks to procure more interesting work for his department. Moreover, the greater the tension and stress at home, the greater the distance between John and the family, the greater Deborah's hostility towards her husband, the more likely he is to distance himself from the family, feeling pushed into the role of outsider, completing the destructive spiral.

It would be all too easy to blame Seth's "behavior problem," Deborah's depression, or John's distancing rather than look at the work-family conflicts operating here. John says that he is working for his family and that work and family are separate. John explains that work is a "jungle" and home should be a comfortable nest. Despite John's wish for the separation of these two spheres, the frustrations of work are often inappropriately displaced onto the family. In addition, John's absence from his family has set off a chain of shifting alignments and reactions resulting in a home that is even less comfortable than work. While John has an ideological commitment to the importance of family life and would probably rate it as first priority on a survey questionnaire, his 12-14 hour work days leave him without the energy to work out interpersonal issues within the family, or the awareness of the interdependence of events in work and family arenas. Moreover, on those days when John does get home and reinvests himself in the family, he is left with no time alone for himself.

In this case the strain created by the reallocation of John's work time was felt along the lines of stress already present, acting catalytically to intensify and shift problematic alignments in the family. It is as if the increased demands of a developing career can send ripple effects along the family "fault line," or point of weakness, resulting in shifts in the family structure which can have either constructive or destructive consequences for the family system.

John's dilemmas are not his alone, and the pressures he experiences in the dual role of worker and committed father are shared by many young fathers of this generation. The demands of these two roles are frequently in direct conflict with each other. Deborah has been considering returning to work. If she does this, the pressures on John for more role sharing will be even greater. They will have new areas of sharing but increased competition for resources within the family. Either way, the work-family issues are complex, and there is the potential for considerable growth as well as conflict.

James Mooney: A Day Shift Father

Although both rising young professionals and factory workers experience conflicts between work hours and family needs, both the nature of the conflicts and the timing of them differ. While John Williams' wife was home full time, hoping to return to part-time work after the children were older, James Mooney's wife went back to work full-time when her youngest was 2. When Jane Hood interviewed them four years later, they had become co-providers and co-parents and were trying, in spite of inflexible work schedules, to make time to be together as a family.

In 1975, James Mooney was 30 and his wife, Jill, 27. They had two boys, Chuck, then 8, and Jimmy, 6. James had been working for the past 9 years as a diemaker in an auto plant and was earning $17,000 a year including overtime pay. Jill, after staying home full-time for 4 years, had gone back to work and had had a variety of unskilled jobs in the past 4 years. At the time, she was doing a routine clerical job in the finance office of a hospital and earning $7,000 a year, about 30% of their gross family income.

"I like to be close to my kids. I think there's too many kids that are on their own nowadays."

Jill remembers the early child-rearing years as a nightmare. Their first son, Chuck, had arrived 9 months after their marriage, interrupting an extended honeymoon. Before that, James would take days off from work and borrow his brother's jeep so that they could go riding through the woods. The

baby ended all of that, and James gradually withdrew to the basement with a set of model trains. Jimmy was born less than 2 years after Chuck, and Jill did the best she could with an infant and a very active toddler. However, by the time the youngest was 2, Jill had developed a bad case of eczema. "A nervous reaction," she told me. "Me and the children, we get along when they're older, but babies?" At age 19 and 21, neither Jill nor James was ready for "babies."

Jill's eczema got so bad that finally a doctor told her that she would have to get out of the house. Because he had less than 10 years seniority, James was still working the afternoon shift. This meant that Jill could leave the children with him while she worked from 7:00 a.m. to 3:30 p.m. A baby sitter could fill in for the hour between the time James left for work and Jill returned. Not only would she be getting out of the house, Jill reasoned, but also, she would be adding to the family income, and money was more important to her than it was to James.

James agreed to try the new arrangement, and suddenly found himself alone all day with a 2 year old and a 4 year old whom the doctors were now calling "hyperactive." Jill remembers that during this period, James frequently called her at work and complained about the children: "I finally told him to stop calling me at work or I'll just quit and stay home. We used to have a lot of arguments about this."

James did not remember it being as hard for him the first year as Jill had described, although he was ambivalent: "I was, kinda mixed emotions . . . kind of an economic deal . . . in our situation. I imagine, somebody with a doctor for a husband, it would be more or less something to do (for the wife to work). . . . It wasn't that much. You know, I helped out before. Just the first time I had them all to myself all day. It wasn't much of an adjustment. Diapers, I never could get used to that."

A Fortunate Man

We will probably never know what really happened in the Mooney family during that first year, but, when interviewed 5 years later, James had just gotten back from a picnic lunch with Jill and the children at her work place. After the interview, he had an appointment to take Chuck to the doctor at 2:00 p.m. so that he could be back by 3:00 p.m. to let the baby sitter in before going to work. Although their work schedules make it difficult for James and Jill to spend as much time together as they would like, James feels that he is more fortunate than men whose wives do not work: "Yea, I see situations like that, where the wife doesn't work. It seems the wife is 'the parent.' The father is always working. Whereas, the situation we have . . . I never really thought . . . it might be just the way the situation was out of necessity. . . . I was brought closer to my kids." In other words, although neither he nor Jill planned it that way, James became a psychological parent because he worked the afternoon shift and was home alone with the children while they were awake. Now, he says: "Some days you feel like knocking their heads together. I think it's good though. I'm thinking that later in life, when I get older, they'll be closer with me. And I like to be close to my kids. I think there's too many kids that are on their own nowadays. And when they get older, they get in trouble and the parents can't figure out why . . . and I figure it's because the parents weren't there when the kids needed them. Now, when they're young and everything, you should be developing their life." "Developing their life" is a responsibility that James takes so seriously that in the past year he has been going to P.T.A. conferences by himself, allowing *Jill* to remain at work.

"Professionals such as John Williams need major changes in the formal and informal standards by which they are evaluated before they can freely choose to spend more time at home."

Although James is delighted with the way things have worked out for him and his sons, he would like more time with Jill and more time together as a family. When interviewed, he was working 7 day, 66 hour weeks. He explained that it was mandatory and that if he didn't come in, he would be subject to reprimand and then a disciplinary layoff. He does not like having to leave Jill in the middle of a week-end afternoon to go to work when weekends are the only time they have together. He does have the option of working days now, but hesitates to do this because of the child care problem they would have when the children are home from school in the summer.

While James would like to reduce his work commitment, Jill would like to increase hers. In between interviews, she had moved up a classification and had a job where, as she put it, she had to use her head. She would like to continue to advance, but that would mean working overtime and/or going to school, and further encroachments on the already too small amount of time she and James have as a couple. Thus, becoming a two-job family has had a positive effect on James' relationship with the children and has increased his role-sharing with Jill, but mandatory overtime and inflexible work-scheduling make it difficult for him to be with his family at the times they are free to be

with him.

If the Mooneys could shape their work lives to fit their personal and family needs, James would work 30 to 40 hours a week on a flexible schedule which would allow him to adjust to both his children's needs and Jill's work hours. Jill would work and/or get additional training 40 to 50 hours per week, and would earn enough money to compensate for James' reduction in overtime pay. The family could also gain flexibility by developing a more widely based social support system. As it stands, they have few friends, partly because James is, as Jill describes him, "a loner," and partly because their time together is so valuable they don't want to share it with other people. This, however, makes them very dependent on each other. Given an emotional crisis in either of them or in the relationship, they have no outside resources to turn to. Although more flexible work scheduling would not in itself break the Mooney's isolation, it would provide them with more opportunities for doing this themselves.

The work/family conflicts experienced by John Williams and James Mooney are not isolated incidents in the lives of the two individuals, but examples of several of the ways work scheduling affects family life. This conclusion will underline some of the important similarities and differences in the two cases, the patterns that emerge from this comparison, and recommendations to family practitioners and policy-makers.

Unintended Consequences

In both cases, work schedule changes had unintended consequences for family roles and the quality of family interaction. In the first case, the choice of an afternoon shift had the unintended negative consequence of increasing the family's stress level and intensifying particular problematic relationships within the family. In the second case, a wife's return to work on the day shift had the equally unintended positive consequence of increasing the father's involvement in the family and investment in the father role. These changes then led him to consider negotiating a new work schedule which would allow him to live in accordance with his new priorities.

The range of work schedule options available, the overt and covert forces which shape the choices the men in these cases make, reflect differences in their social class and occupational prestige, as well as in the structure of specific occupations. For example, working class men marry early and peak in earning capacity and on-the-job responsibility sooner than do professionals. They are also more likely to work predictable shift work schedules within a seniority system and be subject to explicit mandatory overtime requirements. The progression of shift work cycles is sometimes in conflict with the developmental needs of the children and other family members. For example, a shift worker who does not have enough seniority to move from the afternoon shift when his children are school age will see his children only on weekends, leaving his wife to resolve all their daily problems.

Professional men continue to add new occupational responsibilities in their 30's, becoming more focused on upward mobility, and less on leisure time. In contrast, skilled workers have gone as far as they can without becoming foremen, and must look to other areas of their lives for personal development in their 30's. In each occupational and class group, the peaking of work hour pressures for time, commitment, and involvement intersects differently with the changing developmental needs within the family.

"It is especially important for family counselors to consider carefully the reciprocal relationship between work and family life."

For working class men such as James Mooney, the inflexibility of work organizations and the link between seniority and work shifts are major problems related to work scheduling. James needs changes in company policy which would allow him to work day shift during the school year, take time off if a child is sick, reduce his work week to forty hours or less, and abolish mandatory overtime. If James works fewer hours, Jill will need more opportunity for advancement on her job and a higher rate of pay. At present, occupational sex segregation keeps women such as Jill in jobs where they earn an average of 57% of what men do. Professionals such as John Williams need major changes in the formal and informal standards by which they are evaluated before they can freely choose to spend more time at home. In John's case, the nature of the task to be accomplished and the criterion for maintaining his professional reputation and credibility required that he work during the hours Seth was home. Moreover, by the time he got home after a 12-16 hour work day, he did not have the energy left to relate to Seth or other family members. Hence, men's values and ideals about work-family priorities are often not actualized under the pressure of conflicting expectations and pressures.

Family Issues

These work schedule problems also define, in part, the marital issues couples must negotiate. For example, if John Williams continues to commit as much of his time and energy to his work as he has,

it will be increasingly difficult for Deborah to do anything but provide the support services necessary to keep the family going. Such a "two person career" can result in the spiral of anger, resentment, and distance described in the Williams family. While the increased demands of John's job may keep Deborah at home, the limitations of James Mooney's earning capacity sent Jill to work. James, in turn, seeks work schedule changes that will support and accommodate Jill's work requirements. In the process, James, who is not a feminist, has become a staunch supporter of role sharing, and John, ideologically egalitarian, has come to support a very unequal division of labor.

Shifts in work schedules are also reflected in realignments of family coalitions and changing patterns of closeness and distance both in and outside of the family. For John and Deborah Williams, this resulted in destructive rifts between Seth and both his parents, and between Deborah and John, and the intensification of dysfunctional triangles in the family. James Mooney developed a closer relationship both with his children and his wife, but because of their complicated schedule, the family has become more isolated from neighborhood and friends.

Interconnected Spheres

We think that it is especially important that the effects each man's commitments and work schedule had on family interaction were unintended and unanticipated. . . . Work-family problems often go undetected because of the tacit assumption that the two spheres are in fact as separate as John Williams wished they were. The case studies presented in this paper suggest that it is especially important for family counselors to consider carefully the reciprocal relationship between work and family life. Problems experienced by many men within the family are often, in fact, work-family problems which cannot be adequately understood without considering the entire work-family role system.

Jane Hood is an associate professor of sociology at the University of New Mexico in Albuquerque. She has also written the book, Becoming a Two-Job Family. *Susan Golden is a family therapist in private practice in Ann Arbor, Michigan.*

Flexible Work Schedules Will Not Change Family Roles

Halcyone H. Bohen and Anamaria Viveros-Long

Editor's note: The following viewpoint is excerpted from Halcyone Bohen's and Anamaria Viveros-Long's study about flexible work schedules and balancing jobs and family life using employees of the Maritime Administration.

For 95 percent of employed Americans, the places where they live and the places where they work are two separate worlds. Typically a half-hour's travel time lies between job and home. Yet people have daily responsibilities in both settings, especially if they have children who depend upon their care.

Most of the daylight hours, most days of the week and year, the children are one place and their parents are somewhere else. Both parents of a majority of American children are employed, including almost all the fathers and half of the mothers. Depending upon their ages, children are at school, at home, in child care facilities—or in a variety of other places doing things with or without adults other than their parents.

These characteristic circumstances of work and family life in the United States in the late 1970s led to interest in the topic investigated in this study. Would giving employed adults some flexibility in scheduling their hours of work help them to function successfully in both their job and family worlds, for their own sakes and those of their children? . . .

Given the increasing use of flexible work schedules [flexitime] and the claims for their value to families, this study of federal employees on flexitime aimed: first, to contribute empirical data to policy and research on the topic; and second, to experiment with the process of conducting family impact analysis on public policies.

As stated above, the project appeared simple. A

particular workplace innovation of recent years had caught the popular imagination. It seemed to please both employers and employees—and to be of benefit to people's lives beyond the workplace. Observers from many quarters enthusiastically proclaimed that flexible work schedules are good for family life.

Investigating these claims for flexitime required looking behind the cheerful consensus to find out, first, what improvements in family life people expected from flexitime—and for which family members; and second, what differences in family life, if any, there were between a group of workers on flexitime and a group on standard time. Finally, the outcomes of these two inquiries suggested questions about what additional social policies might be useful in helping people balance job and family responsibilities.

Misplaced Optimism

The results of this investigation challenge the predominant optimism about flexitime in five important ways:

• Analysis of the testimony in the congressional hearings on alternate work schedules revealed that various spokespersons had virtually contradictory expectations for how flexitime might help families.

• The survey data in this study revealed that the families most helped by a modest flexitime program are those with the fewest work-family conflicts, namely, those without children.

• More flexibility in work schedules, as well as other programs and policies, probably are required to help families with the most pressing work-family conflicts.

• The supplementary interviews suggest that complicated and unresolved value questions both about men's and women's roles, and about the relative importance of work and a family, underlie the ambiguous expectations for, and effects of, flexitime.

Halcyone H. Bohen and Anamaria Viveros-Long, *Balancing Jobs and Family Life: Do Flexible Work Schedules Help?* Copyright © 1981 by Temple University. Reprinted by permission of Temple University Press.

• Minor changes in the formal conditions of work (like scheduling) will not significantly affect the family variables measured in this study (like sharing of family work). More substantial structural changes, as well as shifts in values and expectations about people's participation both in work and a family must occur first.

Contradictory Expectations for Flexitime

With respect to the hopes of how flexitime may help families, the contradictory expectations appear to have emerged in the following way. At first glance flexitime seems a logical way out of the most frequently mentioned work-family conflict, namely, between children's need for parental time and parents' need for work time. Flexitime seems to respond directly to the incongruence between children's school schedules and adult work schedules. In addition to the traditional conflicts between work and school schedules, other work conflicts—for people with or without school children—include those between the demands of the job and the needs or desires of workers for time alone; time with children, friends, spouses, and other relatives; or time in community activities, recreation, or other interests.

"As desirable as flexible work schedules are for most people, other factors are far more influential in determining how people distribute their time and energy between jobs and family life."

By age three, most American children are away from home part of the day, but usually not as long as their employed parents. If school and work schedules were better synchronized, the logistical conflicts between jobs and schools might be reduced for employed parents. Allowing parents choice in scheduling their work might allow them to coordinate their work-family responsibilities more easily—and permit them to spend more time at home.

But a few pieces of the logistical puzzle are left over. Most workdays are still several hours longer than school days. What should be done with children under age three for whom out-of-home care is not universally available? What should be done when older children are sick and cannot go to school? Or when elderly or infirm family members need attention? How can job demands and schedules accommodate all the activities related to sustaining family life that take place outside job and school hours?

As soon as these questions about family care become concrete, the notions about how flexitime will help families become elusive. Who (meaning men and women), will do what (meaning take care of dependents and household chores), and when (meaning parts of the days or years)? Where will the care take place (at home or elsewhere)? Or what will be gained (meaning satisfactions in time with children, grandparents, and domestic activities) by those who take time from employment (or leisure) to give to family work? Also, who will pay for the time spent in child rearing? Individual families or general taxation? Private or public systems? When both men and women are employed in comparable ways, in terms of hours and responsibilities, can flexible work scheduling affect how and by whom these functions are managed? . . .

The survey findings suggest that the families most helped by flexitime are those with the fewest work-family conflicts, on the basis of the following reasoning. Employed women in the sample continue to bear primary responsibility for family work, as measured by hours spent on home chores and child rearing, whether they or their husbands are on flexitime or not. Women without children have less stress if they are on flexitime; but mothers (i.e., those workers with the most job-family conflicts), with or without spouses, are equally stressed on either work schedule. Thus, . . . women should still bear primary responsibility for family work. . . . But those women presumed to have the most to do—i.e., mothers—have no less stress when they have this modest flexitime option. . . .

Men on Flexitime

Men on flexitime with employed wives do not spend significantly more time on family work than those on standard time whose wives are also employed. But flexitime men whose wives are not employed do spend more time on family work than their standard time counterparts—and they feel less stress.

What can be made of these somewhat confusing trends in stress and the division of domestic responsibilities in the survey data? To those who hoped that employed parents will have less stress, will spend more time with their children, and will share family work more equally, the flexitime program examined in this study seems to have little to offer. Yet recognizing that such social changes are not likely to occur overnight . . . , some encouragement may be found in the fact that fathers on flexitime whose wives are not employed are spending more time on home chores and with their children than their standard time counterparts (but not more time than the two-earner fathers on both schedules whose wives are employed). This trend prevails even when controlling for the fact that the standard time men work an average of two hours a week more than the flexitime group.

Thus, for three groups—fathers with unemployed wives, employed married women without children, and all single people—the MarAd [Maritime Administration] flexitime program [studied here] makes a measurable difference in the ease with which workers can take care of personal and family chores and activities. In short, for people without primary child care responsibilities, a slightly greater degree of control over their time helps a lot.

"Changes that now encourage men and women to have comparable work roles throughout their child-rearing years require policy responses far beyond flexitime."

For those employed adults with the most family-related obligations, however (namely, single mothers and employed parents with employed spouses), the small degree of schedule latitude permitted in the MarAd program does not make a measurable difference in job-family stress, or in the amount of time workers spend on family activities—suggesting, therefore, the necessity to look further than flexitime for ways to help such families.

Sex-Role Expectations

The interviews with a small group of survey respondents and their spouses enrich and enliven the information from the survey in several important ways. Above all, they suggest that as desirable as flexible work schedules are for most people, other factors are far more influential in determining how people distribute their time and energy between jobs and family life. The most powerful influences are sex-role expectations and work expectations—both internalized and institutionalized.

Like the survey respondents at large, the interviewees had different expectations for the work and family roles of men and women. Even when career training was the same, career performance was different: women expected less of themselves in quantity and sustained quality. In turn, they were more absorbed in their family lives than their husbands. Even men who wished to be more engaged in child rearing found it difficult because of their work pressures and commitments. And men who were less work absorbed simply felt less responsibility for day-to-day home and child care—and in turn their wives did not expect it from them.

In short, cultural values about work and family roles for men and women dictated who did what, as well as what stresses were felt by whom—more than the formal work structures like flexible scheduling. For professional men and women, in particular, the

current asymmetry between male and female roles in work and family, plus the heavy time requirements of each, leave enormous uncertainties about where their energies and emphases should be. Flexitime helps them to juggle the choices around the margins, but it does not help decide how to make the choices. For less work-absorbed women with family responsibilities, a little schedule leeway is a great boon in managing the logistics of daily work and family life—but these women are still left with the primary responsibility for most of the home demands.

New Work Policies Needed

Perhaps the major importance of the present study for policymakers and employers is to dramatize the fact that families with the most work-family conflicts may need more accommodations to their dual sets of responsibilities than are currently available. In other words, in light of changing employment, fertility, and life expectancy patterns, even stable, middle-class, civil servant parents—like those in the study—may require more substantial changes in the structure of work than minor schedule flexibility if they are to better balance their lives both as employees and family members. . . .

The popularity of flexitime results, in part, from the fact that it seems to be an easy structural solution to the strains produced by rapid social changes. But its very simplicity obfuscates the competing hopes for what it can accomplish. On the one hand, flexitime is agreeable because it costs very little and changes very little about what employers can expect by way of a day's work from employees—while apparently making people more cheerful about what they get paid to do.

On the other hand, for those who want to alter the traditions which make it difficult to combine "paid work" and "family work," the concept of self-determined working hours seems a step towards a multitude of far-reaching changes in the structure of work. But on the basis of the findings in this survey, modest versions of flexitime alone—like that in the Maritime Administration—cannot be considered significant changes in the existing organization of work, that is, in terms of their impact on work-family conflicts. The complexities of the social, economic, and demographic changes that now encourage men and women to have comparable work roles throughout their child-rearing years require policy responses far beyond flexitime—if the goals for families with children are, in part, those held out for flexitime, namely, to reduce parental job-family stress, to enable parents to spend more time with their children, and to increase equity between males and females in paid work and family work. What other policies might help? . . .

Those which are already in use and could be used more widely in the United States include:

• Parental work-leave policies. In Sweden parents may divide nine months of leave after the birth of a baby. Either parent may stay home with the infant. France and Norway also have national parental leave policies.

• More flexible work schedules and flexiplace. New United States federal flexitime legislation allows people to average eighty hours every two weeks, with more or less than eight hours daily, as they wish (within strictures of agencies who have made use of the new law). Some businesses now allow mothers on maternity leave to work at home, as far as possible in terms of their assignments. Sabbatical leaves are being conceived in terms of redistributing time to education, leisure, family work and paid work over the life cycle.

• Shorter work days for parents (i.e., variations on part-time). Parents may now work six-hour days in Sweden until their youngest child is eight years old, with less pay than for eight-hour days but without jeopardy to their jobs.

• Increased pre-primary school programs and more after school programs. More programs for children from age two to three through age five are desired and in use in some places, for example, in Belgium and France. Expansion of such programs will gradually do away with the artificial historical dichotomy between day care programs and pre-primary care, and will acknowledge the interest of most parents in having their children have some group experience from ages three to five.

• Parental insurance (instead of maternity benefits). Swedish parents may divide between them an entitlement to stay home from work for child rearing, either as an absence of two to four hours per day, or for a period corresponding to three months of full-time absence from work at any time up until the child is eight years of age. They will be paid at 90 percent their actual income for two of the three months. . . .

"Excessive work hours will be reduced for committed professionals only if their criteria and rewards for successful lives are not synonymous with long work hours."

Even if policies and programs like those suggested above are legislated, they will not alleviate work-family conflicts unless they are accompanied by shifts in values about the appropriate connections between work and family life, as well. . . .

For example, flexibility in job schedules will increase time in family work only if people have jobs in which they can earn enough to support their families without excessive overtime; if the jobs are challenging and fulfilling; and if they choose to spend some of the non-work time in family life. Excessive work hours will be reduced for committed professionals only if their criteria and rewards for successful lives are not synonymous with long work hours. More equal sharing of family work between spouses will occur only if expectations about sex role divisions of paid labor and home labor are altered.

Demographic and economic factors are also likely to influence each of the above. For example, as people have fewer children and longer work lives, more time with the children may seem more desirable. As women share more of the economic support of families, and men are encouraged to value their family time more, men may feel less compelled to be absorbed in work. And as women's lives are challenged and diversified by participation in the labor force, they may have greater pleasure and success in their parenting. . . .

Placing a Priority on Family Needs

[Sociologist Joseph] Pleck sees the problems of contemporary families as extending beyond individuals and requiring institutional and value changes:

> It does not seem possible for large numbers of families to function with *both* partners following the traditional male work model. Such a pattern could become widespread only if fertility dropped significantly further or if household work and child care services became inexpensive, widely available, and socially acceptable on a scale hitherto unknown. In the absence of such developments, greater equality in the sharing of work and family roles by women and men will ultimately require the development of a new model of the work role and [a] new model for the boundary between work and the family which gives higher priority to family needs.

Halcyone H. Bohen is the director of the corporate policy project at the Children's Defense Fund. Anamaria Viveros-Long is a social science analyst with the US State Department's Agency for International Development.

"Getting husbands to help at home is an adjustment millions of working wives are making in their families."

Men and Women Should Share Housework

Jean Marzollo

At a conference, because another woman canceled at the last minute, I found myself the only female on a panel of six "experts." Speech in hand, I was ready to rise from my chair. I was nervous. I'm always nervous before speaking. I listened as the moderator mentioned my books, noted that I have two children, and concluded by saying that I am a member of the school board in the town where I live. It was time. I clutched my papers and began to rise. Just as I did, the psychologist next to me leaned over and whispered, "All at the expense of being a supermom?"

A Joke with a Punch

He said this in jest, and I laughed, not inside, but outside because a laugh was socially called for. By this time I was standing at the lectern and felt I had to explain my laugh to the audience. "Dr. so-and-so just said, 'All at the expense of being a supermom!' But I'm not a supermom at all. I make lots of mistakes, I really do. I don't do everything."

I didn't know how to go on. I felt incredibly stupid. Something was wrong, but I didn't know what it was. I just knew that I hated being called a supermom. Finally I gave up and read my speech. Not until the next day when the conference was over and Dr. so-and-so was back in his laboratory researching the mothering instinct did I realize how angry I was. Then I spent hours mentally rewriting my speech, cleverly incorporating his pejorative remark into the opening. Here is what I wish I had said:

"The gentleman to my right has just suggested *sotto voce* that I am a supermom. Recently we've been hearing a great deal in the media about supermoms. Supermoms are mothers who try to do too much. We've heard about the supermom

syndrome, the problems of mothers breaking down because they have overextended themselves. Some supermoms invest too much in their homes and children. They collapse under the burden of ordering perfect draperies, baking perfect soufflés, and raising perfect children. These supermoms are always cooking, cleaning, driving, shopping, and planning. Other moms hate them, and so, when the supermoms start to twitch or drink too much, the other moms shake their heads knowingly and say, 'The trouble with her was that she thought only of others. She had no real existence of her own.' The cure is for the supermom to let things go a bit. She'll probably feel better, and other mothers will like her much better.

Supermom II

"There is another kind of supermom, call her supermom II, if you will, the woman who has an outside job and still tries to be supermom. This syndrome is worse because not only does the woman have no life of her own but she hardly ever does anything well. Her draperies are hopeless, and her children don't take ballet because she can't arrange for them to be picked up afterward. It is *men* who don't like supermom II. Some husbands refuse to help them at home. It is bad enough, these men feel, that their wives have to work, thereby publicizing to the world that the men cannot earn enough to support their families, but if a man then has to come home and cook dinner? No way. His home is his castle. He is a *man*, a king. You won't catch him peeling potatoes. And no mopping either. Housework is for women.

"Of course, many men today help their working wives at home. They realize that it is too much for a woman to work full-time and also do all the housework. Many husbands have started chipping in. Usually they get to pick the jobs they want, but nevertheless they are helping, and that is good.

Jean Marzollo, "Don't Call Me Supermom," *Parents*, April 1984. Reprinted with the author's permission.

"I'll bet that you, the psychologist who just called me a supermom, clear the table in your home. I'll bet you fold the laundry, too. At the same time, I'll bet you often look out the window at the world today and sigh with despair at the thought of children in day-care centers and mothers in mine shafts. If only women didn't work, I bet you think wistfully in your study, the world would be a happier place.

Male Analysts

"It is men like you who love to analyze the supermom syndrome, and when you do, you're not talking about the supermom who drives and bakes and sews all day. You're talking about supermom II. You like to hear how some of us have found the work world cold and artificial, how some of us have asked ourselves in crowded subways, 'Why am I doing this when what I care for most in the world is my family?' How one day one of us bursts into tears at work because she has her period and the school has just called—little Johnny threw up—and there's no way the report can be finished by 2 o'clock! I just can't take it anymore!

"'You don't have to,' you love to say. 'Unless you need and want to work, you shouldn't have to.'

"'I guess I just don't have what it takes,' you love to hear us say.

"'Only a man does,' you don't have to say in reply. The whole world says it for you. Why is there no such thing as a super*dad* syndrome? If you are successful at work and come home to help your children with their homework, the whole world cheers about what a wonderful father you are. 'So busy yet he always finds time for his kids!' When you get up to give your speech, no one whispers in so-called jest, 'At the expense of being an overachiever?'"

"Men can be swell, but that doesn't mean they understand one whit about what a working mother goes through."

"'Supermom,' like 'overachiever,' is a putdown. The word implies that a woman has been foolish enough to go beyond her abilities. Supermom II is especially foolish because by trying to do more than is womanly possible, she may be hurting her children. 'Supermom' is a particularly effective slur to sling at a woman because it fuels her guilt, especially since the insult comes from men, whom most women are trained from childhood to please."

But the day of the conference, of course, I said none of this. What did I do? I stood awkwardly at the lectern and apologized for *appearing* to be a supermom.

As I mentioned, it took me a while to realize how angry I was, and as I write this, I realize I am *still* angry both at the psychologist and myself. *Ms.* magazine calls this sort of mobilizing experience a "click." Here I am, I go along for years taking for granted the inroads feminists have made in a basically sexist world, but if asked, I say, "Who me? I'm not a feminist. I *like* men." I was for E.R.A. when it was alive, but only when I read the papers. I never gave money or time.

Sexism wasn't really a problem for me. My husband and I have always split child care and housework equally. Male friends cook, change babies, grow flowers. Swell guys. But that day at the conference, or rather the day *after* the conference, I realized something: men can be swell, but that doesn't mean they understand one whit about what a working mother goes through. Some men do, yes, but I honestly believe that most men secretly wish women would stay home, tend babies, and bake bread. Click.

Working mothers understand other working women, but working men don't. Yet still we listen to the male "experts," or at least I do. When that charming male psychologist called me a supermom, my first thought was: he must be right. I probably *was* doing too much. My children probably *were* suffering. I *had* been selfish. I probably *would* have a nervous breakdown, and it would serve me *right!* I embraced his insult as God's truth, which was absurd because I *wasn't* doing too much, my children *weren't* suffering, and I *wasn't* going to have a nervous breakdown.

So why did I feel so guilty that day? Because what I share with most other working mothers is a deep well of guilt. Jewish American males, you who have had the literary corner on guilt for decades, step aside. The 80's are for us, the working women of today. *You can define us by our guilt.*

What About Our Husbands?

One of our worst failures is that we don't worship our husbands in quite the same way that women did when they depended on their husbands for money. We know that on some level our husbands yearn for a "real" wife, and truthfully we don't blame them.

Our poor husbands, they're not *used* to housework. It hurts their *egos.* When they have *big* things on their minds, how can they be expected to remember *little* things like margarine? They *try* to help, but they don't know *how* to mop a floor. Housework is beneath them. Is it any wonder that some of them rebel? "All right, look," they say. "I'll change the baby's diaper if it's wet, but not if it's soiled." Or, "I'll vacuum, but I won't clean."

Darling, we say, of course not! You shouldn't have to do that! I'll do that. I may not like it, but I'll do it anyway because . . . because why? Because I know that fecal matter is beneath your dignity but not mine? Oh, for Heaven's sake, Jean, says a woman friend. Why do you get so worked up about it? Cleaning toilets is not worth arguing about. Just do it.

This sort of acquiescence in women is a trait men approve of. It has even been touted as a feminine virtue—the ability to shoulder burdens silently. Women are proud of it and often mock men for their babyish refusals to cope with the simplest hassles. The more women acquiesce, the more feminine women feel. And, really, isn't there something repulsive about the image of a man cleaning a toilet? He doesn't seem quite a man. Any woman who makes her husband do such a job is, well, not quite a woman.

"For some men, the thought of housework makes them feel their manhood is attacked. By their wives, of all people!"

Now, I don't like writing about men, women, and the cleaning of toilets. In fact, I'd rather clean a toilet than write about it. It would be much easier to skip over this tired, old subject and go along with the *status quo:* put up and shut up. It's not worth it. Talking with men who feel they have something to lose is like talking to a stone wall. They don't get it. They don't even try. Why should they? For some men, the thought of housework makes them feel their manhood is attacked. By their wives, of all people!

In other words, that's just one more responsibility to add to the working mother's list: her husband's manhood. What does she do when she realizes this? She backs down. She cowers. Oh, my goodness, she says, horrified at herself. You're right! I'm sorry! I didn't realize! Forget I ever asked! She's guilty again. Before she was an uncaring mother and a sloppy housewife. Now she's a castrating bitch.

She'd rather do *all* the housework than be called that, and I would rather *not* have my credentials mentioned at a conference than be called a supermom. What a bunch of pushovers we are. Never mind sticks and stones, we can't even take name-calling.

Well, we've got to get tougher than that. We've got to stop feeling so guilty about working. If we're good mothers (or wives), we'll be good mothers (or wives) whether we're working or not.

Enjoying Outside Work

Working outside the home may be something we *have* to do, but it can also be something we enjoy. We don't have to feel bad about enjoying it. There is

something very real to enjoy—the company of other adults, the satisfaction of completing tasks, the money we earn. We may have to spend it all on the grocery bill, but still there's no denying that with money goeth power. Without us the bill wouldn't get paid. Women who earn money have more power in the household than women who don't. It's just that simple.

The world we live in today resists women coming to power. It pays us wages grudgingly, but at the same time it lets us know what it thinks of us. We are less than women.

Such treatment makes me want to stand up and shout, "I *love* being a mother and I *love* working and I wouldn't do it any other way!" For that is true. But there are plenty of times, such as the pre-Christmas season, when the juggling of responsibilities makes me wish I were neither working nor a mother, and having thought this, I feel guilty.

Anger in Disguise

But guilt may merely be a disguise for a more unpalatable emotion—anger. Guilt is palatable because it lends us an air of moral striving. I'm trying to please you. I'm so sorry I haven't quite made the grade. But watch me try! Let *me* figure out what to get for *your* mother for Christmas!

Anger is nasty. It makes people dislike us. It hurts people. We're often too frightened of what might happen if we let our anger out. It's much nicer and far more polite to be guilty.

What would have happened say, if at that conference I had turned to that man and said, "Don't call me a supermom. It makes me furious." Well, the moderator would have been shocked, the audience would have been abuzz, and all the male panelists would have groaned, "Oh, no, not a feminist. What a drag."

What would happen if a mother came home from the office and opened a can of ravioli for her family? What if her husband and children refused to eat it? Imagine, just *imagine* that she felt clear enough to say to them, not cruelly but simply, "Then cook something else for yourselves. I'm too tired to do anything else." Not, I'm sorry, please forgive me, but just, This is the way it is. No guilt.

No romantic idealism either. Rare is the man who says, "Darling! I just *got* it! You're under too much pressure! You have to work and run the household, too! Let *me* manage things for a while and do the dirty work, too. And thank you for all those years when you did everything!" No, we must not *need* this kind of approval from men because most of us are not going to get it—whether we demand it or not.

Standing by one's man is all well and good, but we have to stand up to him as well. Getting husbands to help at home is an adjustment millions of working wives are making in their families—and it takes courage. Standing up to men in professional situations takes courage, too. What we have to say to ourselves and each other when we do this is DON'T FEEL GUILTY! because men will play on our guilt for as long as we let them.

Author Jean Marzollo specializes in writing books about children.

*"No other working person but the
housewife is expected to put in forty
hours of work plus overtime each week
in return for room and board."*

viewpoint **68**

Men and Women Should Pay for Housework

Letty Cottin Pogrebin

Housekeeping ain't no joke.

Little Women
Louisa May Alcott

People laugh at a woman who is inept at
housework because housework is supposed to "come
natural" to a woman. God, it's the *least* she can do.
Men who do housework well can't be *real* men,
therefore they are funny, like Felix, the neat partner
of *The Odd Couple*. In cartoons and TV commercials,
men shown doing housework almost invariably do it
badly. That's funny the way Albert Einstein's failing
arithmetic is funny: Housework is the only activity
at which men are allowed to be consistently inept
because they are thought to be so competent at
everything else. For a man to be "all thumbs"
sewing on a shirt button is safely "masculine"
comedy.

A Source of Conflict

On the other hand, Louisa May Alcott was right.
"Housework ain't no joke." In fact, polls and studies
suggest *it is the major source of family arguments
between parents and children, and the primary cause of
domestic violence.* Conflicts related to cooking,
cleaning, and home repairs more often lead to
physical abuse between spouses than do conflicts
about sex, social activities, money, or children.

A refusal to do housework signals feminist
rebellion for women, and resistance to "women's
liberation" for men. As for children, the little ones
want to clean and cook to prove they're grown up,
and the older ones refuse to clean and cook—also to
prove they're grown up. More than a third of all
parents of children over six complain about their
offspring's not doing chores.

When a housewife takes a paying job, getting
someone else to do housework is a financial

problem. For the single parent or two working
parents, finding time to do housework is a logistical
problem. The full-time housewife feels defensive
because so many women have abandoned
housework for paid work. The wage-earning wife
feels overwhelmed because she puts in a "double
day"—on the job and then at home.

To conservatives, the traditional housewife—a
woman serving her man and children—is a political
symbol, a glorified archetype in their pantheon of
Good Americans. To radical economists, housework
confounds their critique of capitalism until it is seen
as the one form of labor linked both to production
and reproduction. To progressives, especially couples
committed to egalitarian family life, housework is
the last battleground for equity. . . .

Heidi I. Hartmann, a staff member of the National
Research Council of the National Academy of
Sciences, says, "Time spent on housework [is] a
measure of power relations in the home.". . .

How much housework time is contributed by
women, men, and children?

• Women who are homemakers spend more than
eight hours per day on house and family work.

• Women who are employed spend just under five
hours on house and family work.

• Men spend about an hour and a half a day on
house and family work *whether their wives are
homemakers or employed.*

• Children spend about as much time on
housework as do men.

In other words, on the average wives do 70
percent of the housework while husbands and
children each do 15 percent. . . .

The Male Contribution

A nationwide marketing survey identified four
groups of husbands:

• Those who believe in the traditional division of
labor and do not help around the house (39 percent)

Letty Cottin Pogrebin, *Family Politics: Love and Power on an Intimate Scale.*
New York: McGraw-Hill Book Company, 1983. Reprinted by permission.

- Those who believe the man should help but whose actions suggest they do not follow through (33 percent)
- Those who have ambivalent attitudes but say they do help with the housework (15 percent)
- Those who regularly perform household chores and have little difficulty adjusting to the role (13 percent)

If this survey is accurate, nearly three out of four American husbands either do nothing or barely lift a finger. And if so, Heidi Hartmann may be right in her suspicion that husbands constitute a "net drain on the family resources . . . that is, husbands may require more housework than they contribute." She makes the case from another direction: a single mother with two children spends considerably *less* time on housework than a woman with one child and one husband. The difference—about eight fewer hours a week—"could be interpreted as the amount of increased housework caused by the husband's presence."

Boyhood Lessons

The average man's conscious resistance to the inconveniences of doing housework is buttressed by an unconscious resistance that originates in the psychoplasm of his boyhood. By age three or four he learned that certain tasks are "appropriate" to his sex and doing them well makes him a "real boy," while certain tasks are not, and doing them well makes him a "sissy." This sex-role imperative is impressed upon him by parents, peers, teachers, children's books, and television, which sex-type his toys (trucks, yes; dolls, no), his fantasy play ("boys can't be nurses"), his emotions ("big boys don't cry"), his interests (math, yes; poetry, no), and his participation in housework ("help Daddy take out the garbage while Sister sets the table"). . . .

In the conventional patriarchal family, what makes life comfortable for the man (and children) is the housework that makes life hard for the woman. Those who wax sentimental about old-fashioned Thanksgivings, for instance, are clearly not viewing the event through the eyes of the housewife who dusted from cellar to attic, made up beds for visiting relatives, went marketing five times in three days, cooked for a week, polished every glass, set the table, served the meal, cleared the table, washed the dishes, and put the house to rights again.

Holidays and every day, that cherished thing known as "family life" is purchased with a woman's time and labor. Warm family memories rest on a network of chores she accomplished, responsibilities she remembered, get-togethers she organized, messes she cleared away, rooms she made welcoming, food she cooked to please. The rest of the family adds the conversation, games, laughter, stories—the seeds of family closeness. But seeds cannot be planted unless the earth has been plowed and cultivated. Like plowing, housework makes the ground ready for the germination of family life. The kids will not invite a teacher home if beer cans litter the living room. The family isn't likely to have breakfast together if somebody didn't remember to buy eggs, milk, or muffins. Housework maintains an orderly setting in which family life can flourish.

If one person on a farm is solely responsible for all the plowing, it stands to reason that she will have a different relationship to the planting and the harvest. For one thing, she will be tired when the others are just beginning. Then too, she will feel separate and estranged for having worked alone before they got there. And, if her plowed field is taken for granted, she will be bitter.

The alternatives are obvious: Either everyone plows as well as plants so that the pleasures of the harvest are more fully shared, or an outside person is paid to do the plowing so that everyone in the family can start even, and together sow the seeds of family life.

Hire Experts

I've described many examples of shared housework in the pages of my previous book, *Growing Up Free.* So, rather than review family sharing, I want to explore the more radical alternative to housewife oppression—professionalizing housework. . . .

In pre-industrial America, wage labor was rare. The typical family was self-sustaining: The wife canned, cooked, made cloth, sewed, baked, and nursed the sick. The husband worked in or near the home, whether as a shopkeeper, artisan, or farmer; he also raised vegetables, chickens, and pigs, milked cows, hunted for game, shoed the horses, built the house and barn, and repaired whatever broke.

"That cherished thing known as 'family life' is purchased with a woman's time and labor."

Today, the average man goes out to one job, brings home a wage, and the wage pays for products and services that replace his skills. A supermarket supplies the food he used to grow, raise, or hunt. A dairy delivers the milk he once squeezed from his cows. Cars have made his horse obsolete and an auto mechanic does his maintenance. His house is built by experts, its repairs parceled out to plumbers, electricians, roofers, tilesetters, and the like. Of course, he acknowledges, the specialists are far more efficient than any one man could be. The average American man is no longer a do-it-yourselfer *unless he wants to be.*

Meanwhile, in post-industrial America, *the*

housewife is still doing it herself, whether she wants to or not. Although some of her chores have been simplified by modern equipment, for the most part "efficiency"—that hallowed aim for men's labor—is a minor consideration for the housewife. She has a vacuum cleaner as well as a broom, but she is still doing the floors. She buys butter instead of churning it, buys bread instead of baking it, but she is still in charge of stocking the house with bread and butter, and she is still the one who butters the children's bread. She may not be making the clothes but she is still expected to wash, iron, and mend them. She has access to miracle drugs and a private pediatrician but she is still on call (or expected to stay home from work) if a child is sick.

"If housework were professionalized, more men would enter the field—which is what must happen . . . to save family women from exploitation in unpaid work."

Comparatively speaking, the effects of "progress" mean less to women. Despite convenience foods and labor-saving technology, today's housewife actually spends the same or more time at her chores as did women forty or fifty years ago. This is because of our heightened standards of cleanliness—for instance, people used to wear a shirt for a week, not a day—and the modern ideal of "creative" homemaking (we need twenty ways to make chicken, not two). What's more, while the paid workday has been shortened through collective bargaining and automation, the housewife's workday has remained spread out over her total waking hours.

Stereotyped Jobs

Although labor itself is genderless, most jobs are still sex-typed in many people's minds and jobs done mostly by men are better paid than jobs done mostly by women. Because men's time has become more valuable than women's (in money terms) we are willing to pay for the "man's work" husbands once did for their families, but we expect wives to keep doing "woman's work" free. But think about it: If our society professionalized housework the way we have professionalized men's chores, would women's time and labor be worth more in the labor market? Why is it okay to hire someone to *fix* the toilet if the husband can't/won't, but not okay to hire someone to *clean* the toilet if the wife can't/won't? Husbands do not make the excuse, "It's silly to pay some man to do my plumbing when that plumber will just have to hire another man to do his carpentry,"

because he will and he does, and that's called commerce. However Art Buchwald can write, "Behind every liberated woman there is another woman who has to do the dirty work for her," because housework is still considered *her* work, and because no woman is ever "liberated" until a man decides housework is his dirty work too. . . .

If housework were professionalized, more men would enter the field—which is what must happen to speed its transition from semi-slavery to a respected occupation, and to save family women from exploitation in unpaid work they may not choose to do as the price of admission to their own homes. A century ago, half of all employed women were household workers; now they total only 3 percent and today, a black domestic worker is likely to be middle-aged, under-educated, and a cleaning woman; a white domestic is usually young, better-educated, and a babysitter. But the reason why cleaning help is inadequate is not because household workers are black or female but because, at barest minimum wage, the job attracts only the unskilled: illiterates, illegal immigrants, people who have no other choice. Then too, housework attracts unskilled labor because it is thought of as unskilled labor. The idea is *any* woman can do it, since *every* woman does it, and does it free. (If every man fixed his own pipes at home, the plumber who hired himself out would have trouble convincing customers his services were worth $17 an hour.)

Extend Cleaning Services to the Home

Given the privacy of housework, it remains difficult to assess its skill levels or establish a standard of excellence. As long as housewives are resigned to "I might as well do it myself," people will never fully appreciate what "it" is, or be able to justify paying upgraded wages to those who do "it" for others. . . .

If James D. Robinson III, Chairman of the Board of American Express, can call the growing service economy "an all-American phenomenon," the rest of us can insist there's nothing *un*-American about de-privatized housework. Already, innovative services called "Renta Yenta," "Homemakers For Hire," and "Support Systems" charge from $8 to $25 an hour to organize closets, do gift-shopping, clean the garage, or manage family finances. Already, one in four meals is eaten out of the house, a practical solution for singles but financially prohibitive for families for whom in-house delivery of meals and housework services is the best answer. "Today this is an accepted practice in public buildings," says sociologist Jessie Bernard. "A firm specializing in cleaning, well-equipped with the most efficient appliances, staffed with trained employees, contracts to keep a building in good shape." It should not be such a major step to extend such services to apartments and houses—if sexist family politics could be swept aside. . . .

I've said that everyone in the family should do some of the housework (plowing), but by the same token, families that cannot manage certain tasks alone should have the option of hiring a domestic specialist. For that to happen, *housework must be given a monetary value.* Then people of either sex who choose to do their family's housework for nothing would know what their labor is worth, and people who are paid to do others' household jobs could command a reasonable wage pegged to each job's skills.

"The housewife is culturally extolled but economically valueless. She's 'just a housewife.' She doesn't 'work.'"

The Economic Value of Housework. The contradictions tell the story:

• A few years back, Funk and Wagnalls Dictionary defined a housewife as "one who doesn't work for a living," at the same time that a Chase Manhattan Bank study found that housewives work up to 99 hours a week at twelve different tasks.

• The U.S. Department of Labor, which classifies jobs according to their skill levels, gives hotel clerks and parking lot attendants a higher rating than homemakers and child-care workers. Yet a 1981 analysis of the kinds of work a typical homemaker does—cleaning, counseling, teaching, cooking, decorating, budgeting—came up with a dollar value of $41,277.08 (which buys three or four hotel clerks.)

• According to traditionalists, being a housewife is the noblest calling for women, and a talent that comes "naturally" to females. I suspect they would also call being a soldier the noblest calling for men, and one that comes naturally to males. Assuming this parallel, we might ask why the United States spends billions to train and equip the supposedly instinctual warrior while no funds are allocated to basic training for the supposedly instinctual housewife.

• *Quote of the Month:* When asked why she didn't stay in the kitchen where she belonged, Bea Farber, harness racing's most successful woman driver, said, "Honey, you show me how to earn over $600,000 a year in the kitchen, and I'm on my way."

• *Quote of the Year:* "MYTH: Most women who live in the suburbs are housewives. FACT: Most women who live in the suburbs work."

Economically Valueless

The point is, the housewife is culturally extolled but economically valueless. She's "just a housewife." She doesn't "work." If she dies, her functions as helpmeet, lover, homemaker, and mother cannot be duplicated for any amount of money. In that sense, she's priceless. But when the widower replaces her services, the wage he pays is substandard and the person he hires is often ill-equipped. Thus, the same work that was so revered and priceless when done "for love" becomes nearly worthless when done for money.

Looking at it the other way around suggests *The Sound of Music* syndrome: A woman who works as a housekeeper, as Maria did for the Baron von Trapp and his children, receives a wage—a pittance, but a wage. When they marry, she becomes, in John Stuart Mill's words, "his bondservant." The services continue but the market value disappears. No other working person but the housewife is expected to put in forty hours of work plus overtime each week in return for room and board. No other worker is asked to consider money for food, housing, kids' clothes, and medicine her "spending money." No other worker toils into the night, on weekends, through illness and vacation (when her chores are just relocated to a trailer or summer cottage), gets no sick pay, disability insurance, or retirement benefits (other than what her husband links to his), or qualifies for Social Security benefits only if she was married to her husband for at least ten years. Yet these are facts of life for the homemaker, and these facts have taught women of every social class that the marriage contract is no guarantee of lifelong security for housewives. Laws that make husbands responsible for support tend to benefit not wives, but creditors. A wife cannot use these laws to compel a husband to support her. She can only sue for separation or divorce. And despite cries of rage from ex-husbands, only 14 percent are ordered to pay alimony and less than half of these remit payments regularly. So the full-time homemaker risks *all* on her husband and his largesse—which means she is only one man away from welfare.

When she is widowed, deserted by her husband, or thrown onto the job market when he is unemployed, a housewife learns the hard economic truth: Her decades of budgeting, mediating, managing, creating, decision-making, nurturing, and physical exertion elicit a sentence that chills the soul. "Aha," says the job interviewer, "I see you haven't worked in years."

No use answering, "But I followed the rules; I worked for my family." That may wave banners at a Moral Majority convention but it doesn't wash in the personnel office.

Letty Cottin Pogrebin is a founding editor of Ms. *magazine. She lectures nationally on non-sexist child rearing and family life. Pogrebin edited* Stories for Free Children *and was a consultant to the book, record, and TV special,* Free To Be . . . You and Me.

"[Women] also should have the right to remain in historically female jobs and earn a fair, non-discriminatory wage for their labor."

Comparable Worth Can Eliminate Discrimination

Ronnie Steinberg

On the Op Ed pages of the *New York Times*, Morris Abrams of the U.S. Commission on Civil Rights decries the arrival of pay equity, asserting that arbitrary wage setting by the federal government is but a step away. George Will, writing in the "My Turn" column of *Newsweek*, threw up his hands at this latest unreasonable demand of feminists, suggesting that management consulting firms retained to do pay equity studies would turn out to be the major beneficiaries. Even Phyllis Schlafly has gotten into the act, testifying before Mary Rose Oakar of the House Committee on Post Office and Civil Service. What are these and others with access to the media so worried about?

The reform creating all this hysteria is equal pay for work of comparable worth. It is also know as pay equity. It has surfaced in the last seven years to address discrimination in wages, a by-product of occupational segregation by gender and by race/ethnicity. Going beyond the earlier policy of equal pay for equal work, it requires that dissimilar work of functionally equivalent value to the employer be paid equal wages.

In Minnesota, for example, the Legislative Task Force on Pay Equity found that Registered Nurse (an historically female job) and Vocational Education Teacher (an historically male job) were equivalent jobs. Yet, Registered Nurses earned, on average, $537 less per month. As a result of the 1982 State Employees Pay Equity Act, this wage gap has been closed, along with other similar identified inequities. This was accomplished at a cost of 4 percent of the personnel budget, with no apparent increase in either inflation or unemployment, and with a 19 percent increase in the number of women entering historically male jobs. . . .

Ronnie Steinberg, "The Debate on Comparable Worth," *New Politics*, Volume I, No. 1, Summer 1986. © 1986 New Politics Associates, Brooklyn, NY.

Pay equity critics make four somewhat inconsistent arguments. A first argument holds that there is no problem, that the wage gap is not a valid indicator of discrimination. A second position contends that you can't measure the problem, even if there were one in the first place. The third suggests that even if you could solve the problem, the solution would have very bad consequences. A final set of criticisms asserts that pay equity is not a serious reform.

1. *There Is No Problem.* The wage gap between women and men has been regarded as one of the oldest and most persistent symptoms of sexual inequality in the United States. For as long as it has been measured, it has hovered, with surprising stability, around 60 cents to the dollar. Recently, a number of studies, funded primarily by the Reagan administration, have begun to question what the wage gap measures.

Ignoring Discrimination

A study by the Rand Corporation . . . attempted to shift the focus from existing inequality to wage gains. It called the recent improvement in the wage gap—from 60 to 64 percent—the swiftest gain in the century. It concluded that, by the year 2000, women will earn, on average, 75 cents to a man's dollar, a dramatic decrease in the wage gap attributed to women's increasing education and job experience. The study ignored the issue of discrimination altogether.

The Commission on Civil Rights went even further in trying to sever the connection between the wage gap and discrimination:

> If the wage gap is in large part the result of non-discriminatory factors—familial and societal socialization, female labor force expectations and labor force participation, or discrimination beyond an employer's control (such as that which may occur in educational institutions)—then an antidiscrimination "remedy" imposed on employers is the wrong answer.

The Commission arrived at these conclusions, partly

by implying that women, and especially married women, choose to earn less money by choosing lower-paying jobs. Evidence for their "choice" argument rests on the spurious finding that:

> the earnings differential varies by marital status. Men and women who have never married exhibit the smallest differential—2.4 percent by one measure—while the largest differential is found between married men and women—61.6 percent by the same measure.

In fact, the reason that the wage gap between single women and single men is so small is because we are comparing the top pool of women earners with the bottom pool of male earners.

Out of Touch

The free choice justification is a frequent refrain of other critics. *Commentary* tells us that women "want jobs permitting easy exit from and re-entry into the labor force, preferences which flow in turn from the average married woman's perception of her family as being her primary responsibility, especially when her children are young." While this may have been true twenty years ago, its use as an argument today by the affluent white male critics writing in these journals only suggests how out of touch with the realities of average America they are.

Their position on the measuring of the wage gap falls apart entirely in light of the available evidence. After a two-year review of existing research, the National Research council concluded:

> Not only do women do different work than men, but the work women do is paid less, and the more an occupation is dominated by women the less it pays. . . . Women are systematically underpaid . . . on the basis of the review of the evidence our judgment is that there is substantial discrimination in pay.

Moreover, white women and white men now have about the same number of years of formal education. Yet, the wage gap between them remains large. Indeed, whatever the educational level and regardless of race, women earn substantially less than men. Why, then, does the Rand Corporation think that further equalization of the level of education will bring about wage equality?

Employers Are Responsible

The assertion that occupational segregation is beyond the control of employers is perhaps the most absurd of all expressed thus far. It flies in the face of study after study showing that artificial barriers are constructed by employers, the impact of which is to profoundly restrict mobility across sex-segregated jobs. A Census Bureau study recently found more discrimination against women entering the labor market in 1980 than in 1970. Taking into account factors like education and experience, entering white women were paid, on average, 83 cents for every dollar earned by white males. In 1970, women earned 86 cents on a man's dollar. Over this decade

when the position of women declined, the average educational attainment of white women increased rapidly. The gap between black women and white men closed slightly but remained substantial in 1980 at 79 percent. The study also showed that, for women who started working in 1970 and were still working in 1980, the gap between their wages and those of men widened significantly. By 1980, those women who had originally earned 86 percent of their male cohorts were now earning only 68 percent of men's wages. It is hard to see how employers bear no responsibility for this deterioration of average earnings. . . .

"A Census Bureau study recently found more discrimination against women entering the labor market in 1980 than in 1970."

---

2. *You Can't Measure the Problem.* This criticism has been called the apples and oranges myth, after an early article in *Fortune* said that comparing dissimilar jobs is like comparing apples and oranges. Of course, *Fortune* forgot that nutritionists daily compare apples and oranges, in terms of minerals, vitamins, and number of calories. The Reagan administration has converted this into the "poets and plumbers myth" even though, with the exception of universities, few workplaces hire both poets and plumbers.

In criticizing pay equity studies, opponents call job evaluation a subjective technique. But when employers use it, job evaluation has an aura of objectivity. Use it they do. The Government Accounting Office estimates that over 80 percent of large public and private sector employers use job evaluation as part of the wage-setting process, and the National Research Council estimates that over two-thirds of *all* employers do.

Job evaluation techniques are built on the assumption that dissimilar jobs can be compared in terms of job content characteristics that cut across jobs. These characteristics include such job features as level of education required, amount of prior job experience necessary, writing skills and other mental demands, fiscal responsibility, responsibility for patients, clients and inmates, degree of supervision required, degree of supervision exerted, and so on. For example, jobs differ in the level of education necessary. But all jobs can be described in terms of a required educational level. In general, jobs requiring more education are paid more.

Even the federal government does job evaluation. The salary structure of its employees is based on one of the largest evaluation systems ever instituted. The

Dictionary of Occupational Titles, published by the U.S. Department of Labor, is a ranking of thousands of jobs from most complex to least complex according to three general job content characteristics. This system has been used by firms throughout the country as an aid to setting salaries. It is only when proponents of pay equity seek to use job evaluation that it becomes an unacceptable approach to wage-setting.

Sexism in Current Job Evaluations

It is important to remember that comparable worth proponents did not create job evaluation. Instead, proponents' studies seek to adjust existing classification and compensation policies to remove their discriminatory aspects. It is not surprising that the way job evaluation has been designed creates pervasive inequities, because sex-and-race-type jobs have implicit compensable job content characteristics that depress the wage rate. Gender and race bias occur primarily because male jobs and female jobs are described and evaluated inconsistently.

For example, the 3rd edition of the *Dictionary of Occupational Titles* rates dog pound attendant or zookeeper as more complicated jobs than nursery school teacher or day care worker.

Labor Department evaluators had overlooked important characteristics of female-dominated jobs, especially those associated with taking care of children. They did not regard these as job skills, but rather as qualities intrinsic to being a woman. They were confusing the content and responsibilities of a paid job with stereotypic notions about the characteristics of the job-holder. Skills like fine motor coordination and rapid finger dexterity, and noisy and public working conditions associated with female-dominated blue collar and clerical work are also overlooked. . . .

Undervaluing Female Work

All job evaluation systems value characteristics associated with historically male jobs and undervalue female work. In a typical system, one set of evaluation charts is constructed so that the number of points in the managerial know-how scale is five times as great as the number of points in the human relations know-how scale. On that same chart, technical know-how may receive seven times the number of points as human relations know-how. Human relations skills are differentially found in jobs held by women and minorities; fiscal responsibility and heavy equipment are disproportionately associated with white male jobs. In other words, the point values contained in the charts reflect a traditional bias against the content of female and minority jobs. A bias in points directly translates into lower salaries.

In fact, these evaluation systems may entirely overlook content characteristics associated with female or minority work. For example, working with mentally ill or retarded persons is often ignored as a stressful working condition, while working with noisy machinery is not. Lifting heavy weights or working out doors may be given a *high* point value, while the eye strain associated with working on Video Display Terminals is uncompensated. . . .

The Chicken Little School

3. *The Consequences Are Worse Than the Problem.* The different criticisms in this category have been called the "Chicken Little" school of opposition. It includes such statements as:

- Pay equity will interfere with the free market system;
- It will cost too much;
- It will result in a permanent national, administrative wage-setting process;
- It will increase unemployment;
- It will increase inflation;
- It will destroy the collective bargaining process;
- It will undermine efforts toward affirmative action; and that
- It will be impossible to implement voluntarily, and inevitably lead to controversy, strikes, and litigation.

These are the same arguments that have been used during organizing drives by anti-unionists and by the political foes of every major labor law reform effort of the late nineteenth and early twentieth centuries. In the 1880s, for example, employers testified before the Massachusetts legislature that a proposed law would lead to chaos in the productive process, that employers would move out of the state, that it would destroy the excellent relationship between employers and employees, and that it would lead the country into socialism. What was this dangerous legislation? It was a Child Labor Law prohibiting children from working more than eight hours a day.

"The 3rd edition of the Dictionary of Occupational Titles *rates dog pound attendant or zookeeper as more complicated jobs than nursery school teacher or day care worker."*

Theories of the free market doom comparable worth, according to some critics. *Commentary* says,

> It is instructive to reflect that comparable worth can never come about through voluntary agreement. If a firm can get secretaries at a market-clearing wage, so can its competitors. Were it to raise its secretarial wage for ethical reasons, its labor costs would rise without any gain in productivity, its products would cost more than those of its competitors, and it would slide into failure. . . .

Ray Marshall, Secretary of Labor under President Carter, points out that a simplistic belief in supply-and-demand theory leads to the notion that,

> women's wages are like any other price, and women's labor is akin to any commodity that is for sale on the market. If women's wages are low, it is because market forces deem that they be low.

Why will pay equity increase unemployment? Again, because economic theory says it will. This is the same economic theory that considers labor market discrimination, and associated occupational segregation, and the wage gap to be a temporary aberration. It is also the same economic theory that would have us believe that women rationally choose low wage occupations because they do not want to invest in training for higher paying occupations when they will be entering and exiting the labor market to meet their family responsibilities. Marshall instead concludes that there are:

> numerous studies to discredit those who refuse to admit that discrimination—both racial and sexual—plays an active role in wage and occupational determination. When examined more closely, theories that may "look good" on paper turn out to be inconsistent with both data and common sense. The problem is that opponents of comparable worth base their arguments on a theory of the labor market that might fit neoclassical, general equilibrium models, but that does *not* fit well with reality and therefore, is an inadequate guide to policy.

The real labor market is filled with imperfections, including discrimination. The real labor market is not perfectly competitive. If it were, all workers would be constantly searching for higher-paying jobs, and workers would compete with each other by lowering their asking pay. Employers would routinely fire employees when they found someone else who would work for less money. But most men and women remain in the same jobs for years if not decades.

The Cost of Pay Equity

What would be the cost of pay equity if it could be implemented? Employer advocacy organizations have estimated that the cost of implementing comparable worth would range from $2 billion to $150 billion. An even more expensive estimate has been put forward by Hay Associates, the largest compensation consulting company in the world. They estimate that comparable worth would cost $320 billion to implement, on the assumption that women would come to earn, on average, 80 percent of what men earn, and that the change in benefits would add 15 percent to the cost of salaries.

There is no doubt that pay equity will be costly to implement. After all, employers have been saving lots of money for years by paying women and minorities less than they would have paid white men for performing identical work. But it will not be costly in the way opponents contend.

Most of the cost estimates are based on the assumption that all wage discrimination in all work organizations is going to be rectified all at once, tomorrow. Most legal reforms that impact upon the labor market have, however, been implemented in stages. The first federal minimum wage law, the Fair Labor Standards Act, for example, called for an increase of the minimum hourly wage rate from 25 cents in 1938 to 40 cents in 1943. Similarly, Title VII of the Civil Rights Act of 1964 limited initial coverage to work organizations in the private sector with at least 100 employees and included a schedule extending coverage over a five year period, so that by 1968 the law covered employers with at least 25 employees. In 1972, the law was amended to cover state and local government employees and firms with 15 or more employees.

"Employers have been saving lots of money for years by paying women and minorities less than they would have paid white men for performing identical work."

Even in those cases where pay equity adjustments have been made, corrections have been introduced a step at a time. In the state of Minnesota, for example, the legislature appropriated 1.25% of its personnel budget or $21.7 million for pay equity adjustments. This represented the first of four appropriations to fully adjust the wage structure to eliminate discrimination. In New York State, over $70 million was set aside by labor and management for initial pay equity adjustments to be made when an implementation plan is finalized. This money, though an enormous sum, represents only 2 percent of the state's annual personnel budget. This is very important to remember: the cost of pay equity is large because the overall wage bill is huge. What Hay Associates and others who make estimates repeatedly failed to do is to place the total cost of pay adjustments in the context of the total wage bill. . . .

The opponents of pay equity, the same people who were fighting affirmative action twenty years ago, now suggest that pay equity could undermine efforts toward affirmative action and increase occupational segregation. While there is not much evidence, we do know from the experience of Minnesota that many women moved into non-traditional jobs *at the same time* that pay equity adjustments were being made. Raising the wages of women's work may actually increase the number of men who enter historically female jobs, an unthinkable outcome given the current wage gap. Imagine a male carpenter leaving his job, going back to school to learn typing and grammatical skills so that he can take a clerical job at a $5000/year salary cut! Or, even a custodian returning to school for several years to earn the same or slightly lower wages. There is presently no economic incentive for most men to seek female-dominated jobs.

Moreover, the segregation of our work force is so extensive that fully two-thirds of all men and women would have to change fields of employment to bring about an equal distribution of the sexes across all occupations. The sheer numbers involved point out the impossibility of integration alone as a reasonable solution to pay inequities.

Pay Equity and Affirmative Action

What is needed is *both* pay equity and affirmative action. Women should be provided the opportunity to move into historically male jobs if they want to. They also should have the right to remain in historically female jobs and earn a fair, non-discriminatory wage for their labor. Men's jobs would not be the only ones that can be done with dignity and fair pay. Our society needs nurses, day care workers, waitresses and typists. It is unreasonable to underpay these workers simply because they had the misfortune not to be born male and not to choose traditionally male jobs.

The final "Chicken Little" criticism actually has the sky falling—that pay equity will result in economic and political chaos. But . . . voluntary pay equity adjustments have been achieved—through unilateral personnel action in Idaho, through legislation in Iowa, Wisconsin and Minnesota, through collective bargaining in San Jose, Connecticut and New York, to name but a few instances. In fact, the Minnesota law was so effective, that in 1984, the state legislature passed a bill requiring a phased-in program of pay equity in cities, counties, and school districts. . . .

4. *It's Not a Serious Reform.* Perhaps the most appalling of all the criticisms of pay equity is that it is not serious because it is *just* a middle-class white women's reform, as high-ranked officials in the Reagan administration have asserted. Comparable worth could hardly be "just" a middle class reform since women are disproportionately concentrated in low status, low pay jobs. Only a small proportion of sole supporting women are part of the middle class. Pay equity studies examine potential wage discrimination in jobs such as food service worker, institutional caretaker, and entry level clerk typist, along with secretary, Registered Nurse, and librarian. Minority women are disproportionately represented in these jobs as well.

Pay equity is being extended to encompass jobs disproportionately held by minority males. This includes such jobs as window washer, elevator operator, janitor, cook, barber, and bus driver. Pay equity is relevant to jobs held by minorities because the processes perpetuating undervaluation are the same, whether the source of differential treatment is race or sex or ethnicity.

Not Merely Middle Class

Like the right, some on the left have a tendency to characterize feminist reforms as merely middle-class. Their reservations about pay equity reflect a misunderstanding of the intersection of gender, race, and class in determining the relative position of different groups of employees. Who falls at the bottom of the class structure in occupational terms? White males? No. One would have to answer black females, unless one wrongly categorizes women workers in terms of their husbands. White women do earn somewhat more than black women, but both dominate the bottom of the occupational hierarchy. Indeed, if we look at the impact of the typical woman worker's salary in the two-earner family, we find that she brings the family income up to a modest, at best middle-class, living standard. As the many feminization of poverty studies show, the lower class is largely made up of women and the children for whom they are responsible.

Pay equity is, therefore, a working class issue at the same time that it is a feminist issue. While it will mean that men's wages will decrease relative to women's simply because women's wages are increasing to eliminate past discrimination, it does not involve an absolute decline in men's paychecks. Instead, it represents an overall increase in family income.

"Comparable worth could hardly be 'just' a middle class reform since women are disproportionately concentrated in low status, low pay jobs."

In several places, the monies for pay equity adjustments are being taken out of what would otherwise be across-the-board wage increases, and not out of general revenues. This might result in a loss of less than one percent of salaries to some male employees. In general, unions are participating in decisions that allow governments to take from Peter to pay Paulette. Perhaps they are doing so because, at least in the public sector, loss in percentage wage increases affects managerial employees to a substantially greater degree than blue-collar employees.

The threat to male workers, then, is less financial than psychological. It means, in essence, that men must adjust their self-images. No longer will women be, in Simone de Beauvoir's terms, the inferior other.

This gender-based conflict is unavoidable. Those on the left must side with feminists who are exposing and correcting this profound source of social inequality.

Pay Equity Will Prevail

Pay equity will not bring socialism to the doorways of American business, but it will require deep changes in attitudes toward women's work and women workers. While change is always difficult, it is also necessary. In the case of pay equity, the fight is no longer over whether there will be change but what the change will look like. How broad will the definition of female-dominated jobs be? To which male jobs will female jobs be aligned? Where will the pot of money for equity adjustments come from? How long can the courts delay the reform? And, to the extent that laissez-faire remains the dominant ideology, it will be a different laissez-faire than operates today.

"Make no mistake, in ten years, pay equity will be a much less controversial reform."

Yet, make no mistake, in ten years, pay equity will be a much less controversial reform. Standards will have been hammered out, studies will have converged on how much particular female jobs are undervalued, implementation plans will be borrowed from locality to locality. It is likely that many private sector firms will have also achieved pay equity in their compensation policies. For this, we have the women's movement and trade unions to thank. No doubt, in the next decade, we will move on to the next set of reforms in the long and controversial road to equality.

Ronnie Steinberg, a sociology professor at Temple University, directed the New York State Comparable Pay Study.

"Comparable worth . . . is not going to move women any closer to equality."

Comparable Worth Cannot Eliminate Discrimination

S. Anna Kondratas

I am strongly in favor of pay equity for women. I know and you know that there is still an awful lot of discrimination and prejudice out there. That is why I am for strong enforcement of laws mandating equal pay for equal work and equal opportunity for women in hiring and promotions. I think we should push for the elimination of barriers to women in non-traditional occupations as well as encourage women to be active in pursuit of their equality.

It does not matter whether you are liberal or conservative. I think we all should be against comparable worth for some logical reasons. Comparable worth has about as much to do with pay equity as astrology does with astronomy. Calling comparable worth pay equity is a public relations ploy that amounts to false advertising. The General Accounting Office, for example, thinks that pay equity is a broader concept than comparable worth. The *Washington Post* says that pay equity is a narrower concept than comparable worth. Ask the average person on the street about comparable worth. He or she does not know what it is. Of course they are for pay equity because they think it means equal pay for equal work.

Supporters of comparable worth do nothing to dispel this misconception because confusion works in their favor. When a comparable worth bill was being debated in the House of Representatives in 1984, the Majority Leader said he could not understand why anybody was against it because, he said, "it affirms the principle of equal pay for equal work." However, equal pay for equal work has been law since 1963. That and the Civil Rights Act of 1964 are all that women need to continue the remarkable progress of the last 20 years.

Some feminists say progress has not been fast enough. They also contend that discrimination is still the rule because most women are segregated in low paying women's jobs and therefore the Equal Pay Act is not sufficient. They think we need new laws, or at the very least, a reinterpretation of the old laws. But that is wrong. Real social progress is never fast because radical change inevitably has unforeseen consequences. Just recall how feminists pushed for no-fault divorce. Now we have ample documentation that that was one of the major causes of the impoverishment of women and children.

Comparable worth would also have many harmful side effects and we should consider them seriously. It is not going to move women any closer to equality. Saying that our present law is insufficient because discrimination still exists is like saying that our laws against murder are insufficent because murder still occurs. It is not the law that is the problem.

The theory of comparable worth says that our society does not value women's work, that scorn for their work runs so deep that any job category dominated by women will certainly and automatically be paid less than it is worth to the employer. There is absolutely no economic explanation for this kind of artificial wage depression. But supporters of comparable worth do not really need an explanation. It is proof enough for them that working women are clustered in certain occupations and that the overall pay gap between men and women has changed very little in the last twenty years. It thus seems patently obvious to comparable worth supporters that women's jobs are undervalued.

The Mysterious Pay Gap

Let us look at this mysterious pay differential. In spite of the famous button that says 59 cents, the real pay gap is more like ten cents and it is mere pennies for younger women. The average annual

S. Anna Kondratas, "Comparable Worth: Pay Equity of Social Engineering," a part of the Heritage Foundation Lectures on February 5, 1986. Reprinted with permission.

earning of women is 64 to 65 pecent of men's, but that figure is misleading because the analysis compares all jobs—which includes a lot of very high-paid doctors as well as a lot of very low-paid file clerks. It is also misleading because men who work full-time jobs tend to work much longer hours than women. Adjusting the study for hours worked reveals that women make 72 percent of what men earn. The figure is much better for younger women. It is close to 90 percent, which shows the progress made in job integration which is the real progress that women need to make.

"There is almost no pay gap between single men and single women."

Not even the most radical feminists say that this very shrunken pay gap is the result of discrimination. About half of the pay gap, and maybe more, is explainable by differences in factors like the skills, education, and work experience of women. Upon analysis these factors are explainable and the pay gap shrinks and shrinks until we find that the part of the pay gap that is even potentially attributable to discrimination shrinks down to nickels and pennies depending on the age group. But the 41 cent gap implied in the slogan "59 cents" is a lot more dramatic. What it amounts to is a manipulative lie in order to elicit sympathy.

However, that is not the whole of it. The pay gap between married men and unmarried men is about the same as between men and women overall. Married men earn far more than unmarried men and married men with children earn even more than married men without children. There is almost no pay gap between single men and single women. Think about that. Married women, on the other hand, earn far less than single women, and married women with children earn less than married women without. Obviously this reflects not labor market discrimination, but the different roles of men and women in the family.

The burden of being the primary bread winner has generally fallen on the man in our society. Sometimes that means overtime and second jobs. Married women, whether they work out of financial necessity or for personal satisfaction, generally perceive themselves as the secondary wage earner. I want to stress that they perceive themselves to be the secondary wage earner in the family. They act accordingly and they plan their lives accordingly. Whether you consider that societal discrimination, as the radical feminists like to think, or simply a practical adaptation to biological reality, two things are very clear. The roles that a man and woman choose for themselves in a marriage are up to the

two of them and no one else. Labor market discrimination is not the cause of the big pay gap. Even if we could accept what some feminists maintain, that the family is an oppressive social institution for women and that women are the helpless victims of social pressures in defining their roles, it would still be unfair to expect employers to pay reparations for the sins of husbands.

The Floating Numbers Game

The second part of the comparable worth mystery is what I call the floating numbers game. I am talking about job evaluations. The comparable worth remedy for the pay gap problem is to have employers compare jobs by assigning points to various job characteristics and then totaling the points and seeing whether the pay scale reflects the point totals. Job evaluations are a very widespread and useful tool for employers. But no one, including job evaluators, claims that the process of evaluating jobs is objective. No one, that is, except the supporters of comparable worth. Giving numerical ratings to job characteristics such as skills, education, responsibility, and working conditions does not establish any kind of mathematical relationship among those factors.

In dollar terms, for example, what is a year of college worth compared to working outside in the winter? The question is meaningless and it does not make it meaningful to express it in numbers. Court after court in this country has rejected the idea that numerical ratings in a job evaluation study can be proof of discrimination. . . .

The original Washington State study—the one that supposedly found inequities among comparable jobs in Washington—was contradicted by a second study done by another reputable job evaluation firm which did not find any inequities in Washington State. A case involving a nurses union and the State of Alaska had both the plaintiff and defendant producing studies that came to different conclusions.

There is a case that really emphasizes how dangerous it would be to allow job evaluation studies to become proof of discrimination. Some months ago the *Washington Post* reported on a study that concluded women are paid fairly in Maryland State jobs. Another *Washington Post* story sometime later said that a study shows that women are not paid fairly in Maryland State jobs. Well you reread each article and suddenly realize that they are talking about the same study. The poor helpless consultants were faced with demands from labor union representatives in Maryland and were asked to reevaluate their data. They did, and the second time the consultants understood it much better. How is a poor consultant to earn a living after all? Conservatives really can believe the *Washington Post*, if not one day then the next.

But ironically, the best case that I have ever heard

against using job evaluations to set fair wages came from a strong supporter of comparable worth. In an attempt to demolish the assertion of her opponents that you cannot compare apples and oranges, she proudly exhibited a chart in which she scientifically and objectively compared apples and oranges. She compared their carbohydrate content. She compared their sugar content. She compared their vitamin content. But what never seems to have entered her head is that none of those factors have anything to do with the relative price of apples and oranges.

Poor Women Will Be Hurt

My most serious objection to comparable worth, however, is that it can end up hurting more women than it will help. And conscientious feminists ought to reject it. Some already have. Emotional rhetoric about poor single women trying to raise a family, and sex discrimination as the reason for the feminization of poverty, makes it sound like comparable worth is going to help poor women. Nothing could be further from the truth. The vast majority of the three and a half million poor female heads of households are poor because they do not work. They are not in the labor force at all. Most of them are on welfare. Only 7 percent of poor female heads of households have full-time jobs. You have read interviews recently with welfare recipients. You know that many of those women would dearly love to have one of those supposedly dead-end secretarial jobs. Very few working women in two-earner families are poor either. Those who are, are most likely to be employed in small retail businesses or as domestics or farm workers. And comparable worth is not going to help them one bit.

Unless America opts for socialism, and sets wages for the entire private sector, comparable worth remedies are not going to help nonpoor working women in low wage jobs either. Comparable worth on a firm-by-firm basis is possible only in the public sector and in large firms. Job evaluation studies for small businesses are not only very expensive, but do not make much sense. Can you imagine a little bakery employing a female bookkeeper, a male delivery man, and two male bakers, doing a job evaluation study? But small business is where the low pay for women is. Only 9 percent of full-time working women work in the public sector. Further, in the private sector 45 percent of women work in businesses that have fewer than a hundred employees. Only a third work for firms that have a thousand or more employees. Women's wages on average are highest in the large firms. In fact, women in large firms earn an average 37 percent more than women in small firms. That is greater than the entire male-female pay gap. Women are also more likely to have fringe benefits in large companies and unions to fight for them. So comparable worth has the perverse effect of helping

those women who least need help while pretending to be the salvation of the struggling poor.

Some women in the public sector and large firms will suffer. Various studies show that comparable worth wage increases for female-dominated jobs are going to have a number of negative effects. I am going to leave aside for the moment all of the economic effects on men in male-dominated jobs and on blue collar workers. I will just concentrate on women.

Increased Unemployment

Comparable worth pay increases will have disemployment effects. Even Heidi Hartman of the National Academy of Sciences, one of the godmothers of the comparable worth idea, admits this, but she hedges by saying that no one knows how big this disemployment effect will be. No one knew how big the poverty effect of the no-fault divorce law would be and now we are stuck with it. There is no doubt that either some women will be laid off as a result of comparable worth decisions or fewer will be hired in the future. Mayor Diane Feinstein is already threatening layoffs if a comparable worth measure is enacted in San Francisco. Naturally those women with the least skills and the least ability will be the ones laid off. Then they are going to have a choice between going on welfare or unemployment. What a wonderful way to promote equality for women.

"My most serious objection to comparable worth, however, is that it can end up hurting more women than it will help."

There are other serious economic costs to comparable worth. But I almost agree with the supporters of comparable worth that the economic considerations must be secondary to the moral and ethical ones. Nevertheless, they totally misinterpret the pay gap and they do not understand the limitations of job evaluation studies. They are proposing remedies that clearly will do nothing for the vast majority of low-paid women and they are going to hurt less fortunate ones. I do not see anything morally compelling about comparable worth. Calling it pay equity is simply unethical. . . .

Better Off Than Most

Comparable worth supporters also do not know who they are hurting. The women who are getting these pay increases are not underpaid and exploited. They are women who are better off than most women in the labor market. Secretaries in the public sector make about 4 percent more than in the private sector even before the pay increases. Due to comparable worth they are now making about 15 percent more. What about the poor secretary in the private sector whose taxes are paying for the increase in the pay of the secretary in the public sector? How do you know prices will not be raised and some poor mother on welfare will not have to pay more for whatever product the company produces? Money does not appear from thin air. Whenever anyone gets a settlement, the money comes from somewhere else. Comparable worth supporters have not been looking at the impact on people who are not affected by comparable worth or the evidence that the vast majority of women who need it the most will not benefit from comparable worth.

"Comparable worth has the perverse effect of helping those women who least need help while pretending to be the salvation of the struggling poor."

Job evaluation studies are used widely but they cannot determine discrimination. All they can show is somebody's opinion of what a job is worth. It is not reasonable to have a law that allows job evaluators and judges to determine that worth. The equal pay act sets a standard so the employer knows whether he is discriminating. As long as he treats workers with similar skills in the same way, he is following the law. If comparable worth is enacted, an employer will have no idea whether he is discriminating. A job evaluator or judge tells him. There will not be one standard because different job evaluations come to different conclusions. Therefore, I do not think that Title VII should be expanded.

Comparable worth settlements have been reached in many areas due to union negotiations. However, that amounts to political pressure and blackmail. It has nothing to do with equity, rationality or any kind of economic analysis. When unions push for something, they want wage increases for their membership. They can call it comparable worth or anything else. It is no different than what has been going on before. As a woman I feel a little bit insulted that unions need to use that argument. Why don't they ask for a pay raise because their membership deserves it, not because Joe Schmo gets more so I deserve more? . . .

Raising a secretary's pay in the public sector will not raise a secretary's pay in the private sector. There will be waiting lines for people wanting to get into public employment. Small businesses will not be able to afford to pay their workers the same and will go out of business.

Under existing equal pay and employment laws, the definition of discrimination is clear. And employers who treat workers with the same skills the same way are complying. Under comparable worth, we are not going to have any such clear standard. Nobody will know what discrimination is and it will be in the eye of the beholder. What is fair to one person is not fair to another.

Supporters of comparable worth are frighteningly blase about the legal and economic mess that it could cause. The remedy proposed does not address the problem they perceive. They believe that poor women are going to benefit most. Most poor women will not benefit from comparable worth because there is no trickle down effect from giving people in the public sector pay raises. We will make more progress if we pull ourselves out of the comparable worth morass and get back on the firm ground of equal opportunity and equal pay for equal work.

S. Anna Kondratas is the Shultz Fellow and a senior policy analyst at the Heritage Foundation, a conservative Washington think tank.

"[Comparable worth] threatens to distort labor markets and to turn societal values away from the principle of nondiscrimination."

Comparable Worth Would Undermine the Free Market

David G. Tuerck

Imagine a future historian who sets out to identify the single most important development to take place in the United States during the last quarter of the twentieth century. Will it be microchips, space travel, or rock videos? Biotechnology, AIDS, or TV evangelism? It will not, in my judgment, be any of these. Rather, it will be litigation that future historians will identify as having weighed most heavily, for better or worse, on life in the United States during this period. . . .

Everywhere we look the litigation craze is in full swing and takes its toll in money, in the quality of life, and, not least important, in respect for our legal system.

The emergence of this craze blends into another penchant that we Americans appear to have acquired—namely, that of blaming every problem on someone's unfairness. . . .

Comparable Worth's Supporters

The idea of "comparable worth" combines the modern American's penchant for litigation and for fairness. Women's groups, Democratic presidential candidates, the *Boston Globe*, and the American Federation of State, County, and Municipal Employees, support the idea. Though extendable to other causes involving pay disparities, comparable worth has surfaced as a slogan for fairness in women's pay. Proponents of comparable worth cite evidence that, on the average, women's pay averages less than two-thirds of men's pay and that men dominate high-paying jobs while women dominate low-paying jobs. This state of affairs, they say, is unfair because it reflects an institutionalized practice of paying less for jobs dominated by women than for jobs dominated by men. The proposed remedy

David G. Tuerck in a speech presented to the Federalist Society at Boston University Law School on March 25, 1986.

consists of wage adjustments that would bring low-paid women's jobs into line with "comparable," high-paid men's jobs. . . .

The comparable worth argument blames individual employers for societal conditions that discriminate unfairly against women. By paying less for jobs held mainly by women than for different but comparable jobs held mainly by men, an employer supposedly ratifies a whole system of discrimination that crowds women into low-paying jobs and men into high-paying jobs. Never mind if the employer pays men who take low-paying jobs as much as it pays the women who take those jobs and if it pays women who take high-paying jobs as much as it pays the men. In paying less for "women's work," the employer contributes to or takes advantage of sexual stereotypes, the existence of which are the underlying cause of the seemingly permanent pay gap that separates women from men—so the argument goes.

The comparable worth argument condemns the marketplace simultaneously for undervaluing women and for not offering a credible standard with which to value men or women. We must substitute objective job evaluation criteria, as handed down by experts in the field, for the subjective, often sexist judgments of employers. Fairness in pay is for consultants and judges to decide. If the marketplace were fair, women would not be paid as little as they are—again, so the argument goes.

The problem with this argument is that it confuses the marketplace with the attitudes—admittedly, the sometimes sexist attitudes—that enter into people's market decisions. The market for labor services must accommodate the preferences of millions of workers, employers, and consumers. To suggest that the process by which it accommodates these preferences is reducible to some gender-based class struggle is, at best, naive. Indeed, by inviting ridicule, comparable worth threatens to undermine the very principle of fair pay for women. One commentator calls comparable worth "A Doctrine of the High Priests." Another calls it "Loony Tunes and the Tooth Fairy."

The case against comparable worth is both clear and strong: Comparable worth can do as much to reinforce sexual stereotypes as to break them down, and it does not necessarily work to the advantage of women. It is less an attack on discrimination than it is the exploitation of our penchant for fairness and of the American legal system as a collective bargaining weapon. It is a gimmick for enriching consultants and politically powerful employee groups at the expense of the general taxpayer and, eventually, the general consumer. It threatens to distort labor markets and to turn societal values away from the principle of nondiscrimination and toward the idea of litigation for profit. It underestimates and undermines the ability of the marketplace to deter discrimination.

The Role of the Market

Of these arguments against comparable worth, the last is perhaps the clearest and strongest. Feminists who simply dismiss the marketplace as an instrument of sexist oppression fail to grasp the role of the marketplace in accommodating the preferences of both women and men.

An economic analysis of comparable worth can begin with the chapter on "Inequalities of Wages and Profit" in Adam Smith's *Wealth of Nations*. Pay differences result in part, said Smith over two hundred years ago, from the "imaginations of men." Some kinds of work are, for subjective reasons, incomparable with other kinds of work. "The wages of labour vary with the ease or hardship, the cleanliness or dirtiness, the honourableness or dishonourableness of the employment." Thus, "a journeyman weaver earns less than a journeyman smith. His work is not always easier, but it is much cleanlier."

Supply and demand do not respect consultants' opinions. Job pay depends as much on subjective, unmeasurable considerations that bear on a person's willingness to take a job as it does on objective, but still-difficult-to-measure characteristics like required skills, accountability, and working conditions. The fraction of all women in the labor force rose from 34 percent in 1950 to 43 percent in 1970 to 52 percent in 1981. Of these, many still put family ahead of work and education, opting for career paths that offer relatively low pay but that accommodate the viscissitudes of husbands' careers and the demands of child bearing and raising.

Although subjective considerations like these are important, they explain only part of the pay gap. Objective considerations explain another part. On the average, women have less education (though this is changing) and exhibit higher turnover rates than men. Women thus come to the labor force with less human capital (schooling and on-the-job training) than men. Jobs held by women do not generally require as much human capital or, therefore, pay as much as jobs held by men.

These considerations do not argue for sex discrimination. They do argue against the idea that society somehow discriminates against women by paying them less, on the average, than men. If women voluntarily concentrate themselves in low-paying jobs on the basis of legitimate subjective considerations and if men generally have more human capital to offer employers than women, there is nothing sinister about a pattern of pay that rewards men more than women.

"As the number of women entering the labor force and getting college degrees rises, it becomes increasingly costly . . . to discriminate against women."

Feminists will laugh at the notion that a young mother voluntarily hires herself out as a clerk typist rather than a brain surgeon. It is, however, to missed careers in gardening, not brain surgery, that comparable worth speaks. There can be little doubt that employers still practice hard-to-root-out forms of sex and racial discrimination that reduce the market options available to women and minorities. Insofar as it is possible to identify and root out such forms of discrimination, the law is clear and should be rigorously enforced. The fact that such forms of discrimination continue to exist in the face of their unmistakable illegality should give pause, however, to those who would condemn the marketplace as the source of the problem or depend on comparable worth formulas to provide a remedy. The marketplace arguably deters discrimination more effectively than any court-imposed alternative.

The marketplace imposes its own punishment on those who would discriminate. Insofar as some employers discriminate and in the process depress women's pay, those employers who do not discriminate will find that they can hire women more cheaply than men. A nondiscriminating employer will then be able to undersell its discriminating rivals, punishing them for their preference for discrimination over profit. This *improves* market conditions for women and narrows the gap between men's and women's pay.

This is no textbook argument of the kind that economics professors conjure up to desensitize students or to fill up class time. Since 1970, women have been taking about half the new jobs in the professional, technical, and managerial fields. They now earn about half the bachelors degrees. As the number of women entering the labor force and getting college degrees rises, it becomes increasingly costly even for otherwise sexist employers to discriminate against women. The result is what we might call the feminization of men's work, or at least of those kinds of men's work that women happen to find attractive.

Sexism and Men

Sex discrimination imposes costs not only on the employers who practice it but also on the men who supposedly benefit from it. During the 1979 to 1982 recession, the number of jobs held by women rose by almost 2 million while the number of jobs held by men fell by more than 1 million. Some women probably took part-time jobs to tide things over while their husbands rode out the recession. Other women, however, continued to take professional, technical, and managerial jobs in large numbers. One explanation is that women were able to outbid men for jobs, owing to a male prediliction to hold out for better times and higher pay.

This is not to suggest that the marketplace will eliminate every vestige of sexism or, in doing so, close the gap between men's and women's pay. Perhaps this gap will narrow only slowly and slightly, owing in part to the "subjective" considerations outlined above. Sexism, too, will not disappear. Unhappily, women are not having much success in penetrating the senior ranks of corporate management. One expert suggests that women may have a management style that men find difficult to accept. This may explain why women entrepreneurs account for a growing fraction of business startups. Perhaps the best women managers often find that they are better off going it alone than trying to overcome stereotypes that would block their advancement.

> "[If women] demonstrate a better management style, the market will reward them accordingly."

Management practices that block a person's advancement owing to sex, race, or some such factor are reprehensible and must be condemned. But the civil rights laws are not likely to be effective against such practices, wherever the advancement process is highly subjective and political, as it is near the top of the corporate hierarchy. Indeed, there probably is no easy cure, inside or outside the marketplace, for stereotypes that refuse to accommodate different management styles.

One advantage of the marketplace, though, is that it provides useful information about the comparative effectiveness of different management styles. Perhaps women offer a management style that is better in some ways and under some conditions than the management style offered by men. If this is so, then women can start their own firms, as they are in fact doing, and manage their firms themselves. If, in this process, they demonstrate a better management style, the market will reward them accordingly. Also, smart investors will buy up male-dominated firms and replace their management with men and women who can implement the better management style. The market might not be nice, but it can be depended upon to put money ahead of sexism most of the time.

Laundry Workers and Truck Drivers

The purpose of comparable worth, someone will argue, is not to protect women with advanced degrees who can't get above the senior vice president level but to protect government laundry workers whose employers do not feel the spur of market forces. The question, however, is why should a government agency or any other employer pin a laundry worker's pay on that of a truck driver?

Suppose that a government agency can hire a laundry worker for less than it could normally hire a truck driver and that this is so in part because government and nongovernment employers generally and wrongfully believe that men are better truck drivers. A business or government agency that hires truck drivers would, if motivated only by economic considerations, recognize that this practice had resulted in the overpayment of truck drivers. It would adjust the pay that it offers truck drivers to some level that is below the pay that employers normally offer truck drivers but above the pay that employers normally offer laundry workers and then plan to replace some men truck drivers with women. We could expect some women to give up jobs in the laundry in order to take jobs driving trucks, and some of the men so replaced to take jobs in the laundry. As other employers caught on to the possibility of thus hiring truck drivers more cheaply, truck driver pay would fall and laundry worker pay would rise. Economic efficiency would rise and the pay gap between men and women would narrow.

Consultants

The advice of a compensation consultant could serve as a catalyst in bringing about adjustments of this kind. Perhaps a report that identifies laundry work as equivalent to truck driver work would spur employers to consider whether they might be able to hire truck drivers more cheaply and thus set off the process just sketched. This would save the employer money (raising "efficiency") and help reduce any distortion in pay scales to which any stereotypes had given rise.

It is wrong, however, to interpret a consultant's

report as revealing some Godlike judgment about the proper relation between laundry worker and truck driver pay. Pay adjustments made on the basis of such a report may or may not increase "efficiency." A policy of trying to substitute women for men truck drivers as a cost-cutting measure may backfire. Maybe subjective considerations will intervene, and women workers will not respond to the opportunity to make higher pay by driving trucks. Or maybe there will be a boom in the transportation industry, and it will be truck drivers who find themselves in a position to demand higher pay.

The same considerations argue, however, against raising laundry worker pay. The problem is not that laundry workers are underpaid but that stereotypes may have led laundry workers to be underpaid and truck drivers to be overpaid. The solution consists of seeing to it that government managers be more careful not to let stereotypes interfere with their business judgment. Properly motivated managers try to hire labor at the lowest possible price, and it is to this end that we should motivate them in framing the laws that govern their actions. As already shown, women and minorities especially benefit from hiring policies that rest on economic factors, rather than discriminatory, noneconomic factors like sex or race.

"[Comparable worth] can be expected to lull some women who could go on to higher-paying jobs into staying on as secretaries."

The claim of comparable worth on our penchant for fairness is a difficult one to defend. The woman traveling to her textile loft derives little comfort from the claim that her job is comparable to that of the better paid subway worker who takes her there. Let a judge decree that she should get a higher wage, and a worker in South Korea will gladly do her job for less. This is not to say that the solution for her lies in limiting textile imports (which regrettably, we do), but rather to point out that comparable worth offers no hope to a substantial number of persons to whom it is logically though not practically extendable.

An Unfair Policy

Indeed, we might question the fairness of a policy that raises the incomes of a particular group of low-paid persons, mainly female government workers, at the expense of the general taxpayer. The real problem would appear to lie in the fact that there are too many low-income families, most of which are beyond the reach of comparable worth adjustments. If this is the real problem, then it is to the solution of this problem, through welfare reform and through similar measures, that we should direct our public resources.

Not even its actual beneficiaries can hope to benefit indefinitely from the comparable worth idea. Raising secretaries' wages above market levels can be expected to attract more men to secretarial work and thus to shrink the number of secretarial opportunities for women. Even worse, it can be expected to lull some women who could go on to higher-paying jobs into staying on as secretaries, thus reinforcing the very stereotype against which the comparable worth idea is supposedly directed.

In our penchant for litigation and for fairness, comparable worth is likely . . . to be around for awhile. Perhaps we get ideas like this because we are a fair and sympathetic people, and so we might be remembered by future historians. I wonder, however, for which it is that we will be remembered: for our fairness or for our having trivialized and politicized our legal system in the name of fairness so that now we compensate burglars for injuries sustained in the line of duty and treat the findings of consultants as if they were the wisdom of Solomon.

David G. Tuerck is the chairman of the economics department at Suffolk University.

"Interventions to eliminate discrimination cause the real market to operate like it's supposed to theoretically operate."

Comparable Worth Would Not Undermine the Free Market

Ray Marshall

While I believe that most of the arguments against the so-called "pay equity" or "comparable worth" notion are overdrawn, I think important issues are raised and those need to be considered. . . .

Let me make three preliminary observations. . . . The first one is that . . . discrimination in compensation—which is what we're talking about here—is expressly prohibited by Title VII of the Civil Rights Act and by Executive Order 11246. I also think it's important to point out, of course, that compensation discrimination is not the only form of discrimination, and all of the others are also covered by this title.

All Thumbs

The second point that I'd like to make is that a lot of the reasons for the disagreements about this issue relate to difference in conception about how the market operates. I am a specialist in labor markets, and I know that labor markets are not like the bean market and they're not like the stock market; people are not commodities, and the labor market works very imperfectly. I've often observed that when Adam Smith's invisible hand moves in the labor market, it's all thumbs. It is not perfect. I think it's an important institution and we ought to try to improve it as much as we can. But it is not perfect and leaves a lot of room for discretion. Wages are not determined by the automatic forces of demand and supply or marginal productivity. It tends to operate imperfectly.

Secondly, it seems to me to be extremely important to distinguish between the internal labor market and the external labor market. The internal labor market is the market within a firm, say, within the Federal Government, within the State of Washington, within General Motors, or within any particular organization. The labor market operates even less perfectly within a large organization. Within an organization you get consideration of equity, custom, and tradition and not the operation of the forces of demand and supply. That doesn't mean that the forces of demand and supply are irrelevant to that internal labor market. However, their relevance is to what labor market specialists call "ports of entry." That's where you go into the external market to hire people. Another way to put the same thing is that in every large organization, every job is not up for bid and you don't go and look on a board like you do the stock market to see how much they're going to pay you today based on fluctuations in the forces of demand and supply. Workers are immobile. There's an assumption in market analysis that people will readily move. Well, it's costly to move. People don't have perfect information and you get discrimination.

The Real Market

I think one of the problems with all the arguments of "let the market do it" is that there is a great intellectual leap in building a picture of an abstract market and how it operates and then leaping to the market that we have and saying this market is perfect and, therefore, whatever it does should be sanctioned and, therefore, we ought not to have any intervention in that market. In fact, I haven't heard an argument yet about nonintervention in the connection with pay discrimination that we didn't have in connection with discrimination against minorities or anybody else. The basic argument of market specialists was that if you had competition in the market, you would eliminate all these forms of discrimination. Now, those of us who believe in intervention in the market believe interventions which would interfere with a perfect market will improve the market that we have. There shouldn't

Ray Marshall in testimony to the US Commission on Civil Rights, comparable worth hearing on June 7, 1984.

be discrimination in the market, so interventions to eliminate discrimination cause the real market to operate like it's supposed to theoretically operate. I believe that if you didn't have those market interventions, we would still have more segregated seniority rosters and other forms of discrimination. We had very tight labor markets during World War II, but these markets stayed segregated within firms, and you would still have the discrimination in compensation and other matters without intervention in the form of antidiscrimination legislation.

"The forces of demand and supply are important, but they function very imperfectly, leaving room for . . . discrimination."

The third point that I would like to make is that there seems to be a great deal of confusion in a lot of the discussion about the effects of comparable worth. Some of the arguments assume that we're talking about the external labor market and that we're talking about people—individuals and their characteristics—and that they get paid according to those so-called human capital characteristics. That's not what we're talking about. We're talking about *jobs* and the pay that gets assigned to those jobs. Now, you hope in the real world there is some correspondence between the characteristics of the people and the skill, effort, responsibility, and working conditions, which are the points usually used in job evaluation in order to assign values to jobs. The point of this is that employers—every day, every State government, Federal Government—assign different pay scales to different jobs. And they don't do it by any kind of market quotation. There are places where they have to go into the market at those so-called ports of entry. . . .

[Let's] examine the arguments for and against comparable worth. . . .

The Demand and Supply Argument

The first argument is that wage differentials between men and women are not based on discrimination, according to the critics, but merely reflect demand and supply. As I've noted, the problem with this argument is that it assumes a model of the labor market which is very different from the way wages are actually determined. The forces of demand and supply are important, but they function very imperfectly, leaving room for discretion, that is, for discrimination. Few would argue that discrimination is the only reason for the pay gap. But few objective analysts could argue that there is no discrimination in the labor market

against women or minorities or others that are in the classes who tend to be discriminated against. Numerous efforts to account for the pay gap by a variety of techniques usually leave a sizable residual that cannot be accounted for by so-called human capital factors.

However, several points should be made about these generally economy-wide studies. The first is that equations cannot prove discrimination or the absence of it. They merely constitute one piece of evidence to be used in arguments over whether or not discrimination exists. It seems to me that an extremely important point is that you cannot, in the abstract, tell us whether discrimination exists in a particular organization or firm. You have to present the evidence on all sides, and then somebody has to make the determination. Comparable worth, as I've mentioned, relates to specific jobs in particular enterprises. Of course, employers use job evaluation techniques to assign values to jobs in different classifications. I was an arbitrator for 20 years and examined these techniques all the time in wage classification cases. The courts have done it. It was done during World War II. In fact, employers are the ones who insisted that you use job evaluation techniques in order to bring some order into the internal labor market. Of course, job evaluation techniques are not precise. They are inherently judgmental. But so are all compensation systems. There are few, if any, perfect markets for labor, or even markets like the stock and commodity markets. As noted, this is particularly true in the internal labor market and also particularly true for government.

Subjective Evaluations

Again, however, these job evaluation techniques leave latitude for discretion. We're persuaded, though, that most job evaluation techniques show a pay gap between predominantly male and female jobs which probably understates the margin for discrimination because they use factors which are more likely to predominate in men's jobs or which are more common among men than women. Indeed, sex bias in job evaluation techniques is a proper concern for any antidiscrimination agency. If it is assumed, as we do, that there is discrimination in the external labor market, then importing that bias into the internal labor market through wage surveys is no defense against discrimination. This is particularly true for government. Governments typically claim to assign wage rates to jobs on the basis of wage surveys from the external market—though I must say the governments rarely use those surveys to exactly determine wages. . . .

Secondly, it is sometimes argued that comparable worth is like attempting to return to the obsolete, medieval concept of the just price. The trouble with this argument is just price or equity still plays an important role in wage determination in internal labor markets, especially in government employment. Governments typically make surveys, but do not translate the results into wage changes, arguing that such survey results are too high or too low—which is an equity and not a market idea. Similarly, most organizations seek to preserve hierarchies of wage payments based on status considerations as when it is determined that Federal employees should not be paid more than Cabinet officers, the President, or Members of Congress; that State employees should not be paid more than their supervisors or the Governor; that wages in one occupation should retain established relationships to other occupations in order to prevent morale problems; or that no wage should be cut, regardless of survey results. These are perfectly valid considerations for wage and salary administration, but they are not automatic consequences of the forces of demand and supply. Unfortunately, these traditional job hierarchies also contain the consequences of traditional attitudes about men's jobs and women's jobs.

This background makes it possible to deal more quickly with typical arguments against discrimination in compensation or comparable worth. First, there is the argument that the wage gap is due to things other than discrimination. We completely agree. But most studies leave a residual unexplained by other things, which suggests a latitude for discrimination.

The Unequal Work Argument

The second argument is that comparable worth would require the government to force employers to pay equal wages for unequal work. A variant of this argument is that comparable worth would lead to government wage fixing. The government would not force the employers to do anything, except not to discriminate in whatever compensation system the organization uses. That should be the objective of any discrimination legislation, to see to it that people are not discriminated against for things unrelated to their merit and productivity. The government would not fix wages though courts might order specific wages where discrimination had been proved after trial.

The Disruptive Argument

The third argument is that the acceptance of the comparable worth principle would be very disruptive and expensive. Our response is, "Who knows?" Since you have to look at each one of these cases on its own merit, it would depend on the evidence in each case. Some critics assume comparable means the elimination of wage differentials between men and women. This is absurd. Not many argue that all of the pay differential is based on discrimination. Moreover, the

critics frequently assume that what is contemplated in antidiscrimination programs for compensation is that you're trying to cause somebody to be paid more than they are worth. That's not the issue. The issue is to cause people to be paid what they are worth and not less than they are worth because of discrimination.

Most of the arguments about disruption start from the assumption that there is no discrimination in the market, that the markets establish the best wage which is nondiscriminatory, and that any interference with that will cause great disruption. If you'll start from the supposition that there is discrimination, that people are not paid what they're worth to that employer in whatever job evaluation system that employer uses, then you do not disrupt the market by causing people to be paid what they're worth—you improve the market. I think it's great that if you increase the wages in some jobs, you would get more men applying for those jobs. That, after all, is the objective, to be neutral with respect to sex. As noted, however, the evidence of discrimination in compensation must be judged in each case. If much discrimination in pay can be demonstrated to the satisfaction of the courts or administrative agencies, there could be some disruption. But that is the price for correcting serious problems of discrimination. If the critics of comparable worth are correct and discrimination cannot be demonstrated, there will not be much disruption.

"Most job evaluation techniques show a pay gap between predominantly male and female jobs."

We have noted, however, that the theoretical and general arguments used by most of the critics prove nothing. If you assume perfectly competitive labor markets and equilibrium conditions, then any intervention would be disruptive. It also should be noted that most critics of comparable worth assume discrimination to be mainly a specific overt act of discrimination and ignore the institutional patterns, which they assume not to be the concern of public policy. I believe that these institutional patterns are extremely important and should be a subject of national policy.

A Useful Remedy

In conclusion, therefore, whether or not there is discrimination in wage payment is to be determined on the basis of the facts in each case. A remedy for pay discrimination does not require that wages be equal for men and women, only that the jobs be valued on a nondiscriminatory basis. This does not lead to central planning or government wage fixing anymore than passage of the Civil Rights Act led to central wage fixing by the Federal Government. The government does not have to fix wages in order to eliminate discrimination. It is true that comparable worth is based on some elements of just price or equity. But in the absence of auctions for labor, a sizable equity element is inevitable in labor markets. Similarly, job evaluaton is not precise. It is inherently judgmental. But it is an established technique in comparable worth cases that would involve no more judgment than ordinarily is involved in wage and salary administration.

Ray Marshall, formerly the Secretary of Labor under Jimmy Carter, is now a professor at the Lyndon B. Johnson School of Public Affairs at the University of Texas.

The Government Should Provide Child Care

Barbara R. Bergmann

Attitudes toward out-of-home child care are determined in part by what people think is good for children. They are also influenced by the importance people give to women's autonomy—whether they think women have the same right as men to be a parent without leaving paid work and thus the right to avoid, if they wish, a stint in the housewife status when they have children. It would be a mistake to imagine that attitudes on such issues are unaffected by economic incentives. To some degree, attitudes follow majority practice, which is apt to change when the economic environment changes.

Only a few decades ago, a mother was considered neglectful unless she waited until her youngest child had graduated from high school before taking a full-time job. A mother was told that it was crucial to her child's development that she be in the house at the moment the child came home from school so that the child might tell her about the events of the school day. Later it became respectable for a mother to go to work when her last child entered elementary school. We appear to be entering a period where mothers have society's permission to avoid any and all full-time housewifery. This last development depends on an acceptance of day care as a satisfactory way of caring for preschool children.

Experts' Changed Thinking

One striking change in the climate of opinion is the turnabout in the thinking of "experts" on the harmful effects of the mother's employment on the child. Prior to 1976, the most widely used baby-care manual, that of Dr. Benjamin Spock, had this to say:

> If a mother realizes clearly how vital [good mother care] is to a small child, it may make it easier for her to decide that the extra money she might earn, or the

satisfaction she might receive from an outside job, is not so important after all.

The 1976 edition and subsequent editions of Spock's *Baby and Child Care* abandoned this attitude completely. The book now advises,

> Parents who know they need a career or a certain kind of work for fulfillment should not simply give it up for their children . . . [but should] work out some kind of compromise between their two jobs and the needs of their children, usually with the help of other caregivers.

One amusing turnaround is in the lessons taught by "monkey research." In the 1960s much publicity was given to the report of a researcher who had deprived a monkey infant of its mother. The monkey mother was replaced in the cage by a heated post swathed in terrycloth, on which was mounted a bottle of milk. The unfortunate infant was wont to cling to the post in moments of stress. To no one's surprise, the monkey brought up by the terrycloth post developed severe psychological problems. From our current perspective, it is hard to see how the results of that experiment could be considered relevant to the effects on children of maternal employment. However, at the time it was considered highly relevant, and the publicity it got strengthened the presumption that the full-time presence of the mother was indispensable if the child were to develop normally. By 1974, however, monkey studies were being quoted to show that even a male monkey might make a splendid "surrogate mother" for a monkey infant.

Rearguard Agitation

There continues to be, of course, some rearguard agitation against purchased child care. Selma Fraiberg's 1977 book *Every Child's Birthright* argues that every child is entitled to full-time mothering. A recent book on day care by Marian Blum, a Wellesley College psychologist, is a compendium of untoward practices and incidents observed in daycare centers: the children who cry when brought to the center, the use of harnesses for taking children on walks, the mass-production feeding, the long hours that children must spend without privacy or quiet, the occasional delinquencies of center staff who may fall asleep or walk off the job. Somewhat facetiously, she invites a comparison of the children at a day-care center to Soviet prisoners in a slave-labor camp. Some of the things that Blum faults seem trivial, such as the color-coded bottles to keep formulas apart. Others seem serious and point to the need for reforms. Such problems include children's unmet needs for quiet and individualized attention, and the difficulties created when parents bring sick children to a day-care center.

Federal and local governments are involved with out-of-home child care on three counts: maintaining quality standards, improving availability, and reducing the price to the parents. In some cities the local authorities themselves run child-care centers. In the past there has been considerable agitation for a more active governmental role in providing or subsidizing preschool child care, and it may well revive once the current wave of conservatism passes.

Governmental regulations on quality are enforced by city and county authorities in the United States. For the most part, they pertain to issues of health and safety: appropriate space, bathroom facilities, the avoidance of overcrowding, and cleanliness of food service. Recent widespread publicity on the sexual abuse of children in a few day-care centers has provoked demands that there be official regulation of personnel selection.

"Government-sponsored child care would help mothers by redressing the traditional difference between the sexes in child-care responsibilities."

In the United States, governmental payments for preschool child care, either through subsidy or through outright provision of free service, is a highly controversial subject. What little has been provided came from programs arising out of the "war on poverty" that began in the mid-1960s. Some child-care programs were aimed at improving the cognitive development and health of low-income preschool children. Others have been designed to encourage low-income single mothers to take jobs, to reduce welfare costs to the public. However, in 1971, a broader program almost became law. The Congress passed a bill setting up a federal child-care program, with universal access and with a sliding-fee schedule based on parents' income. Perhaps to

camouflage the benefits such a bill would confer on mothers, the bill was entitled the Comprehensive Child Development Act. President Nixon vetoed it, declining, as he said in his veto message, to "commit the vast moral authority of the National Government to the side of communal approaches to child rearing over against the family-centered approach."

Despite President Nixon's veto of the 1971 child-care bill, public spending for child care continued to increase. By 1977, the federal government was spending $1.7 billion a year for child-care programs that served about 2 million children. The Reagan Administration starting in 1981, has cut back on these programs to a considerable degree.

Other Countries

Other countries have been far more active in providing governmental funds to finance the care of preschool children. . . . Eastern European socialist countries, believing that their economies need the full-time labor of women, have been particularly active; among capitalist countries, Sweden and France have done the most. France has a large system of public child-care centers. The youngest are cared for in *crèches*, which are highly subsidized. Older preschool children are cared for, free of charge, in *écoles maternelles*, which are provided with accredited teachers who lead the children in activities designed to enhance their enjoyment of the senses—sight, hearing, taste, and smell. A large proportion of French preschool children attend the *écoles maternelles*; even children whose mothers are not employed attend them in considerable numbers. Apparently their educational programs are considered by parents to be beneficial to the children.

Many feminists favor governmental financial support for high-quality child care; they think it would help both mothers and children. The children would be helped by saving them from the inadequate care to which some of them are consigned in the absence of government aid. Government-sponsored child care would help mothers by redressing the traditional difference between the sexes in child-care responsibilities.

Current economic arrangements and social assumptions allow men to fulfill the duties and have the pleasures of parenthood without sacrificing their right or ability to pursue economic and vocational interests. Men customarily go to their jobs unencumbered by the worry that their children will not be well cared for. Those fathers who are single parents usually have salaries high enough to enable them to buy child care.

High-quality child care provided at no charge by government would confer on female parents the right and ability to pursue their economic betterment (and their children's) less encumbered by child-care worries. Single mothers, whose rate of pay is on average too low to stretch to high-quality child care and who lack a husband's financial help, are particularly torn between the needs of their children for care and the need of the family for the mother's earnings. However, the suggestion that mothers need freedom from the encumbrance of child care touches a sensitive nerve. Many people cannot bring themselves to believe that mothers could ever under any circumstances find their children an encumbrance. So most emphasis tends to be put on the benefits to children.

The Opposition

In the United States, the demand for government-run and government-paid-for child care runs up against two sources of opposition. One obvious source is the people devoted to the perpetuation of the system of sex roles that prescribe that women be homemakers, a system that accords the husband primacy in the family on the basis of his role as sole earner. The second source of opposition in the United States is from those who think that as a rule people ought to obtain what they need or want from profit-making private enterprises out of their own incomes rather than from government organizations at public expense. Free or subsidized provision of any product by the government has the effect of forcing those citizens who have no call or need to use the product to subsidize those who do. Advocates for publicly provided and publicly paid-for child care for preschool children have the burden of demonstrating that it is a proper exception to that rule.

Of course, free public schools for children are provided by governments everywhere, including the business-oriented United States. Can the rationale that justifies them also be used to justify free child care? After all, the addition of a public child-care system would simply tack on additional years of attendance at public institutions for children. The common explanation given for public provision of free schools is that it helps the whole country economically and politically to have a literate citizenry. The primary benefit of education does go to the student. But there is an external or spillover effect that benefits everyone taking part in the advanced economy that universal education makes possible. A second, less frequently cited, yet certainly valid argument for free public schools is that they save the children of poor parents from being fatally disadvantaged throughout their adult lives by the lack of an education. The free schools mitigate the rigors of an economic and social system that condemns children of poverty-stricken parents to live in poverty.

The concern for poor children does lend some support to subsidized child care. Research suggests that children from poor home environments benefit from spending time in a high-quality child-care

center. There is a chance to catch and attend to health and emotional problems that might plague the child for its whole life and that might lead later to behavior costly to society as a whole. Helping the children provided part of the rationale for some early-childhood programs, such as Head Start.

"Research suggests that children from poor home environments benefit from spending time in a high-quality child-care center."

However, it would be hard to base an argument favoring the extension of government-sponsored care from poorer children to all children just on the analogy to public schools. Rather, the argument has to depend on the gains to mothers available in no other way and on the structure of the child-care industry. The absence of a high-quality "brand-name product" in child care that operates at a price that parents in moderate circumstances are willing to pay produces situations for mothers exemplified in the following account:

> Last year was a nightmare for Carol Berning. Each day after dropping off her two pre-school children at the baby sitter's, the 34-year-old consumer research manager for Procter & Gamble went to work with a knot in her stomach. Instead of analyzing data for such products as Tide, Cascade and Ivory Liquid, she found herself staring at her youngsters' pictures and worrying. Their sitter had been letting them play in the street, and worse, she was taking them on unscheduled trips across the Ohio River to Kentucky. Then, unexpectedly, the sitter resigned and the chore of finding a replacement was soon absorbing much of Mrs. Berning's workday. . . .

Berning's "nightmare" is without doubt authentic, and experiences like hers must at one time or another be the lot of parents who depend on family day care. But she appears from the context to have a well-paying job. Why doesn't she buy the kind of care that would present fewer or no nightmarish experiences? Is it up to the taxpayers to arrange some better alternative for her children, and for the taxpayers to pay for it?

Risky Daycare

The argument for government provision of child care open to all children is based in the last analysis on its assured quality. Government-run centers would allow parents to bypass family day care of the type used by Berning. Family day care provided by individuals in their homes is rather like the little girls in the nursery rhyme: When it is good it is very, very good, and when it is bad, it is horrid. The problem is that parents cannot with assurance distinguish ahead of time the good from the bad. They hope to be lucky—to take advantage of the low cost, yet to find a provider who will give their child a good environment. More parents choose family day care than choose a child-care center. Most of the providers of family day care probably do a good job. Children can be treated more individually in very small groups, and for very young children the likelihood of catching an illness is lower. Managerial expenses are minor, and the facilities are the living quarters of the provider and therefore are essentially free to the day-care business. (Tax evasion by family day-care operators probably also reduces costs to parents; it is really a stolen government subsidy.)

"Public child care would help women just entering the labor market and those women who become unemployed. It would greatly facilitate their job search."

Family day care may be both best and cheapest as long as things are going normally. However, independent family day care is more risky and less dependable than institutional child care. Unassisted private individuals cannot be as dependable as organizations, which can routinely arrange for backups in case of illness or other problems. The lack of oversight of the independent family day care operator and the defenselessness of the children open them to abuses. Moreover, when a parent has to change providers, finding new providers, evaluating them, and deciding which to use is a nerve-racking and time-consuming task.

Simplify the Working Woman's Life

A government program might provide institutional child care, on a free basis, or with fees geared to family income. It is likely that unsupervised and unaffiliated family day-care providers would be run out of business, and there would be both gains and some losses from that. Some excellent child-care establishments might be eliminated. On the other hand, there probably would be a reduction in the number of children receiving inadequate care in downright dangerous situations. Such a program would simplify the lives of employed mothers, doing away with difficult and costly searches and allowing them the luxury of carrying out their jobs in relative peace. Whether public opinion would support a substantial child-care program on such a rationale remains to be seen. But putting a floor under quality for the sake of both parents and children certainly is a worthy objective of public policy.

Public child care would help women just entering the labor market and those women who become unemployed. It would greatly facilitate their job search. Freely available child care also would permit women with a low potential wage to avoid welfare. Free public child care never could be justified solely or mainly on the ground that it reduces welfare costs. But there would be a gain in independence and respectability for low-earning single mothers. They would have at least a chance to advance to a better job.

Author Barbara R. Bergmann is an economics professor at the University of Maryland.

"Those who clamor for facilities where working mothers can leave babies and children too young for nursery school are ignoring their real needs."

The Government Should Not Provide Child Care

Rita Kramer

In recent years, the American family has been subject to increasing scrutiny by experts in widely divergent fields, all of them contending that the family as we know it is threatened with imminent demise, a kind of endangered species among social institutions. Historians of the family have traced its evolution from an extended band of rural kinfolk to a conjugal pair living in suburban isolation with its offspring—the much-maligned nuclear family. Sociologists have explained the changing nature of the family as a social institution from a producing group to a consuming one. Political activists have deplored the traditional family's failure to foster women's rights, racial integration, tolerance of homosexuality or of economic justice, depending on their particular interests. And various kinds of health and welfare professionals, supported in one way or another by government, are ready to provide services they maintain families can no longer provide for their own members—in particular, their children.

It is hard to pick up a newspaper or magazine, look over the titles in a bookstore, or turn on the television set without being offered diagnoses and prescriptions for the ailing family. The media, a world in constant search of novelty, where one idea is presumed to be as good as any other, gives us reports as up-to-date and as constantly changing as weather reports on what is about to replace the family as we know it—homosexual or lesbian couples with adopted children, open marriages that may or may not be childless ones, cohabiting unmarried singles, groups living together in communes.

The beleaguered couple united in a heterosexual marriage and concerned about its children's well-being has a hard time of it these days. Not only are they assured that the present situation of the American family is precarious and its prospects dim, but who can they trust among the many experts proferring them advice? The trouble is, the experts disagree. And when the authorities say different, and often even opposite things, whom do you listen to?

When writers raise that rhetorical question, the answer, of course, is usually "me." But while this is addressed to the parents in average middle-class American families today, its aim is not to give them specific advice on the problems of child rearing but to make a more general statement: Parents are not helpless before social, political, and cultural forces beyond their control and they need not be overwhelmed by them. . . .

The Test of Common Sense

"Experts" can't tell you anything that applies in specific detail to you or your child; they can only stimulate your own use of reason and intuition. In the end you must trust yourself, be guided by your own values, apply the test of common sense to what you do.

If you listen to everyone you'll find sooner or later that they cancel each other out. The obvious conclusion is to listen to yourself. Yes, but who am I? asks the modern parent. You know who you are in other areas of your life—how you feel about your work, your politics, your religion or lack of it, your expectations in marriage, in friendship, what you owe, or don't, to your own parents. Why not as a parent? Why the fear of inadequacy, of getting it wrong, of failure, of the irreparable moment? What counts in parenthood is not any one action at any given moment. It is the kind of person you are and how that is expressed to your child.

The perniciousness of so much of the advice from experts that pervades the media is that it undermines the confidence of parents in their own abilities and their own values, overemphasizes the significance of specific child-rearing techniques, and grossly misrepresents the contribution the expert in psychiatry or education can make to the conduct of ordinary family life. . . .

Parents can and should make a difference in their children's lives and the most effective way to do so is through the family as it has traditionally been defined—a married couple of different sexes living with their own children by blood or adoption and having certain hopes and expectations for their characters, their education, and their futures. Of course, there are variations on this ideal, especially in the many single-parent families resulting from increasing rates of divorce, and we have to consider ways in which to compensate for the absence of two parents in a child's life, as we do ways of compensating for other kinds of handicaps or deficits. But the traditional nuclear family as we have defined it remains the chief agency—and the best one—for developing character in the individual and for transmitting the values of the culture. . . .

Where Have All the Mothers Gone?

Is it a lost cause?

If, as the demographers tell us, "young adults are establishing quite different life styles from their parents, with later marriage, fewer children, more divorce, more working wives," and if "this diversity in households will increase as we move toward 1990," we have to ask ourselves about the psychological implications for children of having single parents, older parents, fewer siblings, working mothers, other-than-parent grownups living in, two sets of parents, and so on. We have to ask about the consequences if, as family-policy authority Mary Jo Bane tells us, "projections of the 1990 female labor force . . . indicate a new life course pattern for women, one of high and continuing attachment to the labor force even through the childbearing period."

According to the experts, "Married women, especially those with children, show the sharpest increase in participation rates [in the labor force]. Within the group with children, the greatest increase in participation is among those with young children," and "projections call for growth . . . in working compared to non-working single-parent families." In other words, many of the nation's children will soon have only one parent, a mother who works.

While mothers turn to factory jobs or clerical work, who will mind the children? . . . The irony is that the same feminist logic that sends mothers of young children out of the home to fulfill themselves in the labor pool makes it unlikely that anyone but those at the very bottom of the heap would be willing to take their place in the home. It also makes it unlikely that most working women—excepting, of course, the well-educated and well-connected class from which most published feminist writers come— can earn much more than they would need to pay for adequate substitute-mother care.

Is publicly-funded and publicly-provided child care the answer? The authors of the MIT-Harvard report on the state of the American family tell us that the traditional "suburban nuclear-family life style" ("families with children, male workers and female homemakers") is rapidly becoming obsolete. What they expect to take its place is "a new combination of work and family life that uses nursery schools, day care centers and paid child-care help more extensively." They add, "it seems likely that families in 1990 will be looking to nonfamily sources for help with the care of children," by which they mean that some child-care services "may become the responsibility of government." . . .

Private Lives and Public Policies

Mary Jo Bane was one of the co-authors of *Inequality*, the much-discussed "reassessment" of American education in the early seventies that concluded that "neither family background, cognitive skill, educational attainment, nor occupational status explain much of the variation in men's incomes." Since schooling cannot be correlated statistically with economic success, in order to achieve "distributive justice" in society we must forget about indirect antipoverty programs, doomed to failure. "The only way to eliminate poverty is to redistribute income directly." Goodbye, equality of opportunity; hello to a social policy dedicated to ensuring equality of results.

"The same feminist logic that sends mothers of young children out of the home . . . makes it unlikely that anyone but those at the very bottom of the heap would be willing to take their place in the home."

A few years after the publication of *Inequality*, when Mary Jo Bane turned her attention to the American family, she concluded that it was "here to stay." Taking issue with the "myth" of the happy, stable, extended family of the past described by so many writers on the family, Bane found evidence in the reams of statistics from which she quotes to indicate that Americans remain as deeply committed as ever "to the notion that families are the best places to raise children." She has noticed that "when left to their own devices, and even in the face of some severe discouragements, Americans continue to marry, have children, create homes, and maintain family ties." However, she thinks it inevitable that other social commitments—to sexual equality and economic equality—will require changes in the family.

To understand what kind of brave new world the academic policy makers funded by government and foundations envision for us and for our children, we must ask about the nature of those changes and the bases for them. . . .

Working mothers of preschool children rose from 12 percent in 1950 to 40 percent by the mid-seventies. Who, we may wonder, is taking care of these children? Bane finds no evidence that children are less well cared for now than they ever were. Even though fewer children today live with both parents than in the past, more children live with at least one parent than previously—childen are less likely to be orphaned or abandoned than they once were. And the prediction is that the increase in one-parent families will continue.

Returning to the Wet Nurse

The crucial issue would seem to be the working mother—of young children. Bane assumes that with complete economic equality and an increase in "the bargaining power of women within the family," it would be a toss-up which partner in a marriage "should give up his or her income to assume family responsibilities." (Most committed egalitarians assume that all kinds of differences between individuals are artificially imposed and that if the barriers were removed everyone would be pretty much alike and want more or less the same things. They seem to find it difficult to entertain the possibility that partners in a marriage could consider their roles equally important although different. Equal does not mean equally valuable to them, but the same.) In this less than perfect world, however, Bane finds some women opt for being childless rather than giving up their work, others choose to stay home to care for their children, and still others "choose work over child care, though not over maternity." They decide to have children but hire someone else to care for them. Progressive women may thus succeed in returning to the practices of two hundred years ago, when every respectable woman who could afford it hired a wet nurse.

When "vigorous enforcement of equal pay and equal opportunity legislation" finally results "in substantially equal economic status for women . . . " as well as "equal status within the family," Bane thinks it possible that a number (unspecified) of men may prefer to stay home and take care of the children while their wives go out to work for pay. It's an interesting possibility, but there lurks the suspicion that mothering, even if culturally reinforced, can't be entirely without a biological basis. Social scientists tend to talk as though "cultural" meant "arbitrary," when in fact culture, like the heart, has its reasons.

Oddly enough, not all women want to work rather than care for home and children. Most who do so probably have little choice; they are poor or they are unmarried, widowed, separated, or divorced. A few who work have lots of money—and jobs open to them that do not represent realistic choices for most women. Yet feminists assume that any woman who had the opportunity would choose to be employed. Bane dismisses housework as "a wretched job." Compared to what? To factory work on an assembly line? To clerking in an office? To a high-level position in a policy-making organization, perhaps. But not every woman, for whatever reasons of nature or nurture, wants that particular life. Even some well-educated women enjoy cultivating the arts of domesticity, and technology has made housework a matter of relative ease and convenience. The picture of the average American housewife's life painted by militant feminists is as distorted as their view of the average working woman's world is romanticized. . . .

"It's best if a mother can take care of her child as much as possible during his first three years."

We know that the most significant aspects of human development—of character, intellect, and personality—depend on the establishment of ties to parents who both gratify (mostly) and frustrate (somewhat), with whom the child identifies and in order to secure whose love he internalizes a set of rules that become his conscience. Basically optimistic about the world they have surrounded him with, he explores and experiments with his maturing capacities and develops a sense of himself as a separate individual of a specific sex and of a degree of competence that enables him to let his mother go for increasing periods of time.

Mothers Are Needed

It follows that under normal circumstances, it's best if a mother can take care of her child as much as possible during his first three years, the years in which her style of mothering will have such influence on how he faces the world when he is ready to leave her. The better things have gone between them up to then, the smoother that transition will be. A mother who has a choice—who is emotionally and economically able to do so—is laying the foundation for her child's future life by caring for him herself. When he goes off to nursery school is the best time for her to resume or begin working part time. Few jobs and even few professions can offer a woman who is also a mother anything that will turn out to be more important to her in the years to come than what can be accomplished in her interaction with her child in the earliest years of life.

This speaks, of course, to the situation of the woman who is ambivalent—whose natural desire to be with her baby may give way to the social pressure to "be somebody" in a society that is increasingly telling women that what counts is achievement, however trivial, outside the home, just so it is outside the home and apart from child rearing. No woman is really free unless she can follow her nature in defining her life; the point about liberation is having options. But feminism, like some other sociopolitical movements of our day, attempts to substitute one form of tyranny for another. Separating mothers from the daily life of their infants, when preventable, does a disservice to both of them.

And what about the cases where it's unpreventable? Obviously, the best alternative to one source of individual responsive mothering is another responsive individual. Mothers who have to work, and there are increasing numbers of them as the divorce rate rises and so does the birth rate, would ideally provide their child with someone—some *one*—who can meet his needs at the different stages of his growth in such a way as to foster first security and then independence. Despite the undeniable justice and necessity of equal work for equal pay, of equal opportunity (although not necessarily of outcome) for every individual in every sphere of life, the women's movement propagandists tamper with basics they barely seem to comprehend when they encourage attitudes and even legislation that would separate women from their children's early life.

Public Mothering

Public mothering is a contradiction in terms. Those who clamor for facilities where working mothers can leave babies and children too young for nursery school are ignoring their real needs as mothers and those of their infants.

Women who could afford to do so have traditionally brought substitute mothers into their homes when they have been occupied elsewhere; common sense has usually led them to seek someone whose maternal capacities—quality of judgment and degree of empathy for the child— seemed to be in proportion to the extent to which they would be taking a mother's place. Women unable to afford the luxury of chosen paid mother substitutes have turned to arrangements with relatives, friends, neighbors—the more stable and lasting, the better for everyone concerned.

Of course, for women in dire poverty, group care facilities can have another meaning altogether. And there are women whose own resources, emotional as well as financial, may limit their capacity for flexible mothering. If you have not been well cared for by your own parents, it is very hard to feel like a loving parent yourself. The immature, the defeated, the hostile ought to be given the option of placing their children somewhere where a better beginning than they can offer might help to break the cycle of diminished lives.

But these are not the mothers to whom this is addressed. No woman whose interests may clearly be different from her child's should be forced to care for him. It's the many women whose interests are inseparable from those of their infants—who stand to gain along with their children by contributing to their growth, but who are told they are wasting their valuable time and energies, squandering the years in which they could be realizing themselves—who might benefit from being reminded of the old-fashioned idea that sometimes you find yourself through another self, particularly in the process of helping to create one.

A Peculiar Idea

The idea that anyone can be as affectionate, responsive to, and concerned about a baby as its own mother—and that therefore it doesn't much matter who cares for infants—is a peculiarly political one: It focuses on institutional arrangements with no considerations of the complexities that motivate the behavior of real men and women and children. Even more absurd is the assumption that there is a great number of warm, devoted, patient women somewhere waiting to be put in charge of other people's babies for pleasure and profit, and who can discharge that responsibility effectively.

"An average woman with normal emotional resources . . . has no real need to turn . . . [her child] over to anyone else until they both are ready."

Effectively, we have to ask, compared to what? It makes a difference whether the alternative is care by an inadequate parent, by an indifferent or abusive parent, by a parent who really has no choice but to be absent from a child's life because of illness or economic necessity, or whether it is an average woman with normal emotional resources, predisposed to be attached to her child and to appreciate him, who has no real need to turn him over to anyone else until they both are ready. Let's not pretend we need to construct day-care centers in the interest of this woman or her child.

Rita Kramer's books include How To Raise a Human Being *and* Giving Birth: Childbearing in America Today. *She also contributes to* The New York Times Magazine *and other publications.*

The Government Should Mandate Parental Leave

Patricia Schroeder and Albert R. Hunt

Editor's note: Representative Patricia Schroeder wrote Part I of the following viewpoint. Journalist Albert R. Hunt wrote Part II.

I

Numbers rarely speak for themselves; and yet, where women and work are concerned, they have never been so convincing. Between 1947 and 1980, the number of women in the labor force increased by 175 percent, while for men the number rose by only 43 percent. Today, well over one half of all women work outside the home, making up nearly 44 percent of the labor force. The most dramatic contrast between now and 40 years ago, however, is not just the large number of women in the labor force but the growing number of mothers: they account for more than 60 percent of all wage-earning women.

If demography is destiny, a closer look at this burgeoning group reveals an even more striking picture of the future. More than 80 percent of women in the work force are of childbearing age; and 93 percent are likely to become pregnant during their working careers.

The biggest problem that new mothers face is whether they will be reemployed in the same or similar position after the birth of their child. The Pregnancy Discrimination Act of 1978 took one step toward solving this problem, requiring that serious pregnancy-related health conditions be treated like any other serious short-term health condition. Unfortunately, legislation is limited. In the absence of a federal requirement to provide disability coverage to employees, women are treated equally well or poorly, depending on the availability of a disability leave policy. The legislation is further constrained because employers with fewer than fifteen employees are exempt from the law.

A 1980 Columbia University study found that for 250 companies it examined, only 72 percent of the employers guaranteed that a women could return to her job and retain her seniority if she took maternity leave. A more recent preliminary study done by the Catalyst Career and Family Center found that 95 percent of its respondents provided a temporary disability policy; of the women covered, only 39 percent received full wage replacement, while 52 percent were eligible to take an unpaid child-care leave.

Although heartening news is that women in large companies (70 percent of those responding employ more than 2,500) receive important disability and job protection benefits, least protected are women in smaller companies, who work in part-time or female-dominated jobs.

A Family Issue

Pregnancy and parental leave are not, however, simply women's issues; they are a family issue. Women work out of economic necessity. In 1985, both parents had to work to maintain the standard of living that their parents could enjoy on one income. According to 1983 data, 25 percent of married wage-earning women had husbands who earned less than $10,000, while close to 40 percent had husbands earning less than $15,000. The typical family painted by Norman Rockwell is vanishing: women are increasingly responsible for providing family incomes where they are the sole heads of households. In 1984, women headed 10.3 million families, representing 16 percent of American families. One-half of the 45.6 million children in two-parent families have both parents in the work force.

Perhaps the most critical time for a family comes

when a child becomes seriously ill—a time when parents feel the need to be at home or in the hospital with their child. More serious medical conditions require constant care, and parents believe that they are the ones who should provide it. Yet too few parents have the flexibility at the work place to make this decision and are instead faced with having to choose between job security and caring for their children. Thus, for the 24.8 million children in two-working-parent families, flexible options could ensure that parents can continue to provide the care so essential to a child's well-being.

But help for working families is at best uneven. At present, no national policy provides job-protected leave for parents for parental care purposes. A bill that I am sponsoring, the Parental and Medical Leave Act . . . would do just this.

It would establish parental leave for the birth or adoption or serious illness of a dependent son or daughter. It establishes a minimum standard for job-protected leaves below which an employer may not fall. Employees would be permitted to take up to eighteen weeks' leave over a two-year period. The leave is to be unpaid but requires that an employer continue health insurance coverage on the same basis as prior to the leave. Most important, upon returning to work, an employee is to be restored to the same or similar position with benefits and seniority continuing as though the employee had not taken leave. An employee has the option of substituting paid vacation or sick leave for unpaid leave. . . .

Public Policy and Reality

We must promote the stability and economic security of families and American workers. By providing an unpaid leave with job protection, this legislation provides families with essential options to meet familial concerns and responsibilities. It establishes leave where none may have existed before, and it guarantees a degree of economic security by ensuring job protection. Most important, it allows families to plan ahead and gives meaning to a government committed to the American family—a family in which both parents work outside the home. . . .

Policymakers and analysts must work to bring public policy into line with the current reality of the 1980s. By creating more flexible work options for America's working parents, we can begin to bridge the gap between work and home. No longer will job or economic security be traded against the needs of the family.

II

The family is a popular political issue these days, so it isn't unusual to see a consensus forming over a measure proposing to require a limited unpaid leave from their jobs for parents with new or seriously ill children. But the shape of that consensus is surprising.

Conservative Republican Sen. Orrin Hatch of Utah charges that the proposed legislation would "stifle innovation" and says that it's none of the federal government's business. Liberal Democratic Sen. Edward M. Kennedy of Massachusetts shows little enthusiasm, with aides privately arguing that it is politically better to focus on other initiatives, such as increasing the minimum wage.

The National Organization for Women also has shown little enthusiasm for the measure. . . . The U.S. Chamber of Commerce wasn't too distracted to widely circulate its charge that this measure could cost business as much as $16 billion a year.

Talk to the Experts

These critics, who charge that the bill is tantamount to a "national nanny," ought to talk to leading child-care medical experts about the importance of a parent spending initial months with a newly born or adopted child. "Parental leave is critical to the healthy development of children and families," says Edward Zigler, director of Yale's Bush Center for Child Development and Social Policy.

"Critics, who charge that the bill is tantamount to a 'national nanny,' ought to talk to leading child-care medical experts about the importance of a parent spending initial months with a . . . child."

Where sick children are involved the trauma is more striking. "In our experience of caring for over 2,000 children with cancer and other serious blood diseases, we have encountered numerous instances where parents had to choose between bringing their child into the hospital for much-needed treatment and evaluation vs. losing their jobs," says Stuart E. Siegel, the head of the division of hematology-oncology at Children's Hospital in Los Angeles.

When Tom Riley joined Colibri Inc., a Cranston, R.I., maker of men's accessories in mid-1982, he told the company that his son Christopher faced a life-and-death cancer. By Thanksgiving his son's condition worsened. Mr. Riley started taking some time off to spend with his dying boy, though he did considerable work at home. "Chris died on Jan. 6, 1983. Four weeks later, I was fired," Mr. Riley says. "Losing my son was devastating enough. Losing my job totally destroyed my self image.

"I don't want or expect any special favors from anyone—my employers or the government," Mr. Riley says, but "I don't think that giving unpaid leave for families like mine is a lot to ask." (Officials of Colibri didn't return phone calls seeking comment.)

There surely are more complicated and far-reaching issues than parental leave. But with a changing work force now dominated by two wage-earning parents and single parents, this issue is far more important than before.

Simple Facts

A few simple facts: Women constitute 44% of the work force today, and almost 50% of women with children under the age of one work outside the home. Yet more than 60% of women and men have no guaranteed leave when new babies arrive or their kids become seriously ill. The U.S. is the only industrialized nation that doesn't require parental leave.

The parental-leave measure before Congress, pushed chiefly by Democratic Sen. Christopher Dodd of Connecticut in the Senate and Democratic Rep. Patricia Schroeder of Colorado in the House, would provide for up to 18 weeks of leave for a mother or father when a new child arrives or a child is seriously ill. Although the leave would be unpaid, health benefits would be continued and the same job would be guaranteed after the leave. Businesses with 15 employees or fewer would be exempt. The measure still would affect an estimated four million working parents each year. . . .

"85% of all women working outside the home are likely to become pregnant during their childbearing years."

Critics ignore changing realities. Most families don't have two wage earners because it's fashionable; rather, it's essential to pay the bills. Two-thirds of women who work outside the home are either the sole providers for their children, or their husbands earn less than $15,000 a year. Moreover, 85% of all women working outside the home are likely to become pregnant during their childbearing years and, unfortunately, some of them will be faced at some point with a critically ill child.

The Least We Can Do

There certainly is precedent for guaranteed leave. Any worker entering the armed services is guaranteed his job if he returns to civilian life within four years. That, we agree, is the least we can do for those willing to help ensure that our children grow up in a free society. The same guarantee, on a much shorter basis, ought to be available to those who seek to ensure that these children will be better able physically and emotionally to enjoy the fruits of that freedom.

Democrat Patricia Schroeder introduced the Parental and Medical Leave Act in the House of Representatives. Albert R. Hunt is the Washington bureau chief of The Wall Street Journal.

"Flexibility—not new, rigid government mandates—is the most appropriate answer to the work-family problems in today's work force."

The Government Should Not Mandate Parental Leave

Harry Bacas and US Chamber of Commerce

Editor's note: Part I of the following viewpoint is excerpted from an article Harry Bacas wrote for Nation's Business, *a publication of the US Chamber of Commerce. Part II is a briefing paper prepared by the Chamber of Commerce.*

I

Congressional proposals to require lengthy employee leaves for child care or disability are provoking an outcry among small-business owners.

"Whatever we do will be wrong," says Laura S. Cline, president of a property-management firm in Holliston, Mass. "First we'll have to replace the person who takes leave, and then we'll have to fire the replacement and pay benefits to both."

The congressional move to mandate such benefits as health insurance and parental leave, say Cline and other small-business owners, makes it harder for them to offer other benefits their employees may prefer.

Bills in the House and Senate . . . would require every business with 15 or more employees to provide 18 weeks of unpaid, job-protected leave for birth, adoption or serious illness of a child and another 26 weeks for an employee's serious illness. . . .

While almost all large companies already provide leave like that required by the two bills, small companies, with fewer resources, often do not.

Cline's company, Eagle Management, Inc., gives its 25 employees health insurance, paid vacations, holidays and sick leave. Cline says granting leave creates problems because her employees work in small groups at four widely separated locations in New England, and the prolonged absence of one employee creates a noticeable gap.

One woman in the home office has had two children while employed there, and while she was gone "I did her work," says Cline. "It was six weeks each time, and it was clearly understood that she *would* come back."

But under the proposed law, she says, "you could hold the job for 18 weeks and never know whether the employee was coming back. Then if the employee returned, we would be faced with either having to fire the temporary replacement, which means that we would be charged unemployment compensation, or keep that extra person on our payroll."

"It will be totally disruptive," says Frank L. Mason, president of Mason Corporation in Birmingham, Ala., which makes aluminum building products. The company has 180 employees. . . .

Totally Unrealistic

David L. Guernsey, president of an office-products firm in Arlington, Va., with 75 employees, says, "I liken the effect [of this bill] to a roulette wheel. If our number doesn't come up, we'll be all right; but if our number does come up, it could be impossible."

He explains: "If a salesman takes extended leave, we can cover. But if our data-processing manager—the technical person in charge of our considerable investment in data-processing equipment—goes out, what do we do? Could we hire somebody like that as a temporary? I'm not sure such a temporary exists. If there is one, would he be willing to come to work for us for six months knowing the other person was guaranteed his job back?

"From a small-business perspective, it's totally unrealistic. I don't know what planet this bill is designed for, but it's not for the planet I live on."

Winston Weaver, Jr., president of Rockingham Construction Company, Harrisonburg, Va., says

Harry Bacas, "Mandated Leave: Small Firms' Nightmare." Reprinted by permission, *Nation's Business*, August 1987. Copyright 1987, U.S. Chamber of Commerce.
US Chamber of Commerce, "Business Opposes Mandated Parental and Medical Leave Legislation." Reprinted with permission.

finding temporary employees in his business would be very expensive. His firm, started by his grandfather 50 years ago, erects utility poles and maintains lines for power and telephone companies in Maryland, Virginia and the District of Columbia. He has 275 employees, mostly male linemen.

Qualified linemen, all highly paid, are in such short supply in the mid-Atlantic states that Weaver has to advertise for workers as far away as Colorado and Texas. He spent $10,000 on such recruiting in 1985 and $27,000 in 1986 and had laid out $12,000 in just the last three months, even without a mandated leave law to make things tougher.

"Why would somebody take a job with us on a temporary basis when he could get a permanent job elsewhere?" he asks.

Family Responsibilities

Labor unions and other proponents of mandating job-protected leave for disability or the care of a child or parent say it is a simple way of guaranteeing equal treatment while according special priority to family responsibilities.

But this view is "simplistic," says Frances Shaine, chairman of SPM Manufacturing in Holyoke, Mass. Shaine, who has three children, says that "if parental 'bonding' or nurturing after the birth or adoption of a child is the desired goal, it will not result from government coercion. Federal legislation simply cannot make us 'bond' with our children.". . .

The U.S. Chamber was the first business organization to spotlight the small-business impact of parental-leave legislation [in 1986], when the measure was gaining wide support as a family-oriented issue. By rallying small-business opposition, the Chamber halted the rush toward what had been seen as certain passage. . . .

Shaine said a small company has just so much money in its benefits budget, so mandating a particular benefit cuts into the money available for other benefits.

"The proposed legislation would hit small businesses the hardest because they have the least ability to pay."

For example, an individual employee may be more interested in child-care services, educational assistance, relocation assistance, physical-fitness programs, additional vacation days, health insurance, life insurance or retirement benefits, she said.

But mandates "stifle the trend toward flexible benefits."

American business, she pointed out, already pays nearly 40 percent of its payroll costs for benefits, most of them not mandated. And she said business is responding to the changing demography of the work force by developing "innovative solutions to the demands of working parents." She said that is a better way than imposing "rigid, inflexible, costly and probably counterproductive federal mandates."

The proposed legislation would hit small businesses the hardest because they have the least ability to pay, Shaine said. Yet small business is the great generator of jobs.

She pointed out that in 1983 and 1984, small business created nearly three times as many jobs as large companies, and women form the fastest growing component of those new jobs.

"It would be ironic," she said, if mandated parental-leave legislation "winds up destroying the very jobs that have helped to assimilate second-income wage earners into the labor force."

Less Regulation, Not More

Clifton H. Claybourn, general manager of Sunshine Laundry & Cleaners in San Marcos, Tex., wrote to Rep. J.J. Pickle (D-Tex.) that the mandated-leave proposal "is bad legislation."

He said: "We are struggling with our own eight-week leave of absence. It has been used by employees to temporarily work on other jobs for higher pay or to try out for other employment to see if they like the jobs before they resign. It is most discouraging to hold a job for an employee eight weeks and then not have them return."

Claybourn has 46 employees, mostly Mexican-American women. Some have been with him as long as 25 years. He gives workers paid vacations and health and life insurance and allows six weeks' unpaid leave in a calendar year for maternity or health reasons.

He says that if Congress mandates long leaves, he will either hire more help—"and inevitably that will be reflected in our prices"—or he will drop part of his business and let some people go.

"Congress has taken more and more of running a business away from the employer and given us more and more regulation," Claybourn says. "Can't it see that the best benefit for people in this country is a job and that this over-regulation is costing jobs?"

II

Parental and medical leave may be worthy benefits for some people, but flexibility—not new, rigid government mandates—is the most appropriate answer to the work-family problems in today's work force.

The legislation is anti-competitive. Congress is increasingly approaching all perceived social problems with the answer, "Let's simply *require* the employer to provide this new benefit." Whereas other nations may require employers to grant unpaid or paid maternity leave, the U.S. has left employee benefits up to collective bargaining or else the economic discretion of the employer. Such flexibility has created over 18 million new jobs since 1973 compared to a net job loss of one million in Western Europe (those nations with extensive state mandated benefits) during the same period.

Congress is oversimplifying the family problems. Whereas one family may want time off to "bond" with a newborn or newly adopted child, another family may prefer dental benefits so they can get braces for their teenagers, flexible work schedules so they can be home with a "latch key" child, part-time or home-based work, or increased pay! Family needs are diverse and individual.

Laws cannot make us good parents. Ultimately family responsibility is individual responsibility. Granting lengthy leave periods will not guarantee that workers will use that time to "bond" with their child or care for a sick person. This type of new federal "entitlement" is subject to much abuse.

> *"Industrialized nations with the most generous maternity leave policies also have the highest incidences of unemployment for women of child-bearing age or their women are clustered into the lowest paying jobs."*

Mandating any benefit stifles the trend toward flexible benefits. With benefit costs currently about 40% of payroll, many employers have begun offering cafeteria plans allowing each employee to select the benefit package that meets his or her needs. The best possible solution is the flexible benefit package that serves the individual needs of employees and contains costs for the employer.

Most benefits are not mandated. Currently, the only mandated benefits are: Social Security, workers' compensation and unemployment compensation. Health benefits or vacation leave are not federally mandated.

Employers are responding to workers with family responsibilities. Surveys indicate that the majority of medium to large employers offer parental leave. Small businesses typically are as flexible as possible, in a humanistic way, but simply cannot afford generous leave policies.

Existing law is fair and effective. The Pregnancy Discrimination Act of 1978 already requires all employers to treat pregnancy and childbirth the same as any other temporary medical condition. If the employer permits sick or disabled employees to take leave with or without pay, or guarantees the job upon return (for a broken leg or hepatitis for instance), the same type of leave must be available for pregnant employees.

The Supreme Court has recently sanctioned preferential treatment for pregnant women who are disabled by pregnancy; however, the wisdom of making this *federal* law has not been fully considered. California and eight other states treat pregnancy disability with some degree of preference at this time, but often limit leave to the period of actual disability or incorporate flexibility for reinstatement "rights."

An Expensive Policy

This legislation is not cost free. The Department of Labor estimates the cost to administer this new law as over $40 million including the need to hire 948 new employees within the Department of Labor. Any further cost to be incurred would be shifted to the private sector.

Chamber [of Commerce] staff estimates that a worst case scenario would bring about new costs of over $27 billion. Should the bill be expanded to include PAID leave, costs could easily skyrocket to over $75 billion.

Micro-level cost figures indicate the average cost to replace a word-processor employee in the Washington, D.C. area would be more than $5700 for 18 weeks.

The characterization that every other nation provides these benefits is ludicrous.

Virtually no other nation or state in the U.S. offers as generous of benefits as those proposed in the legislation. Most offer state-imposed maternity leave—not time off for child-birth, child-rearing, sick children, sick parents or personal illness!

On the other hand, two-thirds of the working women in the world work in agriculture. The next most populated field of concentration is domestic help. Both women-dominated fields are frequently excluded from the scope of coverage of these generous maternity leave policies in foreign countries.

Those industrialized nations with the most generous maternity leave policies also have the highest incidences of unemployment for women of child-bearing age or their women are clustered into the lowest paying jobs. In the United States, younger women are entering into non-traditional jobs at record rates and the wage gap is closing between those men and women.

Often times, the less developed nations frequently cited by proponents do not have basic civil rights for women, do not give equal pay for equal work, impose separate minimum wages for women or may force women to take time off for child care and child bearing.

Harry Bacas writes for Nation's Business, *a monthly published by the US Chamber of Commerce. The Chamber is a national organization of small businesses.*

Less Government Regulation Is Needed in Child Care

Karen Lehrman and Jana Pace

In the past 15 to 20 years, day care regulation has come to consume $47,000,000 of taxpayers' money. Today, all 50 states and the District of Columbia have some day care regulations. More significant, day care facilities are also subject to a host of local zoning, building, health, fire, and safety statutes. These regulations, which vary from state to state and municipality to municipality, can dictate everything from the time a facility opens to the width of the exit door. The intent of these regulations is to ensure minimum health and safety standards for the children and to guarantee responsible care by the day care provider. Unfortunately, many requirements do little to achieve these aims, while a major effect of regulation has been to raise the cost of day care services, driving providers underground and limiting the number of children who can benefit. Unnecessary regulations are stifling the supply of day care at a time when the need has never been greater and shows every sign of continuing to surge.

High Demand

Once considered an unfortunate necessity for single mothers, day care has become an American institution, used by people of all economic, cultural, and educational backgrounds. This phenomenon is the inexorable result of social and demographic changes that, over the past 20 years, have altered the lifestyle and composition of the American family. No longer are most children raised in traditional, two-parent households, with a father who works and a mother who stays at home; in 1984, both parents held jobs in 52% of American families. At the same time, the traditional form of day care provided by relatives and friends is vanishing. Not only has the increased mobility of American society led to the disappearance of extended families, but the conventional babysitters have themselves joined the workforce.

Yet, the availability of day care services has not kept pace with demand. While there are an estimated 10,000,000 day care spaces available nationwide, there are at least 14,000,000 preschoolers whose parents work full time, according to the Institute for Parent/Child Services in Philadelphia, and that figure is expected to increase 38% by the decade's end. The need for infant care is particularly pressing, since 47% of women with children under one year of age are now in the labor force. According to a day care referral service in California, 40% of its requests are for children under two, while only 13.5% of the licensed day care spaces available locally are for this age group. Another study found that, in 1982, more than 17% of parents searching for day care were not able to find it. Such failure does not necessarily mean that parents forfeit job or education opportunities; rather, it means that young children are often left alone for at least part of the day.

Whether children are better cared for at home by their own mothers, in others' homes, or in day care centers is not a policy question. Day care has become a necessity for most families and should thus be regarded as an essential community service. The question is whether current policy is working to cultivate or suffocate this much-needed resource.

Shortage

Why is there a shortage of day care services? One reason is general—there is usually a lag in any market before supply catches up with demand. Another, more specific, reason is that day care has not proven a particularly lucrative venture, at least not for the 1,500,000 people who provide day care in their homes. According to the Child Care Law Center in California, the economic realities of "family" day care are these:

Karen Lehrman and Jana Pace, "Day Care Regulation: Serving Children or Bureaucrats?" Reprinted from USA TODAY MAGAZINE, May 1987. Copyright 1987 by the Society for the Advancement of Education.

The average fee per child per month for full time care in a large family day-care home is $150 to $200 per month. If there are 12 children (and that is rare for any program to be constantly full due to parents' vacations, delays in replacing a child, collection problems, etc.), the total *gross* annual income would be $21,000 to $28,000. Out of this amount, two full-time salaries and benefits must be paid and expenses must be met, including liability insurance, food for snacks and lunch, equipment, supplies, and so forth.

More typically, a provider cares for only three or four children full time, earning less than $6,500 a year. Another survey estimates that a family day care provider earns an average of $74 a week in profit. For this, most day care providers are required to put in an 11-hour day—from seven a.m. to six p.m.—to accommodate the schedules of working parents.

"The [1979 National Day-Care] study found only a 'slight' correlation between staff-child ratios and quality."

The other major type of day care service—the day care center—usually serves 20 or more children and is run either as a commercial enterprise or as a nonprofit activity of a church or school. Centers charge higher fees and the commercial ones can actually be profitable, but they also tend to price themselves out of the reach of lower- and middle-income families who typically spend more than 10% of their after-tax income on day care. Home care remains the most important for such families, and it is here that the need is greatest.

Of course, home providers do not enter the day care market as entrepreneurs seeking to get rich. Most are in the business because they like children. Many are mothers themselves, who have chosen to stay home with their own children and supplement their families' incomes (or actually support their families) by caring for the children of people who work outside the home. Added expenses or bureaucratic red tape can easily tip the balance for home providers, turning a marginally profitable, but rewarding, endeavor into a frustrating and expensive one.

Clearly, then, if the supply of day care is ever to keep pace with the rapidly rising demand, it is essential that there be a favorable climate for its growth. At present, there is not, and the regulatory obstacle course laid out by state and local officials is in large part why.

Regulatory Barriers

Licensing and regulation. The primary regulation of day care occurs at the state level, where standards are set and licenses are granted. All states require day care homes to be licensed as well. In some

states, if a person cares for even one unrelated child in a private residence other than the child's own, that person is considered to be operating a day care facility and is required to obtain a license.

To monitor compliance, day care facilities are inspected by state licensing officials (usually with the department of social or human services) upon application for a license and, in most states, again each time a license is renewed. Several states only conduct spot checks on a random sampling of licensed family homes.

The Registration System

In response to tightening budgets, some states have replaced the licensing of day care homes with "registration," generally considered to be a mild form of regulation. Registration often does not require inspection by the state, emphasizing instead the participation of parents in monitoring the care of their children. In some states, registration is even voluntary.

Currently, 11 states register family day care homes and three either license or register them, depending on the number of children enrolled and the presence of children receiving Federal subsidies. Five states regulate only those homes that receive Federal funds. Home providers caring for fewer than five children are exempt from regulation in 19 states, while 23 others set more relaxed standards for providers who care for fewer than six or seven children in their homes. These states have a separate classification for large family day care or "group" care facilities. In states without such a category, homes where more than five or six children are cared for are usually defined as day care "centers" and are therefore subject to more rigorous standards.

State standards generally govern the number and ages of children that can be cared for. In a day care home, the most common maximum number is six, of which no more than two can be infants. State standards also regulate the amount of indoor and outdoor space provided, the quality of meals and snacks, program content, parental involvement, etc. In addition, regulations for large family homes and day care centers usually include standards on educational requirements for center directors and teachers and on the ratio of staff to children.

Staff-child ratios. Of all the state regulations, staff-child ratios have the most direct bearing on the supply of day care. Virtually all states have regulations limiting the number of children one staff member can care for in a day care center. The most common staff-child ratios for preschoolers are one-to-10 and one-to-15. Since staff salaries comprise one of the largest components of a center's costs—about 75%—low staff-child ratios limit the number of children that can be cared for in centers with limited budgets. The 1979 National Day-Care Study commissioned by the Department of Health,

Education, and Welfare, the only study that has examined the effect of state standards on quality of care, confirmed that the staff-child ratio was the most important determinant of providers' costs. Moreover, the study found only a "slight" correlation between staff-child ratios and quality.

"When stringent standards are imposed on residences used for day care, providers are discouraged from applying for a state license. . . . 90% of home day care providers operate without a license."

Some states currently require centers to maintain a one-to-three ratio for infant care. Ann Muscari, a spokesperson for Kinder-Care, by far the largest chain of day care centers, says that such a low ratio is not always necessary in a well-equipped center. It is, in part, such costly regulations that have kept Kinder-Care—which opened its 1,000th center in 1985—out of 10 states. According to Muscari, in addition to weighing the demand for day care and the real estate costs in a potential market, Kinder-Care "tends to go where regulations are such that [the company] can make a reasonable profit, while providing affordable and quality child care." The "very, very stringent" regulation in New York is a principal reason for not opening a center in that state. The staff-child ratio for three-year-olds in New York is one-to-seven.

Fewer Children Benefit

Strict standards of this nature also limit the number of children able to benefit from a day care facility receiving Federal funds for children from low-income families. Fifteen states have different standards—generally more stringent—for subsidized care, according to Helen Blank of the Children's Defense Fund. In seven states, family day care homes are subject to a more stringent regulatory process if they accept subsidized children.

Zoning regulations. Although the state's formal permission to operate is the fundamental requirement for most providers of family day care, complying with state standards usually does not prove as costly or complicated as getting past local regulatory obstacles. The highest hurdle facing providers is often the first—obtaining the approval of local zoning officials. Of all local day care regulations, zoning statutes have the least relevance to the quality of care and the safety of the children. Most city zoning commissions consider day care to

be a small business and prohibit programs from opening in residential areas. This prohibition extends even to individuals wishing to use their own homes to care for a few neighborhood children.

The illogic of this restrictive zoning policy was pointed out by one frustrated would-be provider before the Washington, D.C., Board of Zoning Adjustment: "You're telling us that we cannot operate a day care facility in a residentially zoned, middle-class neighborhood with a large number of working mothers, but we can operate a center in a commercial zone between two topless bars."

In most cases, providers can apply for a zoning variance or a conditional-use permit, but the process is generally neither cheap nor easy—nor is it always successful. Fees to process an application for a variance or a use permit typically range from $100 to $1,000, although zoning commissions that are particularly vehement in their desire to keep day care out of residential areas have been known to levy fees as high as $3,000. Before a use permit is granted, some communities also require complex, formal hearings in which applicants may need legal counsel, a further—and not inconsequential—expense. An applicant may also be required to send a written notice of the hearing to neighbors as well as to pay for a public notice in the local newspaper. . . .

Building, fire, and health regulations. Like zoning codes, building, fire, and health codes applied to day care are administered primarily on the local level and vary widely from community to community. In cases where state licensing regulations conflict with local codes, the more restrictive provisions generally apply.

When interviewed, many providers say that a house or apartment deemed safe enough for a family should be considered suitable for the care of five or fewer unrelated children. Yet, this belief is rarely shared by local officials. A home judged safe by building and fire inspectors for private residents must usually meet a host of additional requirements if it is used for day care. . . .

Unlicensed Care

When stringent standards are imposed on residences used for day care, providers are discouraged from applying for a state license and identifying themselves to local authorities. It is estimated that 90% of home day care providers operate without a license, even where it is illegal to do so. Ten percent of the larger, more visible day care centers are unlicensed. The most frequently cited reason for "going underground" is the complex and costly maze of requirements that must be met before obtaining state sanction. For parents seeking day care, this vast underground market can present a problem. When providers choose not to register or apply for a license, they do not appear on public or private information and referral lists. Even more visible (and uncountable) than the providers who go underground, however, are the potential providers who are deterred by state and local regulations from entering the day care market at all.

Child Abuse

Investigations and arrests in New York, California, New Jersey, Illinois, Alabama, and Tennessee have focused national attention on the potential problems of sexual abuse in day care settings. Concern, of course, is well-justified. However, not only could a flood of new state legislation prove inadequate in preventing child abuse, it could deter dedicated and caring individuals from entering the day care market. Added to these risks are the costs to day care providers in time and money and the potential threat to civil liberties. . . .

"In 56,000 cases of reported child abuse, the vast majority—82%— involved abuse by family members. Day care workers and babysitters were involved in only 1.5%."

Congress directed the Department of Health and Human Services (HHS) to provide the states with guidelines for minimum licensing and registration standards. Along with the guidelines, which were promulgated in January 1985, HHS issued a statement on the potential effectiveness of screening:

> Experience to date indicates that criminal record checks for licensing and employment purposes in various occupational categories yield a positive identification rate (*i.e.*, the person being checked has a criminal record) of only five to eight percent of the persons screened. Because child sexual abuse so frequently goes undetected and because the conviction rate for sexual abuse crimes is so low, it is estimated that only one to 15% of sexual abusers have criminal records. In addition, while approximately 95% of child care workers are female, it is males who constitute 80 to 85% of the criminal record cases and 78 to 92% of child sexual abuse cases. It is estimated that only seven to eight percent of reported child sexual abuse is committed by someone other than a relative. It appears likely, therefore, that only a small number of child sexual abusers will be identified in this type of screening of child care workers.

HHS also noted that, while the increase in the reporting of child abuse is a legitimate cause for concern, it may not mean that sexual abuse in day care facilities is actually on the rise. It is plausible that increased attention may have led to increased reporting. In May 1985, HHS released a report on child neglect and abuse that stated that, in almost 98% of known cases, children are abused in the home by close relatives, family friends, or neighbors.

The single largest group of abusers, comprising 77% of the total, is parents. A 1982 survey by the American Humane Association supports these findings. The survey found that, in 56,000 cases of reported child abuse, the vast majority—82%— involved abuse by family members. Day care workers and babysitters were involved in only 1.5%.

The cost of criminal record checks may not be insignificant for day care operators, and the processing time may be more than providers can afford. The FBI charges $12 for each fingerprint card submitted for nationwide screening. The state and local fees vary; for example, Nebraska charges $5, California charge $15.50, and New York City charges $17. A report by the Inspector General's Office of HHS estimates that a nationwide criminal record check of both state and FBI files using two fingerprint cards costs about $25 per person. The FBI estimates that it takes an average of 14 days for a fingerprint check to be processed, while state checks can take as much as six to eight weeks. These are long delays for day care facilities, especially since the day care industry suffers from a staff turnover rate of 40% and must be able to make replacements quickly both to assure adequate care and to meet state staff-child ratio requirements. In addition, while criminal checks can deter job applicants by potential abusers, they can also discourage perfectly acceptable individuals from entering the day care market, particularly when the checks require long delays before employment. "Ultimately," states the HHS report, "the costs of regulating will be borne by the consumer or the taxpayer.". . .

Toward Deregulation

By increasing providers' costs, day care regulations limit the supply of a much-needed service. Many regulations, especially local zoning and building codes, do little to promote quality or ensure safety. Even in cases where regulations might benefit the child's welfare, limited enforcement minimizes any positive effect. For these reasons, states should replace licensing laws with a system of registration for both homes and centers. Registration requirements should include only those that have a proven effect on quality of care and on health and safety and are not so costly that they would cause providers not to operate or to operate illegally. At the time, states and child-advocacy groups should continually reassess standards to determine which ones serve children best in the context of providers' and parents' willingness and ability to pay.

Unlike licensing, registration appropriately would give parents the ultimate responsibility for the quality of their children's day care. Since they come into contact with the day care staff and observe the facility at least twice a day, parents are in the best position to monitor day care homes and centers effectively. Complaints by parents can then form the basis for official action, including unannounced inspections by state and local authorities. In some states, day care providers are permitted to restrict parental visitation; this, obviously, must be changed.

If parental monitoring is to work, parents must take the trouble to learn what good-quality day care is and, especially, how to recognize signs of child abuse and neglect. Until they do, regulations—especially those with only indirect bearing on day-care quality—can do little to ensure good day care. Parents often get a false sense of security from the mere existence of government standards regulating day care—even if those standards are not enforced through frequent inspections. When this happens, regulations not only fail to promote the welfare of children, they jeopardize it. . . .

State preemption codes, which exempt day care homes from restrictive zoning, building, and fire regulations, should be adopted more widely. States also need to address the concerns of group day care homes. Statewide safety standards should take into account the fact that day care programs are usually established in existing buildings. Alterations of existing structures should be required only when they are deemed so essential to child health and safety that their cost is justifiable. A home that local inspectors consider safe for a family should not have to meet any additional requirements to be considered safe for six or fewer unrelated children.

The Private Sector's Role

A number of private-sector services have taken on the accreditation of day care facilities and the certification of day care providers and their staffs. Although most of these initiatives are still in their infancy, it is conceivable that an expanded private role in setting standards and monitoring day care services could eventually take the place of state oversight of day care. Since private certification and accreditation of individual day care programs would give parents the greatest degree of choice in selecting day care, the growth of such agencies is desirable.

One of the most important of the private initiatives, the Child Development Associate (CDA) National Credentialing Program, provides training in child care at more than 350 colleges and universities nationwide. Since 1971, nearly 13,000 child care providers have received CDA certification. An increasing number of states have begun using these credentials to assess day care staff qualifications. (The CDA program is not entirely private, however—it receives half of its funding from a Federal grant.)

Another private initiative starting up in some areas is the "satellite system," which recruits and trains home providers, sets standards for care, and closely supervises programs. At present, satellite day care

systems must be licensed by state authorities and must operate according to state standards, though some develop their own standards as well. At least five states—California, Florida, Michigan, Texas, and Virginia—now have provisions for satellite systems.

It is conceivable that such day care programs could operate effectively in the absense of a state licensing system. Money now spent by states on licensing could be better spent on the education of parents through information and referral services. In addition, a private program to certify day care providers could be established on the model of the American Bar Association and funded through membership fees. However, certification from such an association should be optional, and parents should be able to choose whether or not to place their children in homes or centers with certified day care providers.

"By increasing providers' costs, day care regulations limit the supply of a much-needed service."

As with many services, day care has been plagued by the ill-considered directives of well-intentioned bureaucrats. Laws designed to protect the health and safety of children and guarantee responsible care have, in many cases, proven to be counterproductive. By raising the cost of day care services, would-be providers have been deterred from the business while others have been driven underground. This is aside from the fact that many of the requirements do little, if anything, for the welfare of children.

Counterproductive Regulation

It is vital that children be cared for by competent, dedicated professionals in a safe environment, but this quality of care has been achieved through parental concern, not ineffective and often counterproductive regulations. Without the false sense of security provided by government standards, parents would take more responsibility for the well-being of their children. Moreover, through unregulated competition, day care facilities and services can supply parents with something even more fundamental—freedom of choice.

Karen Lehrman is the managing editor and Jana Pace the associate editor of Consumers' Research *magazine.*

"[Children] are being . . . put into very inadequate child-care. . . . One way to rectify this situation is to have a set of minimum standards for all day-care settings."

78

More Government Regulation Is Needed in Child Care

Robert J. Trotter

It's 3:30. Do you know where your kids are? A lot of parents do, and they aren't all that happy about it:

• Doug and Lisa's 13-year-old daughter, who goes home to an empty house after school, often smokes dope with her friends before her parents get home. She recently announced that she is pregnant.

• Lucy, a single parent, can barely afford to pay $50 a week to an elderly woman who cares for 2-year-old Toby and eight other babies in a one-room apartment.

• John and Julie have to pay $300 a week for a live-in nanny to take care of little Jack.

It's the crisis in child-care. We've all heard about it. Newspapers, magazines and talk shows have turned it into one of the hot social issues of the '80s. *Doonesbury* has turned it into black humor. But is there really a crisis? Yes, if you are a working parent who can't find or afford adequate day-care. Yes, if like Yale University psychologist Edward Zigler you realize that the physical and mental development of millions of children are being compromised by inadequate and damaging day-care.

"We expect these children to grow up, take their place in society and provide the work that's going to make this country competitive and productive," he says. "But these children may not be ready. And that's a very frightening prospect for our society."

Zigler, one of the architects of Project Head Start and for 30 years a researcher in the field of child development and social policy, says, "It's not enough for social scientists to say, 'These are my subjects.' We have to say, 'These are human beings that we study to try to help.'" Combining his research expertise and his experience with the federal government, he is trying to help by developing what he thinks is a practical, affordable solution to the

number one problem of American families.

"We have all the knowledge necessary to provide absolutely first-rate child-care in the United States," he claims. "What's missing is the commitment and the will. First," he says, "we must convince the nation that when a family selects a child-care center, they are not simply buying a service that allows them to work. They are buying an environment that determines, in large part, the development of their children. Remember," he says, "child-care is a day-in-day-out, year-in-year-out phenomenon for a child."

The job of convincing the nation that child-care should be a top-priority issue has been made easier by the sheer size and continued growth of the problem. Fifteen years ago, only 52 percent of mothers with school-age children were in the out-of-home work force. Today, that figure is up to 72 percent, while 57 percent of those with preschoolers work and 53 percent of those with infants and toddlers work. And all indications are that this trend will continue.

A Great Defeat

Zigler and other social scientists saw the problem coming as long ago as 1971 and tried to get the government to take steps to start a national child-care program. Working with Rep. John Brademus (D-Indiana) and Sen. Walter Mondale (D-Minnesota), they helped write the Child Development Act of 1971 and even had the backing of the Nixon administration until right-wing evangelicals, outraged that any self-respecting mother would let someone else care for her child, quashed it with a hate-mail campaign. "That was one of the great, great defeats of my life—for me personally and certainly for the country," Zigler says. "Just think, that bill provided the embryonic child-care system that could have grown up and been fully in place by now. Those of us who knew the demographics knew where we would be now, but there was no outcry from the parents who needed child-care. And no country tries to solve a problem until there is a sense that a problem exists. Demographics drive social policy. Now, the demographics are there."

Many mothers choose to work because they have fulfilling jobs or because they just don't want to be cooped up at home all day, but most work because they need the money. "In the current economic situation," Zigler explains, "a young family needs two incomes if they are to have what we consider a decent level of life. Furthermore, there has been a tremendous shift in the nature of jobs in the United States, with only one job in four paying enough to support a family of four comfortably."

The child-care situation begins to look even worse, Zigler says, when you realize that about one in four children and one in two black children are being reared in single-parent homes. This is actually a euphemism for poverty, he says. "The fact is that 90 percent of those homes are headed by women, and women only earn about 70 percent of what men earn for comparable work." Furthermore, only about 30 percent of the nearly 8 million women rearing children alone receive child-support payments, leading to what we now call the "feminization of poverty." "One of every two children who are living in poverty," Zigler explains, "are from single-parent homes headed primarily by women. These women must work if they are to support themselves and their children, and child-care is their greatest problem."

Economics

Unfortunately, the day-care problem has grown so large and intimidating that it seems insoluble. Even Washington, Zigler says, seems to be saying, "It's too big a job, especially with today's budget deficits. We'd break the bank if we provided child-care for the nation."

Zigler, who was responsible for all the federal programs for children in the early 1970s and has spent many years commuting between Yale and Capitol Hill lobbying for various types of child and family legislation, is well aware of the country's economic situation. "Some people are still arguing for the Swedish model—a day-care center on every corner; the government buys it and you go use it. That's unrealistic," he admits. Zigler estimates that day-care for American children costs between $75 billion and $100 billion a year, and there is no way the federal government can pick up that kind of bill. "But," he says, "there is an affordable alternative. We just have to take the problem apart, look at its various pieces, then find a way to solve each one."

The biggest part of the problem, numerically, is school-aged children. There may be as many as 5 million children who go home to empty houses after school. These so-called latch-key children represent more than 50 percent of the child-care problem and,

according to Zigler, they are the easiest part of the problem to solve.

"I think we have to build a new school in America. We have to change the school system. We have to open schools earlier in the morning, keep them open later in the afternoon and during summer."

Don't think of school as an institution, Zigler says. Think of it as a building—one that's already paid for, one that is owned by taxpaying mothers and fathers who need day-care for their children. Part of the school building would be for teaching and the rest of it for child-care and supervision. This kind of system, Zigler says, could provide working parents with good developmental child-care services. And it should be available to every child over age 3. Zigler does not think children should start formal schooling at age 3. They would only be in the schools for day-care.

"People have got to realize that there is a connection between leaving children unsupervised after school and such social problems as teenage pregnancy, juvenile delinquency and the use of drugs."

At the age of 5, Zigler suggests, children should start kindergarten—but only for half-days. If the child has a parent at home, the child would spend the rest of the day at home. If the parents are working, the child would spend the second half of the day in the child-care part of the school. For children ages 6 to 12 there would be before-school, after-school and vacation care for those who need it.

Social Problems

Keeping the schools open, says Zigler, would solve the problem of latchkey children, but it would do much more. "People have got to realize that there is a connection between leaving children unsupervised after school and such social problems as teenage pregnancy, juvenile delinquency and the use of drugs," he says. "We are really precipitating these problems if we do not provide adult supervision for children and allow them to socialize themselves and each other. Children should be in the care of adults. They do not have the ability, the cognitive wherewithal or the experience to socialize themselves."

Zigler doesn't want teachers to provide child-care. Teachers are trained as educators, and they are expensive. What we need, he says, is something called a child development associate (CDA), a person trained to work with children—but one we can afford to pay. Someone with a degree would run the system, but CDA's, with on-the-job training, would do the bulk of the work. We already have CDA's for infants and toddlers, he says, and we should develop the same kind of professional for school-age children. The teachers would go home at three o'clock, and the CDA's would take over.

In 1971, Zigler suggested that the nation begin developing a group of certified workers that parents could trust to provide proper care for their children. "I still like that idea," he says, "but what I had in mind was to see 200,000 such people by now. Unfortunately, our country has produced only 23,000. Hardly enough to meet the need."

The new school that Zigler wants to build would do more than provide on-site child-care. "I like the Parents as First Teachers program that they have in Missouri," Zigler says, "where trained specialists actually go into homes and help teach mothers and fathers about parenting." This kind of program could be run out of the local schools, which would also provide an information-referral system and resource center for parents. Families, for example, would go to the school to find out about local day-care homes for infants and toddlers. The school would also serve as a resource center for all the day-care homes in the neighborhood.

"If we had that kind of system in place," says Zigler, "the only missing pieces would be child-care needs for infants and toddlers up to 3 years of age. The first chunk of this would be handled by pregnancy- and infant-care leave. South Africa and the United States are the only two industrialized nations in the world that do not provide this option," Zigler points out.

Leave for New Parents

Several years ago, Zigler and a panel of child-development specialists agreed that it is best for parents to care for their infants for the first few months of life and called for an infancy-care bill. The ideal would be six months of leave with three months of it paid at 75 percent of the person's regular salary, Zigler says. This would not be overly expensive for industry, he explains, because there would be a payment plan something like Social Security or workman's compensation, with both employee and employer contributing a set amount of money.

One infant-care plan . . . would provide only 18 weeks of unpaid leave. "This is the most minimal bill of any nation," he says. "But even Yale professors know that something is better than nothing. What we have to do first is get the principle in place. Then we can work toward something better."

Once the mother returns to work, the final piece of the day-care puzzle has to be solved—care for infants and toddlers until they are old enough to enter the school-based system. This part, Zigler admits, is very expensive and will probably call for government subsidies or a negative income tax.

At present, there are three types of child-care available for infants and preschoolers. The first is home care—somebody comes to your home or you take your child to a neighbor or relative. About 31 percent of the day-care in this country is home care. The second type, 37 percent, is family day-care—someone, almost always a woman, takes in four, five or six young children. Another 23 percent is center-based care—parents drop the kids off at an organized day-care center.

"There's a lot of mediocre child-care out there and some absolutely horrible day-care—children tied to chairs being cared for by women so senile that they can't care for themselves."

The problem, as Zigler sees it, is that what's available is very uneven in quality. "There is some absolutely wonderful, beneficial day-care available. Parents with the wisdom to seek it out and the money to pay for it are finding it. But it's like a cosmic crapshoot," he says. "If you are lucky enough to find that loving, committed day-care mother, it's like adding another person to your family and you can count your blessings. But there's a lot of mediocre child-care out there and some absolutely horrible day-care—children tied to chairs being cared for by women so senile that they can't care for themselves. So what we have developing is a two-tier system, with affluent people being able to afford to buy into the first tier and the rest having to accept mediocre or even dangerous care for their children.

"We cannot have a society," Zigler goes on, "in which some children at 3 weeks of age are sent into a child-care system that helps their development while another group is put into a system that is damaging." And it is the children in the second tier who need the most help. "They are already vulnerable, or at risk, because they come from single-parent homes or from families with little money, a lot of deprivation and poor health care. And they are being placed at even greater risk by being put into very inadequate child-care settings. We are talking about hundreds of thousands, if not millions, of children."

One way to rectify this situation it to have a set of minimum standards for all day-care settings. These would include such things as the size of the group, the training of the staff and the quality of the program. Zigler and other child-development specialists have drawn up national standards on several occasions during the past 20 years but have never been able to get them through Congress. One criterion these experts agree on, for example, is that no adult should be allowed to care for more than three infants.

Eight Babies at Once

"That's what it takes to provide proper stimulation," Zigler explains. "But how many states meet that standard?" Only three: Kansas, Massachusetts and Maryland. "It's not uncommon," Zigler says, "to find ratios of eight to one. I don't have to see any research to know that this isn't good. I have visited centers with eight-to-one ratios. When you go there you find overworked women, sweat pouring from them, spending their day changing diapers, placing babies in cribs. They are horrible environments. Visit them. I can tell you without any research that it is impossible for anyone, trained or untrained, to care properly for eight babies."

Beyond the lack of standards, says Zigler, there is another problem. "We are only getting from caretakers what we pay for. If you want quality child-care, you have to pay for it. But 58 percent of the caretakers in day-care centers are earning poverty-level wages or less. And in home care, where I am most concerned, 90 percent of the women are earning at that level. An absolutely number one item for us must be improving the training, the status and certainly the pay for people who decide to give their lives to the care of other people's children."

Zigler's plan to use local schools includes using them as the hub of a network for family day-care homes. They would be a resource center for parents looking for a good child-care home or facility. They could provide training for day-care workers and help make sure that the day-care homes in the local network meet the standards.

"Experts agree . . . that no adult should be allowed to care for more than three infants. . . . 'But how many states meet that standard?' Only three."

Even if every day-care center and home met minimum standards and had trained caretakers, there would still be a question about the overall effects of placing very young children in day-care. . . . Zigler says he finds this ongoing debate interesting but irrelevant for several reasons.

For one thing, he says, much of the research cited in these arguments has been conducted in settings unlike those used by most parents. Even reviews that find day-care to be harmless usually include the caveat that there be no more than three infants per caretaker. "But that standard does not yet exist," says Zigler, "so we ought not be arguing among ourselves."

Furthermore, he says, this argument is not going to end tomorrow. "We will not know the ultimate effects of infant day-care until these infants have grown up and become parents. We have a whole generation that we should be watching."

Paying for Child Care

Finally, for the many parents who have to work, the question is moot. They have no choice but to use the day-care available to them. Their question is, How do we pay for it?

Zigler's answer is, "We have to figure out a package of payers." First, he says, we put the public schools into the system and add a little bit to the local taxes to pay for having them open earlier and later. But even that, he concedes, would not cover the entire cost. There would have to be a realistic fee system built into the plan, like the one incorporated in the 1971 Child Development Act. The exact amount is yet to be worked out, but Zigler suggests that the fee be adjusted according to family income. And for very poor people, the fee would have to be zero.

Some people may complain about paying higher taxes to keep other people's children in day-care, but Zigler says we are in the same situation now as when we started universal education. It is something we decided to pay for for the good of the nation. And as more mothers join the work force and more families begin to use the system, it will seem logical that we all pay for it. "Why do we pay school taxes anyway? Why do we educate children?" Zigler asks. "Because we don't want stupid people. That's why." And for the same reason, he says, we should be willing to pay taxes for day-care. "We don't want to put children into a system that is going to damage them. We don't want them to grow up to be criminals. . . .

"It's a large vision," he says. "We're talking about a structural change in our society, a new face for our school system. But I am optimistic. . . . It still amazes me that between the fall of 1964 and the summer of 1965 we managed to put 560,000 kids into Head Start. We can do the same thing with day-care."

Robert J. Trotter is a senior editor at Psychology Today.

"Because group day-care programs are almost all very new, it's hard to predict their long-term effect on children."

The Effects of Day Care: An Overview

Betty Holcomb

At two and a half, Jeremy Shaw is one of New York City's youngest commuters. Each morning, he boards a PATH train in Hoboken and makes the ten-minute trip under the Hudson, then walks three and a half blocks to Joy McCormack's All Day Nursery in Battery Park City. Most of the time, he doesn't utter a whimper when his mother, Lynn Asinof, drops him at the center and leaves for her job at the nearby *Wall Street Journal*. In the evenings, Jeremy is a pint-size streak of energy, galloping through the World Trade Center, dodging briefcases, and eliciting surprised smiles from the older commuters.

"Day care has turned out to be a wonderful experience for us," says Asinof. "Jeremy has learned a tremendous amount by being with other kids. He's learned how to share and how limits get set. And he has lots of activities he never had at home, like painting and finger painting."

First Day at Day Care

Asinof's opinion was decidedly different last September [1986]. The day after Jeremy began the program, she awoke in a panic, certain she'd made a terrible mistake. Though he was usually confident and outgoing, he'd been miserable at the center, shrieking hysterically when his mother tried to go. Asinof knew he would adapt. What really bothered her was leaving Jeremy with all those other children. "I kept thinking, 'There just aren't enough arms to go around all these kids. There aren't enough laps for all these kids,'" she recalls. "No one's going to hear him talking, no one's going to know who he is."

Yet a search for another child-care arrangement would have plunged the family into crisis for the fourth time in two years. Asinof and her husband, Peter Shaw, had already lost two sitters, and they were reluctant to try another one. Asinof seriously

considered quitting her job. Finally, they decided to give the day-care program at least a month, thinking, "We couldn't do irreparable damage to Jeremy in just a month."

By month's end, Jeremy had grown enthusiastic about the center, and today he's thriving there. Still, Asinof retains doubts about full-time group care for young children. "I think kids need time to just play and be themselves and not have to cope with a group," she says. "I guess I had questions when Jeremy was home with a baby-sitter too. There's no perfect answer to this. It's all compromise."

Like many parents today, Asinof suffers periodic anxiety about her choices for child-rearing. Study after study shows child care to be the key source of stress for today's working parents. A recent survey of 3,200 parents at large corporations found that they typically make a new child-care arrangement once a year and that nearly 40 percent of them considered leaving their jobs because of child-care difficulties. "We only canvass the parents who stick with the job," says Tyler Phillips, president of Child Care Systems, Inc., which did the study. "We think many more drop out because of child-care problems."

Because group day-care programs are almost all very new, it's hard to predict their long-term effect on children. The uncertainty is especially acute for the growing ranks of parents who have to enroll babies. Nearly 50 percent of all working mothers today are back on the job before their child's first birthday, twice the percentage in 1970. Care for children under two is the fastest-growing segment of the business—and also the most controversial.

"There's good reason to believe this whole generation of infants who are spending ten hours a day in groups are going to have trouble relating to another person in a close relationship like a marriage," says Bryna Siegel, a child psychologist at Stanford University Medical Center and author of

Betty Holcomb, "Where's Mommy?" *New York*, April 13, 1987. Reprinted with the author's permission.

The Working Parents' Guide to Child Care.

Others strongly disagree. "When it's done right, good group care certainly does not hinder a child's development, and it can help," says Jan Miller, director of the child-care consultation service at Bank Street College of Education and founder of the Basic Trust Infant and Toddler Center on the Upper West Side. "My fantasy is that we can turn out tomorrow's leaders, people with a strong sense of autonomy."

Perplexed Parents

Parents are understandably perplexed. "It is the most heated debate going on in my field today," says Edward Zigler, a child-development expert and Sterling Professor of Psychology at Yale University. Still, today's debate is part of a fight over child-rearing and women's roles that has raged since World War II. Throughout those 40 years, the status of day care has been closely linked to the role of women. Indeed, the current dispute—and the studies that fuel it—should probably be seen in that context.

In the postwar decade, for example, when mothers were expected to stay home and tend the nest, group day care was almost unheard of. By the late sixties, the women's movement and an inflationary economy had sent many mothers to work, and studies reported that day care was a healthy way of coping. In the Reagan era, with its shift back to older values, day care is again under fire. Many researchers, sympathetic to the plight of working parents and their children, are searching for middle ground. But the current fight threatens to reopen discussion of whether mothers of the youngest children should work at all.

"Scientists have had little more than a decade to study large numbers of children in group care, and they are still arguing over how best to do the research."

Part of the problem is that the research is so new. Scientists have had little more than a decade to study large numbers of children in group care, and they are still arguing over how best to do the research. The real results of this social experiment won't be known for a generation or more, when the first day-care children grow into adults.

What's more, even professionals like Asinof and her husband, who can afford to buy the best, find the choices for their children limited. There's no organized child-care system; the options are informal and in some instances inadequate. Many researchers are concluding that today's working parents are

pioneers.

"We are dealing with a twenty-first-century issue here, looking to a time when child care will be available to everyone, just like any other municipal service," says Jay Belsky, a psychologist at Pennsylvania State University. "Some of us are saying there are some risks out there for kids, and we have to decide which risks we are willing to take and which ones we are not.". . .

Until the late sixties, the most influential studies of infants cared for outside the home were those made by an English psychologist, John Bowlby, who studied homeless babies in British institutions after World War II. These babies were given an adequate diet and were kept warm and clean, but they were rarely cuddled or given the opportunity to develop relationships with the changing army of nurses who cared for them. Bowlby's findings were startling: Without a stable, loving relationship, these infants withered. They retreated into a shell, losing interest in eating, playing, or even looking around. . . .

Psychologists began to talk darkly about a new syndrome, "maternal deprivation," and the press warned that mothers would harm their babies if they worked outside the home. Throughout the fifties, this research formed the backbone of resistance to day care. Prominent pediatricians, such as Benjamin Spock, relied on Bowlby's studies and recommended that mothers stay home with preschool children. As recently as 1968, Dr. Spock's book included the "working mother" under the section on special problems in child-rearing, and he said, "A day nursery or 'baby farm' is no good for an infant. There's nowhere near enough attention or affection to go around." (He has since revised his position.)

New Developments

By the mid-sixties, however, two developments had sparked a dramatic rethinking of child care: A growing number of mothers were working at paid jobs, and new discoveries were shaking up psychology. By 1967, one quarter of all mothers with children under six were working, and they needed someone to care for their children. Families who could afford to hired baby-sitters to come into their homes, the closest they could come to the classic model of the mother. Many more enlisted a grandmother or an aunt. But families were increasingly fragmented, and there were often no relatives nearby. So day care, long tolerated as a necessary evil to help poor women make ends meet, arrived in the middle class.

Meanwhile, psychologists were gaining new insight into how children think, feel, and learn. For the first time in decades, serious debate broke out over the influence the mother has in child development. Scientists had learned more about how the brain works and how memory and awareness develop.

They began to speculate that a child's development may be biologically determined, preprogrammed in the genes like time-release capsules. Many believed these genetic programs to be very strong, buffering children against changes in the environment. These scientists began to describe even the tiniest babies as a sturdy lot who could adapt to a variety of child-care arrangements without serious harm. Feminists and the most radical psychologists used these findings to dismiss psychoanalytic theory as outdated Victorian bias that had been used to keep women at home. . . .

"The Strange Situation quickly became the most prevalent yardstick of an infant's emotional health, and even today, it is often at the heart of studies that raise concerns about the emotional effects of day care."

Psychologists began to take a serious interest in studying the effects of out-of-home care, but from the start, they faced an enormous obstacle: How could they measure the emotional, social, and intellectual life of children too young to talk and barely able to control their bodies? The only known barometer of a child's mental health was a healthy attachment to mom. How could that be quantified?

The Strange Situation

For many scientists, the answer arrived in the form of a fascinating and controversial tool known as the Strange Situation, which was developed by American psychologist Mary Ainsworth, one of Bowlby's protégés. The test is brilliant in its simplicity—all an infant needs is a good set of lungs. A mother and her child, between the ages of twelve and eighteen months, are brought into a laboratory. A stranger enters, and the mother departs. The infant usually shrieks in horror. The mother returns, and upon reunion, the baby is put in one of three categories: Those who are easily comforted by mother are said to have strong, healthy attachments; the others are described as either anxious or resistant. As the children grew older, they were given standard mental and psychological tests. Researchers found that the tots with secure bonds were the most likely to be happy, curious, and confident. Those in the other categories tended to have problems getting along with people, and they were easily frustrated and more withdrawn.

"It was a real breakthrough in psychology. All of a sudden, we had a handle on how to measure the infant-mother relationship," says Belsky, the Penn State psychologist.

The Strange Situation quickly became the most prevalent yardstick of an infant's emotional health, and even today, it is often at the heart of studies that raise concerns about the emotional effects of day care. Initially, scientists using the test gave some of the most optimistic reports on day care. Indeed, as recently as 1978, Belsky issued a widely circulated study that said day care need not be harmful to infants and toddlers. In essence, day care was given a scientific blessing, one that was picked up in the media and in the mountains of child-development books marketed to modern parents.

Disturbing Answers

But the blessing was short-lived. The earliest studies soon came under intense criticism. Most significant, the first studies had focused on centers sponsored by universities, where the care was of exceptional quality and a far cry from what most American children experience in day care. Many researchers began to double back and refine their questions: Do boys react differently from girls? Do six-month-olds react differently from two-year-olds? The answers this time were disturbing.

Since then, a number of studies have found that children under one suffer when taken out of their mothers' care. When tested under the Strange Situation, a disproportionate number of these children have been described as insecurely attached to their mothers. Now some of the same scientists whose studies had helped promote day care just a few years ago—most notably Jay Belsky—are sounding an alarm. In a child-care newsletter, Belsky warned that infants separated from their mothers before their first birthday are more likely to be insecure as infants and aggressive and uncooperative during their preschool and elementary-school years.

"I don't want to be hysterical," Belsky said in a recent phone interview. "But if I had to give a recommendation to somebody who could afford to stay home without terrible consequences, I would tell them to do it."

Belsky's change of heart has deeply upset the day-care community. "Jay's reversal is seen as significant because he was one of the most persuasive voices that said day care was all right," says Alison Clarke-Stewart, professor of social ecology at the Irvine campus of the University of California. "His opinion carries weight."

On the Wrong Track

Still, Clarke-Stewart and other experts who disagree with Belsky claim he is simply on the wrong track—that he has given the mother-infant bond far too much importance. Recent findings in biology indicate that tiny infants can develop sustaining attachments to several adults, not just to their mothers. . . .

These scientists dismiss the Strange Situation as a

strange way to assess a child's mental health. "The idea that a baby can and should only feel emotionally secure in the presence of its mother seems like a rather perverse kind of development to encourage," says Sandra Scarr, chairman of the psychology department at the University of Virginia and author of *Mother Care/Other Care*. "I think it's healthy for infants to discover that other adults can be trustworthy."

These scientists have turned to broader measures of a child's well-being, often relying on simple observation of tots as they are being cared for. When children are under two, the researchers look for signs of attachment to the mother—the distance the child plays from her, for example, or how the child greets her. But they also look at how cooperative, happy, and energetic children are and how long they stay with any one activity. Once children reach the age of two, the researchers give standard tests to see if prior day-care experiences have affected their development.

Studies from this camp have indicated that babies as young at three and a half months do fine inside or outside the home, with or without mother, as long as the care is of high quality. In one study, Scarr and several colleagues went to Bermuda, where many mothers work and infants and toddlers get out-of-home care. The only children to suffer any bad consequences were those in day-care centers where staffers had no training in child development, were poorly paid, or were required to watch more than five infants at a time.

Another important study showed that high-quality day care could actually accelerate a child's social and intellectual development. "My study was one of the first to say not only that it is okay to have kids in day care, but that they might actually do better," says Clarke-Stewart. Overall, she concluded, children in day-care centers raced some six to nine months ahead of children raised at home by mothers or baby-sitters.

Clarke-Stewart's research was important because it was wide-ranging—she used measures as diverse as a child's attachment to his mother, language development, and standard intelligence tests—and because she and her colleagues tested a broad sample of children from a variety of situations.

Middle Ground

Day-care advocates immediately embraced the study as a vindication of out-of-home care, but the story is a little more complicated than that. Clarke-Stewart and her colleagues also found that the differences between home-reared and day-care children disappeared by the time they turned five. She speculates that the toddlers she studied suffered something known as "fade-out" or "washout" of the positive effects of enrichment programs as soon as the programs were over. "If you were committed to

developing your child as fast as possible, you'd just have to keep pouring on the enrichment," says Clarke-Stewart. "One year it would be dance, the next year Suzuki lessons. I'm not sure parents really want to do that."

Indeed, Clarke-Stewart is dismayed that her study is often used as an unconditional endorsement of day care. "I don't want to be portrayed as promoting day care at all costs," she says. She feels especially cautious about infants under a year old. "That is when kids are most vulnerable and our research is most vulnerable."

The most popular pediatricians today straddle both camps, giving cautious advice about the care of very young children. In the latest edition of his book, Dr. Spock stresses the need for individualized care for children under three but recognizes that the best group situations can meet that need.

"[Other] scientists have turned to broader measures of a child's well-being, often relying on simple observation of tots as they are being cared for."

Pediatrician T. Berry Brazelton, whose books have made him a latter-day Dr. Spock, said in recent congressional testimony on parental-leave policies that "we are all stuck with our wish for the mother to be at home." But he added, "We have got to get rid of the old model of attachment" and explore new ones more in tune with today's social patterns. Still, Dr. Brazelton holds the more traditional view that parents and infants forge strong and lasting bonds in even the earliest months. He has become a leading advocate of maternity leaves of at least four months. Beyond that, he argues, an infant can thrive in a group or individualized setting, as long as the care is individualized and loving.

By now, many researchers in child development have acknowledged that strong feelings often color the debate. "My own personal sense is that few individuals are truly open-minded about infant day care," Belsky wrote recently. He chastised politicians and others who sift through research "looking only for ammunition for their arguments," but he conceded that "scientists are susceptible to similar biases, however much we try not to be."

Betty Holcomb is a free-lance writer in New York City who contributes frequently to New York, *a weekly magazine.*

> *"Daycare children of all ages are more comfortable with their peers . . . and they are more cooperative and empathic."*

viewpoint 80

Day Care Helps Children

Jo Ann Miller and Susan Weissman

It's seven o'clock on a fall morning, and the sunlight is just beginning to peek through the windows of the house that Ellen and Mark Randall share with their nineteen-month-old son, Michael. Ellen, a worn teddy bear under her arm and a pad of paper on her lap, sits on the edge of her bed. Today is Michael's first day at the Pine Street Daycare Center, and Ellen wants to be sure not to forget anything.

She checks off her list—extra bottles, Michael's favorite blanket, his bear. Mustn't forget Teddy, she reminds herself, and tucks the bear into her briefcase.

In the kitchen Ellen joins Mark, who's busy preparing breakfast. Michael sits in his high chair, cheerfully smearing applesauce on the wall beside him. Leaning over to wipe the dripping wall, Ellen spots two bottles on the floor—so that's where they went! Silently she multiplies by six. There will be six children in Michael's group. She turns to Mark. "How on earth will they manage six sticky walls and twelve lost bottles?" she wonders aloud. "Not to mention all those soaking diapers!" Mark reminds her, as he carries a squirming Michael over to the changing table.

Ready for Daycare

In less than half an hour, he and Ellen and Michael, who's been freshly changed and dressed in his favorite Superman shirt, will join four other new children and their parents for the first day of "Welcome Week" at the Pine Street Center.

Mark and Ellen looked at two other daycare centers before making their choice. At Pine Street they found a well-organized program and warm, intelligent caregivers who they believe will not only manage sticky walls and lost possessions but give

their son lots of affection and attention. But they still have questions. Will Michael have the right toys to play with? What if he doesn't like the caregivers? Or likes them too much—and forgets about his parents? What if he doesn't eat? Or sleep? . . .

Children go to daycare at different ages—six-week-old infants whose mothers return to work, toddlers who graduate from Grandma's care, preschoolers who move from a small group home to a larger center. A hallmark of good child care, say experts such as Yale University Professor of Pediatrics Sally Provence and University of Virginia psychologist Sandra Scarr, is that it is *developmentally appropriate*. . . .

We divide children into three approximate age groups:

Babies and infants: birth to eighteen months
Toddlers: eighteen months to three years
Preschoolers: three years to five years

Babies are much more interested in grown-ups than they are in other babies. So, there must be enough adults to cuddle and care for them. By the time they become toddlers they are forming warm friendships and can tolerate a little less adult attention. But they still depend on grown-ups to comfort them and help them learn about the world.

Preschoolers seem very independent, and they need challenging activities and materials to prepare them for the more formal schooling that lies ahead. But they too need the affectionate attention of caring adults.

Of course, age doesn't tell the whole story. As every parent knows, children also differ in temperament. *Meeting individual needs* is the second feature that the experts agree is crucial to quality child care. . . .

There are easy babies who nod off dreamily and can be plunked down almost anywhere without a whimper. And there are "difficult" ones who need ten minutes of back-rubbing to fall asleep and who

From THE PARENT'S GUIDE TO DAYCARE by JoAnn Miller and Susan Weissman, MSW. Copyright © 1986 by JoAnn Miller and Susan Weissman. Reprinted by permission of Bantam Books. All rights reserved.

wail in protest when they find themselves in a new situation. Shy toddlers need special encouragement to involve them in activities; aggressive preschoolers must be helped to control themselves. All these children can thrive in daycare if parents and caregivers are sensitive to them as individuals. . . .

Another Family's Decision

Julie Daniels, recently separated from her husband, is visiting the pediatrician with her seven-month-old daughter, Emily. Since Emily's birth, Dr. Stark has been a tremendous source of comfort, patiently dispensing good advice through bouts of colic and new-mother nervousness. Now Julie needs some special counsel from him. The examination is over and Dr. Stark is about the leave the room, when Julie turns to him.

"I think I'm going to have to go back to work," she begins hesitantly. "I can't count on steady money from Paul, and my company offered me my old job back." Julie, a talented commercial artist, has been freelancing since Emily's birth and had not planned to return to full-time work for at least another six months. "I heard about a woman nearby who takes care of babies," she continues, but Dr. Stark starts shaking his head vehemently.

"Oh no," he says, cutting Julie off. "Seven months is much too young for you to leave Emily. She needs her mother. She doesn't belong in a group with other babies."

This is not what Julie had hoped to hear. The last thing she needs to feel now is guilty! Disappointed and angry, she walks out of Dr. Stark's office, vowing never to discuss her personal life with him again.

Now let's rewrite the scenario. How much more helpful it would have been if the doctor had said: "Mrs. Daniels, I know this is a hard decision for you, and before you decide what to do and who should take care of Emily, I want to tell you what I think you should know about the needs of a baby her age. And I want you to consider what you've learned about Emily as a person in the few months you've known her."

For years the debate has raged. Is group care good for children or bad for them? Is there a "best" age to start daycare? Still, there are no clear answers. Maybe that's because we've been asking the wrong questions. A better approach, we think, is for those who know and care about children to ask: "What can we tell parents about child development and about the realities of group care that will help them choose the best arrangement for their children—when they need it?". . .

Care To Fit the Child's Needs

Psychologists consider *developmental appropriateness* a key factor in quality daycare. Let's look at this now from Julie and Emily's point of view.

Had Dr. Stark played out our second scenario he might have told Julie that seven-month-old babies need to be in a small group with babies their own age—ideally, no more than three babies with one adult. In fact, the family daycare home that Julie was about to describe (and in which she did finally enroll Emily) was perfect. Run by Jane Exner, an experienced mother with a son two months older than Emily, it was known in the neighborhood as a warm and caring place for babies. . . .

A Year Later

About a year after their son entered the Pine Street Center, we visited Ellen and Mark Randall again. Michael was then nearly three years old, a chatty little boy, with the kind of self-assurance that we'd come to associate with daycare children. While we talked with his parents, he worked on a puzzle on the living-room floor, frequently interrupting us to ask for juice or to crawl into Mark's lap for a hug. We commented that the Randalls seemed to have adjusted well to the daycare experience.

Ellen agreed. "I wonder, though," she said, "how Mike will be later on, how he'll do in school. We've heard so many conflicting reports—one psychologist on TV said children in daycare are bound to have psychological problems, and that if mothers really cared about their kids they'd stay home for the first three years."

Mark went on: "And then another expert on the same talk show said his research showed that daycare kids grow up with fewer emotional difficulties. We don't know what to believe."

"Daycare children are not removed from their parents or abandoned by them. . . . Mothers of children in daycare give them as much 'attentive care' as at-home mothers do."

When we talked to Julie Daniels, she added another concern: "I read these magazines that said that Emily would love Jane more than me because she started there so young and she was away from me so much." Julie laughed ruefully as she remembered one article. "This child psychologist said a mother should have lunch with her child every day. So I'd rush over to Jane's on my lunch hour—it was crazy." She paused and continued thoughtfully: "I want to do what's best for Emily, but it's hard to see the future. I wish I could be sure she's not being harmed by daycare."

Until recently, answers to questions like these have been conflicting and confusing. This is partly because of the natural limitations of daycare research. It's also a result of extrapolating—incorrectly, we believe—from studies conducted on children in hospitals and orphanages, studies that pointed out the dire emotional consequences of institutionalization. But group care is not institutional care. Daycare children are not removed from their parents or abandoned by them. They still spend a great deal of time together—in fact, some studies show that mothers of children in daycare give them as much "attentive care" as at-home mothers do.

Daycare Research

In the last fifteen years, as group care has become a reality for more and more families, researchers have begun systematic comparisons of home-reared children with those raised in daycare. Their aim has been to answer the very question that Ellen, Mark, and Julie ask: *Does daycare harm children's development?* Scores of investigators have observed children in daycare homes and centers, questioned their parents and caregivers, and evaluated their social, emotional, and intellectual development. Despite the complexity of doing this kind of research, the results have been consistently positive. Most of the research showed that *good-quality daycare itself produced few if any harmful effects.*

Typical among these studies is the important one by Harvard psychologist Jerome Kagan and his colleagues. Their intensive six-year investigation found no important differences in attachment, separation anxiety, and social and emotional development between daycare childen and those reared at home. Kagan concludes: *"If the child comes from a relatively stable family and if the daycare is of good quality, the child's development seems to be normal."*

In recent years, daycare research has become more sophisticated. Investigators have now begun to ask a different question. This "second wave"—as noted researcher Jay Belsky calls it—asks: *Under what conditions do children fare best in daycare?* . . .

Daycare research usually examines daycare's impact on *emotional development*—how children feel about themselves and their parents; *social development*—how they relate to adults and other children; and *cognitive development*—how their thinking and intelligence evolve. . . .

Relations with Parents

The major question in emotional development has been: Will daycare interfere with the mother-child bond? This is what Julie Daniels was worried about, and understandably so, because many researchers believe this bond is the crucial base for a person's emotional security throughout life.

This bond, or "attachment," is usually measured by separating a mother and child, thus creating a stressful situation, and then watching how the child reacts when he's reunited with his mother. How much a child protests when he's separated from his mother and what kind of reunion they have are taken as measures of attachment. In the vast majority of such experiments, daycare children don't differ from home-reared ones, regardless of the age at which they entered daycare. That is, some daycare children are "securely attached" and some are less so, but as a group they are no different from children raised at home.

> *"No matter how much Emily loves Jane, she, like the majority of daycare children, is most likely to prefer her mother."*

Researchers also look at whom children prefer for comfort or stimulation: their parents or their caregivers. Here again, Julie need not worry. No matter how much Emily loves Jane, she, like the majority of daycare children, is most likely to prefer her mother.

Jay Belsky does cite two studies that suggest that some children who begin daycare before the age of one year and have many changes in caregivers may have disturbances of attachment and later behavior problems. Although these findings are in the minority, they should alert us to the need to assess infant programs very carefully.

Social Relationships

Since daycare children interact with more people than home-reared children, researchers have been curious to learn whether daycare makes a difference in social development. When it comes to peer relationships, the answer seems to be an overwhelming *yes.* Daycare children of all ages are more comfortable with their peers—they take more easily to children they don't know than home-reared children do—and they are more cooperative and empathic.

This certainly supports our own observations. We saw many children deeply involved with their groupmates. One of our favorite examples is the little boy who offered his most treasured possession, his thumb, to a hurt friend.

On the negative side, although daycare children have more complex relationships with their peers, they are also more boisterous and aggressive then children reared at home. But Alison Clarke-Stewart points out that although these may seem to be "negative" behaviors, they are really signs of *social maturity,* of children who are "more knowledgeable about the social world." Again, this is what we saw in daycare—children who were unfazed by a stranger, who chatted amiably with a visitor, who exuded self-confidence. As one mother observed: "I have seen my child walk into a room where he has never been before, and he has no fear of being in that room."

Will this social precocity persist through life? Very little research has followed children much beyond the early grades, so it is difficult to answer this question. However, one study found that boys who had been enrolled in daycare before the age of five were more sociable and better liked by their peers when they reached adolescence. In general, though, it appears that daycare children remain more socially mature than their home-reared peers for the first few grades and that the differences then level off.

"In an especially comprehensive study of children . . . [Alison] Clarke-Stewart found children in group care significantly more intellectually competent than those reared at home."

As for social relations with adults, Jay Belsky reports that daycare children seem to be less cooperative with caregivers, more troublesome in classroom settings, and less attentive than children reared at home, probably because caregivers are less concerned about obedience and more tolerant about aggression than parents are. Belsky warns that these results are only suggestive and are by no means inevitable.

Intellectual Development

Ellen and Mark Randall wonder how daycare will affect Michael's performance in school. Here the research is very encouraging. According to both Jay Belsky and Alison Clarke-Stewart, middle-class children in daycare either show no difference in intellectual performance from home-reared ones or show appreciable gains, at least in the short run.

In an especially comprehensive study of children in a variety of home and out-of-home care arrangements, Clarke-Stewart found children in group care significantly more intellectually competent than those reared at home.

For disadvantaged children, the gains may be more dramatic, preventing, as Belsky puts it, the "intellectual decline" that disadvantaged children often suffer in early childhood.

Although Ellen and Mark can be proud of Michael's advanced intellectual abilities, they—and other middle-class parents—won't have too many years to rest on their laurels. By second grade Michael's home-reared agemates are likely to have caught up with him in intellectual competence. But

the most important thing is that the research is unanimous in finding no adverse effect on children's intellectual development.

Jo Ann Miller is a writer and editor who specializes in psychology. Susan Weissman has a master's degree in social work and founded the Park Center Preschools in New York City. She is also a consultant to other child care centers.

Day Care Harms Children

Fredelle Maynard

All parents want the best for their children. The vision of what's best, however, is greatly affected by social climate. Fifty years ago, *best* frequently meant *best behaved*; today it's widely equated with *brightest*. In a 1980 poll of qualities parents most desired in their offspring, "intelligence" topped the list. Harvard University's T. Berry Brazelton, who in his role as pediatrician has observed thousands of families, confirms the trend. "Everyone wants to raise the smartest kid in America rather than the best adjusted, happiest kid."

It's not surprising, then, that day care investigation has so often concerned itself with cognitive development. Do children learn better at home or in surrogate care? In family groups or centres? What is surprising is the relative poverty of research findings. The mountain labours—hundreds of papers from universities across the land—to bring forth a very small mouse. What does research tell us? Send a child to day care or keep him home, provide him with sophisticated educational toys or kitchen tools, as far as intellectual development goes, it doesn't much matter. He will be what he will be, thanks to the genes he inherited and the social class into which he was born.

Stimulation

That's an overstatement of course. In the earliest months, the human brain requires for optimal development certain kinds of environmental stimuli—the kind of stimuli, for example, that a mother (or constant caretaker) provides in a multitude of small daily interactions with her infant. Patting, rocking, smiling, feeding, babbling—all these instinctive responses, by stimulating alertness or pleasure, become part of infant learning. Where they don't occur, says child psychiatrist Humberto

From *The Child Care Crisis* by Fredelle Maynard. Copyright © Fredelle Maynard 1985. Reprinted by permission of Penguin Books Canada Limited.

Nagera, the result is a permanent limitation of brain capacity and function. It follows that an infant in day care from 6:30 A.M. to 6:30 P.M., exposed to shifts of staff and multiple caretakers, will very likely suffer a lack of appropriate stimulation. That's a distinct minus for some children in some day care situations. Conversely, take a child from what sociologists call a "high risk" environment—a chaotic home with depressed or angry parents and a generally low level of competence. Put him in a good day care centre, with a rich program and attentive caretaking, and he will show intellectual as well as social gains. That's a plus for some children in some day care situations.

In general, studies agree that day care of average quality has no apparent ill effects on children's intellectual development. Such positive effects as it produces, substantial gains for "disadvantaged" children, however promising initially, tend to wash out after the program ends. Children from relatively privileged backgrounds—homes with educated parents, books, music, conversation and a lively round of activities—are unaffected by even high-quality enriched programs. They don't lose anything intellectually, neither do they gain. . . .

Social Development

Children accustomed to other-than-parent care, whether in a centre or a neighbour's home, achieve an earlier mastery of social skills: that seems incontrovertible. Watch a group of four-year-olds in a well-run day care facility, and you'll be struck by the highly organized behaviour. These children spontaneously put away their painting smocks and take out their pillows for circle time. They know how to gain entry into an ongoing game and how to stave off trouble by well-timed compromise or surrender. They remember to put the caps back on magic markers, return puzzles to the shelf. They approach and talk to strangers, are eager to show what they're doing. They sing unselfconsciously. "Children with a long experience of day care are notably independent," says Renee Edwards, Director of Toronto's Victoria Day Care Services. "They're skilled in looking after themselves, are fairly sophisticated socially, *competent*. They know how to cope with others, and have a better understanding of their own capacities."

If they've been in care any length of time, children understand and adapt to the daily rhythm. (Now it's time for outside . . . for juice and crackers . . . for toileting . . . for story . . . for Mommy and home.) Parents report with pleasure the day care child's ease in the world, his capacity for mature and complex relationships. "Our child is able to adjust to changes and strangers very easily." "She's socially confident and loves groups." "He has a social sense which seems much more animated than what I've seen in children remaining at home." These comments, from a Michigan survey of parental perceptions of their children's experience, are typical and typically positive. Other parents describe their day care children as more competent, helpful and co-operative than stay-at-homes. "Less timid" and "less fearful" are also often cited, though here the research evidence is conflicting and confused. Some investigators have found day care children more apprehensive in situations involving strange adults— unless they're in the comforting presence of peers. Very early day care (before age two) seems to be associated with *increased* fearfulness, and later day care with *diminished* fearfulness. . . .

Separateness, independence, social confidence and competence . . . so far, so good. The flip side of the coin, however, presents a less reassuring aspect. Bryna Siegel-Gorelick, a Stanford child psychologist, fears what she calls "a negative sense of separateness" in the child, who may feel cut off from the parent, and in the parent who, anticipating early surrogate care, may resist formation of a close bond. . . .

Feeling Their Oats

In general, day care children acquire superior social skills. The other side of this social confidence is often cockiness. Day care children tend to be less tractable, less polite, than children raised at home. They feel their oats, they're less impressed by punishment, less averse to dirt, more prone in the early years to tantrums and toilet lapses. What adults want is not necessarily important to them. They will be loud and boisterous and quarrelsome if they choose. Yes, they enjoy groups, gravitate to groups; often this means that away from the group, they're at loose ends. Accustomed to companions and a highly structured life, children raised in day care may seek constant stimulation and suffer from an impaired capacity for entertaining themselves.

The gravest social development problem presented

by the day care child is increased aggressiveness. On this point all investigators agree: day care children are more inclined to get what they want by hitting, threatening, kicking, punching, insulting and taking possessions without permission. ("Day care may slow the acquisition of some cultural values," one observer says delicately. Indeed.) A recent report found day care children performing *fifteen* times as many aggressive acts as home-reared age-mates. Other studies says that these children enter school more hostile to both teachers and peers and that their aggressiveness is accompanied by (or is part of) much greater impulsivity and distractibility. School performance may well be affected. A British study conducted by the Tavistock Institute, reporting the progressive acceleration of aggressiveness in day care children (the longer in care, the feistier), found that of eight day care graduates, all average or above average in intelligence, only one achieved average levels in reading, language and ability to concentrate.

"Day care children are more inclined to get what they want by hitting, threatening, kicking, punching, insulting and taking possessions without permission."

This is bad news, particularly in view of evidence that male aggressiveness, once developed early, is likely to persist. . . .

Child Care for Infants

Addressing the question of surrogate care for the very young children of working parents, Dr Annette Silbert, a Boston child psychologist, observes that each case is individual, no pat prescriptions apply. "Many people are unhappy when they hear that, but it is better to face this truth than to encourage the illusion that perfect, all-purpose prescriptions exist." The real question, she says, is not job or no job, day care or home care, but "What does it take to live in our society? If we want our children to become adults who can cooperate with one another, who have flexibility so they can adapt to changing situations, who can work, if we want people who are capable of affection, devotion, constancy and who will be wise parents when they are of age, then there are certain things we have to put into the care of these children when they are young." Only the family, Dr Silbert maintains, can provide children with some semblance of cohesion and harmony, with the basis for trust in other people and in themselves. What about the option of a mother-substitute? If the substitute is affectionate, responsive and loyal (in other words, stays on the job) the child may flourish, will love both caretaker and mother. But—"the values he will incorporate will most likely be those of the chief caretaker, the conscience he will develop will be influenced as much by the caretaker as the mother—and if the value systems of the principal characters in his little life's drama are not harmonious he has some ready-made conflicts." Consider for example, the infant daughter of professional, academic parents who value intellectual distinction, industry, self-discipline and achievement. Put her for the first four years in the care of (a) a European nanny (b) a loving, aging matron (c) an active young *au pair*. The result, depending on care, may be a beautifully mannered social being, a relaxed carefree spirit, a wholesome skier or tennis player. . . Certainly her parents cannot count on genetic endowment and some judicious "quality time" to mould this child in accordance with their own value system.

Day Care's Lessons

Children learn what they live with. "If a child lives with hostility he learns to fight. If he lives with criticism he learns to condemn," Dorothy Law Nolte wrote in a well-known collection of aphorisms. "If a child lives with fairness he learns justice. If he lives with approval he learns to like himself. And if he lives with acceptance and friendship he learns to find love in the world." What of the child who lives in some form of surrogate care from infancy until school-starting age? "A day care centre that ministers to a child from his sixth month to his sixth year has more than 8,000 hours to teach him values, beliefs and behaviours and, potentially, is an enormously powerful influence over what that child will become," says Harvard's Jerome Kagan. All day long, in care, the child is learning—and not just what's in the curriculum. When three-year-old Kelly draws faces on the fingers of her left hand—"Look, puppets!"—a teacher snatches the felt marker with a reproving, "We draw on paper, not fingers!" (Lesson: *Do what you're told. Experiments get you into trouble.*) Jason wants to finish his block tower but is propelled into the circle for "Show and Tell." (*Your own work is not important. Fitting into the group is important.*) Charlie—whose mother is in hospital with a new baby—is having a bad day and the caretaker, suddenly tired of his whining, says, "That's enough now. I want to see a smile on your face." (*It's not safe to show your feelings.*) After juice the children are given collage materials to make greeting cards. "Let's see who can finish first!" the caretaker says. (*Speed matters more than quality. Get ahead of the next guy.*) Both Margie and Steve are having difficulty with their Easter basket handles. The day care worker briskly attaches a handle to Margie's basket—"There, isn't that pretty?"—and tells Steve, "You're a big boy. Put more paste on the handle and try again." (*Girls need a lot of help. Boys can manage*

on their own.) Ellen interrupts the story with an earnest question, "Why can't boys have babies?" and is silenced with "This isn't talking time, it's listening time." A particularly horrifying example of unintentional values-teaching appears in *Children and Day Nurseries.* A group of four-year-olds is being taught numbers and colours and days of the week as part of their school preparation. Mention of school triggers in one small boy a passionate outburst: "My Daddy's dead, but I've got a grandfather and he's going to take me to school!" "Is he?" says the teacher. "Now, everyone, after me: It-is-Wednesday-the-30th-of-June."

"Working parents may fantasize delightful quiet times at day's end when they hold a little one close and share their thoughts about life. . . . Reality is tired parents collecting a tired child."

But surely parents have the last word in value-teaching? In theory, yes. Working parents may fantasize delightful quiet times at day's end when they hold a little one close and share their thoughts about life. Reality is somewhat less idyllic. Reality is tired parents collecting a tired child (who has been away from home as much as ten hours). Child is cross, also angry at mother in the sheer nervous excitement of seeing her again; mother, all set up for tenderness, feels a surge of guilt and anger too. ("I work hard all day and this is what I get.") There's dry cleaning to collect, a stop for milk and coffee, supper to prepare, bath and bedtime still to come. . . Who wants to talk (or hear) about Beauty, Truth and Goodness?

And of course, values—like sex education, like any kind of complicated learning—are not taught in orderly segments at selected times. (Today, honesty. Tomorrow, fair play.) Values emerge continuously in the course of daily life. "It's rude and unkind to stare at a child who has trouble walking. That girl has cerebral palsy, and it's hard for her to get around. Why don't you hold the door open for her?" "No, you can't keep the Smurf you found on the school steps. Give it to your teacher and she'll try to find out whose it is." "Yes, I know you'd like to go to McDonald's with the kids. But you promised to go to Grandma's this afternoon. You mustn't break a promise." Value issues are raised constantly in a child's questions—about war, about people who are different, about sex and divorce and the TV commercials. "Children do not make notes about their questions to bring up at a more convenient time," Rita Kramer writes in *In Defense of the Family.* "They wonder about things according to the rhythm of their inner life, and ask whoever is there at the moment. Being there more often than not when they're constructing their view of reality, their outlook on life, is a value to be seriously weighed against the reasons any mother may have for not being there.". . .

Tied to a Schedule

Consider now the child in a large fairly typical day care centre—not wonderful, not terrible. There are eighty children here, mostly ages two to four, with eight caretaking adults whose job at times may be simply to prevent mayhem or co-ordinate boots with boot-owners. Noise level is high; activity constant. A shy child or an unhappy one goes virtually unnoticed. If he requires attention—somebody hits him on the head with a block—there's time for a bandage but not, probably, for close holding, a gentle explanation of *why* Mike hit him ("You knocked over his space station. I know, you didn't mean to.") and reintroduction to the scene ("Let's go over and see if you can help.") As for feeling in charge of his own life—the freedom of a day care centre is illusory. At home, maybe, he can have a snack or go outdoors when he pleases. Here, of necessity, the schedule decides. At home he inhabits an adult environment where he must learn what can and cannot be done. The stove is hot, knives dangerous, the china vase fragile, the garage and the baby's room off limits. So he practices the art which is at the core of moral behaviour, making choices. If he has been well parented, he becomes, in Milton's grand phrase, "sufficient to have stood, though free to fall." The child in a day care centre, an artificial child-centred environment, is in a sense not free to fall—at least he can't fall very far. His choices are all trivial: puzzles or paints? Apple juice or orange?

"Compared with their counterparts who had experienced substitute care, the boys [raised at home] . . . expressed a stronger interest in academic subjects."

The child in a centre is also poorly provided with adult models. The ratio [usually is] one adult to eight, ten, sometimes fifteen children. Albert Bandura and his colleagues have shown that children learn moral standards (as well as general coping skills) by observing others in a wide range of situations. Research also demonstrates what most of us know from experience: that we admire and strive to emulate adults whom we love and who love us. Separated from parents for almost all of his playing-working day, tended by adults who may be kind, devoted, conscientious but cannot be expected to *love* all their charges, the child in day care chooses

models from the most plentiful source of supply—other children. In the generally neglected area of moral development, fraught as it is with imponderables, research agrees on one crucial, alarming point: day care children tend to acquire values and standards from their peers. . . .

To date, the only research tracking the effects of substitute care beyond the pre-school years is an eleven-year English study conducted in London. T. Moore compared development in two groups of children from pre-school up through age fifteen. One group consisted of children who had experienced early substitute care (beginning at an average age of three and continuing for two years). The other group, up to age five, had apart from occasional baby-sitting been in full time mother-care. Both children and mothers were observed and interrogated at regular intervals (child ages, six, seven, nine, eleven, fifteen), and the first-hand assessments supplemented by school evaluations.

In the first assessment (1964), when the children were six years old, those who had experienced substitute care were judged significantly more self-assertive with both other children and their parents, less conforming and less impressed by punishment, less averse to dirt and more prone to toilet lapses than their home-reared counterparts. The differences by mode of care were far more pronounced for boys than for girls and became increasingly marked as the children grew older. Moore calls this a "sleeper effect."

Teenage Males

Compared with home-reared boys, teenage males with a history of substantial substitute care were more likely to be described by the mother on a behaviour checklist as telling lies to get out of trouble, differing with parents about choice of friends, using parents' possessions without permission and taking "things they knew they should not have." As a group, Moore concluded, these boys are characterized by "fearless, aggressive nonconformity."

Boys raised primarily in their own families were described on the checklist by items like the following: "Can be trusted not to do things they should not do," "Slow to mix" with other children. Compared with their counterparts who had experienced substitute care, the boys themselves expressed a stronger interest in academic subjects, "making or repairing things," and "creative skills." The boys also read significantly better at age seven and were more likely to remain in school and pass their final examinations.

The differences among girls were similar but much less marked. The girls experiencing substitute care before the age of five "revealed more aggression and ambivalent feelings." They showed more confidence in the standardized task situations but revealed considerable unease about their adult sexual roles. Girls raised exclusively at home described themselves as "active" and expressed a positive attitude towards sex. . . .

Anti-Social Peers

At this point some readers, those perhaps who once saluted the greening of America as the dawn of a new day, may ask, What's bad about that? Is peer-oriented by definition a less admirable, less moral stance than adult-oriented? It all depends upon the peers. In the Soviet Union every educational agency, from nurseries to universities, embodies the ideals of obedience, self discipline, co-operation, industry, sharing, loyalty to the state, and it is to these ideals that the peer-oriented young Russian conforms. In Israel the peer-oriented young kibbutzniks embrace similar values but with a higher priority given to initiative, independence and physical daring. Both in Israel and in the Soviet Union, the peer group is heavily influenced by adult society. In North America and in Britain the peer group is relatively autonomous, cut off from the adult world and in fact defining itself by opposition and difference. Writing in 1970, [social psychologist Urie] Bronfenbrenner described peer-oriented young Americans as defiantly antisocial, off-hand about playing hookey, lying, teasing and "doing something illegal." He found young Americans *more* likely to break a rule or law if they thought their peers would know about it. His gloomy prediction: If parents are removed from active participation in the lives of children, and the resulting vacuum is filled by the age-segregated peer group, "we can anticipate increased alienation, indifference, antagonism and violence on the part of the younger generation in all segments of our society—middle class children as well as the disadvantaged."

Fredelle Maynard studied at the University of Toronto and received a doctorate degree from Radcliffe College in Cambridge, Massachusetts. She has written several books and articles about raising children.

"For too long we have worshiped a God of only male characteristics, denying God's female aspects."

God Should Be Seen as Female

Mary Louise Howson

The images of reality on which we base our lives are often more essential to our understanding of truth than are our intellectual constructs. We may speak and write on an intellectual level, but it is within the living landscape of these pictures that our spiritual journey is shaped and our understanding of reality is rooted.

Psychologists tell us that these images are a passageway to God, that through them, not around them, we will be led to meet the God who overwhelms all our images. As a picture becomes a passageway and we enter the gap on the other side, we find ourselves in a new relationship with God who calls us on to still newer imagery. But when we smash these images into propositions or dogmatic truth statements, we absolutize them so that they become walls instead of doors. For a proposition denies the possibility of its opposite. If, for instance, God is male, God cannot, by definition, be female.

Throughout history we Christians have asserted intellectually that God is neither male nor female, while simultaneously picturing God only as male. For many of us these male images have contracted into a dogmatic truth statement so that God has indeed become male. We have conceived him to be impassible, active and independent. Always in control, he is the ultimate monarch who merely speaks in order to accomplish. He is the one who is subject to no other power, who is utterly self-sufficient because he is not in any way needy. He initiates; we respond. He orders; we obey. This God has none of the stereotypical feminine traits; he is not responsive, emotional, flexible or passive.

Such an excessive emphasis on the maleness of God has not only led us to absolutize an idol, but it has also laid a foundation upon which we as a

society have built a lopsided construct of the nature of power as self-assertion, self-expansion, invulnerability, control and dominance. Consequently, one of the most difficult biblical texts for us to understand is: "Blessed are the meek for they shall inherit the earth." What could possibly be good, desirable or godlike about being meek? Our security, health and life itself have been rooted in a God whose attributes are the very opposite of meekness. Perhaps if we could begin to reclaim the "feminine" qualities of God's power such as meekness and responsiveness—placing them alongside the "male" qualities of initiative, calm rationality, impassibility and independence—we could begin to learn how they are integrated into a whole. Then we might be able not only to meet God in new and life-giving ways, but also to bring healing to our fractured selves and our broken world.

Feminine Power

Giving birth is a useful paradigm for a feminine understanding of power that can illuminate how meekness and responsiveness may be qualities of God that could reshape our understanding of power. In this process of giving independent life, power in the sense of coercion, domination, control, force, autonomy, impassibility, dispassionate rationality and self-expansion play little, if any, constructive role. For the embryo to grow into a fetus and finally into a child, it needs hospitality: empty space that responds to its growth; quiet, dark warmth; responsive caring.

As the mother increasingly recognizes the otherness of this growing child she must (if she desires the full health of her child) limit herself by its needs. That is, she must rest, exercise appropriately and eat properly—whether she feels like doing so or not. By restricting herself, she increasingly empowers the embryo to grow, to become more than it is, and, ultimately, to achieve life independent of her. Most mothers will tell you that while these restrictions may frequently be annoying and/or inconvenient, they are not life-denying.

As the time for birth approaches, the mother will find herself increasingly dominated by this growing child. As it wakes her at night, sends her to the bathroom every hour and makes her increasingly unwieldy, her hospitality will doubtlessly be strained at times. No matter. The time for releasing this new creature—letting it go so that it may breathe on its own—is at hand.

"[God] chooses to give of her own being in order that human beings may have life and have it more abundantly—just as a mother gives of herself that her child may have life."

Again we women learn that to give birth most easily and effectively, we cannot seek to control or dominate the process. Rather we must cooperate with it, responding attentively to the new needs of this child trying to be born. Care, not equality, must dominate this birthing process, for self-expending love, not reciprocity, is the source of life. In this renunciation of control and in the conscious effort not to use force, the mother voluntarily becomes the child's servant. By submitting herself to the rhythms of another, the mother renounces her power to dominate while maintaining her dignity and authority. By limiting herself, by letting the womb release its treasure, she gives life. Such responsive cooperation is self-giving servanthood, which, while it may be self-limiting rather than self-expanding, is in no way self-denying or self-denigrating. On the contrary, it is life-enhancing for the mother as well as life-giving for the child.

The Bible's Feminine Imagery

In this context, then, power can no longer be equated simply with the ability to control, dominate or manipulate. Instead, it must also include the ability to give life, to call into being, and to summon toward wholeness and health. Nor can servanthood be understood as defective, inferior or subordinate.

To comprehend this mystery more fully it is perhaps helpful to examine some of the Bible's feminine imagery for God. In Genesis 2, God, seeing that Adam is lonely, causes a deep sleep to fall upon him and makes for him a "help meet"—woman, called Eve. The Hebrew words translated here as "help meet" are *ezer neged. Neged* means suitable or appropriate for, while *ezer* can be translated helper or assistant.

The traditional, patriarchal interpretation of this passage was that the female was joined to the male to serve him. Thus she was inferior both by derivation and by design, and she had no integrity or authority of her own. This interpretation assumes that connectedness is inferior to autonomy, that servants are subordinate to rulers.

Virginia Ramey Mollenkott points out, however, that *"ezer"* is used 21 times in the Hebrew Scriptures. Three times it refers to vital human assistance in moments of extreme need; 16 times it speaks of God's direct assistance to humans; and twice it is applied specifically to Eve, the human female (*The Divine Feminine: The Biblical Imagery of God as Feminine*). Thus as Eve is Adam's *ezer,* so God is humanity's *ezer.*

How God is our *ezer* is reflected in the following texts that Mollenkott analyzes:

> But I am poor and needy
> O God, hasten to my aid.
> Thou art my help [*ezer*], and my salvation;
> O Lord, make no delay
> [Ps. 70:5].
> There is none like the God of Jeshurun
> who rides the heaven to your help [*ezer*]
> [Deut. 33:26]
> O Israel, thou hast destroyed thyself;
> but in me *is* thine help [*ezer*]
> [Hos. 13:9]

These and similar passages in no way connect inferiority, weakness or lack of internal integrity and authority with being a helper—an *ezer.* Rather one senses in these passages that the *ezer* is strong, competent, reliable and capable of self-determination and initiative. The God who is *ezer* chooses to give of her own being in order that human beings may have life and have it more abundantly—just as a mother gives of herself that her child may have life.

The Value of Meekness

Now, perhaps, we can begin to understand the value of meekness and why the meek will inherit the earth. Meekness gives life and empowers others. It receives others openly and hospitably, giving them space in which to become. It waits attentively for the right time, instead of constantly projecting itself onto others. It reflects the other back to itself so that it may grow. Meekness is servanthood, and from it comes life itself. It is a love that is intimately involved, but not possessive, manipulative or controlling. It uses the stuff of its own being so that the other may have life and have it more abundantly. Is this not the very power by which God acts in our lives? Is it not at the heart of the Good News as proclaimed in the loving self-expenditure of Jesus?

If, indeed, love is made manifest in meekness, if

wholeness develops in vulnerability to the other, if servanthood is life-giving, then are we not challenged to a new pattern of acting and a new way of being? Must we not begin to ask whether our salvation lies in our "strength" or in what we had previously defined as weakness? Perhaps our so-called strength is actually weakness, because, by its very nature of domination, it diminishes. If, indeed, the authority of service is life-giving and enabling, does not true power then come to perfection in meek weakness rather than in domineering strength?

In order to be clear, we must distinguish between servanthood and what we might call servitude—the perversion of servanthood. Servanthood is the model of love that Jesus illustrated for us. It embodies an inherent authority and gives birth to growth. It nurtures and nourishes a soul, conferring dignity upon both giver and receiver. It moves us toward the wholeness that God wishes for us and for his creation. It holds and reflects another as the calm sea holds and reflects the image of the sun.

"By expanding our imagery [to include feminine images of God], we hope to cultivate a fuller knowledge and love of God."

But when self-expending love is absent, when pride or dominating, coercive power are the goals, or when service is demanded or expected, then servanthood becomes servitude, demeaning the humanity of both giver and receiver. When power is equated with dominance and self-expansion, one cannot receive and reflect back the other but can only reflect a stereotype, a prejudice or a self-image. Such activity is ultimately self-denying, for it denies mutuality, relationship and true selfhood to both parties. Likewise, when dispassionate objectivity is the goal, servanthood is perverted into servitude as one refuses to engage and reflect back anything. Such a position allows one to retain a different type of dominance—that of the calm, superior observer. We cannot receive the other unless we are willing to be vulnerable.

Vulnerability

Perhaps a key lies in this vulnerability. Ours is a God who for our sake is willing to be vulnerable. God created us free so that we might love freely and reflect God's very essence. In doing this, God risked our disobedience and the expansion of evil.

And because evil spread, God became a human being, vulnerable to all that we suffer to show us once again that servanthood and meekness are the source of life. Indeed, the crucifixion and resurrection demonstrate starkly and clearly that the mastery and control that we think are the essence of power can bring only death. God's way of patient, self-giving love offers life, and ultimately triumphs over coercive power.

For too long we have worshiped a God of only male characterics, denying God's female aspects. Thus in reducing our image to an idolatrous proposition, we have lost the complementary half. By expanding our imagery we hope to cultivate a fuller knowledge and love of God and, as a result, more faithfully reflect this God into our world.

Mary Louise Howson is the Protestant chaplain at Western Connecticut State University.

viewpoint 83

God Should Be Seen as Male

James R. Edwards

In the last 50 years it has been customary in academic circles to do theology "from below." From below means that we begin to speak of God from where we are rather than beginning "from above" with such things as the attributes of God or the Trinity, which can be known only by revelation. From below is primarily a method. It has enabled theologians to break away from older approaches, often rooted in rationalism, and freed them to discuss theology from contemporary perspectives, which today are largely social and ethical.

As a method, from below is both justifiable and desirable. Calvin began his *Institutes* by discussing how we can know God, Luther launched the Reformation because of his deep struggle to find a merciful God, and Augustine discovered grace only after despairing over his sinfulness. Jesus' parables and Paul's wrestling with sin and law (as recorded in Romans 7) began from below, too. This is proper, for the meaning of the Incarnation is that God meets us where we are.

A problem arises, however, when from below is not only a point of departure but determines all that comes after it. When that happens, we are told we may speak properly of God or the Bible *only* when such statements agree with human experience.

Limited Understanding

Take the understanding of Christ as an example. Recent biblical scholarship has concentrated on the human side of Jesus—his identification with sinners, his involvement in the process of liberation, or his death as an example of suffering love. But contemporary scholarship has been reticent about discussing his divine nature—including the performance of miracles and atonement for sin.

On the positive side, understanding Christ from below has helped us not to overemphasize his divine nature at the expense of his humanness, and hence his radical identification with sinners. It has helped us accept that Jesus "pitched his tent among us," to render the Greek of John 1:14 literally.

A Christology done only from below, however, has the negative effect of limiting Christ to less than the complete biblical report about him. It is like a ham operator who limits his reception to those radio frequencies which he has discovered on his own. If he were more trusting of his manual he could learn other frequencies, which would enlarge his reception from the transmitter.

Feminist theology, likewise, starts from below. In doing so it offers promise in providing a new and needed "radio frequency" from Scripture. But it is also dangerous—if Scripture and theology are judged by that "frequency" alone.

Feminist theology concerns itself with woman's role in Creation, redemption, and the church. Such questions are intensified by the fact that, in two millennia of church history, women have rarely been allowed to tell their own story. Within the Judeo-Christian tradition, half the human race has been spoken for (or to), but essentially deprived of a voice in behalf of its own image, faith, and community.

Promethean Aims

Feminist theology, however, has gone beyond its origins in women's suffrage and civil rights. With Promethean intimations it is clamoring for a resymbolization of Christianity, based on categories of feminism. Such theology, to quote Elizabeth Achtemeier of Union Theological Seminary (Va.), is "in the process of laying the foundations for a new faith and a new church that are, at best, only loosely related to apostolic Christianity." Feminists who desire to change the names of God from Father, King, and Lord, to "Womb of Being," "Immanent Mother," "Life Force," "Divine Generatrix," or

James R. Edwards, "Does God Really Want to be Called 'Father'?"
Christianity Today, February 21, 1986. Reprinted with the author's
permission.

"Ground of Being" are not merely switching labels on a product. They are advocating a shift from a transcendent God to a creation-centered deity. God is no longer our father in heaven, but a "womb covering the earth."

Donald Bloesch tackles the issue of feminist resymbolizations in a recent book, *The Battle for the Trinity*. Following his earlier *Is the Bible Sexist?*, Bloesch, who considers himself pro-woman, sees the Achilles' heel (should we say "Penelope's loom"?) of radical feminism as determined by and limited to thinking from below (although he does not use that expression). "For nearly all feminists, the final court of appeal is human experience, particularly feminine experience," he writes. "The Bible . . . is treated not as an inspired witness to a unique and definitive revelation of God in the history of the people of Israel culminating in Jesus Christ, but as an illuminating record of the struggles of the people of Israel for liberation from political and economic enslavement. . . ."

"Many women, in their dedication to the feminist movement, are being slowly wooed into a new form of religion, widely at variance with the Christian faith."

Bloesch argues that such resymbolizations of God are, intentionally or not, moving in one of two directions. They lead to making God an abstraction (as opposed to a person) and light-years removed in transcendence. Or, with their insistence on an androgynous Godhead ("God/dess," "Creator/Creatrix," "Father/Mother"), they augur a return to fertility worship.

To quote Elizabeth Achtemeier again, "I am sure that much of feminist theology is a return to Baalism. . . . Many women, in their dedication to the feminist movement, are being slowly wooed into a new form of religion, widely at variance with the Christian faith. Most such women have no desire to desert their Christian roots, any more than many German Christians had when they accepted National Socialism's resymbolization of the faith in Nazi Germany."

God's Judgment

The crucial question arises when from below conflicts with from above, when our isms differ from God's Word. Consider this question from Katharine Sakenfeld in *Feminist Interpretation of the Bible:* "How can feminists use the Bible, if at all?" The structure of the question determines that the Bible is a lesser authority than feminism. But surely this cannot be the proper question. The Bible is not a tool to be used by a special-interest group. What if we rephrased the question, "How can Madison Avenue use the Bible?" or "How can the Ku Klux Klan use the Bible?" Then the Bible would depend on the means and ends of free-enterprise economics or racism.

To be biblically proper we must reverse the question. God does not bear our image; we bear his. It is God's Word, Jesus Christ, who tells us who we are and what we may become. If the Bible is the record of God's redemption of estranged and disobedient creation, then *all* life—and all life's institutions, philosophies, isms, and ideologies—stand under God's judgment and grace. In the light of revelation we are revealed for the sinners and idolaters that we are, and in its light we are promised transformation according to the image of Jesus Christ.

The Bible is the story of God's judgment on all human prospects and institutions, and also of his transformation of them by grace in Christ. It judges all forms of pride and serves none. No endeavors—in this case feminism—stand apart from God's judgment.

Appeasing Ideologies

This was precisely what the confessing church intrepidly declared at Barmen in 1934 against the rising tide of the German Christianity. The Barmen Declaration rejected the "false doctrine" that there was a source of the church's proclamation other than the Word of God, that some areas of life might not belong to Jesus Christ, or that the church might change its message to appease current ideologies.

What radical feminists are proposing—and what the church must reject—is that biblical language (and hence thought) about God are simply products of human experience and may vary as conceptions of human experience vary. To this the church must say, with the clarity of Barmen, that it cannot place "the Word and work of the Lord in the service of any arbitrary chosen desires, purposes, and plans."

When, for example, Jesus called God "Father" he was not merely following convention. True, Jewish society of his day was patriarchal (though less so than its neighbors), but this does not account for Jesus' use of "Father." Prof. Joachim Jeremias undertook a massive study of the Aramaic behind the Greek *patér* ("father"). Two of his conclusions belong to the assured results of New Testament scholarship—whether liberal or conservative. First, no evidence has yet been found in the literature of Palestine of "my Father" being used by an individual as an address to God—a remarkable fact considering the Jewish Talmud extends nearly to the length of the *Encyclopaedia Britannica!*

It was the custom in postexilic Judaism to avoid out of reverence the name of God whenever possible. Sometimes, for example, the passive voice was used; or ''Adonai'' was substituted for the ineffable ''Yahweh''; or ''blessed be he'' was repeated when God's name could not be avoided. In startling contrast, Jesus not only called God ''Father,'' but ''Abba,'' an Aramaic diminutive equivalent to ''papa'' or ''daddy.'' Not just on certain occasions did Jesus call God Abba, but on every occasion.

Why Not Mother-God?

This is Jeremias's second conclusion. The Jews of Jesus' day would have been scandalized to presume such familiarity with the Almighty and Holy One. Jesus, however, not only addressed God with the warmth and security of a child addressing his father, but he taught his disciples to do the same. Most important for our purposes, the fatherhood of God was determinative for Jesus' self-understanding—and for that of his disciples. In his study *The Teaching of Jesus*, T.W. Manson puts it succinctly: ''For [Jesus] the Father was the supreme reality in the world and in his own life; and his teaching would make the Father have the same place and power in the life of his disciples, that they too may be heirs, heirs of God and joint-heirs with Jesus Christ.

''Abba-theology'' calls into question a purely *transcendent* God-concept (''Eternal or Divine Spirit,'' ''Ineffable Force,'' ''Omnipotent One,'' and so on) as well as an *impersonal* God-concept, such as ''Parent'' (with Jesus as corresponding ''Offspring''). ''Parent'' may do for functional objectivity, but ''Father'' or ''Abba'' involves the speaker in a relationship of intimacy and trust, as Jesus both exemplified and taught his followers.

Some ask, ''Why not then a Mother-god concept?'' Motherhood, after all, avoids exclusive transcendence and impersonality (perhaps better than fatherhood). Several metaphors in the Bible speak of God in feminine imagery: Wisdom in Proverbs 8, love in Isaiah 49 and 66, or Jesus' likening himself to a mother hen, or God to a woman cleaning house. The question is whether or not these occasional images are to be understood as normative teaching about God. While recognizing their partial validity, they are not the norm in Scripture. They are not the preferred speech of the Pentateuch, Prophets, Jesus, or apostolic church. The Hebrew language does not even have a word for ''goddess.''

A Mother-God concept is further imperiled because the Judeo-Christian tradition knows nothing of an androgynous Godhead; that is, God does not need a female counterpart to complete his identity. When a female counterpart is present, fertility worship, or neo-Baalism, lurks beneath. Elaine Pagels notes, ''Unlike many of his contemporaries among the deities of the ancient Near East, the God of Israel shares his power with no female divinity, nor is he the divine Husband or Lover of any. He scarcely can be characterized by any but masculine epithets: King, Lord, Master, Judge, and Father.''. . .

The Kingdom of God

''Abba'' is not the only important theme in Jesus' language. More significant is the theme of the kingdom of God. The kingdom—or better, the active reign of God—is the dominant theme of the Gospels, the single reality for which Jesus lives, teaches, and dies. God's reign means kingly rule as well as faithfulness to the covenantal relationship with Israel and the church.

Although the idea of God as king is present in the Old Testament, oddly enough, the expression ''kingdom of God'' occurs neither in the Old Testament nor Apocrypha. In the speech of Jesus, however, it is a necessity—occurring 51 times in Matthew's gospel alone.

In *Is the Bible Sexist?* Donald Bloesch asserts, ''The debate over sexist language is ultimately a debate concerning the nature of God.'' What God's nature is *in itself*, the Bible does not say. Presumably God's nature is beyond gender. Nevertheless, according to the biblical tradition, God chooses to relate to creation in a masculine way, as Abba and King.

This is supported not only by Jesus' use of ''Abba'' and ''kingdom of God,'' but especially by the use of ''Lord'' in the Bible, a term of sovereign freedom and authority that occurs nearly twice as often as a reference to God does than the word ''God'' itself. As Creator, God is sovereign initiator; as Sustainer, kingly ruler; and as Redeemer, he is self-sacrificer in Christ—and ultimately Consummator. Paul makes it clear there can be no doubt that God's initiative and power alone effect salvation. To shift this emphasis from a sovereign theocentrism to creation-centrism—whether feminist or otherwise—is no longer innovation but error.

''To say that God relates to creation in a masculine way does not mean that men are superior to women.''

Feminists reject masculine nomenclature for God, as I see it, generally for one of two reasons. Some see masculine images and nomenclature used by men to exclude women from ministry and (worse yet) from bearing God's likeness. Whenever men do this they tacitly claim that they are more like God than women. This, of course, is heresy—indeed the oldest of heresies, attempting to make God in our image. Women bear God's image equally with men, and biblical scholarship increasingly is revealing the important role women played in salvation history and must regain in the life of the church. But to reject masculine imagery of God for this reason is to take a right step in the wrong direction, so to speak. The error lies in the misuse of truth, not with the truth.

To say that God relates to creation in a masculine way does not mean that men are superior to women. The Bible characteristically speaks of God's covenant relationship with his people with three paired images: husband/wife, father/child, king/subjects. *But note that the latter halves of these pairs include both male and female.*

In the first image, both Israel and the church are feminine in relation to God. The chief metaphor of the prophets to castigate Israel's apostasy, for example, was that of ''adultery,'' and in the New Testament, the church can be referred to in the imagery of a bride. The father/child image stems from the Exodus when Yahweh first called Israel his son. Because of Israel's failure to live in filial obedience to God, Israel's redemption would come, not surprisingly, from an obedient Son who would call God ''Abba'' and teach his disciples likewise.

The final image has a long history in the Bible. In early Israel, Yahweh alone was king. During the monarchy, the king ideally was Yahweh's vice-regent, and in Jesus, as we have seen, God's kingly rule is present in the person of his Son. In each image, Israel and the church (again, including both men and women) are responsive, filial, and obeisant to God.

The idea of subordination may lead to a second reason why feminists reject masculine imagery for God. This reason is not unique to feminists: some process thinkers and liberation theologians reject subordination with different names and reasons. The rejection is especially prevalent in thinkers committed to democratic or egalitarian ideals, for whom the idea of ''lordship'' is seen with reserve or repugnance. Underlying this attitude is the belief that man (especially the individual) is the cosmic fulcrum upon which reality balances. The chief end of man has become himself.

Revolt from Below

I think of it as a revolt from below because it subordinates all other realities, including God, to human experience and self. The result, as Elizabeth Achtemeier rightly sees, is a different faith and church.

Ultimately, the question of feminist resymbolization of God—or any resymbolization—depends on one's view of revelation. If one believes the biblical story to be primarily a record of an evolving consciousness of God, or that the revelation, if it has occurred, was determined by patriarchal norms, then the proposed resymbolization is permissible and perhaps demanded. If, however, one believes that Jesus Christ is the self-disclosure of God within the fullness of time, then this once-for-all historical act is itself the norm for all human experience.

We begin from below with all life's questions and possibilities, for this is the meaning of the Incarnation—God become man, God meeting us in human experience. But we need not remain below: indeed, we cannot remain below. To paraphrase Jesus' words to Nicodemus, we are invited to receive from above that which chastens and completes our existence.

James R. Edwards is a religion professor at Jamestown College in North Dakota.

"Marriage and motherhood do bring God-given distractions from self, calling us to give for the sake of others, but we receive as we give."

viewpoint 84

Christianity Fulfills Women

Dee Jepsen

The family is the basic unit and backbone of society. Historically, when the family has disintegrated the society has fallen. The family, in spite of all its worthy attributes, is under attack today in a variety of ways. Divorce, causing the breakup of the family, is, of course, one of its most obvious foes. In that area, however, there is good news: after a pattern of increase, for the second consecutive year, the divorce rate declined in 1983.

Families Under Attack

There are those radical elements within the women's movement who have targeted marriage and the family as natural enemies of women's rights and fulfillment. It is true that some husbands have not treated their wives with the respect and the fairness they are due, and that society has denied them the recognition they have earned for service. However, to label the institution of marriage and family as detrimental to the well-being of women on that basis is not only short-sighted, but villainous. . . .

Though the family is under fire by some in the secular world, I firmly believe the family will not only survive, it will flourish. For in this cold and impersonal world, which moves faster and faster, where so few things are without change, the comfort and support found in the community of the family will become increasingly prized. Most women are not going to harden themselves against the importance of family. No title, scholastic recognition, or salary check can match the inner joy of the soul when a mother hears her child say, "I love you, Mom," or her husband say, "I don't know what I would do without you, honey"—and she knows he means it.

When women come to realize that the "highest quality" life is measured in terms of human relationships rather than in terms of material things, they will begin to fully appreciate that their impact on the family has an influential effect on society as well. . . .

Need for an Ultimate Authority

One of the greatest rewards for me as a mother, in recent years, is hearing my grown children repeat as truth some of the things I taught them long ago, things they may have disagreed with as younger children. Many of those principles I employed to train them they are now using to train their own children. The influence of mothers continues into the generations of the future.

There has been much talk in the Christian community about what the Bible has to say regarding the relationship of husband and wife in marriage. Teaching on "submission" by a few in the evangelical and fundamental church communities has at times given the impression that wives are to be the equivalent of "doormats" for their husbands to rule over. This teaching implies that wives should always stay home and never develop any of their talents and abilities. Sincere as has been the intent of this message, it has at times been overstated to the extent that some Christian women, unfortunately and incorrectly, see themselves as second-class citizens. In reality the Bible does not teach that women are to be *subordinate* to their husbands, and certainly not to all men generally; additionally, both women and men are not only biblically allowed to develop their talents, they are mandated to do so.

What the Bible does teach concerning family relationships is that in the government of the family there must be one person who has ultimate authority. In God's established order of authority, that is the husband. It makes the wife no less important, just as Christ is no less important because He was made subject to the Father in God's order of authority. Though we are to submit to one another,

Dee Jepsen, *Women: Beyond Equal Rights.* Waco, TX: Word Books, 1984. Reprinted with permission.

the wife is to willingly submit to the headship of her husband. This is logical and orderly. Every successful corporation has one chief executive officer, though there is input from others before final decisions are made. Generally, in a harmonious marriage it is not very often necessary for the husband to overrule his wife in a final decision. Most decisions can be made in agreement. In fact, more often than not, the wife initiates many of the decisions that are made. Authority establishes order and harmony, when it is not abused.

Christian Marriage

The Bible gives the husband definite instructions on how to treat his wife, to love her as he would a part of himself. If both partners in a marriage follow the biblical guidelines, the relationship functions in the most satisfactory and fulfilling manner. God designed marriage, and when it is lived by his perfect plan, in his order, it is a blessing in every way to the husband, the wife, and the children.

In the February 1983 *Moody Monthly*, Sandi Frantzen wrote about women in Christian marriage.

> As a wife, she is to work alongside her husband, blessing him spiritually, physically, mentally, and emotionally.
> Obviously, God designed women to complement man. In the home they are to work together as partners. . . .
> Scripture, however, does not deny a woman her individuality or coerce her into obedience, the essence of subordination.
> It allows her to submit by choosing to do so. . . .
> As women look to the Lord Jesus Christ, they find a perfect model of willing submission to the Father. Christ's absolute submission in no way diminished his personhood. . . .
> But as women exercise biblical submission and as men exercise biblical headship, they will demonstrate to the world, as they work side by side, what Christ has already lived out—leadership can be conducted with compassion and sensitivity, and submission can be assumed with honor.

The husband is to be the benevolent leader of the home, and husbands and wives should become one another's advocates. Some women become concerned about this order, especially if they have had domineering fathers. Such women often rebel because they fear their husbands will dominate them, as their fathers did.

Games of manipulation have no place between husbands and wives. Real love does not exploit. Trying to control a relationship by manipulation or domination only destroys intimacy. Though the husband may have the ultimate authority in marriage, there is often more power, or impact, in women's influence. Men and women are created distinctly different. Each gender is equipped to perform certain functions better than others within life, and certainly within marital relationships.

In the creation story in Genesis, woman was the completion of God's creation. God said it was not good for man to be alone, that he needed a help-mate. God did not create Eve from the dust of the earth, as He did with Adam. Rather, God drew Eve from Adam, and Adam said, "This is the bone of my bone, and flesh of my flesh. She shall be called woman, because she was taken out of man" (Gen. 2:23). I think it has great significance that the Bible says, "And God created man in his own image, in the image of God created he *him; male and female created he them* (Gen. 1:27). In Genesis 5:1-2 we are additionally told, "In the day that God created man, in the likeness of God made he *him; male* and *female* created he *them,* and blessed them, and called their name *Adam,* in the day they were created." There is no sign of inequality there: in fact, I believe that the fullness of the character of God is present when both men and women, in harmony, have developed the attributes of character with which they have been especially gifted. God Himself must have *both male and female attributes,* as we identify them, or He could not have made us *both in His image.*

We are also told in Galatians 3:28," . . . There is neither male or female, for you are all one in Christ Jesus." Men and women have equal spiritual worth before God. . . .

Women and Children

As more and more women have entered the marketplace and the women's movement has stressed pursuing out-of-the-home careers, mothers are faced with the dilemma of whether to leave their children. One woman, telling me of her personal decision to stay home with her children, said, "What working mothers leave is not just an empty house, but lonely children."

"The question that modern-day mothers have to ask themselves is, what price are my children paying for my lifestyle?"

Presently, nearly two-thirds of the mothers with children older than six have left the home to enter the work force. I believe that most of us would agree that in each heart there is one special corner that only a mom can fill. Responsibility requires that some of the negative results of mothers working be honestly assessed. Numerous articles have been written about the loss of the age of innocence for children today. Many of America's children no longer have a childhood, because many are required at a young age to meet adult responsibilities and care for themselves.

Ron and Lynette Long, co-authors of *The Handbook for Latchkey Children and Their Parents,* estimate that in this country there may be as many as fifteen million children left routinely unattended for some period most days. Latchkey children are children who unlock and enter an empty house everyday in their working parents' absence. The Longs found in their interviews of former latchkey children that more than half felt there was some negative carry-over. . . .

Dee Jepsen is an author and was President Reagan's liaison to women's organizations from 1982 to 1983.

"Within the family unit, if we are willing to give freely and fully for the sake of the other members, the family can be a 'cocoon of love' in which individuals grow, develop, find fulfillment."

The question that modern-day mothers have to ask themselves is, what price are my children paying for my lifestyle? If mother is working to add to the family income to raise the standard of living, she and her husband must weigh that "high-cost family living" against the true cost of that "high living." Is the price too great? . . .

Joys of Motherhood

The joys of motherhood more than compensate for the sacrifices. Motherhood also builds character. In sacrifice, freely given, mothers stay up nights with sick children, put on and pull off winter clothes, change diapers and wipe runny noses, all the while developing patience, perseverance, and a strength that is of great benefit when applied in any other life situations. Mothers lay down their lives for their children out of love. I believe the denigrating of motherhood, in recent times, is self-deception, an attempt to camouflage selfishness. Not only children, but women and society are the losers. . . .

It is true, marriage and motherhood do bring God-given distractions from self, calling us to give for the sake of others, but we receive as we give. In the family, solitary individuals can be bound together by love into community and into nurturing relationships. Within the family unit, if we are willing to give freely and fully for the sake of the other members, the family can be a "cocoon of love" in which individuals grow, develop, find fulfillment—and then go out into the world from that supportive environment. Loving relationships not only sustain us in life but affect us in death. For when that time comes for each of us to leave this world, as it surely will, what will matter will not be the power we acquired, the money we made, or the honors we received. What will matter will be relationships. First, what is our relationship to the God to whom we will return? Then, what is our relationship to our family, to our friends, and, yes, to our enemies?

"I will not succumb to the sex roles dictated in our society which stem from Judeo-Christianity. I am not here to cater to the male ego."

Christianity Oppresses Women

Dagmar Loring

So, there she was, and there she is in her eggshells and lace. What was the experience of this woman married off at seventeen to a man ten years her senior? How could she know about love—falling in it, receiving it, giving it, and sustaining it with a man of her choice? All she knew was that she must submit to the patriarchy: first to her pious, self-righteous father and now to the stranger who would be her husband. Her guidelines for interacting with men were set: the appropriate behavior for women (Armenian women raised in the Middle Eastern chauvinist patriarchy) is submission. Submit to the male: "Wives, submit yourselves unto your own husbands, as unto the Lord" (Ephesians 5:22). The male is superior; he is next to God: "For the husband is the head of the wife, even as Christ is the head of the church: and He is the saviour of the body" (Ephesians 5:23). Obey your husband; he knows more: "Even as Sarah obeyed Abraham, calling him Lord . . . " (1 Peter 3:6). And in her naiveté and desire to please God, father, and husband (Father, Son, and Holy Ghost?), she submitted willingly as verses from the ancient past echoed in the hollow chambers of her mind.

Celebrating Males

Soon, a child is born, a male child, a son-king: "For unto us a child is born, unto us a son is given . . . and His name shall be called 'wonderful' . . . " (Isaiah 9:6). She will not submit to him as she did to her father and husband (at least not in the same way). However, she delights in his maleness, she praises it, and rejoices that the first born is son and not daughter. And in this uplifting praise, the motif of submission emerges yet again: she lies subservient to her celebration of male. Now there are two men in her life by which to procure

self-identity: the minister-husband and the first-born son. She almost says, "I am woman taken from Adam's side and just to the left of him and slightly behind will I stand, sanctioned and certified by father-god."

Time passes, a second child is born, but this time a daughter. The daughter is not praised for being second-child, female, so she grows up somewhat independently but in the shadows of the first-born. The messages are subtle but are there. "Older brother, must I submit to you as mother submits to father and to you?" No, never. I will not submit. Before female, before male, there is only human. I am a human being who happens to be female; you are a human being who happens to be male. We are different. We are equal.

The mother does not understand the second child. The second one does not submit. She would rather climb trees and race bikes in denim blue instead of play doll and house in pinafore white. What is the problem with number two? Read Bible verses: "Daughter of Sarah, obey!" (Ephesians 3:6). Indoctrinate her in the way of the Lord and proper sex roles. Accept your status, number two. You are female, you are second (second-fiddle, second-guess, second-hand, second-rate, second-string, Cain and not Abel).

Resisting the Role

Adolescence is a time when most conform to the peer rituals and social castes of dating. The daughter does not date nor does she care to socialize. From school to house, house to school, in her room she sits and reads, reads and sits. Not accepted by her mother, she is not accepted within her peer group. Mother is anxious. There is no trace of feminine conformity. "Where is your dress, your lipsticks and rouge and subtle perfume? High heels and nylons? Where is your identity?"

As the daughter emerges into adulthood, the

Dagmar Loring, "Female, Second Person Singular." This article first appeared in THE HUMANIST issue of January/February 1988 and is reprinted by permission.

mother is concerned: "When are you going to marry?" "I don't know. Maybe never." (Too much education will intimidate prospective Christian, Armenian, male partners.) "What is this senseless talk about going to graduate school?" Absolutely incredible. She is socializing me to repeat the same toxic life-patterns that incarcerated her in an abusive association with my father, a pathetic excuse for a man. Perhaps this is what is meant by the sins of the fathers (mothers) being passed onto the children.

"Feelings of impotence overwhelmed me, for I knew there was nothing that I could do to unleash [my mother] from the oppressions [she] experienced in the name of God."

Dear mother, quiet mother, fragile mother. All your attempts to create the illusion of the perfect family are shattered. So far, no child has married, no grandchildren born. You ask, "Why?" You feel a failure. I cannot speak for son-king, only for myself. In your desperate attempts to please God and minister-husband, you forfeited your rights as a living, thinking human being. You remained quiet when you should have spoken. You chose to remain the weak vessel when you knew you were the stronger. And all the time, I watched and quietly wondered why you succumbed to a man one thousand times your inferior. Gentle mother, loving mother, what happened to your dignity, and why did you allow your freedom of thought to be usurped by the vacant beliefs in a dead god? Kind mother, sad mother, who are you, and where are you going? Patient mother and suffering mother, how disappointed you must be that your silent father-god did not rescue you from your pain, did not wipe your tears when you wept, did not hold you in your broken vulnerability.

Women Losing Themselves

And now I am saddened by the thought of you and your attempts to restore unity and peace to a family shattered by the sick proposals of ancient religions. You cared too much about what others might think and not enough about what you knew to be true. By your silences you committed the gravest sin of all—the sin of omission. And now, as you look at yourself, what do you see? Broken relics of a darkling past and not much hope for the futures which you conceived. Your confusion is understandable. In quiet moments I hear your questions: "But I did everything that I was supposed to do: submitted to my husband, supported him in his schooling and ministry, attempted to raise three children in the fear of the Lord, and nothing has turned out the way I imagined."

Sweet mother, gentle spirit, there were too many voices and not enough were your own. First your father, then your husband, always your God, forever your Jesus, Bible verses, hymns, sermons—from one authority to another. But where were you in all this? Didn't you understand that your identity was not in the male—not in your husband, not in your son, not in your Jesus, not in your god—nor in the Western and Eastern constructions of the feminine but rather within yourself? How much pain you must feel. I remember seeing your grief, your turmoil, and being saddened by it. You never saw my sadness. I lamented alone for the distress that was yours. Feelings of impotence overwhelmed me, for I knew there was nothing that I could do to unleash you from the oppressions you experienced in the name of God by your minister-husband.

Even now, the bittersweet warmth of sorrow creeps into my throat from beneath my heart and swells into my eyes, and there it is transformed into tears. Quiet tears, easy tears, for the emotional scars that are yours. I recall the night that I had to call emergency. Your nerves had exploded; you could no longer abide his ranting, his raving. There, lying on the hospital bed you looked so weak, so small, so fragile, and my childhood fear that your death would precede his was looming before me. But you did not die; you lived. Strong mother, faithful wife, intelligent woman, will you now learn to live for yourself?

Rejecting Ancient Traditions

Yes. Time has passed, and he has mellowed. I see within you an acceptance, no matter how difficult, of the way things are. Your children are grown now and out on their own. And I live with your memory in appreciation and anger: appreciation for your love and care, and anger that you suffered needless pain and abuse from a sick man to whom you were betrothed without much choice and who you could not leave due to senseless religious codes. It is disturbing to me how many sins are committed in the name of God and family and tradition.

And so now I hope you can accept me as I have accepted you. For I will continue in my independence and autonomy. I will not submit to ancient traditions which demand that I obey nonexistent gods and sons of gods. I will not succumb to the sex roles dictated in our society which stem from Judeo-Christianity. I am not here to cater to the male ego nor to kowtow to it, for this eventually leads to sick interdependence between male and female. Nor does the male exist to patronize me. And as I grow as human, as I become more of whoever I am, as I discover the self that is "I," then I allow men to also grow as human and to discover the self that is theirs.

I am tired of the games and will not play. You

must understand that there is no such thing as masculine or feminine. There is simply human, and one's ''maleness'' or ''femaleness'' is the vehicle by which feminine and masculine are expressed: an assertive female is feminine by virtue of her gender, and an artistic male is masculine by virtue of his gender. Love, self-respect, dignity, and care are neuter, and by their neutrality they speak universally to all who submit to them.

Shedding the Faith

So, careful mother, I have chosen to submit myself to my emotions and foremost to my ability to reason; for as the self submits to the Self, one begins to emerge as person. Unlike you, I did not search for my identity in gods, fathers, sons, and ancient documents. Rather, I decided to discover changing truths as they were revealed to me by life experiences. And now I have shed the faith which you so consistently taught me and in which I so fervently believed. I am not the daughter which you envisioned, nor could I ever be. But maybe somewhere, sometime, we will talk with each other from our own places. Until then, I leave you with a Bible verse: ''There is neither Jew nor Greek, there is neither bond nor free, there is neither male nor female. For ye are all one . . . '' (Galatians 3:28).

Dagmar Loring teaches writing at the University of Southern California.

"As Women-Church we claim the authentic mission of Christ, . . . the real agenda of our Mother-Father God who comes to restore and not to destroy our humanity."

The Church Must Embrace Feminism

Rosemary Radford Ruether

What does it mean theologically to be Women-Church? That is what I want us to think together about. How can women, the excluded half of the human race, the excluded gender from the tradition of the Church, claim to *be* Church, claim to speak as Church? Is this not, in the most basic sense, schismatic, sectarian, breaking the whole into only one of its parts, tearing the "seamless robe of Catholic unity," as the fathers are wont to say? I would contend that we as women can indeed speak as Church, do speak as Church, not in exile from the Church, but rather that the Church is in exile with us, awaiting with us a wholeness that we are in process of revealing.

Reject Patriarchy

First of all, to speak as Women-Church means we speak to denounce, to cry out against the smothering of Church in the temples of patriarchy. We have a controversy with the representatives of patriarchy who claim to be the authentic spokesmen of the Church. We say that the temples of patriarchy have disfigured and hidden our true Mother and Teacher, and replaced her with a great mechanical idol with flashing eyes and smoking nostrils who spews out blasphemies and lies. What does this idol say? How speaks this monstrous robot of the temples of patriarchy? Let us recall the words that come from its mouth, the deeds that come from its hand.

This is the idol of masculinity, the idol of father-rule. And it claims all the earth as the creation and domain of father-rule. It monopolizes the image of God, claiming that God can only be spoken by the name of Patriarch, can only be imaged in the image of Father-rule. God is Sovereign, King, Warrior, God of Power and Might, who magnifies the rule of the powerful and abases the degradation of the lowly,

who gives the scepter to the mighty and teaches the little ones of the earth to cower in fear and self-hatred. This God is not to be imaged as Mother, as Helper, as Friend, as Liberator. It cannot be imaged in the faces of women, or children, of the poor, of the timid and gentle creatures of the earth.

Men are the proper and fitting image of this mighty God, especially powerful men—rulers who command, warriors who kill, judges who punish. These are the ones who are most like God, who most exemplify the image of God. To see them is to see God. To obey their word is to obey the Word of God. To criticize their power, to rebel against their rule is to rebel against God. Women are not in the image of God. In themselves, women can only image that which is degraded, disgraced, that which is to be subordinate, that which is to be ruled over. Women image the body, the passions, the shameful bloody process of birth and death, of finitude and mortality, of corruptibility, of all those foul and stinking limits from which this mighty transcendent masculinity seeks to escape into eternal life and power forever and ever. Women cannot image God, the mighty and eternal One. They are the image of all that is *not* God, of all that must be crushed and reduced to silence so that men can be as God.

Blasphemies and Lies

Let us hear further the blasphemies and lies of this great idol of patriarchy with its flashing eyes and smoking nostrils, its inhuman mechanical voice whirring out from its internal computer. "Christ has come, the great savior, for us *men* and for our salvation." Who is this savior and from what does he save us? This savior of men comes to free men from birth, from women, from earth, and from limits. This savior can only come in the image of the male. As God can only be imaged as male, as the male is the proper image of God, so the savior too must be male. Woman is misbegotten man, the defective and imperfect expression of the human species. Only the male represents perfect humanity.

In turn, only the male can represent Christ. There must be a physical resemblance between the priest and Christ, and this does not mean that the priest should look Jewish. No, it means that the priest should have balls, male genitalia, should stand erect as the monument of phallic power. Only the male can rise in the phallic pulpit to bring down the seminal word upon the prone body of the people, the women and children waiting passively below to receive it; only the male can confect the Eucharist with this same seminal power. Women are impotent, castrated, lacking in divine seminal power. They cannot act; they can only receive and should be grateful for what they receive.

"Pope, patriarch, and prelate join hands in fraternal alliance over the prone body of woman."

Let us hear further what deeds come forth from the hand of this idol. "If women are not grateful, they shall be punished. Indeed, they have never been grateful, but have always been rebellious. In the very beginning woman was the cause of all of our troubles. It was she who brought sin and death into the world; she who caused us to lose paradise and to be forced to earn our living by the sweat of our brow. For this reason woman is to be punished through all of history. She is to be silent and to serve us in all meekness, knowing that this is her place and she deserves no better. If she talks back, she is to be muzzled, shamed, and ridiculed into silence. If she will not be shamed and silenced, she will be taught by force." A million women, twisted on the racks of Christian torture chambers, were bound in sacks and tossed into rivers, hung on gibbets or thrown into fires to teach them this lesson of shame and silence. In every minute of the day and night, women scream and stifle sobs of pain as they are beaten, stabbed, and raped in back alleys and in their own homes, to teach them this lesson, this lesson of shame and silence.

Exploiting Women's Bodies

Women's bodies should be ever sexually available to those who own them, never sexually available to those who do not own them. Their wombs and ovaries belong to their husbands who impregnate them; to priests and doctors who make the rules of birth and death. Let women not think that they are in charge of their own bodies, that they may decide when to conceive and when not to conceive, when to give birth and when not to give birth. "If a woman dies in childbirth, it matters not, because it

was for this that she was created by God." So spoke the great reformer, Martin Luther. And all the voices of patriarchy echo his teaching in ecumenical accord. Pope, patriarch, and prelate join hands in fraternal alliance over the prone body of woman. Solemnly they meet together to agree that woman is no part of their tradition. Her voice is not to be heard from their pulpits; her hands are not to be raised in blessing at their altars.

As Women-Church we repudiate this idol of patriarchy. We repudiate it and denounce it in the name of God, in the name of Christ, in the name of Church, in the name of humanity, in the name of earth. Our God and Goddess, who is mother and father, friend, lover, and helper, did not create this idol and is not represented by this idol. Our brother Jesus did not come to this earth to manufacture this idol, and he is not represented by this idol. The message and mission of Jesus, the child of Mary, which is to put down the mighty from their thrones and uplift the lowly, is not served by this idol. Rather, this idol blasphemes by claiming to speak in the name of Jesus and to carry out his redemptive mission, while crushing and turning to its opposite all that he came to teach. In its hands, his transformative redemptive mission is overturned or, rather, turned back to the ways of Babylon. The *first* shall be first and *last* shall be last. This is the way God made the world, and this is the way it shall ever be. The powers and principalities of rape, genocide, and war achieve their greatest daring by claiming to be Christ, to represent Christ's mission. The Roman Empire clothes itself in the mantle of the crucified and seats itself anew upon its imperial throne.

Authentic Mission

As Women-Church we cry out: Horror, blasphemy, deceit, foul deed! This is not the voice of our God, the face of our Redeemer, the mission of our Church. Our humanity is not and cannot be represented here, but it is excluded in this dream, this nightmare, of salvation. As Women-Church we claim the authentic mission of Christ, the true mission of Church, the real agenda of our Mother-Father God who comes to restore and not to destroy our humanity, who comes to ransom the captives and to reclaim the earth as our Promised Land. We are not in exile, but the Church is in exodus with us. God's Shekinah, Holy Wisdom, the Mother-face of God has fled from the high thrones of patriarchy and has gone into exodus with us. She is with us as we flee from the smoking altars where women's bodies are sacrificed, as we cover our ears to blot out the inhuman voice that comes forth from the idol of patriarchy.

As Women-Church we are not left to starve for the words of wisdom, we are not left without the bread of life. Ministry too goes with us into exodus. We learn all over again what it means to minister, not to lord over, but to minister to and with each other, to teach each other to speak the words of life. Eucharist comes with us into exodus. The waters of baptism spring up in our midst as the waters of life, and the tree of life grows in our midst with fruits and flowers. We pluck grain and make bread; harvest grapes and make wine. And we pass them around as the body and blood of our new life, the life of the new humanity that has been purchased by the bloody struggles of our martyrs, by the bloody struggle of our brother Jesus, and of Perpetua and Felicitas, and of all the women who were burned and beaten and raped, and of Jean Donovan and Maura Clarke and Ita Ford and Dorothy Kazel [churchwomen murdered in El Salvador], and of the women of Guatemala, Honduras, El Salvador, and Nicaragua who struggle against the leviathan of patriarchy and imperialism. This new humanity has been purchased by their blood, by their lives, and we dare to share the fruits of their victory together in hope and faith that they did not die in vain. But they have risen, they are rising from the dead. They are present with us as we share this sacrament of the new humanity, as we build together this new earth freed from the yoke of patriarchy.

An Exodus from Patriarchy

We are Women-Church, not in exile, but in exodus. We flee the thundering armies of Pharaoh. We are not waiting for a call to return to the land of slavery to serve as altar girls in the temples of patriarchy. No! We call our brothers also to flee from the temples of patriarchy; we call our brothers [American bishops] Maurice Dingman and Frank Murphy and George Evans; Raymond Hunthausen and Charles Buswell and Tom Gumbleton, and even our brother Karol Wojtyla [Pope John Paul II] and all our fathers and sons and husbands and lovers, to flee with us from the idol with flashing eyes and smoking nostrils who is about to consume the earth.

"We call our brothers to join us in exodus from the land of patriarchy."

We call our brothers to join us in exodus from the land of patriarchy, to join us in our common quest for that promised land where there will be no more war, no more burning children, no more violated women, no more discarded elderly, no more rape of the earth. Together, let us break up that great idol and grind it into powder; dismantle the great Leviathan of violence and misery who threatens to destroy the earth, plow it into the soil, and transform it back into the means of peace and plenty, so that all the children of earth can sit down together at the banquet of life.

Rosemary Radford Ruether is a theology professor at Garrett-Evangelical Theological Seminary in Evanston, Illinois.

The Church Must Reject Feminism

Michael Novak

"The more one becomes a feminist," Rosemary Reuther has been quoted as saying, "the more difficult it is to remain a Catholic." To which some will reply: "But of course!"

Many of the claims of contemporary feminism are as radically opposed to orthodoxy as were similar gnostic claims in the second century, in the first few generations after the death of Christ.

By the end of the second century, the tradition of a male priesthood—parallel to the selection Jesus made of his apostles—was decisively made canonical. An all-male priesthood was seen to be the institutional expression of orthodoxy, as a female priesthood was seen to be the appropriate institutional principle of gnosticism. . . .

Feminism a Heresy

What is at stake in feminism? Like any heresy, it carries within it some truth. But it advances by associating itself with a "popular front," trying to add to its hard core every possible sympathizer for any remotely connectible constituency. Part of the reason for this is to inflate its numbers, part to disguise what really is at stake.

Since a "popular front" advances by a false principle of inclusiveness, the only sensible response is to demand that it clarify its positions by negative exclusion. One must ask, in short, what are feminists who wish to remain orthodox prepared to repudiate?

Consider the invitation issued to the convention of 1200 women in Chicago called "Woman Church." The invitation was explitly directed to women "of every sexual orientation." (*Every*?) It appealed to the collapse of "sexual taboos." (*Which* taboos, one wonders: rules against homosexual activity, extramarital activity, abortion?) The invitation

expressed remarkable hatred for our own society, for its alleged sexism, racism, militarism and systemic injustice. It did not fail to mention the cherished cause of the domestic left, "the feminization of poverty" (which the facts suggest ought to be called "the poverty consequent on feminization"). Its decription of the role of story, myth, ritual, ecstasy and play was also pagan. The liturgy of the day, as described in the *Washington Post*, seemed to be closer to the "mystery cults" of the early Mediterranean basin than to the orthodox Christian sacraments, of which the distinctive mark is clerical order.

Question Settled by the Early Church

The call to Woman Church, moreover, is couched in hostility to "patriarchy." Is its alternative "matriarchy?" Probably not, since the feminists who "called" the gathering called their conference "Woman Church," not "Mother Church." Is the alternative, then, "anarchy"? The liturgy created by the Chicago women was a ritual derived from "our own power," as one leader defiantly declared afterwards. This suggests that the proper sacramental order in Woman Church would be neither patriarchy nor feminarchy but equal rule by one and all.

Most of us of middle-age and older, when we studied the heresies of the first two centuries of the church, had little expectation that those bizarre cults and beliefs which then bedevilled the young and vulnerable church had much chance of being resuscitated during our lifetime. We were wrong.

In particular, the debate of the early church concerning the proper ordering of sex (and the sexes) has been renewed with quiet force today. There is no doubt how the early church answered it. Female goddesses and female priestesses were powerfully attractive to the ancient world. The gnostic spirit, asserting in part that sexual differentiation entailed no essential difference in the ordering of natural or

Michael Novak, "Women Church Is Not Mother Church." Reprinted with permission from *Crisis* magazine, February 1984, PO Box 1006, Notre Dame, IN 46556.

supernatural life (and, consequently, none in ecclesiastical life), also asserted that, in a sense, the ultimate force in nature is the mothering force of spiritual inclusiveness. Matriarchal religions blur differences; patriarchal ones insist upon distinctions. The female principle is oceanic; the male principle insists upon discriminations. *Anima* expresses openness, abandonment, contemplation, receptivity; *Animus* expresses drive, distinctions, active differentiation, forward thrust. There are in all sexual concepts biological materials, psychological materials, cultural materials, and materials of social organization.

"[Many men] scrutinize feminism seriously, seeking some possible way, absurd as it seems, in which the will of God might actually be expressed in it."

Let us try to imagine Woman Church. If the ideals of some of its proponents could be realized, Woman Church would make no moral distinction between active heterosexuality and active homosexuality; it would favor approval for abortion; it would insist upon female priests, bishops, and popes; it would open up the liturgy to spontaneous song, ritual, dance, ecstasy, and feeling, issuing forth from "inside"; it would render the concept of heresy useless, except for those who manifested the spirit of exclusivity and clear differentiation. It would dissolve hierarchy in equality, objective criteria for membership into qualitative criteria.

There is some truth, of course, hidden within feminism. That truth, known to Jesus, is that in God's eyes women are equally dear to Him; moreover, that women are always likely to be at least as faithful to Him as men, and on many occasions visibly more so. Jesus did not come to abrogate nature but to fulfill it. Furthermore, the specifically new virtues that He taught—in the *agape* of his own life; in the Sermon on the Mount; and in the Beatitudes—are a clear rebuke to the masculine, warrior cultures of his (and every) time. Meekness, humility, seeking to be last rather than to be first, service, and submission to the will of God are not the virtues which feminists today proclaim.

Where Jesus teaches meekness, feminists teach self-assertion; where humility, pride; where seeking to be last, seeking equality up front; where service, command; where submission, their own will. It is possible to show how this feminist "transvaluation of values" is necessary in certain cases. It is not possible, alas, to call it orthodox.

Indeed, feminists clearly say that orthodoxy as it exists is a source of the repression they claim to feel.

In their eyes, orthodoxy is a bastion of patriarchy; feminism is true orthodoxy, recently discovered.

These absurdities go unchallenged, in fact, for reasons precisely the reverse of those feminists allege. If men and non-feminist women were to respond as feminists allege that they do—with decisiveness, competitiveness, and repression—these absurdities would long since have been laughed out of currency. But in the presence of feminists, most men are meek, humble, and submissive. They scrutinize feminism seriously, seeking some possible way, absurd as it seems, in which the will of God might actually be expressed in it. It is males who typically smile wanly while pinning "I'm a male Feminist" buttons on their lapels. In Chicago, it was bishops who exhibited meekness, humility, and submission.

The latter are, perhaps, not to be blamed for walking the last mile—so long, as least, as they do not use the good name of evangelical virtues as a cover for abandoning the orthodoxy it is their manly duty to defend. The real power in this world is not that of the male.

The rage of feminists is partly to be explained by the weakness of the males they encounter. Men find it more difficult to stand up to the fury of a woman than to any other thing on earth; nothing so tests their manhood. In our age, as much as Adam before Eve, men fail this test.

No Appeasement

In this lies an important clue. The Catholic Church will not quiet the fury of feminists through appeasement. Appeasement will induce yet more scathing contempt. For what feminist[s] are seeking are not womanly models like Margaret Thatcher, Jeane Kirkpatrick, Indira Gandhi, Golda Meir—or even Teresa of Avila, St. Therese of Lisieux, Catherine of Siena, and Mary the Mother of God. The agenda of feminism is not *woman* but politics. Hard-core feminists call themselves "persons," not "women," as if hating their own sex, as if hating women's traditional cultures, traditional roles, and traditional virtues and spiritual witness. They demand a world made over. That is why the hatred they manifest is so unbelievably intense. It is not so much radical as total.

I do not think, as Hans Kung does, that feminists are orthodox and the pope heretical. Nor do I think that appeasement will work. What is needed, instead, is not a decisive use of teaching authority but decisive *teaching*. Why is it that the creed says "Father Almighty" in relation to "only begotten Son"? Why is it that Jesus prayed, "Our Father"—not in some abstract Greek way, but in the familiar way of the intimate family, Abba? Is it important that God be conceived of in masculine rather than in feminine symbolic contexts? Is it important that when God sent the Messiah, the Messiah came not as a daughter but as a son? Is it important that the sacraments of Catholicism should not be imagined as inclusive and oceanic, but fenced in by male images? Is it important that only males are called by God to be "other Christs," and to say "This is my body" in a sexed and incarnate way? *Why* such things are so needs to be *taught*; merely asserting them to be so is plainly insufficient.

Historical Precedents

Further, it is crucial that the Church be known, as it has for centuries been known, as "holy Mother Church." This is not the same as "Woman Church." Woman Church is a church for feminists, who feel estranged from orthodoxy. It is quite honest of them to feel estranged. It would not be honest to alter orthodoxy to suit their agenda.

The Church is called mother because it includes all of us sinners, non-judgmentally as regards our sins, but quite jealously as regards our orthodoxy. Without orthodoxy, the church is not of God. For it would then be subject to any pressure group and any powerful gnostic movement. Since all groups and every movement contain some element of truth, discernment is called for. Also prayer. And, finally, due reflection on prior historical precedents.

The Christian movement in its earliest years showed a remarkable openness towards women, Elaine Pagels notes in *The Gnostic Gospels*. "But from the year 200, we have no evidence for women taking prophetic, priestly, and espiscopal roles among orthodox churches." Her evidence makes clear that the battle over sexual images and sexual order in the early church formed one of the most important foundational battles of the first 150 years of the church's existence. In this sense, the issue of feminism is not new; it is paradigmatic and permanent.

"It is crucial that the Church be known . . . as 'holy Mother Church.' This is not the same as 'Woman Church.'"

Gnostic Christians, Professor Pagels tells us, "assert that that which distinguishes the false from the true church is not its relationship to the clergy, but the level of understanding of its members, and the quality of their relationship to one another." The gnostics and the orthodox both claimed to speak for God about sexual doctrine, ritual, and clerical hierarchy, in the years leading up to 200 A.D. Professor Pagels again:

> From the bishop's viewpoint, of course, the gnostic position was outrageous. These heretics challenged

his right to define what he considered to be his own church; they had the audacity to debate whether or not catholic Christians participated; and they claimed that their own group formed the essential nucleus, the "spiritual church." Rejecting such religious elitism, orthodox leaders attempted instead to construct a *universal* church. Desiring to open that church to everyone, they welcomed members from every social class, every racial or cultural origin, whether educated or illiterate—everyone, that is, who would submit to their system of organization. The bishops drew the line against those who challenged any of the three elements of this system: doctrine, ritual, and clerical hierarchy—and the gnostics challenged them all. Only by suppressing gnosticism did orthodox leaders establish that system of organization which united all believers into a single institutional structure. They allowed no other distinction between first- and second-class members than that between the clergy and the laity, nor did they tolerate any who claimed exemption from doctrinal conformity, from ritual participation, and from obedience to the discipline that priests and bishops administered. Gnostic churches, which rejected that system for more subjective forms of religious affiliation, survived, as churches, for only a few hundred years.

Catholicism or Feminism

Gnosticism, like all powerful heresies rooted in human nature, does not really die; periodically, sparks leap from its ashes and its ancient glow suffuses dark corners. Like gnosticism, modern feminism is difficult to define; its elusive content is part of its purpose, part of its appeal, and part of its duplicity. It speaks of "the person," "equality," "maturity," "raised consciousness." Seeing through its claims is not easy. Doctrine, ritual, and clerical hierarchy are at stake. On all three, at the end of the twentieth as at the end of the second century, feminism and orthodoxy are in fundamental disagreement.

It is, indeed, difficult to go deeper into feminism without rejecting Catholicism; and the reverse. The issue, now that it has been raised, should not be treated as political. It goes to the substance of the symbols of faith.

Michael Novak is a resident scholar at the American Enterprise Institute and the publisher of Crisis *magazine.*

"Paul laid down a universally normative regulation that prohibits women from ruling and teaching men in the church."

viewpoint 88

The Bible Limits Women's Role in the Church

George W. Knight III

When we focus on the question of the role relationship in the teaching-ruling functions in the church, it is appropriate to ask if that question is dealt with explicitly in the New Testament. If it is, we must concentrate our attention on such didactic passages. That is basic to the proper handling of the Scriptures and the resolution of any question, and will prevent us from drawing erroneous conclusions from passages that treat the subject only incidentally. In that case we have three passages: I Timothy 2:11-15, which most clearly gives both the apostle Paul's verdict and his reason for that verdict; I Corinthians 11:1-16, which explains the significance of that reason; and I Corinthians 14:33b-38, which presents the apostle's command and his reason for it in more general terms.

Women Must Not Teach

The setting for I Timothy 2:11-15 is a letter in which Paul instructs Timothy about the life of the church. Paul says explicity that he is writing so that Timothy may "know how one ought to conduct himself in the household of God, which is the church of the living God, the pillar and support of the truth" (3:14-15). While the limits of this reference may extend to the whole letter, it certainly encompasses at least chapters 2 and 3. In chapter 2, Paul first writes about prayer, referring particularly to the responsibility of men. Then he turns to women and speaks of the need for modesty in dress, for a repudiation of ostentatiousness and a concentration instead on the adornment of good works.

After a general statement that requests women to learn in quietness and all subjection (pasēi hypotagēi; hypotagē, or subjection, is also the keynote found in the wife-husband relationship [Eph. 5; I Pet. 3]), he

then makes that aspect of subjection more explicit by a definite negative: "But I do not allow a woman to teach or exercise authority over a man, but to remain quiet." That which is prohibited is teaching (didaskein) and having dominion (authentein). The prohibition is not that a woman may not teach anyone (cf. Titus 2:3, 4), but that within the church she must not teach and have authority over a man (andros). . . .

The reason for such a vigorous prohibition ("I do not allow," epitrepō) follows immediately in verses 13 and 14: "For it was Adam who was first created, and then Eve. And it was not Adam who was deceived, but the woman being quite deceived, fell into transgression." The first statement is that the order in which God created man and woman (Adam and Eve) expresses and determines the relationship God intended and the order of authority. The one formed first is to have dominion, the one formed after and from him is to be in subjection. . . .

Reversing Roles Leads to Sin

The second statement is related to the Fall and the fact that Eve (woman) was beguiled. Paul does not expand and develop this argument, and we must be content with his brief statement of it. One may only conjecture that the apostle cites this foundational incident to indicate that when the roles established by God in creation were reversed by Eve, it manifestly had a disastrous effect. It is noteworthy that no cultural reason is given or even alluded to in this passage; Paul gives instead only the most basic, foundational reason, one that is always germane to men and women—namely, God's creation order and the dire consequences of reversing the roles, as evidenced in the Fall. No more basic and binding reason could be cited. Paul thus follows the example of Jesus Christ who, when He dealt with the basic question of the permanence of the marriage relationship, cited the Father's creative action.

The reason Paul gives in I Timothy 2:13-14 is

developed in I Corinthians 11:1-16. In I Corinthians 11, Paul discusses the freedom that the Corinthian women felt they had to abandon the order that God has ordained and expresses in nature. Paul argues that our freedom in Christ does not allow us to overturn that order and the particular expression of it in Corinth and the apostolic age. But he is careful to insist at the end of his argument that God Himself has, by means of long hair, provided the covering needed. So he ends: ". . . but if a woman has long hair, it is a glory to her? For her hair is given to her for a covering" (I Cor. 11:15). We thus have two things intertwined in this passage: the expression of the principle at stake in a particular practice, and the natural provision, long hair, that God has given and that expresses at all times the principle.

"Just as Christ is not a second-class person or diety because the Father is His head, so the woman is not a second-class person or human being because man is her head."

Paul begins his argument about the role relationship of men and women by placing it in the hierarchy of headships (*kephalē*). "But I want you to understand that Christ is the head of every man, and the man is the head of a woman, and God is the head of Christ" (v. 3). He establishes the propriety of headship by appealing to that of Christ to man and God to Christ. At the same time, he shows that such headship is not derogatory to one's person, being, or essence. He sandwiches the disputed relation (that of man and woman) between undisputed ones to set it in a proper framework.

Equal But Subordinate

It needs to be noted that Paul speaks not only of Christ as the head and authority of every man, but also of God as the head of Christ. The headship of God the Father in relation to the incarnate Christ in no way detracts from or is detrimental to Christ's person as incarnate deity. His full deity, His being of the same essence as the Father, is not at all denied, nor must His deity be affirmed in such a way that the Father's headship must be denied to maintain it. The headship of God in reference to Christ can be readily seen and affirmed with no threat to Christ's identity. This chain of subordination with its implications is apparently given to help answer the objection some bring to the headship of man in reference to woman. Just as Christ is not a second-class person or deity because the Father is His head, so the woman is not a second-class person or human

being because man is her head. . . .

We turn now to I Corinthians 14:33b (or 34)-38. These verses come in the midst of a chapter in which the apostle authoritatively regulates the use of spiritual gifts according to the norms "Let all things be done for edification" (v. 26) and "Let all things be done properly and in an orderly manner" (v. 40). He requires any man who speaks (*lalei*) in a tongue to keep silent (*sigatō*, v. 28) unless there is one to interpret, and then only two, or at the most three, may speak in turn. Likewise the prophets are to speak (*laleitōsan*) in turn, and if another is given a revelation, the first is to keep silent (*sigatō*, vv. 29-30). It is this section dealing with speaking and silence that provides the setting for Paul to speak about matters in regard to women, using the same two key words (*laleō* and *sigatō*). And just as the order of God, who is not a God of confusion but of peace, must prevail for tongues speakers and prophets, so it must prevail for women.

The speaking prohibited to women in verse 34 and the silence demanded is to be interpreted by two factors. First, the speaking (*laleō*) must be, considering the light of the immediate context and previous usage, public communication. Second, the correlation of speaking and silence found here is paralleled in I Timothy 2:11-14, where what is prohibited is women teaching men. Such an understanding seems most appropriate for I Corinthians 14. Therefore, women are prohibited from speaking in church because it would violate the role relationship between men and women that God has established. In the event that the prohibition against speaking and teaching in the church be circumvented by women who say that they are only asking questions and learning, the apostle points in verse 35 to another solution that clearly will not violate the prohibition of verse 34.

Upholding God's Law

Now we need to note the reasons for this prohibition. The appeal is to the need for subjection (*hypotassesthōsan*, v. 34), which would be violated by speaking. This subjection is taught by "the Law" (*honomos*, v. 34). It is most likely that "the Law" refers to God's law, and to the same passage cited in I Timothy 2:11ff. and I Corinthians 11:1ff.—namely, the creation order described in Genesis 2. The violation of the subjection taught in God's law is what makes it shameful for a woman to speak in the church. The apostle rebukes any disobedience by asking in verse 36: "Was it from you that the word of God first went forth? Or has it come to you only?" With these pointed and crisp questions, Paul shows that the Corinthians must not suppose that they originated God's Word and order, or that they alone have some word from God contrary to the understanding and practice of the apostle and all the other churches. . . .

We conclude from our survey of these three key passages that the apostle Paul laid down a universally normative regulation that prohibits women from ruling and teaching men in the church. These passages are not illustrations but commands; the commands are grounded not in time-bound, historically and culturally relative arguments that apply only to Paul's day and age, but in the way God created man and woman to relate to each other. . . .

Conclusion

Two facts emerge. The first is that none of the passages recognizing and encouraging women in their service in the church recognize or encourage them in the public and authoritative teaching-ruling offices or functions in reference to the church as a whole or to men in particular. The data has reinforced, not minimized or refuted, that teaching. The second fact is that the New Testament and the apostles do recognize and encourage women to use their gifts in various other capacities in the life and service of the church. Those two facts must be seen in correlation, and neither should be used to negate or overturn the other. . . .

Christians and churches faithful to Scripture and to the Creator-Redeemer who reveals His will in Scripture should encourage both the role relationship of men and women that God ordains and the free exercise, in harmony with the role relationship, of the gifts He gives to both men and women.

George W. Knight III is a professor of New Testament at Covenant Theological Seminary, St. Louis.

The Bible Does Not Limit Women's Role in the Church

Jacques Ellul

It has become commonplace to affirm that Christianity has been antifeminist, that it has kept women in bondage, that it has treated women as minors, and more. Many appeal to texts in the Old Testament and in Paul. Some have even tried to portray Paul as the founder of antifeminism.

Others have tried to justify the Bible and Christians by saying that they were simply following the patriarchal customs of the period. This excuse is in fact a terrible condemnation, for it testifies to the lack of Christian freedom relative to the customs and ideologies of the age. . . .

Women Play Important Role

The biblical texts are very favorable to women—or are at least neutral, according to local circumstances. Yet in later Judaism and in certain strands of Christianity, these texts have been taken in such a way as to become completely hostile to women. This poses a serious difficulty.

In the Hebrew Bible, women occupy an important place, as witness the political role of Esther, Judith, and Rahab, the prophetic role of many prophetesses, the role of Rebekah, and the role of the female "judges" in Israel. Texts such as the Song of Songs and Proverbs 31 display the essence of feminine symbolism.

More theologically, if we return to the Genesis text, we are astonished at the usual misunderstandings: Eve is inferior, it is said, because she is created *after* Adam. This superb logic makes Adam inferior to the great lizards after which he was created. Creation is in fact an ascending act, and Eve, who is created last, comes at the climax as its crown and completion. Again, it is said that Eve is inferior because she is not made out of primal clay but out of a part of Adam. This is equally absurd

reasoning, for Adam, who carries the name Earth, is made out of inanimate matter, but Eve, who carries the name Life, is made out of animate and hence superior matter.

There remains, of course, an argument that is repeated again and again in later Judaism and in some branches of Christianity. Eve, it is said, was the first to sin. She gave sin an entry into the world. She is thus guilty and must be subject to her husband. Again, this is absurd reasoning, for it is hard to see how Adam can have any claim to superiority when in this test he shows himself unable to rule his wife, falls into the simplest of traps, and is in no way worthy to be the head. But was not woman tempted first? Indeed she was. And this leads to the invoking of absurd arguments according to which she is less intelligent, easier to seduce, weaker, and the like.

There is in fact a better theological reason for her being tempted first. If she is the supreme achievement and perfection of creation, it is through her that the serpent must attack the rest. She does not resist. But neither does the man. We may simply recall the famous Chinese proverb that it is by the head that the fish decays.

The Glory of Man

A second basic truth, as Paul reminds us in I Corinthians 11:7, is that woman is the glory of man. (Many modern versions do not use the word *glory*. They show a concern to attenuate and weaken the biblical text, making it more banal. Thus they do not translate *doxa* here as glory but as reflection, which is basically the opposite theologically of the Hebrew conception of glory.)

Now this passage has often been misconstrued as teaching a hierarchy from God to man and man to woman. But this is not its point or its purpose. Following [theologian Karl] Barth and others, I have often recalled that glory is revelation. God is glorified when God is revealed as God is. Jesus Christ glorifies God when he reveals God to us as the God of love who is also the Father. We ourselves are called upon to be the glory of God as we live in God's image, as we show by what we are who is the God to whom we bear witness. In this passage then, Paul adds that the woman is the glory of the man; she reveals him; she shows what a human being truly is.

> "[Paul] affirms total equality when he says that in Christ there is neither Greek nor Jew, male nor female, slave nor free."

Relating this to the temptation, we see that Eve brings to light the fundamental reality of Adam. She shows him to be weak, undiscerning, fluctuating, ambitious, and desirous of equality with God. She simply reveals this. Both are equally at fault, and the condemnation (as commentators and theologians should remember) is more severe for the man, since he is given no hope. The woman, on the other hand, has a double promise that carries a double hope: that she will transmit life and that her posterity will crush the serpent.

To Jesus, Women Are Equals

Insistence has often been placed on the positive attitude of Jesus toward women. Jesus receives both men and women on an equal footing. He cures sick women as well as men and does not repel the adulterous woman or Mary Magdalene. Naturally, it has been noted that he chooses only men as his disciples. But to this one may make the radical reply that he first reveals his resurrection to women. Both in the Synoptic Gospels and in John, women are the first to receive this supreme revelation. Women become the "evangelists" of this resurrection by carrying the news of it to the disciples. Women receive the first witness to eternal life. This is theologically consistent, for it is a fulfillment of the name Eve and of the promise about the serpent. Compared to this, all else is secondary.

It is important that Jesus affirmed monogamic marriage and its indissolubility. But this pales in comparison with his complete reversal of the judgment of his age concerning the transmission of truth by women. We should also not forget the decisive role of women in the primitive church. Women are its founders and pillars. They act as missionaries, as Paul often shows, and they bear responsibility for churches. Externally, we have curious testimony in the famous letter of Pliny to Trajan in which he writes about female ministers.

We should also remember that women have spiritual gifts, such as deaconhood, prophecy, and speaking in tongues. One may thus say that there is a clear-cut accession to utterance and to equality with men. Paul, too, recognizes that women have the gift of public prayer and prophecy. Finally, he affirms total equality when he says that in Christ there is neither Greek nor Jew, male nor female, slave nor free.

Making Moral Laws

The opinion soon arose, however, that Paul is a frightful misogynist and that we should focus only on those other texts in which he speaks about the obedience of women to their husbands, their inferiority, and the need for reservations about them in certain church affairs.

Fundamentally, the mistake has been to make moral laws out of these passages. Cutting one's hair was a sign of prostitution. So Paul tells Christian women not to do it, since they are not prostitutes. But we must not make of this an imperative.

The matter of subordination is more important. When Paul speaks about hierarchy, it is in the context of what Jesus himself said and showed, namely, that the greater must be the servant of the lesser, that the hierarchal superior must serve the hierarchal inferior. The stronger must not exercise power and authority but put them, and self, at the disposition of the weaker. Paul calls no one to a macho life style. He calls us *all* to a life of nurturing and caring, a life modeled on Christ's self-giving love of the church. Tragically, the church has often misunderstood Paul's theology, retaining only half his teaching and transforming this half into a moral duty and a type of legal organization in which women inevitably find themselves on the bottom, the exact opposite of what Paul intended.

Jacques Ellul is a retired law professor at the University of Bordeaux, France.

The Bible Is Unclear About Women's Role in the Church

Pheme Perkins

Over the past century, historical critical study of the Bible has taught scholars to look for the history and development of its traditions. We have learned to see that there is a close relationship in the Bible between various expressions of faith and the concrete social and historical experience of the believing community. Some parts of the canon disagree with other parts in the rendering of God or of faith.

All of the canonical traditions took shape in cultural contexts that presumed women were inferior to men. This inferiority was evident in the greater restrictions placed on women, their inferior education, their youth and inexperience relative to males to whom they were married, their greater mortality and their dependence upon males to negotiate the public world outside the home. Though women may have enjoyed more or less independence at different times, the fundamental perception of "female" as both different from and inferior to the "male"—especially in any activities involving the public and political world—continued to be the norm.

Scholars have noted that the Bible contains stories in which women act with great initiative. The mothers and wives of Israel's patriarchs are remembered for clever schemes that insure that the promise passes to the son for whom it is destined. This scheming may involve prejudice and oppressive behavior that represent other social prejudices, as in Sarah's treatment of the Egyptian slave woman Hagar.

Several stories of women from the post-exilic period present women whose initiative shatters the conventional roles assigned them. Ruth, the foreign wife, refuses to return to her people. At a time when many were becoming hostile to Gentile wives, her story defends the right of such outsiders to be incorporated into the people and to be treated according to Israel's standard of justice. Esther and Judith "show up" the faith of weak and vacillating males. Through them, the people are delivered from powerful foreign enemies. Unlike the males in Israel's story, all of these women act without any divine promises to assure their success. Their unconventional behavior is tolerated because it preserves the tradition in a time of crisis.

A similar assessment might be made of the stories of women as presented in the New Testament canon. For example, the genealogy of Mt. 1:2-16 breaks the line of patriarchal descent in four places: Tamar, Rehab, Ruth, and the wife of Uriah. These examples of divine initiative outside the established ordering of society can be seen to vindicate the adoption of Mary's child into the Davidic tradition by Joseph. Mary Magdalene and the other women disciples who discovered the empty tomb may also have proclaimed the Easter message. But the Gospel narratives dissociate the revelations of angels, and even the appearance of Christ to them, from the mission-initiating and church-founding manifestations of the risen Lord to Peter and the male disciples. A Gnostic author of the late second century, seeking to establish Mary Magdalene as the source of authentic teaching by Jesus, challenged this canonical bias by presenting Mary (not Peter) as the one who rallied the disciples to the task of mission.

Women Active in Early Church

Women appear in the Gospel narratives as recipients of healing and praise for their faith. Often they are women who bear a further burden of marginalization due to their disease (woman with hemorrhage) or non-Jewish origin (Syro-Phoenician woman) or social stigma as "sinner" (woman who anoints Jesus out of love). Jesus defends Mary's position as a disciple learning from the teacher when Martha attempts to call her away to a more traditional "women's place," preparing an elaborate meal for the honored, male guests. The despised Samaritan woman becomes both a believer and missionary who calls others to Jesus. She repeats a pattern established for the male disciples in Jn. 1:35-51.

Women were among the larger group of followers who accompanied Jesus and are witnesses to His passion and death. Even more evidence for the active participation of women in the earliest days of the Christian movement comes from the Pauline letters. Some, like Chloe and Phoebe headed household churches and sent both reports and assistance to the apostle. Others like Prisca and her husband Aquila, and other women and men mentioned in Rom. 16:3-16, seem to be involved in missionary, community-founding and community-nurturing activities independent of the apostle. Paul asks the Philippians to help reconcile two women who had worked side by side with him in the mission in that area.

Women's Role Restricted

Though reflected in some stories, and in the greetings of Pauline letters, this picture of women as "fellow workers" in the spread of the Gosepl is not established by the New Testament canon taken as a whole. Markan narrative confines Jesus' interactions with women to "private" areas like the home. The Evangelists never secure them a place as followers of Jesus even in the group larger than the "Twelve."

"Neither feminist nor anti-feminist can claim [the Bible] as ally."

Within the Pauline churches, the apostle and his followers responded in conventional ways to tensions created by the activities of women. Women are not to upset the "good order" of society. Women prophets show by their dress (and subordination to Paul's authority?) that God's Spirit does not challenge the subordinationist order of creation. Women are to learn from their husbands and other males; they are not to speak or teach in public. Christian wives are to demonstrate the "non-threatening" character of the movement in their modesty and subordination to their husbands ([I Pet. 3:1-6] where obedience to one's husband is the lesson a woman is said to learn from Sarah). Most of these injunctions could be paralleled in popular Greco-Roman moralists many times over. They represent a shared cultural consensus about how things ought to be. The canon takes a similar position with regard to slaves. Yes, they are equal brothers and sisters to freed and freeborn persons in the Christian community. No, the community will not challenge the conventions of slave-ownership. Better for women and slaves to achieve their salvation in patterning themselves on their suffering Lord.

A Double Bind

It is no wonder that increasing numbers of women today find that the biblical traditions place them in a "double bind." The Bible's message of justice, equality, entitlement of the oppressed, and its strong images of women of faith are an inspiration. But sometimes the canon seems to preserve these messages "in spite of itself." Women are to do what is extraordinary and heroic when their witness preserves the tradition in times of crisis. They are not to use such traditions to challenge the cultural ordering of gender relationships inherited from earlier times. Women are puzzled by the hypocrisy of churches that loudly condemn South Africa and willingly admit that canonical texts about slavery are culture-bound, while some of the same churches just as loudly proclaim "separate but equal" doctrines for women based on "timeless truths" found in canonical texts no different from those about slavery.

It should be evident from our brief survey that the Bible does not take anyone's side in the difficult questions facing women today. Neither feminist nor anti-feminist can claim it as ally. What we do have from the Bible is not a social or ecclesial blueprint, but the stories of faith that sustained our ancestors. What it means to be faithful to the God who is represented there continues to be a new challenge for the believing community in every generation. And if we believe the biblical witnesses, many of our experiments may prove to be more human than divine. We still live in a creation that "groans" along with us as we await the completion of redemption.

Pheme Perkins is a theology professor at Boston College who has published several books on the New Testament.

"When it came to participation in the temple itself, these gifted multitudes of faithful women were systematically excluded."

viewpoint 91

Women Should Be Priests

Women's Ordination Conference

Editor's note: The following article is in the form of a parable. It was presented to a committee of Catholic bishops writing a pastoral letter on women in church and society.

Parable of the Faithful Women and the Deaf High Priests

There was in the land of gospel living a multitude of faithful women who in their lifetimes had experienced great religious renewal. These women came from all walks of life, all ages and races and cultural backgrounds. Their common heritage was in the fact that they shared the same faith and belonged to the same religious temple, a temple of long tradition and influence in many lands.

But the temple itself was in great tumult and confusion. Over the centuries it had come to pass that the high priests only were allowed to make policy, determine budgets and conduct the sacred rites of the temple. These rites were called sacraments. And to be a high priest, one must not only be a man, but a man who would promise never to love a woman in marriage. A man, thus distanced from and renouncing women, became a high priest through a ritual called ordination.

"It Has Always Been So"

Now the high priests claimed all this was God's will because it had always been so. They remained adamant about this despite the temple's own scholars, who had for years documented another tradition—one of equality and equal sharing, a discipleship of equals, a tradition of diversity in early communities who followed Jesus and perhaps, most important, a tradition of the fundamental equality of women as persons made in God's image. Temple scholars called the high priests' policy (of

exclusion based on gender) sexism. They said it was sinful and likened it to other great evils that excluded categories of people on arbitrary and unfounded bases (like race or creed or sexual preference).

Now the high priests were a curious lot. They were sincere men who when speaking about things outside the temple wrote decrees calling for justice. They said they would "read the signs of the times" . . . "seek to detect the meaning of emerging history" . . . "listen to the cry of those . . . oppressed by unjust . . . structures." The high priests even said they had found the process necessary to bring about this justice. They said it was "dialogue."

Women in Pain

Meanwhile, inside the great temple of tradition and influence, there was terrible pain. Women, living out Jesus' mission, were advocating for the poor, healing the sick, comforting and anointing the dying, discerning means of peace with justice coalitions, providing support to the many agonizing with moral decisions. But when it came to participation in the temple itself, these gifted multitudes of faithful women were systematically excluded.

It's not that the high priests weren't informed— their representatives had met repeatedly with representatives of the faithful women. Some women felt the high priests didn't care; others accused them of loving power and control more than their own principles of dialogue and justice; still others felt genuine consternation and concluded perhaps they must be deaf.

But regardless of what analysis or conclusions were drawn about why the high priests persisted in their ways, faithful women renewed their involvements with the mission of Jesus and the land of gospel living was the richer for it.

But in the temple rituals and day-to-day life, they

Women's Ordination Conference, "A Parable on Deaf High Priests," *Origins*, March 21, 1985.

experienced greater and greater alienation. The self-contradiction and violence of sexism were so great in the temple rites that increasing numbers of faithful women stopped worshiping there altogether. Many left temple jobs, forced out by the double standards and trivializing of their experiences (a logical and direct consequence of sexist policy).

Battered, anguished and spiritually homeless, they began to find each other. Faithful women began to share their stories, their tears of rejection suffered at the hands of temple policy. They also shared their gifts and discovered that this sharing energized each other and renewed their strength for mission in the land of gospel living. Hungry for the nurturing supper of Jesus, they celebrated it themselves. Not only was Jesus' presence recognized among them, but they discovered rich new symbols of prayer and liberation; they found language and images of God that spoke the truth of their bodies, their lives, their relationships and their experiences. There was new hope and new life now as more and more faithful women sought out, rediscovered, reconstructed and shared what was a part of the temple tradition all along, but lost or overlooked or unvalued because over time all records and laws were written in the words of men, with male images and language.

A Letter on Women

Then one day, as the faithful women were about their ministries, they got word that the high priests were going to write another decree. The confounding thing was that this "letter" was to be about women!

Some of the faithful women were outraged at the high priests' arrogance, knowing they didn't know or understand women's experience. Others didn't care because nothing about the temple made sense or spoke to faith anymore—at least not to women's faith. Many said that a letter written by men about women would only alienate more of the faithful, especially because a temple newsletter had reported that some high priests were insistent that the decree be "written within the teachings of the (church) temple." And the faithful women knew this meant that the very issues that caused the pain and alienation would go unacknowledged or summarily dismissed. But most of the faithful women didn't know about the proposal at all—they had long since left the temple, weary of its patronizing ways, seeking elsewhere for models of equality for their daughters and support of equal sharing for their sons.

And lo, it came to pass that the high priests decided to ask some women about their decree. Those invited felt compromised taking part in a closed temple meeting. But acknowledging that the alleged deafness of many of the high priests may have influenced the exclusive context, one of the bands of faithful women collaborated with others on the best means of speaking their truth.

The designated scribe set about gathering stories of faithful women. But her heart grew heavy and her spirit greatly sad as she heard the cries of so many hurt by injustices and rejected by the very temple they had once known as home.

"Tell them to put into practice their own words about justice," many cried out.

"Ask them why when they write about nuclear armament and issues of economy they can consult with military advisers and proponents of control by force, but when faithful women want to meet in one of the temple buildings to talk about the very issues of women's faith that are pressing today, the local high priest forbids the meeting there," another said.

"Tell them as long as women are excluded from ordination and thus any role of decision making in the temple, the high priests continue great scandal to those of other religious traditions—and they intensify the crisis of faith within," many said.

"Tell them the ultimate insult was welcoming married high priests from another temple—men who left their temple precisely because their temple was beginning to ordain women," several others offered.

"Ask they why, if dialogue is their means to justice, when faithful women sign a public statement calling for dialogue about issues of justice, the high officials of the high priests threaten expulsion from these women's communities of faith," was another inquiry.

"[Many women] had long since left the temple, weary of its patronizing ways."

"Tell them that Jesus in dialogue with a woman (the Syrophoenician woman of Mark 7) learned from her that his mission was broader than he had hitherto understood, and that maybe if they dialogued with women, they too would learn," offered one of the faithful women, herself a great scholar.

And on and on went similar cries for an end to sexism in the temple. Some women even came to speak for themselves.

A Possible Conclusion

And it came to pass that as the faithful women spoke, the ears of the high priests were opened, the hearts of some of the high priests were moved. They too felt pain, but even more remorse for the role their own harshness of heart had played in allowing temple policy to serve only some and impose such harsh exclusion on others.

Some of the high priests set about to do the things faithful women had suggested. They sought out women trained in discernment of the Spirit and sought their help as their own personal counselors.

They delegated many temple matters to others and freed time to listen and to be about dialogue with others. To their amazement, throngs and multitudes barely seen or known to high priests before, who at one time had been staunch temple members, came forth to share their stories. Women and men poured out their hopes, their dreams, their experiences of God, their needs, concerns, their prayers.

"Promises of justice were applied to temple practice, and untold gifts of the faithful were freed for the mission of Jesus in the broader world."

At first the high priests didn't understand and were troubled at the diversity of views and the depth of feelings. They panicked at times at the seeming disarray in temple offices and the mutterings of staff who minced no words telling them they spent too much time talking! But calling on the Spirit of wisdom and truth and bolstered by the responsiveness of the faithful, the process of dialogue healed deaf ears and challenged faithful hearts. Promises of justice were applied to temple practice, and untold gifts of the faithful were freed for the mission of Jesus in the broader world. Outside the temple the high priests and the temple itself were taken more seriously, and many of those long alienated began to return.

Nor was dialogue without its pain, both in the process and the changes it enabled. The high priests and the faithful women found that not all who dialogued wished to collaborate. Indeed, for some, fear of change and loss of control triggered attacks on the entire process. Alas, high priests from higher temples sought to silence the whole affair. But the high priests accompanied groups of faithful women to the highest of the high priests in the imperial city.

Equality Will Bring Vigor

There was insecurity to deal with, economic questions, a host of troublesome procedures. The tension between the dialoguing temples and those entrenched in the old ways grew more passionate and foreboding. When Jesus' Supper was celebrated now, women broke bread together with men. The cost of discipleship had new meaning and the death-resurrection paradox was experienced daily.

All this took place as Jesus promised. And as he said, his word continued to empower many to bring freedom and justice to those trapped in oppression and pain. The temple practice was alive with the vigor equality brings. And equal sharing practiced there gave flesh to the good news that faithful women and men took to all the surrounding nations.

The Women's Ordination Conference is an organization of men and women who believe women should be Catholic priests.

"For His purposes—you can quarrel with His choice but He made it—the Lord God chose, not the most hospitable, most peace-loving sex, but the male sex."

Women Should Not Be Priests

Belloc

Noel, Noel, Noel, Noel!
May all my enemies go to hell!

The straight premise of feminist talk is that sex involves serious differences. What is resisted, what causes anger, restlessness, and frustration, is not said to be particular disciplines but their originating sexual source. This is a hard teaching, "Womanchurch"—the feminist heretical version of the Catholic Church, a parody of the Catholic Church, like that practiced by free thinkers during the French Revolution, in which sourdough bread is broken in the name of women priests past "and yet to come," in which (*Newsweek* tells us) a goblet of wine is held aloft by a woman, offering her sisters a "chalice filled with the blood of those who have given birth and are giving birth today"—it is not the Christ who is remembered but woman.

In place of the sermon, a taped lecture of a woman theologian is read, ridiculing Rome's declaration that only men can "image" Christ. This does not mean "that the priest should look Jewish," the feminist theologian explains. "It means the priest should have b_____." I couldn't have said it better. Belloc lives, I say again!

Now—to lapse into male logic—either sex is significant or it is not. If it is, Christ being male, Peter being male, the apostles and their successors being male, is a matter of significance. If sex is of significance, then Rome is correct, and Womanchurch heretical. If sex is not of significance, wherein lies the anger? Males and females being interchangeable, all males or all females or a mix of both is a matter of indifference.

I can understand complaints by women that priests and successors of Peter are not holy, not competent, not admirable human beings. That, by

the way, has often been true. I cannot understand the complaint that they are male. Not, at least, when this complaint is based upon the premise that sex does, in fact, make a difference.

Sex Makes a Difference

Perhaps feminists intend a different premise. Sex is of serious significance, they may say, only not the current "patriarchal" significance. Patriarchal values must be turned upside-down, either into matriarchal values or into sex-neutral values. The last alternative lands us back at "Sex is not significant, any more than looking Jewish or being tall." But that is clearly not intended. For feminists want *women* priests. Having *women* in the priesthood is significant to them. So sex does make a difference. Therefore, each sex does "image" itself and not the other. This lands us back at "Sex is significant."

I believe I can assent to this. Having an anatomical appendage of the sort described, with all its attendant miseries, does, most assuredly, make a difference. It got the church in a peck of trouble under Alexander VI, for example. It has often gotten the church—the whole human race—into very deep trouble. Would that men were angels. We would all like the church better that way. Maybe. In reality, alas, humans aren't any angels. Men are different from women. No males, alas give birth. Males shed no blood giving birth. That much is true. Men shed quite a lot of blood, however. When Sister Quinn says that "feminist vows" are likely to run toward "hospitality and working for peace," there may be a residue of "the feminist mystique" in that, but there is some truth in it, too. By holy heaven, many a warrior has come home to a woman of peace, down the long slide of the centuries, to have his wounds bound and his spirit restored.

So which is it, now? Are women different from men, or not? If they are not different at all, why, then, the rule of angels should be the rule of the

Belloc, "All Hail the Feminist Hour!" Reprinted with permission from *Crisis* magazine, April 1984, PO Box 1006, Notre Dame, IN 46556.

church. If, on the other hand, being sexed male or female does make a difference, then how deeply into the rule of the church should that difference run? And who should decide? . . .

God Chose Males

Let us call things by their names. One cannot have both a feminist church and the Roman Catholic Church. One must choose. Just as, in choosing in which sex to be incarnated, and to which sex to turn in choosing a Vicar, the Lord God himself, our Father who art in heaven, had to choose, and did choose. For His purposes—you can quarrel with His choice but He made it—the Lord God chose, not the most hospitable, most peace-loving sex, but the male sex, the patriarchal sex, the dominating sex, the warrior sex: and bade that sex to imitate the other in gentleness, meekness, hospitality, and peace. The Lord did indeed plan for the feminization of humanity. He did not do so through founding a feminist church, however, but through founding, and confounding, a masculinist church. To miss that irony, to bowdlerize that paradox, is to miss what is as plain, when we are naked, as the nose on a face.

"Whoever speaks of the equality of the sexes tells a lie."

Moreover, the males of the late twentieth century are desperately in need of the masculine ideal. Wimpiness is gaining everywhere. Males are being told that having an anatomical appendage is a deformation, that they ought to act like angels, that they ought to be sensitive, caring, tender, and supportive, while their female colleagues teach them anger, militance, dissent, and revolt in the name of hospitality and peace. Females are angry, males are told. Males should be meek, males are told. Now is the female hour. All bow down before our Mother, who art in heaven, God the Mother almighty. All hail the feminist hour.

Equality of Sexes a Lie

Whoever speaks of the equality of the sexes tells a lie. But one thing I will concede. Men who have the anatomical appendage, but who act as if they do not, who act, that is, like wimps, deserve Womanchurch. They should proudly (or wanly) say that they cannot be Roman Catholics. A church ruled by men, they should say, is no church of theirs. For twenty centuries it has served men and women well; no more. It must become, now, other than it has been.

Was God unfair in making Christ a male? Could no male die for the sins of females? Can only a female savior redeem the female sex? God must have made a fundamental error. He should have sent a female Redeemer. Better, He should have sent an angel, sparing twentieth-century enthusiasts confusion about their sexual identities, anxieties, and ambitions. . . .

From where I sit in Heaven—Purgatory, I may warn you, is infinitely more painful than I can describe, though all things pass as in an instant—I already see the church of the earthly future. The days ahead are far darker than parochial Americans imagine. Pope John Paul II sees farther, by far, than the American enlightened class. I cannot, of course, expect any American to believe that. Let me leave you only with a warning.

Let us suppose that your fondest feminist dreams come true, and that the Roman Catholic Church shortly will capitulate to feminism. For a while, there will be women priests, bishops, cardinals, popes; then *married* women priests, bishops, cardinals, popes. Soon more than half the leadership of the church will be female. Rules for nepotism will be codified, no mother's son preferred. According to your dream, women religious will no longer be angry, restless, or frustrated. They will enjoy upward mobility. Males and females will cooperate harmoniously, in relationships of mutual esteem, equality, and sharing. Mother Church will reverberate as one happy family. Women will do everything that men now do, and they will also (most of them) bear children. *Machismo* will have perished; feminism will have wilted away, a transitory cause in a victory won.

A Short-Lived Triumph

Like all such triumphs in history, a worm will eat at it. *Male* religious may then grow angry, restless, and frustrated. They may claim that females do not understand them, that females exclude them, repress them, and insist that they act like females, which like schoolboys males obediently try to do but fail. Males will appeal to the early church, to Scriptural traditions, to centuries of practice, and to rigorous logical (male) argument. They may become militant. They may begin to raise one another's consciousness; to incite sexual envy, and to stimulate ambition. The spark of the warrior sex may ignite. They may treat civilization as a fraud, a sham, an instrument of their oppression. They may claim the Christian God has become effeminate. They may turn to pagan gods, to Thor, to Woden. They may drink the blood of animals and enemies. They may begin to sing my song:

Noel, Noel, Noel, Noel!
May all my enemies go to hell!

History may repeat its many cycles. The coming days, I say, may be darker than anyone imagines.

Belloc is a pseudonym used by a writer with Crisis *magazine. Hilaire Belloc (1870-1953) was a British Roman Catholic writer and satirist.*

"The church needs married priests."

Priests Should Be Allowed To Marry

Michael O'Connell-Cahill

This crisis in vocations leads to an obvious conclusion and conviction: the Catholic Church needs married priests. There are many reasons why this is true, but the most obvious reason stems from the hard fact that the celibate priesthood doesn't work anymore.

The numbers tell a big part of the story. Half of the world's Catholics do not participate in weekly Eucharists due simply to the shortage of priests. While the causes of this shortage are complex, certainly mandatory priestly celibacy contributes to it. Catholics run the danger of becoming less and less a sacramental and eucharistic church as long as the church places priestly celibacy ahead of sacramental preparation in the order of important priorities.

The numbers also point to another fact: burnout and low morale among priests. Many of the best and the brightest have fallen victim to fatigue and loneliness in their efforts to do their jobs well for so many with so little priestly support. Others have given up and left the priesthood. When today's young Catholics see this, most choose not to enter seminaries where they perceive, often all too correctly, that unhealthy communities exist.

This of course leads to the question, what young men do enter the seminary today? While once the decision to enter the priesthood garnered strong support from Catholic communities, this is not often so today. It is hard enough to live a celibate priesthood with solid support. In today's climate, celibacy becomes not so much a Christian countersign but a discipline whose meaning—or lack thereof—is questioned frequently even by those practicing it.

Like it or not, the church faces a problem of

priests who inadequately perform their duties. In a speech to Catholic journalists in 1985, Father James Burtchaell of Notre Dame labeled this a "problem of national proportion." Burtchaell pinpointed "pathologies involving sexual maturity and materialism" as those affecting priests today. It's certainly true that some priests today live self-indulgent, materialistic lives, show signs of sexual immaturity sometimes of a severe nature, and actively break the celibacy discipline.

This leads to disillusionment not only among the Catholic community, but particularly among the priests and seminarians still trying to make the celibate priesthood work in today's society and church.

Beyond the numbers, other reasons for a married clergy stand out. Sixty thousand marriages are annulled each year by church marriage tribunals. Something is wrong with the state of Catholic marriage. I'm not one to argue that only a married person or couple can understand and counsel another married person or couple. I think that is nonsense. And certainly married couples already minister to others in all sorts of Catholic programs.

So why married priests? A married priest and spouse can bring to married couples in a parish something the celibate priest cannot; they can share the experience of their marriage and do so precisely as ministering priests in the community. While this takes nothing away from a celibate priest's ministry, it adds another dimension that married Catholics desperately need, especially from the pulpit. Also, a priest with a child would stand as a powerful sign in a church that emphasizes family life and abhors abortion.

Called to Married Priesthood

But perhaps the best reason to form a married priesthood arises when one looks at all the ex-priests, ex-seminarians, and just good Catholics who

Michael O'Connell-Cahill, "The Church Needs Married Priests," *U.S. Catholic*, December 1987. Reprinted with permission from *U.S. Catholic*, published by the Claretians, 205 W. Monroe, Chicago, IL 60606.

live in the married state who would simply make good priests. While most may not and need not feel called to the priesthood, many do feel called. "I'm ready to serve the minute they change the discipline. I feel called to the priesthood, but not to celibacy. And I'm not alone," says a former priest. Indeed he is not. The discipline of celibacy forces many Catholics to turn away from the call to the priesthood that they hear from their God.

Many Catholics fear the structural and economic changes the church would undergo if a married clergy became a reality. But the alternative also looks bleak: a nonsacramental church with monthly Masses from a celibate priest who covers five to ten parishes, attempting to keep them sacramentally alive.

Perhaps more important, some Catholics believe the state of marriage is antithetical to the state of priesthood and that celibacy is intrinsically part of Catholic priesthood. The facts state otherwise. Peter was our first married priest and pope. The church instituted mandatory celibacy only after its first 1000 years. Even today, married Episcopal priests convert to Catholicism and serve as priests. No one asks them to leave their wives.

Also, among the many who fit into the "called to priesthood, not to celibacy" category are minorities. Many Catholics in the black and Hispanic communities simply don't value celibacy the way the Irish and Polish once did and to some extent still do. For blacks, Hispanics, and others to enter the priesthood according to their numbers, the celibacy law will have to change.

Celibacy a Discipline

Many Catholics, priests and lay, have expressed concern about a married clergy not because they disagree with it theoretically, but because they believe the gift of celibacy to be a valuable gift they don't want to see disappear. The Catholic memory and imagination remember and envision the celibate priest, the priest who loves his people and his parish so much, who loves his God so much, that he chooses freely to be celibate for the Kingdom of God. Who can deny the beauty and the power and the experience of celibacy when we have seen it work? No one.

Yet the question for today is how many priests today have this gift of celibacy? How many feel called to celibacy as well as the priesthood? In fact, many priests say that God called them to the priesthood and that they see celibacy as nothing more than a church discipline imposed on them because of that call. Thus, many celibate priests today resent their celibacy as the wrapping paper that covered their priestly present from God. . . .

For those priests who feel called to be celibate for God's kingdom, let's hope the church always supports them and loves them as they love the

church. And let's hope the church always has more of its young who feel called to celibacy by a community that values that state as a gift anyone can receive from God.

"For those many persons—priests, former priests, seminarians, married couples, and more—who want priesthood but do not want celibacy, let's ease the yoke and allow them into the Catholic priesthood."

But for those many persons—priests, former priests, seminarians, married couples, and more— who want priesthood but do not want celibacy, let's ease the yoke and allow them into the Catholic priesthood. Granted, to do so will initiate by necessity even more radical change in a church that rarely catches its breath of late. But not to do so may well mean the continued demoralization and perhaps even death of the priesthood itself.

Into the Future

I don't believe that 50 years from now we can afford to look at the church and the priesthood and say:
• In most parishes weekly Mass is a thing of the past.
• A bright, energetic, intellectual priesthood no longer exists.
• Catholic seminaries are empty of healthy, mature young individuals.
• Many of the remaining clergy are an embarrassment and scandal in their defiance of church teaching on celibacy.
• Marriage and family life in the church still receive inadequate attention. Couples still can't hear preaching by others who share their marriage experience.
• Minority priests are nonexistent, and their congregations have by and large left the Catholic Church.
• Talented and willing Catholics who feel called to the priesthood are still denied ordination.
• The celibate priesthood is a sad remnant of what it once was, standing alone and unsupported by a married clergy.

Many of these conditions have already come to pass. Imagine the destruction if the present situation continues unchanged. What is the remedy for this worst-case scenario? The church needs married priests. Let's ordain them now.

Michael O'Connell-Cahill is a financial planner in Chicago and a former Catholic seminarian.

"The church's leadership over the centuries has discerned that only those with the gift of celibacy should be called to priesthood."

Priests Should Be Celibate

Daniel Pilarczyk

The scriptural *locus classicus* [passage that explains] on celibacy is Matthew 19:10ff. Jesus has been talking about the indissolubility of marriage and the apostles say, "If that's the way things are, it is better not to marry." Jesus says, "Well, that is not for everybody either. Remaining unmarried may be better, but only for those who have received a special gift from God. These are the ones who are eunuchs for the sake of the kingdom of heaven. If someone is able to embrace this gift, he should do so by all means."

Historically, celibacy for the kingdom has always been highly regarded in the church. Over the centuries, the church of the West has made dedication to celibacy a defining precondition for ordination to priesthood.

Vatican II dealt with celibacy in *Presbyterorum Ordinis* 16 and *Lumen Gentium* 42. Both of these places speak of celibacy principally in terms of pastoral availability. Celibacy "signifies and stimulates pastoral charity . . . (Through celibacy priests) more easily hold fast to (Christ) with undivided heart. They more freely devote themselves to him and through him to the service of God and man. They more readily minister to his kingdom and to the work of heavenly regeneration, and thus become more apt to exercise paternity in Christ, and do so to a greater extent."

In 1967 Pope Paul VI issued his encyclical *Sacerdotalis Coelibatus*. There he offered three reasons for the celibacy of priests. The first is Christological. Celibates image Christ in a special way in that they reflect Christ's own exclusive dedication to the kingdom by sharing his very condition of living. The second reason is ecclesiological. The celibate loves and dedicates himself to all the children of God. He is best disposed for a continuous exercise of a perfect charity. The third reason lies in the eschatological significance of celibacy. It proclaims the presence on earth of the final stage of salvation where our life is hidden with Christ in God.

Not a New Controversy

I would like to try to say in my own words what I think the commitment to celibacy is all about in the church, but first I want to remind us of something.

The controversy about priestly celibacy is not new in the church. It has been around at least since the Spanish Council of Elvira in 306. It took centuries to achieve universal application of the discipline in the Western church. It was discussed again and again at general councils: Lateran II (1139), Lateran IV (1215), Vienne (1311-12), Constance (1414-18), Florence (1431-45), Lateran V (1512-17) and Trent (1545-63). The discipline was reaffirmed by Vatican II.

It is a question which will not die, perhaps because there is no apodictic, rational proof that things have to be that way or even that they should be that way. There is no essential, inherent connection between priesthood and celibacy which would make their separation absurd. And yet, at the most solemn moments of the church's teaching and legislating activity, i.e., at general councils, the church's leadership has consistently come down in favor of celibacy as a condition for priesthood. A cynic might say that it is merely a case of the bishops trying to maintain control over their priests. Someone else might say, though, that it is the Spirit guiding Christ's church in his own often incomprehensible ways. It may also be that the charismatic kernel of priestly celibacy manifests itself differently at different times and so requires a constant effort of identification and explanation. In any case, we are not the first bishops in the history

Daniel Pilarczyk, "The Changing Image of the Priest," *Origins*, July 3, 1986.

of the church to face the question of the connection between celibacy and priesthood.

What is the church trying to say, then, when it determines that priests must be celibate?

I would like to start from secular human experience. It is not unreasonable, though it is not common, for people to be so taken up with certain values as to want nothing else for their lives. They do not say that other values are bad, but only that they themselves wish to give all their energies to a specific human good—politics, science, the arts, sports. In the lives of people like this there is room for only one major commitment, not because of the smallness of their life but because of the size of that one commitment.

It was not too long ago that most large families had at least one of the children who chose not to marry for the sake of taking care of his or her parents as they grew older. I suspect you have had people ask you, as they have asked me, why they never hear any preaching in church on the value of a single life in the world. Remaining unmarried for a specific purpose is not monstrous or unreasonable.

Celebacy a Gift

The New Testament speaks of those who remain unmarried for the sake of Christ and his kingdom. This is not for everybody. It is a special gift which some are given for the good of the church at large. Such people are so enchanted, so fascinated by Christ and his kingdom, so caught up in their spell that they do not want to do anything else but work directly for Christ and the kingdom. They want their lives to have complete availability for apostolic service. In the process of living out this dedication to Christ and the church, they image him in a unique way. They offer special energies to the life of the church. They teach with their lives that there is a future way of living in which everyone will be fully and definitively taken up in Christ.

Here we are in the realm of charismatic enthusiasm. It is not so much a matter of giving up marriage for the sake of giving up something as it is a matter of extraordinary joy at finding a different treasure.

The Western [rite of the Roman Catholic] church has decided over the centuries that men of this type, and they only, would be ordained priests. Few in numbers? Perhaps. A fitting decision? I believe so.

Having said this, though, we have not yet said everything. I would now like to offer five caveats about celibacy and the way it is understood.

First, it is not the case that people have a vocation to the priesthood and then the church forces them to be celibate. Vocations come from a certain combination of human and divine gifts and from the discernment and call of the church through the bishop. The church's leadership over the centuries has discerned that only those with the gift of

celibacy should be called to priesthood. Logically, celibacy comes first, then priesthood. The two are separable things. We do not force priests to be celibate. We only invite those who are committed to celibacy to be priests.

Psychologically, it may happen the other way around. Men first become attracted to the priesthood and then consent to a life of celibacy because of the church's law. But even at that, the commitment to celibacy comes before priesthood is conferred.

Not a Man-Made Burden

In this context I would observe that when we speak of "the gift of celibacy" we can do so in two senses. From one point of view, it is a charismatic gift from God to certain individuals. From another, it is a gift from the candidate to the church, viz., a pledge of a lifetime of full and individual ministerial witness and service to God's people. The church has discerned that only those should be ordained to priesthood who are willing and able to offer this gift to the church.

"The celibate priest should be able to say, 'I love my people, and I do not love anybody else as much,' . . . as sincerely and straightforwardly as a married man would say it about his wife and children."

I would also observe that the very real pain, burdens and frustration that sometimes come with celibacy are not necessarily a sign that it is a man-made burden, unjustly imposed. All God's gifts, beginning with life itself, are heavy.

Second caveat. Celibacy does not play down matrimony. Such would be the case if being a priest were in itself and always better than being a lay person. If being a priest is "better" than being a lay person, and if you cannot be married and be a priest, then something is wrong with marriage. In fact, as I have said earlier, ordained priesthood exists for the sake of the church at large and cannot be properly envisaged except as a service to the people of God. (Note that Vatican II and other recent church teaching about celibacy do not speak of cultic purity on the part of the priest, a purity arising from sexual abstinence.)

Third. Celibacy is not so much a giving up, a discipline, but a style of life, indeed a style of loving. It is primarily positive. It implies an intensity of focus in the celibate's psychic energies. The portion of the church community entrusted to the priest is to play something of the same role in his life that family plays in the life of those who are married.

Celibacy needs affective expression. It is not true that the celibate gives up human affection. On the contrary, the celibate priest should be able to say, "I love my people, and I do not love anybody else as much," and he should be able to say this as sincerely and straightforwardly as a married man would say it about his wife and children. In fact, *Presbyterorum Ordinis* 14 tells us that the bond of priestly perfection which unifies the life and activity of the priest is nothing other than pastoral love. (This is not to deny, of course, that the priest requires the support of intimate friends beyond the limits of his ministry.)

Unseen Problems

Fourth. Celibacy is not a gift that comes all packaged and wrapped, requiring only to be used. Rather, celibacy is a willingness to risk, to risk everything on the direct service of Christ and the church. It is a wager that the celibate makes on the validity of his work for the kingdom. It is not a guarantee, but a call, a challenge, an opportunity. It requires constant attention and constant nourishment and development through contact with the Lord in prayer and through deliberate and explicit personal dedication to priestly ministry. Consequently, it is possible to cheat on celibacy, not just by sexual activity, but by self-indulgence, by selfishly limiting one's availability, by making the priesthood a job instead of a love affair.

Fifth caveat. Changing the church's policy of ordaining only celibates to priesthood could bring with it as many problems as it proposes to solve. These problems include those of financial support, of mobility, of numbers, of marriage strain and divorce, of tension between married and celibate priests. What effects would come from the necessary sense of loss which parishioners would feel as they learn that the priest is no longer "theirs" in the same way he was before? What implications about the church's teaching on human sexuality, about matrimony, and, indeed, about the nature of priesthood itself lie hidden in such a change?

To conclude, a case can be made for priestly celibacy. It is not the case that can be made for a geometry theorem, but rather the case that can be made for falling in love, for falling so in love with Christ and the service of his church that one is willing to take the position that nothing else in life really matters.

Daniel Pilarczyk is the Roman Catholic Archbishop of Cincinnati.

"The feminist response that justice requires equal sharing of all domestic responsibility by men and women is not a solution."

Feminism's Impact on Sex Roles Has Been Negative

Allan Bloom

Relations between the sexes have always been difficult, and that is why so much of our literature is about men and women quarreling. There is certainly legitimate ground to doubt their suitability for each other given the spectrum—from the harem to Plato's *Republic*—of imaginable and actually existing relations between them, whether nature acted the stepmother or God botched the creation by an afterthought, as some Romantics believed. That man is not made to be alone is all very well, but who is made to live with him? This is why men and women hesitated before marriage, and courtship was thought necessary to find out whether the couple was compatible, and perhaps to give them basic training in compatibility. No one wanted to be stuck forever with an impossible partner. But, for all that, they knew pretty much what they wanted from one another. The question was whether they could get it (whereas our question today is much more what is wanted). A man was to make a living and protect his wife and children, and a woman was to provide for the domestic economy, particularly in caring for husband and children. Frequently this did not work out very well for one or both of the partners, because they either were not good at their functions or were not eager to perform them. In order to assure the proper ordering of things, the transvestite women in Shakespeare, like Portia and Rosalind, are forced to masquerade as men because the real men are inadequate and need to be corrected. This happens only in comedies; when there are no such intrepid women, the situation turns into tragedy. But the assumption of male garb observes the proprieties or conventions. Men should be doing what the impersonating women are doing; and when the women have set things right, they become women

again and submit to the men, albeit with a tactful, ironical consciousness that they are at least partially playacting in order to preserve a viable order. The arrangement implicit in marriage, even if it is only conventional, tells those who enter into it what to expect and what the satisfactions are supposed to be. Very simply, the family is a sort of miniature body politic in which the husband's will is the will of the whole. The woman can influence her husband's will, and it is supposed to be informed by love of wife and children.

Reason To Fear the Worst

Now all of this has simply disintegrated. It does not exist, nor is it considered good that it should. But nothing certain has taken its place. Neither men nor women have any idea what they are getting into anymore, or, rather, they have reason to fear the worst. There are two equal wills, and no mediating principle to link them and no tribunal of last resort. What is more, neither of the wills is certain of itself. This is where the "ordering of priorities" comes in, particularly with women, who have not yet decided which comes first, career or children. People are no longer raised to think they ought to regard marriage as the primary goal and responsibility, and their uncertainty is mightily reinforced by the divorce statistics, which imply that putting all of one's psychological eggs in the marriage basket is a poor risk. The goals and wills of men and women have become like parallel lines, and it requires a Lobachevskyan imagination to hope they may meet.

The inharmoniousness of final ends finds its most concrete expression in the female career, which is now precisely the same as the male career. There are two equal careers in almost every household composed of educated persons under thirty-five. And those careers are not mere means to family ends. They are personal fulfillments. In this nomadic country it is more than likely that one of the partners will be forced, or have the opportunity, to take a job in a city other than the one where his or her spouse works. What to do? They can stay together with one partner sacrificing his career to the other, they can commute, or they can separate. None of these solutions is satisfactory. More important, what is going to happen is unpredictable. Is it the marriage or the career that will count most? Women's careers today are qualitatively different from what they were up to twenty years ago, and such conflict is now inevitable. The result is that both marriage and career are devalued.

"Neither men nor women have any idea what they are getting into anymore, or, rather, they have reason to fear the worst."

For a long time middle-class women, with the encouragement of their husbands, had been pursuing careers. It was thought they had a right to cultivate their higher talents instead of being household drudges. Implicit in this was, of course, the view that the bourgeois professions indeed offered an opportunity to fulfill the human potential, while family and particularly the woman's work involved in it were merely in the realm of necessity, limited and limiting. Serious men of good conscience believed that they must allow their wives to develop themselves. But, with rare exceptions, both parties still took it for granted that the family was the woman's responsibility and that, in the case of potential conflict, she would subordinate or give up her career. It was not quite serious, and she usually knew it. This arragement was ultimately untenable, and it was clear in which way the balance would tip. Couples agreed that the household was not spiritually fulfilling for women and that women have equal rights. The notion of a domestic life appropriate to women had become incredible. Why should not women take their careers as seriously as men take theirs, and have them be taken as seriously by men? Terrific resentment at the injustice done to women under the prevailing understanding of justice found its expression in demands seen as perfectly legitimate by both men and women, that men weaken the attachment to their careers, that they share equally in the household and the care of the children. Women's abandonment of the female persona was reinforced by the persona's abandoning them. Economic changes made it desirable and necessary that women work; lowering of infant mortality rates meant that women had to have fewer pregnancies; greater longevity and better health meant that women devoted a much smaller portion of their lives to having and rearing children; and the altered relationships within the family meant that they were less likely to find continuing occupation with their children and their children's children. At forty-five they were finding themselves with nothing to do, and forty more years to do in it. Their formative career years had been lost, and they were, hence, unable to compete with men. A woman who now wanted to be a woman in the old sense would find it very difficult to do so, even if she were to brave the hostile public opinion. In all of these ways the feminist case is very strong indeed. But, though the terms of marriage had been radically altered, no new ones were defined.

The Inadequate Feminist Response

The feminist response that justice requires equal sharing of all domestic responsibility by men and women is not a solution, but only a compromise, an attenuation of men's dedication to their careers and of women's to family, with arguably an enrichment in diversity of both parties but just as arguably a fragmentation of their lives. The question of who goes with whom in the case of jobs in different cities is unresolved and is, whatever may be said about it, a festering sore, a source of suspicion and resentment, and the potential for war. Morever, this compromise does not decide anything about the care of the children. Are both parents going to care more about their careers than about the children? Previously children at least had the unqualified dedication of one person, the woman, for whom their care was the most important thing in life. Is half the attention of two the same as the whole attention of one? Is this not a formula for neglecting children? Under such arrangements the family is not a unity, and marriage is an unattractive struggle that is easy to get out of, especially for men.

And here is where the whole business turns nasty. The souls of men—their ambitious, warlike, protective, possessive character—must be dismantled in order to liberate women from their domination. Machismo—the polemical description of maleness or spiritedness, which was the central *natural* passion in men's souls in the psychology of the ancients, the passion of attachment and loyalty—was the villain, the source of the difference between the sexes. The feminists were only completing a job begun by [Thomas] Hobbes in his project of taming the harsh elements in the soul. With machismo discredited, the positive task is to make men caring, sensitive, even nurturing, to fit the restructured family. Thus once again men must be re-educated according to an abstract project. They must accept the "feminine elements" in their nature. A host of Dustin Hoffman and Meryl Streep types invade the schools, popular psychology, TV and the movies, making the project respectable. Men tend to undergo this re-education somewhat sullenly but studiously, in order to avoid the opprobrium of the sexist label and to keep peace with their wives and girlfriends. And it is indeed possible to soften men. But to make them "care" is another thing, and the project must inevitably fail.

The Old Moral Order

It must fail because in an age of individualism, persons of either sex cannot be forced to be public-spirited, particularly by those who are becoming less so. Further, caring is either a passion or a virtue, not a description like "sensitive." A virtue governs a passion, as moderation governs lust, or courage governs fear. But what passion does caring govern? One might say possessiveness, but possessiveness is not to be governed these days—it is to be rooted out. What is wanted is an antidote to natural selfishness, but wishes do not give birth to horses, however much abstract moralism may demand them. The old moral order, however imperfect it may have been, at least moved toward the virtues by way of the passions. If men were self-concerned, that order tried to expand the scope of self-concern to include others, rather than commanding men to cease being concerned with themselves. To attempt the latter is both tyrannical and ineffective. A true political or social order requires the soul to be like a Gothic cathedral, with selfish stresses and strains helping to hold it up. Abstract moralism condemns certain keystones, removes them, and then blames both the nature of the stones and the structure when it collapses. The failure of agriculture in socialist collective farming is the best political example of this. An imaginary motive takes the place of a real one, and when the imaginary motive fails to produce the real effect, those who have not been motivated by it are blamed and persecuted. In family questions, inasmuch as men were understood to be so strongly motivated by property, an older wisdom tried to attach concern for the family to that motive: the man was allowed and encouraged to regard his family as his property, so he would care for the former as he would instinctively care for the latter. This was effective, although it obviously had disadvantages from the point of view of justice. When wives and children come to the husband and father and say, "We are not your property; we are ends in ourselves and demand to be treated as such," the anonymous observer cannot help being impressed. But the difficulty comes when wives and children further demand that the man continue to care for them as before, just when they are giving an example of caring for themselves. They object to the father's flawed motive and ask that it be miraculously replaced by a pure one, of which they wish to make use for their own ends. The father will almost inevitably constrict his quest for property, cease being a father and become a mere man again, rather than turning into a providential God, as others ask him to be. What is so intolerable about

the *Republic*, as Plato shows, is the demand that men give up their land, their money, their wives, their children, for the sake of the public good, their concern for which had previously been buttressed by these lower attachments. The hope is to have a happy city made up entirely of unhappy men. Similar demands are made today in an age of slack morality and self-indulgence. Plato taught that, however laudable justice may be, one cannot expect prodigies of virtue from ordinary people. Better a real city tainted by selfish motives than one that cannot exist, except in speech, and that promotes real tyranny.

Biology and Nature

I am not arguing here that the old family arrangements were good or that we should or could go back to them. I am only insisting that we not cloud our vision to such an extent that we believe that there are viable substitutes for them just because we want or need them. The peculiar attachment of mothers for their children existed, and in some degree still exists, whether it was the product of nature or nurture. That fathers should have exactly the same kind of attachment is much less evident. We can insist on it, but if nature does not cooperate, all our efforts will have been in vain. Biology forces women to take maternity leaves. Law can enjoin men to take paternity leaves, but it cannot make them have the desired sentiments. Only the rankest ideologue could fail to see the difference between the two kinds of leave, and the contrived and somewhat ridiculous character of the latter. Law may prescribe that the male nipples be made equal to the female ones, but they still will not give milk. Female attachment to children is to be at least partly replaced with promissory notes on male attachment. Will they be redeemed? Or won't everyone set up his own little separate psychological banking system?

"It is indeed possible to soften men. But to make them 'care' is another thing, and the project must inevitably fail."

Similarly, women, due to the unreliability of men, have had to provide the means for their own independence. This has simply given men the excuse for being even less concerned with women's well-being. A dependent, weak woman is indeed vulnerable and puts herself at men's mercy. But that appeal did influence a lot of men a lot of the time. The cure now prescribed for male irresponsibility is to make them more irresponsible. And a woman who can be independent of men has much less motive to entice a man into taking care of her and her children. In the same vein, I heard a female lieutenant-colonel on the radio explaining that the only thing standing in the way of woman's full equality in the military is male protectiveness. So, do away with it! Yet male protectiveness, based on masculine pride, and desire to gain the glory for defending a blushing woman's honor and life, was a form of relatedness, as well as a way of sublimating selfishness. These days, why should a man risk his life protecting a karate champion who knows just what part of the male anatomy to go after in defending herself? What substitute is there for the forms of relatedness that are dismantled in the name of the new justice?

Setting the Social Machine in Motion

All our reforms have helped strip the teeth of our gears, which can therefore no longer mesh. They spin idly, side by side, unable to set the social machine in motion. It is at this exercise in futility that young people must look when thinking about their future. Women are pleased by their successes, their new opportunities, their agenda, their moral superiority. But underneath everything lies the more or less conscious awareness that they are still dual beings by nature, capable of doing most things men do and also wanting to have children. They may hope otherwise, but they fully expect to pursue careers, to have to pursue careers, while caring for children alone. And what they expect and plan for is likely to happen. The men have none of the current ideological advantages of the women, but they can opt out without too much cost. In their relations with women they have little to say; convinced of the injustice of the old order, for which they were responsible, and practically incapable of changing the direction of the juggernaut, they wait to hear what is wanted, try to adjust but are ready to take off in an instant. They want relationships, but the situation is so unclear. They anticipate a huge investment of emotional energy that is just as likely as not to end in bankruptcy, to a sacrifice of their career goals without any clarity about what reward they will reap, other than a vague togetherness. Meanwhile, one of the strongest, oldest motives for marriage is no longer operative. Men can now easily enjoy the sex that previously could only be had in marriage. It is strange that the tiredest and stupidest bromide mothers and fathers preached to their daughters—"He won't respect you or marry you if you give him what he wants too easily"—turns out to be the truest and most probing analysis of the current situation. Women can say they do not care, that they want men to have the right motives or none at all, but everyone, and they best of all, knows that they are being, at most, only half truthful with themselves.

Allan Bloom is the author of The Closing of the American Mind *and co-director of the John M. Olin Center for Inquiry into the Theory and Practice of Democracy at the University of Chicago.*

"The women's movement has been one of the few vital movements that really stems from life."

Feminism's Impact on Sex Roles Has Been Positive

Betty Friedan

Editor's note: The following viewpoint is Betty Friedan's response to The Closing of the American Mind *by Allan Bloom. The previous viewpoint is excerpted from that book.*

In a talk I gave to the women's movement very early on, I said that our revolution is unique. True, our revolution was motivated by the seemingly abstract values of every revolution, by those values which have been a part of American ethos from the beginning: equality, freedom, the worth of the individual, the right to have some say and some control of our own destiny. But I asked then, and I have asked ever since, when have those values been wedded to the concrete reality of daily life? What was unique about the women's movement was that it wedded these values to life. An abstract concept of equality, the male model of equality, was never right for the women's movement.

If anything, the women's movement has always promoted a concept of equality that goes beyond the male model of equality, and the abstraction of male dominance this model represents. We had to bring nurture and compassion, which come from the service of life and which women live in their private lives, into larger society. Now, in theology, in medicine, in psychology, in education and politics and other areas, we have value that comes from female experience ejected into public and professional spheres.

Women's Advances

In theology, some of these brilliant new women rabbis and ministers bring values of life into theology that didn't exist when only men defined theology. Before, these women just cooked the church supper and weren't supposed to notice that

Betty Friedan, "Fatal Abstraction," *New Perspectives*, Winter 1988. Reprinted with permission.

the language of the prayer book insulted them.

In education, women were never considered as capable of moral, philosophical development as men. This is true whether we talk about Plato, Socrates, or Freud. But, for example, a few years ago Harvard professor of education Carol Gilligan used real life situations to test women and men on their moral development. She found that women are more capable of moral development than men when moral development is applied to real life.

In politics, women vote in higher percentages than men. Significantly, before women had a basis of independence, they voted like their husbands. Now, in the years since the women's movement, women vote very differently than men, and not just on questions of women's rights. Take child care. Child care is a crying need because in America today, either both parents work or a single parent works. But only Patricia Schroeder and the women's movement are really pushing legislation that would grant up to 16 weeks of job-protected parental leave to both mother and father for the birth, adoption, or serious illness of a child.

And, women tend to vote much more sharply against the candidate who seems to threaten life in terms of nuclear war, pollution of the environment, or the destruction of social programs.

So Bloom must be completely unaware of the reality of the feminist movement and of what has happened to women's lives and women's needs. He ignores the reality of life. In the last 15 years, the women's movement has been one of the few vital movements that really stems from life. Women, at least, have a sense of power and purpose beyond themselves.

The Neanderthal Family

Let's not kid ourselves about what the nuclear family used to be like when women had no freedom. Let's not kid ourselves about the compassion men had for that Neanderthal family of years gone by which now makes up less than 7% of the American populace. Men used to be the ones who had the freedom to get divorced and they got divorced. In the 50s, the divorce rate was already climbing, but women almost never sought divorce. Men had the right to beat their wives and children. Forget all this caring that men used to do!

And forget the image of the housewife, happy in her home. We have to consider, what is the nature of woman? Woman is not just a uterus. Woman is a uterus, but woman is also a brain. And woman is all the human abilities she shares with man.

This isn't new. Think of pioneer women, or of immigrant women in New York and Chicago who worked in sweat shops and factories; who kept their families alive and sent their children to school to learn a language that was not their own. These were strong women and their strength was good for their families.

"It was absolutely necessary that women define themselves as more than child-bearers, or as men's wives."

Only when men came home from World War II, demanding that women who had been working out in society return home, was women's strength perverted. Properly channeled feminine strength was then heaped onto the little suburban family.

As a result, women became monsters. Under the frills and curls and lilting laugh of Tennessee Williams' southern belle was a cannibal eating up her son. Women needed to fill their lives with more than shopping or mah jong or volunteer work that insulted their abilities. Jokes were made about Jewish mothers following their sons to college. Suppressed, women's strength became a cancer to the family.

New Roles for Women

So it was absolutely necessary that women define themselves as more than child-bearers, or as men's wives. Considering the 80-year life span modern American women can anticipate, these old roles can't possibly define a woman's whole life. When women started living longer, their life roles had to change. Now, women as well as men have a degree of access to every profession, have the opportunity to move up and articulate concrete values of life in many fields.

Tellingly, there is all kinds of research that proves women's mental health improved enormously after women ventured out of the home to expand their life roles. Twenty years ago, the Midtown Manhattan Longitudinal Study and the National Center for

Health Statistics showed that women's mental health consistently decreased after age 20, dramatically after age 40. When those studies were repeated a few years ago, women in their forties, fifties and sixties were as mentally healthy as women in their twenties and thirties. This is clearly important to the family as a whole.

Bloom is wrong. Feminism was not formed as a way to be free of family responsibilities. The family had to change when women came into the family as equals, as more than family servants, as people who are entitled to their human and American birthrights of equal opportunity to move in society. But this change was for the better. Feminism has been and will continue to be necessary for the strengthening of the family because women, healthier when participating in society, and men, enriched by giving more at home, make the family a more stable institution.

Where We Went Wrong

If you go back and reread *The Feminine Mystique*, you will see that I consider child bearing and child rearing an enormously powerful part of life. This is not a mystique; it's reality. In the face of hard economics, the choice to have a child becomes a profound statement of human values, an assertion of human priorities in defiance of pressures for material success. That women were faced with an impossible either/or choice between family and career was a mistake.

When women won the right to vote in 1920, they didn't take into account how the people who gave birth to children were also going to move in society and use the political rights they had won. All their energy had been geared to proving women were equal to men, to getting the vote and the right to control their own earnings and their own property. It was hard to face the real differences between women and men, and painful to face the fact that very few women were taking advantage of their rights on paper.

In the 60s, when I entered the picture, women still needed to focus on equality because not only women's rights, but the history of women's rights, feminism, and the "career woman"—the very terms of the women's movement—were all condemned in a society still defined by men. Women were expected to stay home and give up their careers because the post-World War II feminine mystique, which was powered by Freudian psychology and the economic structure of society, told them to do this. Symbolically, the spirited heroines of the 30s, like Katherine Hepburn and Betty Davis, were replaced by dumb, dreary housewife heroines like Doris Day who lost their husbands and whose children were cursed with pneumonia when they ventured away from the home, but who repented by getting pregnant again.

We were insulted by this image of the dumb housewife. We were insulted that nurses who may have taught three generations of surgeons had to stand when the doctor entered the room and were paid a tenth of the doctor's salary. We were insulted by the competent woman at home on her pedestal and the competent secretary who ran the office but who could not dream of being an executive. Women weren't supposed to apply the idea of equality to their situations. The term "sex discrimination" didn't even exist. We were angry, and we had to break out of the feminine mystique that defined us solely in terms of the child bearer.

A Distorted Message

But not to the repudiation of child bearing. That was never my message. There were some extreme, radical feminists who applied the doctrine of class war to the situation of women and men, and who chanted, "Down with men! Down with the family!" The media harped on this because it made good copy and diverted attention from the basic reality that was affecting every woman's life: we were finally taking ourselves seriously.

If the media distorted feminism's message, so does Bloom distort serious feminism when he implies that feminism repudiates the values of white Western male society. The values of freedom, equality, and human dignity originated in such a society, and have been crucial to the women's movement itself—even though today, the cutting edge of society's evolution may well come from the experience of women, and from people of cultural and religious origins who have not played a central part in our culture up to now.

I used to tell feminists long before I wrote *The Second Stage*, "If this really were a war of women against men or against the family, we would never win. Nor would we want to." There are profound biological, psychological, social, emotional, human bonds that connect men and women.

The real leaders of the feminist movement knew this all along. We always wanted more than "dressing for success." Now, in the Second Stage, we have to move beyond the male model of equality. We can't even live equality when the structures of the work world are based on men who have wives to take care of the details of life.

A Changed World

The economy has changed. Living in the old family form where you have the restricted-to-the-home mother and bread-winner father now means that father has to be making quite a bit of money. More and more, a family needs two incomes to survive. This is the reality of the family today.

We must restructure home and work so women can freely choose to have children, and also move freely in society. This will entail articulating life

values in the public and political sphere: this time not only by women, but by men, who will have more concrete life-oriented values and not fall into the abstract trap of Bloom as they begin to share in the daily responsibilities of child rearing.

Forget women, forget women's rights for a moment. Polarizing the family is dangerous in today's world. We have to have values of the larger human family. Polarizing the family would doom the family to a terrible economic crisis by keeping women at home or locked into low-paying jobs, divert attention from real economic problems that require new solutions, and leave men free to play win-lose games with dangerous weapons. We can't send women home again.

What we need are more real choices. Men were always supposed to aim for as much choice as possible. Women weren't. Women were the passive face of Eve. The women's movement aims to gain a greater degree of human freedom for women so they can move as full people and have more choice, including really responsible human choices about having children. There is a price attached to having a child today, because if you want to bond with your child and need parental leave of four or six months to do this, you can lose your job. We don't have enough options concerning child care.

Men, too, want more real choices. Men have been absolutely chained to their bread winning role. They don't have as many choices that have to do with the values of life. In a sense, the woman's movement made men aware that they can choose to affirm the values of life.

> "The women's movement aims to gain a greater degree of human freedom for women so they can . . . have more choice, including really responsible human choices about having children."

And there is great need for new forms of family, and new forms of family commitment. The reality of the family today is diversity. The American Home Economics Association gave a really good definition of family some years ago at the White House Conference on Family: The family is two or more people who commit themselves to caring for each other, who are responsible to each other, and who share a common future. The family is who you come home to. And it is these bonds, the mutuality, the sharing, and the responsibility that define the family, not blood.

So in the US today, families are as diverse as trees with their many branches. Family is mother and father, with both of them working, or divorced.

Family is also single parents and children. Family is many older people living together because the tax and social security laws make it easier economically for them not to marry. And it's more and more people who are going to be living into their 70s, 80s, and 90s. It is people, with or without sexual bonds, pooling resources and sharing homes.

I am not denying that there is a biological basis of human nature. But we can also choose our families, and what we choose is based on the options open to us, and on the way our perception of these options is molded by society. Attempting to define what the family should look like is an abstraction.

Back to the Girdle

I would like to tell Bloom about the metaphor I use when I talk to the young girls who have grown up taking women's rights for granted. These young women of today say, "I am not a feminist, but I'm going to be an astronaut. I am not a feminist, but I am going to be a Supreme Court Justice."

I ask them, "How many of you have ever worn a girdle?" They laugh. I tell them that not long ago, every woman from the age of 12 to 92, whether she weighed 70 pounds or 270 pounds, pasted her flesh into rigid plastic sausage casing that made it hard for her to breathe and move. No woman questioned wearing one; it's what being a woman meant.

"We know that it is so much better being a woman . . . when you can be yourself and use your voice and use your eyes and let your heart feel fully and affirm your own sexuality."

"How can you know what it felt like when being a woman meant you always wore a girdle," I challenge, "when you wear nothing but panty hose under blue jeans, or nothing at all, or bikini briefs? How can you know what being a women meant when you wore a girdle over your head, over your eyes, over your mouth, over your heart, over your sexual organs, to say nothing of over your belly itself?"

But we knew. We lived through the change. We know that it is so much better being a woman when you don't have to wear that girdle, when you can be yourself and use your voice and use your eyes and let your heart feel fully and affirm your own sexuality. And I say, "You better be careful, as you struggle to move in your new high heels and super short mini skirts, that they aren't going to put you back in that girdle." Bloom is trying to put them back in that girdle.

This would be mad. With the new economic problems of today, with the serious complexities of our world, it would be dangerous to go back to the girdle. We have to go forward. We have to be able to move, and live, and raise our families and choose to have children, and if we must, help our families survive. Men and women need to share parental responsibilities as well as responsibility to the future. In this Second Stage, we need to take on, not retreat from, a complete restructuring of the nature of power.

Betty Friedan, a founder of the modern women's movement, is the author of The Feminine Mystique *and* The Second Stage.

"The modern women's movement has not just been anti-men; it has also been profoundly anti-children and anti-motherhood."

Feminism Has Harmed the Family

Sylvia Ann Hewlett

The feminists of the modern women's movement made one gigantic mistake: They assumed that modern women wanted nothing to do with children. As a result, they have consistently failed to incorporate the bearing and rearing of children into their vision of a liberated life. This "mistake" has had serious repercussions. . . .

Some feminists rage at babies; other trivialize, or denigrate them. Very few have attempted to integrate them into the fabric of a full and equal life. When Betty Friedan wrote *The Feminine Mystique* in 1963, she described the deep well of frustration faced by homemakers as "the problem that has no name." One might say that *motherhood is the problem that modern feminists cannot face.*

My own experience at Barnard College illustrates this point very well. The college, in refusing to develop a maternity policy, exhibited a profound indifference to the whole issue of reconciling professional and maternal responsibilities—this despite Barnard's reputation as a bastion of women's rights. My colleagues, many of whom were active feminists, were hostile toward such a policy and accused me of trying to "take a free ride." At the time I felt bewildered and betrayed. It was somehow a lot more difficult to take this kind of treatment from Barnard College than from some stronghold of male privilege. After all, if my liberated female colleagues did not think I deserved any time off to deal with miscarriage or premature birth, maybe they were right and I was just being self-indulgent. I have since discovered that their reaction to my predicament was part of a larger trend. The modern women's movement has not just been anti-men; it has also been profoundly anti-children and anti-motherhood. . . .

It is well known that the first targets of radical feminist rhetoric were men. According to the Redstocking Manifesto, "*All men* receive economic, sexual and psychological benefits from male supremacy. *All men* have oppressed women." Men were enemy number one, but family, marriage, and children also came under direct attack because they were the mechanisms through which women's second-class status was perpetuated through time. "Freedom for women cannot be won without the abolition of marriage." However, since women as wives and mothers play a central role in all aspects of family life, they too became prime targets of the movement. To be a nurturing and empathetic mother and to be a loving and supportive wife—the overriding goals of women who grew to maturity in the 1950s—were seen as signs of weakness and inadequacy. These attributes and these roles were to be stamped out in the brave new world of liberated women. The problem with being a woman could not be taken care of by getting rid of oppression or even by destroying the oppressors; it was wrapped up in *being a feminine woman.* In the late sixties and early seventies significant numbers of young feminists rejected the whole package—marriage, motherhood, and children—as a bad life choice for any woman. To be liberated came to mean wiping out all special female characteristics, leaving behind an androgenous shell of abstract personhood. Stripped of their men and their children, these unfettered women could then join the mainstream and clone the male competitive model in the marketplace.

Fleeing the Domestic World

At least some of the new wave feminists were fleeing from the ultradomestic world of the 1950s. Betty Friedan was typical. When she wrote *The Feminine Mystique*, she was struggling to free herself from fifteen years as a suburban housewife, years which featured three children and a failed marriage. Her own salvation was wrapped up in dismissing homemaking as comprising "tasks for feeble minded girls and eight year olds," and it was to be twenty years before she could look motherhood in the eye again. In her 1982 book *The Second Stage*, written when she was enjoying the pleasures of grandmotherhood, she acknowledges the central role of children and family in women's lives. Then she was able to say that "the failure of the women's movement was its blind spot about the family. It was our own extreme reaction against the wife-mother role."

A Blind Spot

Gloria Steinem is an example of another genre—the modern feminist leader who has chosen not to have children. This decision is undoubtedly colored by her personal history. In her powerful and touching essay "Ruth's Song," Steinem describes her mother, Ruth, as "a spirited and adventurous young woman who struggled out of a working-class family and into college, who found work she loved." But all this was before "she gave up her career to help my father." Ruth's first bout of mental illness "followed years of trying to take care of a baby [and] be the wife of a kind but financially irresponsible man." Ruth's daughter Gloria has obviously done her best to avoid such traps as marriage and babies, and this is reflected in her feminist perspective. In her 1983 book *Outrageous Acts and Everyday Rebellions* Steinem collects together twenty-seven essays. They represent the best of her writing and are impressively diverse, ranging from a piece on "The International Crime of Genital Mutilation" to a poignant essay entitled "In Praise of Women's Bodies." Aside from the description of her mother's life, not one page is devoted to motherhood, family, or children.

"The failure of the women's movement was its blind spot about the family."

Most of the women who were on the cutting edge of the women's movement in the late sixties and seventies were trying to obliterate those bright and smiling housewife-mothers of the 1950s with their "unique femininity" and their devotion to the bearing and raising of children. They were not impressed by women's "God given sensationally unique ability to wear skirts." In many instances the doll-like creatures of the fifties did not wear well. During the countercultural rebellion of the 1960s millions of them were tossed on the scrap heap by their husbands and became pathetic "displaced homemakers"; others dealt with the "empty nest syndrome" by the liberal use of Valium and alcohol.

If the lives of our mothers had been less artificial (or more viable), modern women might not have had to rebel so radically. In any event, contemporary feminists "threw the baby out with the bathwater." Twenty-five years of the feminine mystique and a birthrate rivaling that of India meant that anything which smacked of motherhood became anathema to the modern women's movement.

Attacking Motherhood

We are often told that those "libbers" alienated ordinary women because of their extravagant rhetoric and behavior. They burned their bras, called respectable men chauvinistic pigs, and ordinary folks tuned out. I don't find this explanation very convincing. Every revolution requires its polemics since oppressors are usually deaf to reasoned whispers. Much more negative than the language of the movement has been the fact that is has alternately ignored, reviled, and lashed out at the most widely shared experience of women (after sex), motherhood. In so doing the movement alienated its main constituency. The great majority of women have children at some point during their lives, and few of these women ever cease to love their sons and daughters. For the majority of mothers their children constitute the most passionate attachment of their lives. It is absurd to expect to build a coherent feminist movement, let alone a separatist feminist movement, when you exclude and denigrate the deepest emotion in women's lives. It is difficult to build a women's movement on an anti-men platform, but it could probably be done. The modern world is, after all, populated with divorcées, widows, gays, and singles, many of whom bear grudges against the male sex. But it is impossible to build a mass women's movement on an anti-child, anti-mother platform.

Despite this logic, modern feminists have not been restrained in their treatment of women with children. The views of feminist Juliet Mitchell are typical. In *Women's Estate* she describes women with families as inclined to "small-mindedness, petty jealousy, irrational emotionality and random violence, dependency, competitive selfishness and possessiveness, passivity, a lack of vision and conservatism." It is almost necessary to remind oneself that this is a portrait drawn not by a misogynist but by a feminist. Mitchell goes further: If women in families are despicable, the family itself is, "By its very nature . . . there to prevent the future.". . .

An Ignored Topic

It is easier to find feminist positions on abortion, rape, the female orgasm, the rights of lesbians, and genital mutilation in the third world than to find out what feminists think about motherhood. In a popular anthology of writing from the women's liberation movement, *Sisterhood Is Powerful*, only one out of seventy-four essays has anything to do with motherhood. One can read an essay on "The Politics of Orgasm". . . but it is difficult to find anything on childbearing or childraising, which are the central issues of most women's lives.

It is important to note that hostility toward children has not been limited to the radical wing of the feminist movement. The mainstream of the women's movement has been indifferent to motherhood and family, and at times this indifference has shaded into antipathy.

"It is impossible to build a mass women's movement on an anti-child, anti-mother platform."

For the last fifteen years the national feminist organizations (such as NOW and WEAL) have given top priority to the ERA and abortion. Issues such as access to credit, equal educational opportunities, and getting women elected to political office have constituted a second tier of goals. Child care has been at the bottom of the scale of priorities, and . . . maternity leave hasn't even made it onto the feminist agenda.

The various platforms of the movement generally include child care, but treatment of this issue is always perfunctory. For example, at the 1977 International Women's Year conference in Houston, child care was hardly touched upon. The burning issues of the conference were the ERA, abortion, and sexual preference. In the thirty-page "National Plan of Action" that resulted from this conference, child care occupied half a page. At other meetings child care has been mixed up with issues of reproductive freedom and control over one's body. For example, the Congress to Unite Women called for the "elimination of all laws and practices that compel women to bear children against their will." This congress also strongly advocated "research in extrauterine gestation." Mainstream feminists have generally treated motherhood as something most women want to avoid.

Low Priority

In an interview, child-care expert Dana Friedman talked to me about the six years she spent in Washington, D.C., lobbying, trying to get various pieces of child-care legislation through Congress. As Dana puts it, "The feminist groups never took the lead on child-care issues. It's not that in the end they didn't sign off on child-care initiatives, but they never put any real effort into this area." Dana paused and then said reflectively, "It's as though they wanted to look good—they didn't want to be accused of not supporting government funding for child care. But they viewed child care as an issue that was too connected to motherhood—too related to the role they were trying to downplay. At the Houston Conference, child care was number fourteen on a list of goals that had fifteen items on it. It think that's a pretty accurate reflection of the importance of child care to feminists—it is priority number fourteen."

Sylvia Ann Hewlett is an author and the vice president for economic studies at the United Nations Association.

*"Feminists and the progressive
movement have done more for families,
real flesh-and-blood families, than the
right will ever do."*

viewpoint 98

Feminism Has Helped
the Family

Noreen Connell

For the past few years, first quietly and now
vociferously, critics have called for the women's
movement to focus more on "pro-family" issues.
With the publication of Sylvia Ann Hewlett's *A
Lesser Life* and the controversy over a case
challenging California's pregnancy-leave law, the
debate has drawn national attention.

Criticism comes from several directions. Some of
our friends advocate a midcourse correction in our
movement's priorities. They caution that our defense
of legal abortion and civil rights for lesbians and gay
men is alienating us from the mainstream. The crux
of their argument is that by developing a national
family policy, the National Organization for Women
and other women's rights groups could take back
ground lost to the right wing.

A convincing case can be made that feminists and
the progressive movement have done more for
families, real flesh-and-blood families, than the right
will ever do. We've lobbied, demonstrated and
campaigned for child care, flexible work schedules,
changes in insurance coverage, parental leave, food
stamps, the enforcement of child-support judgments,
work sharing, housing, decent working conditions
and good health care. The right's reaction to these
family support measures is that they're too
expensive—something that doesn't trouble them
about new weapons.

Definitions of "Family"

Yet efforts by feminists and progressives to
convince the electorate of this case have not
succeeded. The sterling records of vice President
Walter Mondale and Representative Geraldine
Ferraro on family issues did not sway the voters
who say they hold traditional family values. Thus,

this hypothetical feminist "pro-family" strategy that
our friendly critics advocate has already been played
out in the day-to-day world of politics without much
success. Having engaged in numerous shouting
matches with right-wingers on who is more pro-
family, I have come to the conclusion that "family"
means something different to each side. When
feminists and progressives talk about the family, we
mean working parents with high mortgage payments
and college costs, single heads of households, and
homemakers who freely choose to work in the
home. We envision a unit bound together by love
that must be strengthened against economic hardship
and harsh employment practices.

When rightists talk about the family, they are not
talking about the diversity of families in late-
twentieth-century America, or even about the
romanticized family of Norman Rockwell. Their call
for a return to traditional family values is a much
darker vision and more counterrevolutionary than
most of us want to understand. By "family" they
mean a relationship based on male authority and
female economic dependence. In their eyes there is
no contradiction between being pro-family and
slashing budgets for child care or for programs to
prevent child abuse, or limiting food stamps for
single women who head their households.

Their call for a return to traditional family values
means eradicating all programs that lighten the
burden of child care for women or that allow them
the economic support to raise children without a
male breadwinner. Unfortunately, some women,
emboldened by education and the American
tradition of individualism, aspire to a life beyond
staying home and caring for their husbands and
children. To keep such women from sabotaging the
social ideal, the right strenuously opposes
comparable worth, careers open to merit, affirmative
action, flexitime, child care, abortion, social and

financial support for raising children out of wedlock and the enforcement of laws concerning husbands' violence against wives. This is the right's pro-family agenda.

The modern women's movement has made remarkable, if uneven, progress over the past twenty years. We have secured legal rights to equal employment and education, birth control and abortion, and have seen restrictive "protective" labor legislation struck down. None of these actions have been anti-family, including our advocacy of civil rights for lesbians. These activities have been a seamless web, all part of a movement to recognize the individuality of women, to make child rearing a voluntary option and to end the centuries-long sacrifice of the needs of women to the responsibilities of the family.

Regression

The right's agenda is also a seamless web. In the past decade it has attempted to checkmate the women's movement in every area, with considerable help from the Reagan Administration. It has cut government support for families, especially those headed by single women; it has attempted to make abortion illegal again and has harassed women who get abortions and doctors who perform them; and it has tried to eliminate Federal funding for battered-women's shelters. The Administration has backed away from affirmative action and equal employment opportunity laws.

"The modern women's movement has made remarkable . . . progress over the past twenty years. . . . None of [our] actions have been anti-family."

Recently a new set of critics of the women's movement has entered the debate over the role of women and the family. These are the neofeminists—represented most clearly by Hewlett but also by Dorothy Wickenden, in an article in the May 5 [1986] *New Republic* titled "What NOW?"—who claim that the American women's movement has not only failed women but has made life harder for them. They argue that while European feminists secured maternity leaves and child-care programs for women, American feminists have ignored the needs of working mothers in pursuit of an ideal of equality that disregards the biological differences between the sexes. This is no call for a midcourse correction. Rather, neofeminists say, feminist leaders should step aside. Instead of their misguided quest for equality, we need laws that "protect" the working mother and the family.

The case made by neofeminists is based on what

could charitably be called misinformation, or uncharitably called lies. All European governments implemented maternity-leave policies and most had child-care programs long before the modern European women's movement emerged. Feminism had nothing to do with those policies. Postwar labor shortages, the election of democratic socialist governments, a desire to limit the influx of workers from other countries and the European tradition of legislating employment practices for the private sector all contributed.

The neofeminist portrayal of the American women's movement is just as inaccurate. Even a cursory review of the activities of American feminists reveals that the neofeminist version of them is a straw woman. Demands for child care and leaves of absence for parents have been on the political agenda of NOW since its founding. Although the Equal Rights Amendment and abortion, both under right-wing siege, were its priorities, twenty-three out of fifty policy statements adopted by NOW at national conventions over the past twenty years have dealt with family-related issues. In Washington, organizations like the Women's Equity Action League lobby day after day for extended insurance coverage, parental leave and civil service flexitime and work sharing. If neofeminists do not bother to research the modern American women's movement, they could at least look through an issue of *Ms.*, which typically contains articles about child rearing and reproductive health. After all, most women in the women's movement are, or will be, mothers.

Feminists' Success

But the most insidious argument of the neofeminists is not their distortion of recent European and American history but their attack on the women's movement for not achieving the rights they advocate. Here, too, they are misguided. Day care in this country is limited and inadequate because President Nixon vetoed the Comprehensive Child Development Act in 1971, not because the women's movement was obsessed with the E.R.A. Representative Patricia Schroeder's modest bill providing for unpaid parental leaves is being opposed by the U.S. Chamber of Commerce, not by feminists. If the women's movement in the United States had ever had the access to a President that the right does to Reagan, we might justifiably be blamed for neglecting working mothers. But since 1966 the best the feminist movement has ever secured from the White House was Jimmy Carter's lukewarm support for the E.R.A. That the women's movement has made the gains it has is testimony to two decades of hard work on the local, state and Federal levels, not evidence that feminists have refused to use some kind of magic wand for the benefit of working mothers. Our victories have cost the government nothing (abortion) or very little (battered-women's shelters). The neofeminists blame the women's movement for its lack of power. But it will take more than the women's movement to achieve a multimillion-dollar national child-care program or a law requiring employers to provide parental leave. It will take the concentrated and combined energies of feminists, trade unionists, the liberal business community, elected officials and progressive activists.

"Day care in this country is . . . inadequate because President Nixon vetoed the Comprehensive Child Development Act in 1971, not because the women's movement was obsessed with the E.R.A."

Neither our friendly critics nor the neofeminists seem to understand—nor do the journalists who barrage us with articles and television programs about the problems of the working mother—that the women's movement advocates child-care and family responsibilities shared by both parents. Women will never escape the double burden of work and family unless men assume the day-to-day hard work at home. Both our friendly and unfriendly critics share the traditional assumption that child rearing and homemaking are the exclusive responsibility of women; by extension, they also assume that pro-family activism is the exclusive responsibility of the women's movement.

Men Must Become Pro-Family

Our critics are wrong. It is not the women's movement that needs to be more pro-family; it is men. Despite an occasional diaper change or a young lawyer's refusal to work on weekends, Betty Friedan's second stage has not occurred. Why should it? Working fathers already have a system of child care, their wives, and they are not interested in giving it up. Only when men become pro-family at the most basic level, at home, will male union leaders and business executives and politicians and, yes, progressive activists be ready to stop ponificating about the need for child care and do something about it. We'll know the time has come when *Esquire* runs articles about the tough lot of working fathers, and political commentators question whether a male candidate should run for office while his children are still so young.

Noreen Connell is New York State president of the National Organization for Women.

"There is no more important task before us than to respond to the challenge feminist women have set before us."

Men Should Embrace Feminism

Chris Brazier

Editor's note: The following viewpoint originally appeared in a special magazine issue focusing on the subject of men and masculinity.

My grandfather died as I was putting this issue together. He was 84 and illness had led us to expect the worst. And I knew when I visited him the weekend before his death that I was speaking to him for the last time. As I stood beside the bed he looked shrunken into himself, helpless and weak though still mentally alert; he seemed like a little boy, lost inside a withered frame. I couldn't say anything meaningful to him—about whether he was afraid at the prospect of death, perhaps—since neither his wife nor his son, my father, were able to have such conversations with him.

A Promise

But then it had always been so. Intimate talk about anything that went much deeper than the surface level of work and everyday happenings always made him profoundly uncomfortable. In this he was typical of many men, though there is no such thing as 'a typical man'. And as I meditated at his funeral on what he had meant to me I kept coming back unavoidably to this one image of him standing by the fireplace, his hand jangling the coins in his pocket as a way of absorbing his embarrassment at the experience of one-to-one communication. Once I remember he and my father stood together at the fireplace talking, both of them jangling the coins in their pockets. And I promised myself that I'd never be like that with my father or my sons, that I'd work to change the patterns of masculinity laid down for the male members of my family. . . .

'Masculinity' is itself something of a taboo area in

our culture. True, it is a culture dominated by men, and we will sound off endlessly about most things under the sun. But, as Simone de Beauvoir once pointed out, men are always the subject rather than the object of discussion. We never talk about what it is actually like to be a man. Instead we simply react when forced to by the urging of our female partner or a feminist at work. We wait for women to raise the issue and then adjust accordingly. This is why almost all heterosexual men who have thought seriously about masculinity have been obliged to do so by entering a relationship with a feminist—at which point they are doing it for the sake of their own comfort.

This is understandable but it is time we stopped seeing 'women's concerns' as only being relevant to us when they smack us in the face. Women have enough trouble dealing with their own problems in a sexist world without having to take all the responsibility for changing men, too. It's time we stopped relying on their emotional strength, their knowledge of relationships and built up some of our own.

Recognizing Oppression

But we can't begin to do that until we recognize that masculinity as it is currently constructed is oppressive to women. . . . We earn 90 per cent of the world's income and own 99 per cent of its property. We commit around 90 per cent of crimes of violence, and 100 per cent of rapes.

When I say 'we' do these things you may think I strike a false note. After all, it is probable that you, like me, have only a modest income and little or no property; that you have never committed a violent crime, let alone a rape. Why should we be equated with men who run countries and corporations, men who rape and kill?

We can ask women not to lump us indiscriminately together with hostile men. But in return we

Chris Brazier, "Birth of a New Man," *New Internationalist*, September 1987. Reprinted with permission.

need to recognize that we benefit from sexism every day of our lives, whether we like it or not. There is, for instance, the way that male-dominated workplaces tend to reproduce themselves by appointing more men. The way even sympathetic men leave more of the burden of childcare and housework on women. But there are also more everyday, less obvious benefits, such as the confidence and power we can feel in public situations because they are populated and defined mainly by men.

This is true even when we walk down a street, especially at night. On rare occasions we might find this frightening—when we have to pass a group of aggressive or drunken men, for example. But a women is likely to experience this feeling as an almost everyday experience. Some don't go out at night at all. Others make elaborate transportation arrangements to avoid walking alone. Those who do will often have a nagging fear in the back of their minds—trying not to think about the shadows, worrying about those male footsteps echoing behind her which just might be those of an attacker. This might seem exaggerated. But if so it probably only shows how safe we feel by comparison. The echoing footsteps are quite likely to be ours, after all. *We* know that nothing is farther from our minds than rape or attack. But the woman ahead of us does not. By simply crossing the street or waiting we could put her mind at rest.

Beyond Guilt

Guilt, guilt, guilt. If we manage to get past our initial threatened reaction, this is often the next phase—despair sets in. If anything from walking along the street to taking a job in an already male-dominated setting can be seen as a contribution to the problem, then aren't we all hopeless cases?

I don't believe this for a moment. Guilt is a negative emotion which paralyses us, makes us feel worthless and incapable. And a lot of the early writing and thinking done by anti-sexist men in the 1970s was redolent of this guilt. But there is so much we can do and so much to be done if we are serious. . . . In order to be usefully anti-sexist we have to listen to what women are saying and take political action to help their cause. But we must also be prepared to change ourselves, often in quite painful ways. This is a tough business. But it might also be a great adventure. To understand why, we need to go back to the beginning.

What Kind of Baby?

Imagine you're encountering someone else's baby for the first time. You look at the strange, scrunched-up little face, you push your finger into its grasping hand and your heart melts at the vulnerability of this tiny human being. But something is nagging at you and you feel uneasy until you know one key

thing—whether this is a girl or a boy. Why should this be? I think it can only be because we need to slot the baby into a box marked 'male' or 'female' in our minds—*and to respond accordingly*. This may result in the most imperceptible changes in attitude and behaviour—particularly among those of us who consciously try to be anti-sexist. But I can't see any other reason for that small movement of relief in us when we find out a baby's sex.

"Masculinity and femininity are not written down in tablets of stone or of DNA."

The world at large, of course, is much more crass and unashamed in its preconceptions. And the result is that boys and girls are set out along different routes. Some argue that biology has something to do with it. This may well be true but it almost doesn't matter, since it is clear that society and culture, which are human creations, fully capable of change, have an overwhelming influence upon us. If this were not so then you would have to say that Iranian women, for example, were more genetically predisposed than Canadian women to wear veils and be submissively invisible, which is clearly absurd.

Masculinity and femininity are not written down in tablets of stone or of DNA. And that is a message of hope. Because although no parents can exclude all the sexist influences upon their children, they can certainly alter the mix. Indeed every one of us, parents or not, can do our bit to change that mix of influences by our own example. Minute and undiscernible it may be, but this is one area in which we all have an effect.

Boys learn how to behave by hint and example from parent and peer group, television and teacher. They learn to be more interested in activity and competition than in communicating and listening, than in being sensitive to the moods and rhythms of people and places. This is often quite a painful process for them. Very few boys are as rough, tough and unfeeling, for example, as the often violent culture of the playground expects them to be.

Two Michaels

Take eight-year-old Michael, the son of a friend, who is torn between the macho boy his schoolfriends expect him to be and the more sensitive creature required at home. We settled down to talk one night as an alternative to a bedtime story and the novelty of having his words recorded helped him respond very well to the challenge of an adult conversation.

I mean there's a bad side of me and a good side of

me and sometimes the bad Michael comes out and sometimes the good Michael comes out. Because they're fighting . . . to come out.

What happens when the bad side comes out?

I just start to fight.

What makes you start to fight?

What my body says to me. It says you've got to do the things that you want to do. When someone does something bad to you you've got to do what you want to do to them. Like if they hurt your feelings you have to do something, not just walk off. You have to do something, tell somebody or just punch them.

Where do you feel more like the real you?

At home.

Do you think one day there'll only be one Michael?

Mmm. Maybe when I'm grown up.

Not all of us would express this so starkly—in the classic terms of the split personality. Nor did most of us, coming as we did from homes and parents with conventional assumptions about boys and girls, have to face up to this conflict quite so early as Michael. But it is a drama we have nevertheless all undergone. Learning to be a man is partly learning how to hide and cover the more sensitive side of ourselves. This, we are taught, we have to do in order to survive in a violent world. We have, as the Sergeant says every week in *Hill Street Blues*, to 'do it to them before they do it to us'. This helps us to 'get on', to fix our eyes on the far horizon in the interests of 'getting the job done'.

"Our preoccupation with doing and achieving things is a real hindrance when it comes to understanding our own inner selves."

People around us can be damaged by this 'far horizon' approach. But we are damaged by it, too. A man, as Elvis Costello once sang, is 'shot with his own gun'. The same weapons in his personality which protect him in the big wide world also leave him lost in his own personality. Our preoccupation with doing and achieving things is a real hindrance when it comes to understanding our own inner selves or forming and maintaining close relationships. This is why we rely on women to unlock this area for us, and where the common saying arises that a man 'has his rough edges knocked off by a woman'.

Back in the 1970s some men concluded from this that they were just as much victims of their 'sex role' as were women. They conceived the idea of 'men's liberation', when there can't really be any such thing. What they forgot is that men have power over women and not the reverse. It is men who have constructed a world for their own benefit—and men who must be prepared to relinquish their power by supporting women's rights in the home, the workplace and society at large.

Light Years Away

But at least these men were putting some serious thought into what had made them men. Most men are still light years away from understanding the issues, let alone from embodying the newly popular marketing image of 'the new man' which is referred to on the tongue-in-cheek cover of this magazine. We could all come up with depressing evidence that we have a long way to go. My own mind goes back to the bar at Johannesburg's Jan Smuts airport. I was joined by a white man keen to engage me in conversation. As most of us will, he chose what he thought would be uncontentious shared ground for his opening comment. He said: 'There are some tasty pieces of meat on this flight, aren't there?' What he meant, since you may well be in need of an interpreter, was that he found some of the women sexually attractive.

I should perhaps have answered that I was a vegetarian. I should certainly have done more than splutter apoplectically into my orange juice and then pointedly ignore him. But, like most men, I am often weak when it comes to telling other men that their sexism is unacceptable to this one, at least, of their brothers. I've had some successes along the way too. But somehow it's always easier to opt for a quiet life and keep your head down than to confront that sexist joke at work, that casual aside about a woman's appearance.

Sexist Pressures

I'm sure you know the pressures I mean. Ever since adolescence, socializing with other men has meant being drawn into this kind of banter. Yet another part of learning to be 'a regular guy' in this society is learning the codes of conduct that are acceptable between men, knowing the right prejudiced levers to pull. We joke about straight sex to prove we're healthy red-blooded males who lust after women. We joke about gay sex to prove we're not homosexual—and so scared are we of being thought so that when we're in a public toilet we stand in lines, eyes straight ahead in case that man in the next urinal might think we have an abiding interest in his lower anatomy.

I'd be surprised if there was a single man reading this who is genuinely free of complicity in this kind of sexism. We have to be brave and leap in there to pull up other men on their sexist witticisms and remarks, no matter how much social discomfort this causes us. Taking responsibility for our own sexism and that of other men is a bottom line—but it has positive spin-offs too. By accepting responsibility for other men we are holding out the hope of another kind of communication and relation with them, beyond the backslapping banter. At the moment our male friendships too often subsist on a ritualized level—we rarely expose in them our deeper feelings and anxieties, saving those instead for one or two selected women. But our male friends should be worth more to us than this.

"Taking responsibility for our own sexism and that of other men is a bottom line."

There may be a long way to go but I think there are still grounds for hope. Men are already experiencing some of the beneficial effects of feminism, whether they realize it or not. They are finding themselves in more equal relationships with strong, independent women. Such relationships may require painful compromise at first but they ultimately provide a mutual understanding undreamed of in the past. And men are also beginning to participate more actively in fatherhood, from their presence at birth through to a more intimate involvement with their children later on.

Benefits of Fatherhood

This renovated fatherhood could be very important. The special feeling of intimacy it offers with small, vulnerable people whose needs and emotions are very much on the surface is a unique experience which might well change men almost of itself. It might make them that bit readier to be gentle, that bit more responsive and sensitive to the other people around them. Certainly there are new frustrations involved. But the joys of a more active kind of parenthood which are beginning to ripple through men's lives are joys which few of their fathers and grandfathers ever knew. And that leads me back to where I began, seeing the changes I manage to effect in my masculinity as something I hold in trust from my father and grandfather for my own sons and daughters.

That is the hopeful message about masculinity. This issue presents a pretty grim picture of man's inhumanity to women from Kenya to Cairo, from New South Wales to Nova Scotia. But it also shows men who are beginning to change. Believe me, there is no more important task before us than to respond to the challenge feminist women have set before us. And no more exciting one either.

Chris Brazier is an editor for New Internationalist, *a British magazine which focuses primarily on world poverty.*

"The men's movement . . . is most certainly not feminist—that would be a contradiction in terms."

viewpoint **100**

Feminism Has Little Relevance for Men

Richard Haddad

I want to present some ideas on the nature of the men's movement—a presentation that will include a re-examination of feminist sex-role theory. I will refer to feminism frequently and not flatteringly, and it is important for you to understand that I draw a very sharp distinction between women's rights (or equal rights in general) on the one hand, and feminism on the other. Equal rights is a concept with which I presume few will quarrel. I support the concept and its application without reservation on any subject you care to name.

I do have some problems with feminism—not with feminist advocacy of equal rights, but with feminist sex-role theory, feminist portrayal of men, feminist rhetoric, and feminist naivete. My problems with feminism extend to feminist men because of their blanket adoption of feminist sex-role theory, their acceptance of the negative portrayal of men which feminism advances, their parroting of feminist rhetoric—which for some reason sounds sillier coming from a man than from a woman, and their equally naive posturing about how society is currently ordered or should be ordered.

Once a Feminist

True confession: I was once a feminist. I stopped considering myself a feminist several years ago, shortly after an incident in which an acquaintance who was an officer of a local chapter of the National Organization for Women was refused entry to a local feminist coffee house because he was a male. Denying him entry on the basis of his sex was a violation of the county human rights law, and on threat of legal action the coffee house sponsors ultimately rescinded their women-only rule. The incident, however, had a big effect on me. It was not

THE reason or even the major reason I abandoned feminism, but it occurred at a time when I was doing a lot of thinking about how relevant feminism was for men, and the incident was very symbolic for me—mostly of the hypocrisy I had begun to sense in feminist women.

Since then, as a result of much reading on the subject, a lot of talking with friends, a lot of reflection on my own life, and my observations of the lives and behavior of other people, I have developed some fairly strong opinions on the origins of sex-roles, the nature of what I call the sex-role contract which has existed between men and women, the role of the feminist movement in what I feel is an unprecedented and extremely significant period for our society, and the inevitability of a men's movement which will complete the sex-role revolution which feminism began.

My thinking has led me to conclude that men as a class do *not* oppress women as a class. Nor do I believe that women as a class oppress men as a class. Rather, I feel that men and women have cooperated in the development of contemporary male and female sex-roles, both of which appear to have advantages as well as disadvantages, but which are essentially restrictive in nature, growth inhibiting, and, in the case of the male, physically as well as psychologically lethal.

I argue that in a society in which the roles of both sexes have not only been rigidly defined for so long, but originally complemented each other as well, it is ludicrous to hold either sex responsible for the condition of the other. It seems somewhat obvious to me that women have traditionally been reared to be the nurturing, sensitive, noncompetitive people because these characteristics were most suited to the domestic, child-rearing role they assumed in the order of things. It seems equally obvious to me that man, the hunter, the physically stronger of the sexes, has traditionally been reared to be the aggressive,

Richard Haddad, ''Concepts and Overview of the Men's Liberation Movement'' in *Men Freeing Men* edited by Francis Baumli, PhD. Copyright 1979 by Richard Haddad.

male / female roles   433

unemotional competitor because these characteristics were vital to his early role as protector and provider.

The problem, I think, is that somewhere along the line, we (men and women both) lost sight of the purpose of stressing different characteristics in the rearing of our male and female children. And so, for instance, long after physical strength ceased to be a major factor in providing food and shelter, women continued to rely on men to take care of them; and long after it was unnecessary for men to be away from their families much of the time, they continued to rely on women to raise their children and keep their homes. Even today, after almost two decades of modern feminism, men jealously guard their economic and political roles, resenting and ridiculing the intrusion of women into "man's business"; just as women, who jealously guard their child-rearing role, only lately assigning men to "helper" status in the home, will undoubtedly resent and resist the full and equal participation of men in the child-rearing process.

I argue that men do not dominate society—do not have a monopoly on power, nor do they rule the world. They are certainly over-represented in decision-making positions in certain of our social institutions like government and industry, but that is because it has always been their role to perform in those arenas. And I argue that they have no more used their position in these institutions for their own benefits as men, than women have used *their* position as the primary parent for their own benefit as women.

As far as power is concerned, a dictionary definition is "a position of ascendency; an ability to compel obedience." Someone defined it for me once as the ability to say no and get away with it. Either definition seems to have very wide application to both sexes. But if that is so, then why do we generally associate power with men and not with women?

Two Kinds of Power

I think the answer is two-fold. For one, we frequently fail to modify the term power by the set of social transactions we are labeling. For another, we do not look for power everywhere it exists. Maybe we are afraid.

For instance, if the subject is political power, we might conclude that men have more of it than women. And if we are discussing economic power, we might come to the same conclusion. But aren't there other kinds of power? Don't we generalize about men and power based on the apparent political and economic power they have?

How about domestic power—power in the home, where virtually all of us spent our most formative years? And what of the female's power over men by virtue of his more socially acceptable (i.e., expected) sex drive? We are all familiar with the manner in

which women are perceived as using sex to reward the male for good behavior—and to punish the errant male by withholding it. I ask you to consider which kind of power it is—economic, political, sexual, domestic—that has the most significant impact on us as individuals and as a society. Does the chairman of IBM have more power over you than your wife? Is our president's imprint on you stronger than your mother's? Doesn't it seem to you also that the power wielded in interpersonal relationships makes all other forms of power seem puny in comparison?

"Men do not enjoy a life of privilege."

I argue that men do not enjoy a life of privilege. Far from it, a look at the life of the average man is a fairly depressing sight. What kind of privilege is it that bestows on men a ten-year-shorter lifespan than women, and a higher incidence of disease, crime, alcoholism, and drug addiction? What kind of privilege is it that blesses men with a frequently self-destructive need to achieve? What kind of privilege is it that honors a man with the duty to spend a lifetime supporting others, more often than not at an unsatisfying job?

Whether or not we choose to look, the effects of sexism are all around us, in plain sight. What the feminists, in their proper concern for women, have neglected to point to our attention is that for every woman who is discouraged from working (by the whole of society, not just its economic or political components) there is a man forced by social convention to work; and for every bored and unfulfilled woman, there is a man burdened with the responsibility that only a primary wage-earner knows, who will die early, in part, from sex-role poisoning.

Men's Liberation

Men's liberation recognized that society lays oppressive roles on *both* sexes, a fact which feminism tends to ignore. Because its subject is men, not women, men's liberation is no more likely to dwell on the way society oppresses women than is feminism likely to dwell on the way society oppresses men. The objective of the men's movement can only be to free men of the restrictive roles in which they find themselves, and to foster the conditions under which they can define and choose for themselves the behaviors and relationships with which they are most comfortable and free. This simply cannot be done within the context of feminist theory, which proposes an oppressively negative view of men: the dominant gender which has it all and keeps it by exploiting women. . . .

It is fashionable to subscribe to the theory that men oppress women. It is also convenient to do so if one happens to be a women, and flattering if one happens to be a man. What is fashionable, convenient, and flattering has, of course, a much larger audience than what is unfashionable, inconvenient, and unflattering.

And so it goes until enough men tire of the flattery and turn back to the reality of their lives, and find something different than they did the last time they looked. First one, then another, asks himself why he is supporting his wife . . . or why he got married in the first place . . . or why he had children . . . or why he doesn't spend more time with his children . . . or why he continues to labor at a job which bores him . . . or why his wife got custody of the kids after the divorce . . . or why he pays alimony . . . or why his sons will go to war but not his neighbor's daughters . . . or why his wife will probably outlive him.

And suddenly, what flattered him yesterday angers him today. He turns further inward to examine his life, and feminism becomes irrelevant to him, as it should, because he is a man and feminist theory does not comprehend the male experience nor does it address his problems. . . .

Every day another man realizes that if women are not in charge, then *no one* is running the social machine because he is *sure* that men are not in charge; and all of the theories about his behavior be damned, he will live the rest of his three score and ten exactly as he pleases.

And *that* is what the men's liberation movement is all about.

Reasons for Anger

I am an angry man. Not quite as angry as I was a few years ago, but still angry. What is at least as important as my anger, however, is the fact that I am comfortable with my anger—comfortable with feeling it and with expressing it—and am not the least bit inclined to apologize to anyone for that anger.

I am angry because of the way I lived my life for some 30 or 35 years—the way I was conditioned to behave, the advantage that was taken of me in my conditioned state, the many self-destructive games I was taught to play, the life decisions I never got to make, the control over my life I gave generously to others, the guilt I allowed to be instilled in me, and my tolerance of exploitation through manipulation of my guilt.

Very specifically, I am angry because my father, who was conditioned in precisely the same manner I was, was so preoccupied with his role as bread-winner that he never had the time—or maybe the inclination—to develop the relationship with me I needed and wanted so badly.

I am angry because in my rush to select a career—or at least to find a job—right after finishing school, so that I could start earning a good living so I could get married so I could have a family so I could demonstrate to my parents and relatives and the rest of the world that I was a "mature and responsible adult male," I abandoned some dreams I am now sorry I never pursued.

I am angry because I was never really convinced that I had the option of not getting married, and never really convinced that once married I had the option of not having children. I am also angry because no one ever prepared me in the slightest for either marriage or parenting, and so not only feel that I was forced by social pressure into getting married, but was also led to believe that no special skills or preparation were required to function and to be happy in that esteemed institution.

Angry at Women

I am angry because of the sometimes defensive and sometimes self-righteous denial of most of the women in my life that they had anything at all to do with my conditioning and the reinforcement of my conditioning to think, behave, and react in certain prescribed ways, and that they have benefited as well as suffered by my conditioned reactions.

I am angry because women have been blaming and dumping on men for close to fifteen years now, harping on the privilege and power we theoretically have and have used to exploit them and keep them subservient, forgetting and overlooking that our so-called privileges and powers were foisted on us by social customs which *they also* helped to maintain, and that these same customs have exacted from us an outrageous price for a very questionable male advantage.

"Feminist theory does not comprehend the male experience."

I am angry that in the name of eliminating sex-stereotyping, feminism has reinforced some of the most fundamental and devastating stereotypes of all: the man as predator . . . stalking . . . powerful . . . base and insensitive . . . exploitive and untrustworthy . . . driven by uncontrollable and animalistic urges; the woman as victim . . . noble . . . pure . . . caring . . . selfless . . . loving . . . trusting . . . sensitive . . . suffering . . . used, battered, and reused for man's unspeakable purposes.

I am angry over the hypocrisy of too many women I know—their assertion of strength and independence *except when it is convenient* to be weak and dependent; their insistence that I and other men change, but *only* in ways and to a point which will please them; cries for affirmative action in employment but not in the domestic relations court; a thousand press releases from NOW on abortion but "Let's not press the draft issue because that's 'politically unwise.'"

I am angry because of the broken bodies and spirits of good men who spend their lives locked in a death dance, driven by compulsions they do not understand, filled with fear of not meeting the masculine ideal, buffeted by the frequently contradictory expectations of the women whose approval they desperately need. . . .

No Guilt

So the men's movement in which I am involved will have none of the nonsense about oppressed and victimized women; no responsibility for the conditions of women, whatever that condition might be; none of the guilt or self-loathing that is traditionally used to keep men functioning in harness.

It does not buy the line that men rule the world or that, all things considered, they have any more power than women do.

It will hear nothing of the male's life of privilege, or of his advantages as a male unless those advantages be balanced against the disadvantages of the male role.

"We need to forget what women will have us be, and to figure out first what we are."

The men's movement is rooted in the male experience, not the female experience or the female perception of the male experience.

It is positive, not negative, on the subject of men, and is supportive of men who dare to break out of self-destructive roles. . . .

The men's movement, however, is most certainly *not feminist*—that would be a contradiction in terms. Feminism will have nothing of the male experience and will not recognize it as valid. It downplays the relative importance of male concerns and insists that women's problems and struggles be given top priority. . . .

Not Political

Lastly, the men's movement must not be aligned with any particular political party or philosophy. I feel I have to say this because it looks more and more like the women's movement has aligned solidly with left-of-center Democratic politics, and because most male feminist groups have a very silly habit of mixing leftist politics and an anti-corporate attitude with men's issues.

The men's movement can no more be Marxist in

its orientation than it can be capitalistic; no more liberal than conservative; no more Democratic than Republican. Men of all political persuasions, of all income levels, of all classes, the black and the WASP and the Catholic and the Jew; the laborer and the corporation executive; the urban and the rural dweller; all suffer the same conditioning as men, the same self-destructive tendencies; the same need to achieve at all costs; the same provider burden; the same guilt; the same dependence on women and distance from other men. . . .

We need to listen to each other for the cries of pain and to recognize the fear we all have. We need to approach each other cautiously but steadily, holding out a hand of understanding and trust and support. We need to acknowledge our anger and help each other turn it into a source of energy for positive change. We need to talk with each other openly and stop worrying about how "cool" or knowledgeable we will appear. We need to forget what women will have us be, and to figure out first *what we are* and what *we* want to be and how *we* choose to live our lives, and that—and only that—is what will make for a genuine men's liberation movement.

Richard Haddad is a Maryland human resources manager. He founded Free Men, a men's liberation group, in 1977.

organizations

American Family Communiversity
5242 W. North Ave.
Chicago, IL 60639-4430
(312) 637-3037

The Communiversity works to promote, strengthen, and conserve American family life based on Judeo-Christian values. It is especially concerned with upgrading the effectiveness of agencies, laws, and institutions that serve families. It publishes pamphlets, including *Needless Government Day Care*, and books, including *Positive Divorce Reform for America*.

Business and Professional Women's Foundation
2012 Massachusetts Ave. NW
Washington, DC 20036
(202) 293-1200

The Foundation is a research, education, and grant-making organization that works for equity and self-sufficiency for women in the workforce. It provides financial assistance to women seeking to improve their employment and education opportunities. It publishes brochures, bibliographies, information digests, and research summaries on women and work issues. These materials are available from BPW Supply Service, 11722 Parklawn Drive, Rockville, MD 20852.

Catalyst
250 Park Ave. S
New York, NY 10003-1459
(212) 777-8900

Catalyst is a national research and advisory organization that helps corporations foster the career and leadership development of women. It publishes a wide variety of reference tools, manuals, and reports, including *Beyond the Transition: The Two-Gender Work Force and Corporate Policy* and *New Roles for Men and Women*. It also offers a monthly update of workforce issues called *Perspective*.

Catholics United for the Faith (CUFF)
45 Union Ave.
New Rochelle, NY 10801
(914) 235-9404

CUFF is a conservative organization whose purpose is to support, defend, and advance the orthodox teachings of the Roman Catholic Church. The Catholic Church's teaching on a variety of issues is presented in the monthly *Lay Witness*.

Center for the American Woman and Politics
Eagleton Institute of Politics
Rutgers University
New Brunswick, NJ 08901
(201) 828-2210

The Center engages in research, education, and public service aimed at developing and disseminating information about women's political participation in the United States. It also encourages women's involvement in public life. The Center publishes numerous reports and fact sheets on women in politics. Its book publications, including *Women as Candidates in American Politics*, are available from various commercial publishers.

Center for the Family in Transition
5725 Paradise Dr.
Bldg B, Suite 300
Corte Madera, CA 94925
(415) 924-5750

The Center researches the effects of divorce on children and family relationships and publishes reports on its findings. It also provides counseling services for divorcing families with children. The list of reprints available from the Center is extensive.

Center for Research on Women
Clement Hall
Memphis State University
Memphis, TN 38152
(901) 454-2770

The Center conducts, disseminates, and promotes research in the field of women's studies focusing on southern women and women of color in the United States. It operates a computerized information retrieval service called the Research Clearinghouse which contains more than two thousand entries of books, journal articles, chapters in books, unpublished manuscripts, and multimedia materials. The Center publishes *Newsletter*, research papers, and bibliographies.

Child Care Action Campaign
99 Hudson St., Suite 1233
New York, NY 10013
(212) 334-9595

The organization is a coalition of leaders from other organizations. Its goal is to establish a national system of quality, affordable child care. It provides advocacy, education, and information for corporations, child-care organizations, and the media. Its publications include a bimonthly members' newsletter called *Child Care ActioNews*, as well as various fact sheets, including "Who's Caring for Your Kids?—What Every Parent Should Know About Child Care."

Child Care Employee Project
PO Box 5603
Berkeley, CA 94705
(415) 653-9889

The Project is an advocacy organization working to improve the wages, status, and working conditions of the child-care profession. It believes that such improvement is the key to quality child-care. It also serves as a clearinghouse and consultant for child care work issues. It publishes handouts, articles, and pamphlets including *Comparable Worth: Questions and Answers for Child Care Staff*, and a monthly newsletter, *Child Care Employee News*.

The Coalition of Free Men
PO Box 129
Manhasset, NY 11030
(516) 482-6378

The Coalition of Free Men is a non-profit, educational organization that examines the way sex discrimination affects men. It brings male gender issues to the attention of the media and the public through research, conferences, and video productions. It publishes a bimonthly newsletter called *Transitions* for its members, and it promotes pertinent publications like the book *Men Freeing Men*.

Commission on the Economic Status of Women
Rm. 85, State Office Bldg.
100 Constitution Ave.
St. Paul, MN 55155
(612) 296-8590

This legislative advisory commission was established to study matters related to the economic status of women. It conducts research, holds public hearings, and publishes reports on issues including divorce laws, employment rights, and child-care support.

The Council on Women and the Church (COWAC)
Presbyterian Church-USA
475 Riverside Dr., Room 1151
New York, NY 10115
(212) 870-2025

COWAC is the women's rights group of the Presbyterian Church in the United States. Its purpose is to identify issues and monitor policies related to the status of women in the church and society. It publishes *A Woman's Resource List*, a bibliography of literature on women's and gender issues.

Displaced Homemakers Network
1010 Vermont Ave. NW, Suite 817
Washington, DC 20005
(202) 628-6767

The Network provides information, technical assistance, and other related services to ex-housewives who are now single and seeking employment. It also compiles statistics, monitors legislation, and maintains a program data library. It publishes the bimonthly *Network News*, as well as an annual Displaced Homemaker Program Directory.

Eagle Forum
Box 618
Alton, IL 62002
(618) 462-5415

The Forum is a politically active group that advocates traditional family values. It opposes the Equal Rights Amendment and any other political forces that are anti-family, anti-religion, or anti-morality. It publishes the monthly *Phyllis Schlafly Report*, as well as various brochures, including "Will 'Comparable Worth' Freeze Your Wages?"

Family Research Council of America, Inc.
515 2nd St. NE
Washington, DC 20002
(202) 546-5400

The Council is a research, resource, and educational organization. Its purpose is to ensure that the interests of the traditional family are considered and respected in the formulation of public policy.

It publishes numerous reports from a conservative perspective on family, education, youth, child care, pornography, and other issues affecting the family. These reports include *The Importance of the Family to Society* and *Infant Day Care: A Cause for Concern*.

The Family Resource Coalition
230 N. Michigan Ave., Suite 1625
Chicago, IL 60601
(312) 726-4750

The Coalition is a national information and advocacy group. It works to meet the changing American family's needs which are not yet recognized by current social and governmental structures. It also provides technical assistance, educational conferences, and a parent referral service. In addition to books like *Working with Teen Parents* and *Programs To Strengthen Families*, it also publishes a journal, *FRC Report*, three times a year.

Men's Rights, Inc.
PO Box 163180
Sacramento, CA 95816
(916) 484-7333

MR, Inc., is dedicated to ending sexism in a way that recognizes the social, psychological, physical, legal, and economic problems of men. It conducts research and programs on health and community education. It publishes news releases on divorce, custody battles, men's relationships and the treatment of men by the media.

National Association for Family Day Care
815 15th St. NW
Suite 928
Washington, DC 20005
(202) 347-3356

NAFDC is a volunteer organization comprised of family day-care providers and advocates. It was established to study the needs of family day-care providers nationwide. The Association has a national directory of day-care agencies, associations, and support groups, and publishes *The NEW National Perspective*, a quarterly newsletter.

National Committee on Pay Equity
1201 16th St. NW, Suite 422
Washington, DC 20036
(202) 822-7304

NCPE advocates eliminating wage discrimination and achieving pay equity by raising the salaries of women and people of color so their wages are the same as white men for work of comparable value. The Committee provides studies, public education, and congressional testimony on pay equity.

National Council for Children's Rights (NCCR)
2001 O St. NW
Washington, DC 20036
(202) 223-6227

NCCR helps children of divorced parents maintain healthy relationships with *both* parents by working to change divorce and custody laws which have institutionalized the single-parent family. The Council publishes legal briefs, model bills, audio-visual materials, and reports, including, "Crisis in Family Law: Children as Victims of Divorce," and "Sixty Rapid-Fire Points in Favor of Joint Custody."

National Council on Family Relations
1910 W. Co. Rd. B, Suite 147
St. Paul, MN 55113
(612) 633-6933

The organization consists of family services professionals. Its objectives are to encourage research on families, promote family life education, foster dialogue and interaction among family services professionals and organizations, and provide information on family life through education and publication. It publishes books, bibliographies, a quarterly newsletter called *NCFR Report*, and two quarterly journals called *Family Relations* and *Journal of Marriage and the Family*.

National Council for Research on Women
Sara Delano Roosevelt Memorial House
47 E. 65th St.
New York, NY 10021
(212) 570-5001

The Council is a network of organizations representing the academic community, policymakers, and others interested in women's issues. It uses institutional resources for feminist research, policy analysis, and education, and acts as a clearinghouse. It publishes a member list, reports, and research papers, and an annually updated compilation called *Opportunities for Research and Study*.

Priests for Equality
PO Box 5243
West Hyattsville, MD 20782
(301) 779-9298

Priests for Equality is an organization of Roman Catholic clergymen who have endorsed a seventeen-point charter of equality. They believe that equality between men and women is essential for social justice in the world and in their Church. They advocate ordaining women to the priesthood. The organization engages in sociological studies and surveys and sponsors research on equality. It publishes tabloids, a quarterly newsletter called *News and Notes*, and pamphlets like *Toward a Full and Equal Sharing*, a pastoral letter on equality in the Church.

Project on the Status and Education of Women
c/o Association of American Colleges
1818 R St. NW
Washington, DC 20009
(202) 387-1300

PSEW provides information concerning women students, faculty, and administrators, and works with institutions, government agencies, and other associations and programs related to women in higher education. It develops and distributes materials that identify and highlight institutional and federal policies as well as other issues affecting women's status on campus. These publications include a quarterly newsletter called *On Campus with Women* and information packets on sexual harassment, minority women, and nontraditional careers.

Select Committee on Children, Youth, and Families
US House of Representatives
385 House Office Building Annex 2
Washington, DC 20515
(202) 226-7692

The Committee was created by the 98th Congress in 1983 to conduct an ongoing assessment of the condition of American children and families and to make recommendations to Congress and the public about how to improve public and private sector policies. It publishes reports and transcripts of hearings it holds on family issues.

Society for Research in Child Development
University of Chicago Press
5801 Ellis Ave.
Chicago, IL 60637
(312) 702-7470

The Society is an organization of professionals including doctors, educators, sociologists, psychologists, and statisticians. It exists to further research in the area of child development. It publishes the bimonthly journal *Child Development* and the triannual *Child Development Abstracts and Bibliography*.

Stepfamily Association of America, Inc.
602 E. Joppa Rd.
Baltimore, MD 21204
(301) 823-7570

The Association acts as a national advocate for stepfamilies and their special needs. Its goals are to expose myths about family relations, to educate the public, and to provide information that will improve the chances of success for remarried families. It also serves as a clearinghouse for literature related to stepfamilies. In addition to a bibliography on stepfamily issues, it publishes the quarterly *Stepfamily Bulletin*.

Tradeswomen, Inc.
PO Box 40664
San Francisco, CA 94140
(415) 821-7334

Tradeswomen, Inc. is a non-profit membership organization for peer support, networking, and advocacy for women in nontraditional, blue-collar jobs. It publishes the quarterly *Tradeswoman Magazine* and the monthly *Trade Trax* newsletter.

United States Department of Labor
Office of Information and Public Affairs
200 Constitution Ave. NW
Washington, DC 20010
(202) 523-8165

The US Department of Labor is part of the executive branch of the federal government. The Office of Information and Public Affairs publishes extensively on various labor-related topics like equal employment, women, youth, and labor-management relations. These materials are listed in *Publications of the U.S. Department of Labor*, available from the Department.

Wider Opportunities for Women
1325 G St. NW
Washington, DC 20005
(202) 638-3143

WOW works to achieve economic independence and equality of opportunity for women and girls. It focuses on, among other issues, the economic status of women, education and employment training for women, occupational segregation and affirmative action, and child care for working mothers. The organization publishes legislative alerts and issue briefs, bibliographies, and a quarterly newsletter called *Connections*.

Women for Racial and Economic Equality (WREE)
130 E. 16th St.
New York, NY 10003
(212) 473-6111

WREE is a political activist organization. It strives to end racism and economic inequality for all through the enactment of a Women's Bill of Rights. It is affiliated with Women's International Democratic Federation which publishes the quarterly journal *Women of the Whole World*. WREE publishes the bimonthly journal *WREE-View of Women*.

Women's Equity Action League (WEAL)
1250 I St. NW, Suite 305
Washington, DC 20005
(202) 898-1588

WEAL is a national membership organization that specializes in women's economic issues. It is committed to the economic development and advancement of women. It conducts research and education projects, supports litigation, and engages in legislative advocacy. It publishes fact sheets, reports, and kits, including a *Special Attorney's Packet on Divorced Spouse Legislation*.

Women's Ordination Conference
PO Box 2693
Fairfax, VA 22031
(703) 255-1428

The Conference is an international grassroots movement of women and men committed to the ordination of Roman Catholic women to the priesthood. It networks with other feminist groups, lobbies with Church leaders, and offers workshops and seminars. It publishes a bimonthly newspaper, *New Women/New Church*.

Women's Research and Resource Center
Spelman College
Atlanta, GA 30314-4399
(404) 681-3643

The Center publishes *Sage: A Scholarly Journal on Black Women* which deals with black women in education, black women in the workplace, health and gender, mothers and daughters, and other issues related to black women. It also publishes bibliographies on these topics.

Work and Family Information Center
The Conference Board
845 Third Ave.
New York, NY 10022
(212) 759-0900

The Center is a national clearinghouse for information related to employment and family issues. It publishes material on work and family, child care, parental leave, and alternative work schedules.

bibliography

The Nature of Sex Roles

Franklin Abbot, ed.
New Men, New Minds: Breaking Male Tradition. Freedom, CA: The Crossing Press, 1987.

Duncan Maxwell Anderson
"The Delicate Sex," *Science 86*, April 1986.

Anthony Astrachan
How Men Feel: Their Response to Women's Demands for Equality and Power. Garden City, NY: Anchor Press/Doubleday, 1986.

Francis Baumli, ed.
Men Freeing Men: Exploding the Myth of the Traditional Male. Jersey City, NJ: New Atlantis Press, 1985.

Beryl Lieff Benderly
The Myth of Two Minds. New York: Doubleday Books, 1987.

David F. Bjorklund
"What Are Little Boys (and Girls) Made Of?" *Parents*, February 1987.

Susan Brownmiller
Femininity. New York: Linden Press/Simon & Schuster, 1984.

Clarence B. Carson
"Saws for the Gander," *The New American*, March 16, 1987.

R.W. Connel
Gender and Power: Society, the Person and Sexual Politics. Stanford, CA: Stanford University Press, 1987.

Faye J. Crosby, ed.
Spouse, Parent, Worker: On Gender and Multiple Roles. New Haven, CT: Yale University Press, 1987.

James E. Dittes
The Male Predicament. San Francisco, CA: Harper & Row, 1985.

Riane Eisler
The Chalice and the Blade. San Francisco: Harper & Row, 1987.

Anne Fausto-Sterling
Myths of Gender. New York: Basic Books, Inc. 1985.

Peter G. Filene
Him/Herself: Sex Roles in Modern America. Baltimore: The Johns Hopkins University Press, 1986.

Gary Alan Fine
"The Dirty Play of Little Boys," *Society*, November/December 1986.

Daniel Goleman
"As Sex Roles Change, Men Turn to Therapy To Cope With Stress," *The New York Times*, June 21, 1984.

Janet L. Hopson
"Boys Will Be Boys, Girls Will Be . . ." *Psychology Today*, August 1987.

Michael S. Kimmel
"Real Man Redux," *Psychology Today*, July 1987.

Doreen Kimura
"Male Brain, Female Brain: The Hidden Difference," *Psychology Today*, November 1985.

Gerda Lerner
The Creation of Patriarchy. New York: Oxford University Press, 1986.

Michael Levin
"The Return of Human Nature," *The World & I*, November 1987.

Gail F. Melson and Alan Fogel
"Learning To Care," *Psychology Today*, January 1988.

Allan Parachini
"Demise of the Tomboy," *Los Angeles Times*, March 22, 1988.

Ethel S. Person
"Some Differences Between Men and Women," *The Atlantic Monthly*, March 1988.

Letty Cottin Pogrebin
Growing Up Free. New York: McGraw-Hill, 1980.

Phyllis Schlafly
"Yes, Virginia, There Is a Difference," *The Phyllis Schlafly Report*, December 1987. Available from the Eagle Forum, Box 618, Alton, IL 62002.

Wendy Schuman
"When Girls Act Like Boys," *Parents*, January 1986.

Sara Bonnet Stein
Girls & Boys: The Limits of Nonsexist Childrearing. New York: Charles Scribner's Sons, 1983.

Mimi Swartz
"Who Wants To Think Like a Man?" *Glamour*, March 1986.

Mary Roth Walsh
The Psychology of Women. New Haven, CT: Yale University Press, 1987.

Relationships Between the Sexes

Bebe Moore Campbell
Successful Women, Angry Men. New York: Random House, 1986.

Sey Chassler
"Listening," *Ms.*, August 1984.

Bryce J. Christiansen
"America's Retreat from Marriage," *The Family in America*, February 1988. Available from The Rockford Institute, 934 North Main St., Rockford, IL 61103-7061.

Connell Cowan and Melvyn Kinder
"Fear of Intimacy: Not for Men Only," *Glamour*, October 1987.

Barbara Ehrenreich, Elizabeth Hess, and Gloria Jacobs
Re-Making Love: The Feminization of Sex. Garden City, NY: Anchor Books, 1987.

Warren Farrell — *Why Men Are the Way They Are*. New York: McGraw-Hill, 1986.

Suzanne Fields — "Battlefront Update in War of Sexes," *The Washington Times*, December 31, 1987.

Suzanne Fields — "Orange Blossom Revival," *The Washington Times*, July 29, 1986.

Anne Taylor Fleming — "The American Wife," *The New York Times Magazine*, October 26, 1986.

Herbert J. Freudenberger — "Today's Troubled Men," *Psychology Today*, December 1987.

Trip Gabriel — "Why Wed?: The Ambivalent American Bachelor," *The New York Times Magazine*, November 15, 1987.

Sandra M. Gilbert and Susan Gubar — "Sex Wars: Not the Fun Kind," *The New York Times Book Review*, December 27, 1987.

Glamour — "Why Is All the Relationship-Repair Advice Aimed at Women?" February 1987.

Daniel Goleman — "Two Views of Marriage Explored: His and Hers," *The New York Times*, April 1, 1986.

Rosanna Hertz — *More Equal Than Others*. Berkeley: University of California Press, 1986.

Shere Hite — *Women and Love: A Cultural Revolution in Progress*. New York: Alfred A. Knopf, 1987.

Rita D. Jacobs — "Gut-Spilling Is Being Used by Men as a Shortcut to Intimacy," *Glamour*, March 1986.

Cloé Madanes — "Marriage in the '80s: Altered States," *Vogue*, August 1987.

Elizabeth C. Mooney — *Men and Marriage: The Changing Role of Husbands*. New York: Franklin Watts, 1985.

Joe Mysak — "The Endless Chase," *The American Spectator*, December 1987.

Bernice Cohen Sachs — "Changing Relationships Between Men and Women," *Vital Speeches of the Day*, October 1, 1984.

Claudia Wallis — "Back Off, Buddy," *Time*, October 12, 1987.

Ira Wolfman — "The Closer You Get, the Faster I Run," *Ms.*, September 1985.

Connie Fourré Zimney — *In Praise of Homemaking*. Notre Dame, IN: Ave Maria Press, 1984.

Family

Paul Bohannan — *All the Happy Families: Exploring the Varieties of Family Life*. New York: McGraw-Hill, 1985.

Allan Carlson — *Family Questions: Reflections on the American Social Crisis*. New Brunswick, NJ: Transaction, 1988.

Clarence B. Carson — "Government Fragments the Family," *The New American*, December 9, 1985.

Dennis L. Cuddy — "The American Family Under Attack," *Lincoln Review*, Winter 1987.

Dollars & Sense — "It's All in the Family: How Government Influences Family Life," March 1987.

David Gelman — "Playing Both Mother and Father," *Newsweek*, July 15, 1985.

W. Norton Grubb and Marvin Lazerson — *Broken Promises: How Americans Fail Their Children*. New York: Basic Books, 1982.

Michael H. Hodges — "Children in the Wilderness," *Social Policy*, Spring 1987.

John A. Howard — "The Family: America's Hope," *Vital Speeches of the Day*, January 1, 1984.

Barbara Kantrowitz — "The Clamor To Save the Family," *Newsweek*, February 29, 1988.

Barbara Kantrowitz — "Three's a Crowd," *Newsweek*, September 1, 1986.

Robert W. Lee — "How Government Has Made War Against the American Family," *Conservative Digest*, February 1988.

Michael Levin — "Feminism, Stage Three," *Commentary*, August 1986.

Sar A. Levitan and Richard S. Belous — *What's Happening to the American Family?* Baltimore: The Johns Hopkins University Press, 1981.

Eleanor D. Macklin and Roger H. Rubin — *Contemporary Families and Alternative Lifestyles*. Beverly Hills: Sage Publications, 1983.

Wilma Berry Mann — "Reclaiming the Family: Parents Must Reassert Responsibility for Their Children," *The New American*, November 9, 1987.

Joanne M. Martin and Elmer P. Martin — *The Helping Tradition in the Black Family and Community*. Silver Spring, MD: National Association of Social Work Inc., 1985.

James McGhee — *Proceedings of the Black Family Summit*. New York: National Urban League, 1985.

Steven Mintz and Susan Kellog — *Domestic Revolutions: A Social History of American Family Life*. New York: The Free Press, 1987.

Daniel Patrick Moynihan — *Family and Nation*. New York: Harcourt Brace Jovanovich, 1986.

Arthur J. Norton — "Families and Children in the Year 2000," *Children Today*, July/August 1987.

Joseph R. Peden and Fred R. Glahe — *The American Family and the State*. San Francisco: Pacific Research Institute for Public Policy, 1986.

Society — March/April 1987 issue on the family.

Peter Uhlenberg — "Reinforcing the Fragile Family," *Christianity Today*, January 16, 1987.

Working Group on the Family — *The Family: Preserving America's Future. A Report to the President from the White House Working Group on the Family*. Washington, DC: The Group, 1986.

Women and the Family

Deborah Baldwin — "The Part-Time Solution: How One Parent Is Working Less and Enjoying It More," *The Washington Monthly*, December 1984.

Barbara Berg — "The Guilt that Drives Working Mothers Crazy," *Ms.*, May 1987.

Katharine Byrne — "Varieties of Working Mothers," *America*, March 9, 1985.

Deborah Fallows — *A Mother's Work*. Boston: Houghton Mifflin, 1985.

Maureen F. Gallogly — "Growing Up as a 'Latchkey' Child Made Me More Independent and Confident—I Loved It!" *Glamour*, April 1985

Kathleen Gerson	*Hard Choices: How Women Decide About Work, Career, and Motherhood*. Berkeley: University of California Press, 1985.
Ellen Goodman	"Office or Home? Either Is Anxious Choice for Women," *Los Angeles Times*, September 20, 1985.
Sheila Graham	"Myths of Motherhood," *The Plain Truth*, April 1988.
Phyllis A. Hall	"All Our Lonely Children," *Newsweek*, October 12, 1987.
Jenkin Lloyd Jones	"Able Women Face Career-Family Dilemma," *Conservative Chronicle*, September 3, 1986.
Barbara Kantrowitz	"A Mother's Choice," *Newsweek*, March 31, 1986.
Kaye Lowman	*Of Cradles & Careers: A Guide to Reshaping Your Job To Include a Baby in Your Life*. New York: New American Library, 1984.
Wally Metts Jr.	"Home-Grown Kids Need a Full-Time Mom," *Christianity Today*, March 6, 1987.
Julie Trocchio	"Ten Rules for Working Mothers," *Parents*, December 1986.
Pamela P. Wong	"No Babies!?" *Eternity*, June 1987.

Men and the Family

Mary Kay Blakely	"Calling All Working Fathers," *Ms.*, December 1986.
Anthony Giardina	"Confessions of an Ex-Superdad," *Glamour*, December 1986.
Pete Hamill	"Great Expectations," *Ms.*, September 1986.
Ron Hansen	"The Male Clock," *Esquire*, April 1985.
Ronna Kabatznick	"Nature/Nurture," *Ms.*, August 1984.
Larry L. King	"Fatherhood Yesterday, Today and Tomorrow," *U.S. News & World Report*, June 3, 1985.
Michael Lamb	"Will the Real 'New Father' Please Stand Up?" *Parents*, June 1987.
Robert A. Lewis and Marvin B. Sussman, eds.	*Men's Changing Roles in the Family*. New York: The Haworth Press, 1986.
Diane Manuel	"A New Generation of Fathers," *The Christian Science Monitor*, June 13, 1986.
Robert B. McCall	"Homemaker Dads," *Parents*, April 1987.
Samuel Osherson	"Finding Our Fathers," *Utne Reader*, April/May 1986.
Jerrold Lee Shapiro	"The Expectant Father," *Psychology Today*, January 1987.

Divorce

Teresa Amott	"Put Responsibility Where It Belongs," *Dollars & Sense*, October 1987.
Terry Arendell	*Mothers and Divorce*. Berkeley: University of California Press, 1986.
Andree Brooks	"Divorced Parents and the Neglected Child," *The New York Times*, July 26, 1986.
Jennet Conant	"You'd Better Sit Down, Kids: Parents Should Help Children Cope with Divorce," *Newsweek*, August 24, 1987.

Richard F. Doyle	*What Everyone Should Know To Beat the Racket*. Forest Lake, MN: Poor Richard's Press, 1988.
Frank Ferrara	*On Being Father*. Garden City, NY: Doubleday & Company, Inc., 1985.
Susan B. Garland	"New Deal for the Children of Divorce," *Business Week*, September 1987.
George Gilder	"The Princess's Problems," *The Human Life Review*, Spring 1986.
Phyllis Gillis	*Days Like This: A Tale of Divorce*. New York: McGraw-Hill, 1986.
Bernard R. Goldberg	"Love and the Deadbeat Dad," *The New York Times*, August 20, 1986.
Fredric Hayward	"In Defense of a Monster," Part I, *Los Angeles Times*, August 6, 1985. "Deadbeat Dads? Not So," Part II, *Los Angeles Times*, August 7, 1985.
Marsha Kline, Janet R. Johnston, and William Coysh	"Outcomes in Joint and Sole Custody Families: Findings from Different Populations and Social Policy Implications," research summary papers, 1988. Available from Center for the Family in Transition, 5725 Paradise Dr., Bldg. B, Suite 300, Corte Madera, CA 94925.
John Leo	"Men Have Rights Too," *Time*, November 24, 1986.
Ms.	"Beneath the Surface: The Truth About Divorce, Custody, and Support," February 1986.
James L. Peterson and Nicholas Zill	"Marital Disruption, Parent-Child Relationships, and Behavior Problems in Children," *Journal of Marriage and the Family*, May 1986.
George Rekers	"Fathers at Home," *Persuasion at Work*, April 1986.
Kay Richards	"Phantom Fathers," *The Progressive*, August 1987.
C.W. Smith	*Will They Still Love Me When I Leave?* New York: G.P. Putnam's Sons, 1987.
Marianne Takas	"Divorce: Who Gets the Blame in 'No Fault'?" *Ms.*, February 1986.
USA Today	"Victims of No-Fault Divorce," December 1986.
Yvette Walczak and Sheila Burns	*Divorce: The Child's Point of View*. New York: Harper & Row, 1984.
David Whitman	"The Children Who Get Cut Out," *U.S. News & World Report*, October 12, 1987.
Joy Ann Zimmerman	"Failed Marriages, Vulnerable Children," *ABA Journal*, January 1, 1988.

Work

Judith Buber Agassi	*Comparing the Work Attitudes of Women and Men*. Lexington, MA: Lexington Books, 1982.
Grace Baruch, Rosalind Barnett, and Caryl Rivers	*Lifeprints: New Patterns of Love and Work for Today's Women*. New York: McGraw-Hill, 1983.
Laurie Baum	"Corporate Women: They're About To Break Through to the Top," *Business Week*, June 22, 1987.
Mary Kay Blakely	"Fathering," *Ms.*, August 1984.
Srully Blotnick	*Ambitious Men: Their Drives, Dreams, and Delusions*. New York: Viking Penguin, 1987.

Srully Blotnick — *Otherwise Engaged: The Private Lives of Successful Career Women.* New York: Facts on File Publications, 1985.

Bebe Moore Campbell — "Working Wives, Threatened Husbands," *U.S. News & World Report,* February 23, 1987.

Janice Castro — "More and More, She's the Boss," *Time,* December 2, 1985.

Carol Crosthwaite — "Working in a Man's World," *Vital Speeches of the Day,* January 1, 1986.

Liz Roman Gallese — "Women Like Us," *Working Woman,* February 1985.

Edith Gilson — *Unnecessary Choices: The Hidden Life of the Executive Woman.* New York: William Morrow, 1987.

Sandra Hardesty and Nehama Jacobs — *Success and Betrayal: The Crisis of Women in Corporate America.* New York: Franklin Watts, 1986.

William Hoffer — "Businesswomen: Equal but Different," *Nation's Business,* August 1987.

Ann Hughey and Eric Gelman — "Managing the Woman's Way," *Newsweek,* March 17, 1986.

Michael S. Kimmel — *Changing Men: New Directions in Research on Men and Masculinity.* Beverly Hills: Sage Publications, 1987.

Jeane J. Kirkpatrick — "Why I Think More Women Are Needed at the Pinnacle of World Politics," *Glamour,* September 1985.

Elinor Lenz and Barbara A. Myerhoff — *The Feminization of America.* Los Angeles: Jeremy P. Tarcher, Inc., 1985.

Charlotte Low — "Time Off for Motherhood," *Insight,* April 27, 1987.

Samuel Osherson — *Finding Our Fathers: The Unfinished Business of Manhood.* New York: The Free Press, 1986.

John Podhoretz — "Career Women Lash Out," *The American Spectator,* January 1988.

Charles E. Rice — "The Legality of Equality," *The New American,* July 6, 1987.

Karen Rubin — "Whose Job Is Child Care?" *Ms.,* March 1987.

Felice N. Schwartz — "Corporate Women," *Vital Speeches of the Day,* January 1, 1988.

B.F. Smith — "Women and Children First," *Crisis,* March 1988.

Lester Thurow — "A Surge in Inequality," *Scientific American,* May 1987.

William Tucker — "Condemned to Liberation: The Woman as Breadwinner," *The American Spectator,* November 1984.

Amy Wilbur — "Working Women and Weak Men," *Science Digest,* July 1986.

Leah Yarrow — "Fathers Speak Out," *Parents,* September 1985.

A Case Study: Comparable Worth

Henry J. Aaron and Cameran M. Lougy — *The Comparable Worth Controversy.* Washington, DC: The Brookings Institution, 1986.

Carole and Paul Bass — "Yale Teaches a Valuable Lesson," *The Progressive,* March 1985.

William R. Beer — "Real-Life Costs of Affirmative Action," *The Wall Street Journal,* August 7, 1986.

Barbara Bergmann — "Pay Equity—How To Argue Back," *Ms.,* November 1985.

Walter Block — "Equal Pay Legislation," *Vital Speeches of the Day,* February 1, 1985.

Beth Brophy and Maureen Walsh — "Women's Pay: The Catch-Up Game Quickens," *U.S. News & World Report,* September 14, 1987.

Linda Chavez — "Pay Equity Is Unfair to Women," *Fortune,* March 4, 1985.

Commission on the Economic Status of Women — *Pay Equity: The Minnesota Experience.* St. Paul, MN: Commission on the Economic Status of Women, 1985. Available from 85 State Office Building, St. Paul, MN 55155.

Commonweal — "Woman, Work, and the Question of 'Comparable Worth': Is It Really Worth It? Two Views," May 31, 1985.

LouEllen Crawford — "Comparable Worth: Precedent or Appeasement?" *The Humanist,* March/April 1988.

Dollars & Sense — "In Pursuit of Pay Equity," September 1986.

Margaret Engel — "Comparable Worth: How Is the Battle for Salaries Going?" *Glamour,* April 1985.

The Humanist — "Comparable Worth: What Is *Its* Worth?" May/June 1986.

National Review — "The Comparable-Worth Story," December 5, 1986.

Clarence M. Pendleton — "Comparable Worth Is Not Pay Equity," *Vital Speeches of the Day,* April 1, 1985.

Anne Phillips — "Doing What Comes Naturally," *New Internationalist,* March 1988.

Robert Rector — "The Pseudo-Science of Comparable Worth," *Backgrounder,* February 29, 1988. Available from The Heritage Foundation, 214 Massachusetts Ave. NE, Washington, DC 20002.

Phyllis Schlafly — "The Current Feminist Follies," *The Phyllis Schlafly Report,* November 1987. Available from Eagle Forum, Box 618, Alton, IL 62002.

Kathryn Steckert — "Why Aren't You Earning More? The Real Reasons Behind the Wage Gap," *Glamour,* June 1986.

George F. Will — "A Doctrine of the High Priests," *Newsweek,* September 30, 1985.

Child Care

Brigitte Berger and Peter L. Berger — *The War Over the Family.* Garden City, NY: Anchor Press/Doubleday, 1983.

Mary Kay Blakely — "What Kind of Childhood Is This, Anyway?" *Working Woman,* February 1985.

Marian Blum — *The Day-Care Dilemma: Women and Children First.* Lexington, MA: Lexington Books, 1983.

James G. Bruen Jr. — "Surrogates and Spinsters," *Fidelity,* February 1988.

Changing Times — "Child Care: Get Your Boss To Help," October 1986.

Fern Schumer Chapman — "Executive Guilt: Who's Taking Care of the Children?" *Fortune,* February 16, 1987.

Alison Clarke-Stewart — *Daycare.* Cambridge, MA: Harvard University Press, 1982.

Daughters of Sarah	"Working and Parenting: Can We Do Both?" March/April 1988.
Louis Dehmlow	"A One-Size-Fits-All Leave Policy?" *U.S. News & World Report*, December 7, 1987.
Carol Dilks and Nancy L. Croft	"Child Care: Your Baby?" *Nation's Business*, December 1986.
Edith Fierst	"Careers and Kids," *Ms.*, May 1988.
Dana E. Friedman	"Child Care for Employees' Kids," *Harvard Business Review*, March/April 1986.
Kathleen Gerson	"Briefcase, Baby, or Both?" *Psychology Today*, November 1986.
Martha Humphreys	"A Place for Kids," *Parents*, December 1986.
Brenda Hunter	"Breaking the Tie that Binds," *Christianity Today*, February 21, 1986.
In These Times	"Bringing up Babies," January 27/February 2, 1988.
Mark D. Isaacs	"The Home Wreckers," *The New American*, November 9, 1987.
Peter C. Kratcoski	"Is Motherhood Becoming a Devalued Career?" *USA Today*, January 1985.
Kathy Palen	"Family Leave: A Needed Guarantee," *The Christian Century*, April 22, 1987.
Jane Bryant Quinn	"A Crisis in Child Care," *Newsweek*, February 15, 1988.
Robert J. Samuelson	"Uncle Sam in the Family Way," *Newsweek*, August 11, 1986.
Leonard Silverman	"Corporate Child Care," *USA Today*, May 1987.
Lester C. Thurow	"The New American Family," *Technology Review*, August/September 1987.
Claudia Wallis	"The Child-Care Dilemma," *Time*, June 22, 1987.
Burton L. White	"Should You Stay Home with Your Baby?" in *The Psychology of Women: Ongoing Debates*, Mary Roth Walsh, ed. New Haven, CT: Yale University Press, 1987.
Michael W. Yogman and T. Berry Brazelton	*In Support of Families*. Cambridge, MA: Harvard University Press, 1986.
Edward F. Zigler	"Parental Leave for Men, Too," *The New York Times*, June 14, 1986.
Edward F. Zigler and Meryl Frank	*The Parental Leave Crisis: Towards a National Policy*. New Haven, CT: Yale University Press, 1988.

Religion

Ronald and Beverly Allen	*Liberated Traditionalism*. Portland, OR: Multnomah Press, 1985.
Henry G. Brinton	"The Pastor's Problem," *The New York Times Magazine*, January 17, 1988.
Kim Chernin	*Reinventing Eve*. New York: Times Books, 1987.
Joan Chittister	"Yesterday's Dangerous Vision: Christian Feminism in the Catholic Church," *Sojourners*, July 1987.
Carol P. Christ and Judith Plaskow, eds.	*Womanspirit Rising*. New York: Harper & Row, 1979.
Stephen B. Clark	*Man and Woman in Christ*. Ann Arbor, MI: Servant Books, 1980.
Commonweal	"Dear John," April 22, 1988.

Elisabeth Schussler Fiorenza	*Bread Not Stone: The Challenge of Feminist Biblical Interpretation*. Boston: Beacon Press, 1984.
Elouise Renich Fraser	"The Church's Language About God," *The Other Side*, December 1987.
Mary Gerhart	"Women Doing Theology," *Commonweal*, December 26, 1986.
Manfred Hauke	*Women in the Priesthood?* San Francisco: Ingatius Press, 1988.
George G. Higgins	"The Women's Challenge," *America*, January 10, 1987.
Jacquelyn A. Kegley	"Gender and Religion," *USA Today*, July 1985.
Vincent P. Miceli	*Women Priests & Other Fantasies*. San Francisco: Ignatius Press, 1984.
Frank Morriss	"Substituting the World's View for the Gospel," *The Wanderer*, April 28, 1988. Available from 201 Ohio St., St. Paul, MN 55107.
Ms.	"Special Section: Finding Spiritual Strength," December 1985.
Mary O'Connell	"Is Feminism God's Gift to the Catholic Church?" *U.S. Catholic*, June 1987.
Mary O'Connell	"Why Don't Catholics Have Women Priests?" *U.S. Catholic*, January 1984.
Effie Alley Quay	"It Was the Woman You Put with Me," *Fidelity*, February 1988. Available from 206 Marquette Ave., South Bend, IN 46617.
Derk Kinnane Roelofsma	"Cover Story: Women in the Pulpit," *Insight*, April 6, 1987.
Adrianus J. Simonis	"Some Reflections About Feminist Theology," *The Wanderer*, February 11, 1988. Available from 201 Ohio St., St. Paul, MN 55107.
Karen Sue Smith	"'Claiming Our Power': Dialogue, Worship, & Development," *Commonweal*, November 6, 1987.
Elaine Storkey	*What's Right with Feminism?* Grand Rapids, MI: William B. Eerdmans, 1985.
Gordon Thomas	*Desire and Denial*. Boston: Little, Brown and Company, 1986.
Mary Luke Tobin	"Women in the Church Since Vatican II," *America*, November 1, 1986.
Mary Stewart Van Leeuwen	"The End of Female Passivity," *Christianity Today*, January 17, 1986.
Max J. Walz	"Some Reflections on Priestly Celibacy," *The Wanderer*, May 20, 1985. Available from 201 Ohio St., St. Paul, MN 55107.
Peter White	"God and Women," *World Press Review*, January 1988.

Feminism

Bella Abzug and Mim Kelber	"Let's Use 'Wise Women'," *The New York Times*, December 20, 1986.
David Behrens	"Confusion," *Ms.*, August 1984.
Nijole V. Benokraitis and Joe R. Feagin	*Modern Sexism: Blatant, Subtle, and Covert Discrimination*. Englewood Cliffs, NJ: Prentice-Hall, 1986.
Allan Bloom	"Liberty, Equality, Sexuality," *Commentary*, April 1987.
Noreen Connell	"Feminists and Families," *The Nation*, August 16/23, 1986.
Nicholas Davidson	*The Failure of Feminism*. Buffalo, NY: Prometheus, 1988.

Suzanne Fields   "Friedan's Equation Reworked," *The Washington Times*, February 25, 1988.

Leslie Garis   "Suburban Classic," *Ms.*, July/August 1987.

Stella G. Guerra   "Women in America Shooting for the Stars: As We See Ourselves So Do We Act," *Vital Speeches of the Day*, September 15, 1986.

Sylvia Ann Hewlett   "Feminism's Next Challenge: Support for Motherhood," *The New York Times*, June 17, 1986.

Ruth Hubbard   "Facts and Feminism: Thoughts on the Masculinity of Natural Science," *Science for the People*, March/April 1986.

Beverly LaHaye   "Why Feminism No Longer Sells," *The Heritage Lectures*, March 10, 1987. Available from The Heritage Foundation, 214 Massachusetts Ave. NE, Washington, DC 20002.

Madeleine L'Engle   "Shake the Universe," *Ms.*, July/August 1987.

Charles Lynch   "Power," *Ms.*, August 1984.

Ed Marciniak   "The Impact of the Women's Movement(s) on the Family: A Father's Perspective," *America*, March 7, 1987.

Mary O'Connell   "Isn't That Just Like a Woman," *Salt*, March 1988.

Nancy R. Pearcey   "Why I Am Not a Feminist (Any More)," *The Human Life Review*, Summer 1987.

Vermont Royster   "Musings of a Male Chauvinist," *The Wall Street Journal*, June 8, 1987.

Eloise Salholz   "Feminism's Identity Crisis," *Newsweek*, March 31, 1986.

Society   "Patriarchy and Power," September/October 1986.

Gloria Steinem   "Humanism and the Second Wave of Feminism," *The Humanist*, May/June 1987.

Lawrence Wade   "Getting What We Ask For," *The Washington Times*, August 22, 1986.

Walter Williams   "What Women Stand To Lose If Feminists Have Their Way," *The Washington Times*, September 13, 1984.

and role modeling, 176-177, 178-179, 183
  difficulties of, 192-193
  economic penalties for, 200
  feminism is against, 421-423
    con, 125, 417, 425-427
  importance of, 133-134, 135, 183-184, 335-336
  is compatible with a career, 167-169
    con, 181-184
  origins of, 116-117
  sacrifices of, 134-135
Moyers, Bill, 151, 152, 154
Moynihan, Daniel Patrick, 108, 115
Mudd, Emily H., 111, 113
Murray, Charles A., 115, 151, 162

Neely, Richard, 237
Nelton, Sharon, 167
Nixon, Richard M., 330, 426
Novak, Michael, 389

O'Connell-Cahill, Michael, 407
Osborne, David, 91

Pace, Jana, 345
Pagels, Elaine, 375, 391
parental leave
  government should mandate, 337-339, 353
    con, 341-343
parenting
  importance of, 335-336, 338
  noncustodial
    a father's view, 243-248
    a mother's view, 249-253
  shared
    benefits of, 145
    difficulties of, 144-145, 148-149
    is possible, 143-145
      myth of, 147-149
    psychological responsibilities in, 148
  see also fatherhood; motherhood
patriarchy
  alternatives to, 37-38, 386-387
  as oppressive, 7-9, 385-387
  definition of, 7-8
  in Western thought, 33, 40
  is universal, 25-26
    myth of, 31-33
  origins of, 30-31, 33
Perkins, Pheme, 399
Pilarczyk, Daniel, 409
Plato, 33, 163, 415
Pleck, Joseph, 66, 67, 199
Pogrebin, Letty Cottin, 108, 307
poverty, feminization of, 204, 352
priests
  shortage of, 407
  should be allowed to marry, 407-408
    myth of, 409-411
  vocations of, 410-411
  women should be, 401-403
    myth of, 405-406

rape, 7-8, 387, 429
Reagan, Ronald, 140, 162, 426
Research and Forecasts, Inc., 125
Rich, Adrienne, 7, 8
Roback, Jennifer, 259
Robertiello, Richard, 88, 89
Rogak, Lisa, 249
Rossler, John, 227, 230

Rubin, Gayle, 9, 10
Ruether, Rosemary Radford, 385, 389

Salholz, Eloise, 99
Sanderson, Jim, 83
Scarr, Sandra, 177, 358, 259
Schroeder, Patricia, 108, 337, 339, 417, 426
Schwartz, Pepper, 199, 200
sex roles, see gender roles
Shaevitz, Morton H., 47
Sherman, Marilyn, 197
Shreve, Anita, 175
Siegal, Bryna, 355, 364
Sills, Judith, 96, 97
Smith, Adam, 322, 325
Smith, C.W., 243
Solnit, Albert, 233, 234, 238
Spock, Benjamin, 329, 356, 358
Steinberg, Ronnie, 311
Stempler, Allan, 249, 252

Taubin, Sara B., 111, 113
Tavris, Carol, 19
Thatcher, Margaret, 19, 271
Thompson, Cooper, 55
Thompson, Keith, 59
Trask, Haunani-Kay, 7
Trotter, Robert J., 351
Tucker, William, 115
Tuerck, David G., 321

US Chamber of Commerce, 341

Velson, Ellen, 285
Viveros-Long, Anamaria, 299

Wade, Carole, 19
Wade, Lawrence, 75
Wallerstein, Judith S., 104, 211, 227, 234
Walsh, Joan, 108, 110
Ware, Ciji, 231
Weissman, Lenore J., 201
welfare, see families
White, Randall P., 285
women
  and dating, 75-81, 95-97
  and divorce, 201-203, 221-225, 249-253
  and government aid, 160-162, 165-166
  and marriage, 100-101, 105-106, 134-135, 203
  and the priesthood, 401-403, 405-406
  as single mothers, 101, 201-204, 337
  belong in the home, 137, 181-183
    con, 167-169, 175-179
  Bible's teaching on, 393-400
  Christianity's impact on, 377-383
  civilizing role of, 4, 134-135, 417
  gender role of, 79-80
    and matriarchies, 35-41
    as negative, 7-9, 89, 415
    as positive, 1-5
    feminism has improved, 417-419, 425-427
      con, 413-415, 421-423
    in marriage, 133-141
  misunderstand men, 76-77
  over thirty
    are unlikely to marry, 99-102
      benefits of, 105-106
      myth of, 103-106
    Harvard-Yale study on, 99, 104, 105
  sexual identity of, 2-4

want liberated men, 44, 79-82
  con, 75-77
working
  and networking, 272-273
  are not taken seriously, 269-270
  as role models, 176-179
  balance work and family, 167-169, 179, 305
    con, 171-174, 282, 284, 287, 378-379
  benefit children, 175-179
    con, 181-184
  discrimination harms, 70, 255-258, 268-269, 290, 311-316
    is exaggerated, 259-262
  earnings of, 199-200, 203-204, 255
  guilt of, 303-304
  housework and, 199, 300-310
  in corporations
    and job requirements, 286-289
    are accepted, 263-266
      con, 267-270, 283, 285-287
    boredom of, 289-291
    drop-out rate of, 76, 268, 281-282, 289-290
    humanize business, 277-278
      myth of, 273-274
  men's support of, 168-169
  wage gap of, 257-258, 288, 311-312, 326-327
    is exaggerated, 259-262, 317-318, 322
  see also comparable worth; divorce; families; feminism; management styles; motherhood
Women's Ordination Conference, 401

Young, Jane, 227

Zigler, Edward, 338, 351-354, 356